Biographical Fiction

Biographical Fiction

A Reader

Edited by
Michael Lackey

Bloomsbury Academic
An imprint of Bloomsbury Publishing Inc

B L O O M S B U R Y
NEW YORK • LONDON • OXFORD • NEW DELHI • SYDNEY

Bloomsbury Academic
An imprint of Bloomsbury Publishing Inc

1385 Broadway
New York
NY 10018
USA

50 Bedford Square
London
WC1B 3DP
UK

www.bloomsbury.com

BLOOMSBURY and the Diana logo are trademarks of Bloomsbury Publishing Plc

First published 2017

Library of Congress Cataloging-in-Publication Data
A catalog record for this book is available from the Library of Congress.

ISBN: HB: 978-1-5013-1799-6
PB: 978-1-5013-1800-9
ePub: 978-1-5013-1801-6
ePDF: 978-1-5013-1803-0

Cover design: Daniel Benneworth-Gray

Typeset by Deanta Global Publishing Services, Chennai, India
Printed and bound in the United States of America

In memory of my mother,
Janice Nora Lackey
(1940–2012)

CONTENTS

ACKNOWLEDGMENTS

For more than four years I have been working on this anthology, and I have been fortunate to have the support of so many people and organizations. Without their assistance and insight, this anthology would not be possible. I would like to start by thanking my university. The University of Minnesota, Morris, supported this project with a single-semester research leave and a number of grants for travel to archives in the United States and Europe. I am immensely grateful to the university and Roger Wareham in particular, who works passionately, tirelessly, and aggressively to secure funding for faculty. I would also like to thank our dean, Bart Finzel, who has taken much interest in this project and very generously supported it. In my experience, the University of Minnesota system has done more to support humanities research than any other university I have ever seen. Without its generous funding to travel to archives and to interview writers, I could not have even imagined this book. But my biggest thanks go to the University of Minnesota's Institute for Advanced Study, which has done so much to promote and advance scholarship about biofiction. In particular, I want to thank Susannah L. Smith, who has always been willing and eager to create forums about biofiction.

Over the last few years, many of my colleagues have patiently listened to me discuss the nature and evolution of biofiction, and I would like to both thank and credit them: Julie Eckerle, Pieranna Garavaso, Brook Miller, Brad Deane, and Dan Demetriou.

Working on biofiction has put me in contact with some wonderful scholars and writers who have given me much direction and corrected my missteps. In particular I would like to thank Stephen Banks, Anindya Bhattacharya, Mary F. Burns, Rupert Dörflinger, Annette Gordon-Reed, Monica Latham, Gill Lowe, Laura Marcus, Martin Middeke, Julia Novak, Carl Rollyson, Max Saunders, Valentina Vannucci, and Mark Wenger.

In doing this project, I have met many wonderful biographical novelists. For their generosity in working with me, I would like to thank Julia Alvarez, Russell Banks, Madison Smartt Bell, Mark Allen Cunningham, Michael Cunningham, Anita Diamant, Bruce Duffy, David Ebershoff, Ron Hansen, Sherry Jones, Rebecca Kanner, Kate Moses, Barbara Mujica, Joyce Carol Oates, Lance Olsen, Jay Parini, Joanna Scott, and Edmund White.

To those scholars who are also friends, I want to say thank you for working with me on this and all my other projects: Pamela Caughie, John Ernest,

Mark Hussey, Dana Nelson, and Jim West. For all their assistance with this project, I want to thank my student assistants Kelsey Butler and Katie Brown.

Finally, I would like to thank my editor, Haaris Naqvi, who always gives me insightful and useful direction and feedback.

I would like to thank all the contributors for their kind permission to reproduce their work. Every effort has been made to trace copyright holders and I apologize in advance for any unintentional omission. I would be pleased to insert the appropriate acknowledgment in any subsequent edition.

Alvarez, Julia. From *In the Time of the Butterflies*, published by Algonquin Books of Chapel Hill. Copyright © 1994 by Julia Alvarez. By permission of Susan Bergholz Literary Services, New York, NY and Lamy, NM. All rights reserved.

Alvarez, Julia. “Fixed Facts and Creative Freedom in the Biographical Novel” from *Truthful Fictions* (2014). Reprinted with the permission of the interviewee and Bloomsbury Academic.

Banks, Russell. “The Truth Contract in the Biographical Novel” from *Truthful Fictions* (2014). Reprinted with the permission of the interviewee and Bloomsbury Academic.

Barrett, William E. From *Woman on Horseback: The Biography of Francisco Lopez and Eliza Lynch* by William E. Barrett. Copyright © 1938 by William E. Barrett.

Bode, Carl. “The Buxom Biographies” by Carl Bode from the journal *College English*. Copyright © 1955 by the National Council of Teachers of English. Reprinted with permission.

Bradbury, Malcolm. “Preface” from *To the Hermitage*. Copyright © 2000 by Malcolm Bradbury. Published in 2011 by the Overlook Press, New York, NY. www.overlookpress.com. All Rights reserved.

Buisine, Alan. “Biofictions” from *Revue des Sciences Humaines*. *Revue des Sciences Humaines* 224 (1991): 7–13. Reprinted with permission.

Chase-Riboud, Barbara. Afterword copyright © 2009 by Barbara Chase-Riboud. *Sally Hemings* copyright © 1979 by Barbara Chase-Riboud. Reprinted by permission of Chicago Review Press.

Cunningham, M. Allen. “Author’s Note” from *Lost Son*, by M. Allen Cunningham (pp. 469–70). Copyright © 2007 M. Allen Cunningham. Reprinted by permission from Unbridled Books. All Rights Reserved. unbridledbooks.com.

Duffy, Bruce. "In the Fog of the Biographical Novel's History" from *Truthful Fictions* (2014). Reprinted with the permission of the interviewee and Bloomsbury Academic.

Duffy, Bruce, Michael Lackey, Lance Olsen, and Jay Parini. "The Uses of History in the Biographical Novel" (2012). From a round-table conversation moderated by Michael Lackey at the University of Minnesota's Institute for Advanced Study (September 20, 2012): http://ias.umn.edu/2012/09/20/duffy-parini-olsen-biographies/. Reprinted by permission.

Ebershoff, David. "An Introduction to The Danish Girl," from *The Danish Girl: A Novel* by David Ebershoff, copyright © 2000 by David Ebershoff. Used by permission of Viking Books, an imprint of Penguin Publishing Group, a division of Penguin Random House LLC.

Ehrlich, Leonard. *God's Angry Man* by Leonard Ehrlich. Copyright © 1932 by Leonard Ehrlich. Permission obtained from Simon and Shuster, Inc. All rights reserved.

Ellison, Ralph, William Styron, Robert Penn Warren, and C. Vann Woodward. "The Uses of History in Fiction." From *The Southern Literary Journal*, Volume 1, Number 2. Copyright © 1969 by the Department of English and Comparative Literature of the University of North Carolina at Chapel Hill. Published by the University of North Carolina Press. Used by permission of the publisher. www.uncpress.unc.edu.

Endore, S. Guy. "A Final Word" from *King of Paris* by Guy Endore. Published with permission of Marcia Endore Goodman and the Henrietta Endore Trust.

Enright, Anne. Acknowledgments from *The Pleasure of Eliza Lynch*, copyright © 2002 by Anne Enright. Published by Vintage Books, 2003.

Hall, Brian. "Author's Note," from *The Fall of Frost* by Brian Hall, copyright © 2008 by Brian Hall. Used by permission of Viking Books, an imprint of Penguin Publishing Group, a division of Penguin Random House LLC, and The Wylie Agency, LLC.

Keener, John F. Adaption from Chapters 4 and 5 of *Biography and the Postmodern Historical Novel*. Copyright © 2001 John F. Keener. Used by permission of Edwin Mellen Press.

Kendall, Paul Murray. From *The Art of Biography*, copyright © 1965. Reprinted with permission from Caroline Kendall Orszak and Gillian Murray Kendall.

Latham, Monica. "'Serv[ing] under two masters': Virginia Woolf's Afterlives in Contemporary Biofictions" from *a/b: Auto/Biography Studies* (2012). Copyright © The Autobiography Society, reprinted by permission of Taylor & Francis Ltd, http://www.tandfonline.com on behalf of The Autobiography Society.

Lukács, Georg. From *The Historical Novel* by Georg Lukács, copyright © 1962 by the Merlin Press Limited. Reprinted by permission of Beacon Press, Boston.

Mallon, Thomas. "The Historical Novelist's Burden of Truth" from *In Fact: Essays on Writers and Writing* by Thomas Mallon, copyright © 2001 by Thomas Mallon. Used by permission of Pantheon Books, an imprint of the Knopf Doubleday Publishing Group, a division of Penguin Random House LLC. All rights reserved.

Middeke, Martin. "Introduction" from *Biofictions: The Rewriting of Romantic Lives in Contemporary Fiction and Drama*. Copyright © 1999 by Martin Middeke. Used by permission of Camden House Press, an imprint of Boydell & Brewer Inc.

Mujica, Barbara. "Going for the Subjective: One Way to Write Biographical Fiction" from *a/b: Auto/Biography Studies* (2016). Copyright © The Autobiography Society, reprinted by permission of Taylor & Francis Ltd, http://www.tandfonline.com on behalf of The Autobiography Society.

Nünning, Ansgar. "Fictional Metabiographies and Metaautobiographies: Towards a Definition, Typology and Analysis of Self-Reflexive Hybrid Metagenres" from *Self-Reflexivity in Literature*. Republished with permission of Verlag Königshausen & Neumann GmbH.

Oates, Joyce Carol. "Enhanced Symbolic Interiors in the Biographical Novel" from *Truthful Fictions* (2014). Reprinted with the permission of the interviewee and Bloomsbury Academic.

Parini, Jay. "Fact or Fiction: Writing Biographies versus Writing Novel" from *Some Necessary Angels: Essays on Writing and Politics* by Jay Parini. Copyright © 1997 Columbia University Press. Reprinted with permission of the publisher.

Schabert, Ina. "Fictional Biography, Factual Biography, and their Contamination" from *Biography: An Interdisciplinary Quarterly* 5.1 (Winter 1982). Copyright © by the Biographical Research Center. Reprinted with permission.

Scott, Joanna. "On Hoaxes, Humbugs, and Fictional Portraiture" from *a/b: Auto/Biography Studies* (2016). Copyright © The Autobiography Society, reprinted by permission of Taylor & Francis Ltd, http://www.tandfonline.com on behalf of The Autobiography Society.

Sellers, Susan. "About *Vanessa and Virginia*." Reprinted with permission from Susan Sellers.

Stegner, Wallace. Foreword from *Joe Hill* by Wallace Stegner, copyright © 1950 by Wallace Stegner. Copyright renewed © 1977 by Wallace Stegner. Used by permission of Doubleday, an imprint of the Knopf Doubleday Publishing Group, a division of Penguin Random House LLC, and Brandt & Hochman Literary Agents, Inc. All rights reserved.

Stone, Irving. "The Biographical Novel" from *Three Views of the Novel* (1957). Reprinted with permission from The Bancroft Library, University of California, Berkeley (call number: BANC MSS95/2015 cz).

Styron, William. "Nat Turner Revisited" by William Styron from *American Heritage* (October 1992). Used by permission of Inkwell Management on behalf of the estate of William Styron. Copyright © 1992.

Tóibín, Colm. "Henry James for Venice." *The Henry James Review* 27.3 (2006), 192–201. © 2006 The John Hopkins University Press. Reprinted with permission of John Hopkins University Press.

Tuck, Lily. Authors Note [pp. 247–48] from *The News from Paraguay* by Lily Tuck. Copyright © 2004 by Lily Tuck. Reprinted by permission of Harper Collins Publishers.

Vannucci, Valentina. "The Canon and Biofiction: The Subjects of History and New Literary Worlds" from *altri canoni/canoni altri: pluralismo e studi letterari* (2011). Vannucci Valentina, *Canone e* biofiction, *i soggetti della storia e i nuovi mondi letterari*, in De Zordo, Fantaccini (eds), *altri canoni/ canoni altri*: pluralismo e studi letterari (2011). Florence: BSFM 10, FUP: 125–51. This is an open access text through the publishing house catalogue (http://www.fupress.com/catalogo/altri-canoni---canoni-altri/1871) and through the institutional archive of UNIFI (http://www.fupress.com/catalogo/altri-canoni---canoni-altri/1871).

Yolen, Jane, and Harris, Robert J. From *Girl in a Cage* by Jane Yolen and Robert J. Harris, copyright © 2002 and 2004 by Jane Yolen and Robert J. Harris. Used by permission of Philomel, an imprint of Penguin Young Readers Group, a division of Penguin Random House LLC and Curtis Brown, Ltd.

Michael Lackey

Introduction: A narrative space of its own

Two separate factions have tried to own biofiction in order to disown it. In 1937, Georg Lukács published the groundbreaking study *The Historical Novel*, which does a masterful job defining what he refers to as the classical historical novel, a literary form that pictures the social, political, and economic forces that shape and determine consciousness and thereby gives readers an accurate view of the essential factors that gave birth to major historical collisions. Within Lukács' framework, the biographical novel is a bastardized version of the historical novel, because the biographical novel's excessive focus on the psychological subject's interiority necessarily distorts and misrepresents the objective proportions of history. Therefore, Lukács considers the biographical novel an irredeemable aesthetic form.

In 1965, Paul Murray Kendall authored *The Art of Biography*, and like Lukács, he totally denounces biofiction. But instead of analyzing and assessing the narrative form in relation to fiction, he defines it in relation to life writing. For Kendall, the biography seeks to breathe life into figures from the past, picturing them as they were "in the days" they "lived."[1] The biographical novel, which Kendall refers to as "the novel-as-biography," is ultimately doomed to failure because it is "almost wholly imaginary."[2] Thus, instead of giving readers a living picture of figures from the past, as capable biographers do, it projects the wayward vision of wannabe novelists, thus disqualifying it as a legitimate biography.

In the battle for intellectual jurisdiction over biofiction, the life writing tradition has dominated, leaving Lukács and his fiction approach so far behind that scholars since the 1960s rarely if ever entertain the possibility that his work could play a productive role in analyzing the narrative form. To illustrate, let me mention just a few prominent scholars who have foregrounded the biographical in their approach to biographical fiction. In 1990, Ina Schabert published *In Quest of the Other Person: Fiction as*

Biography, a title which indicates that biofiction is really just a form of biography. As Schabert claims, her project examines how fictional biographies and biographical fictions enable readers "to get knowledge of the real, other person."[3] In 1991, Alain Buisine published his essay "Biofictions." But this essay does not examine the aesthetic form as fiction. Rather, Buisine specifies how postmodernism led to the rise of a new type of biography, one that acknowledges via its form as fiction the fact that an accurate representation of the biographical subject is no longer possible. In a 2012 essay, Monica Latham argues that biofiction is a hybrid narrative form that straddles two separate worlds, but she ultimately suggests that the genre seeks to picture the biographical subject's "life story,"[4] thus subordinating the fictional to the biographical. All these scholars define biofiction primarily in relation to the goals and techniques of biography, and not one of them cites Lukács.

What makes all this so unsettling is the fact that from the earliest days authors of biofiction have emphatically stated that what they write is not biography. As Leonard Ehrlich claims in the author's note to *God's Angry Man*, which was initially published in 1932: "This work is a *novel*, not a biography or a history."[5] Subsequent biographical novelists make an almost exact claim. For instance, in the foreword to *Wife to Mr. Milton*, Robert Graves says that "this book is a novel, not a biography"[6]; in the note to *Death of the Fox*, George Garrett says that "this is a work of fiction," and he goes on to claim that "it is not supposed to be in any sense a biography of Sir Walter Ralegh"[7]; and in the afterword to *An Imaginary Life*, David Malouf states that what he "wanted to write was neither historical novel nor biography, but a fiction."[8] In 1960, Nikos Kazantzakis authored the daring biographical novel *The Last Temptation of Christ*, in which he explicitly and unambiguously claims that the "book is not a biography."[9] More prominent, contemporary biographical novelists who have unequivocally stated that their works are to be considered fictions and not biographies include Bruce Duffy, Joyce Carol Oates, Anne Enright, Jay Parini, Margaret Atwood, Madison Smartt Bell, Joanna Scott, Ilya Troyanov, Anita Diamant, Jerome Charyn, Hilary Mantel, David Lodge, Laurent Binet, Colm Tóibín, and David Ebershoff, just to name a notable few.

Let me specify why so many authors stress the fact that biofiction and biography are separate and distinct. Thomas Mallon has authored a number of biographical novels, and in two of them he has issued the following warning: "Nouns always trump adjectives, and in the phrase 'historical fiction' it is important to remember which of the two words is which."[10] What Mallon writes is fiction, not history and not biography. Therefore, when categorizing and evaluating his work, it is important to keep in mind that biographical representation is subordinate to fictional creation.[11] Given Mallon's claims, it would be inappropriate and even inaccurate to refer to biographical novels as fictional biographies, as some scholars do, because this would subordinate the fictional to the biographical.

Russell Banks, in particular, goes out of his way to underscore the fact that there is an irreconcilable difference between the two narrative forms. In 1998, Banks published *Cloudsplitter*, a biographical novel about John Brown's son Owen. In his "Author's Note," Banks says that his "book should be read solely as a work of fiction, not as a version or interpretation of history." Immediately after making this claim, Banks lists the biographies of John Brown that he consulted and used in order to construct his narrative, but to emphasize the fact that he authored something separate and distinct, he draws a sharp distinction between biography and biofiction. Discussing the biographies he just mentioned, Banks says: "They are excellent, deep works of biographical history. This, it bears repeating, is a work of fiction."[12] Banks is basically saying: "Do not hold me bound to the laws of biography, because what I write is fiction, not biography." This is a point that Banks makes so clearly in his interview about the novel: "It seemed to me a given that I could write from inside a historical figure. I could write a 'life' of that figure, using that figure's life, but I would be writing a dramatic narrative, a work with a dramatic shape and intent, rather than a biography of that character."[13] Notice how Banks strategically sets his work off from biography. The two genres cannot be confused with one another, because they do very different things.

Julia Alvarez best clarifies why biographical novelists are so adamant about calling their work fiction and distancing it from biography. *In the Time of the Butterflies* pictures the lives of the Mirabal sisters. But in her postscript to the novel, Alvarez says that what readers get in her novel "are not the Mirabal sisters of fact." What leads Alvarez to make this claim is the fact that she lacks "the talents and inclinations of a biographer to be able to adequately record"[14] the lives of the Mirabal sisters. Authors of biofiction and biography have very different abilities, methods, approaches, and objectives. Therefore, Alvarez wants readers to assess the quality of *In the Time of the Butterflies* for what she writes, which is fiction, rather than for what she does not write, which is biography.

This anthology symbolizes the official arrival of biofiction, which has finally emancipated itself from both historical fiction and life writing and has charted a narrative space uniquely its own.

A new literary symbolism

The objective at this point is to define some of the distinctive features of biographical fiction. To begin, I want to discuss briefly the major debate and controversy surrounding the publication of William Styron's biographical novel *The Confessions of Nat Turner*, as this work signals a decisive shift in literary symbolism. Standard among prominent writers of the early twentieth century is the tendency to base their protagonists on actual historical figures, but to change the characters' names in order to give the writers more liberty to alter facts and to use the protagonists to do social and political critique. One thinks, for instance, of F. Scott Fitzgerald's Daisy Buchanan, who is based on Ginevra King; Willa Cather's Bishop Jean-Marie Latour, who is based on Bishop Jean-Baptiste Lamy; Aldous Huxley's Mark Rampion, who is based on D. H. Lawrence, and Virginia Woolf's Mr. and Mrs. Ramsay, who are based on Woolf's parents. One of the most notable authors to do this is Robert Penn Warren, who based his novel *All the King's Men* on the life of Huey Long, but changed the protagonist's name to Willie Stark. Making this change enabled Warren to convert his character into a literary symbol that could represent Long as well as other prominent politicians.

Styron committed an unpardonable sin in 1967 by naming his protagonist after the actual historical figure, and in a roundtable forum about "The Uses of History in Fiction," he was viciously criticized for this aesthetic choice. Participants in the forum included Ralph Ellison and Warren, and while it might seem that Warren would have had the most compelling reason to fault and attack Styron, since Styron clearly rejected the Warren approach of changing the protagonist's name, it was Ellison who led the charge against Styron. But there was a clear reason why. Styron, intentionally or not, authored a form of fiction that subtly but decisively rendered the kind of novel Ellison wrote less effective and perhaps obsolete.

Admittedly, Ellison's 1952 novel *Invisible Man* is a work of genius, which brilliantly pictures the political psychology that leads so many in positions of power to marginalize a wide range of people. Because of "the construction of their *inner* eyes,"[15] many leaders, especially in major organizations, have glaring blinds spots, which is why they fail to see others and explains how and why they can violate others with emotional, psychological, and sometimes legal impunity. To expose the individual and communal psychology that make such political blindness possible, Ellison invents the Brotherhood, an organization with leaders who cannot see those who exist outside of its history-making agenda. Over the years, scholars have suggested that the Brotherhood is really the Communist Party. But Ellison consistently rejected this view, because he purposely created a symbol that could represent the Communist Party, but also the Democratic Party, the Republican Party, and many other organizations. To equate the Brotherhood with the Communist Party would render his literary symbol too narrow, specific, and reductive, which is why Ellison consistently rejected the view that the two were one and the same.

During the roundtable forum, Ellison praised Warren for changing the name of his protagonist from Huey Long to Willie Stark. However, this surface praise was merely Ellison's backhanded way of faulting Styron for not doing the same. It was in a contentious exchange with Styron that Ellison clearly formulated why he considered Styron's aesthetic approach a mistake. As a novelist, Ellison's task "is to create symbolic actions which are viable specifically, and which move across all of our differences and all of the diversities of the atmosphere."[16] To expose and critique a social and/or political mentality, authors create symbolic figures that can be used to illuminate a wide array of cases. "This is why," Ellison tells Styron, "you must lie and disguise a historical figure."[17] The implication is this: to name the character after an actual person renders the protagonist too historically specific, thus divesting the potential literary symbol (figured in and through the protagonist) of its power to signify a wide variety of people and cases across all of our "differences" and "diversities."

For Ellison, the aesthetic stakes of Styron's choice were high indeed. Novelists play a crucial role in critiquing the sociopolitical mentalities underwriting culture and in reshaping that mentality. Were writers to adopt the aesthetic approach Styron deployed in his biographical novel, creative writers would no longer be able to fulfill their roles as the culture's most insightful critics. But for Styron and many authors of biofiction, there is a potential flaw in the kind of symbolism found in novels like *Invisible Man*. To understand why this is the case, let me clarify how postmodern shifts in our theory of knowledge impacted the literary symbol. Postmodernists hold that there is an arbitrary element in the construction of a system of knowledge, so all conceptual systems, no matter how insightful and/or compelling, are limited, flawed, and untrustworthy. This view significantly impacted the traditional literary symbol. For instance, in *Mrs. Dalloway*, Woolf created the character of Sir William Bradshaw, who represents a pervasive patriarchal psychology in the medical profession. This character as symbol may be effective and even accurate, but biographical novelists want to avoid the charge of manufacturing an arbitrary symbol that serves their ideological or political agenda, so they base their characters on actual historical figures. In short, the rise of postmodernism led to a need for a more historically specific and empirically based literary symbol.

What Ellison did not understand or anticipate was the way biographical novelists could combine fact and fiction in order to create a literary symbol out of a historical figure, a symbol that could expose and critique the culture exactly as Ellison did in *Invisible Man*. To illustrate, let me briefly discuss Bruce Duffy's spectacular biographical novel *The World as I Found It*. Ludwig Wittgenstein was one of the most famous and influential philosophers of the early twentieth century. What few people know, however, is that he and the Nazis had strikingly similar views about Jews. In his novel, Duffy spends a lot of time picturing Wittgenstein, who was part Jewish, struggling with his Jewish heritage and anti-Semitism. To give readers a visual symbol of Wittgenstein's anti-Semitic impact, Duffy creates a character named Max, who is a close friend of Wittgenstein's, has similar experiences as the philosopher, and adopts Wittgenstein's anti-Semitic ideology. To suggest that Wittgenstein played a role in advancing the Nazis' anti-Semitism, Duffy has Max become a member of the SS. By the end of the novel, Duffy indicates how Max symbolizes not just a racist dimension of Wittgenstein's thinking, but also a racist psychology pervasive throughout the West. In essence, Duffy, just like Ellison, exposes and critiques a sociopolitical mentality through the portrayal of his protagonist, and he clearly creates a symbolic figure (Max) that could be used to illuminate a wide array of figures and cases across our "differences" and "diversities."

What makes Duffy's novel different from Ellison's, and I would even say more effective, is his historically specific and empirically rooted literary symbol. Ellison created with the Brotherhood a powerful symbol, but it was one that was so general and abstract that some could accuse him of concocting a symbol that conveniently served his ideological and/or political agenda. In our postmodern age, we have become more suspicious of such overarching, ahistorical symbols. Consequently, biographical novelists have reimagined the literary symbol by making it more historically specific and empirically rooted. Readers of Duffy's novel can see specifically how Wittgenstein's anti-Semitic ideas, symbolized in and through the character of Max, align with and sometimes advance the Nazis' ideological and political agenda. Put simply, it is far more difficult to accuse biographical novelists of manufacturing a symbol that suits their ideological agenda, because their works are based on actual historical figures and events.

In essence, postmodernism mandated a new type of literary symbol, the nature, function, and value of which we can best see in biographical fiction.

Inverting the historical novel

Lukács insists that the protagonists of historical novels are fictional figures that represent "historical-social types."[18] Within this framework, actual historical figures can appear in the novel, but only on the periphery. The central figure must be invented so that he or she can function as a symbol to portray "a great crisis in society."[19] However, for the protagonist to fulfill this symbolic role, he or she must not be a typical Romantic hero glowing with quasi-supernatural virtues, but a "mediocre, prosaic hero,"[20] who, in a momentary flash of greatness, commits a truly spectacular act that has an enormous historical impact. Given this aesthetic law, the biographical novel is doomed to failure because the author of such a work idealizes the protagonist and, therefore, fails to portray the representative struggles and tensions of the historical-social type.

Mediocre figures play a prominent role in Lance Olsen's brilliant biographical novel *Nietzsche's Kisses*, but instead of being construed as heroes, he inverts the historical novel by portraying them as the culture's primary culprits. Olsen's Nietzsche first starts thinking about the mediocre when teaching at the university. After discovering that many academics mechanically mouth dominant systems of thought rather than thinking and imagining their way toward a new and original conceptual system, Olsen's Nietzsche concludes: "It was a terrible thought to contemplate: how an immense number of mediocre minds were occupied with remarkably influential matters."[21] Note that the problem is not just that there are so many mediocre people. The problem is that so many are involved in remarkably influential matters.

Nietzsche's brother-in-law, Bernhard Förster, numbers among the mediocre. A Berlin high school teacher, Bernhard made a name for himself by authoring an anti-Semitic "petition demanding the limitation of Jewish immigration, registration of all Jews, and the exclusion of Jews from positions of authority in government and education."[22] Nietzsche vehemently opposed anti-Semitism, as he states explicitly and unambiguously in a letter to his sister Elisabeth: "It is a matter of honor to me to be absolutely clear and unequivocal regarding anti-Semitism, namely *opposed*, as I am in my writings."[23] Therefore, it should come as no surprise that Olsen's Nietzsche detests Bernhard. But what is most significant is Nietzsche's claim that Bernhard's "anti-Semitism was a mutiny of the mediocre."[24]

Unfortunately, Bernhard is one of those mediocre who has a remarkable impact on influential matters. In the 1880s, Bernhard had an idea about building a Jewish-free colony in Paraguay, and his biggest helpmate was Elisabeth. The colony did not do well, which, in part, led Bernhard to commit suicide. Shortly before Bernhard's suicide, Nietzsche had a mental breakdown from which he never recovered. For a couple years, Elisabeth devoted herself almost exclusively to her husband's cause. But in the 1890s, she shifted her focus from the Paraguay colony to Nietzsche and his work—she founded the Nietzsche Archive. This had devastating consequences, for Elisabeth, having adopted Bernhard's anti-Semitism, sought to conceptually remake her brother into her husband. And since she founded the Nietzsche Archive, she had the power to do so—in both Olsen's novel and real life, Elisabeth altered and even forged some of Nietzsche's writings. To signify what Elisabeth would ultimately do, Olsen has Nietzsche imagine Elisabeth "*förstering a new idea that will cull us all*."[25] In other words, Elisabeth *försterized* her brother (on paper, she transforms Friedrich Nietzsche into Bernhard Förster), making him into an anti-Semite whose work anticipated the Nazis and even contributed to their making. As Olsen says in an interview about the novel, one of his objectives was to clarify how "Elisabeth had begun to rewrite her brother, gain control over him by narrativizing him."[26] To expose the catastrophic historical consequence of Elisabeth's move, Olsen pictures Hitler visiting the Nietzsche Archive in 1934, where Elisabeth passes "the torch"[27] to Hitler. The symbol of passing the torch suggests that Nietzsche and his thought contributed to the making of Hitler and the Nazis. But, as Olsen so aptly dramatizes, the reality is that Elisabeth did not pass the torch of Nietzsche to Hitler and the Nazis. By *försterizing* Nietzsche, she passed her husband's torch to them.

Lukács rightly believes that the novel can answer some major historical questions, such as: "how was the Hitler regime in Germany possible?"[28] This question, Lukács avers, can best be answered through "the classical type of historical novel,"[29] and it emphatically cannot be answered through the biographical novel, because in the latter, "the character is inevitably exaggerated, made to stand on tiptoe, his historical calling unduly emphasized while the real objective causes and factors of the historical mission are inevitably omitted."[30] Lukács wrongly assumes that the biographical novel focuses on the protagonist's groundbreaking ideas and their subsequent translation into sociopolitical action. But in *Nietzsche's Kisses*, the exact opposite is the case: the novel focuses on the way the mediocre misunderstand, misappropriate, and then disseminate the protagonist's ideas. In the process, Olsen offers, at least in part, a plausible way of thinking about not the role that Nietzsche played but the role Elisabeth's *försterized* "Nietzsche" played in the making of Hitler and the Nazis.

By portraying the pernicious relationship between the mediocre and the protagonist, Olsen inverts the historical novel, thus giving readers a new way of thinking about some of the historical forces that made the Hitler regime in Germany possible.

Fictionalizing the biographical subject

At this point, it would be instructive to think about the differences between biographical fiction and life writing. What should immediately stand out is the fact that authors of biofiction unapologetically change facts. Take, for instance, the protagonist of Banks' novel *Cloudsplitter*, Owen Brown. The actual Owen died in 1889. But in Banks' novel, he tells his story in 1903. In an interview, Banks explains that he let his character "live on into the twentieth century so that his story, John Brown's story, would lose some of the antique quality it might have had otherwise and would point toward the twentieth century, to our own time."[31] There are two separate things here that clearly distinguish the author of biofiction from the author of biography. Imagine, for a moment, that you are reading a biography about Virginia Woolf, and on the first page, the author says: "On January 27, 1900, Julia Stephen gave birth to Virginia, who did more to reshape our sensibilities about human and sexual identity than any other author of her generation." Many readers would rightfully feel violated after reading this sentence, and some would certainly request a refund, because the author makes a claim that is not only false but also could not be true, as Woolf was born in 1882, and Stephen died in 1895.

According to Banks, authors establish a tacit contract with their readers, and for authors of biographical fiction and life writing, the terms of that contract are very different. Biographers cannot simply alter established facts in order to make what they consider a more important intellectual point, because the contract they tacitly enter into with readers prohibits such liberties. There is an expectation that biographers will represent the life of the subject with as much accuracy as possible. Now, of course, an informed reader will know that the authors' ideological orientation will inflect their representation of the biographical subject, so what readers get in a biography is a biased version of their subject's life. But there is a big difference between an inadvertent misrepresentation and a purposeful and strategic alteration of fact.

Malcolm Bradbury, who authored a biographical novel about Denis Diderot, articulates the matter most clearly and comically in his Preface to *To the Hermitage*. Describing himself as a "wee postmodern Haussman," Bradbury says that he has drawn "a great deal on history," but he confesses that when history seems "dull or inaccurate," he decided to improve on it. As he claims: "I have quietly corrected errors in the calendar, adjusted flaws in world geography, now and then budged the border of a country, or changed the constitution of a nation."[32] In biofiction, history and biography take their cue from the vision of the creative writer rather than from the reality of the external world.

But what would motivate authors to strategically misrepresent historical or biographical facts? As authors of fiction, biographical novelists seek to represent a different type of truth from biographers. Styron's biographical novel about Nat Turner will prove useful here. Turner organized a bloody rebellion in 1831, which led to the death of many white people in Virginia. Writing in the 1960s, Styron was interested in the socioeconomic and psycho-political structures that led marginalized and oppressed people to stage violent rebellions, because such rebellions were commonplace in Styron's time. Therefore, examining the forces that led Turner to rebel was as much about understanding the 1960s as 1831. As Styron says, "I'm sure that my early fascination with Nat Turner came from pondering the parallels between his time and my own society."[33] To bring into sharp focus the bi-temporal structures and conditions of oppression, Styron altered many facts about Turner's life. For instance, there were no major plantations where Turner lived, but Styron put him on one anyway, because it enabled him to expose one of the structures of oppression at work in both times and places. As he says:

> The plantation was an integral and characteristic part of Southern life in slave times; it was the very metaphor for the capitalist exploitation of human labor, and the plantation owners often represented the best and worst of those whom history had cast as masters in the peculiar institution, carrying within themselves all the moral frights and tensions which slavery engendered. I needed to dramatize this turmoil, and so I contrived to have Nat Turner grow up on a prosperous plantation which

> might have existed fifty years before far up the James River but could not have flourished in poverty-racked Southampton.[34]

In an effort to expose the essential structures of oppression that have led to mass rebellions in both periods, Styron had to alter what he considered many less significant truths.

This example brings into sharp focus some of the key differences between biofiction and biography. Given the tacit contract between biographers and readers, altering established facts about the subject's life is unacceptable—readers of a Turner biography would feel violated were the author to say that Turner was raised on a plantation that did not and could not exist in Turner's place and time. But because authors of biofiction are interested in a socioeconomic or psycho-political truth, they feel free to take liberties with the established facts in their effort to represent what they consider something more substantive. This more substantive truth is not temporally restricted to a specific figure or time from the past. Rather, it is consciously and strategically bi-temporal—the structures and conditions in the past obtain in and can therefore be used to explain the present. To signify this, biographical novelists convert their protagonist into a literary symbol. Consequently, instead of exactly representing who and what the biographical subject is, authors of biofiction use the biographical figure in order to picture the subject in such a way that it can simultaneously represent people from other places and times. Within this narrative framework, if altering minor details about the actual biographical subject's life is necessary in order to project the creative writer's more substantive truth, then that is what the author must and will do.

It is this art of transforming the biographical subject into a literary symbol that most distinguishes authors of biographies and biofiction. Biographers seek to represent the life of the subject as accurately as possible, while authors of biofiction use the life of their subject in order to create their own vision of the world. This idea of using a life is of crucial importance, for it shifts the emphasis from biography's sacred art of accurate representation to the creative writer's sacred art of imaginative creation. Artists see in a certain event or life something that has the power to make sense of the world. They then use that event or life to communicate their own vision. Thus, they do not feel bound to the biographer's law of accurate representation.

Given that what they write is more fictional creation than biographical representation, authors of biofiction want their works to be compared and measured in relation to creative works. As Banks says: "my contract with the reader is that *Cloudsplitter* is a novel because it says so on the cover and title page: some of it is drawn from history, some of it is drawn from biography, and a lot of it is made up. Some of it is drawn from my own personal life. But for my purposes, the way it should be read is as a novel, and the books against which it should be measured are novels."[35]

Comparing *Cloudsplitter* to a biography would be a grave mistake because the two genres have radically different methods and objectives, and as such, they are premised on very different truth contracts.

To put the matter very simply, biographical fiction fictionalizes rather than represents the biographical subject.

Anthology contents and choices

This anthology contains a wide variety of writing about bioficiton. The first section consists of authors' reflections on their own works, which is most commonly found in prefaces, afterwords, and authors' notes. Most are simple statements claiming that their work is loosely based on an actual person's life and that the authors have taken some liberties with established facts. Sometimes authors specify the changes they have made and cite the sources they have consulted and used in order to construct their narratives. These statements are extremely useful because they bring some clarity to major discussions about disciplinary constructions of knowledge. For instance, historians were very critical of Styron's *The Confessions of Nat Turner* and Barbara Chase-Riboud's *Sally Hemings*, because the authors presumably made historical errors in their biographical novels, thus discrediting their works, according to the historians. But both Styron and Chase-Riboud knowingly and strategically altered historical facts in order to picture what they considered a more substantial truth. Statements from Styron and Chase-Riboud enable readers to clearly define the tacit contract that the authors established with their readers. Within this framework, we could say the following: it is inappropriate for historians to use the tacit or explicit contract within the field of history to critique and fault biographical novelists for altering established historical facts, just as it would be inappropriate for biographical novelists to critique and fault historians for not converting their historical subjects or events into a literary symbol that could represent a wide variety of people and cases in other places and times. Through this section, readers can get a sense of the variant ways authors think about and understand their work and the tacit contract underwriting it.

However, we should not think of biographical fiction as some sort of Platonic Form. This is a genre of fiction that has evolved, so what it was in the 1930s might be very different from what it is today, which is why I specifically include the section about Eliza Lynch biographical novels. In the foreword to his 1938 novel *Woman on Horseback*, William E. Barrett claims that he has "been faithful to time and place and sequence." Moreover, he states that in no case did he distort "the true chronology of events for dramatic effect."[36] Barrett's approach is very different from the one in Anne Enright's *The Pleasure of Eliza Lynch*, which calls the reader's attention to the fact that her work "is a novel" and therefore "Not True."[37] Lily Tuck makes a similar claim in the "Author's Note" in her biographical novel *The News from Paraguay*. These two authors unapologetically invent characters and events and alter established facts. So who has the right definition of or approach to biofiction? In my estimation, this is an ill-conceived question. Better questions would be these: what are the conditions of knowledge that led authors to think of biofiction in one way during one period of time and another way during another period of time? Or, how has a particular author reimagined or invented an original approach to biofiction?

As should be clear, then, the objective in this anthology is not to lay down an absolute definition of biofiction, but to examine the variant mutations of the literary form and to identify conflicts and contradictions in the way authors and scholars understand and approach it. This is precisely what we see in the Lectures and Forums section. More than any other twentieth-century author, Irving Stone popularized the biographical novel. But as Stone rightly notes in his lecture "The Biographical Novel," most academics had nothing but contempt for the form. But the question is why. Ellison provides a compelling explanation in the forum with Warren and Styron, as I have already discussed. However, by the early twenty-first century, biographical fiction has become so dominant with well-respected authors that it is no longer possible to dismiss it as an inferior, misguided, illegitimate, or irrelevant form. Given the formal acceptance of the aesthetic form (authors of biofiction have now won the Pulitzer Prize in fiction, the National Book Award, the Man Booker Prize, the Pen/Faulkner Award, and many others), it was time to get prominent biographical novelists into substantive debates about the nature and value of biofiction, which is what I tried to accomplish with my roundtable forum ("The Uses of History in the Biographical Novel") with Duffy, Olsen, and Jay Parini.

With regard to biofiction, Alvarez (*In the Time of the Butterflies*), Banks (*Cloudsplitter*), Duffy (*The World as I Found It*), and Oates (*Blonde*) have written spectacular works that bring into sharp focus what this aesthetic form is uniquely capable of doing. It is for this reason that I include a section of interviews with these four novelists. In these conversations, each one of these writers clarifies his or her understanding of biofiction and gives us specific insight into their individual works. But more importantly, these interviews enable us to see if there is a gap between what authors of bioficiton believe they are doing and what scholars of biofiction say they are doing.

The last section consists of scholarly works about biofiction. The first work is from Lukács, who is extremely critical of the form, but who also gives us some useful ways of thinking about it. In a sense, Lukács' *The Historical Novel*, which is a groundbreaking study that had an enormous impact for many decades, led scholars to dismiss biographical fiction as an irredeemable aesthetic form, which partly explains why it took so long for scholars to start writing about biofiction in a positive and insightful way.

Ironically, what led to the rise of biofiction scholarship was the explosion of work done in biography, life writing, and autobiography studies, which is why I include so many works from such scholars. But it is important to note that the work on life writing did not necessarily have the best outcome for biofiction, since these scholars tended to foreground the role of biographical representation rather than fictional creation. Many scholars are still struggling to understand the relationship between biography and biofiction, and students will have to consult and engage a wide variety of texts in order to draw their own conclusions. In my estimation, a lot of work still needs to be done in order to clarify the nature and role of the biographical within biofiction.

One question is of particular importance for contemporary students of biofiction, and it is David Lodge who best articulates it (I would have liked to include Lodge's work in this volume, but his chapter is much too long for such an anthology. However, it is definitely worth reading.). In the year 2004, there were a number of biographical novels about Henry James, including one by Lodge. Lodge wonders why James never appeared in a fictional work as a protagonist under his own name before Emma Tenant's 2002 novel *Felony*, but that in the year 2004, he was the primary subject of Alan Holinghurst's *The Line of Beauty* and the protagonist of Tóibín's *The Master*, Lodge's *Author, Author*, and Michael Heyns' *The Typewriter's Tale* (Heyns' novel was submitted to publishing houses in 2004, but because it was the last in the line of James-inspired novels, it was rejected until 2005). This development is fascinating because Lodge could not imagine writing a novel about an actual historical figure, since his "concept of what constituted a novel ... did not include the possibility of writing one about a real historical person."[38] Lodge, of course, is wrong to suggest that biofiction is a relatively recent aesthetic development. But his question is both relevant and important. What changed within the communal psyche that led so many contemporary writers to author biofiction and so many readers to accept such works? This is one of many questions that still needs to be answered.

In short, there is still much work to be done, because there is still no consensus about the nature of biofiction. It is for this reason that I have strategically included in this anthology sources that are in deep conflict with each other so that students and scholars of biofiction can work through the debates on their own. Thus, what students, scholars, and teachers get in this anthology is not a settled definition of or vocabulary about biofiction. Instead, they get numerous documents, theories, and approaches, which are calculated to inspire further conversation and thinking. And this is a conversation for which there can be no end. Indeed, there can only be conversations that inspire new developments in biofiction or the scholarship. The hope is that this anthology will serve the purpose of growing, expanding, and advancing the aesthetic form as well as the scholarship about it.

Bibliography

Included is a bibliography of biographical novels as well as scholarship about biofiction. But it is important to keep in mind that some works do not qualify as biographical novels or biofiction. For instance, Virginia Woolf's *Flush* and Truman Capote's *In Cold Blood* cannot be technically considered biofiction—*Flush* is a version of the historical novel, while *In Cold Blood* is a version of fictional biography. However, these hybrid works pose unique challenges to our definitions and have contributed to the aesthetic and genre innovations that made contemporary biofiction both possible and popular. The same applies to some scholarly works. Some scholars have confusing and faulty conceptions of biofiction, but because their works anticipate some key intellectual developments in biofiction scholarship, I have included them nonetheless. The goal is to provide students and scholars of biofiction with a resource for clarifying the origin and evolution of this very rich genre of fiction.

Notes

1 Kendall (1967), *The Art of Biography*. New York: The Norton Library: ix.
2 Kendall (1967): 126.
3 Schabert (1990), *In Quest of the Other Person: Fiction as Biography*. Tubingen: Francke Verlag: 1.
4 Latham, "'Serv[ing] under two masters': Virginia Woolf's Afterlives in Contemporary Biofictions." *a/b: Auto/Biography Studies* 27(2) (Winter 2012): 355.
5 Ehrlich (1941), *God's Angry Man*. New York: The Press of the Readers Club: ix.
6 Graves (1962), *Wife to Mr. Milton: The Story of Marie Powell*. New York: The Noonday Press: vii.
7 Garrett (1971), *Death of the Fox*. New York: Doubleday & Company, Inc.: 9.
8 Malouf (1978), *An Imaginary Life*. New York: George Braziller: 153.
9 Kazantzakis (1998), *The Last Temptation of Christ*. Translated by P. A. Bien. New York: Simon & Schuster: 4.
10 Mallon (2001), "The Historical Novelist's Burden of Truth," in *In Fact: Essays on Writers and Writing*. New York: Pantheon Books: 291.
11 Problematic, of course, is Mallon's suggestion that what he writes is historical fiction rather than biographical fiction. However, if we know and use the definition that Lukács establishes, and I think we should, then there is good reason to characterize his work as biographical rather than historical fiction.
12 Banks (1999), "Author's Note," in *Cloudsplitter*. New York: HarperPerennial.
13 Banks (2014), "The Truth Contract in the Biographical Novel," in *Truthful Fictions: Conversations with American Biographical Novelists*. Editor and Interviewer Michael Lackey. London and New York: Bloomsbury: 43–44.

14 Alvarez (2010), *In the Time of the Butterflies*. Chapel Hill: Algonquin Books of Chapel Hill: 324.
15 Ellison (1995), *Invisible Man*. New York: Vintage Books: 3.
16 Ellison, et al., "The Uses of History in Fiction." *Southern Literary Journal* 1(2) (Spring 1969): 74.
17 Ibid.
18 Lukács (1983), *The Historical Novel*. Translated by Hannah and Stanley Mitchell. Lincoln and London: University of Nebraska Press: 35.
19 Lukács (1983): 36.
20 Lukács (1983): 34.
21 Olsen (2006), *Nietzsche's Kisses*. Normal/Tallahassee: FC2: 95.
22 Olsen (2006): 163–64.
23 Qtd. in Walter Kaufmann (1974), *Nietzsche: Philosopher, Psychologist, Antichrist*. Princeton: Princeton University Press: 45.
24 Olsen (2006): 164.
25 Olsen (2006): 179.
26 Olsen (2014), "The Biographical Novel's Practice of Not-Knowing," in *Truthful Fictions: Conversations with American Biographical Novels*. Editor and Interviewer Michael Lackey. New York and London: Bloomsbury: 195–96.
27 Olsen (2006): 207.
28 Lukács (1983): 344.
29 Ibid.
30 Lukács (1983): 314.
31 Banks (2014): 47.
32 Bradbury (2000), *To the Hermitage*. Woodstock, New York: Overlook Press: ix.
33 Styron (1993), "Nat Turner Revisited," in *The Confessions of Nat Turner*. New York: Vintage International: 438.
34 Styron (1993): 442–43.
35 Banks (2014): 50.
36 Barrett (1938), "Foreword," in *Woman on Horseback: The Biography of Francisco Lopez and Eliza Lynch*. New York: Frederick A. Stokes Company: viii.
37 Enright (2003), *The Pleasure of Eliza Lynch*. London: Vintage Books: 231.
38 Lodge (2006): 10–11.

PART ONE

Authors' Reflections

1

Leonard Ehrlich

"Author's Note" from *God's Angry Man* (1932)

This work is a *novel*, not a biography or a history. But this is not to say that it is a flight of "fancy." Throughout, it moves scrupulously within a frame of historical fact. The main lines of the narrative are those of Oswald Garrison Villard's monumental biography (to which an unpayable debt is hereby recorded)—save that herein certain lesser events have been telescoped in the interests of dramatic continuity, and occasional letters are either composites or mosaics of John Brown's most vital and moving utterance. The names of certain minor characters have been slightly altered—first, to avoid confusion where repetitions occur in the nomenclature of the Brown family; second, so that freedom might be gained to work out their destinies more richly. But nowhere has their essential spirit been distorted; the historical originals can be easily discerned. The episodes dealing with Thoreau are written almost entirely in his own words, gathered from his journals and speeches—with the idea of presenting as directly as possible his very thought and emotion. There is little included which he did not actually say and think; and nothing which he might not have said and thought.

L. E.

2

Wallace Stegner

"Foreword" from *Joe Hill: A Biographical Novel* (1950)

No thoroughly adequate history of the IWW exists. The standard histories are factual and doctrinal summaries, valuable for the record of the IWW's organization and activities but stopping short of the real climax of the movement just after World War I, and lacking in the kind of poetic understanding which should invest any history of a militant church.

From 1905 to the early twenties, the IWW was just that—a church which enlisted all the enthusiasm, idealism, rebelliousness, devotion, and selfless zeal of thousands of mainly young, mainly migrant workers. Its history is a chronicle of strikes, free-speech fights, riots, trials, frame-ups, and martyrdoms. It began in the industrial-union notions of Vincent St. John and Big Bill Haywood and the Western Federation of Miners. It was born of union and compromise in a national convention in 1905. It suffered its schisms and its withdrawals, especially when the Socialist Labor Party and the Socialists of De Leon and Debs withdrew in protest against IWW violence. It followed its own star of direct action, One Big Union, and the solidarity of all labor, applying its own industrial weapons of the strike, sabotage, free-speech fights. It won its great victories, as in the Lawrence strike when Joe Ettor and Arturo Giovannitti not only broke down the mill owners to the workers' demands, but won their legal fight against a murder charge in the Salem court. It had its magnetic leaders—St. John, Haywood, Ralph Chaplin, the Magon brothers, Frank Little, Elizabeth Gurley Flynn—and its areas of power, as in the lumberwoods of the Northwest and the harvest circle from Oklahoma to eastern Washington. It had its legendry, its lore, its songs. A singing union, volatile, mobile, "with more guts than good sense," it made itself in its short life the most militant and dramatic organization in the history of American labor.

It represented the very dissidence of dissent, the rebelliousness of rebellion, and it lived an increasingly violent life, battered at by all the power of industry and industry's local law, from 1905 to the series of anti-syndicalism trials that broke its back in the twenties. By the time its back was broken many of its founders and leaders were in jail, and had been since 1918, on charges of resisting the draft. Chaplin, Haywood, the Magons, dozens of others, shared the fate of Eugene Debs in those years. And others of the leaders were dead, like Frank Little, whose crippled lynched body swung from a Butte bridge a long time before anyone cut it down. Still others had drifted into the orbit of the newly formed Communist Party, headed for the sad manipulation and eventual disillusionment that awaited Haywood. Others hung on, and still hang on, belligerent as ever, dissenters to the end of a long resistant life, hating the ballotboxers as dupes, despising yellow socialists for their gradualism, loathing the Communists for the way they have taken over IWW methods and twisted them to perverted uses. The IWW now is an exclusive and somewhat mellowed club, but it can still rise up when it is stepped on, it can still muster pickets before the doors of the *New Republic* when it prints an article by me implying that Joe Hill, one of the great martyrs, could have been guilty. An injury to one is still an injury to all; the union doctrine has not changed by a hair's breadth. But now it is a church of old men.

They were militant in a period when militancy meant floggings, jail, bloodshed. They fought fire with fire, dynamite with dynamite. Police, newspapers, the middle-class citizenry, were all against them. Organizers disappeared, were run out of town, flogged through gauntlets, threatened with death. Towns passed laws against their speaking on street comers, and the word went out so that every loose Wobbly in five hundred miles grabbed the next freight, intent on climbing up on a soapbox long enough to get himself arrested. They jammed the jails, wore out the police, used up the city funds, and they kept on coming till the authorities buckled or they themselves were overwhelmed. And sometimes, as at Everett, they were mowed down by the guns of special deputies. Sometimes, as at Centralia, they were rushed by Armistice Day paraders, and out of that riot came another martyr, Wesley Everest, beaten and castrated and lynched and pumped full of bullets.

The IWW was a fighting faith. Its members were the shock troops of labor. Its weakness was that it really liked a fight better than it liked planning, negotiations, politicking. It won victories and attracted thousands of new members and let them drift away again for lack of a concrete program. Its ideas were vaguely the anarcho-syndicalist ideas that had stirred France a little earlier; its methods and shibboleths, even the "wooden shoe" symbol of sabotage, were the same. Its membership was an utterly American mixture, with a good percentage of the foreign-born because the foreign-born were often the most migrant, the most economically adrift, and also the most politically awakened. But in the best American tradition, it took its orders from no one, was ripped by internal quarrels of policy, and fought the battles that were most immediate and most concrete.

It was conflict of the bloodiest kind that kept the IWW together. It existed for the prime purpose of making the first breaches in the resistance of entrenched industry so that later organizations could widen and deepen them. Its greatest single contribution was the production of martyrs.

The Preacher and the Slave is in no sense a history of the IWW, even by implication. It is not history, though it deals here and there with historical episodes and sometimes incorporates historical documents; and it is not biography, though it deals with a life. It is fiction, with fiction's prerogatives and none of history's limiting obligations. I hope and believe it is after a kind of truth, but a different kind from that which historians follow.

For turning sometimes-historical people and sometimes-historical events to the purposes of fiction I have two justifications. One is that all fiction is made this way and cannot draw upon any other material than actual material. The other is that fact and fiction bad already become so entangled around the controversial figure of Joe Hill that it seemed permissible to leave him as tangled as I found him. Innocent or guilty, he was already legend, thanks to his own flair for self-dramatization and to the campaign that built him into a martyr. Murderer or martyr, he was certain to resist absolute definition. So I contented myself with trying to make him a man, such a man as he might have been, with his legend at his feet like a lengthening shadow.

The people who have contributed to my knowledge of both the legend and the facts are many, and I thank them all. But they are surely not in any way responsible for the interpretation I have given to IWW history, the events that led to Joe Hill's death, or the ambiguous personality of Joe Hill himself. Joe Hill as he appears here—let me repeat it—is an act of the imagination.

3

S. Guy Endore

"A Final Word" from *King of Paris* (1956)

What shall we call this book anyhow? Novel? Biography? Is there any truth to it whatsoever? And if so, how much?

The answer is that it is exceedingly true. For it is a work of fiction not only solidly based on research, but going beyond research.

To illustrate, take one of the very minor episodes concerning Dumas' love for medals. The painter Paul Huet did actually, according to the records, come upon Dumas standing guard duty in a uniform so dazzling with medals that Huet felt impelled to spin the man around to see if perhaps he did not have some extra medals hung on his backside.

And there our recorded story stops.

But this is outrageous! A landscape painter such as Paul Huet may consider that a good story, but not a writer. It just isn't funny enough. One feels hung up in mid-air. One wants to know if Dumas really did have medals pinned to his rear end. And if so, how did he explain it? Dumas was of course quite capable of hanging medals on the seat of his pants, but he would certainly never let himself be caught without an appropriate explanation. Very likely some simple, convincing and at the same time touching remark such as I lend him—namely that the medals on his backside came from kings who had since lost their thrones.

Now the anecdote is complete.

Was it wrong of me to have corrected this little story? With a man like Dumas, of whom so many delightful stories have come down to us, surely it is a harmless assumption that many more stories, and perhaps better ones, would have survived had his friends been more diligent in collecting and recording them. No doubt it cannot be given to every man to have his Boswell, but are we to hold that against Dumas when it is obviously not his fault but the fault of his friends?

Occasionally Dumas himself cannot be trusted to do his own anecdotes, even when acting as his own Boswell. As for example in the bear-steak story. There he omits so obvious a curtain line that I have felt compelled to supply it: I refer to the line in which he tells the innkeeper that he will do for the widow of the man eaten by the bear more than merely give her some money; he will give her back her husband.

Was it wrong for me to have corrected Dumas' oversight in this matter? And if so, may I know, please, whom I am wronging?

Dare we show ourselves less generous toward Dumas than Dumas showed himself toward his historical characters in his own books? Surely not. And thus if at times throughout my book I have done a little touching up of the tales of Dumas' cookery, his uniforms, his remarks about women or about writing, and so forth, consider it as nothing more than writers have been doing since the dawn of literature, gradually boosting some anecdotes from India into the tales of Boccaccio and from there into Shakespeare's plays, and, who knows, someday perhaps beyond that.

All this, so far, has concerned itself only with the passementerie of my book.

More serious are my inventions of conversations that never took place. For example the conversations between Dumas and Véron, between Dumas and his business manager, between Dumas and Viel-Castel, Dumas and William Wells Brown, etc. But note that in each instance these are conversations that should have taken place! Take the case of William Wells Brown, that free Negro from America who tried so hard to have a conversation with Dumas. And then there he was one evening in the same theater with Dumas. He in the orchestra, Dumas in a box.

What did Brown do?

He did nothing.

But how criminal of this colored man from America to have come thirty hundred miles, and then to have failed to take just thirty more steps to talk to the most famous colored man in the world. And apparently all because of mere pique: because Dumas had failed to answer his letters! It's obvious that Brown had jumped to the conclusion that Dumas was ashamed of his Negro blood. What Brown probably didn't know was that Dumas was constantly being subjected to practical jokes about his Negro ancestry. For example, when Barnum's circus came to Paris some wag hired the entire Negro troupe to burst in on Dumas at his apartment, crying, "Cousin, we are here!" and dumping their baggage on the floor, prepared for a long stay. Naturally Dumas had become wary.

Thus it was left me to supply a conversation that should have taken place but didn't. Lies? Well, yes. But the question is not whether I lied, but whether the conversation, had it taken place, would not have been pretty much as I give it. Fact is that my conversation goes beyond a real conversation, since actual recorded conversations, even between men of genius, often fail to touch upon essential points, due to accident, lack of time, embarrassment, tiredness, who knows what. While imaginary conversations are able to go at once to the point.

Dumas' contemporaries are unanimous in calling him a brilliant conversationalist. Shall we fly in the face of these authorities simply because we fail to find certain conversations recorded, and others recorded but lacking somewhat in brilliance?

You see, the more one studies the Dumas material, the more one is forced to the conclusion that research alone will never do justice to the man. Personally, in my reading of Dumas biographies, I always seemed to hear deep subterranean groans, as if Dumas were there in the cellar, struggling against the shackles of research.

And yet it was not without some trepidation that I dared follow the lead of Goethe and combine truth and invention, Dichtung und Wahrheit, for the sake of a closer approach to reality. After some groping around I found my way to a novel that would rely on research without being bound by it. And I hit at last on a novel written in the form of research, as other novels have been written in the form of letters, or extracts from diaries, and so forth.

For this I had some justification in Dumas' own statement to the historian Michelet: "Admit, my dear Michelet, that historians are better the more their works read like novels, while novels are better the more they read like history."

And for my motto I adopted the Italian expression Se non è vero, è ben trovato; roughly: If it isn't the exact truth, it's at least a valid lie. My goal, you see, being a book in which the lie would be indistinguishable from the truth.

This proved indeed the only solution of the problem of writing Dumas' life. For note that if one were to stick to research and nothing but research, then it would be impossible to write five full pages about Dumas' duels, and much of that would be mere speculation. Such episodes as the saliva duel at two paces, the dinner discussion of duels and epigrams, the story of the thirteenth duel—all that has for its actual historical support only this one small incident: Dumas fils, smarting from the insults flung at his father by De Mirecourt, had his seconds go to the journalist's apartment to arrange for a duel. But the door was opened by De Mirecourt himself, carrying in his arms his two-year-old boy and saying, "If Dumas sends his son to fight for him, then here, I offer you my son, who will fight for me."

That ended that. And no encounter ever took place.

Obviously this is not much of a scene properly to illustrate the immense devotion and love that, in those early days, young Dumas had for his papa. And this climax, a mere line of dialogue, is neither sufficiently startling nor sufficiently bitter to give the reader a sense of the tragic rebuff that it must have occasioned Alexandre. The affair cries for more light and shadow. The metal of truth wants bumping up here to a higher and sharper relief.

Nor was any great amount of invention required to achieve this. Only that De Mirecourt should delay his pronouncement regarding his son fighting for him until the appearance of the principals on the dueling grounds. Then only one thing more was needed to produce the grotesque performance that convulsed Paris: the age of De Mirecourt's son had to be raised from two to eight. And the little scamp had somehow to be supplied with a real sword.

However small, these are no doubt serious deviations from the truth, especially when they are allowed to expand into the scenes they evoke. But the question is: in what direction do they deviate? Is it in the direction of more truth? Or less truth?

Perhaps this question lets itself be examined best in connection with the scene in which Delacroix makes a masterpiece of an omelet in a frying pan. Here we have not one iota of truth on which to base ourselves. Nothing but research. And from that research we know first of all that such cooking sprees were a feature of Dumas' life, and, in the second place, that Delacroix was often present. Now, if you will look into Delacroix' diary, you will discover that Dumas plays an important role in Delacroix' private emotional life, because the painter both envied him for his enormous popularity and scorned him for his cheapness.

To have limited myself to the truth as it is given to us in the records would have prevented me from bringing these two great personalities to grips in my book, and their strange friendship and antagonism would have had to remain something in the shadows, unlived, without benefit of climax, a matter of a few words scattered here and there in Delacroix' private journal.

Ask yourself which brings these men more to life—the strict truth, or the invention based on that truth?

This same question of whether the lie tends in the direction of more truth or less truth comes up particularly strongly in the romance between Dumas and his first Parisian mistress, Catherine Lebay, where the absence of information is nothing less than shameful. Only eight words and a few sentences to cover everything: the romance, Catherine's pregnancy, the birth and registration of the child, the various events of a boy's schooling and growing up to manhood.

Who will say that those eight words from Dumas' Memoirs, those few sentences from a letter by Dumas fils, are closer to the truth than the expansion that I have given them out of my imagination?

One would of course have no excuse for adding a word to the existing records if human beings were not so obstinately determined to conceal the truth about themselves. Even writers, who do not shrink from exposing the characters of their stories to the public gaze in their most intimate moments, insist on preserving for themselves large areas of mystery. Why this happens to be so is not for discussion at this point, but its prevalence is such that today there exists a whole branch of medicine that bases itself on the theory that the only truly honest and trustworthy fiber left in man has taken refuge in his dreams, where it is almost beyond his will power to destroy it.

Thus, in order to restore to Dumas' life the truths that belong to it, one is called upon to supply material that is not to be found in any research however thorough.

And something more.

For there is often a vast amount of documentary material that by its sheer quantity tends to distort a man's life especially where other facets of his life have left little or no record.

An outstanding example is the question of Dumas' plagiarisms. Here one can easily be snowed under. Nothing is more certain than that Dumas was hauled into court again and again on charges of literary fraud and was repeatedly forced to pay damages and make good in other ways. And in addition to the attacks on him during his lifetime, only recently there have been renewed investigations, for example, of his books on Spain, where a student was able to demonstrate with parallel columns how ideas, sentences, even whole paragraphs had been copied from previous travel books.

And then there is Quérard. In my novel I have had the nerve to dismiss Quérard out of hand. Can that be justified on any grounds?

Quérard was that indefatigable book salesman turned bibliographer who in the first half of the nineteenth century, in the course of amassing his huge lists of French books, ran across so many cases of deceit, so many instances of fraudulence and plagiarism, that he eventually devoted a separate five-volume work to this subject all by itself.

Seemingly nothing could escape the microscopic eye of this dry, mousy man with the sour and furtive air. And Dumas—yes, our good friend Dumas—rates the biggest entry of all in Quérard's Supercheries littéraires devoilées, his Literary Frauds Unveiled. Quérard sets aside for Dumas not less than 150 closely printed columns! So enormous is this listing of Dumas plagiarisms and Dumas deceits that Quérard felt it necessary to furnish this colossal article with its own private index so that the reader might find his way around in it.

Quérard is no cheap scandalmongering journalist such as Eugène de Mirecourt. He's no ambitious political charlatan like Granier de Cassagnac, a man determined to make a big name for himself no matter over whose dead body. You cannot brush aside his work as you can the short sketch by Loménie, who pictures our hero sitting at his desk turning over with his left hand the printed pages of a published work as fast as his right hand can copy out another original Dumas story, handwritten and ready now for the printer.

No, Quérard is one of France's great bibliographers, whose works are in every major research library of the world.

So when it comes to the facts about Dumas' literary frauds, there you have them. Written out in detail by a famous scholar who lived in Dumas' day and whom Dumas never dared sue. There are the facts. But for me they don't count. They don't add up. I wipe out all those 150 columns, just like that. And for this reason: from Quérard you will learn that one of the ghost writers most frequently deprived of his rightful author's credit by Dumas was his old boyhood friend Adolphe de Leuven (son of the Swedish regicide), whose plays Dumas put on the stage time and time again under his own name, eventually including them in his twenty volumes of collected plays with no acknowledgment to their true author.

But what Quérard couldn't possibly know was this: that when Adolphe de Leuven would die at the ripe age of over ninety, surviving both Quérard and Dumas by many years, he would leave his considerable estate, including a house and grounds . . . well, to whom do you suppose? Why, to the son of the very man who, according to Quérard, had so vilely misused and defrauded him.

Yes, he made Dumas fils his heir!

Now-ask yourself what truth about Dumas there really is in all the 150 columns of Quérard? Facts, yes. Plenty of facts. But truth? Obviously not a shred of it.

Oh, to be sure, one wants and needs facts. All the facts one can get. And compilations of facts are very valuable. But at the same time one must never forget that all the facts about any person will never add up to the living man or woman. That is why the living Dumas somehow never leaps out of the pages of his biographers in the same way as Dumas' own creations leap out of his pages. Which is no reflection on Dumas' biographers, for he has had several excellent ones.

It is rather because when an author has absorbed all the available facts on the subject he is going to write about, he is still nothing but a supersaturated solution. And everyone knows that nothing can crystallize out of such a solution unless some foreign matter manages to get into it. For a snowflake to grow, more is required than the existence of water vapor and freezing temperatures in the upper atmosphere. Each and every snowflake requires a grain of dust or some other impurity around which to develop.

This foreign matter, this impurity—call it a lie, call it imagination, or truth beyond research—call it whatever you prefer, but without it all the research in the world will never produce anything. It must always remain sterile.

Now to come to the heart of my book: the father-son duel during the masquerade party. We will have to admit at once that there is absolutely nothing in the records even remotely suggesting such a father-son combat. And yet, once one has accepted the theme of dueling as eminently befitting a tale on Dumas (and I don't see how this could be avoided), then the eventual father-son explosion is in the cards.

In the records all we have is this one isolated fact—a fact, however, that like the fact of Adolphe de Leuven's will speaks volumes: one day Dumas fils found himself, knife in hand, about to enter a room where his father lay asleep. Dumas fils afterward pleaded illness and exhaustion as the cause of a temporary aberration of his mind.

But was this really no more than a temporary aberration of the mind? Was it not more likely a bit of that really honest and trustworthy fiber of man revealing itself in this walking nightmare?

We know that between these two men there existed not only a deep bond of affection but also certain hidden feelings, such that for years on end they never saw each other except at funerals.

How intolerable, then, to an author who wishes to portray the real Dumas that this powerful mixture of emotions existing between father and son should have found expression in nothing more overt than this little knife incident, a lapse so slight that it isn't worth more than a sentence or two in any Dumas biography.

Here are two men in whose novels and plays there are uncounted duels. Two men therefore whose imaginations ran riot in gunplay and swordplay. Is it fair that history should forever deny such men the one big encounter of their lives?

We know from any number of witnesses that Dumas really lived his stories to the hilt, played them out so intensely that he would sit up all night at his little deal table, busily moving his pen and all the while keeping up a constant shouting, groaning, weeping, laughing. At such moments he was not merely Dumas; he was also Ange Pitou storming the Bastille, he was the Queen Mother slinking through the corridors of the Louvre, he was the Iron Mask staring through the barred window of his prison, he was Cagliostro scheming up the affair of the diamond necklace, he was the future Count of Monte Cristo letting himself be buried alive in order to escape from the dungeons of the Château d'If.

Surely a man deserves as much as he gives. How can the hero of your book be the real Dumas if you yourself will not feel like shouting, groaning, weeping, laughing while you write about him? That this father-son rivalry should have eventually dissipated itself in other ways than one grand piece of swordplay is just one of those accidents of life whereby many a potentially heroic man never finds the opportunity of demonstrating his real size.

Thus the crucial importance for me of Dumas' criticism of Jean-Léon Gérôme's painting "Le duel à la sortie du bal masqué." This criticism is not out of my imagination. True, he did not make it before a crowd at the Salon, but he did write and publish it, and you will find an excerpt from it in Larousse's Grand Dictionnaire Universel du XIXème siècle, in the D volume under the title of the painting.

All other art critics of Paris—Saint-Victor, Gautier, Pesquindoux, Delescluze—had nothing but paeans of praise for Gérôme's canvas. Only one critic, Dumas, took it upon himself to lecture Gérôme on what is reality in a duel and what is not reality. Could one ask for better proof of the fact that Dumas was eaten with scorn and envy, to see this painter get away with so obvious a fake duel, while he could not make the sophisticates of his day believe in his real ones?

Here is part of what he says: "The conception of the scene in Gérôme's painting is dramatic. But not so the result. And the failure stems from this one factor: the artist did not concern himself sufficiently with the problem of the real and the false.

"In brief: it is absolutely unbelievable that anyone could leave a masquerade party to go out into the snow to fight a duel and not in some way mar his fancy dress costume. And no matter how you may imagine this quarrel to have arisen, no matter how anxious the principals may have been to effect an immediate and bloody settlement, even to the point of denying themselves time to go home and change clothes, still the scene remains incredible because merely to leave the hall the combatants would have to pass the cloakroom and they could not have failed, in midwinter, to redeem their overcoats. And even had their headlong thirst for the clash of steel prevented them from stopping for a moment at the cloakroom, they still would have found time to divest themselves at least of wigs and ribands, tear off some of the hampering cloth, if only to feel freer to kill.

"But here we see nothing of the sort. The artist is determined that his Pierrot and his Harlequin shall appear on the field of honor as flawlessly attired as if they were about to go into their dance on the stage of the Paris Opéra. Now do not accuse me of being a stickler for inconsequential details. I say this is basic to the declared purpose of the artist. And I say furthermore that precisely the effect he hopes to achieve is nullified by the complete absence of anything that might call to mind the life of our day and the usual dress of our times.

"In fine, standing before this painting I do not feel myself the spectator at a tragedy, but rather in the theatre at the final tableau of a pantomime. Oh, a well-staged pantomime to be sure. Pierrot handles his role with talented mendacity. No one could possibly play dead any deader. I applaud enthusiastically. Really I am thrilled—but you don't catch me shuddering. For I can see with my two eyes that this Pierrot has only been stabbed with a trick sword. And that the stain of blood on his white doublet was done by himself with a sponge previously soaked in red paint. Not for a moment do I doubt that when the curtain has dropped for the final time, our Pierrot will leap to his feet, rush to his dressing room for a quick change and then home and to bed. Bravo Pierrot!"

Is not this the sarcastic cry of a man who had to suffer under the suspicion of faking his duels? And just as Adolphe de Leuven's testament opened my eyes to all the gossip and even the facts about Dumas' literary frauds, so this bit of art criticism opened my eyes on the subject of Dumas' supposedly staged duels.

And rightly, or wrongly, around this impurity my snowflake grew.

Whether I have done a good job of growing my snowflake, that is another matter. Time will tell whether the lie I have constructed is just an ordinary lie, or whether it is one of those special lies that are truer than the truth. Because there are such lies. For instance, the ostrich who hides his head in the sand is a lie, for no such ostrich exists. And yet that non-existent ostrich is just about the only one we talk about, and it has more reality for us than the ostrich who still goes on providing man with those useless and unfashionable plumes.

If my Dumas should eventually become the real Dumas in the minds of people, dimming or even blotting out the Dumas of the facts, just as Edmond Rostand's Cyrano de Bergerac has blotted out the real Cyrano, or for that matter just as Dumas' own d'Artagnan has blotted out the real d'Artagnan (who was Cyrano's contemporary), then that will be the proof that the lie can sometimes be truer than the truth.

Guy Endore

4

William Styron

"Nat Turner Revisited" from *American Heritage* (1992)

Twenty-five years ago this November, I found myself in Ohio, where I was being awarded an honorary degree at Wilberforce University. The university, one of the few all-Negro institutions in the North, was named after William Wilberforce, the great British abolitionist of slavery, and so I marked the special appropriateness of this honor when I accepted the invitation a few weeks earlier. My novel *The Confessions of Nat Turner*, based on the Virginia slave revolt of 1831, had been published early in October to generally glowing reviews, had received a vast amount of publicity, and had quickly ascended to the top of the best-seller lists, where it would remain for many weeks. Only the most disingenuous of writers would, I think, fail to confess being pleased by such a reception.

I was also gratified to have the blessing of both the Book-of-the-Month Club and *The New York Review of Books*. There was a lavish movie contract from Twentieth Century-Fox and an admiring review in the *New Republic* from one of America's pre-eminent historians. I am stressing these outward signs of success only to point up the reversal of fortune the book would soon undergo. Like any writer who is honest with himself, I knew that *Nat Turner* had defects and vulnerabilities—Faulkner remarked that we novelists will be remembered for "the splendor of our failures"—but that it was hard not to feel a certain fulfillment that fall, more than five years after having sat down at my desk on Martha's Vineyard, determined to re-create, out of an extremely sketchy and mysterious historical record, the life of a man who led the only significant slave revolt in our history, and to try to fashion in the process an imagined microcosm of the baleful institution whose legacy has persisted in this century and become the nation's central obsession. In 1962, when I began writing the book, the civil rights movement still had the quality of conciliation; Martin Luther King, Jr.'s grand and impossible dream was dreamed in a spirit of amity, concord, and the hope of a mutual understanding. The following years demonstrated the harsher truths: Birmingham, the bombings, Selma, the death of Medgar Evers, the three youthful martyrs of that Mississippi summer, churches set on fire, unbounded terror. James Baldwin, who was a friend of mine and who had made notes for his great essay *The Fire Next Time* while living in my house, had seen his prophecy come to pass in the smoke and flames of Watts and of Newark and Detroit. I've often been surprised, reflecting on this time, at the naiveté or perhaps blindness that prevented my perceiving in that tumult a suggestion of the backlash that awaited *Nat Turner*.

But on the campus of Wilberforce University there was no hint of the gathering storm. The angry word had not yet gone out. In a sea of smiling black and brown people, I was greeted with good will, thanks, praise. During lunch the university's president publicly expressed his appreciation for my story, for the way I had illuminated some of slavery's darker corners. At the convocation ceremony I made a brief talk in which I expressed the hope that an increased awareness of the history of the Negro (I used this word, which, though moribund and about to be replaced within months by black, was still acceptable), especially of Negro slavery, would allow people of both races to come to terms with the often inexplicable turmoil of the present.

There was much applause. George Shirley, a Wilberforce alumnus who was a leading tenor with the Metropolitan Opera, gave a spine-chilling rendition of "The Battle Hymn of the Republic," in which the audience joined together, singing with great emotion. Standing in that auditorium, I was moved by a feeling of oneness with these people. I felt gratitude at their acceptance of me and, somehow more important, at my acceptance of them, as if m literary labors and my plunge into history had helped dissolve many of my pre-conceptions about race that had been my birthright as a Southerner and allowed me to better understand the forces that had shaped our common destiny. For me it was a moment of intense warmth and brotherhood. It would have been inconceivable to me that within a short time I would experience almost total alienation from black people, be stung by their rage, and finally be cast as an archenemy of the race, having unwittingly created one of the first politically incorrect texts of our time.

The story of Nat Turner had been long gestating in my mind, ever since I was a boy, in fact, since before I actually knew I wanted to be a writer. I could scarcely remember a time when I was not haunted by the idea of slavery or was not profoundly conscious of the strange bifurcated world of whiteness and blackness in which I was born and reared. In the Virginia Tidewater region of my beginnings, heavily populated by blacks, society remained firmly in the grip of the Jim Crow laws and their ordinance of a separate and thoroughly unequal way of life. The evidence was blatant and embarrassing even to some white children, like myself, who were presumably brought up to be indifferent to such inequities as the ramshackle black school that stood on the route we traveled to our own up-to-date and well-equipped edifice, with its swank state-of-the-art public-address system, very advanced for the late 1930s. Many black schools in Virginia at that time had outside privies.

Despite our own fine local facilities, Virginia-in the era of the hidebound Harry Byrd political machine-ranked in public education among the lowest of the states, down there with Arkansas and Mississippi, and the quality of instruction in the black schools had to be even worse than what we white students were given, which (except for a few individually outstanding teachers) was desperately mediocre. I was painfully sensitive to this disparity, just as I was conscious of the utter strangeness of this whole segregated world: the water fountains and rest rooms marked "White" and "Colored," the buses in which black folk were required to sit in the rear, the theaters with blacks seated in the balconies (in the larger towns there were actually separate theaters); even the ferryboats crossing the rivers and bays enforced a nautical apartheid, with whites starboard and Negroes portside. I was perpetually bemused by this division and the ensuing isolation.

It was a system both ludicrous and dreadful, and I sensed its wrongness early, probably because of my parents, who, while hardly radical, were enlightened in racial matters, but also out of some innate sense of moral indignation. Although of course I was an outsider, I fell under the spell of *négritude*, fascinated by black people and their folkways, their labor and religion, and especially their music, their raunchy blues and ragtime and their spirituals that reached for, and often attained, the sublime. Like some young boys who are troubled by their "unnatural" sexual longings, I felt a similar anxiety about my secret passion for blackness; in my closet I was fearful lest any of my conventionally racist young friends discover that I was an unabashed enthusiast of the despised Negro. I don't claim a special innocence. Most white people were, and are, racist to some degree, but at least my racism was not conventional; I wanted to confront and understand blackness.

Then there was the incomparable example of my grandmother. In a direct linkage I still sometimes find remarkable, I am able to say that I remain separated from slavery by only two generations and that I was related to and was familiar with and spoke to someone who owned slaves. Born in 1850 on an eastern North Carolina plantation, my father's mother was the proprietress of two slave girls who were her age, twelve or thereabouts, at the time of the Emancipation Proclamation. Many years later, when she was an old lady in her eighties and I was eleven or twelve, she told me at great length of her love for these children and of the horror and loss she felt when that same year, 1862, Union forces from an Ohio regiment under General Burnside swept down on the plantation, stripped the place bare, and left everyone to starve, including the little slave girls, who later disappeared. It was a story I heard more than once, since I avidly prompted her to repeat it and she, indulging her own fondness for its melodrama, told it again with relish, describing her hatred for the Yankees (which remained undiminished in 1937), the real pain of her starvation (she said they were reduced to eating "roots and rats"), and her anguish when she was separated forever from those little black girls, who were called, incidentally, Drusilla and Lucinda, just as in so many antebellum plantation novels. All of the deliciously described particulars of my grandmother's chronicle held me spellbound, but I think that nothing so awed me as the fact that this frail and garrulous woman whom I beheld, and who was my own flesh and blood, had been the legal owner of two other human beings. It may have determined, more than anything else, some as-yet-to-be-born resolve to write about slavery.

Nat Turner entered my consciousness through brief references to his revolt in my text on Virginia history. But most memorably he appeared in the form of a historical highway marker adjoining a peanut field in Southampton County, where I traveled with our high school football team in the fall. This was a remote, down-and-out farm region, whose population was 60 percent black. I was transfixed by the information conveyed by that marker, paraphrased thus: *Nearby, in August of 1831, a fanatical slave named Nat Turner led a bloody insurrection that caused the death of fifty-five white people. Captured after two months in hiding, Nat was brought to trial in the county seat of Jerusalem (now Courtland) and he and seventeen of his followers were hanged.* I recall how this sign set off in my mind extraordinary resonances, which were clearly in conflict with my grandmother's story: What was the connection, if any, between her loving memories and this cryptic notation of terror and mayhem? Perhaps more important, I remember wondering whether that bygone moment of sudden disaster didn't reflect something sinister in the divided white and black world in which I lived, so outwardly peaceable yet, except to the blind, troubled and jumpy with signs of resentment, sullenness, covert hostility and anger. The Virginia of my boyhood, like virtually all the South, was a place where the amiable, if often edgy, relations between the races rose from an impulse that was mutually self-protective, keeping in abeyance much white fear and much black rage.

Daily life produced an unstated precariousness. There were strong, even passionate bonds of affection between individuals, black and white, but the social arrangement was a different matter; in the vast rural areas a form of pseudoslavery prevailed, and the white man's whim was law. Urban existence, not much better, gave rise to ghettos where crimes by black against blacks went ignored and unrecorded. At its worst, the South was filled with intimidation and brutality on a terrifying scale; in the Deep South lynchings were still more than occasional. At its best, kindheartedness and decency, along with genuine love spontaneously reciprocated, were the rule, but even so, the South suffered, in its Jim Crow shackles, from the sickness of alienation. It was a bizarre, culturally schizoid world with falsity at its core, not to speak of a glaring inhumanity. I'm sure that my early fascination with Nat Turner came from pondering the parallels between his time and my own society, whose genteel accommodations and endemic cruelties, large and small, were not really so different from the days of slavery. I think I must have wondered whether this tautly strained calmness might not someday be just as susceptible to violent retribution.

I wrote several works of fiction before I finally tackled *Nat Turner*. Then in the early 1960s I decided that the time was ripe; certainly I was never anything but intensely aware of the way in which the theme of slave rebellion was finding echoes in the gathering tensions of the civil rights movement. Although it didn't dawn on me at the time, I later realized that one of the benefits for me in Nat Turner's story was not an abundance of historical material but, if anything, a scantiness. This was a drama that took place in a faraway backwater when information gathering was primitive. While it may be satisfying and advantageous for historians to feast on rich archival material, the writer of historical fiction is better off when past events have left him with short rations. A good example might be the abolitionist John Brown, who made his prodigious mark on history only thirty years after Nat Turner but whose every word and move were recorded by enterprising journalists, producing documents enough to fill a boxcar.

The novelist attempting John Brown's story is in conflict with the myriad known details of the chronicle, and his imagination cannot simply run off in a certain direction—which is what fiction writers need their imaginations to do—because he is fettered by already established circumstances. He is in danger of being overwhelmed by an avalanche of data. That is why the writing of novels about plentifully documented figures—Lincoln, say, or John F. Kennedy—is a risky matter, constricting for the writer himself who, while quite free to take liberties with the known facts (the shopworn but sound concept of artistic license), must still take care not to violate the larger historical record. (Although even here the convention has often been broken; history has taught us, for example, that Richard III was not an unmitigated villain, nor a hunchback, but only pedants carp at Shakespeare's nasty portrayal.)

The single meaningful document having to do with the Turner revolt was a short (seven-thousand-word) transcript that gave the title to my own work. The original *Confessions of Nat Turner*, which comprised both Nat's account of his upbringing and a description of the events leading up to the revolt, as well as the details of the revolt itself, was put in writing by a court-appointed lawyer named Thomas R. Gray, who took down the words from

Nat's lips as he sat chained in his jail cell during the October days before his execution. From the first word this discourse poses serious questions of veracity. At a time when justice for slaves was at best a sham, and in the aftermath of a sensational trial where the state's absolute authority must have prevailed, how reliable or authentic was anything Nat said, when filtered through the mind of this minion of the state? Still, despite this problem, the bulk of the document appeared genuine—Nat himself had nothing to lose at this point by telling the truth, and while some of Gray's interpretation is doubtless suspect, he had little to gain by substantially altering Nat's statement—and n Pond. So I was generally disposed to use it as a guideline, a *loose* guideline, for my own narrative.

Aside from Nat's own *Confessions* and a number of contemporary newspaper articles, most of which added little to Gray's account (except to emphasize the immediately devastating psychological effect the event had on Southern society), there was virtually no material of that period that was useful in shedding further light on Nat Turner as a person or on the uprising. Such a near-vacuum, as I say, seemed to me to be an advantage, placing me in the ideal position of knowing neither too much nor too little. A bad historical novel often leaves the impression of a hopelessly overfurnished house, cluttered with facts the author wishes to show off as fruits of his diligent research. Georg Lukacs, the Hungarian Marxist critic whose monumental *The Historical Novel* should be read by all who attempt to write in the genre, views the disregard of facts as a state of grace; the creator of historical fiction, he argues convincingly, should have a thorough-perhaps even magisterial-command of the period with which he is dealing, but he should not permit his work to be governed by particular historical facts. Rather, his concern "is to reproduce the much more complex and ramifying totality with historical faithfulness." At the time of writing *Nat Turner*, I felt that as an amateur historian I had absorbed a vast amount of reading on slavery in general, not only by way of a great number of antebellum books and essays but through much recent scholarship in the exploding field of the historiography of the slave period; thus, while my command may scarcely have been magisterial, I felt I reasonably fulfilled the first of Lukacs's conditions. It was perhaps serendipitous that Lukacs's other condition, regarding the relative unimportance of facts, made my task easier since I had chosen a man about whom so little was known.

Yet the facts can never be simply ignored, and the principal item I had to deal with, and freely reject, was that which involved the character of Nat Turner himself. The fact: He was a person of conspicuous ghastliness. I eventually read the original *Confessions* countless times, trying to pick up useful clues about the man and his background, but early on I was struck by the impression that our hero was a madman. A singularly gifted and intelligent madman, but mad nonetheless. No attempts on my part of sympathetic reinterpretation could alter this conclusion: his apocalyptic and deranged visions, his heavenly signs and signals, his belief in his own divinely ordained retributive mission, his obsessive fasting and prayer, his bloodthirsty megalomania and self-identification with the Deity (to a provocative question about himself by Gray, he replied, "Was not Christ crucified") there was no shaking the fact that on the record Nat Turner was a dangerous religious lunatic. I didn't want to write about a psychopathic monster. While the institution of slavery was so horrible that it could readily produce psychopathology, and often did, I wished to demonstrate subtler motives, springing from social and behavioral roots, that could drive a young man of thirty-one to embark on his fearsome errand of revenge. So, without sacrificing the essence of Old Testament vengeance that plainly animated Nat, I attempted to moderate this aspect of his character and in doing so give him dimensions of humanity that were almost totally absent in the documentary evidence. When stern piety replaced demonic fanaticism, the man could be better understood.

I took an enormous liberty with historical actuality when I began to deal with Nat's childhood and upbringing. I placed the boy in a milieu where he could not possibly have belonged. During the course of Nat's brief life, Southampton County, where he was born and reared, had already suffered the impoverishment that had come to Virginia long before as the result of the overcultivation of tobacco and other crops, leaving a surplus of slaves who were constantly in danger of being sold off to the thriving plantations of Alabama and Mississippi—the "Far South." Virginia's Southside, as the region below the James River is known, was in those days dotted with small farms and modest holdings, patches of cotton and corn for home use (peanuts had yet to come into their own), apples grown for cider and brandy, pigs in their wallows or rooting in the wild. This bore no resemblance to the romantic view of Old Dixie. The average farmer owned one or two deprived slaves. It was a forlorn, down-at-the-heel section of the Tidewater, where there never existed the celebrated plantations that gave the South its sheen and legendary glamour.

But I felt I had to create a plantation anyway. The plantation was an integral and characteristic part of Southern life in slave times; it was the very metaphor for the capitalist exploitation of human labor, and the plantation owners often represented the best and worst of those whom history had cast as masters in the peculiar institution, carrying within themselves all the moral frights and tensions that slavery engendered. I needed to dramatize this turmoil, and so I contrived to have Nat Turner grow up on a prosperous plantation that might have existed fifty years before far up the James River but that could not have flourished in poverty-racked Southampton. In this way I was able to expose young Nat Turner (from whose point of view the story is told) to the intellectual tug-of-war between the two Turner brothers, owners of the plantation and men diametrically opposed in their views on the morality of slavery. Such a strategy, while disdainful of the facts, enabled me to demonstrate certain critical philosophical attitudes I couldn't have done otherwise, except didactically, yet still allowed me to remain, in the larger sense, historically faithful.

Two of the most carefully pondered decisions I made regarding Nat's fictional character were ones that later provoked the greatest outrage from many of those people who became bitter enemies of the book. As is the case with disputes involving so many heroes, contemporary or departed, the bone to pick here was over the matter of sex. Why, came the bitter demand, hadn't I linked Nat with a black woman? First, in the process of using the *Confessions* as a rough guide, I was struck by the fact that Nat referred to his relationship with quite a few people-grandmother, mother, father, master, disciples—but never to a woman in a romantic or conjugal sense; apparently he had neither a female companion nor a wife. This absence was quite significant, and I had to use my intuition to guess at its meaning. A wife or companion would have had important resonance, and his mention of such a woman would have forced me to create her counterpart. But since no other reliable source ever spoke of Nat's being married (a pointless connection in the formal sense, slaves being legally forbidden to wed) or even being involved with a woman, it made it all the more plausible for me to portray a man who was a bachelor, or at least womanless, a celibate with all the frustrations that celibacy entails. Further, such a portrayal was entirely compatible with both the real Nat Turner's revolutionary passion and his religious zeal; chastity, combined with a single-minded devotion to a cause, has been the hallmark of religious rebels and reformers throughout history, and I saw a commanding reasonableness in having Nat share their condition, in which austerity clashed with feverish sexual temptation.

But by all odds my most crucial choice, as I picked my way through the facts and factoids of the original *Confessions*, was the one that also gave rise to the most furious misinterpretation later—and this was to invent a relationship between Nat Turner and a teenage white girl, the daughter of a small landowner. No decision I made shows so well the pitfalls waiting for the historical novelist who, however well intentioned, creates a situation or concept repugnant to ideologues; at the same time, nothing so deftly illustrates the invincible right of the novelist to manipulate historical fact and pursue his intuition concerning that fact to its artistically logical conclusion. Here are two intertwined facts, recounted by the perpetrator and recorded by Thomas Gray with the clinical dispassion of a modern-day homicide report: During most of the course of the revolt, in which fifty-five people were slaughtered, the leader of the murderers could not kill or inflict a wound on any of the victims although he confesses that he tried more than once. This is the second fact: Toward the end of the bloody proceedings Nat is finally able to kill, and he kills-seemingly without qualm—a young woman named Margaret Whitehead, once described as "the belle of the county." It is his only murder. And after that murder his insurrection seems to quickly run out of speed. Why?

These are two of those undecipherable facts so consequential that they can't be sidestepped; indeed, for me they acquired such importance that my need to fathom their meaning became a dominant concern. And here it may be interesting to comment on the roles of the historian and the novelist, each of whom would be presented with different but overlapping opportunities to make sense of this terrible moment. Hewing more or less to the written record, both the historian and the novelist would be able to set the same scene, although the novelist would probably allow himself more descriptive breadth: the tranquillity of a hot August day in the still countryside; the band of black marauders bursting out of the pinewoods and engulfing the simple whitewashed frame house where the sunbonneted mother is swiftly decapitated by a muscular, screaming black man; the pretty young girl fleeing across the field, falteringly pursued by the Negro-irresolute at first, then determined—who, when she stumbles down in a heap, stabs her with his sword, then batters her head with a fence rail until she moves no more. Who was this Margaret Whitehead and what brought her together with Nat Turner? The facts tell us nothing else.

For this reason the historian's concern with Margaret Whitehead would most likely end here, and he would pass on to other matters. Let us pause for a moment. The killing of Margaret is near the climax of Nat Turner's chronicle, and it might be a convenient place to reflect on the immense effect the uprising had on American history and how its violence may have helped churn up a larger violence undreamed of by even the most obdurate slaveholder in 1831. Throughout that year the Virginia legislature had been engaged in a debate concerning the abolition of slavery; because of strong antislavery feeling in the Piedmont region and the western counties, where slaves were few, it appeared likely that abolition would become a reality, if not immediately, then in the near-future. The Turner cataclysm caused a wave of fear to sweep through the state, as well as much of the rest of the South, and may have been the most important factor in assuring the continuation of slavery in the Old Dominion. A legislator is reported to have said in public, "We're going to lock the niggers in a cellar and throw away the key." Had Virginia, with its great prestige among the states, abolished slavery during that critical time, the impact on the future (especially in terms of the possible avoidance of events leading to the Civil War) is awesome to contemplate.

But as a novelist I couldn't abandon the relationship of Nat Turner and Margaret Whitehead to the vacuum into which it had been cast in the *Confessions*. It was nearly inconceivable that in the tiny bucolic cosmos of Southampton the two had not known each other, or had not been acquainted in some way. And if they had known each other, what was the nature of their affinity? Had she been cruel to him, slighted him, snubbed him, subjected him to some insult? Since she was his sole victim, could the entire rebellion have been conceived as his retribution against her? Far-fetched perhaps, but history is full of catastrophes in which many have been sacrificed because of one person's lethal wrath against another. Or was it something else entirely that bound them, something absurdly obvious, the very antithesis of hatred? Had they been lovers? This seemed unlikely, given one's conviction about his basic asceticism. Perhaps, however, she had tempted him sexually, goaded him in some unknown way, and out of this situation had flowed his rage.

Perhaps nothing at all had occurred between them, and her death came merely as a needful act on the part of a man who, having been unable to kill, having failed to prove his manhood in front of his followers, desperately sought to destroy the nearest living body at hand. This I very much doubted, and rejected, though no one, of course, could ever know the truth. But it was my task—and my right—to allow my imagination to range over these questions and determine the nature of the mysterious bond between the black man and the young white woman. In *The Confessions of Nat Turner* I strove to present a complex view of slavery, and Nat and Margaret's story would occupy a relatively small place in the larger scheme. But from the first page I was drawn irresistibly to that final scene of horror in the August heat, knowing that, to my own satisfaction at least, I had discovered a dramatic image for slavery's annihilating power, which crushed black and white alike, and in the end a whole society.

Several years after my novel appeared, two historians named Seymour L. Gross and Eileen Bender published a long essay entitled "History, Politics and Literature: The Myth of Nat Turner." The essay was a carefully argued defense against the attacks on *The Confessions of Nat Turner*, which were chiefly embodied in a polemical book called *William Styron's Nat Turner: Ten Black Writers Respond*. Professors Gross and Bender made the interesting point that as a result of the extraordinary denunciation I had received, my book had been cast, as far as blacks were concerned, into the abyss. "Like the white schoolchildren in South Carolina at the turn of the century," they wrote, "who had to take an oath never to read *Uncle Tom's Cabin* because there was no truth in Mrs. Stowe, present-day blacks are being similarly assured that they can safely despise Mr. Styron's book without having to read it." There was a curious element of prophecy embedded in this statement, because much of the limbo status of *Nat Turner* (again insofar as black readers have been affected) has extended until the present day; as recently as the mid-1980s Paule Marshall, a fully grown black writer and a reputable one, was quoted in *The New York Times Book Review*—where she was playing a game in which writers were asked to name "Books I Never Finished Reading"—as saying that she never even *started* reading *The Confessions of Nat Turner*, since she had been assured that the work was "racist."

The racist tag was affixed to the novel soon after the publication of *Ten Black Writers*, which appeared the summer after I spoke at Wilberforce. The book was published by Beacon Press, under the auspices of the Unitarian Universalist Association, a high-minded group ostensibly dedicated to preserving the truth. This collection, which contained critical pieces by largely well-known black intellectuals from various disciplines (English, sociology, psychiatry, history), along with several critics and fiction writers, was an extraordinary book by any standard; a collective *cri de coeur* of throbbing pain and rage, its overall lament was that I had written a malicious work, deliberately falsifying history, that was an affront to black people everywhere. The volume received much attention: the front page of *The New York Times Book Review*, two consecutive reviews in the daily *Times*, and so forth. There was nothing restrained about the assault; in the splenetic tone of the sixties I was labeled "psychologically sick," "morally senile," and was accused of possessing "a vile racist imagination." The major complaint was apparent from the book's first sentence: How dare a white man write so intimately of the black experience, even presuming to *become* Nat Turner by speaking in the first person?

Following close upon this indictment were other charges: that (aside from the outrageous business about the young white woman) I had "missed the beauty of the Afro-American idiom," that I had created an indecisive and emasculate wimp rather than the stalwart figure of history, that the text reflected an approving view of the paternalism of slavery, that my description of a fleeting homoerotic episode in adolescence meant that I regarded Nat as a "raving homosexual," that I had failed to give him a wife, that the secret agenda of the entire work was to demonstrate how the black struggle for freedom was doomed to failure—the bill of particulars was interminable. Virtually nothing in my work, according to these inquisitors, had merit; the most innocuous and tangential aspects of the novel received scathing treatment.

A couple of the essays, a bit less irate than the others, were at least well considered; they had in common the conviction that I had somehow missed the religious and emotional center of the black experience—and they may have been right. I knew from the beginning the hazards of setting foot in exotic territory and was aware that even though I was dealing with long-ago Virginia, instead of, say, Harlem or Watts (about which I would never have been able to write with authority), my stranger's perspective might not always ring true to black people. One of these more rational critics, who called *Nat Turner* a "tragedy" (in the noncomplimentary sense) and my figure of Nat "a caricature," expressed the general hurt and frustration he shared with his fellows by saying that "[Styron] has done nothing less ... than create another chapter in our long and common agony. He has done it because we have allowed it, and we who are black must be men enough to admit that bitter fact. There can be no common history until we have first fleshed out the lineaments of our own, for no one else can speak out of the bittersweet bowels of our blackness." Right or wrong, this was a civilized sentiment that I could take seriously.

But the prevailing tone was strident and crude, sounding very much like the agitprop flatulence of the 1930s. Over the entire enterprise hovered the spirit of the historian Herbert Aptheker, the official United States Communist party "theoretician," who had done pioneering work on Nat Turner and American slave revolts in the 1930s and 1940s. A militant quotation from Aptheker set the tone of the book. Aptheker's work had been ground-breaking and useful at a time when Negro history was almost totally neglected, but it was badly skewed by party dogma; his thesis that the institution of slavery was threatened by constant rebellion simply did not, and does not, hold up under scrutiny. He underestimated slavery's suffocating might. My own view, shared by many students of the history of slavery, was that the institution in the United States was almost uniquely despotic, a closed system so powerful and totalitarian that organized insurrection was almost entirely precluded, though, of course, rebelliousness on an individual level was always present.

This overview necessarily dominated my *Nat Turner* Aptheker, upon whose preserve I had so seriously poached, was incensed by my book and for a while trudged around the university circuit preaching a gospel in which I was cast as one of the supreme liars ever to write about American history. (He never seemed to grasp the fundamental fact that I had written a *novel.*) It was unfortunate that in *Ten Black Writers Respond* so many recklessly unprovable allegations were made; they were also written in shabby and slipshod rhetoric that even permeated the essays of well-thought-of black figures like the political scientist Charles V. Hamilton and the psychiatrist Alvin F. Poussaint; the impression left upon many people (including myself and those sympathetic to the black cause) was of intellectual squalor. For me the most frustrating aspect of *Ten Black Writers Respond* was that writing filled with so much overheated absurdity should have acquired real authority in black America, causing my work to be lodged in a kind of black *Index Expurgatorius* from that point on, along with such overtly racist novels as *The Clansman* and *Mandingo*. Lest such a notation appear overstated, I would point out ample evidence of *Nat Turner*'s being not only unread by blacks but in perpetual quarantine. This came from reports filtering back to me from black studies programs in the years up to the present. Several times I learned the dismal news that in specific courses *Ten Black Writers Respond* would be required reading, while *The Confessions of Nat Turner* was not listed. This has echoes of Alice chatting with the March Hare. I have often felt perversely gratified that my work could inspire such fear, though scarcely such stunning mindlessness.

In my few ill-considered public appearances that year, when I was unwise enough to accept invitations to defend my fictional choices in front of predominantly young black audiences and tried to show the inner logic that dictated my interpretation of Nat Turner and some of his relationships, the result was disastrous. Writers of novels should never defend themselves, but this was a somewhat special case. In these often raucous sessions, where the gathering was drenched with hostility, I would attempt to explain why I had made certain decisions. I observed, for example, that in the matter of one of the most inflammatory issues—that of Nat's wife—the ten black writers had simply got it wrong. There was no documentary evidence of a wife, or the equivalent, and if there had been, my conscience would have compelled me to give him one, even though as a novelist I had no such strict obligation. Likewise Margaret Whitehead. A careful reading, I insisted, would show that Nat's motivation was complex, flowing from a relationship containing hatred as well as love, but not the simple-minded lust claimed by the critics. This made little impression, the response was pitched between sneering disbelief and incomprehension, and for the first time in my life I began to share the clammy chagrin of those writers and artists who have stood before whatever intimidating tribunal, hopelessly defending their work to cold-eyed political regulators. By this time I was being stalked from Boston to New Orleans by a young *dashiki*-clad firebrand, who unnerved me. Somewhat belatedly, I realized that *Nat Turner* was not, in this case, an aesthetic object but a political whipping boy—the most prominent one that the black activists possessed at the moment—and I quickly backed off from public view, letting others act as counsel for the defense.

I received as strong and vigorous a defense as a beleaguered writer could expect. I was especially well served by Eugene D. Genovese—who was then on his way to becoming the preeminent historian of American slavery and whose devotion to the black cause could scarcely be questioned—when he issued a massive rebuttal to the black essayists in *The New York Review of Books*; clearly as much dismayed as angered by the book's irrationality and philistinism, Genovese took up its main arguments one by one and effectively demolished them. This inflamed the black critics and their colleagues even more, and in counter-rebuttals that filled the back pages of the *The New York Review* the ugly debate raged on. Inevitably the storm died down, but the controversy has remained at a slow simmer until this day. Literally hundreds of articles have been written about the dispute, and at least four full-length books have appeared, including a ponderously comprehensive study of the entire affair that appeared only this year. Amid this vast scholarly debris it is possible to salvage at least a few commentaries whose insight and wisdom are worth preservation, and one of these is the GrossBender essay. Like Genovese, the historians deal harshly with the ten black writers and briskly dispose of their charges, but they have further illuminating things to say about the perennially enigmatic figure of Nat Turner and his place in our history.

They make the point that while Nat Turner was relatively obscure until my book appeared, he had "always belonged to those who used him—as a myth, as an imagined configuration of convictions, dreams, hopes and fears." What has helped make the man such a fascinating subject for speculation is his very inaccessibility. Neither historians nor writers of fiction have ever been able really to make much sense of the original document or to draw from it an identity with which everyone can agree by concluding: This is the historical truth. No firm truth can be established from such an incoherent text, or from the silhouette of the man, and, therefore, Nat has been the subject of wildly varying interpretation. One of the most prominent black historians of the nineteenth century, William Wells Brown, sallied forth on an ostensibly historical account but ended up drawing an elaborate imaginative portrait that resembled fiction; like me, he was repelled by Nat's religious mania, and like me, he minimized or softened his biblical bloodthirstiness. In most other respects this chronicle by a historian plainly baffled by the obscurities and paradoxes of the record is as novelistic as mine. And Brown makes no mention of a Mrs. Nat Turner.

On the other hand, the illustrious Thomas Wentworth Higginson, ardent champion of black rights, was fascinated by Nat Turner and did supply the hero with a spouse in his account, which was quasi-historical or semifictional, depending on the reader's definition of this blurred region, but in any case almost totally fanciful. Harriet Beecher Stowe, George Washington Williams, and numerous other writers of the last century, both black and white, tried to pin Nat down, but this "black Spartacus," as he was termed by one commentator, utterly evaded a consistent portrayal; the fabled insurrectionist, mad or sane or simply beyond comprehension, was truly a chameleon. As recently as this year, in an off-Broadway play about the insurrection by a black playwright, Nat Turner's ultimate motivation for violence is the rape of his "wife" by slaveholder-acceptable enough if one subscribes to the principle of artistic license, but a far more flagrant deviation from prima facie evidence than anything in my own work. Gross and Bender conclude that my own attempt was "very much part of a tradition. Styron has 'used' Nat Turner as Gray, Higginson, Wells Brown, and, indeed, the accusing critics themselves have used him—reading into him, and out of him, those usable truths which seemed to him to coalesce about the image he was contemplating."

When I mentioned James Baldwin earlier, it was with the memory of our friendship and of the time when he was encouraging me to do what at first caused me hesitation, and that was to take on the persona of Nat Turner and write as if from within this black man's skin. Baldwin was wrestling with his novel *Another Country*, which deals intimately with white characters, and we both ultimately shared the conviction that nothing should inhibit the impulse that causes a writer to render experience that may be essentially foreign to his own world; it is a formidable challenge and among an artist's most valuable privileges. Baldwin's determination to pursue this course aroused the ire of many militant blacks, who saw such a preoccupation as frivolous and a betrayal of a commitment to the black cause. He stuck to his belief though his conscience and his persistence brought him rebuke and bitter alienation. My attempt, of course, was an even greater effrontery, and after *Nat Turner* was published, Baldwin told an interviewer most accurately, "Bill's going to catch it from black and white." Some months later, when I saw him, he offered me congratulations on the book's success and commiseration on the uproar, adding with the voracious full-throated Baldwin laughter that was one of his trademarks, "If you were just darker, it would be you, not me, who was the most famous black writer in America." It was at least partly true: my problem was less that of my work than that of my color.

Color and its tragedy, in this troubled year of 1992—which so resembles the troubled year of 1967—has made me think often of James Baldwin and the stormy career of *The Confessions of Nat Turner*. Naturally I didn't create the book with a political or social agenda in view, but as Georg Lukacs points out, historical novels that have no resonance in the present are bound to prove of only "antiquarian" interest; certainly in the back of my mind I had hoped that whatever light my work might shed on the dungeon of American slavery, and its abyssal night of the body and spirit, might also cast light on our modern condition and be understood by black people, as well as white, as part of a plausible interpretation of the agony that has bound the present to the past. But while the book remains alive and well and widely read by white people, it is, as I say, largely shunned by blacks, sometimes with amazing hostility neither articulated nor explained, as if the admonitions of those ten black writers a generation ago still provided a stony taboo. I am less bothered by this boycott in itself—for despite what I've just said, I am far from believing that my book, or any novel, has any real relevance to the contemporary crisis-than the way in which it represents a continuation of that grim apartness that has defined racial relations in this country and that seems, from all signs and portents, to have worsened over the twenty-five years since *The Confessions of Nat Turner* appeared. That year much of Newark and Detroit burned down; this year the fires of Los Angeles seem anniversary fires too cruelly symbolic to accept or believe.

It was typical of Jimmy Baldwin's intransigent spirit that he never truly abandoned hope. I doubt that he would give up hope, even today. A recent essay on Baldwin quoted some brave and lovely words of Jimmy's that reminded me of the time when he and I, with our boundless and defiant ambitions, were both setting out to break through the imprisoning walls of color and into the alluring challenge of alien worlds: "Each of us, helplessly and forever, contains the other-male in female, female in male, white in black, and black in white. We are part of each other."

5

Julia Alvarez

"A Postscript" from *In the Time of the Butterflies* (1992)

On August 6, 1960, my family arrived in New York City, exiles from the tyranny of Trujillo. My father had participated in an underground plot that was cracked by the SIM, Trujillo's famous secret police. At the notorious torture chamber of La Cuarenta (La 40), it was just a matter of time before those who were captured gave out the names of other members.

Almost four months after our escape, three sisters who had also been members of that underground were murdered on their way home on a lonely mountain road. They had been to visit their jailed husbands who had purposely been transferred to a distant prison so that the women would be forced to make this perilous journey. A fourth sister who did not make the trip that day survived.

When as a young girl I heard about the "accident," I could not get the Mirabals out of my mind. On my frequent trips back to the Dominican Republic, I sought out whatever information I could about these brave and beautiful sisters who had done what few men—and only a handful of women—had been willing to do. During that terrifying thirty-one-year regime, any hint of disagreement ultimately resulted in death for the dissenter and often for members of his or her family. Yet the Mirabals had risked their lives. I kept asking myself, What gave them that special courage?

It was to understand that question that I began this story. But as happens with any story, the characters took over, beyond polemics and facts. They became real to my imagination. I began to invent them.

And so it is that what you find in these pages are not the Mirabal sisters of fact, or even the Mirabal sisters of legend. The actual sisters I never knew, nor did I have access to enough information or the talents and inclinations of a biographer to be able to adequately record them. As for the sisters of legend, wrapped in superlatives and ascended into myth, they were finally also inaccessible to me. I realized, too, that such deification was dangerous, the same god-making impulse that had created our tyrant. And ironically, by making them myth, we lost the Mirabals once more, dismissing the challenge of their courage as impossible for us, ordinary men and women.

So what you will find here are the Mirabals of my creation, made up but, I hope, true to the spirit of the real Mirabals. In addition, though I had researched the facts of the regime, and events pertaining to Trujillo's thirty-one-year despotism, I sometimes took liberties—by changing dates, by reconstructing events, and by collapsing characters or incidents. For I wanted to immerse my readers in an epoch in the life of the Dominican Republic that I believe can only finally be understood by fiction, only finally be redeemed by the imagination. A novel is not, after all, a historical document, but a way to travel through the human heart.

I would hope that through this fictionalized story I will bring acquaintance of these famous sisters to English-speaking readers. November 25th, the day of their murder, is observed in many Latin American countries as the International Day Against Violence Towards Women. Obviously, these sisters, who fought one tyrant, have served as models for women fighting against injustices of all kinds.

To Dominicans separated by language from the world I have created, I hope this book deepens North Americans' understanding of the nightmare you endured and the heavy losses you suffered—of which this story tells only a few.

¡Vivan las Mariposas!

6

Barbara Chase-Riboud

"Afterword" from *Sally Hemings* (1994)

Fifteen years ago, when I first published *Sally Hemings,* many factors differed greatly from what they are today. My first book of poetry had just been exquisitely and lovingly edited by Toni Morrison, who was not yet the Nobel laureate. Black studies were in their infancy in American universities and the name Sally Hemings was totally unknown to the general public. Everyone involved with publishing *Sally Hemings,* including the author, underestimated the emotion and controversy that would swirl about a novel that gave flesh, blood, and sinew to a long-held and much discussed conviction that Thomas Jefferson had a slave family by the half-sister of his dead wife. This conviction was long held by his contemporaries, from John Adams, who received Sally Hemings and Jefferson's daughter at the American Embassy in London, to Gouverneur Morris, a New York Congressman who was with Jefferson in Paris in 1789, and long, long denied by others.

I had wanted to illuminate our overweening and irrational obsession with race and color in this country. I would do it through the man who almost single-handedly invented our national identity—and through the woman who was the emblematic incarnation of the forbidden, the outcast; who was the rejection of that identity. I would use the form of the nineteenth-century American Gothic novel, whose very essence is embedded in the American psyche.

But I was a poet, a sprinter in literature, not the long-distance runner that the novelist is. Timidly, I began *Sally Hemings* as an epic poem. Then I discarded that and wrote an outline of something I called *Diary of a Slavegirl, Paris 1788.* Discouraged, I begged Toni Morrison to write this story. Had that happened, the rest would have been history; but she was busy with her own work. I tried to convince every writer I knew to take up my task. They all had their own lives and Sally Hemings wouldn't let me alone, nor I her. Finally, Morrison advised me that the only solution was the historical novel. When I protested, she smiled the most incisive and irreducible smile in American letters and said, "Stop talking about it. Just do it, Barbara."

I do believe that if this story had not begun in France, where I have lived since the early sixties, I would never have attempted to unravel the morass of legend, disinformation, evasion, hostility, symbolism, and false perceptions of almost mythical dimension that it encompasses. I don't know that I myself would have believed the story of Thomas Jefferson and Sally Hemings if it had begun in a field at Monticello, as many have chosen to imply, rather than in the revolutionary Paris of 1787. And never knowingly would I have taken on the old-guard Jeffersonians, powerful, southern white men with an agenda: to protect the good name of Jefferson, by any means and at all cost, from their greatest fear—the accusation of race-mixing, or as it was misnamed around 1864, miscegenation, a term that originally had nothing to do with race, but referred to the intermixing of heathen and Christian motifs.

But what makes the story believable is precisely that these two personages were taken completely out of their racial and social context and redefined in a France fermenting with ideas of social and personal liberty. Sally Hemings, described in the memoirs of Isaac, a Monticellian slave, as "mighty near white" with long black hair hanging down her back and known as dashing Sally, was white enough to pass as white in Paris and most probably did so. Otherwise, Jefferson's circle in that city would have remarked that in his household he had a blackamoor, a coveted and fashionable status symbol among the European aristocracy at the time, who cultivated the exotic "Moorish" style. Jefferson's friend Maria Cosway had such a blackamoor in her residence in London. On the other hand, Thomas Jefferson had, for the first time, ventured beyond the provincial and racist slave-holding plutocracy he had been born and raised in. He could perceive Sally Hemings for what she truly was. In France, both of them were free. And then consider the astounding blood ties between them that reached back through three generations of slave mistresses and made Sally Hemings the half-sister of Thomas Jefferson's wife, aunt to his legitimate daughter, and sister-in-law to Jefferson.

Moreover, I had to find a way to elevate a member of the most despised caste in America to the level of the most exalted. I had to do that in order to make believable Sally Heming's liaison with America's most famous historical name: Thomas Jefferson. Linguistically, I solved the problem by always referring to Sally Hemings by her full name. I felt that neither the author nor the reader had the right to call Hemings "Sally," much as Hemings dare not call Jefferson "Thomas" until they were equal in love.

This subtlety was sometimes lost on my copy editor, who wanted to know what difference it would make if a few "Sally's" slipped in. But as far as I know, over fifteen years (and counting), no one has commented on this styling and its efficiency—apparently, and gratifyingly, because the supposed artifice seems natural to readers. It simply lifts Sally Hemings well out of her role as a slave and helps make a minor historical figure the equal, as a genuine archetype, of Thomas Jefferson.

Perhaps that was one reason the novel was railed against from the pulpit, from CBS "Sunday Morning" and from Monticello itself. Three months after the publication of *Sally Hemings,* on the night of July 3, 1979, the stairway at the foot of Thomas Jefferson's bed was removed, leaving a huge, gaping hole to greet the dawning of the Fourth of July. I was not told why the stairway was removed; I was only ardently assured that it had *not* been removed because it was mentioned in *Sally Hemings* and tourists were asking to see it.

The book itself had gotten the Jeffersonian scholars and enthusiasts up in arms; now they were roiled by news that God forbid, *Sally Hemings* was going to be a movie. And, in fact, my eyewitness to the removal of the stairway had been a screenwriter working on his movie adaptation of my book. On the third of July, when the screenwriter had been at Monticello, the staircase had existed; and when he returned on the fifth, it had disappeared.

Two months later I discovered the unplastered, uncamouflaged hole where the stairway had been. When I stormed into the curator's office, he rather shakenly assured me that the removal of the stairway and its demolition had nothing to do with me or Sally Hemings. I was being "paranoiac," I was assured. "The staircase was not authentic," he explained; I asked what was authentic and received the answer "steps." That man's present, excellent successor as research director explained that indeed, the staircase had been removed in seventy-nine and that they had been proved "right" in their presumption that it was false because they had found Victorian nails and a discarded Victorian tool under the stairs.

The original analysis may have been proven correct, but on the basis of the act that followed it, one might soon hear the experts say: "Next let's break all the Victorian windowpanes at Monticello and never replace them, because they are not authentic." As of this writing, the staircase has never been replaced, by "steps" or anything else. Nothing has been placed in the stairwell because any structure there, I was told, would be "misleading to the public." One would have to believe that America's greatest architect built a stairwell not meant for a staircase from the foot of his bed to nowhere for no earthly reason.

But now all the old-guard Jeffersonians of our century, including the most illustrious, Dumas Malone, have disappeared. In his last interview with *The New York Times,* Malone admitted (as, I suppose, a kind of testament) that he could accept that "it" (a clandestine liaison between Thomas Jefferson and Sally Hemings) had taken place "once or twice." I am not sure if he meant one or two *children,* or if this most fervent admirer and greatest biographer of Jefferson preferred to accept the idea of Jefferson as a casual seducer or rapist of slave women, rather than to consider the possibility of a long-standing human relationship between "his" president and Sally Hemings. He also never addresses Jefferson's sexual life between the ages of 39, when his wife died (he was 43 when Sally Hemings arrived in Paris) and 81, when his life ceased.

Now the Jeffersonians have a different stratagem from the pained silence of old: categorical, sound-bite denial; in certain cases, fudging of dates and of historical evidence; and disinformation. These Jeffersonians also contend that Jefferson never changed his mind about race. They cite his *Notes on the State of Virginia* ad nauseam to prove his racism, and incidentally, to reinforce their assertion that an intimate human relationship between a slaveholder and a "black" slave was impossible.

Yet, as the "strident," "enraged," and "blasphemous" detractor of Jefferson, I think otherwise. The *Notes on the State of Virginia* were not written for publication; they were letters to a Frenchman in 1784 when Jefferson lived in a backwater, oppressive, slaveholding Virginia society, and had never ventured outside this closed environment. Twenty years later, Jefferson wrote to another Frenchman, Condorcet, concerning the black mathematician Benjamin Banneker, whom he had hired along with L'Enfant to lay out the city of Washington, D.C.

> . . . I procured him to be employed under one of our chief directors in laying out the new Federal city on the Potomac, and in the intervals of his leisure, while on that work, he made an almanac for the next year, which he sent to me in his own handwriting . . . I have seen very elegant solutions of geometrical problems by him. Add to this that he is a very worthy and respectable member of society. He is a free man. I shall be delighted to see these instances of moral eminence so multiplied as to prove that the want of talents, observed in them, is merely the effect of their degraded condition, and not proceeding from any difference in the structure of the parts on which intellect depends.

Could he have been any clearer? Are we to believe the provincial Thomas Jefferson of 1784 or the President of 1804? The Jefferson before his only voyage outside America, or the Jefferson after? That notable absence of one indispensable American from the newly independent United States lasted for five years. Yet even today there exists not one serious volume dedicated to Jefferson's activities or thoughts during those years he spent in France.

Whom would we elect the true Thomas Jefferson? The man on record before Sally Hemings came into his life, or the one that spoke and wrote after she had produced her third daughter, Harriet, the subject of my 1994 book *The President's Daughter*?

The debate between the new Jeffersonians and me abides, and not without incident. A fitting, ironic piece of evidence came to light in February 1993, the 250th anniversary of Thomas Jefferson's birth. The Monticello research department discovered in their own archives a letter dated December 19, 1799, in Jefferson's own hand, addressed to his son-in-law, Francis Eppes, in which he announces the birth of still another child of Sally Hemings, born December 7, 1799—nine months after Jefferson returned to Monticello from Philadelphia. Indeed, we know he was present in the life of Sally Hemings nine months before the births of all the children now known to have been born to her. But, for me, the true, heart-stopping, hair-raising shock came when I asked for the name of the child and was told that it was Thenia, and that she had lived just beyond her second birthday. In my novel *The President's Daughter*, which had already been delivered to the printer's, I had *invented* a Thenia, who is rescued by Harriet Hemings from the Monticello slave auction and taken north with her, into her new life and oblivion. (To this day, I do not know why I called her Thenia.)

So there is a real Thenia, one who really existed and was Sally Heming's daughter; and there is the Thenia of my imagination, Harriet Hemings's alter ego. Where is "truth" and where is "fiction"? Who is real and who is unreal; who false and who genuine? What is history and what is romance?

In *Romancing the Shadow*, Toni Morrison writes:

> It has been suggested that romance is an evasion of history (and thus perhaps attractive to a people trying to evade the recent past). But I am more persuaded by arguments that find in it the head-on encounter with very real, pressing historical forces and the contradictions inherent in them . . . Romance, an exploration of anxiety imported from the shadows of European culture, made possible the sometimes safe and other times risky embrace of quite specific, understandably human, fears: Americans' fear of being outcast, of failing, of powerlessness . . . In short, the terror of human freedom—the thing they coveted most of all. Romance offered writers not less but more; not a narrow ahistorical canvas, but a wide historical one; not escape but entanglement . . . It offered platforms for moralizing and fabulation, and for the imaginative entertainment of violence . . . and terror's most significant, overweening ingredient: darkness, with all the connotative value it awakened.
>
> There is no romance free of what Herman Melville called "the power of blackness," especially not in a country in which there was a resident population, already black, upon which the imagination could play. . . .

In other words, nineteenth-century Romance has always served in America for what I would call the metaphysics of race.

If Thomas Jefferson offers himself up as a surrogate for meditation on the problem of human freedom, then Sally Hemings is available for meditation on terror, darkness, invisibility, dread of failure, guilt, and powerlessness. Even her "whiteness" is perceived as blackness.

It is this *perception* of race and blackness that is at the hidden core of early American literature and early American history. It is as if we were desperately trying to tear out this heart of darkness that is an integral part of the American identity—a part that cannot be excised, but must be absorbed, reconciled, and above all, recognized.

Sally Hemings and Thomas Jefferson are a most poignant, tragic, and irreducible addendum to the enigma at the very heart of our history and our literature; that of the races and the sexes in our country.

Barbara Chase-Riboud
Paris, April 1994

7

Malcolm Bradbury

"Preface" from *To the Hermitage* (2000)

This is (I suppose) a story. It draws a great deal on history; but as history is the lies the present tells in order to make sense of the past I have improved it where necessary. I have altered the places where facts, data, info, seem dull or inaccurate. I have quietly corrected errors in the calendar, adjusted flaws in world geography, now and then budged the border of a country, or changed the constitution of a nation. A wee postmodern Haussman, I have elegantly replanned some of the world's greatest cities, moving buildings to better sites, redesigning architecture, opening fresh views and fine urban prospects, redirecting the traffic. I've put statues in more splendid locations, usefully reorganized art galleries, cleaned, transferred or rehung famous paintings, staged entire new plays and operas. I have revised or edited some of our great books, and republished them. I have altered monuments, defaced icons, changed the street signs, occupied the railway station. In all this I have behaved just as history does itself, when it plots the world's advancing story in the great Book of Destiny above.

I have also taken the chance to introduce people who never met in life, but certainly should have. I have changed their lives and careers, allowed them fresh qualities, novel opportunities, new loves. To my chief character – Denis Diderot, the most pleasing of all the philosophers, though alas now generally remembered only as a Parisian district or a Metro stop – I have been particularly kind. Diderot suspected himself that it was his fate to be a transient figure, a toy of Posterity: that strange form of collective memory that remembers and forgets, buries and retrieves, celebrates and defaces, constructs and deconstructs. He knew history was the future's complaint against the present; but that past, present and future eternally interfere and interface with each other. In this book I have been Posterity's spin-doctor. I have reshaped his life, adjusted his fame; I have granted him (as he would have liked) some pleasant extra months of existence, extended some of his ideas, developed some of his plots and mystifications. In fact I have amended and reorganized his entire website in the big Book of Destiny above.

I have been just as bold with our so-called contemporary reality. There really is a Boris Yeltsin. And there really is a Diderot Project: a splendid set of international conferences (organized by Professors Bo Goranzon and Magnus Florin of the Royal University of Stockholm) which over the years has encouraged some of our most splendid dons, writers, philosophers, scientists, actors and craftspersons to extend Diderot's educational and intellectual heritage, and for that purpose brought them comfortably together in some of the great cities of the world. I too have taken part in these congresses. In October 1993, when, as so often, Russian history trembled, I took a voyage with them over the Baltic. So this story began.

As all you practised readers of stories know, this means there can be no possible resemblance between the real pilgrims, our real hosts in Petersburg, or the real Diderot Project itself and the imaginary people and plans you find depicted here. This is, as I mentioned, a story. But I dedicate it to those real people (Bo Goranzon, Jon Cook, Stephen Toulmin, etc.), many of whom are my friends. I hope they remain so. My debts continue. This story was greatly encouraged by my splendid late editor John Blackwell who had much help to give me, if from another perspective, having once lived as a spy in a submarine under the Baltic. Another friend, Martin Hollis, late Professor of Philosophy at the University of East Anglia, contributed greatly. A believer in the cunning of reason, he often led me, wandering and peripatetic, up the Enlightenment Trail, aiming for the pub at the top, The Triumph of Reason. I fear we never reached it.

Many fine books helped me (see the coda), but one above all: P.N. Furbank's wonderful portrait of my deceptive hero in *Diderot: A Critical Biography* (1992). It was Furbank who recalled the difficulty of pinning down not just Diderot but his splendid writings. 'Diderot's stories present enormously complicated textual problems, since the manuscript copies all display all degrees of accuracy or carelessness, and Diderot continued to tinker with his texts . . . until the end of his life; moreover, new manuscripts have continued to turn up in quite recent years,' he notes in his edition of Diderot's *This Is Not a Story, And Other Stories* (OUP, 1993). So they do; that explains why I crossed the Baltic in the first place. And that explains how I came to write this . . . well, shall we call it a story?

M. B.

8

David Ebershoff

"Introduction" to *The Danish Girl* (2000)

On a gray April day in Dresden many years ago, I climbed the forty-one steps to the Brühlsche Terrasse to have a look at the view. The river Elbe was running dark and fast, and the city, a ghost of its former self, sat sternly beneath a sky sagging with a late snow. The city bustled with electric trams and subcompact cars and bicycles with wicker baskets and a police van in a chase with its blue light flashing. Across the river were stucco apartment complexes with washing tubs on the terraces and slab-concrete shopping arcades where garbage blew in a cold wind.

The city was shaking itself alive after a century of terrible history. From that view it was nearly impossible to imagine the former Dresden, once called the Teutonic Florence. At the beginning of the 20th century, before the decades of horrors and misery, the terrace where I sat in the chill was known as the Balcony of Europe. "The most beautiful city on the Continent," proclaimed a 1909 English guidebook, *Romantic Germany*, the sort of book with hand-tinted illustrations of half-timber houses and water wells with little thatched roofs. And now this, a city bombed and burned and then choked for more than fifty years by the grip of the Communist East, startled by its recent freedom and the early green shoots of prosperity. Little remained to remind one of Dresden circa 1930. The view from the terrace spoke only of the air raids of February 1945, of the quartering of the German nation a few months later, of the long haul through the Soviet domination, and of the wall a few hours to the north that had crumbled in November 1989. But I was there to research the beautiful past, an almost forgotten past, the history through which Lili Elbe walked, first as Einar Wegener, then as herself.

The wind was sharp and I sealed my eyes against its bite, and there, in the half-instant of a blink, lay the old Dresden where Wegener arrived one cold day in 1930 to complete the journey of becoming Lili. My job was to imagine the past, to hunt through the remnants that lay in the streets and in the library archives that could suggest a world, and a mood, that once was. I was in Germany alone, and other than the librarian at the Dresden Hygiene Museum and my hired translator who scrolled through the microfiche, I spoke to no one during my stay. I did not want to be in the present. I wanted my mind and the materials of research to take me back to the time Lili walked these streets, herself lonely, but more excited than afraid. And it was that day on the Brühlsche Terrasse that I came to recognize one of the fundamental tasks of writing a novel inspired by history such as *The Danish Girl*.

Every novel has its own internal memory, the organic creation that the reader and the writer recall, directly or indirectly, as the story propels itself along. But as I sorted out the story of Lili and Gerda, whom I would call Greta, I began to wonder whose memory was relevant to my role as novelist. For Lili Elbe, that beautiful Danish woman whom Greta first welcomed into their studio, had a history and a memory that belonged to someone else—but did it? Lili spoke of her past as if it belonged to another, as if Einar's memories were not her own. But can we jettison the parts of our past that we no longer feel represent us? A novelist mines the emotional interior of his or her characters. But what was I to do with a historical figure who claimed her early life was not hers? A figure from history who believed the person she had once been was now deceased. Gone to the world, and gone to her. On that gray day I began to understand some of the novel's questions: whose memory informs our own; how does the past, seemingly obliterated, infuse our vision of the world at hand, and of ourselves?

Dresden was gone, razed by an impressively American combination of firepower and efficiency, and yet the city, all of it, lay at my feet, beneath the terrace where lovers rented paddleboats, in the square outside the Semperoper, in the young grass growing along the banks of the Elbe, the river that gave Lili her new last name. Nineteen Thirty was within my grasp, and so was Lili Elbe conjuring memories of a person she claimed was gone. It led me to this: on the day Lili Elbe emerged from the Dresden Municipal Women's Clinic, Einar Wegener, she claimed, fully, finally disappeared; yet where did Einar go? From that point, who would house those memories? Einar was dead, Lili said, but unburied. Einar was gone, she insisted, but Lili failed to reconcile that Einar had no grave. Lili, who very much believed she was a different soul than Einar, had to live with a history that was and was not her own.

But don't we all?

I asked myself if this is any different than what humanity shoves upon all of us. Each of us is defined not just by our own past but also by that of our family and lovers and friends and enemies, as well as our country and civilization, and the forces of history that bring us to our own particular present. On that April day the wind crossed the terrace with an iciness that nicked the eyes, and the novel that I was writing about Lili Elbe, still untitled and far from complete, took shape.

Identity—the loss and acquisition of it, the borrowing, the stealing, the rejection, the embrace; we grow up and declare ourselves, yet the beautiful and awful past lingers forever. Beneath the rubble and the char, inside the prefab concrete and the asbestos tiles, swirling amid the factory belch and the cough of the car, rising in the wind, in the face of a daffodil bending beneath the last snow of the year, history and memory are held aloft by imagination and the sun as bright as a white kite above the river. Nothing is lost, I told myself that day in Dresden. A novel is written so nothing can be lost.

9

Thomas Mallon

"The Historical Novelist's Burden of Truth" from *In Fact* (2001)

At a time when important filmmakers and serious novelists are turning to historical subjects with unusual frequency, their audiences find themselves left to ponder and preserve the distinctions between facts and fabrications. Some years ago, in connection with this subject, I noted Marianne Moore's advice that the poet stock his imaginary garden with real toads. After a decade of writing historical fiction, I'm almost inclined to say what Moore famously declared about poetry itself: "I, too, dislike it." The genre is often done badly, and its practitioners have sometimes made grandiose claims for it. In the afterword to my two most recent novels, I've preferred to strike a cautionary note: "Nouns always trump adjectives, and in the phrase 'historical fiction,' it is important to remember which of the two words is which."

I don't believe that the genre, even when done well, rises to a higher truth than perceptively written history. The literal truth, of things judicial as well as historical, is preferable to any subjective one. However differently experienced by its participants, and prejudicially interpreted by their heirs, historical events happened one way and one way only. It's only their meaning that's open to interpretation.

Then why, in considering history, even apply the fictional imagination? Why not rely upon scholarly investigation, which in its rare eloquent manifestations can be quite as powerful and satisfying? Two occasions, I think, best call for the historical novelist: when the facts have been lost to time, and when a time has been lost to the facts.

My novel *Henry and Clara* concerns the engaged couple who accompanied the Lincolns to Ford's Theatre on April 14, 1865. One can find a small collection of published facts about them, often in the footnotes of Civil War histories. And my own best efforts to unearth more—in pension files, alumni records, private diaries and correspondence, contemporary newspapers and diplomatic dispatches—yielded the outlines of a gripping, but by no means wholly connected, story. So I made a pact with myself: insofar as I could discover the facts about Henry Rathbone and Clara Harris, I would pretty much stick to them. In the pages between the facts, I would allow a novel to grow—by imagination, inference and extrapolation. The book that resulted cannot be called history, and yet in places it is more accurate than some of those supposedly nonfiction footnotes about my characters' lives. Clara, for example, is usually said to have been five years younger than Henry. In fact, according to two sets of census records in Albany, she was three years older—hardly an insignificant matter when considering young lovers.

I was well into a draft of the book before I found this out, and the decision to part with what I had already written did not come easily. I could have stuck to the lie about her age that I suspect Clara herself told for many years. I was, after all, writing fiction. But as I considered the matter, I realized how much more interesting—both psychologically and erotically—the truth would be. Having a Victorian heroine fall for the older stepbrother she acquires through her father's remarriage conforms to all sorts of expectations and archetypes. Having her fall for her new *younger* brother, as Clara did, has a bit of a kink to it. This discovery of her real age is the best justification for the rule I've come to write by: don't fight the facts. They'll almost always give you a better story than invention does. It's only after gathering the facts that the historical novelist earns his imaginative elbow room, the right to suggest and invent the rest of his reality.

In a more recent book, *Dewey Defeats Truman,* I again wrote about a real time and place—the Republican candidate's Michigan hometown of Owosso during the months leading up to his "inevitable" 1948 victory—but I tried something quite different from what I did in *Henry and Clara.* However authentically I attempted to reconstruct Owosso, all of the main characters in *Dewey* are inventions. It was as if I'd dropped a neutron bomb (the one that kills people but leaves everything else intact) on the town and then repopulated it with my own imaginings. It's important to remember that the historical novelist's principal obligations are to literature (telling a good story), not to history, but I also wanted to re-create a specific period that history, particularly the televised kind, has rendered rather poorly.

We all know how the "postwar period" gets introduced in documentaries. There's the shot of the atom bomb's mushroom cloud; then the famous Eisenstaedt photo of the sailor kissing the nurse on V-J Day; and then Levittown, TV aerials and baby carriages. But the world did not turn on quite such a dime. In 1948, the bodies of servicemen killed overseas were still being repatriated for home burial; the war continued to lay heavy on many hearts, and towns like Owosso were enjoying a last year without television.

Historical fiction has the leisure to present a more finely sliced and subtly textured time than even good "social history" does. To do the job, a social historian must eventually resort to statistics and comparisons and context; a novelist, in rendering speech and behavior and even the brand names on the breakfast table, can give a more palpable picture of, to paraphrase Trollope, the way we lived then.

Accuracy counts, of course, and the best readers are the ones on alert. I have gotten letters pointing out how, in *Henry and Clara,* no march by Sousa could have sounded at Col. E. E. Ellsworth's funeral in 1861, since John Philip Sousa only turned 7 that year. I'm pleased (and relieved) to respond that the Sousa in question is John Philip's father, Antonio. All the microfilmed newspapers, slang dictionaries and trademark registers in the library won't keep you from making some mistakes, but if you too often fall back on the excuse that, well, it is after all a novel, the accumulated feeling of plausibility is unlikely to hold up.

The other danger is laying it on with a trowel, or what reporters call "emptying your notebook." If you put an antimacassar on what you've already said is a horsehair sofa, the effect will be more pedantic than persuasive. The reader will be fatally aware of the present-day consciousness pulling the strings. *Titanic,* now and forever playing at your local theater, has some hilariously overdone moments: the philistine fiancé can't just sneer at his bride-to-be's newly acquired paintings; he has to chortle that this Picasso chap will never amount to anything.

When *Henry and Clara* came out, I made an appearance at the Abraham Lincoln Book Shop in Chicago. I was the first novelist they'd hosted in some time, pleased to be asked but not surprised at the lack of a turnout. The serious readers of history who make up the shop's clientele feel toward historical novels roughly what silent-movie enthusiasts felt for the talkies: who needs this loudmouthed stuff? Recently, however, a movement toward "counterfactual" or "what-if" history has been gaining ground among academic historians. Reporting on this trend in *The New York Times,* William H. Honan notes the serious attention being paid to what might have happened, if, for example, the Spanish Armada had emerged victorious. He quotes Niall Ferguson, author of *Virtual History,* on how counterfactualism can "recapture the chaotic nature of experience and see that there are no certain outcomes." I can't help feeling that all this is better left to novelists, for whom the "chaotic nature of experience" is, sentence by sentence, a stock-in-trade. If historians, with their interest in defending a thesis, begin trafficking in the what-if, I'm afraid that what-might-have-been will soon get presented as what-would-have-been.

The historical novelist must grapple with moral considerations, not just aesthetic ones. "Don't you fear the dead?" the Chilean writer Ariel Dorfman once asked me about the dark motives and conduct I ascribed to my character Henry Rathbone. I don't suppose I fear the *long*-dead participants in an event that is by now as much a myth as it was once an occurrence. Immediate families would be, I think, another matter. Thomas E. Dewey's son is justifiably agitated about the portrayal of his honest, crime-busting father as a corrupt prosecutor in the recent movie *Hoodlum*. One cannot libel the dead, but one can refrain from distortions as hurtful as they are preposterous.

Why historical material should be increasingly attractive to both moviemakers (Steven Spielberg) and writers of literary fiction (Russell Banks and Jane Smiley join the ranks of Civil War novelists this season) is the subject of some curiosity. There are those who connect the proliferation of "period" dramas to the way nothing much has been going on in the mid- and late-'90s.[1] But I think the cause is deeper. The cyber and fiber-optic revolutions have made every person and place on the present-day globe absurdly and instantly accessible to every other person and place. It's not enough that we no longer walk down the street or ride a train without talking on the cell phone. We can E-mail and instant-message a thousand people we've never met in Katmandu, and if we're nostalgic for Paris, we can log on to an EarthCam Web site and watch live, real-time images of the traffic. There is less and less need to imagine anybody or any place; we can just access them. We are, as a result and more than we yet realize, becoming sick of one another. The past is the only place to which we can get away, and if I had one prediction for the millennium it would be that all of us, including novelists, shall be spending a lot of time—more than ever before—looking backward.

Note

1 This essay was drafted just a few weeks into the Lewinsky scandal and a year before Kosovo. So much for Francis Fukuyama and *The End of History*.

10

Jane Yolen and Robert J. Harris

"What Is True About This Story" from *Girl in a Cage* (2002)

The starting point of this story is the actual decree issued by King Edward I of England that three of the ladies who had been captured at Tain should be imprisoned in cages. These were Isabel of Buchan, Robert Bruce's sister Mary, and his eleven-year-old daughter, Marjorie.

We know for a fact that Isabel and Mary were caged in Berwick and Roxburgh respectively, in cages that match the description of the one we use in our story. Orders were given for a cage to be prepared at the Tower of London to hold the young Princess Marjorie as well. In the end, Marjorie was never sent to London but was instead made a prisoner at the Gilbertine nunnery at Wotton in England.

We speculate that as the other two ladies were caged on the Scottish borders, that Edward may well have subjected Marjorie to a similar fate at Lanercost, where he lay sick. Certainly enough of an outcry was raised against his treatment of her that he abandoned the idea of removing her to London.

Edward I of England was called Longshanks because he was an enormously tall man for the period—over six and a half feet tall. He liked to refer to himself as "Hammer of the Scots," proudly, vowing to bring that proud northern nation to heel. In fact, Edward had not been a bad king for much of his reign, but after his beloved wife Eleanor died, something went wrong and the dark side of his personality took hold. He became cruel, vindictive, unceasing in his hatred of the Scottish people, and of Robert Bruce, his erstwhile friend, in particular.

In the months following the events portrayed in this book, Robert Bruce (or in the Norman French of the day, Robert de Brus) recovered from his defeat at Methven and waged a brilliant guerilla campaign against his enemies. A series of victories over the English brought the Scots flocking to his banner to oppose Edward's cruel treatment of their country. Even the Earl of Ross, who had sent the royal ladies as prisoners to England, eventually joined Bruce's cause and became one of his most loyal followers. Though history does not tell us why Ross made such a reverse, we have speculated on it with the scene between Elizabeth and her captor.

When Longshanks died in July 1307—begging his son to take his bones into battle—the weak-willed Edward II was unable to prevent Robert Bruce from establishing control over the whole of northern Scotland. The two kings finally met in battle in 1314 at Bannockburn in sight of Stirling Castle. In spite of being outnumbered three to one, Bruce inflicted a crushing defeat on his enemy that guaranteed Scotland's freedom for centuries to come.

So many English nobles were captured at Bannockburn that Bruce was finally able to ransom his family back. After eight years in captivity, Marjorie and the others made a joyful return to Scotland. Only Isabel of Buchan was not repatriated, and she disappears from history at this point. Did she die in prison? No one knows.

The following year Marjorie—now twenty—married Walter Stewart, one of the heroes of Bannockburn. She soon became pregnant. Tragically, she was badly injured in a fall from her horse and did not survive the birth of her son. He, however, went on to become King Robert II. So Marjorie's son became the first of the long line of Stewart Kings who not only ruled Scotland, but eventually became the rulers of England as well.

King Robert never forgave himself the murder of Comyn in the church. When as an old man he knew himself to be dying, he asked that his heart be taken to the Holy Land and buried there, as a sign that he begged forgiveness for the deed. The soldiers carrying the heart in a gilded and bejeweled casket were set upon and many were killed, so the stragglers returned home, where the casket was buried in a Scottish abbey.

The only real tinkering we have done with the historical facts are these: Marjorie's actual term of captivity in a cage, which is still debated by scholars; Isabel of Buchan crowning King Robert on his coronation day (she actually arrived two days later with her husband's destriers, and crowned him then). Also, Marjorie was probably not present in Dumfries right after the murder of Red Comyn. Christina is called Christian in various records, and Neil is also called Nigel. We do not know if Marjorie was called Jo by her intimates, but as that is a common Scots endearment meaning "loved one," we thought it appropriate.

Writing a novel is, of course, different from writing history. The storyteller fills in the interstices of the historical record with guesses and judgments.

We have worked hard to stay in keeping with what is known, while still telling a stirring story.

The life of a hero like Robert Bruce inevitably becomes surrounded by legends. The most famous of these is that, while he was in hiding from his enemies, sheltering in a Highland cave, he saw a spider repeatedly working at its web in spite of setback after setback. He took this as a sign that he too must per-severe if he was to achieve his goal of becoming king.

We do not know whether this spider-in-the-cave tale really happened to Bruce. Recent scholarly thought is that the incident actually happened to his lieutenant, Jamie Douglas, in a field, and simply attached to Robert's story. No one knows for sure. If it did not happen to King Robert, or Jamie Douglas, perhaps—as we have suggested here—it happened to his Marjorie. Certainly both father and daughter found the courage to survive many hardships and finally fulfill their destinies.

11

Colm Tóibín

"Henry James for Venice" from *The Henry James Review* (2006)

Some years before the time I am describing, my mother changed the rooms around, the dining-room to the front of the house, the sitting room to the back. She bought a new carpet for the back room, new curtains, lamps, a new fireplace, a new three piece suite, and a first stereo. She painted the walls white and put up Impressionist prints. Her children were almost grown up; her pension, too, had slightly grown. She could afford it.

She was mainly absent that summer I came home from college, as were my siblings. I was nineteen. I should have gone to London and worked in a bar or a factory but didn't. Instead, I got a job in the local motor taxation office and spent the summer, under sporadic supervision, checking that every file was in place. It was dusty work, drudgery really, but I liked my co-workers and did not kill myself. In the evenings I came back to this strange room that had no clear, pure, direct associations with childhood. Every single object was new; only the echoes were old. Among the records there were three I listened to over and over—the first three Bach cello suites played by Janos Starker, the Beethoven Violin Concerto, and a collection of German, French, and Spanish songs sung by Victoria de los Angeles.

I began, for no special reason, to read *The Portrait of a Lady* by Henry James. I do not think I had read anything by him before, even in school. It was clear from the beginning that this was a novel of pure style, where style itself, prose style, style of dress and manners and gesture, was a sort of high morality. It was clear that Isabel Archer's innate stylishness would allow her to do justice to this rich new world to which her aunt had taken her. These ideas of style were not current in Ireland at the time, and I found them deeply interesting and absorbing.

Thus I was not prepared for the plot of the book, which I found shocking, not only for itself, but because the idea of style as morality, so perfectly set up, had been so summarily shattered. James as dramatist had decided that his conflict should not be between style and failure of style but between right and wrong, truth and lies, deception and honesty. I had misunderstood everything and that realization, as well as the drama surrounding duplicity, seemed to give me pleasure.

In the meantime, Victoria de los Angeles seemed to win out over Bach and Beethoven. There was a great yearning in her voice, a grace of expression mixed with acknowledged pain. Slowly, I began to associate these songs by Schubert and Debussy and Falla with Isabel Archer. I looked forward to coming home every evening to this back room and these two women who wanted something rich from life which life was slowly denying them.

I never once thought about Henry James himself. He seemed beautifully absent from his own novel, which was another aspect of his power. Over the next few years I read all of his novels and some of his stories. I could not find him in his books, and this was strangely more satisfying than finding James Joyce's life and his city all over his books, or George Eliot's opinions all over hers.

More than twenty years later, I had to review *A History of Gay Literature* by Gregory Woods for the *London Review of Books*. James loomed large in this. I was concerned about the argument that his novels were merely a way of disclosing or concealing his homosexuality. I went and read about his life in Leon Edel's biography. Sometime later, in Yaddo, the artists' retreat in upstate New York, I found another set of Edel's five-volume biography of James. I took it to my room, believing that reading it from beginning to end might keep me busy and bore me at the same time, might occupy me without disturbing me so I could get on with finishing my novel *The Blackwater Lightship*. It was, of course, fascinating.

Over the next year I began to imagine James. He came to me as the protagonist of my novel *The Heather Blazing* had come—a distant, refined, mostly silent figure, middle-aged, haunted by flickering figures from the past, animated mostly by work. The life of the novel that slowly grew in my dreams would be the life of his mind.

In my five novels, I have worked only with one main character, one interior life, one intimacy. I could not imagine writing a novel with two main characters. Maybe this was what mattered to me so much when I read James first, his use of the third person intimate, his gathering of detail after detail all observed and experienced by one character, mediated by one consciousness until that consciousness slowly works on the reader until the reader becomes, or half-becomes, or almost becomes, that central consciousness. This character comes to me slowly and gradually, over a year maybe, or more. It soaks itself into my imagination. But the structure and plot do not come in this way. They can come in a flash or not come at all. I never take notes. If something cannot be remembered, then it is not important.

Waiting for a character to emerge is lazy work. You can go to the Himalayas and dream him or her up, you can stay in bed, go for a walk. All of this is work and it would be easy to feel that you could continue like this for years and the book would somehow not only imagine itself, but write itself. But there comes a time in the imagining process when you must pounce. Early in the year 2000 I decided it was time to pounce. I had arranged, in any case, to go to the Santa Maddalena Foundation outside Florence, but I knew now that I was going to begin the novel there close to places that James had known and loved. When they asked me before I arrived if there was anything special I would need, I said yes, I, as a boy from a provincial town in Ireland, was in urgent need of meeting some posh people. That, I was told, could easily be arranged.

It was strange, despite the wars, how much the idea of society, an intact aristocracy, had survived in Italy. Many of them came to the house. They believed in ideas of good families, they believed in old money and spoke with equal awe about newly acquired wealth. Some days I wandered in Florence, looking at pictures, visiting churches. I was in my mid-forties, bald, unattached, bookish. I liked company and I liked being alone. This meant that the house at Santa Maddalena worked wonders for me. There was company for lunch and supper, but my own quarters were sacrosanct. I was meant to be working and could not be disturbed. I loved closing my door.

I worked first on a short story set in provincial Ireland, but I knew this was a form of idling, that I would have to start the book, which had formed in my head as beginning in January 1895 and ending on New Year's Eve 1899. The working title was *The Turn of the Century*. So I wrote down "Chapter One: January 1895." Then I idled once more, went into Florence, looked at the Masaccios and worked on my short story.

One day I decided that no matter what happened it would become the opening of my novel. Anything that day would be made into drama. The sun rose and made its way across the sky as far as I could see, and then it grew dark. That could be an opening. I had my breakfast, I dreamed, I idled, I ate more, I slept. That might be enough. When my fellow guest announced that he was going to Siena, I announced that I was going with him. He knew the city, and I did not. We left too late. It was dark when we arrived. He wanted to walk up to the main square, the famous Campo. We were on a side street, lit by lamps in the wall, there were shops and cafes and restaurants, we were in a hurry, needing to get to a museum or a church before it closed at a certain time, six or seven. He was suggesting that we hurry. There were people on the street, students maybe, half blocking our way and we had to push past them. I wanted to go into the square by the first available entrance but my friend said no. He insisted that we should walk up further, to enter the square by the most perfect route. It was very beautiful when we entered, like something from a painting, and there were figures in the middle of the square and they were, I think, workers and there was some sort of demonstration and one or two of them turned towards us but for no special reason. Our museum was closed but we looked at a few churches and then we went home. I had my opening. The scene became the first pages of my book.

The next day as I worked, a piece of video art by Bill Viola, which I had looked at very closely when it showed in Dublin, came into my mind. It was of three figures of women in an Italian square and they were seeking something, or beseeching someone for something. Slowly, they made their way into the scene as well.

Soon, with the first scene nearly finished, the second scene came. Helen Volkonsky, the Princess Volkonsky, came to lunch. She was the granddaughter of Tolstoy's Prince Bolkonsky and also Stolypin, the Russian reformer. She had been born in Italy and was now, in a changed political climate, about to go to Russia for the first time. I studied her closely and soon I was back in my room working out a way of having her visit Henry James in January 1895, bringing with her a whiff of his years in Paris and a sense of a worldliness and a cosmopolitan, almost decadent, life that he seemed to have abandoned in London, despite his social success. My Princess, of course, had nothing to do with the real visitor, who was a most respectable person, but it stirred an image which I then used.

In those days I was also reading books by and about James, and I had beside the bed one of the most useful books on Henry James called *The Legend of the Master*, edited by Simon Nowell-Smith, published in 1948. This consists of quotes about James taken from books by his friends and family. On page 119 of that book there is an extraordinary passage from Edmund Gosse, with a note to say that James had told Hugh Walpole the same story. Gosse was staying with James in Rye and, on going for a walk with him, found that the master was

> in profuse and enigmatic language . . . recounting to him an experience. . . . He spoke of standing on the pavement in a city, in the dusk, and of gazing upwards across the misty street, watching, watching for the lighting of a lamp in a window on the third storey. And the lamp blazed out and through bursting tears he strained to see what was behind it, the unapproachable face. And for hours he stood there, wet with the rain, brushed by the phantom hurrying figures of the scene, and never from behind the lamp was for one moment visible the face.

Gosse then wrote:

> The mysterious and poignant revelation closed, and one could make no comment, ask no question, being throttled oneself by an overpowering

> emotion. And for a long time Henry James shuffled beside me in the darkness, shaking the dew off the laurels, and still there was no sound at all in the garden but what our heels made crunching the gravel, nor was the silence broken when suddenly we entered the house and he disappeared for an hour.

It is easy for the reader to find echoes of this passage in the work of James, as it is difficult to make any direct connections between a sound and the echoes, which may be, in fact, echoes of another sound. Yet there is a story from 1878, one of James's very worst stories, and that is, in my opinion, saying a great deal for he wrote some very bad stories. The story is called "Rose-Agathe," and it is set in Paris and begins as a man from a window watches a woman in the street, noting her beauty. He then watches a male friend stand in the same street watching, he supposes, the same woman through the window of her husband's hairdresser's shop. All the time our narrator is at his Parisian window studying the scene below, even as "the lamps were lighted in the hairdresser's shop."

The other scene involving a window in Paris with an observer and an observed is one of James's most moving dramatic moments. It is in Book Two of *The Ambassadors* when Strether comes to the street where he knows that Chad lives: "Two or three windows stood open to the violet air; and, before Strether had cut the knot by crossing, a young man had come out and looked about him, had lighted a cigarette and tossed the match over, and then, resting on the rail, had given himself up to watching the life below while he smoked."

The Princess in my first chapter reminds James and the reader of an earlier life, one of easy duplicity; she reminds him too of a resonant name and a resonant moment, which he wishes briefly to set down on paper and then destroy and conceal forever. James is my character and I want him haunted, uneasy but charming; I want his sexuality to be concealed, unspoken, with no private sexual moments shared with the reader, the reader must be like the wider world, kept at arm's length. This is the nineteenth century. This is a reticent man from a Puritan place, ready to do battle on behalf of freedom for his characters, but more skilled at allowing them to renounce what freedom might come their way for the sake of other things that are harder to define.

These scenes, so aleatory in their origin, were merely preparations for the larger drama of the first chapter of my book, which was the failure of Henry James's play *Guy Domville* on the London stage in January 1895. These few months offered a drama which any novelist would work with. The failure of James's play, the replacement, using the same theater and the same producer, by the first production of *The Importance of Being Earnest*. James's attending of another Wilde play *An Ideal Husband* on his own opening night. Wilde's two successful plays on the London stage helping

Wilde to believe that he was invulnerable. James, within days of his own failure, getting the story that became "The Turn of the Screw" from the Archbishop of Canterbury. James going to Ireland, staying one week each with the Lord Lieutenant and the Commander of her Majesty's Forces. Then the Wilde trials.

Thus I had the opening of the book, and the intensity with which I could handle James's failure in the theater might have been greatly assisted by an event that occurred to me four months before I began to write the opening chapter of the book, although I did not realize this until later. In September 1999, my previous novel *The Blackwater Lightship* was short-listed, with five other books, for the Booker Prize. There is an interval of six weeks between the announcement of the shortlist and the announcement of the winner. This last event is done at a long, long dinner in London where many happy people eat a huge dinner and guzzle great quantities of wine and champagne. No one knows as we eat our dinners who has won. The six short-listed authors try and eat too, but it is easier to drink and it would, if drugs were available, be easier to take drugs. At some point towards the end of the dinner the five judges march into the hall, a cross between a pared-down jury and a horde of desperately willing executioners. For six weeks you have been waiting for this moment, what James called "the enraptured moment" when finally your talent is recognized, when your book will become, as it richly deserves, a best-seller all over the world. In order to increase your hope and expectation, there are six cameras and sets of lights in the vast ballroom, one camera is focused on each author. It seems like each of us have won. There is much fanfare and a long speech. And then the cameras come closer, right into your face, as the name is about to be read out. It is time. You are ready, despite the vast quantity of wine and champagne you have been drinking. Sudden fame, a speech to the world, cameras, lights, and much applause is a great way of making you sober. And then the name is read out and it is not yours. Within an instant, the lights are turned off and the cameras packed up and no one is looking at you. You feel a strange guilt and shame. You wish you were at home. Alone. But now you have to brave the night, speak to your publishers, accept commiserations, smile. You are an outsider in London and you wish you were sitting in lamplight with a fire lighting and the servants all asleep, and you leafing through Flaubert's letters.

Instead you will have to do what James did in my novel when his play failed: "He could not give in to his own horrible urge to be in the darkness, to escape into the night and walk as though he had written nothing and was nobody. He would have to go to them and thank them. . . . In the half-light he stood preparing himself, steeling him, ready to suppress whatever his own urges and needs might be." I wrote that section without realizing that the Booker experience was still raw, still preying on my mind. I do not know whether the many accounts of that evening in London in January 1895, including James's letters describing his anguish and his humiliation and his determination to recover, or my own experience in London a few months before, mattered more to me as I composed the first chapter of my novel.

Over the months that followed I went to look at some places in Italy associated with James. I thought it was astonishing that his friends Constance Fenimore Woolson, John Addington Symonds, and William Wetmore Story were buried so close to each other in the English cemetery in Rome where James had buried Daisy Miller years earlier. I stood in front of those graves as he must have done. Once, it was a beautiful June morning, and the place had an aura of beauty and peace. I remember feeling something I had never felt before: death as a sort of completion. I stood by Keats's grave and let the feeling sink in, and I wondered if I could put that into the novel somewhere, allow my character to have that feeling on such a morning in this place. Around this time, too, I read two books that made me feel that I should stop writing now that I had the first chapter done and keep thinking, imagining, and planning. One was Lyndall Gordon's book *A Private Life,* about Henry James's relationship to his cousin Minny Temple and his friend Constance Fenimore Woolson; the other was a book called *Amato Ragazzo,* edited by Rosella Mamoli Zorzi, the letters of Henry James to Hendrik Andersen, which I bought in Rome at the Museum near Piazza di Populo dedicated to the work of Hendrik Andersen, where my book, in its Italian edition, would be launched in 2004.

As I walked in Venice, or in the area around Piazza di Spagna and Via Margutta in Rome, which was lovely work and sure beat looking into my own heart or walking around rainy Irish provincial towns, I became as suspicious of Lyndall Gordon's version of James as I had a number of years earlier of those who tried to explain James's artistry and his genius as a form of neurosis arising from his homosexuality. I realized slowly that her blaming of James offered me a great subject that I could dramatize ambiguously, without judgment, building up detail but making no comment. James, here, could be both good and bad to the extent that neither of those words could mean anything. This, I knew, would require some care because the reader's first instinct is to judge. I knew that all of my novel, every single thing observed and understood, would be seen through James's eyes. Lyndall Gordon had seen things through the eyes of Minny Temple and Constance Fenimore Woolson, who were the innocent parties. But what if James were innocent too, or if such a term could also be rendered meaningless by the careful application of slow detail?

In September 2001 I began to work in earnest on the novel. I had nothing else to do. Each day I would take down the books I needed. Since I was writing the Alice chapter, which was to be Chapter 2 (and later became Chapter 3), I had her diary and her letters and Jean Strouse's biography beside me, as well as a copy of *The Bostonians* and *The Princess Casamassima* in case I needed them. But I needed, more than anything, just to start. Once I had asked a painter how to start a painting and he said: "Just make a mark." I was working in longhand in a notebook, leaving the left hand page blank for corrections. So I just made a mark.

It is, I think, possible to exaggerate the amount of the secret self that goes into any book. Sometimes, I hope, you can work on a surface level, inventing if you need to invent, using given material if the novel is about a set of events that have been already charted, or imagined material otherwise. By the end of *The Master* I simply did not know if certain moments of the book took their bearings from things that were important for me or were merely inventions, images made to satisfy the pattern I was making in the book, or images made in my own likeness. In the time I was writing the chapter on James and Oscar Wilde, I was hearing stories about priests whom I had known personally going to court for sexual abuse of minors. A few days I was like James himself, sitting at home writing a book, waiting curiously for a phone call to keep me informed about the case against Father X. But maybe this had nothing to do with the Wilde chapter; maybe the book needed such a chapter, whether I needed to tell the story or not. So, too, in those months, I was involved in the plight of two children, or rather young adults whom I had known as children, and was deeply alert to the problems and dangers facing them, and that they had faced. I think it is impossible that some of this did not make its way into the creation throughout the first half of the book of images of children in danger, children left alone, which become the young girl Mona in Ireland, who is an invention, Henry James and his sister Alice, Henry and William, Miles and Flora in "The Turn of the Screw," and the two sons of Oscar Wilde. I knew I was patterning as I dramatized these pairs of children, but whether the underlying impulse to pattern so densely was entirely artistic I do not know.

The days passed. I was working, typing each chapter as it was finished, making changes between the holograph manuscript and the typed version. I read some James or something about James every day.

I was interested in placing a set of images throughout the book of what I should call sexual almostness. Hammond the servant in Ireland is invented, one of the few fully invented characters in the book, for that purpose. The scene I outlined earlier in the street in Paris staring up at a window is another. The naked figure of Gus Barker; the scene in bed with Oliver Wendell Holmes; the arrival in Rye of Hendrik Andersen. I found myself hungrily watching out for more such images I could use. One day I was idly rereading Sheldon M. Novick's book *Henry James: The Young Master* when I came across an astonishing sentence at the very end of Chapter 3 about the Jameses' sojourn at Boulogne sur Mer: "When Father was at home, Harry sometimes joined him on walks, as he had done long ago in New York; and one afternoon they walked near the beach, Father talking as usual, his eyes following a young fisherwoman as with fine stride and shining limbs she waded from the sea with her basketful of glistering black shrimps." The footnote for this tells us that it was a letter Henry James Senior wrote to Anne Ward on November 2, 1857, which is in the Houghton Library. It is unpublished.

I knew, as I worked on the opening of Chapter 5, which was going to deal with sexual desire in all its almostness, with Grey and Holmes and Minny Temple, with Holmes and Henry James, I knew what I could do with that one sentence. This is the passage I produced in response to it:

> In the time they lived in Boulogne, Henry walked with his father on the beach. On one of those occasions, it was a windless and calm day, the beginning of summer, with a long sandy expanse and a wide sweep of sea. They had been to a café with large clear windows and a floor sprinkled with bran in a manner that gave it for Henry something of the charm of the circus. It was empty save for an old gentleman who picked his teeth with great facial contortions and another gentleman who soaked his buttered rolls in his coffee, to Henry's fascinated pleasure, and then disposed of them in the little interval between his nose and his chin. Henry did not wish to leave, but his father wanted his daily walk on the beach and thus he had to abandon his delight in observing the eating habits of the French.
>
> His father must have talked as they went along. The image in his mind now, in any case, was of his gesticulating, discussing a lecture or a book or a new set of ideas. He liked his father talking, especially when William was elsewhere.
>
> They did not paddle or walk too near the waves. His memory was that they walked briskly. His father may even have carried a stick. It was a picture of happiness. And for a stranger watching, it might have remained like that, an idyllic scene of a father and son at ease together in the late morning on the beach in Boulogne. There was a woman bathing, a young woman being watched by an older woman on the beach. The bather was large, perhaps even overweight, and well protected from the elements by an elaborate costume. She swam out expertly, allowing herself to float back with the waves. Then she stood facing out to sea letting her hands play with the water. Henry barely noticed her at first as his father stopped and made as though to examine something on the far horizon. Then his father walked forward for a while, silently, distracted, and turned back to study the horizon once more. This time Henry realised that he was watching the bather, examining her fiercely and hungrily and then turning away, observing the low dunes behind him, pretending that they also interested him to the same intense degree.
>
> As his father turned away once more and began walking towards home, he sounded out of breath and did not speak. Henry wanted to

> find an excuse to run ahead and get away from him, but then his father turned again, the expression on his face vivid, the skin blotched and the eyes sharp as though he were angry. His father was now standing on the shore, trembling, watching the swimmer who had her back to him, her costume clinging to her. His father made no further effort to seem casual. His stare was deliberate and pointed, but no one else noticed it. The woman did not look behind, and her companion had moved away. It was important, Henry knew, for him to pretend that this was nothing; there was no question that this could be mentioned or commented on. His father did not move, and seemed unaware of his presence, but he must have known he was there, Henry thought, and whatever this was, this keen-eyed drinking in of the woman bather, it was enough to make his father not care about Henry's presence. Finally, as he turned and set out on the journey home, his father stared back regularly with the look of someone who had been hunted down and defeated. The woman, once more, swam out to sea.

Alert readers will know that before I began to write, I crossed the room and searched for a book. It was, of course, *What Maisie Knew,* which has a long sequence set in Boulogne sur Mer. I needed something to anchor this passage I was writing, to make a bridge between James's experience and his work, as the book I was writing was a bridge between my experience and James's work. If I could draw your attention to the opening thirteen lines of Chapter 30 of *What Maisie Knew*:

> After they were seated there it was different: the place was not below the hotel, but further along the quay; with wide clear windows and a floor sprinkled with bran in a manner that gave it for Maisie something of the added charm of a circus. They had pretty much to themselves the painted spaces and the red plush benches; these were shared by a few scattered gentlemen who picked teeth, with facial contortions, behind little bare tables, and by an old personage in particular, a very old personage with a red ribbon in his buttonhole, whose manner of soaking buttered rolls in coffee and then disposing of them in the little that was left of the interval between his nose and chin might at a less anxious hour have cast upon Maisie an almost envious spell.

This was a way of anchoring my images and phrases in those of James, by riffing on them, referring to them, stealing them.

The image of his father on the beach in Boulogne was recorded not only by the father himself, but it remained in Henry James Junior's mind for forty years. He used it in *What Maisie Knew* when he came to the scenes set in Boulogne. In Chapter 22, Sir Claude "with a kind of absent gaze . . . followed the fine stride and shining limbs of a young fishwife who had just waded out of the sea with her basketful of shrimps. His thought came back to her [Maisie] sooner than his eyes."

In other words, an event in 1857, a tiny moment by the sea, is remembered and used by Henry James forty years later in a novel. We knew the event occurred by a stray reference in a contemporary letter. We presume that James's novels are peppered with such raids on the real as a way of anchoring them in time, as a way of restoring what is lost to the publicity of the printed page. We will never be able to know which of his images were from memory and which from imagination. But the scene in Boulogne and its rendering in a novel make clear, in any case, that personal experience for James, as for most novelists, was the bank from which some of his images were borrowed.

I am pointing this out—much of it is obvious—merely to show that my own method of merging the deeply personal with the imagined, matters which come deliberately and also unwillingly and unconsciously, belongs to the main method by which novelists work and by which James himself, the supreme novelist, also worked. It allows for Freudian reading of novels and for novels to be read as a form of neurosis, but it is often much simpler: things that have mattered emotionally, often for the quality of their pattern, their beauty, their emotional shape, things that are not necessarily traumatic, lodge in the mind, becoming shadows until you sit at a desk and begin to work out a pattern of words and images and then they become substantial and they block the way of narrative progress until they are allowed on to the page, or they offer the narrative great body and substance until they become the secret subject of the book.

The importance of the five years I chose is not that Henry James had a failure in the theater, or not that he moved to Rye, or not that he wrote "The Turn of the Screw," or not that he began to dictate his fiction, although all of these things are of interest and can be dramatized. The importance of the years 1895 to 1900 is that Henry James was building up the images and figures that would constitute the three masterpieces he was gathering all his strength to write: *The Ambassadors, The Wings of the Dove, The Golden Bowl.* As I worked, I was acutely alert to the idea that small moments, recurring memories, a sudden realization, something half understood, random matters, all of these can make their way into the foreground or background of a novel. As you are working on one book, material can occur to you that you will not use for years, you may not plan to use it, or realize its significance—and in James's notebooks, a novel often appears as a very small idea for a short story, or just the name of a character—and the more intensely you are working, the more easily these images will come.

In my book, I offer him some of the images he will need for his last great novel *The Golden Bowl.* The antique dealer in my book, whom the fictional James sees in 1897, will soon be his antique dealer in *The Golden Bowl.* The whiff of sexual secrecy and intrigue in the antique shop in my book will soon be part of the strange web that catches images and moments and prepares them to become part of a pattern, a more elaborate web, being spun in the imagination with care and precision and cunning but also being made by forces hidden from the artist, helped by the great complexity and perhaps the great white blankness of the unconscious mind, the secret self where memories are stored and where what matters looms large.

12

M. Allen Cunningham

"Author's Note" from *Lost Son* (2007)

My driving ambition during the several years spent writing *Lost Son* has been to give readers an entirely human rendition of Rainer Maria Rilke the man and artist. While I've sought to render the poet's remarkable life as accurately as possible, I've been constantly in service to the narrative demands of a novel. *Lost Son,* therefore, should not be taken as biographical inquiry. Still, it is worthwhile to state that the lineaments of Rilke's life have been, with certain needful if substantial excisions as noted below, rendered accurately here.

A few characters in the novel are wholly imaginary: Karl of Saint Pölten, for example, as well as Rilke's young colleague in the Stiftskaserne, Wenzel; both, however, stand in for impressions or experiences Rilke spoke of, or is believed to have undergone, and represent several biographical figures or influences collapsed into a single character. At points I've been compelled to manipulate the order or substance of factual minutiae: Rilke's father, for instance, did not remain in residence at 19 Heinrichsgasse till his death but took quarters elsewhere in Prague, nor was Princess Marie von Thurn und Taxis single-handedly responsible for the poet's release from the Austro-Hungarian infantry—a petition drafted by Katherina Kippenberg and signed by numerous noteworthy literary figures of the day was of greatest effect in bringing about Rilke's transfer to the Vienna Imperial War Archives. Here and there I've shuffled the dates and details of correspondence or events, as well as the dates of certain poetical compositions. Immediately conspicuous to those familiar with Rilke's biography will be the omission in this novel of the poet's later love affairs, or near love affairs, with such women as

Lou-Lou Albert Lasard, Magda von Hattingberg, Mimi Romanelli, and Baladine Klossowska. Despite their absence, I've endeavored to create a Rilke who is almost absurdly vulnerable and nevertheless relentlessly single-minded—which, I believe, is the ultimate impression derived from study of these romantic liaisons. If the overall thrust of *Lost Son* takes Rilke's autobiographical (and sometimes embellished) commentary as its basis, it is a portrait no less true to the poet's inner character for doing so: his impressions, fears, ambitions, failures, friendships, and triumphs. In the end, of course, as Rilke translator Willis Barnstone has put it: "The true Rilke is the poem." I might humbly amend Mr. Barnstone's comment: ". . . or the letter or the prose."

Finally, it is particularly important to note that *Lost Son* takes up a kind of direct discourse with Rilke's novel, *The Notebooks of Malte Laurids Brigge* (published in 1910 by the Insel-Verlag, Leipzig), being in many respects modeled upon *Malte,* which germinated from the poet's initial experience of Paris in 1902. The heart-piercing scenes here, for example, are inspired directly by those in *Malte,* as are the hospital vignettes and various other story elements. It's inevitable, then, that *Lost Son* should pay homage to the fine English translations of *Malte,* first by M. D. Herter Norton and later by Stephen Mitchell; readers are urged to explore Rilke's masterful novel in these rich renditions. All Rilke translations here, save two instances noted in the index below, are my own.

Lost Son was started in the summer of 2001 at the Hôtel de la Poste in Sierre, Switzerland; continued through the subsequent four years in northern California's Diablo Valley—and in the Quartier Latin of Paris in spring of 2005; and completed in Portland, Oregon, in autumn 2006.

—*M. Allen Cunningham*

13

Susan Sellers

"About *Vanessa and Virginia*" from the Two Ravens Press UK website (2008)

I didn't set out to write a novel about Virginia Woolf. *Vanessa and Virginia* began as a short story based on an anecdote: a friend confided in me that when her second daughter was born, her eldest (then a toddler of two) tried to throw the baby away. I have always found it puzzling that while Freud has so many illuminating things to say about the role parents play in child development, he virtually ignores the presence of siblings. Yet for most of us those early relationships with brothers and sisters have at least as much impact on who we are as anything our fathers or mothers said or did. So when I heard this tale my imagination was fired. I pictured the toddler lifting the baby from its Moses basket, and staggering with it to the place she had learned to put things that were unwanted – the kitchen bin. My friend was understandably upset by her daughter's behavior, but to me it seemed an intelligent solution to the problem. After all, what was interrupting the pleasures of mother's attention here was not the Father – but the arrival of a new sibling.

I started a story about this toddler, but though I got a long way with it I never finished it. This may have had something to do with the fact that during this period my mother told me that my friend's daughter was not alone, and that I too had tried to bin my sister, born when I was about eighteen months old. Yet I couldn't leave the story alone. At the time, I was reading a great deal of material about Virginia Woolf and her family for an academic project, including Frances Spalding's wonderful biography of Virginia's elder sister Vanessa Bell. Their relationship intrigued me. They were born at a time when few girls were sent to school, and as a consequence spent most of their days in each other's company. How, I wondered, was it settled between them that while Vanessa would become a painter, Virginia would write? In 1901, when Vanessa was just twenty-two, she was selected as one of twenty students to enter the Painting School of the Royal Academy; Virginia, on the other hand, did not publish her first novel until she was well into her thirties. Yet it was Virginia who became famous, while Vanessa frequently found it difficult to make enough money even to pay her models. I could not help asking myself: what must it have been like for Vanessa living in the shadow of this successful younger sibling? Many contemporary descriptions of Vanessa contrast her reticence in speech with Virginia's loquacious brilliance. If Vanessa had written in anything like the detail Virginia did, what would her story have been?

We have millions of Virginia's words. We have her novels and her non-fiction, as well as a great deal she did not publish in her lifetime, including diaries, notebooks, letters, autobiographical sketches and discarded drafts. Some of Vanessa's words also survive – many letters, an essay or two – but only a small percentage is published and when contrasted with her sister their volume is comparatively slight.

We may not have access to many of Vanessa's words, but what we do have are her paintings. I realized that if I wanted to get to know Vanessa as a character, I would have to do so from this perspective. Consequently, I bought or borrowed every book I could that contained reproductions of her art. I visited the house she settled in at Charleston, almost every inch of which is decorated. For an entire year, as I worked on the first draft of what became the novel, the walls of my study were covered with Vanessa's images. Given the close relationship that existed between the two sisters, I wanted my writing to echo Virginia's interior, poetic, lyrical style – but I did not want to produce a pastiche, and whatever I did had to be with a painter's voice. Since I am not a visual artist myself, I visited friends who are and watched them work. I talked to them about what went through their minds as they decided on a subject, prepared their materials, and set about creating their images. The more I listened, the more I was convinced that if I wanted to imagine Vanessa this process would figure prominently. In the end, I think it was this shared ability to make works of art that enabled both sisters to surmount so many of the difficulties in their lives.

As well as spending time with artists, I continued to read. This raised as many questions as it furnished answers. For example, what role did Thoby – the brother who came between Vanessa and Virginia and who died when he was just twenty-six – play in the sisters' lives? His presence haunts Virginia's novels and he also appears in her diary; Vanessa names her adored eldest son after him (her letters to him as a young man read more like those of a lover than a mother). Why did Vanessa spurn Roger Fry – someone she loved – to pursue a lifelong liaison with the homosexual painter Duncan Grant – a man who could never love her in return? What were Vanessa's motives in writing to Virginia's husband shortly after their marriage, to tell him she thought her sister was frigid? And perhaps the most perplexing question of all: why, having successfully survived so many periods of distress and illness, did Virginia drown herself by weighing her coat pockets with stones when she was almost sixty?

If I had wanted to write an accurate biography of Vanessa and Virginia based on the available evidence, I would only have been able to pose these questions. But fiction is not biography: it does not have to quote its sources and it can take liberties with the truth. It can stage interpretations that arise from the imaginative endeavor of attempting to get inside a character's head. Hélène Cixous – another writer whose work inspires me – quotes Kafka's understanding of what a good book should be in her essay 'The School of the Dead'. Kafka maintains that a book should be an axe to crack open the frozen sea inside us, a phrase I take to refer to the way our view of the world is limited until reading makes us look anew. A good biography changes perceptions by presenting fresh information and challenging interpretations – but fiction has resources which I would argue shatter that frozen sea more profoundly.

To quote one of Vanessa and Virginia's contemporaries, the writer E. M. Forster: fiction shows, it doesn't tell. The more I discovered about the sisters, the more I became intrigued by the desires and compulsions I thought I could see developing in their childhoods, and reverberating through their adult lives. To convey these, I needed a novelist's palette: I gave myself permission to select, stage and heighten; I used metaphor, not fact.

Concocting our life stories and those of others is one of the things that mark us as human. It is a consequence of our existing as linguistic beings. Even biographers in full possession of the evidence must then write it into a story – though the best try to avoid the blunders made by the biographer in Virginia's comic novel *Orlando*, who is lazy, prejudiced and a prude. During the process of drafting *Vanessa and Virginia*, there came a point where I consciously had to let go of my research, in order to allow my characters to come alive on the page. Every fiction writer will know what I mean when I say this: I had to reach a point where my familiarity with the sisters ignited their voices inside my head – so that at times I felt almost as if I were writing to Vanessa's dictation. Once this started to happen, the choice of what to include and what to omit seemed self-evident; I was free to discard, dramatize and invent.

To cite just one example: in the biographies, Virginia's adolescent request for a lectern so that she can emulate Vanessa at her easel and write standing up is included only as a detail – whereas to me it is highly significant. By staging the scene, I was able to give this detail greater prominence. I imagine the differences between straight biography and what I have done with the sisters' story are similar to those between a photograph and a painting: where the photographer aims for a true likeness, the painter offers an individual view – focusing, highlighting, and sometimes adding lines or colors that are not in the original but which the composition appears to call for.

Earlier this year I heard the novelist Rose Tremain read from her novel about Polish immigrants, *The Road Home*. She prefaced her reading by explaining that before she began writing she interviewed migrant workers and collected their stories. Someone in the audience asked her if she felt she had the right to use real people's lives as the basis for her fiction. It is a question I imagine I will be asked about *Vanessa and Virginia*.

As a writer, I believe you have a responsibility towards your subject, but this responsibility is not that of a historian or biographer. Fiction's strength is its ability to make people see, hear, feel, taste, smell its subject: as I have suggested, this process frequently involves deviations from or embellishments of any underlying facts. Though I often asked myself: 'would the real-life Vanessa or Virginia have said or done this' as I worked, my overriding impetus was whether what my characters said or did felt right within the context of my narrative. Every work of art must have its own integrity: I think you have to be true to the book you are writing.

Virginia Woolf's novel *To the Lighthouse* culminates with one of the characters, a painter Lily Briscoe, finishing a picture by drawing a single line down its center. It is a powerful climax because Lily (whom many critics believe is based on Vanessa) has been struggling with this painting for years. Though she senses no one will ever look at her work, or that if they do they will not understand it, she experiences a moment of epiphany as she realizes she has succeeded in portraying her vision. My own feelings on finishing *Vanessa and Virginia* are similar. It is a story about two remarkable women: it is not the only story, and it is certainly not entirely true. My hope in publishing it is that it will prompt readers to return to the extraordinary wealth of writing and painting by the historical sisters, and perhaps offer fresh insights into their troubled, passionate relationship. If it does, it might crack a little of the ice Kafka believed means we see the world through an unquestioning (Cixous would say 'dead') lens. And if it doesn't – if is to be hidden in the attic or destroyed as Lily in Virginia's novel feared her painting would be – well, at least I have kept faith with my vision.

14

Brian Hall

"Author's Note" from *Fall of Frost* (2008)

Although this work is properly called a novel, I've approached it in the spirit of a biographer who wanted to stretch his usual form to accommodate more speculation than nonfiction generally allows. None of the known facts of Robert Frost's life have been changed; all of the letters quoted or paraphrased are real; Frost's public utterances are drawn from transcripts; most of the private conversations are either close paraphrases of reported interchanges or elaborations of a participant's description of a conversation. (Exceptions are noted below.) My contribution, for the most part, has been confined to selecting a few events from a very long and full life to trace what I consider important contours of Frost's extraordinarily lush and difficult mental landscape; adding concrete detail, drawn as much as possible from facts gleaned from a wide variety of sources; and, of course, presuming to guess what Frost might have been thinking during those incidents. In particular, my interest has been to suggest how a great writer's language flows out of his life and back into it, how certain mysteriously fecund words and their associated ideas are turned under in the writer's mind, whence they sprout daughter ideas, seedlings that are turned under again, until the mind "can contain itself no more, / But sweating-full, drips wine and oil a little." Because this subject is perforce highly speculative, straightforward literary biographies tend to undertreat it.

I should point out that what might seem to be the least plausible aspect of my text—i.e., Frost's ability to remember flawlessly hundreds of lines of his own and other poets' verse, so that *le vers juste* seems always to be dancing on the tip of his tongue—was attested by many witnesses during his lifetime. Everything by another poet or writer that I put into Frost's mind was mentioned, quoted, or identified as important to him by the real Robert Frost; the few exceptions are poems or prose works that seem to have inspired a poem of his own.

"The Younger Poet" is not a composite character, since I've changed no facts and thus have not suppressed inconsistencies; rather, it's a common label for various poets, some well known and some not, who could be considered at least in part to have been influenced by Frost's poetry and personality. Presented in the plural, they might have been a chorus called Legacy. I've rendered them in the singular to stand for that perfect Other that most of us hope for, that artists pursue with such ardency, and that Robert Frost hunted with his own peculiar tragic force.

In the chapter notes that follow, I mention only my more unusual sources. Most of the straightforward biographical facts, such as the deaths of children, family histories, well-attested incidents, purchases of farms, and so on, are drawn from Lawrance Thompson's three-volume biography, *Robert Frost* (I: *The Early Years*; II: *The Years of Triumph*; III: *The Later Years,* Thompson and R. H. Winnick). Other excellent sources of biographical information that in general I don't specify are Jay Parini's *Robert Frost: A Life*; William Pritchard's *Frost: A Literary Life Reconsidered*; and John Evangelist Walsh's *Into My Own: The English Years of Robert Frost.* Much of the detail regarding Frost's time in Russia is drawn from F. D. Reeve's *Robert Frost in Russia.* Unless otherwise mentioned, all letters quoted can be found in the biographies, or in one of the following sources: *Selected Letters of Robert Frost,* edited by Lawrance Thompson; *Family Letters of Robert and Elinor Frost,* edited by Arnold Grade; *The Letters of Robert Frost to Louis Untermeyer*; edited by Untermeyer; *Elected Friends: Robert Frost and Edward Thomas to One Another,* edited by Matthew Spencer. Lesley Frost's delightful juvenile writings appear in *New Hampshire's Child.*

Where I've followed a source in unusually close detail, I say so. I also name the various faces of the Younger Poet, and acknowledge my debts for particular insights. If I don't specify a conversation or an incident as an invention, then it is based on fact.

Plagiarism police, take note: if I name a book or article as a source, it means I've felt free to use any reported dialogue therein, and in some cases I've taken the written thoughts of the writer and converted them into spoken expression—or, in the cases of the chapters that are not told from Frost's point of view, the thoughts of my narrator occasionally incorporate phrases that the real person in question wrote in his or her account of the incident being described. Frost's own thoughts throughout the novel are extensively larded with phrases from his letters, and with lines and fragments of lines from his own and other people's poems. (Poetry lovers: happy hunting.) I've tried in the notes that follow to raise the white flag at all those places where my larceny has been grand rather than petty. If I've failed to mention anything, the omission has been unintentional (in other words, don't shoot!); just as whatever factual mistakes I have surely made can be laid at the door of my ignorance and sloth, rather than evil intent.

Finally, a word about Frost's copyrighted poems. Readers may have noticed occasional awkward spots in my text, where I quote only a brief snippet from a poem and then paraphrase the rest. Works first published after 1922 will not enter the public domain until 2018 at the earliest (and perhaps not even then, given the interest of powerful corporations in extending copyright), and anyone wishing to print more than a small fraction of any of Frost's later poems must secure permission from the Estate of Robert Frost. That permission was not forthcoming for this work. I was never granted the reasons for the refusal, but I suspect they were a combination of discomfort over a complex portrayal of a man who has already been unfairly mauled by his official biographer, and nonspecific unhappiness with the genre of biographical fiction. The irony is that I could legally invent a scene in which Frost commits murder (since in American law you can't libel the dead), and I could just as legally fill this novel with my own atrocious doggerel that I insisted, hand over heart, was Frost's, but I'm not allowed to freely quote his actual, still-copyrighted poetry, much of which is widely available (despite copyright) online.

The ever-lengthening arm of copyright protection is proving to be a burden and often a bane to more and more scholars and creative artists. At least in this case I can comfort myself with the thought that my difficulties have been metaphorically apt. Frost really did write to Lionel Trilling, "No sweeter music can come to my ears than the clash of arms over my dead body when I am down." The fight over Frost—plaster saint, monster, or human being?—has always been, and continues to be, Homeric. My ears are still ringing from the ax-blow to my helmet, but I'd like to think that somewhere Frost—or maybe I just mean Poetry—is enjoying the music.

15

Barbara Mujica

"Going for the Subjective: One Way to Write Biographical Fiction" from *a/b: Auto/Biography Studies* (2016)

Abstract

Biographical fiction is necessarily subjective, since authors must filter their protagonist's experience through their own. In her own novels—*Frida, Sister Teresa,* and *I Am Venus*—Barbara Mujica incorporates the unavoidable subjectivity of biographical fiction into the story through the creation of unreliable narrators who force the reader to question the authenticity of the text.

Given the difficulties involved in portraying accurately any human experience, even one's own, authors of biographical fiction necessarily face particular challenges when attempting to bring to life the experiences of others. Inevitably, they must come to terms with their own inability to see the world through their protagonist's eyes. Even if they have access to their subject's diaries and letters, as I did when I wrote *Frida* and *Sister Teresa,* they are limited by the subject's self-representation, which may occult or distort information, as well as by historical realities that are alien to the twenty-first century. Furthermore, authors cannot always know for certain the underlying motives that trigger another's decisions or the effects those decisions will have on others. Thus, modern authors are constantly confronted with the possibility of misrepresenting their characters, for they are acutely aware of their own subjectivity.

Daniel Kehlmann, author of the biographical novel *Measuring the World,* notes that all historical novels "indulge in the great game of narrating the past afresh and of diverging from the official version of the past offered by historians into the realm of invented reality." For Kehlmann, historical fiction does not really exist because writers must always filter history through their own Weltanschauung—a notion I find liberating because it frees writers to embrace their own subjectivity rather than struggling to purge it from their novels. One way to deal with this issue is to accentuate the subjective element that is unavoidable in all historical writing by inventing an unabashedly opinionated narrative voice. This technique provides the author with an angle or point of view that is clearly not the protagonist's and allows the author to interpret his or her material freely with no pretense to objectivity.

The subjects of two of my novels, Frida Kahlo and Saint Teresa of Ávila, are separated by time and place. The wife of Mexican muralist Diego Rivera, Frida was a painter, a social rebel, and a card-carrying communist, known for her dirty mouth as much as for her self-portraits. She was a bisexual who held strong anti-bourgeois and anti-Catholic views, although many of her paintings reveal a profound affinity for family or nature and a deep spirituality. Teresa was a sixteenth-century Spanish mystic who founded a new religious Order, the Discalced Carmelites. A fervent defender of Catholicism, she was canonized in 1622 and declared a Doctor of the Church in 1970. Frida and Teresa were both intelligent, shrewd, tough, and determined fighters who persevered in the face of adversity. Furthermore, both were outsiders living in intensely nationalistic, xenophobic environments, to which they responded by proclaiming their orthodoxy: Frida, her *mexicanidad* and Teresa, her loyalty to the Church.[1] Both women suffered from physical ailments during most of their lives. Both were professionals who broke new ground for women. Finally, today both are cult figures, whose stories are fairly well known. In order to tell those stories in a new and engaging way, I had to define a specific viewpoint, but when I began writing, I was not sure what it would be.

My first attempt at *Frida* was a third-person narrative. After five chapters, I realized I had produced a biography instead of a work of fiction. As an academic, I attached immense importance to historical accuracy and so read extensively before embarking on my novel. However, facts can bog you down. They can overpower your characters and drain them of their vitality. I had wanted to write a novel rather than a documentary about Kahlo precisely because I found her to be such a dramatic and contradictory character. I had wanted to capture the essence of Frida—victim and victimizer—but I had not yet overcome my obsession with facts.

Mario Vargas Llosa argues in *La verdad de las mentiras* that reportage and the novel are two opposing systems for approaching truth. Journalists (and academics) must reconcile what they write with the facts that inspire it. The success of a documentary article or book depends on the accuracy of its data. However, the success of a novel depends on its ability to persuade through the communicative force of fantasy—that is, to spin magic that engrosses and convinces the reader (Vargas Llosa 10). Novels do not merely tell the story; they fill in the blanks. The lies in a novel are never gratuitous, argues Vargas Llosa. They are essential to the construction of a truth. They supplement the insufficiencies of life (12). They grapple with the how and why of things. When I realized that I had produced chapters in which data overwhelmed Frida's larger-than-life personality, I chucked the whole thing and began again.

What fascinated me about Frida—the truth I wanted to convey—was the utterly paradoxical nature of her personality. All human beings hold contradictions, but in Frida antithetical forces reached extremes. Frida was needy yet manipulative, vulnerable yet calculating, naive yet cunning, insecure yet arrogant, big-hearted yet egotistical. She triumphed over pain from disease and injury, but also used her invalid status to control others. She channeled her pain into a successful career in art, yet painted irregularly. She claimed to be a champion of the poor, but relished hobnobbing with the likes of the Rockefellers, whom she both adulated and scorned. She claimed to want children, yet sterility, like illness, became a means of eliciting pity. Although she could be considerate, she could also be cruel, as when she hurled insults at some art students who brought her a Mother's Day gift. In order to capture the "truth" of Frida, I needed a narrator who not only experienced her contradictions, but also responded conflictingly—someone who cherished her yet found her insufferable, someone with strong feelings who made no pretense to objectivity. I asked myself what it would be like to know someone like Frida. What feelings would someone close to her harbor? And who could articulate those feelings?

In *Recasting Historical Women,* an exploration of German biographical fiction, Stephanie Bird points out the need for the authors of biographical fiction to define their own relationship to their subject:

> A problem which relates both to constructing the identity of another person and to constructing an identity in the past is that of authorial identification with the protagonist. Identification is often presumed to be a positive reflection on a relationship, an indication of sympathy and understanding of another's situation. It is arrived at either through the recognition of what is perceived to be a common experience, or by the imagined projection of one self into the other so as to participate in fantasy in the other's experience. (19)

Yet biographical fiction can be born of the author's grappling with the subject. Sometimes the author actually dislikes his or her subject and strives to explore the dark, destructive, or ugly recesses of the subject's mind. Bird writes, "to accept moments of identification at face value and to interpret them as transparent examples of greater understanding by one person or the other is effectively to participate in a process where difference is ignored or underestimated, and potential conflict and ambivalence is denied" (19). In order to devise an effective narrator for my story, I had to come to terms with my own ambiguity toward Frida.

It sometimes comes as a surprise to readers to learn that I do not love Frida. Although I admire her brilliance, creativity, determination, and joie de vivre, I find her whiny and self-serving. Her obsession with her own image and her tendency to portray herself as a sacrificial victim—a Christ figure with a necklace of thorns or a fawn pierced with arrows like Saint Sebastian—strikes me as self-aggrandizing and melodramatic. Her treatment of Cristina, whom she urged to pose nude for Diego and then censured for having an affair with him, seems hypocritical. My narrator would have to be both knowledgeable and perceptive, but also as ambivalent as I toward Frida.

Diego Rivera was out of the question. Abusive, narcissistic, deceitful, and lecherous, Diego was too self-centered to ponder Frida's psyche. He was much too concerned with his own career. Furthermore, he was often away from Frida—traveling, working, or wooing other women. Finally, too much is known about Rivera, making him difficult to "invent." In his book *My Art, My Life,* he describes his relationship with Frida, but, like all autobiographies, Rivera's is an exercise in self-fashioning. He bypasses almost entirely the psychic pain that he caused Kahlo, which eventually caused her to divorce him.

Eventually, I hit on the idea of giving Frida's sister, Cristina, the narrative voice. Just eleven months Frida's junior and her inseparable companion, Cristina was both a constant and a catalyst in Frida's life. She and Frida were so close that Frida called her "my twin," yet they were rivals for the affection of their parents, Cristina's children, and Diego. From a writer's perspective, Cristina was an ideal narrator because she is an almost invisible yet permanent shadow in Frida's life. Every biography of Frida mentions her, yet her inner thoughts remain a mystery. Even *Frida Intima,* by Isolda Pinedo Kahlo, Cristina's daughter, leaves her vague. Because so little is known about Cristina, it was easy to invent a voice for her. Cristina's intimacy with Frida would enable her to comment on all aspects of Frida's life. The ambivalence suggested by her betrayal with Diego and her subsequent submissiveness to Frida made her an appropriate narrative vehicle. While I wanted the book to be accurate with respect to verifiable facts, I also wanted to imbue it with a certain haziness with respect to motives and feelings.

Thus, I made Cristina into a blatantly unreliable narrator. Her narrative voice stresses her subjectivity. The real Frida had a low opinion of her sister's intellect, but the character Cristina is highly perceptive, if insecure. Drawing on the styles of early modern women writers such as Saint Teresa, who strove to convey humility through repeated expressions of self-doubt, I created a Cristina who is observant, yet distrustful of her own observations. Often she contradicts herself, backtracks, or admits to exaggeration. "This is what really happened," she says repeatedly, only to rectify her statement later: "at least, this is what I think happened," or "this is how I remember it." My objective was not only to give my character a distinct voice, but also to convey the utter irretrievability of the past.

When I began *Sister Teresa,* I already had the experience of writing *Frida* and so had a better idea of what I wanted to do. Even so, I fell into the trap of overwriting. I read not only histories and biographies, but also all of Teresa's writing, including all her extant correspondence. I did so much research on Teresa that I wound up producing over six hundred pages, making the book unpublishable.

I had not yet grasped the importance of distancing myself adequately from my subject. Although I always begin a novel with an outline determined by the biography of the protagonist, I have learned not to include every detail, but rather to focus on the *story.* Determining which material is pertinent requires detachment, a willingness to sacrifice (callously!) historical completeness (but not historical accuracy) for effective narrative. Not just the highlights of the subject's career, but the quirky anecdotes that "fill in the gaps" give form to the novel. Often these are developed through the fictional secondary characters whose interaction with the protagonist reveals her inner truth. My agent urged me to cut the manuscript to about three hundred and fifty pages, which I did. In addition, I wrote a scholarly study of Teresa's letters.

Biographies of Teresa tend to be tedious and dry. Even one of the best, Cathleen Medwick's *Teresa of Avila: The Progress of a Soul,* fails to capture the real drama and complexity of Teresa's story. And then there are the hagiographies, whose objective is to enhance Teresa's saintly image. These read like medieval romances: a hero favored by God embarks on a series of adventures and ultimately triumphs over dreadful obstacles.

Grammatiki Karla points out that already in antiquity a dichotomy existed between fictionalized life histories and romances. The former explore complexities of character, while the latter present a more idealized image of the subject. The former depict the whole life, ending with the death of the hero, while romances tend to conclude with a "happy ending." And fictionalized lives often use a narrator, while romances assume an omniscient author. From Teresa's correspondence, I formed a clear idea of her personality. Teresa was a strong-willed, temperamental woman, who was deeply spiritual, yet practical and shrewd. She was warm and loving, but she could be manipulative and imperious. The multifaceted portrait of Teresa I wanted to paint required that I write a biographical novel, not a hagiography or a romance.

Yet, because of my own reverence for Teresa, whom I consider a spiritual guide and mentor, I wanted to avoid staining her character. Frida was easier to "novelize." Everyone knows that bad girls make for more engaging reading than saints. Frida really was a sexual and social rebel, so turning her into a colorful wild-child was easy. In the case of Teresa, I had to humanize the saint without defiling her, yet build into the plot the adventure, romance, sexual tension, and mystery a novel requires.

I once again asked myself: what would it be like to know this woman? On the one hand, Teresa was a mystic, a visionary, and an ecstatic. But her writings show that she could also be a vain, bossy, impatient woman. She herself admits that nuns at the Incarnation Convent resented her demonstrations of excessive piety. When she left Incarnation to found a new Order, they thought her pretentious and proud. What would it be like, I wondered, to be close to a person who went into trances and saw visions? What would it be like to know someone who spoke to God and became impatient with you because you could not? Someone who struggled with prayer while you were struggling to put bread on the table? Someone who made a fetish of self-deprivation when all you wanted was a good meal? Instead of looking for a real person in Teresa's life to narrate her story, I invented a character, Pancracia, who later enters the convent with Teresa as Sister Angélica. I wanted a narrator who was close to Teresa, yet very different from her. Teresa is rich and beautiful, the belle of Ávila. Angélica is poor and plain, but smart and perceptive. When Teresa begins to have visions and claims to converse with God, Angélica grapples with how to react. Because Teresa's flights of mysticism are so alien to her, Angélica often loses patience. Down to earth and somewhat cynical, Angélica was an excellent foil for Teresa. She loves Teresa as a mentor, friend, and sister, but observes her raptures and mortifications with skepticism. Like Cristina, Angélica offers a subjective response to the protagonist's actions. As a fellow nun, she is close enough to Teresa to observe and narrate her life story, yet distant enough to provide a personal commentary that, at times, conflicts radically with Teresa's own perceptions.

And she could provide the sexual tension that this novel about nuns needed. In her *Vida,* Teresa mentions a relationship with a male cousin, but remains vague about the details. Although some critics have speculated that she had an affair before entering the convent, I preferred to respect her ambiguity on this issue. But, unlike Teresa, Angélica is a woman of strong carnal appetites. Weaving sexual tension into this character's narrative came easily. The Carmelite chronicles I had read were full of stories of seduction and deceit. Angélica's tale of an in-convent affair with a friar, who rapes her when she tries to end the relationship, is perfectly plausible, and her subjective voice allowed me to comment on an abusive situation that has parallels in today's society.

The Church and the Carmelite Order have provided "official" narratives of Teresa's life, but through Angélica I was able to examine the ambiguities and fill in the gaps. I was also able to explore what it might have been like to live in a sixteenth-century convent, where girls as young as three could be cloistered for life so that families could avoid paying a marriage dowry. What did that mean for the victims? Angélica's involvement with a young girl who escapes the convent to get married brings the situation to life for readers. And Angélica's comments on the bustle in the convent parlor help to create atmosphere and enrich the plot.

Before Teresa founded the Discalced Carmelites she lived in a convent in which rules were lax. Nuns were free to leave for meals with family and friends, and men routinely brought them gifts of food and flowers. The elite of Ávila society met in the salon to gossip. We know what Teresa thought about these practices because she decries them in her *Vida,* but Angélica gives us an alternative point of view. And because Teresa and Angélica often present opposing perspectives, the subjectivity of not only the fictional voice but also the historical voice, what has become the "official" voice, also comes into focus—that is, the alterity of the unreliable narrator diffuses the authority of the official narrative, reminding us that Teresa, like the chroniclers of the Church and of her Order, represents a particular point of view among many possibilities.

The subjectivity of Cristina and Angélica was a natural outcome of their personal perspectives and storytelling, but in my third biographical novel, *I Am Venus,* I wanted to do something different. Rather than a first-person narrative, I wanted to fashion a third-person account, yet still convey the fluidity of historical truth—something that is difficult to do with an omniscient, omnipresent third-person narrator.

Based on the life of the seventeenth-century Spanish court painter Diego Velázquez, *I Am Venus* explores the circumstances around the creation of the *Rokeby Venus,* Velázquez's only extant female nude. The painting was created during a period when the Spanish Inquisition forbade the painting of nudes, although King Philip IV and his courtiers had sizeable collections of them. The paucity of concrete information about the painting gives ample leeway to the novelist. Who was the model? Who commissioned the work and under what circumstances? How did Velázquez get away with painting it?

In order to tell this story, I decided to give voice to the model herself. Because she is in danger of having her identity discovered, she narrates in the third person, although occasionally, in a burst of anger or excitement, she slips into the first person. This strategy enabled me to retain the subjectivity of the narrator and also to broaden the focus of the story, because, as a woman and rule-breaker, Venus naturally provides unconventional views on events of the period.

Certain similarities between seventeenth-century Spain and the present-day US fascinate me. The Spanish monarchy had bankrupted the nation by overspending and through involvement in multiple foreign wars, then resorted to overtaxing the citizenry (but not the nobles). In order to continue conducting business, it borrowed extensively from foreign lenders, who eventually refused to extend credit, forcing the government to manufacture increasingly worthless money. Veterans returning from the Thirty Years' War faced unemployment and poverty. The ruling class exalted conventional morality while sinking into decadence. Although Spain had once been one of the most powerful nations in the world, by the end of the seventeenth century it was a political and economic shambles. More than Velázquez, who was protected by the King, Venus experienced how macropolitics affected individual Spaniards. Her activities bring readers into contact with nobles, artisans, soldiers, servants, beggars, nuns, priests, and even prostitutes. Through her, readers enter into the birthing room where Velázquez's wife is having his baby and the chapel where neighbors attend a funeral for an infant. They observe the devastating impact of the plague, the details of food preparation, the commerce of fashion, the suffering of returning war veterans, and the intermingling of Old Christians and Moriscos.[2] Venus is an astute observer, but as Velázquez's model she is highly vulnerable and therefore guarded.

Although, for me, finding an effective narrator has always been key to the process of writing biographical fiction, researching the period is what I find most enjoyable. Although I am aware that there are diverse opinions on the subject, to my mind biographical fiction is one form of historical fiction, and to reproduce the historical moment in which my characters lived is vital to the creation of a convincing biographical novel. I love the myriad details of daily life. What did people eat? How did they furnish their homes? What did they wear? How did they spend their leisure time? What toys did children play with? Not only historical studies, but also letters, diaries, paintings, and newspapers can provide clues, whether I am seeking to reproduce the world of the Mexican Revolution or of a sixteenth-century monastery. Knowledge of such minutiae is essential not only to create "period flavor," but also to understand the worldview of the characters. Features such as clothing styles reflect values and ways of thinking. When I write a biographical novel, I spend years researching my subject. Often I am teaching a course or writing a scholarly book on my protagonist.

Although I write in English, my characters are all Spanish or Latin American, and are therefore removed from readers not only chronologically but also linguistically. All historical fiction, including biographical fiction, is, in a sense, translation. The author must "translate"—that is, make intelligible—one culture to another, but, in the case of historical fiction about non-English speakers, language issues are paramount. A key question that dominates translation theory is whether translators should strive to preserve the inherent "foreignness" of the original work or attempt to make the translated version read as naturally as if it had been written in the second language. As Friedrich Schleiermacher puts it, "Either the translator leaves the author in peace as much as possible and moves the reader toward him; or he leaves the reader in peace as much as possible and moves the writer toward him" (49). With regard to historical fiction, we could rephrase Schleiermacher as follows: the author deliberately creates a world that is either uncomfortable and foreign for readers or comfortable and easily accessible. Those who favor the first option argue that, by retaining what is "other" or "strange," the author takes readers out of their comfort zone and enables them to expand their cultural horizons. Those who opt for the second argue that bizarreness can make a book inaccessible or off-putting for audiences, who should be able to enjoy a good read without being subjected to lessons in comparative sociology. I think that writers of any kind of historical fiction, including biographical fiction, always struggle to find the right balance between historical accuracy and readability. This tension is evident in Geraldine Brooks' *Year of Wonders,* in which the author emphasizes the "otherness" of her subject through the use of archaic language, but appeals to contemporary feminist sensibilities in the book's dénouement. In contrast, Dan Brown appeals unabashedly to a popular contemporary audience by casting *The Da Vinci Code* as a mystery in which modern detectives explore historical clues and by patently disregarding historical accuracy.

For me, neither Brooks' stilted language and superimposed feminism nor Brown's cavalier treatment of history works. I have sought to be faithful to history, including the personal history of my protagonists, while at the same time producing books that are readable and characters and situations that, in spite of being particular to specific times and places, speak to widespread human concerns. My characters speak colloquial English, since they would be using colloquial Spanish, easily comprehensible to their interlocutors, if they were speaking their native language. I strive to maintain a sense of linguistic "otherness," however, through the occasional insertion of Spanish words. The imperfection of this solution bothered me for a long time. It did not seem quite kosher to me that Frida, Teresa, and Venus, who spoke Spanish in my head, were speaking English on my pages. I eventually overcame my compunction about language by accepting English, the language in which I choose to write, as one of the inevitable filters that constitute my own world view and inevitably color my depictions of historical subjects.

Frida, Teresa, and Velázquez are all prominent figures who have been defined by institutions, the popular press, and the public. By stressing the subjective in all historical writing, I hope to ignite the imagination of readers and encourage them to explore new and unconventional ways of seeing our cultural icons.

Georgetown University

Notes

1 Frida claimed to be the daughter of a German-Hungarian Jew, although a 2005 book, *Fridas Vater,* asserts that her father, Wilhelm, was actually from a German-Lutheran background (Franger et al.). Teresa was the granddaughter of a Jewish convert.

2 Moriscos were converted Moors, many of whom continued to live in Spain despite their official expulsion in 1609.

Works cited

Bird, Stephanie. *Recasting Historical Women: Female Identity in German Biographical Fiction.* Oxford: Berg, 1998. Print.

Brooks, Geraldine. *Year of Wonders: A Novel of the Plague.* New York: Viking, 2001. Print.

Brown, Dan. *The Da Vinci Code.* New York: Doubleday, 2004. Print.

Franger, Gaby, et al. *Fridas Vater: Der Fotograf Guillermo Kahlo; von Pforzheim bis Mexiko.* Munich: Schirmer Mosel, 2005. Print.

Karla, Grammatiki. "Fictional Biography vis-à-vis Romance: Affinity and Differentiation." *Fiction on the Fringe.* Ed. Karla. Leiden: Brill, 2009. 13–39. Print.

Kehlmann, Daniel. "Out of This World." *Guardian* 21 Apr. 2007. Web. 25 July 2015.

Medwick, Cathleen. *Teresa of Avila: The Progress of a Soul.* New York: Knopf, 1999. Print.

Mujica, Bárbara. *Frida: A Novel.* New York: Overlook, 2001. Print.

—. *I Am Venus.* New York: Overlook, 2013. Print.

—. *Sister Teresa.* New York: Overlook, 2007. Print. New York: Overlook, 2013. Print.

Pinedo Kahlo, Isolda. *Frida Intima.* Bogotá: Dipon, 2004. Print.

Rivera, Diego, and Gladys March. *My Art, My Life: An Autobiography.* New York: Citadel, 1960. Print.

Schleiermacher, Friedrich. "On the Different Methods of Translating." *The Translation Studies Reader.* Trans. Susan Bernofsky. Ed. Lawrence Venuti. New York: Routledge, 2004. 43–63. Print.

Teresa de Jesús. *Libro de la vida.* Ed. Dámaso Chicarro. Madrid: Cátedra, 1993. Print.

Vargas Llosa, Mario. *La verdad de las mentiras.* Barcelona: Seix Barral, 1990. Print.

16

Joanna Scott

"On Hoaxes, Humbugs, and Fictional Portraiture" from *a/b: Auto/Biography Studies* (2016)

Abstract

From its origins, fiction has made a paradoxical claim on readers, presenting its inventions as actual history. In particular, biographical fiction often blurs the boundary between verifiable fact and its imagined material. Like an expertly executed hoax, a strong fictional portrait that borrows from history invites fascination with its uncanny reality.

On 6 June 1868, a cigar manufacturer named George Hull picked out a large block of gypsum from a quarry in Fort Dodge, Iowa. After shipping the block to Chicago, he hired sculptors to shape the gypsum into a huge figure of a man. When they were done, Hull had the stone giant doused in sulfuric acid and pounded with darning needles. Then he sent it by train to a relative's farm outside Cardiff in upstate New York, where it was planted, at Hull's direction, in a five-foot-deep hole.

Hull proved to be a patient man, waiting a full year before conspiring with his relative to unearth the giant. The farmer announced that he wanted a well dug on his property, specifying the precise location beside his barn. All went according to Hull's plan, and the men hired to dig the well were amazed to discover the stone figure. Word spread rapidly that a petrified giant from a prehistoric race had been found in Cardiff. So many people flocked to see the curiosity that an eating establishment was erected nearby, advertising "Warm Meals, Oysters, and Oats." In the weeks that followed, the Newell farm averaged 300 to 500 visitors daily. On one Sunday alone, 2,600 tickets were sold, at fifty cents each.

It was not long before scientists began to weigh in on the find. A local physician examined the figure and concluded it was a stone statue that had been carved hundreds of years earlier by a Jesuit missionary. Others discredited it as a more recent confection. Yet people still came in droves, drawn by the object's notoriety and by the force of their own persistent credulity. "What is it?" they kept asking.

The Cardiff Giant is one example of the many hoaxes perpetrated in the nineteenth century and widely disseminated with the help of steam-powered printing presses. No matter how outrageous the story, if it appeared in the newspaper it had the imprimatur of truth. The public read about a hyena on the run in Ohio, a balloon powered by coal gas that crossed the Atlantic in three days, and a poor woman who was devoured by a carnivorous tree on Madagascar. And did you hear that a scientist with a powerful telescope discovered bison on the moon?

The hoax is its own genre, distinguished, according to the historian Lynda Walsh, by the audience's assumption that the source is trustworthy.  Hoaxes gain credibility when they are reported by reputable sources and verified by experts. Good hoaxes are memorable because they are effectively convincing. The best hoaxes, though, are more than mere tricks. Like any artful performance, they give us a chance to reflect on our willingness to be deceived.

P. T. Barnum maintained that the true meaning of humbug is "to take an old truth and put it in an attractive form" (Saxon 357). A worthwhile fake—with an old truth at its center—needs theatrical flair even more than it needs a semblance of authenticity, in Barnum's view. And he knew what he was talking about. When he could not buy the Cardiff Giant, he had an imitation made and exhibited it at his American Museum two blocks away, boldly advertising the very possibility of trickery: "Is it a Statue? Is it a Petrification? Is it a Stupendous Fraud? Is it the remains of a former Race?" (Jacobs 352) Barnum challenged curiosity-seekers to make their own judgment about the Cardiff Giant and, in doing so, lured the public away from the rival exhibition with his own inimitable fake.

While people generally do not welcome being cast as suckers, Barnum persuaded his audience to appreciate his hoaxes. More recently, the writer William Boyd tested the public's gullibility with his biography of the artist Nat Tate. The publication of the book was celebrated on 1 April 1998 at a party hosted by David Bowie in the studio of the artist Jeff Koons. It was a glittering affair, and the guests were eager to appear stylish and knowledgeable. Many of them spoke with journalists about their impressions of Nat Tate. They remembered shows featuring his work and lamented his tragically premature death. There was one enormous problem with Boyd's book, however: Nat Tate never existed. He was the product of Boyd's lively imagination, a fictional character who was introduced to the world as real, with Bowie and Koons playing along. Boyd came clean and admitted the hoax a week after the publication party, explaining that he had set out to write a modern fable about the "unending brouhaha" of the art world. Today, you can find the book catalogued as a "fictional biography." Safely shelved in its proper place, the book no longer pretends to stick to the facts.

Tellingly, Boyd has said that his main aim was "to prove how powerful and credible a pure fiction could be." He must have known it was a doomed effort. Take the fiction out of fiction and what are we left with? Something other than fiction. But that does not make the ambition any less commendable, or even unfamiliar to novelists. There is a long tradition among novelists of pleading for the stature that comes with verifiable truth. Daniel Defoe set an influential precedent in his preface to *Moll Flanders*. Contrasting his book to the novels and romances crowding the world of eighteenth-century English literature, Defoe called it a "private history" and claimed that the original true story was merely recast in the words of a more learned narrator: "The pen employed in finishing [Moll's] story, and making it what you now see it to be, has had no little difficulty to put it into a dress fit to be seen, and to make it speak language fit to be read" (v).

Nearly three hundred years have passed since Defoe published *Moll Flanders*. We should know by now what we are getting into when we pick up a novel. We embark on a game of pretend characterized by an imaginative freedom that is uniquely appealing to those of us who do not want to be beholden to the rules governing reality. We just have to remind ourselves—or be reminded on the copyright page—that any resemblance to real persons is only coincidental. Yet, from its origins, fiction has made a paradoxical claim on readers, presenting made-up tales as history and asking readers to believe without suspicion. The story of Moll Flanders differs from fact only in the manner of its dress, Defoe assures us. It is autobiography in costume, on a stage that is not always clearly visible. Sometimes, as happened to the first readers of Boyd's novel, we may not even know we are in a theater. As soon as the word "fiction" is attached to the story, however, we are back in the audience, watching a performance where fancy and fact mix, diluting the purity of both.

Fiction and hoaxes both perform in disguises that have been carefully designed by their creators. The story of the Cardiff Giant suggests that even once the specter of duplicity has been raised, a hoax can remain fascinating in its uncertain state. By the time the imitation giant took its place in Barnum's museum of curiosities, the public knew that at least one of the figures was a fake, but they were willing to pay the price of a ticket. In the simplest sense, Barnum's copy of a fake offered the appearance of authenticity—this was what a petrified giant would look like, if one were found.

After getting over our embarrassment when a spectacle is revealed as a hoax, we might enjoy a wry, humbling admiration for the trickster's ingenuity. Similarly, much of the pleasure of fiction comes from the ingenious creation of illusion. Fiction's costume is made of words. As Henry Fielding, echoing Defoe, counseled readers at the beginning of his novel *Tom Jones,* "the excellence of the mental entertainment consists less in the subject than in the author's skill in well dressing it up" (28). Even better than a clever hoax is a fictional character who is so well dressed up with expressive language that he gains a tantalizing existence, like a dream that is so real that we are tempted to remember it as a physical experience.

The fiction that has given me the most pleasure as a reader tends to be full of portraits that are vividly available to my imagination and end up taking an insistent hold in my memory. I have savored Charles Dickens for this reason. Having been introduced, say, to Maggie in *Little Dorrit,* I will not forget her: "A great white cap, with a quantity of opaque frilling that was always flapping about, apologised for Maggy's baldness, and made it so very difficult for her old black bonnet to retain its place upon her head, that it held on round her neck like a gipsy's baby. A commission of haberdashers could alone have reported what the rest of her poor dress was made of; but it had a strong general resemblance to seaweed, with here and there a gigantic tea-leaf. Her shawl looked particularly like a tea-leaf after long infusion" (142). How surely Dickens creates his portraits, with quick strokes of a perfect set of sentences, every word fitting neatly to form a distinct, unified personality. I also relish the way a more jarring presentation can coalesce to make up a character, as with James Joyce's Bloom ("he liked thick giblet soup, nutty gizzards, a stuffed roast heart, liver slices fried with crustcrumbs, fried hencod's roes" [55]), William Faulkner's Dilsey ("The door of the cabin opened and Dilsey emerged once more, this time in a man's felt hat and an army overcoat, beneath the frayed skirts of which her blue gingham dress fell in uneven balloonings" [266]), or Virginia Woolf s Septimus ("He lay very high, on the back of the world. The earth thrilled beneath him" [68]).

When a character is rendered with spirited precision, the complexity of the portrait extends beyond expressible attributes. Consider, for example, the character of Lucy Cabrol, the protagonist of the final story in John Berger's *Pig Earth.* I close my eyes and can see her roll a cigarette, gulp her *gnôle,* comb blueberries on a slope above the tree line. And yet I recognize from the misjudgments of other characters that I cannot really know her, not fully. She is vivid and elusive, a little woman defined by her nickname, the Cocadrille, who defies definition.

As I consider the powerful experience of reading about singular characters, I realize that they are hardly distinguishable in my mind from the real subjects I have been introduced to in fine biographies. Who is more real, the Milly Theale of *Wings of the Dove* or the Henry James of Leon Edel's biography? If I did not know better, I would call Peter Gay's Sigmund Freud and Hermione Lee's Virginia Woolf both fictional characters. And I keep getting them mixed up: do Defoe's *Moll Flanders* and *A Journal of the Plague Year* belong to different genres?

The territories of fiction and history are demarcated by a border that is jagged, maybe even porous in places. Biography gives actual lives a fictional tinge, and fiction gives invented lives an uncanny presence. Precariously balanced on the line between them is the hoax, incorporating elements of both genres and inviting fascination by recasting an old truth in a new form.

When I embarked on my first foray into biographical fiction in my novel *Arrogance,* I was not thinking about what biography and fiction may share, nor was I thinking about hoaxes. I was thinking primarily about portraiture. I named my main character Egon Schiele because I wanted to make a portrait of him, in the same spirit, if not with the same methods, as he had made his own portraits of women, children, family members, friends, and himself. I was not interested in measuring the resemblance of Schiele's painted figures to the models. What ignited my imagination was the richness of human experience conveyed by shapes suspended on a canvas. While I appreciate the surface work of the brush strokes, I could not keep myself from conjuring an interiority for these figures. They were fictions to me before I began my novel. I imagined their intentions, their moods, their hunger, and their dreams, even as I considered the evidence of a singular mind expressing itself through choices made about color and composition.

A strong portrait from any period will draw me across the space of a gallery so I can take a closer look. For example, I see in one of Schiele's most provocative self-portraits from 1911 (now at the Metropolitan Museum of Art) a potent combination of explicitness and mystery, with the naked, contorted figure completely available to our gaze, present inside the frame, and yet disclosing nothing. Sure, the portrait is just watercolor, gouache, and pencil on paper, but it is hard not to be curious about the person represented.

A successful fictional portrait will have a similar effect, presenting a reader with the force of presence and, at the same time, inciting curiosity. Usually, these characters come with made-up names, sometimes as composites borrowed from living people. Less common in fiction are the characters who share names with notable individuals from the past. Their presence on the page tenders a special challenge. I am not talking about the frustrating challenge of figuring out where the facts end and imagination begins. Rather, a character who borrows a real name from history asks us to believe in the fiction for its own sake and, at the same time, to keep the biographical model in mind.

"Sounds are impostures," reflects Joyce's Stephen Dedalus. "Like names, Cicero, Podmore, Napoleon, Mr Goodbody, Jesus, Mr Doyle. Shakespeares were as common as Murphies. What's in a name?" (509). Whether a character is drawn from life or history, whether she is named Moll Flanders or Eleanor Roosevelt, she will not have forceful presence if the author has not succeeded "in well dressing up." Once she is wearing a worthy costume of effectively arranged words, the fictional Eleanor can have as much presence in our imagination as Moll. There is one important difference, though. The names have the effect of reminding us that a reality exists elsewhere, in an actual past—a contrast that, perhaps surprisingly, emphasizes the invention of the fiction.

Gore Vidal, a writer known for creating vivid fictional portraits of historical figures, was asked in a *Paris Review* interview to speculate about what set him apart from other writers. He replied, "I value invention highly, and hardly anyone else does" (156). A typical American novelist, he went on to say, was "terrified that you might think he actually made up a character, that what he writes might not be literally as opposed to imaginatively true" (156). While writing his novel about Aaron Burr, he created space in the story where he could "breathe and make up new things" (158). He did not set out to write a biography. "My *Burr* is not the real Burr" (158), he declared.

What if Aaron Burr had been Vidal's contemporary? There is a special concern when a fictional character is based on a living person: it is known as libel. Publishing a false statement of fact that is injurious to the reputation of an identifiable living person may get a writer into trouble, which is all the more reason to make sure that the character exists fully within the frame of the fiction. Successful fiction must convince the reader to believe in the existence of a character as an independent entity, present and forceful, vivid and mysterious. And for those portraits connected by their names to models borrowed from history, the news, or the neighborhood, there is extra incentive to make the work "imaginatively true." I may not have been considering this when I made my portrait of Egon Schiele, but I know that I gave myself lots of room to "breathe and make up new things." And I kept looking for any opportunity to call fixed judgments into question by introducing contrary views. I aimed to present a mosaic of portraits that were, like Schiele's portraits, simultaneously present and elusive enough to stir the reader's imagination. I was not trying to pretend that my Schiele was the real Schiele. I just wanted him to be real.

University of Rochester

Works cited

Boyd, William. "How I Fooled the Art World." *Telegraph* 13 Nov. 2011. Web. 24 July 2015.

Defoe, Daniel. *Moll Flanders*. 1722. New York: Signet, 1964. Print.

Dickens, Charles. *Little Dorrit.* 1857. London: Penguin, 1967. Print.

Faulkner, William. *The Sound and the Fury.* 1929. New York: Vintage International, 1990. Print.

Fielding, Henry. *Tom Jones.* 1749. New York: Signet, 1963. Print.

Jacobs, Harvey. *America Goliath, vol 1.* New York: St. Martins. 1997. Print.

Joyce, James. *Ulysses.* 1922. New York: Vintage, 1986. Print.

Saxon, A. H. *P. T. Barnum: The Legend and the Man.* New York: Columbia UP, 1989. Print.

Vidal, Gore. "The Art of Fiction L." *Paris Review* 59 (1974): 131–65. Print.

Walsh, Lynda, *Sins against Science: The Scientific Media Hoaxes of Poe, Twain, and Others.* Albany: State U of New York P, 2006. Print.

Woolf, Virginia. *Mrs. Dalloway.* 1925. San Diego: Harvest, 1981. Print.

PART TWO

The Case of Eliza Lynch

17

William E. Barrett

"Foreword" from *Woman on Horseback: The Biography of Francisco Lopez and Eliza Lynch* (1938)

Paraguay is the country of prophecy.

One of the two smallest nations on the American continent, it was the first American communistic state, the first American nation to be governed by an absolute dictator (in the modern sense of the term) and in 1936—a year before the Brazilian coup—Paraguay became a totalitarian state with a Fascist form of government.

In 1864, while the United States was fighting its war between the states, Paraguay produced the World War of 1914-1918 in miniature; a prophetic picture of the great war that was to come. Engaged against three foes which were identified in the press as "the Allies," Paraguay found it necessary to commit "outrages" against shipping as an offset to a blockade which had forced it to the production of synthetic food and clothing. Paraguay's dictator, Francisco Lopez, brought one of his most powerful foes into the war against him when, at the suggestion of Ella Lynch, his mistress, he crossed the territory of a neutral to engage a belligerent. Fighting against odds, Lopez resorted to trench warfare and, in preparation for inevitable retreat, he constructed a "Hindenburg Line" of trenches in three parallel rows, each trench vulnerable to the fire of the trench behind it.

Inevitably, too, the Allies were victorious and the terms of the peace were a foreshadowing of Versailles. The conquered nation was disarmed, occupied, regulated, bound to observe disarmament and boundary treaties for a period of years—and economically ruined.

Ella Lynch remains the only prophecy unfulfilled. The peculiar talents that were hers could never have been put to her own use; she held them in trust for the man who could command them. Without her, Lopez was erratic and uncertain despite his great gift to command; with her he became a perfectly balanced weapon that threw a shadow over South America.

There are many stories in Paraguay that are worth the telling. There is drama in the communistic state of the Jesuits, a taxless state in which every human being received the simple necessities of life and where competitive stress did not exist. There is drama in the story of the Spanish governors who took the excess of production over consumption, used it for export and struck a balance in gold; gold which they preferred to keep in South America for a new Spanish aristocracy in preference to shipping it to old Spain. Then Francia, the half-breed dictator "without a human passion or a human vice save the vice of Lucifer, pride"; the man who made a footstool out of church and state and human dignity.

The stories could be told, and should be told, but the story that matters in the history of Paraguay, because it is the story that affected the destiny of all South America, is the story of Francisco Solano Lopez.

The years that preceded Lopez prepared for him, the years that followed him paid the price of his having lived.

This is the story of Francisco Lopez and of Elisa Alicia Lynch. The story of one cannot be told without the other. They built together in the years of peace and they rode together through the years of an incredible war. In the bloody saga of Francisco Lopez, Ella Lynch shared both authority and responsibility, and she is aptly described by Hector Varela as "a beautiful sinner vitally linked to calamitous events."

The writer of an historical narrative incurs countless debts in the course of the writing; his greatest obligation is to History itself.

In the preparation of "Woman on Horseback," I discarded many romantic legends which would have delighted a novelist and which would have outraged fact. In the writing, I have been faithful to time and place and sequence; in no case distorting the true chronology of events for dramatic effect. Bearing in mind General McMahon's statement that "There never was a war in reference to which there was so much lying as this Paraguayan War," and Hilaire Belloc's phrase that "readable history is melodrama," I have documented more heavily than is the custom in a work of this kind and have striven to keep from melodramatic material the curse of melodramatic writing.

I have not enlisted with the defenders nor the attackers of Francisco Lopez and Ella Lynch. I have tried first to understand them and then so to assemble my material as to convey my understanding of them to the reader. If they emerge from the book as human beings and if they awaken an interest in the colorful and astonishing history of the South American nations, I will be more than content.

To the Library of Congress, and to the many members of its staff who gave me such splendid assistance, I acknowledge my debt and express my most sincere thanks. I wish, also, to make grateful acknowledgment to the Ibero-American Library of the Catholic University for the splendid facilities placed at my disposal and for permission to examine many rare items of the Lima Collection; and to the Library of the Carnegie Endowment for International Peace which afforded me access to much material unobtainable elsewhere and under conditions which made the research most pleasant.

To the following individuals, I owe an especial debt of gratitude: Mr. William Louis Dunne, who knows South America as he knows his United States and who shared his correspondence and his recollections with unstinted generosity; Mr. Charles Gauld, Ph.D. candidate in Latin-American studies, University of California, whose capable assistance was invaluable in the translation of many papers and documents; Mr. Paul A. McNeil, the custodian of the Lima Collection, whose friendly interest was not confined to library hours; Mrs. Florence Jackson Stoddard, who knew the sons of Francisco Lopez and Ella Lynch in Buenos Aires and who contributed many anecdotes and incidents from personal recollection and from her correspondence; and to those, anonymous by request, who generously permitted me to examine the private correspondence of one who played a vital part in the drama of the "Woman on Horseback."

William E. Barrett.

18

Anne Enright

"Acknowledgments" from *The Pleasure of Eliza Lynch* (2002)

I must acknowledge the work of Josefina Plá (*The British in Paraguay in the 19th Century*, Richmond, 1976) and of Helene Clastres (*The Land-Without-Evil: Tupí-Guaraní Prophetism*, University of Illinois Press, 1995). As for the rest: Eliza Lynch seems to provoke in her English-speaking biographers all kinds of sneering excess. Some facts seem to remain constant and it is around these facts that this (scarcely less fictional) account has been built. This is a novel, however. It is Not True.

Thanks are due to The Arts Council/An Comhairle Ealíonn; to the ever-wonderful staff at the Tyrone Guthrie Centre at Annaghmakerrig; and to the library of Trinity College Dublin.

Special thanks to Mario Rosner of Buenos Aires for a likely picture of the *Tacuarí*, to the friends who read the manuscript, and to Shane Enright for additional library work.

19

Lily Tuck

"Author's Note" from *The News from Paraguay* (2004)

Of course there was an Ella Lynch who was beautiful and misguided, there was a Francisco Solano Lopez who was cruel and ambitious, there were family members, generals, good and bad diplomats and their wives (even so I have taken certain liberties: for instance, I have no idea what Mrs. Charles Washburn looked like, I have her blond and fragile but she might well have been a strapping brunette), and of course there never was a Doña Iñes or Fulgencio and his brother, Gaspar. Nonetheless, I have tried to keep to historical facts where I find them to be important and necessary. The events that take place, especially those dealing with the war, are complicated and, for the most part, not well known, which means that the need to explain and the need to dramatize are often at odds. What then, the reader may wonder, is fact and what is fiction? My general rule of thumb is whatever seems most improbable is probably true. Also I would like to quote a friend who cautions his readers with these words: "Nouns always trump adjectives, and in the phrase 'historical fiction' it is important to remember which of the two words is which."

I am particularly indebted to the following works: *Letters from the Battle-fields of Paraguay,* by Captain Richard F. Burton, F.R.G.S., etc., whose keen observations on flora and fauna and human nature were most edifying; *Seven Eventful Years in Paraguay: A Narrative of Personal Experience amongst the Paraguayans,* by George Frederick Masterman, whose quaint anecdotes and quirky illustrations greatly animate his woeful tale; *The War in Paraguay,* by George Thompson, C.E., to whom I am grateful for much, including his appreciation of the Whitworth cannon and Paraguayan cigar; and *The History of Paraguay,* by Charles A. Washburn, where I found much valuable information, including the journal excerpts quoted.

PART THREE

Lectures and Forums

20

Irving Stone

"The Biographical Novel" from *Three Views of the Novel* (1957)

The biographical novel is a true and documented story of one human being's journey across the face of the years, transmuted from the raw material of life into the delight and purity of an authentic art form.

The biographical novel is based on the conviction that the best of all plots lie in human character; and that human character is endlessly colorful and revealing. It starts with the assumption that those stories which have actually happened can be at least as interesting and true as those which have been imagined. Alexander Pope said that the proper study of mankind is man; the biographical novel accepts that challenge and sets out to document its truth, for character is plot; character development is action; and character fulfillment is resolution.

The biographical novel attempts to fuse not only its parent sources of biography and the novel, but that of its grandparent, history, as well. It must tell the story of its main character, not in the bulk of millionfold detail, but in essence; it must recreate the individual against the background of his times, with all of its authentic historical flavor; and it must live up to the exacting demands of the novel structure.

Let me joyfully proclaim that basically the biographical novelist is a yarn-spinner, and the biographical novel a vigorous medium that has been created in order to tell the fine stories that have been lived. The form is fortunate in its opportunity to utilize the single greatest virtue of the novel: growth of character. This growth may be into good or evil, into creativity or destruction; it cannot be static. There are few joys for the reader to surpass that of watching an interesting story unfold through growth of character; and in this field no form surpasses the biographical novel, which by the very definition of its nature is always about people rather than impersonal forces.

The biographical novelist has a greater freedom to interpret than has the biographer, and the reader has a greater chance of coming away with a more personal understanding of human motivation. If there is a tendency to oversimplify, it is in the same fashion that man's memory does as he looks back on his span of time, forgetting nine-tenths of the bulk, remembering only the distillation which has meaning. For the biographical novel is based not merely on fact, but on feeling, the legitimate emotion arising from indigenous drama. Facts can get lost with almost too great a facility, but an emotional experience, once lived, can never be forgotten. Nor can this emotion be artificially induced for the sake of raising the reader's temperature. While a biography can be written purely out of a life's worthiness, with details of important names, places and dates, the biographical novel must emerge naturally and organically from the conflicts of man against himself, man against man, or man against fate. Since an experience shared will remain with one forever, it is the aim of the biographical novel to bring the reader into the very heart of the emotion being engendered so that he will make that emotion his own. For the feelings have a memory and a wisdom of which the mind could well be covetous.

In the fields of straight biography and history, the reader stands on the sidelines. What is transpiring on the page is something that happened long ago, and to other people. When reading the biographical novel he is no longer a spectator, but a participant. He starts to live the story as though its first incident had its inception at the instant he opened the book. Perhaps the biographical novel has become so popular because the reader is allowed to participate intimately in history, to become one of its prime actors and motivators. Thus all history becomes contemporary, as in truth it is. The old joke about the man who thought he was Napoleon can come true.

In the biographical novel therefore, the reading and the doing, through identification, become synonymous; the reader can live a thousand different lives during a relatively brief span of years. Therein lies the genius of the form, therein lies its enchantment and its hope for a permanent place in the literary heavens.

With the exception of Merejkowsky's *Romance of Leonardo da Vinci* and Gertrude Atherton's novel of Alexander Hamilton, *The Conqueror,* the biographical novel was unknown and unaccepted in the United States thirty years ago. Yet today it can be found in the catalogue of every major publisher. Now that the biographical novel has come of age, a few ground rules can perhaps be laid down for its practitioners.

The first of these must surely be that history is not the servant of the biographical novelist, but his master. No biographical novel can be better than its research. If the research is deep and honest, the novel will be deep and honest; if the research is sleazy, shallow, evasive or sensation-seeking, the novel will be sleazy, shallow, evasive, sensation-mongering.

Not every life will fit into the form of the biographical novel. There are specific dramatic elements that must be present, recurrent themes of conflict and accomplishment woven through its entirety, an overall, perceivable pattern into which the parts can be fitted to make an organic whole. There are many lives, important and significant in their end results, which are nonetheless diffuse, their content and design antithetical to the nature of the novel; others seem to have been lived as though the subject himself were constantly aware that he was creating a dramatic structure.

While the biographical novelist is assuredly licensed to search out and select those lives which make good copy, the basic demonstrable truth cannot be pushed around to serve a plot purpose. The writer who must twist or pervert the historic truth to come out with what he thinks is an acceptable or saleable story is a tragically misplaced person in his field. The biographical novelist, on the other hand, who becomes moralistic or political, turns into a pamphleteer. We have had experiences of American biographical novelists twisting history out of shape and proportion in order to make it conform to a preconceived line. What has emerged has been neither legitimate biography nor authentic novel, but propaganda. Biography is rich in materials which can be used to serve a purpose; and the biographical novel, young as it is, has not been free from those who would use the form unscrupulously. But this is a danger incident to all of the arts, particularly in a time of war for man's mind; our nostrils must become aware of the rancid smell of such books. In the biographical novel, as in all art forms, personal and professional integrity lie at the base of lasting accomplishment.

An integrated, successful, first-rate biographical novel can emerge only from a union of the material chosen and the author of the choice; from a free, mutually respectful and frequently self-sacrificing partnership in which the story that has been lived and the author who is recreating that story in print, must be equal, and the final product remain more important than either of the contributing partners. If either one assumes an ascendancy the novel will lack for balance: the material will dominate the author, take directions in defiance of the structure; or the author will dominate the material, make it a creature of his own will and desiring. Few authors are qualified to write equally well or profoundly on all subjects. The wise author waits, or searches, for that meaningful story which he can understand, which moves him, and which he senses he can bring vividly to life. If the author chooses unwisely, perhaps because he does not know his material well enough before he starts, or does not know himself well enough, the result can only be false and fragmentary or at best a dismal regurgitation.

The author has a right to ask, as he looks at the outline of a human life, "Can this story serve my purposes?"—but only after he has demanded of himself, "Can I serve the purposes of this story?"

Because of the principle of selection, the biographical novel will inevitably end up as much a portrait of the author as of the subject, for the biographical novelist is a distiller, deriving his spirits not from rye, and we hope not from corn; but from the boiling-pot of human experience. It follows that the biographical novel, even though it leans so heavily on biography and history, can be no better than the mind of its author. If the author is dull, the novel will be dull, and neither biography nor history can save him. If the author is cold, the novel will be cold, no matter how flaming the material being handled. If the author is humorless, the novel will be humorless; if the author is narrow in his interests, his novel will be narrow in its interests, no matter how wide a slice of life it may be reflecting. And if the author is dishonest, what emerges from the pages must be a dishonest novel, regardless of the integrity of the character being portrayed.

How is a reader unacquainted with the field to distinguish between the honest and dishonest biographical novel, the complete and the fractional? How can the question, "How much of this is true?" be answered? Only by insisting that the biographical novel must be as complete in its documentation as the most scholarly history and biography, and as honest in its interpretation.

If it takes four years to train a schoolteacher or engineer, five years to train a pharmacist, six a dentist, seven a lawyer, and eight a doctor, is there any reason to believe that it can take less time to develop a qualified and professional biographical novelist?

He must become experienced in the writing of imaginative novels, wrestling with this form in order that he may come up against the challenging complexities of structure, mood, master scenes, dialogue, with its accompanying lyricism of language, the mounting involvement and suspense of the fictional tale. He would be well advised to write a half-dozen plays to absorb the superb economy of the form, and learn how to stage his tale under a proscenium instead of in the wings: for what the reader does not see with his eyes he never really knows.

He must be trained as a biographer, working at the assembling of materials about one man or group of men, mastering the technic of close-knit organization of these materials, the perceiving and the weaving back and forth of the life theme, evolving a style, personality, and manner of writing by means of which one man's story can be brought to life all over again by black hieroglyphs on white paper: the eternal miracle of literature: for each life has a distinctive face and figure; and this must be captured in order to differentiate this one special story from the hundreds of millions that have been lived.

The biographical novelist must become as scientific a researcher as was Dr. Jonas Salk in his medical laboratories. During the six years that I attended the University of California there were no courses in the fascinating science of research. I had to stumble my way toward a modus operandi. Today most colleges give courses in research which make the tools of this exciting trade as available and usable as those in accounting or electronics. The biographical novelist must be as dedicated to his digging as the archaeologist who uncovers ancient cities after years of pick and shovel work; and he must be grimly resolved that there is absolutely nothing in the historic record which cannot be found if one will search for it long enough, arduously enough and adroitly enough. Fresh and daring ideas about where and how to look are as important to successful research as are the extracting of fresh and daring drawings by painters from their own minds. Parenthetically the biographical novelist must be as stout of heart as the most ardent lover, for important new materials are frequently buried deep, yielding their charms and protected virtues only to importunate courtship.

Though research is as fascinating as the resolution of a crossword puzzle or a murder mystery, it is also hard work, thoroughly exhausting and unending in its demands. The researcher sometimes gets lost in his forest of facts. To change the metaphor, the biographical novel must be built like an iceberg, about one ninth of solid substance showing above the literary water line, and the other eight-ninths submerged, but giving a solid base to that which is permitted to appear. If the biographical novelist does not know nine times as much as he reveals, the substance of the print he spreads over the page will be painfully thin: for the eight-ninths which he does not reveal permeates the whole, giving to the pages a discernible bouquet, a subtle emanation which enables the reader to feel comfortable and secure.

For every printed page has a feel and a smell to it, just as surely as does a piece of fruit; it is the research which gives the page of the biographical novel its consistency, which enables the reader to feel that this particular piece of literary fruit is sound at its core, and will not soon decay if allowed to sit on the library table. In the biographical novel, research is the hard firm flesh under the surface skin of the printed page.

The biographical novelist must also be uncrushable in his faith that the truth will out, for when he finds three differing versions of the same happening, accompanied by three different sets of dates and circumstances, he must not become disheartened, but must believe that if he will continue to dig he will find a fourth, authentic version based on irrefutable documents. As Charles A. Beard, one of America's most brilliant historical researchers, told me in his library in New Canaan while helping me with an elusive problem, "Every day I find new source material which controverts something I have believed for thirty years."

To the biographical novelist history is not a mountain, but a river. Even when there are no new facts to be found, there are fresh insights, modern interpretations which can give an old story new focus and meaning; for the biographical novelist, like the archaeologist, is not just a pick and shovel man. The sweat on the forehead and the callouses on the palm are the merest preparation for the real work to come: interpretation of the uncovered materials which will throw light on a story long since lived.

The biographical novelist must also be a perennial skeptic and challenger of the printed word. My confrere, Robert Graves, recently told me in his workshop in Majorca that his biographical novel *I, Claudius* was born at the moment when, reading Tacitus, he cried out, "That's a lie!"

The number of lies and part-truths still resting comfortably and respectably in history is a constant source of astonishment to me; as I am equally amazed at the whole areas of history, even American history as late as the Civil War, or the turn of the twentieth century, that are inadequately researched, or simply not researched at all. It is here that the biographical novelist has his magnificent opportunity: for the vigor and enthusiasm, and a fresh point of view, he can change "That is a lie!" into "That is the truth!" just as he can throw beams of light into areas of history which have remained dark and damp through sheer neglect and want of a champion to rescue them from oblivion.

It also follows that the biographical novelist must be a fighter. Frequently the best stories, and the most meaningful, are those of the underdog, of the man or woman who has been vilified and traduced. From the body of my own work may I suggest as examples the stories of Eugene V. Debs, Rachel Jackson and Mary Todd Lincoln. All efforts to cut through the jungle of prejudiced print, to find the balanced, sympathetic yet judicious truth will be met not only with opposition but frequently with ridicule: for man is as unwilling to give up his vested interest in his prejudices as he is any other of his possessions.

Lastly, the biographical novelist must believe that first there came the Book; he must love books with an unflagging ardency, for he will spend the greater part of life with his nose inside one volume or another: and some of them will be mighty tough customers. He must be able to survive the eyestrain engendered by tiny type, the headaches brought on by handling crumbling yellow pages, the fading ink of aged diaries and letters; and worse, the bottomless depths of Dead Sea writing which would break the teeth of any man imprudent enough to read it aloud.

I would like to outline some specifics.

Having determined that he is going to write a biographical novel about the life of Leonardo da Vinci or Alexander Hamilton, the biographical novelist must put out of his mind for six months or a year any illusion that he is a writer, and become a library mole. He must read all the books and articles written by his subject, study the works created by him, be they art or engineering, read every findable word that has been written about the man or work. He must read all the letters that have passed between the hero and his contemporaries, as well as his private notes, journals and memoirs; or, in the case of a heroine, those wonderfully confiding diaries that are kept locked in the middle drawer of a desk. If the subject is of recent times, there will be a need to interview or correspond with everyone who has been involved in the drama, no matter how slightly.

Having grasped more fully the outlines of his story, the biographical novelist then takes to the road, seeing with his own eyes the places his hero has lived, the quality of the sunlight, the native earth beneath his feet, the personality of the cities and the feel of the countryside: for only then can he write with the intimacy and knowledgability of tactile experience.

This is the first and direct line of attack. The second is equally important: the biographical novelist must now begin the study of his hero's times, its fads and fancies, its majority and minority ideas as well as the prevailing conflicts in religion, philosophy, science, politics, economics and the arts; in short, the overall social, mental, spiritual, esthetic, scientific and international climate in which his characters lived and evolved their codes of conduct. He must read the source books of the period in order to absorb its background, the old newspapers, pamphlets, magazines, the novels, plays and poetry of the times, in order to learn the uncountable thousands of illuminating details which he must have at his fingertips in order to recreate the period: what people wear, the architecture of their houses as well as the fabric on their furniture, how they heat their homes, cook the foods they eat at the various hours of the day; what they are buying in the shops and why, how much it costs as well as how it tastes and smells and feels; what ailments they are suffering and how they are treating them; what colloquialisms they are using to enrich their conversation; what their preachers are preaching on Sunday morning and their teachers teaching on Monday morning.

If the biographical novelist has any feeling for his job he will eventually find emerging out of this seemingly vast and inchoate mass of material certain recurrent patterns, strains of character and action that provide a dominant motif and rhythm for the story he will tell, even as the dominant strains of a symphony are enunciated early. Above all, the biographical novelist is looking for those interwoven designs which are perceivable in every human life: for nearly every life works out its own tightly-woven plot structure. Any action forced upon the participants which does not arise indigenously, which arises instead from the author confusing motion with direction, tears the fabric of the story.

Yet by the same token the biographical novelist must be the master of his material; the craftsman who is not in control of his tools will have his story run away with him. For after his research labors, the biographical novelist must then expend as much time and energy as the writer of fiction to create a novel structure which will best project his material, and be unique to the particular story to be told.

And all this new knowledge must never come between the reader and the narration. In the biographical novel a basic tenet is that the author must stage his story as though it were happening right now; he may not emerge at intervals to inform the reader of what will happen two or twenty or two hundred years later. The reader may never be in possession of information which is not available to those who are acting out the day-by-day passion of their lives. The story must unfold for the reader even as the pageant of events unfolds for the participants. There are few soothsayers; the biographical novelist may not turn himself into an a posteriori prophet. Whatever the reader may divine about what lies ahead must arise from his own perception, and not from the biographical novelist fudging on time sequence. If there be wisdom in the author (and God grant that there may sometimes be!) it will emerge from the nature of the story he wants to tell, from his selection of materials within the framework of that particular story, from his understanding of what motivates his people, and from the skill with which he shapes the unassimilated raw action of human life.

Perhaps a glimpse of my own approaches and technics from *Lust For Life* through *Immortal Wife* and *Love is Eternal* may shed further light on this still nascent form. I first stumbled across the paintings of Vincent Van Gogh when taken to an exhibition by insistent Parisian friends. Seeing a whole room of Vincent's blazing Arlesian canvases was an emotional experience that I can liken only to my first reading of *The Brothers Karamazov.* I left the exhibition hall determined to find out who this man was who could move me to such depths. I read all the fragments I could find about him in English, French and German; when I returned to New York and to the writing of my plays, I would spend my evenings at the public library at Forty-second Street and Fifth Avenue, reading the three volumes of Vincent's letters to his brother Theo. I had no intention of writing about Vincent; I was only trying to understand him. But slowly over the months the Van Gogh story took possession of me; I found myself waking at three in the morning, writing dialogue passages between Vincent and Theo, or describing Vincent's death scene at Auvers sur Oise. Vincent's ordeal became for me one of the world's most meaningful stories. At the end of a year, when I found myself unable to think of anything else, I decided that I would have to write Vincent's story if for no other reason than to clear it from my mind.

My background for writing such a story was inadequate, for I had grown up in San Francisco where art was a portrait of two dead rabbits hanging by their feet. My first task then, was to read all the books I could find about art and modern painters, and then to search out the canvases that were available. I returned to Europe with a rucksack on my back and followed the trail of Vincent, going down into the mines of the Borinage where he had descended, living in his bedroom at Madam Dennis's bakery, writing notes in the parsonages where he had lived with his family in Holland, and going to the south of France to work in the Yellow House, to live in the asylum at St. Remy where he had been incarcerated, and finally to sleep in the same room and bed in the little hotel in Auvers on the fortieth anniversary of his death.

Since I did not know how much I did not know about the writing of a biographical novel, I sat down to my first morning's work with a little calling card in front of me on which I scribbled four strictures: 1. Dramatize. 2. Plenty of dialogue. 3. Bring all characters to life. 4. Use anecdotes and humor.

It is somewhat chastening to me, these many years later, when I write myself fifty pages of notes on precisely how the new book must be written and, collaterally, how it must not be written, to find that I emerge with a product which a lot of people feel is no better than *Lust for Life*. I sometimes wonder if I have spent the past twenty-five years enunciating intellectually the things I knew intuitively at the beginning.

It is also a source of considerable astonishment to me that I waited through three biographies to get back to the form in which I had achieved such a happy result; and that only a fortuitous accident pushed me back into the field.

Through my chapter on John C. Frémont in *They Also Ran*, the story of the men who were defeated for the presidency, I once again came across the woman with whom I had fallen in love in college, and in whose image I married: Jessie Benton Frémont. Jessie's story came to possess me, even as Vincent's had.

In the spring of 1943 I wrote myself a list of sixty-two specifics for *Immortal Wife*. I should like to read a few of them as samples of how one biographical novelist sets the boundaries and dimensions of his task.

I quote directly from my notes:

> *The story must flow swiftly, smoothly, lyrically. It is a story of people, not history. People come first, history follows. It must be at least half dialogue. Jessie's interior monologue and thinking must be quietly done, understated. Everything must be seen through her eyes. All characters must be brought sharply and vividly to life. Every scene, every word, must be contemporary. Every reader must identify himself with Jessie. Panorama of a changing world: 1840, 1900 through one woman's eyes. Nothing described for description's sake, only as seen by Jessie and as important in her life. No fact for fact's sake, everything human. Material constantly new, refreshing, yet fitting into life pattern. Humor as constant leaven. Patience in developing and revealing major themes. Must be primarily a love story. Constantly changing nature of their love, yet fundamentally same. Always the third dimension of failure, error, human failing. The fourth dimensions of mysticism: faith in each other and the world, undying hope as wellspring of human life. Thorough and penetrating job on love and marriage. Keep language universal. Never the whole story; always the essence. No skimping of material; no overblown presentation. Vivid imagery of detail of times, rich contrast of changing scene: Washington, St. Louis, Mariposa. Use interesting mechanisms for history, not just plumped down. Should embrace the whole of a life, one life, as symbolic of all.*

Seven years later, when I came to the formulating of *The President's Lady*, I wrote myself advice under the heading of "What devices can be used to get inside Rachel?" some of which may prove germane at this point:

> *We must react to situations with her mind. We must see people through her eyes, our sense of values must be her sense of values. We must suffer from the things that disturb her, and want (at least for her) the things that she wants. We must share her love for Andrew, endure with her the long terrifying loneliness. The form of our anxieties must be identical with the form of her anxieties; we must evaluate all events through the focus of her needs. We must cling to, and love, the friends and relatives she does. We must want fame and greatness for Andrew, and yet fear them terribly too. We must turn religious, need and justify that religion when she does. She must be the stage upon which history is acted out. We must tremble, then rejoice in her few social triumphs, and die when she dies, acknowledging the lethal blow. We must like Rachel, care about her, understand, sympathize with her. We must enjoy her life from inside her mind and heart.*
>
> *This can be achieved by warmth of approach; by the author liking her, himself. By a simple, honest directness of storytelling, by understatement, so that the reader builds up his own emotions. By keeping her clear; by moving her swiftly through events, almost too swiftly for her. By finding and portraying the illuminating detail about her. By finding in her the universal elements of suffering in love and marriage. By discerning the basic structure of her life, and sticking to that; by particularizing her, distinguishing her from all other women. By making her a tool and victim of fate; as we all are. Yet proving that her story has never been lived before; or since.*

At the end of eighteen months of work, just before beginning the penultimate chapter, I also wrote a five-page note asking "What is the cement that holds this book together?," reviewing the whole meaning and purpose of the book to make sure that nothing that had been enunciated at the beginning had gotten lost in transit, and saying to myself, "This book doesn't have to prove anything but doesn't it have to illuminate a great deal?"

I had been interested in the Lincoln story for many years, and had read rather widely in the field, but had never been able to achieve a point of departure, for I had always said to myself, "Poor Abraham Lincoln, married to Mary Todd." After some ten years of incubation (most biographical novels come out well only if they have been incubating at least five years) while I was doing a magazine article about the Lincoln marriage, I came across some obscure source material which threw the marriage and its daily workings into high relief, particularly in relation to Mr. Lincoln in his role as a husband. I found myself exclaiming, "Poor Mary Todd, married to Abraham Lincoln." From that moment of understanding of the truly equal nature of the marriage I was able to begin work on the thesis which Abraham Lincoln inscribed inside the wedding ring he purchased in the square on the Sunday morning of his wedding, "Love Is Eternal." A little of the detail I sought before starting Chapter IV, just after the Lincoln marriage, may give an idea of the tens of thousands of questions a biographical novelist must ask: for his curiosity must be insatiable:

What changes have taken place in Mary, in Abraham Lincoln? How much time does Abraham spend with her? Where is Mary's room located in hotel? Front, back, side, corner? Does it get some sun? Is it warm or cold? Does she rearrange the room, or leave it as it was? (Rearrange to make it her own?) What are the dimensions? What does it look out over? Is it painted, or wallpapered? How much time does she spend in her room, in the parlors? Does she ask for special things, i. e., reading table; buy a few little things, i. e., lamps? How does she occupy her time in the mornings? Reading, sewing, writing letters? What kind of service is available? How does she arrange her money affairs? Does A give her money for incidentals: drugs, materials, etc. Does she have any money of her own? Does she pay at stores, or do they have credit accounts? Since Abraham wants to live economically, does she spend, or follow his wishes? Does she have visitors at hotel? Family, friends to dinner and supper? Is it expensive? She is later accused of being stingy, but if so, does she learn economy from A? Where is dining-room of Globe? How big is it? How decorated? Does Lincoln suggest they eat with others at big tables, or do they have the same table for two? Who was next to, or across from the Lincolns? We know of Bledsoes—what kind of piano, and what pieces, would Mrs. Bledsoe be playing? Would she invite Mary to play?

As I was preparing the last two chapters, I wrote myself a long, stern directive, of which the following lines are typical:

Let's get simple, and stay simple. Do only symptomatic scenes; step up pacing and speed; in perspective distant scenes are always foreshortened. Don't fight the entire Civil War, only those elements that come into the White House. Avoid name-calling, side-taking, prejudice, bitterness. Awaken no hatred, only pity and compassion. Underwrite the grief, underplay the emotion. Don't stack cards, either for or against Mary. Keep the author out, let the story tell itself.

But beyond the specifications for any one particular book, I found the following obiter dicta to be essential to all biographical novels:

No use of names because they later become important elsewhere. No asides, or smart whisperings. No fixations, or prejudices carried over from past feelings or readings. No harpings, or preconceived "theories, into which all history and happenings must fit." No name-calling, let the reader call the proper names. No fiery passions, for or against; they cloud judgment. No assumptions as to the reader's tastes, opinions, ideas, education. No writing for any one class, age or geographic group. No condemnations of people or events; give them their rightful place in the story, and let God judge them. No seeking the sensational for its own sake; and no philosophizing. No concealing of important evidence, no lies, cheating or defrauding the reader. No dullness; throw out the

> *slow, meaningless passages. No striving for effects, no manifest anger or hatred, no browbeating. Watch comparative materials and balance them; no disproportions about materials where I happen to know more. No inheriting of other people's prejudices, hatreds, blindness. No details that illuminate little but themselves. No posturing, no exhibitionism: "See what I know!" No striving for novelty for its own sake. No doctrinairism, or fitting material into one school or pattern. No destructivism, nor defeatism. No pugilism or blind spots. No lethargy. No weasel phrases; all space is needed for direct lines. No meandering down pleasant paths. No use of material that does not tie into focal core of book.*

Because of the tender youth of the biographical novel there has as yet been little discussion of its particular character, of its strengths as well as its limitations. Is it a history, a biography, or a novel? Is it none of these? Or perhaps all three? If in this paper I presume to provide a beginning critique, standards of judgment against which the biographical novel may be viewed, it is done with the happy reassurance that all such strictures will be altered, expanded and materially improved by later practitioners of the craft.

Professor Carl Bode of the University of Maryland recently wrote in the magazine *College English,* in the first serious study of the biographical novel to be published, "In the last ten years several prominent people have been doing their best to make an honest woman of the biographical novel. Considerable progress has been made, but not quite enough. The biographical novel still goes its bosomy way, its flimsy clothing tattered and torn in exactly the wrong places." "Sometimes powerful and often picturesque, it deserves much more attention than it has received from the critics."

When Professor Bode speaks of the biographical novels going their bosomy way, their flimsy clothing tattered and torn in exactly the wrong places, I am afraid he is concerned with such books as *Forever Amber or Kitty,* whose writers took the license of combining sensational material from a hundred different sources, letting their fictional fancies run wild, a privilege not accorded to the biographical novelist, who must remain inside the confines of the life he is writing about. They are certainly not biographical novels, and I doubt very much that W. R. Guthrie or Robert Penn Warren would consider them historical novels.

If anything, the biographical novel has suffered from an excess of good taste and respectability, perhaps because the biographical novelist has been awed by the fact that his characters once actually lived, and hence were endowed with certain inalienable rights, not of concealment, but of privacy and decorum. Bedroom scenes of which critics complain in the lurid, so-called historical novels are not to be found in the biographical novel, a sometime limitation to the sale of the genre, but one which calls forth the subtlety of the biographical novelist if he is to convey to the reader the all-important love and sex life of his subject.

I am going to take the liberty of quoting Professor Bode's analysis of my own work because I believe he has drawn an architectural blueprint for me, and for other biographical novelists, to follow in the future. Speaking of my own five biographical novels that followed the story of Vincent Van Gogh, he writes:

> *Each volume showed the advances in novelistic technique. The scholarship deepened too, though less steadily. The peak for the present day biographical novel was approached with the publication of Stone's book on Mary Todd Lincoln and her marriage. The scholarship is just as sound, according to a leading Lincoln specialist, as it is in the recent and respectfully reviewed biography of Mrs. Lincoln by a trained historian. It deserves to be called meticulous. Many an example can be found of Stone's deep scholarly concern with the life he was writing. He painstakingly prepared a floor-plan of the White House of Lincoln's day—one has never been reconstructed before—as a piece of independent research, and he created most of his dialogue out of skilled paraphrases of historically accurate source material. Furthermore, the handling of the data is judicious. Mrs. Lincoln is always a controversial figure, and Stone could be excused if he slanted his information one way or the other. But he does not. Rising above his declared intention to vindicate her, he portrays her bedeviled neurotic character with fairness. She and Abe emerge as memorable human beings, one great and the other not, but human beings both. The minor characters are carefully differentiated, very seldom are they mere historical names. The scenes are well handled, with pace and suspense to some of them in spite of the fact that historians already know how they come out . . . The descriptions give rich color to the picture Stone creates . . .*
>
> *The aim behind the best writing of this kind is a noble one. It is to see beneath the surface reality of facts and to reveal the true reality to others. It is to use historical data more daringly but more penetratingly than the professional historian can.*

Samuel E. Morison, professor of history at Harvard University, writes in an essay called *History As A Literary Art*: "The historian can learn much from the novelist. The best writers of fiction are superior to all but the best historians in characterization and description. When John Citizen feels the urge to read history he goes to the novels of Kenneth Roberts or Margaret Mitchell, not to the histories of Professor this or Doctor that. Why? American historians have forgotten that there is an art of writing history. In this flight of history from literature the public got left behind. American history became a bore to the reader and a drug on the market."

It is to this mournful state of affairs that the biographical novel addresses itself.

It is important, too, to set down the discernible differences between the biographical novel, the fictional novel, the historical novel, and the straight biography.

A few years ago when I was visiting with Ernest Hemingway in Key West, we discussed the approaches to our two novels in progress. Hemingway said, "There is no such thing as fiction. Everything we write is based on the lives we have lived, and other lives we have observed." Yet the fictional novelist has the opportunity to regroup and rechannel experience, to combine portions of a dozen different lives, to imagine a better world, or a more evil one, if that suits his temperament, and of conjuring up varying resolutions to the human situations he has evoked.

The biographical novelist is a bondsman to the factual truth; yet he will succeed very little if he remains a mere reporter. As Robert Graves said to me, "The biographical novelist who does not have strong intuitions about his subject, and later finds from the documents that his intuition has been substantiated, is not likely to get far in understanding his subject."

Inside the skeletal outline imposed on him, the biographical novelist is free to soar to any heights which his own inner poetry and perception will allow him. There are few if any differences of structure between the two types of novel; with the biographical novel the reader asks, "Did this happen?" and with the fictional novel, "Could this happen?" Therein lies the major distinction between them. Credibility lies at the base of both. A chance reader, unacquainted with the material, setting and character of the two stories, should not be able to tell them apart; he should be able to think that the fictional novel actually happened somewhere, or that the biographical novel was invented by the author. I remember with considerable satisfaction the day in September 1934 when Mrs. Stone asked the telephone operator in her office how she had liked *Lust for Life,* and the girl replied, "Fine, but why did Irving have to kill off the poor man?"

The historical novel is the closest to the biographical novel in its nature and scope; again the difference is not of form but of approach. In the biographical novel all of the characters have lived; in the best historical novels, such as *War and Peace,* only the history has actually happened, while the characters are invented, or built up by accretion, and then set in the authentic framework of the period and the action being written about. The main characters of the historical novel become the apotheoses of their times; they are true in that such characters did live in this particular period, and this dramatic series of events did take place, but to other people, perhaps half a hundred of them, in modified form and sequence. Sometimes the historical novel will be so close to the biographical novel, such as with *All the King's Men,* the story of Huey Long, that little is changed except the names of the characters and a few incidental pieces of personal action. In H. G. Wells' *The World of William Clissold,* Clissold and his various loves were imaginary, but the protagonists were called by their right names, and once again put through their roles in history. In still another type, roughly half of the characters are real people who act out their own historicity, while the other half, more often than not the "heroes" of the tale, are invented.

I would like at this moment to interject, with less bitterness than puzzlement, I hope, the question of why the historical novel, with its accurate background but fictional characters, should have been more acceptable to the academicians than the biographical novel, which is accurate not only in background but in the people involved? The answer to this riddle has remained a mystery to me.

The differences between the straight biography and the biographical novel are considerable, not in substance, since both draw their nourishment from the same source, but in structure, manner, attitude, and relationship between the author and the reader.

The biography has traditionally been in indirect discourse, a chronicle told by a second party, the writer, to a third party, the reader. The biographer, for example, relates what his principals have said; the biographical novelist enables the reader to listen to the conversations as they develop. The biographical novelist, in order to recreate a character, must not only understand his every motivation, but must write of it from behind the eyes of his protagonist. Only then can the reader feel everything that he feels, know everything that he knows, suffer his defeats and enjoy his victories. The biography has been expected to be objective; too often it has been written in cool blood. The biographical novel must be written in hot blood.

Even so, the form of biography is changing, and perhaps the wide public acceptance of the biographical novel has had something to do with this change. The biographies I read in school contained as many footnotes as lines of text, while the quotations were indented in small type in the center of the page, presenting a pedagogical, dull and fatiguing sight to the eye as well as to the emotional interest of the reader. When in 1937 I wrote *Sailor on Horseback,* I put my quotations from Jack London on a continuing line with the main text, separated only by a comma and a quotation mark, so that there would be no break in the reading mood and the typographical page would remain unified and interesting. When I received the first half of the galleys from my then publisher in Boston, all the quotations had been centered in tiny typeknots in the middle of the page. In answer to my anguished telephone call, the proofreader said that he had set my manuscript according to the standard form, since I obviously had not known how to do so. At that point the editor broke into the conversation and ordered the manuscript reset as I had written it. By now the practice has become almost universal.

Up to recent times it was not permitted in biographies to stage dialogue sequences, even when such dialogue was completely documented, evidently on the grounds that recreated dialogue might be less true, or might lead the reader to think he was reading a novel instead of a biography, and hence not believe that what he was reading was factually accurate. This never appeared to me to be a tenable point of view, and, in 1940, when I wrote *Clarence Darrow For the Defense,* I staged, as though they were being acted under a proscenium, all of the conversations that seemed interesting and important; at the back of the book I listed my documentation for every spoken word. I feel sure they had considerably more emotional impact than if I had related at second hand what the conversations had been about.

When I was growing up, few except scholars read biographies. It is my opinion that the biographical novel arose, and has become popular, because of this failure of the biography to reach a reading public that was hungry for authentic human stories. It is also my opinion that the biography will continue to learn from the biographical novel, and lean on its technics. A book is written for purposes of communication; it does an author no service whatever to have his book unreadable and hence unread. It must also be said that the biographical novel will be eternally indebted to the straight biography, for it has learned from it the science of research and the organization of materials.

The biographical novel, like all living creatures, was born in pain. It was called a bastard form, the result of an unfortunate indiscretion on the part of its otherwise eminently respectable parents, biography and the novel.

What are the criticisms that have been and still are, in some unconvinced corners, levied against the biographical novel? It is said to debase the biography and the novel, discrediting both and adding to the stature of neither. Allegedly it mines biography without regard for the verities, strains history through the author's personality, reshapes that history to fit the novel form, oversimplifies, prevents the reader from separating fact from fiction, chooses only those subjects which allow for a lively sale, violates the privacy of people long dead, and makes character the victim of plot.

All of these criticisms have sometimes been true, and probably a good many more of which the critics happily have not yet thought. But to decide that any art form is untenable because of its weakest example or its potential for error is similar to saying that the human race should be obliterated because of the shortcomings of its least admirable percentage. I find that in the course of my twenty-three years in the field most major critics have become reconciled to the fact that the biographical novel is here to stay. The more courageous and perceptive of them now welcome it to the literary boards; by the same token they insist that each volume achieve standards of literary and historical excellence. Instead of categorically damning the form without bothering to read the book, they are judging each succeeding biographical novel on the basis of its writing, research, storytelling, perception.

One of the assets of the human race is said to be that it can learn from experience; history and biography constitute the greatest mine of lived experience; and it is the fond dream of the biographical novelist to bring the wisdom of that experience to the problems and complexities of the modern world.

My own biographical novels have had two motivations: I have hoped to feel deeply about simple things; and I have wanted to tell the story of man, against obstacles, for man.

21

C. Vann Woodward, Ralph Ellison, Robert Penn Warren, and William Styron

"The Uses of History in Fiction[1]" from *The Southern Literary Journal* (1968)

WOODWARD

In introducing novelists into the formal deliberations of historians, I really feel no need to apologize, except perhaps to the novelists. For if apologies are due, they should come, I think, from the side of the historian. Historians have too long cultivated a rather priggish, Nineteenth-Century cult of fact, a creed that borrowed its tenets and prestige from the sciences and the heyday of their ascendency. Like scientists, we said, historians stuck to facts, preferably to hard facts. This conception, this prestige of hard facts, derives especially from the English. It was Oscar Wilde who said that the English are always degrading Truth into Fact, and he went on to say that when a Truth becomes a Fact, it loses all its intellectual value.

Since fiction was conceived to be, in this usage, the opposite of fact, and since novelists dealt exclusively in fiction, historians were inclined to be rather priggish about novelists, especially if they ventured into historical subjects. Historians have been much more eager to claim kinship with scientists, notably social scientists. When the social sciences turn to historical subjects, historians appear flattered rather than offended. We were, or have been, inclined to embrace them as cousins, to offer joint courses, to hold conferences. Our kinship is actually much closer to novelists. We are in fact siblings, historical siblings. The novel is the youngest of the literary forms—the only one the Greeks didn't invent. It was born only in the mid-Eighteenth Century, not long before professional historiography first saw the light of day in Germany. Both sprang from a common parentage of storytellers. Both grew up together in an environment permeated with the growing historical consciousness of western man, and competed with each other to satisfy the demand for historical understanding.

In their mutual attitudes there has been a good deal of sibling rivalry—though, it is, I think, more manifest in the historians than in the novelists. Actually, I find among novelists more respect for and awareness of good history than I find among historians a proper respect for and awareness of good novels. Over the last two centuries novels have become increasingly saturated with history, and novelists have been becoming ever more deeply historically conscious.

In a sense, all novels are historical novels. They all seek to understand, to describe, to recapture the past, however remote, however recent. They might all be described by the title of Marcel Proust's great work, *Remembrance of Things Past.* In his own efforts to understand, describe, and recapture the past, the novelist uses no more specialized a vocabulary than the historian. As Isaiah Berlin has said, history employs few if any concepts or categories peculiar to itself, but broadly speaking, only those of common sense, or ordinary speech—in other words, the same speech the historian himself uses. If the historian feels free to borrow concepts and insights from the psychologist, the analyst, the sociologist, in his efforts to explain human motivation and behavior, the novelist is equally free to use the same resources in doing much the same thing.

An historian stands in no less need of imagination than the novelist; if anything he needs rather more. There are firm rules, of course, about what his discipline permits and forbids him to do with his imagination. He cannot, for example, as the novelist can, invent characters, invent motives for his characters. I certainly have no wish to relax those rules or to confuse or blur the distinction between the historian and the novelist. But over the years, as I have watched my novelist friends at their work, as I have read their books and talked with them about their problems, I have learned to appreciate more and more how much we have in common in our uses of the past, our interest in it, our demands upon it, our concerns with it.

This is, I think, especially true of Southern writers, and particularly of the three who take part in this discussion. Allen Tate has spoken of the peculiar historical consciousness of Southern writers, and described their work as a literature conscious of the past in the present. Tate could hardly have called to witness a better illustration of his thesis than his friend Robert Penn Warren. Warren's books have dealt with virtually every period of American history since the time of Thomas Jefferson, including that time and including also the period of Jackson, the Civil War, the early years of the 20th Century, the 1920's, the 1930's, and on down to the present. These books constitute for some of us a good part of our intellectual autobiography. His first book was not fiction at all, but a biography of John Brown. It seems to me that in that book of "straight" history, he announced the basic themes of all his novels: man's confrontation with evil, and the conflict between good and evil within the human heart. Together, these books constitute a moral history of the South.

William Styron's early novels dealt with contemporary themes and characters, though never without a characteristic consciousness of the past in the present. Only in this latest novel, on Nat Turner, has he turned to the more remote past for his subject, and in this "meditation on history," as he calls his book, he comes very close indeed, given the license of the novelist, to doing what the historian does in reconstructing the past. Here he is concerned with the particular, rather than with the universal, which is, I believe, the distinction that Aristotle made between poetry and history.

Ralph Ellison has declared his allegiance to history, as well as his Southern identity, most clearly in his warning to a critic about the abstraction he would impose upon American reality. With characteristic Southern fear of abstraction, and abhorrence for it, he declared: "the Negro American consciousness is not a product (as so often seems true of so many other American groups) of a will to historical forgetfulness." Rather, it is the memory of slavery and the hope of emancipation, and the myths, both Southern and Northern.

I will call on these speakers in the order of seniority, and that will put Mr. Warren first.

WARREN

I want to say that I am appalled and honored to be invited to a group of historians. It makes you feel that the writing of fiction is more important than you thought it was, and that your writing is, too. I am honored to be here and it is a great pleasure to be among my friends—three old and dear friends.

What I want to do now is simply to try to state a few principles that occur to me about the relation between history and fiction—in a way, between history and art, as I see the problem, as a background to what may happen later.

First I should like to say that the word History is a very ambiguous word. Clearly it means on one hand things that happened in the past, the events of the past, the actions of the past. And the word also means the record of the past that historians write. So whenever the word is used, we have to sort out its meaning. I myself use it differently, in each sense, as the occasion may demand, and I'm afraid my friends do the same thing.

As Vann has said, history is in the past tense. That sounds simple enough. It is about the past. But it is not simple, because it is not merely about what happened in the past, it is also the imaginative past. History and fiction are both in this past tense. History is the literal past tense. The historian says, "It was in the past; I prove that it happened." The fiction writer says, "I'll take it as it has happened, if it happened at all—which it probably didn't." But the mode of the past tense is the past tense of a state of mind—the feel of the past, not the literal past itself. It is a mode of memories. It's the mind working in terms of memory. The history of the past that the historians write is the racial past, the national past, the sectional past, all kinds of pasts, including economic history—but the past, always. To the novelist, say Thackeray, writing about Becky Sharp, the past may be merely a little personal past. But it is past. Even science fiction is about the past; the writers tell about the future as though it were past. In science fiction, you get yourself to a point beyond the story that you are telling. It is never in the future tense. It is in an assumed future which has become a past.

This fact points to a particular stance of mind: it has *happened,* and we are trying to find its meaning. It's a mode of memory we are dealing with, an actuality as remembered. History is concerned with actuality; its past must be provable. The fiction writer's past is not provable; it *may* be imagined. His characters *may* be imagined. But historical characters are imagined, too. They are brought into the picture of an imagined world. For how do we know the world of "history," unless the historian has "imagined" it?

Now the big difference here between history and fiction is that the historian does not know his imagined world; he knows *about* it, and he must know all he can about it, because he wants to find the facts *behind* that world. But the fiction writer must claim to *know* the *inside* of his world for better or for worse. He mostly fails, but he claims to know the inside of his characters, the undocumentable inside. Historians are concerned with the truth *about,* with knowledge *about,* the fiction writer with the knowledge *of.* And neither of these "knowledges" is to be achieved in any perfect form. But the kinds of "knowledge" *are.* This is a fundamental difference, it seems to me.

This leads to another distinction. Fiction is an art, one of the several arts. I want to read a little passage—the most radical passage I could find—about art as distinguished from other human activities. "Either art is a pure, irreducible activity, one that provides its own peculiar content, its own morality—it includes itself in its own meaning; or art is, on the other hand, a pleasanter form of presenting facts, meanings and truths pertaining to other realms of reality like history, sociology, morality, where they exist in purer and fuller form." This states the distinction quite coldly. For fiction is an art, like painting or music—with one difference. Its materials are more charged with all the human commitments and recalcitrances and roughnesses.

Now here is where the rub comes, I think. The materials that go into a piece of fiction may be drawn from history or human experience, but their factuality gives them no special privilege, as contrasted with imagined materials. They have, as "materials" for it, the same status, and nothing more than that. But they come in with all the recalcitrances and the weights and the passions of the real world. The simplest example I can think of is this. Take *Hamlet,* or any tragedy we all admire and respond to. It is dealing with the recalcitrances of human pain, confusion and error. We know these things all too well: the pain, confusion, and error of our own lives. But we come out of the play not weeping, but feeling pretty good, and we go down to the beer parlor and talk about it. Something's happened to the pain, confusion, error. It has happened only because we put the pain and error into perspective, and look at it—to see it and at the same time not quite feel it. We see it as if it had happened a long time ago—to us, but to somebody else, too.

There is, however, always a point where the exigencies and the pains of the materials of fiction or drama or poetry are too great to be absorbed. This recalcitrancy, which is the basis of contention between the form and the content of literature, can become too great. The really bigoted Catholic cannot read Milton; the really bigoted Protestant can't read Dante. In reading literature we have to make allowances for our theologies and our beliefs. But there is a point where it cracks. Let's recognize that. There is a form in which the recalcitrant material—that is, the practical commitment in relation to it—violates the vision of humanity, the long-range beauty of contemplation that is art. Let's leave it there for the moment.

ELLISON

I think I'll go back and try to talk about American historiography and American fiction. I would start by suggesting that they're both artificial; both are forms of literature, and I would suggest further that American history grows primarily out of the same attitudes of mind, and attitudes toward chronology, which gave birth to our great tall stories. Constance Rourke reminded us that we began to define ourselves and to create ourselves through the agency of the word, of the imagination, the fictional imagination—and that basically we are liars. I would suggest that historians are responsible liars. Liars are not bad people; I am by profession a liar. The role of lying is like the role of masquerading. Yeats has a quotation, which I have used somewhere, about the necessity of putting on the mask in order to achieve one's dreams, one's idea of one's self. So when I put a scar on my face or part my hair, you understand that I'm trying to achieve some idealistic image; or if I wear it in Afro-style or conk it, you understand that that too is simply a human assertion against the flux and flow of time and a desire to modify that which was given. And it is here that the novelist and the historian appear to part company. The historian is dedicated to chronology. He can suppress, he can emphasize, he can project, and he can carve out his artifact; and this helps us to imagine ourselves, to project ourselves, to achieve certain goals, certain identities; but he must obey the order of the calendar and the tides of political fortune. I can't, here in New Orleans, fail to point out that so much of American history has turned upon the racial situation in the country. This is a given and accepted fact now. It's argued over and over again. The problem that we have to deal with on the side of history is: How much did you choose to put in, how much did you leave out, what did it lead to, and how to interpret the results. I'm going to be a little nasty here and suggest that our written history has been as "official" as any produced in any communist country—only in a democratic way: individuals write it instead of committees. Written history is to social conduct and social arrangements in this country very much like the relationship between myth and ritual. And myth justifies and "explains" facts. Now it's all human, it is understandable and it has to be evaluated, because complex personal and political interests are involved in such intricate ways that arriving at objective evaluations is extremely difficult. But, thank God, there have been a few novelists who decided to tell the "truth" in their own unique and devious ways. Isn't that nasty?

For here the novelists have a special, though difficult, freedom. Time is their enemy, and while chronology is the ally of the historian, for the novelist it is something to manipulate or even to destroy. And this, I think, is why we wish that historians, within the limitations which they embrace and to which they dedicate themselves, could do a little better by chronology, by events as they actually unfold. Because in certain ways the historians have, thankfully, taken a broader cut of the American experience than the novelists. By nature they possess a greater patience before facts, before events. If you really want to find out what happened in the United States over all these years, you know that *some* historian has written something about it. That is one of the glories of historical writing in this country; there has always been somebody who, for some reason, has tried to say, "Well, the consequences of this fact actually exist, this event actually occurred, and I think it is related in such and such a way to the total reality." But too often history has been an official statement, and it has danced attendance to political arrangements.

Fiction, on the other hand, as it manipulates reality, as it tries to get at those abiding human predicaments which are ageless and timeless, has fought with time, has fought with the realities as envisioned by official history, and by rearranging experience in artful ways it has tried to tell us in small ways the symbolic significance of what actually happened. If you want to know something about the dynamics of the South, of interpersonal relationships in the South from, roughly, 1874 until today, you don't go to historians; not even to Negro historians. You go to William Faulkner and Robert Penn Warren, or you go to the popular arts. You have to read the latter very carefully of course, because they are the biggest liars of all. But somehow the novelists try to deal with unpleasant facts, difficult facts, and Faulkner dealt with the most unpleasant facts of race. I suppose that's why

American history has not been ultimately concerned with tragedy, while literature, at its best, always has. It's always trying to find ways of dealing with the unpleasant facts, and the only way, the profoundest human way, of dealing with the unpleasant, is to place it in conjunction with the pleasant. Thus fiction, at its best, moves ever toward a blending of the tragic with the comic—or towards that mode which we know as the Blues.

I would suggest, then, that American novelists have a special role which should not be confused with the role of the writer of history; which for them is *verboten.* The moment you say something explicit about history in a novel, everybody's going to rise up and knock the Hell out of you, because they suspect that you are trying to take advantage of a form of authority which is sacred. History is sacred, you see, and no matter how false to actual events it might be. But fiction is anything but sacred. By fact and by convention fiction is a projection from one man's mind, of one man's imagination. An American novelist tries to integrate all of the diversity of our people and our regions, our religions, and so on, into an imaginative whole. And through that imaginative integration he attempts to seize the abiding circumstances, the abiding problems, the abiding and time-tested forms of humanity—heroism, truth and failure and love and death—all of the ramifications of those experiences which make us human.

I think that we have something very important going here. We work the same side of the street. So keep us honest and we'll keep you historians honest. I think that Red Warren, who has always been concerned with history, has offered us an example of how to confront the problem of history as the novelist should. I think that when he wrote about a great American politician who governed his state and refused to intrude into the area of the historian, he refused because he was canny enough to realize that he could never get *that* particular man into fiction. And yet, I believe that he did use that man to bring into focus within his own mind many, many important facts about power, politics and class and loyalty. So today we possess an essence of that man presented in a highly imaginative, moving and enduring way, without the novelist having taken anything away from that man And without his having added anything to one who we know was an important historical figure—except the art-created possibility of looking at him through the enriching eyes of Red Warren's imagination. Thanks to Warren's art we may now view that man through that heightened sense of the past which both history and literature grant to all who are truly involved with the mystery of human existence.

STYRON

I have never talked much in public. I don't mean to sound shy, but I haven't, nor have I taught, and I admire the eloquence that has preceded me, and only wish that I were able to speak in an impromptu manner as well as my good friends have done. As a consequence, I have resorted to a composition, fairly brief, some of it composed on Eastern Airlines today, with a terrible and ominous post-election traumatic blues all over me. So I'm going to read it, and if you shut your eyes, perhaps I can give you a subtle feeling that I am not reading it.

Last spring in an exchange in the *Nation,* I quoted at some length from a volume called *The Historical Novel,* by the great Hungarian Marxist critic, Georg Lukács, in an effort to explain my attitude toward the freedom of movement and choice any good novelist must exercise when writing historical fiction. Historical fiction has been largely discredited in this country, doubtless due to the fact that its practitioners, most of them, have aimed at titillating a predominantly female audience, an audience one hopes that has now been preempted by the Late, Late show. What I am speaking about, of course, is the serious historical novel: literature in the tradition of Scott, Stendhal, Tolstoy, Pushkin, Faulkner, and Warren, and it is to this great genre that Lukács has addressed himself, in my opinion, with more intelligence, passion, and penetration than any other modern literary critic. As Irving Howe has written of Lukács, "Unlike so many Marxist critics, Lukács turns to literature not because it provides him with political opportunities but because he has been involved with it for a lifetime and has experienced the passion of the true scholar. . . . Repeatedly Lukács turns to 'the increasing concreteness of the novel in its grasp of the historical peculiarity of characters and events,' repeatedly to that self-reflectiveness in the dominant characters of the modern novel, which he sees as the sense of history become part of experience and thereby transformed into a dynamic agent reflecting and acting upon the dialectal contradictions of the outer world."[2]

It seemed to me that some of Lukács' observations on the historical novel and the novelist's responsibility are more trenchant and wise than any I could make about the matter, and certainly record as well as I could my own feelings about the intricate and subtle relationship between historical fact and fanciful conjecture, between historical faithfulness and literary license, along with other troubling problems that beset the unhappy wretch who dares tackle this literary form. Let me then quote again from Lukács, hoping that these maxims will serve as representative of my own sentiments regarding the fiction writer's very difficult obligation to make sense out of history.

"The deeper and more genuinely historical a writer's knowledge of a period," Lukács says, "the more freely will he be able to move about inside his subject and the less tied will he feel to individual historical data." Speaking of Sir Walter Scott, for instance, he observes: "Scott's extraordinary genius lay in the fact that he gave the historical novel just such themes as would allow for this 'free movement,' and so cleared the way for its development; whereas the earlier traditions of his so-called predecessors had obstructed all such freedom of movement, preventing even a genuine talent from developing. Naturally, a special difficulty is involved in the treatment of specifically historical subject-matter. Every really original writer who portrays a new outlook upon a certain field has to contend with the prejudices of his readers. But the image which the public has of any familiar historical figure need not necessarily be a false one. Indeed, with the growth of a real historical sense and of real historical knowledge it becomes more and more accurate. But even this correct image may in certain circumstances be a hindrance to the writer who wishes to reproduce the spirit of an age faithfully and authentically. It would require a particularly happy accident for all the well-known and attested actions of a familiar historical figure to correspond to the purposes of literature. . . ."

In another context, Lukács expands on this theme of what is not merely the likelihood but the necessity of the writer being allowed great latitude in structuring his vision of the past. He says, "What matters in the novel is fidelity in the reproduction of the material foundations of the life of a given period, its manners and the feelings and thoughts deriving from these. This means, as we have also seen, that the novel is much more closely bound to the specifically historical, individual moments of a period than is drama. But this never means being tied to any particular historical facts. On the contrary, the novelist must be at liberty to treat these as he likes,"—and this is an important phrase, I think—"if he is to reproduce the much more complex and ramifying totality with historical faithfulness. From the standpoint of the historical novel, too, it is always a matter of chance whether an actual, historical fact, character or story will lend itself to the particular method by which a great novelist conveys his historical faithfulness."

Finally, quoting Pushkin, Lukács remarks: "Truth of passions, verisimilitude of feelings in imagined circumstances—that is what our mind demands of the dramatic writer." And he declares, "the writer's historical fidelity consists in the faithful artistic reproduction of the great collisions, the great crises and turning-points in history. To express this *historical* conception in an adequate artistic form the writer may treat individual facts with as much licence as he likes, for mere fidelity to the individual facts of history without this connection is utterly valueless."[3]

Needless to say, the foregoing thoughts merely skim part of the surface of Lukács philosophy of history and its relation to literature. Yet in his unyielding insistence that a writer's responsibility is not to the dead baggage of facts, but to the unfettering and replenishing power of his own imagination, that imagination which at its best can alone reveal ultimate truths, Lukács' observations seem to me enormously provocative, and I hope they provide substance for further discussion this evening.

WOODWARD

Thank you very much, gentlemen. As an historian, I gather from the comments of Mr. Warren that the novelists deal with the inside of history, leaving the outside, I suppose, to the historian; from Mr. Ellison, that historians are essentially liars, and this leaves the truth to the novelists; from Mr. Styron that fidelity to fact is not an obligation of novelists, and this *emancipates* them. Am I too far off base, gentlemen, in saying that it seems to me that you are saying you are going to write a "super-history," or at least a better history than historians can write?

ELLISON

No. I'm suggesting that we have reached a great crisis in American history, and we are now going to have a full American history. You, Vann, began to initiate this movement, as far as I am concerned. We're beginning to go back and to evaluate those realities of American historical experience which were ruled out officially. Henry Steele Commager and a lot of other people, such as Samuel Morison, have turned flip-flops in recent years. I used to be outraged when I read some of the stuff that they wrote, because there is, certainly in the Negro part of the country and in the Southern part of the country, a stream of history which is still as tightly connected with folklore and the oral tradition as official history is connected with the tall tale. I think that we are beginning to realize that.

For instance, the only public school I ever attended was named after Frederick Douglass. The people who walked there from Tennessee and the Carolinas have a sense of history which is only now beginning to get into the history books. Part of this is legend. Part of this is myth. But so much of it—so very much of it—is what actually happened, happened to them. And if official history, if conscious historians do not take cognizance of this experience, then what a critic like Lukács says has very little validity. He was, after all, writing about European countries, with no divided history. Of course I know that the Owen Glendower that Shakespeare gives us in the historical plays is certainly not the Owen Glendower of the Welsh, it's the Shakespearean and Elizabethan notion of Owen Glendower. But here we are dedicated to a different kind of democracy. We have all of these things which happened, and they happened in such great variety. I'm afraid to say what Louisiana experience is, what Louisiana history is, even of the period of Huey Long, because I used to hear things—and highly favorable things, about Long, for instance—from Negro students that I attended college with at Tuskegee.

I think that one of the things that we want to discuss here is the rhetoric of fiction. If you project in fiction a version of history, then you have an obligation to think about these other feed-ins from the common experience which are going to put to question your particular projection of history. I don't think that history is Truth. I think it's another form of man trying to find himself, and to come to grips with his own complexity, but within the frame of chronology and time. Here in the United States we have had a political system which wouldn't allow me to tell my story officially.

Much of it is not in the history textbooks. Certain historians and untrained observers did their jobs, often very faithfully, but many of them have been forgotten except by scholars and historians, and the story they recorded was altered to justify racial attitudes and practices. But somehow, through our Negro American oral tradition and through the names given to children and to public institutions—those places with which white society was not too concerned as long as they did not challenge the public order—these reminders of the past as *Negroes* recalled it found existence and were passed along. Historical figures continued to live in stories of and theories about the human and social dynamics of slavery, and about the effects of political decisions rendered during the Reconstruction. Assertions of freedom and revolts were recalled along with triumphs of labor in the fields and on the dance floor; feats of eating and drinking and of fornication, of religious conversion and physical endurance, and of artistic and athletic achievements. In brief, the broad ramifications of human life as Negroes have experienced it were marked and passed along. This record exists in oral form and it constitutes the internal history of values by which my people lived even as they were being forced to accommodate themselves to those forces and arrangements of society that were sanctioned by official history. The result has imposed upon Negroes a high sensitivity to the ironies of historical writing and created a profound skepticism concerning the validity of most reports on what the past was like.

And so, when a novelist moves into the arena of history and takes on the obligations of the historian he has to be aware that he faces a tough rhetorical problem. He has to sell *me*, convince me, that despite the racial divisions and antagonisms in the U. S., his received version of history is not drastically opposed to mine. Because I am conditioned to assume that his idea of the heroic individual is apt to violate my sense of heroism;—for instance, Bedford Forrest is considered a hero by many whites but it would be a heroic task for me, or for most blacks, to see him so. I can, however, accept Sam Feathers or Lucas Beauchamp in Faulkner, in ways that I couldn't accept Jim in *Huckleberry Finn.* For me, Jim was not rounded enough. And yet, he was involved fictionally with serious historical matters. But Lucas Beauchamp was involved with serious historical and personal matters—*but* (and this is an important *but*) he was mainly involved in those things which historians would not talk about, and this is one of the important roles which fiction has played, especially the fiction of southern writers: it has tried to tell that part of the human truth which we could not accept or face up to in much historical writing because of social, racial and political considerations.

WARREN

Our little girl, who is about 11 years old, was studying for an exam in American History, and she said to me, "hear my lesson." I heard her lesson and she said things I thought were pretty preposterous, but I didn't say anything about it, because I knew she was saying her lesson for an exam. I was too smart to say anything about it, but she was watching my face. "Oh, poppy!" she said, "this is for an exam; this is not the truth. I know better than this."

Now this is not the historians' fault. This is the people who write text books of history. It's very different. Official histories may be tests, or orators at the Fourth of July, or textbook makers, but not historians. They are very different, you see. And girls of ten years old get this point quickly; they understand it perfectly. By the time they are seventeen or eighteen, in college, they may lose it. But they know it at ten years old. They watch things much more shrewdly than their elders; they have no stake in it except truth—truth, and grades. They are quite different: they know this, you see.

The historian is after this truth, and it's a good truth. So is the novelist. They are both trying to say what life feels like to them. They have different ground rules for it. Let's assume that both are conditioned by their societies at every given moment—at every moment in history, in time. Now, the breaking out process is always an act of imagination both for the historian and the novelist. The rules are different, though, in this sense: the historian must prove points, document points, that the novelist doesn't have to document. Yet without that sense of documentation, the knowledge that It Is Possible, the novelist can't operate either. He is conditioned always by the sense of this documentation—that it is historically possible. He himself is tied to the facts of life. He must respect them. Insofar as he departs from them by imagination, he departs in terms of the possibilities laid down by these ground rules of fact—psychological fact, historical fact, sociological fact, all the various kinds of fact. Those are his ground rules. He can take a new view of them, but he cannot violate any one of them to a point which invalidates acceptance. That's the big proviso here. It varies a great deal. The materials that go into his work come from the rough-textured life around him, made up of beliefs and facts and attitudes of all kinds. A bigoted Catholic can't read Milton, and a bigoted Protestant can't read Dante, but a civilized Catholic can read Milton with joy. There's a point, though, where one's commitment to basic ideas and basic materials, by reason of bigotry or something else, makes one incapable of accepting the total vision of an art—of a novel or a poem, or whatever. Let's face this fact. The autonomy of the art is always subject to the recalcitrance of the materials and to your own lack of self-understanding.

STYRON

I don't know what I'm going to say to add to this confusion. We've been dealing in very intelligent abstractions, all of which make me feel that maybe we should get a little bit more concrete. I like that phrase of Red Warren's just now: "the autonomy of the art is subject to the recalcitrance of the materials." This is something that I have had preying on my mind for some time, in regard to a private argument, which became extraordinarily public, having to do with a book I wrote not too long ago. It occurred to me in thinking of this particular book, *The Confessions of Nat Turner,* that in all of the extraordinary flak and anti-anti-missile barrage that has surrounded it, no one, insofar as I know (and I don't mean only people who criticized it from the black point of view, but a number of my white commentators as well; and I bring this up not out of any immodesty, but simply because I'm more comfortable in talking about particulars rather than aesthetic abstractions)—no one has conceived of this book, which does deal with history indeed, as a separate entity which has its own autonomy, to use Red Warren's phrase, its own metaphysics, its own reason for being as an aesthetic object. No one has ventured, except for several people in private (bright people, whom I admire), to suggest that a work which deals with history can at the same time be a metaphorical plan, a metaphorical diagram for a writer's attitude toward human existence, which presumably is one of the writer's preoccupations anyway—that, despite all the obfuscation which surrounds the really incredible controversy about the rightness and wrongness of racial attitudes, wrong readings of Ulrich B. Phillips, Stanley Elkins, and so forth, a work of literature might have its own being, its own fountain, its own reality, its own power, its own appeal, which derive from factors that don't really relate to history. And this is why, again, I'm intrigued by Red Warren's phrase, "the autonomy of the art is subject to the recalcitrance of the materials."

I would like to suggest that, in the endless rancor and bitterness which tends to collect and coalesce around controversial literary works, it might also be wise to pause and step back (I'm not speaking of my own work alone)—and regard a work as containing many metaphors, many reasons for being. This is true for all the literary works I admire. They are works (and I would include, among modern works, books by my distinguished contemporaries to my right) which do exist outside of history, which gain their power from history, to be sure, which are fed by a passionate comprehension of what history does to people and to things, but which have to have other levels of understanding, and have to be judged by other levels of understanding. It may be that in our perhaps overly modern and desperate preoccupation with history, which can be so valuable, we lose sight of the ineffable othernesses which go to make a work of art. At the risk of repeating myself once more, I would like to say that these factors have been forgotten.

WARREN

May I say something, Vann? It strikes me that the question is one of the basic tensions of our whole lives. We can't have an easy formulation for this, an easy way out of the question. We are stuck with the fact that life involves passions and concerns and antipathies and anguish about the materials of life itself—whatever goes on in our hearts and outside of ourselves. This is what good literature involves. If you couldn't carry these things into literature, literature would be meaningless. It would be a mere parlor trick. All this—the concerns, the confusion—goes into literature; it goes into the arts. It exists in terms of the experience that the writer describes in literature, presented there in and of himself. They are not the same thing for everybody; a little different, you know, for each person, frequently quite different. But they all go in as passion, as commitments of various kinds. Yet at the same time the thing described must be made objectively itself. Now take Glendower, to whom Ralph was referring. Now nobody here is a Welsh nationalist, I trust. If there is one here . . .

ELLISON

Ralph Ellison is.

WARREN

No. you're not; *you* aren't Welsh.

ELLISON

I'm a Welsh nationalist. But I also admire art.

WARREN

I'm a Confederate. So here we are. We have personal loyalties and problems, you see. But in *Henry IV, Part One,* Glendower didn't bother us in terms of the great theme of the play. People are not living and dying over Glendower today. This is a purely pragmatic approach to it, you see; what can we surrender, what immediate needs can we give up, how can we withdraw our commitments in a given region of this play—in materials of the play—to gain a larger view? Now I couldn't care less who won the battle, at Shrewsbury, personally. It was a long time ago, and it isn't very important now. . . .

What I care about is the pattern of the human struggle there—as we know it in relation to Hotspur on one hand, and to the cold calculators on the other hand, and to Hal, as a kind of Golden Mean, and then, at last, to Falstaff, with all of his great tummy and great wit, and his ironic view of history and morality—outside of all schematic views. We are seeing a pattern of human possibility that bears on all of our lives, a pattern there that we see every day—the Hotspurs, or those cold calculators like Westmoreland, and then the people like Hal, who try to ride it through and in their perfect adaptability be all things to all men, and drink with Falstaff and kick him out at the end (in the next play, of course). We see this happening all the time. Shakespeare wrote a great vision of human life, but it's not about Welsh nationalism.

ELLISON

Yes. And I'm all for the autonomy of fiction; that's why I say that novelists should leave history alone. But I would also remind us that the work of fiction comes alive through a collaboration between the reader and the writer. This is where the rhetoric comes in. If you move far enough into the historical past, you don't have that problem. I don't give a damn what happened to Owen Glendower, actually, but as a writer, if I were to write a fiction based upon a great hero, a military man, whose name is Robert E. Lee, I'd damn well be very careful about what I fed my reader, in order for him to recreate in his imagination and through his sense of history what that gentleman was. Because Lee is no longer simply an historical figure. He is a figure who lives within us. He is a figure which shapes ideals of conduct and of forbearance and of skill, military and so on. This is *inside,* and not something that writers can merely be arbitrary about. The freedom of the fiction writer, the novelist, is one of the great freedoms possible for the individual to exercise. But it is not absolute. Thus, one, without hedging his bets, has to be aware that he does operate within an area dense with prior assumptions.

WARREN

Quite right.

ELLISON

This I say without any discussion of Bill's personal problem. I haven't read his book, and he knows that—well, maybe he doesn't. Our house burned down so I didn't get to read it at first, and after the controversy I deliberately did not read it. One thing that I know is that he isn't a bigot, he isn't a racist, and all of that. That's beside the point. But there are very serious problems involved. I am known as a bastard by certain of my militant friends because I am not what they call a part of the Movement. That is, they figure I don't cuss out white folks enough. All right; I cuss them out in my own ways. But this isn't the real problem. The real problem is to create symbolic actions which are viable specifically, and which move across all of our differences and all of the diversities of the atmosphere, and allow us to say, "yes," just as Red is saying about Shakespeare. This tells us something of what it means to be a man under these particular circumstances. But at the same time you don't have the freedom to snatch any and everybody, and completely recreate them. This is why you must lie and disguise a historical figure. You cannot move into the area, or impose yourself into the authority, of the historian, because he is dealing with chronology. The moment you put yourself in a book, the moment you put any known figures into the book, then somebody is going to say, "But he didn't have that mole on that side of his face; it was on *that* side. You said that he had a wife; he didn't have a wife. You said that he beat his wife at three o'clock in the afternoon; no, he beat her before breakfast, and they got up at five." Facts are a tyranny for the novelist. Facts get you into all of this trouble. On the other hand, Bill, I would suggest that whether you like the dissonance you picked up, you've written a very powerful novel, and it's very self-evident. Don't kick it. Don't knock it. Just leave history alone.

STYRON

I'm not kicking, Ralph. I'm not. No. I'm glad you authenticate what I said through the voice of Lukács, that facts *per se* are preposterous. They are like the fuzz that collects in the top of dirty closets. They don't really mean anything.

WARREN

I wouldn't go that far.

ELLISON

They *mean* something. That's why you're in trouble.

STYRON

I'll dispute that.

ELLISON

Okay.

STYRON

It depends on what facts you're talking about. Let's pare this down. Obviously when somebody like Lukács, or somebody like myself, claims that it's necessary to dispense with facts, it's not to say that promiscuous blindness, a disavowal of evidence, is what the novelist has as a dirty little secret all of his own. It's not that at all. It's simply to say that with a certain absolute boldness, a novelist dealing with history has to be able to say that such and such a fact is totally irrelevant, and to Hell with the person who insists that it has any real, utmost relevance. It's not to say that, in any bland or even dishonest way, a novelist is free to go about his task of rendering history with a complete shrugging off of the facts. This is not what Lukács says; it is not what I say. It is simply that certain facts which history presents us with are, on the one hand, either unimportant, or else they can be dispensed with out of hand, because to yield to them would be to yield or to compromise the novelist's own aesthetic honesty. Certain things won't fit into a novel, won't go in simply because the story won't tell itself if such a fact is there. This is what Lukács meant. It's what I mean when I say that a brute, an idiotic preoccupation with crude fact is death to a novel, and death to the novelist. The primary thing is the free use and the bold use of the liberating imagination which, dispensing with useless fact, will clear the cobwebs away and will show how it really was. This is all I mean about fact and its use or misuse.

ELLISON

You mean really what was in your imagination, not in historical reality, don't you, Bill?

STYRON

Well isn't that what we're talking about? I mean, when we read *War and Peace* we are reading about Tolstoy's imagination. I don't want to make any invidious comparisons; I'm just saying that anybody who deals, any creative imagination which deals with the fabric of history leaves you, if he's a good novelist, with a sense of an imaginative truth which transcends, in this case, what the historian can give you. An historian can tell you just what happened at Borodino, but only Tolstoy, often dispensing with facts, can tell you what it really was to be a soldier at Borodino. This is what the distinction is, and this is what I insist is the novelist's prerogative when he is faced with the materials of history.

WOODWARD

I'm interested in this question of fact myself. One of our distinguished novelists present, Red Warren, has written a novel about an historian. I think that Jack Burden was an historian, really. At least he was the narrator of *All the King's Men,* and he had two historical investigations in his career. One of them, you'll remember, was the investigation of the truth about an ancestor, I believe a great-uncle named Cass Mastern, and he said that the investigation was a failure. It was a failure because he was simply looking for the truth. The second investigation was about a man who turned out (though he didn't know it at the time) to be his father, Judge Irwin, and this investigation proved to be a great success. And he said that the reason for that success was that he was only looking for facts. The facts resulted in the suicide of his father, and a tragedy. So an interesting distinction was made there between facts and truth. Jack Burden, incidentally, was an historian, a seeker for a Ph.D., as some of us have been.

WARREN

He didn't get it.

WOODWARD

He didn't get it, and the reason, as you say, was he did not have to know Cass Mastern to get the degree. He only had to know the facts about Cass Mastern's world. I would be interested in hearing you discuss this distinction between fact and truth. I think it's to the nub of our discussion, perhaps.

WARREN

I'll tell you how it happened. I'll do it in two ways. One is how it happened to me, and the other is what could be said about it afterwards; they are quite different things. Jack Burden himself was a pure technical accident, a way to tell the story. And you stumble into that, because you are stuck with your problem of telling a story; you have to make him up as you go along. But that's another problem. The question about his peculiar researches, as I look back on them, is simply this. Being a very badly disorganized young fellow, he really didn't want the Ph.D. anyway. He stumbled on his family history, involving a character in his family, a couple of generations back, who had devoted his life to trying to find a moral position for himself. And this young man, without any moral orientation at all that I could figure out (he's an old-fashioned lost boy, not the new kind—there have always been these lost boys), didn't want his Ph.D., and he didn't know what to do with himself. He didn't know his mother, he didn't like his father, and so forth. At first he couldn't face the fact that in his own blood, there was a man who *had* faced up to a moral problem in a deep way. He couldn't follow it through, could not bear to face the comparison to the other young man. Then, he couldn't face the truth otherwise, without this piece of research. Later, when he had the job of getting the dirt on a character in the novel, he did get all the facts. He gets all the facts, and the guy turns out to be his father, who commits suicide. It's a parable, I didn't mean it to be one; I wasn't trying to make a parable of truth and fact. It just worked out that way. You sort of stumble into these things. It's a parable, as you pointed out to me tonight; I hadn't thought about this before. Well, the facts Jack Burden gets are deadly things. Facts may kill. For one thing, they can kill myths.

WOODWARD

We're working here toward a distinction between fact and fiction. Fact comes, I believe, from the Latin: *factum est,* a thing done, an event. It has acquired a lot of prestige in historical circles; it gets talked about all the time—facts, something you dig up like gold, you unearth. Fiction is something that's created, something that's made, something that is made up perhaps of facts and a lot of guesses. I think of two protagonists in Faulkner's *Absalom, Absalom!,* Shreve McCannon and Quentin Compson, who are really seeking historical truth, and they are doing it with facts and evidence, and bits and pieces, and they go on and on, trying to create this image and to discover the truth about Colonel Sutpen. What they are trying to do seems to me very similar to what the historian is trying to do. He gets together a lot of evidence, and he "creates" the truth.

ELLISON

But they are characters in a fiction, Vann, not historians. So there's a difference.

WOODWARD

Yes, but the historian seems to me to be doing much the same thing with the evidence he gathers. He puts it together. Cleanth Brooks has put page after page of the evidence of *Absalom, Absalom!* together to show how this truth is arrived at.

There are some people here who came to ask questions of these writers, and I think we ought to give them an opportunity.

FIRST QUESTIONER

I would like to direct my question to Mr. Styron. Mr. Styron, Mr. Ellison said that the novelist doesn't have the right to distort facts completely. He said his power is not absolute when it comes to fact. Then you also talked about imaginative truth, and that certain things don't fit into a novel. I'd like to know about the fact that Nat Turner was married—didn't that fit into your novel?

STYRON

It seems to me I've heard this before. I can only reiterate what I have said despairingly in public and even more despairingly in cold print, that in the evidence which was available to me when some years ago I began to collect the few basic materials to write this book, there was no evidence which told me he had such a wife.

FIRST QUESTIONER

Didn't Thomas Gray's *Confessions* say that?

STYRON

No. I'm very sorry. Or is that a rhetorical question?

FIRST QUESTIONER

No, I read an article in *Ebony* by Lerone Bennett.

STYRON

I read it, too. He's wrong. No, if you read the *Confessions* yourself, the original *Confessions,* this is one of the amazing things about it. He mentions all the rest of his family, but mentions no wife. Once again, in an essay I wrote about this controversy, I said that, without laying aside my belief in the irrelevance of certain facts, this on the other hand would have been so important that if I had been given any kind of substantial evidence that he had a wife, then as a novelist I would have felt compelled to create a wife for him. But I only ask again, certainly not for the last time, that people who, like yourself, constantly castigate me for leaving his wife out, consult the evidence yourself, and use a little reason.

FIRST QUESTIONER

Is Margaret Whitehead, in the evidence, completely obsessed in his mind?

STYRON

Margaret Whitehead is a part of my fictional imagination. I have no apologies for her. But as for the fact of a black wife, I submit to you, humbly, that the evidence does not show that he had one; and therefore, I think reason dictates that it was perfectly all right for me to leave her out.

FIRST QUESTIONER

I have a number of other questions, but I'm only going to ask one more. You said that a novel has its own reason for being. What's the reason for being for *The Confessions of Nat Turner?* Because I read it and I couldn't find any.

STYRON

Well, I don't know how to answer a question like that. In fact, I don't think I'll try. It's so majestic a question that I don't think I'm able to answer it.

SECOND QUESTIONER

Seeing as though calling historians liars tonight has been quite popular, I can remember that the last time I called you a liar, it became very bitter. It seems as though we confront each other from the North to the South. I met you in Massachusetts this summer, and now all the way down in New Orleans I'm here to call you a liar again.

ELLISON

Which one of us, please?

SECOND QUESTIONER

I'm primarily concerned with Styron. I met him this summer at Harvard. I think possibly we need to take a look at the revolutionary black figure, Nat Turner, to see what he actually represents to black people. I think when we talk about slavery and revolution that it has to be looked at from a psychiatric or a psychological viewpoint. Okay, we take a look at the ten blacks who responded to your book on *The Confessions of Nat Turner.* In this group we have C. V. Hamilton, we have Alvin Poussaint. These men have really delved into the thing; they have looked at it from a psychological viewpoint.

I heard Warren say a few minutes ago that fact can destroy, that fact can be deadly. I contend that imagination and lying can also be deadly and can also destroy. Now let's take a look at this a bit further. First of all we see two major bases from which this book was written. We see some religious ties with Nat Turner—that he was a preacher or something, who had some vision about killing white folk. Secondly, I remember your statement that the white woman was a higher symbol or goal for the black man or the black slave—something that he looked up to and wanted and desired. Okay, I remember asking you that question up North, and I want you to tell these Southern whites this same thing. I want to know this: if the white woman was the symbol for Nat Turner to look up to and this was why he wanted sexual relations, and had all these desires, then, since that black woman [in the novel] was below the white man, what kind of image was she?

STYRON

Have you paused for a question now? Well, let me tackle all of these again, one by one. Indeed you have haunted me. You're my *bête noire,* I'm afraid. I recall you from Harvard Summer School with terror. Now here you are again. I won't reply to your *ad hominem* remarks about my "lies," and so on, but I will try to reply directly to you about what I conceive to be the essential truth about Nat Turner's relationship with white women. Forgive me if I paraphrase you badly, but I think you are asking me if I sincerely believe that Nat Turner really yearned, carnally and otherwise, for a white girl. Am I right?

SECOND QUESTIONER

No, you're wrong.

STYRON

Well then, would you please rephrase it?

SECOND QUESTIONER

My thing was, if you placed the white woman above the black slave—the male slave, and said that this was something that he wanted because she was above or higher than him, then how do you explain the white man reaching below him to go back in the quarters, to get the black women out of those slave quarters, which is the cause of many of my brothers and sisters sitting here tonight being of different pigmentation of skin?

STYRON

I don't think at any place in the book did I for an instant deny the very implicit fact that white men were down in the quarters at all times. The reason that I didn't necessarily describe this happening in any great detail is simply that it didn't suit my artistic needs. But if you are implying that somewhere in the book there is a vacuum, that somewhere in the book there is an implication that Negro women were not violated more or less systematically by white men who ruthlessly went down in the cabins, then you have totally misread the book. Because it's there.

SECOND QUESTIONER

You see, the facts you included would *sell*. The whites *wanted* to read that Nat Turner was not a strong, black, revolutionary figure, but that he had certain sexual desires that drove him on. All right, you talk about his killing women and children. Let's take a look at the *Ten Black Writers* and how they analyze that. It seems that most of the men were away at a meeting. This made no difference. You talk about children; you make me believe that Nat Turner walked up and just stabbed babies or beat them in the head—which possibly would have been all right, because possibly he had the insight to know that these same little white babies would one day be the slave masters of his children, wherever they were. So wiping out the white children would be the very same thing as wiping out those adult honkies. When he burned down a house, he got white women and children and anybody else who was in the house. It made no difference who was in the house; when the house went up in flames, everybody and everything in the house went up, not just women and children.

STYRON

What is your complaint?

SECOND QUESTIONER

My complaint is this: don't just say he killed women and children, like the man had a hang-up or was afraid of white men, because explicitly the ten blacks tell you how he knocked some honky down and beat him to death, and then laid his wife down and killed her, right next to him. He wasn't afraid of white men; he killed white men, white babies, white women, white cats, white dogs, everything that was in the neighborhood.

STYRON

Indeed he did. I tried to point out something to you, I think. I shall try again. (You reappear in my dreams; I knew somehow that you'd find me here. From Cambridge to New Orleans; it's more than the mind can encompass.) Anyway, if I may quote, in a sort of contradistinction to your ten black critics, one of the people who criticized the ten black critics, in this case Eugene Genovese. I think he pointed out, at least to my satisfaction, that if you will read the evidence—if you read the crude evidence of Nat Turner and his insurrection, and you can read it in twenty minutes—you will get the impression, and any rational person will get the impression when he is finished, of a ruthless and perhaps psychotic fanatic, a religious fanatic who, lacking any plan or purpose—admittedly, because it is in the testimony, lacking any plan or purpose—takes five or six rather bedraggled followers and goes off on a ruthless, directionless, aimless forty-eight-hour rampage of total destruction, in which the victims are, by a large majority, women and little children.

SECOND QUESTIONER

But *white.*

STYRON

No. Wait a minute. This is the crude evidence; this is what Lukács would say. These are the facts. Deal with them. I submit to you—I submit to any rational intelligence in this room who would allow himself twenty minutes—that this is the impression you would get. A deranged—

SECOND QUESTIONER

It isn't the impression that I got.

STYRON

Well, I'm sorry.

SECOND QUESTIONER

It may be a white impression.

STYRON

I don't think so.

SECOND QUESTIONER

Quite clearly.

STYRON

I don't think so. What Genovese was generous enough to grant me, in my dealings with this man, was that I supplied him with the motivation. I gave him a rationale. I gave him all of the confusions and desperations, troubles, worries.

SECOND QUESTIONER

But look. Let's stop here.

STYRON

Excuse me. Will you hear me out?

SECOND QUESTIONER

He was a slave, and that gave him enough reason.

STYRON

All right. Listen to me, will you, please?

SECOND QUESTIONER

That gave him enough reason, right there.

STYRON

All right.

SECOND QUESTIONER

You didn't have to create anything for him. He saw brothers and sisters being killed all around him. He saw families being broken up.

STYRON

The evidence . . .

SECOND QUESTIONER

I notice your other point, that these were kind slavemasters. It doesn't matter how kind they were; they were slave-masters.

STYRON

I'm sorry, you haven't read it carefully. The evidence doesn't show any . . .

SECOND QUESTIONER

I've read it quite carefully.

STYRON

Well, then, we're at an impasse, my friend, because you say it's one way, and I say it's another.

SECOND QUESTIONER

Yes, but everytime we meet, you always jibe, and say that I miss your point. You ought to stop lying.

WOODWARD

Are there other people who want to ask questions?

THIRD QUESTIONER

I have a question about another Southern novel, an older one. Perhaps I have read you, the panel, wrong, but I gather you would be willing to predict that in a hundred years *Gone with the Wind* will be an obscure or forgotten novel. From listening to what you have said about using historical facts and about catching the essence, I gather that you would think that *Gone With the Wind* has failed.

STYRON

You must be crazy; I didn't say any such thing. I admire *Gone With the Wind* very, very much. I reread it about four years ago. It's a remarkable novel. I don't think it's a great novel, but it's a remarkable novel, precisely because this little woman from Atlanta had a fire of an imagination, which captured her and somehow allowed her to breathe some kind of miraculous spirit through and around the rather threadbare facts about antebellum Georgia. I certainly would not say that it's going to be dead in a hundred years. If I led you to believe that, you misunderstood me.

WOODWARD

Yes sir?

FOURTH QUESTIONER

As long as we call ourselves black and white, then even if we gain black power, unless we censor that movie I'm sure all white folks will go to it. They love that myth. But I think it's slightly beside the point. [*to Styron*] I would suggest, by the way, that I'm very sorry that Mr. Ellison didn't read your book. I'm extremely sorry, because of the putdown that you did on the young man. I think that intellectually you would have had a little bit more trouble with Mr. Ellison. I didn't stand up here for a putdown, so I'm not going to ask you anything at all. I have a whole lot of trouble with that book. I must say that, like every other black man, I resented it. I do think that the book must not be valid if all the black intellectuals put it down. If it salves the conscience (salves; how do you spell that word?)—if it salves the conscience of whites, and they want to read it, well, then you can make some money. But in view of this, I want to ask Mr. Warren this: since we all felt that *All the King's Men* had to do with Huey Long, why didn't *he* say Huey Long, or King Fish, or something like that? I wonder what would have happened to *The Confessions of Nat Turner* had it just been called the *Confessions of a Revolt Leader,* or something like that. I doubt if anybody would even have paid any attention to it. So I'd like to ask Mr. Ellison—he disguises his characters—

ELLISON

I made them up; they were all me.

FOURTH QUESTIONER

Yes, I know, but you've lived through [the period] since Rinehart, you've lived through Malcolm—

ELLISON

Yes.

FOURTH QUESTIONER

We've had some different experiences [since then.] I don't suggest that you follow in the footsteps of Leroi [Jones] really, as a lot of my militant friends would suggest, but since you are older, and you did live through something, I'd like to know—I mean, it was different, you know; everybody was trying to get along with whitey during that time, and now it's kind of six one way, half-a-dozen the other. But since you've lived through Malcolm, and I've heard that you are writing now, how do you see guys like Rinehart? Would you fictionalize Malcolm, disguise him, or would you feel free to say, well . . .'

ELLISON

I would be ashamed to tell the truth about Malcolm in fiction.

FOURTH QUESTIONER

Ashamed to tell the truth about him?

ELLISON

Yes. Well, I think you're getting at a much more important problem which . . .

FOURTH QUESTIONER

You see, I'm concerned with *using* work . . . , Malcolm versus fiction for instance. I'm saying, leave off the word Nat Turner on that book, and just make it the *Confessions of a Slave Leader,* and nobody would read it. (Which I don't think they should, anyway.) But what would you do with Malcolm?

ELLISON

Well, wait a minute. You throw too many things at me at once, when you're really bouncing them off me to hit Bill.

FOURTH QUESTIONER

Yes, I'm trying very hard.

ELLISON

All right . . .

FOURTH QUESTIONER

He [Styron] put down that other young man so skillfully. I think I'd be a little bit more trouble because I don't think that that young man was aware of the fact that Mr. Styron was trying to put him down.

ELLISON

Maybe the young man . . .

FOURTH QUESTIONER

I thought that was cute and extremely unfair. Nine million people in this country voted for Wallace—I take that rather seriously. A fascist. I mean, you see, we haven't accomplished the revolution—

ELLISON

May I . . .

FOURTH QUESTIONER

Yes, please.

ELLISON

I think that there is a basic question of what all arts attempt to do, or what art should attempt to do. Through depicting the real, fictionally, imaginatively, by abstracting from the historical process, reducing it to a controlled situation where the imagination can load each character, each scene, each mood, even each punctuation mark with the individual writer's sense of life, art can give man some transcendent sense of his complexity and his potentiality—of his possibilities—and convey something of the wonder of human life, and I must say, without reducing man to what Malraux would call a handful of secrets . . .

FOURTH QUESTIONER

That's why I'm sorry you didn't read the book.

ELLISON

. . . posited in his negative potentialities. I think that there is something else here which *you* might think about. I don't know whether you are a writer, or whether you should write, intend to write, or what not. But I think that there is a world of art, a world of fiction, and this must be protected against assaults. Not because we are black or white, or because we are oppressed and fighting for more freedom in this country, but because we seek to express ourselves. I want to say, I want the freedom to depict, to recreate Robert E. Lee in terms of my own vision of human possibility, human failure, and so on. So we cannot reduce this thing, really, to the struggle, which is very important on the political level. This distinction is very important, and I point out that two of the ten critics tried to stick to the literary, to the artistic problems involved. Beyond this, of course, as you and the other young man have dramatized so vividly for us, there *is* a problem. Damn it, there is a *problem* about recreating historical figures. That's why I said it's poison to the novelist; he shouldn't bother them. Don't appropriate the names. Don't move into the historian's arena, because you can only be slaughtered there. But you can also be very, very powerful, and I think that this should not be missed: this book, whatever its literary qualities—and I will stand up for Bill's personal qualities and his . . .

FOURTH QUESTIONER

Malcolm said that most whites in America, deep down in their toes, are racists, even when they don't think so.

ELLISON

I would suspect that all Americans, black and white, are racists.

FOURTH QUESTIONER

Well, we . . .

ELLISON

That isn't the problem here, you see. You asked me then what would I make of Malcolm. Well I wouldn't dare to tell the truth about him, because it would destroy the same myth, and this myth is a valuable myth. But I don't want Malcolm telling me what American history is, and I don't want him to tell me what my experience has been, and so on, any more than I want or I would allow Bill or anybody else to do that. You see, there is a world of fiction, and there's a world of politics. I think it's very important for your own position that you keep these things in clear perspective.

FOURTH QUESTIONER

Are you suggesting that we are still invisible?

ELLISON

I am by no means. I was not invisible, and I would think that you, speaking with your inclination, would remember that old joke: The Negro is unseen because of his high visibility.

WOODWARD

Well, I hope that enigma will satisfy questions. There are people here who have been standing patiently for over two hours, and I feel that I am obliged to bring the meeting to a close after one more question.

FIFTH QUESTIONER

I was going to ask two questions, but I'll condense them. Mr. Styron has stressed several times what I think is probably the quintessential bone of contention this evening; he said—I think I quote him accurately—that the fiction writer's obligation is to make sense out of history. I was going to ask, whether he thinks that is the fiction writer's primary, or one of his primary, obligations. I'd like to address my central question to Mr. Ellison, and step back to a novel that is not as recent and, at present I assume, not as controversial as *The Confessions of Nat Turner.* Mr. Ellison, you said that Jim of *Huckleberry Finn* was not grounded enough, and I think many of us would probably agree with that, but I'd like to ask whether you feel that this was because of a failure of creative imagination, or a failure of historical imagination, on the novelist's part. Or do you see the two as one problem?

ELLISON

I think the author was too much a victim of the history of his times. Artistically, you see, fiction isn't written out of history, it's written out of other art forms. The going art form for depicting Negroes, the one freshest on the minds of people during Mark Twain's time, was the popular art form of the blackfaced minstrel, and it was that tradition which Mark Twain was very much involved in. His own values managed to project through Jim, but I still insist that it was not grounded enough in the reality of Negro American personality. I know of no black—Negro—critics (I'm a Negro, by the way) who wrote criticisms of *Huckleberry Finn* when it appeared. It was all a dialogue between, a recreation, a collaboration, between a white American novelist of good heart, of democratic vision, one dedicated to values—I know much of Mark Twain's writing—and white readers, primarily. What is going on now is that now you have more literate Negroes, and they are questioning themselves, and questioning everything which has occurred and been written in the country.

FIFTH QUESTIONER

Well, then, in a sense his creative imagination was limited in fact by the historical moment, and that is what has changed.

ELLISON

Limited, too, by his being not quite as literary a man as he was required to be. Because he could have gone to Walter Scott, to the Russians, to any number of places, and found touchstones for filling out the complex humanity of that man who appeared in his book out of his own imagination, and who was known as Jim.

FIFTH QUESTIONER

But were any of the, let's say, less socially favored characters of novelists who were his contemporaries or his predecessors any more fully recreated historically than he managed to do with Jim? You know, with someone with whom he could not directly identify?

ELLISON

Aren't you making this too much of an objective matter? It's a collaboration. It was a successful book. I read it years ago. In fact, it was so successful and so painful that they made it a boy's book, a children's book, in order to be able to deal with the moral pain which it aroused. Nevertheless, part of the discomfort which we feel—and the questions which those slaves (when was this? the 80's), those people of my background, would have asked about it—was not Mark Twain's central concern. What I am suggesting is that *everybody* reads now. *Everybody* is American whether they call themselves separatists, black separatists, secessionists or what not. And everybody is saying: Damn it, tell it like *I* think it is. And this is a real problem for the novelist.

WOODWARD

Ladies and gentlemen, we are limited to two hours and we have exceeded our limit. Let me thank you for your patience and good humor, and our fellow members for their contribution.

For permission to record and transcribe the foregoing we are indebted to Professor C. Vann Woodward, the moderator; the three panelists; and to Professor Bennett H. Wall, executive secretary of the Southern Historical Association.

Notes

1 The exchange that follows is edited from the transcription of a panel discussion at the thirty-fourth annual meeting of the Southern Historical Association in New Orleans, Louisiana, at the Jung Hotel, November 6, 1968.

2 Irving Howe, "Preface to the American Edition," Georg Lukács, *The Historical Novel* (Beacon Press, 1962), pp. 9-10.

3 All quotations are from Georg Lukács, *The Historical Novel,* trans. from the German by Hannah and Stanley Mitchell (Beacon Press, 1962), pp. 166-168.

22

Alain Buisine

"Biofictions" from *Revue des Sciences Humaines* (1991)[1,2]

To each his own bad readings. For me, these are the *Life and Death of X.*, *The Strange Destiny of Y.*, these bastard re-workings that have no great revelation, despite some exceptions and transgressions. Doesn't every famous man remain as secret and poorly known as Homer, Shakespeare, Lautréamont, and Salvatore Giuliano?

Pierre Mertens, *Clandestine Letters*

"Do you like science fiction?"

I smile. I say I like it well enough. [...]

"I like Bradbury above all. But off the top of my head, there is a very nice novella, I can't remember anymore by whom... A young man is invited to dinner at the house of a couple of friends. Dinner is over and then they say to him: 'So, are you ready?' And he says yes. 'You have the camera?' 'Yes, you have the tape recorder?' 'Yes.' 'Something to write with?' 'Yes.' 'Then, go ahead.' He says, 'Ok but some coffee? I haven't yet had my coffee.' The others say, 'You'll have it when you get back.' They see a flash, a lightning bolt. A moment passes and he comes back. He had gone thousands of years into the future. They say, 'So, what's going to happen?' He says, 'I have no idea.' 'But you don't remember anything?' 'No.' They look at the pages. He wrote nothing. Nothing on the tape recorder, nothing on the film. They say, 'Come on. Try to remember something.' After a moment, he says, 'Oh yes, now I remember. Someone gave me the choice of whether I would want to remember or not.'

Daniele Del Giudice, *Wimbledon Stadium*[3]

Here we are gathered today around something no one can deny. It is obvious that biographies have never known such success in France, and nothing seems to be able to check this growth—a growth which is truly carcinogenic because it ends by touching and absorbing all the domains of writing and knowledge. These metastases of the biographic progressively contaminate each domain of the human sciences, and they become the essential parameter of all production we call cultural.

Each month, on the tables of our bookshops, we find an ever-growing new delivery of biographies in all genres—of artists, singers, writers, athletes, historical figures, and actors. These are mass-produced stories written to sell, most often appallingly mediocre, with an incurable intellectual naïveté. But they are enough to satisfy the questionable tastes of their audience, insatiably fervent to know the life of the other in all its details and all its failures, fervent to go into the intimate parts of another's life, to become a *voyeur*.

But now that I have ritually pronounced this official excommunication of our cultural sub-products, it is possible to begin our real work. In other words, let us pass from the complaisant good conscience of a pure and simple denunciation (useless because of its infinite repetition) to the complexity and to the efficacy of a symptomatic analysis.

Because literature, even in some of its best fiction and critical works, by no means escapes this biographical curiosity. It is to the point that in the latest book reviews at the end of *La Quinzaine littéraire*, the literary pieces announced by the magazine are more and more often none other than impressive biographies, each more knowledgeable and better-documented than the last. We therefore see a very revealing phenomenon: top researchers who have spent their lives studying a particular writer—after having dedicated decades of many ideological, aesthetic, stylistic, and literary analyses to him or her—have decided to crown their critical effort with a biography that in many cases betrays their former desire. Previously they had openly stated that they were interested in nothing other than the work itself. But after a lifetime of exclusive attention to the author's writing, the literary critic now has no desire other than to become his or her great biographer.

For these literary critics alone, this flood of biographies whose *vogue* comes to us incontestably from the Anglo-Saxon world, this return to the biographic certainly merited a colloquium specifically dedicated to this irresistible growth in power of a genre so denigrated by the guardians of the temple. Particularly, in this place, in this library of the Cerisy-la-Salle chateau, where, in the seventies, some of the glory days of textual self-referentiality were celebrated. How could I not admit that twenty years ago, I, myself, would never have imagined—or at least would have believed myself destined for the worst of critical betrayals—that I would lead a day of a colloquium titled "the biographic"! We are far from the times when our desire for modernity easily conquered us—"that the notion of an author belongs to the reactionary discourse—the discourse of the individual, private property, profit—and that the work of the writer is, on the contrary, anonymous: merely a matter of combinations that could, in a pinch, be left to a machine, since they seem so easily programmable, the human intention being depersonalized in its turn so that it only appears now as a particular phase of the class struggle, which is the mainspring of History in general, as well as the history of the novel." (Alain Robbe-Grillet, *Ghosts in the Mirror*).[4]

Similar "*niaiseries*"[5] (the term is from the author of *For a New Novel*[6]) have been completely overwhelmed and blown away by a powerful comeback, both of the biographic and autobiographic, from the writer in person. Still it is suitable to avoid transforming this return of the biographic into an instrument of revenge against the gains of our modernity. If the rebirth of the author should favor, as many certainly hope for, a strict return to "normality", that is to say a return to the previous way of life after a period so disastrously troubled that it would be necessary for one to forget it quickly, I would force myself to cancel this colloquium. It is not even about returning to Sainte-Beuve after more than twenty years of the new novel and psychoanalysis. It is not about bringing into question the subject and his or her identity illusions. Of this whole era of suspicion, the subject did not escape intact and identical to himself (i.e., the same as he was). This means that the biographic, in its literary forms, will not be able to be anything other than totally different from what it was in the past.

This is because the biographic itself, at the very least in its most interesting contemporary iterations, has not forgotten the lessons of our modernity. Thus, it appeared essential to me to dedicate an entire week of analysis to it. What would appear to me decisive from this point forward is that the biographic is no longer separate from fiction. There is no longer on one side the novelistic imagination that can royally grant itself all different aspects of creativity, and on the other side the biographic construction laboriously constrained to submit itself to the referential exactitude of its sources. Biography has itself become the producer of fictions, and, even more, it is beginning to show that fictionality necessarily plays a part in the biographic retelling. It is a producer of fictions on the most basic level because the face of the biographer (and his ridiculous determination for wanting to discover the "truth" of a given existence) begins to become a typical character of the contemporary fiction universe. See for example *The Paper Men* by

William Golding in 1984 or, more recently still, in 1988, *The Truth about Lorin Jones* by Alison Lurie. More fundamentally from my point of view, similar fictionality is now becoming more and more substantive in many biographic undertakings.

It would be necessary here to consider at length Pierre Mertens' exemplary approach, which offers us seven moments in the life of the German expressionist poet Gottfried Benn[7], interestingly, in the Fiction & Cie collection (by Denis Roche, at Seuil). This poet, despite all of his visionary and revolutionary qualities of being a brilliant trailblazer, committed the worst of errors by becoming, for just one moment, a traveler on the road of Nazi barbarism. In his acknowledgements at the end of *Shadowlight*,[8] Pierre Mertens, emphasizes the importance of the imagination: "But only the novelist's imagination is responsible for the essential meaning of the book. It is a reverie circling around a particular destiny. Intuitions and hypotheses. A 'controlled skid' of the kind all fiction is entitled to."[9] Mertens, however, is fond of showing his gratitude to Ilse Kaul, the poet's final companion, and to Nele Soerensen, her daughter, "whose secrets were precious." Thus, there are no entrenched oppositions between the literary imagination and the authentic source, between functional fiction and the "truth" of a life, the personal intuitions of the biographer and the revelations of close friends and family members, the inevitable autobiographic projections of the biographer and the existence actually lived by the other.

Pierre Mertens wholeheartedly embraced this paradox: "It's fiction, of course. Nothing other than fiction. He who recounts the error of someone's life, recounts the life of an error. The shortest road between History and story is still imagination. The biographer, here, has no other choice than to make himself a historian, and the historian has no other choice than to become a novelist. But the novelist, in his turn, has no chance of seeing clearly except by discovering himself a poet." In his afterword to the *Clandestine Letters* (which dramatizes the last moments of Alban Berg, in 1935, at the Rudolf de Vienne hospital) titled *Credo qui absurdum*, Pierre Mertens develops his thesis on biography as fiction by showing clearly that "the majority of biographers *are writing novels* but hardly give themselves a chance of writing a good one, because they maintain, rightly, that they are not giving into this temptation..." It is not up to me, on the threshold of this colloquium that I am but introducing, to wonder theoretically about the complex relationships of the biographical and fictional. I want to simply highlight that from now on, it is no longer possible to restrain the biographic to the sphere of classic biographies that believe that only the accumulation of exact and verified sources, arranged in a narrative which goes unequivocally from birth to death, will be able to guarantee the literary resurrection of a life.

The idea of biography as fiction is hereby sufficiently established in order to constitute the principle of the collection, "*L'un et l'autre*,"[10] by Gallimard, under the direction of J.-B. Pontalis. We read on the flap of the dustjacket: "Lives, but such lives that memory invents them, our imagination recreates them, a passion animates them. Subjective accounts, a thousand leagues from the traditional biography. / *L'un et l'autre*: the author and his secret hero, the painter and his model. Between them, an intimate and strong tie. Between the portrait of another and the self-portrait, where do we draw the line?"

The biographic is ever more engaged in fiction. Until this borderline situation, there is this strange reversal where biographical fiction will precede the work itself. In 1983, at Einaudi in Italy, the first novel of Daniele Del Giudice appeared, titled *Lo stadio di Wimbledon*. This book tells us how a young man leads an investigation about a dead intellectual almost twenty years earlier. This scholar has the particularity of having published nothing during his own lifetime. This is the paradoxical face of the intellectual whose literary demands drive him to divulge none of his work. Nothing other than private writing ever existed. The man's name was Roberto Bazlen. He was born in Trieste in 1902 to a German father and an Italian mother, and he died in Milan in 1965. In Trieste he often visited Umberto Saba and Italo Svevo, whom he made rich with his own editorial efforts. He was friends with Eugenio Montale, Giacomo Debenedetti, and Sergio Solmi. Being an editorial counselor his whole life brought him to frequent the best writers and the greatest editors. Daniele Del Giudice's book is not, properly speaking, a biography recounting the life of a man from his birth to his death. And yet under the form of a novel it asks how one can recreate the face of a writer without books, or at the very least of a writer who only writes secretly.

One follows the narrator who tries to find everyone who had previously known Roberto Bazlen, first in Trieste, then in London. Every meeting was more disappointing than the one before. Each new encounter with one of his old friends or with a woman from one of his most intimate relationships results in nothing more than making Bazlen even more ghostly, always escaping the writer. The more the narrator tries to capture him, the more he shies away. And the reasons he doesn't publish become less and less obvious. In this sense, Daniele Del Giudice's novel seems to me to be an exemplary witness of what the biographic is in this postmodern regime. It ends with the positivist illusion of a possible literary resurrection of the subject as a whole coming to take meaning in an ordered account. The biographic is thus necessarily dependent on the autobiographical subjectivity of his biographer. Only a decentered, dispersed, thinned out, fragmented, scattered Roberto Bazlen remains. This nevertheless makes him, the subject, eminently particular and singular in his individuality, as the author of his own life which was without doubt his *chef d'oeuvre*.

In 1984 *Il capitano di lungo corso* was published by Adelphi Edizioni, originally written in German by Roberto Bazlen. This means that the biographic novel preceded the literary work in its current form. It is as if in the final analysis of the work, published posthumously, was the product of biographical fiction itself. May this marvelous reversal inspire our work throughout this entire week!

Alain Buisine
Translated by Lisa Shugert Bevevino

Notes

1 Because a colloquium is an event that is not rewritten retrospectively, I have left this text in the exact state in which it was pronounced on August 3, 1990 as a means of introduction. It is up to the reader to determine if the program that it traced was confirmed or denied. (Author's note, Alain Buisine).

2 Because this was given as a talk, there were many sentence fragments and disconnected pieces that the author clearly knew how to connect. The translator has liberally connected these sentences and ideas to make it accessible for the English reader. (Translator's note, Lisa Shugert Bevevino).

3 *Lo Stadio de Wimbledon* (Italy).

4 Alain Robbe-Grillet, *Ghosts in the Mirror*, trans. Jo Levy (New York: Grove Weidenfeld, 1988), 5-6.

5 Idiocies, nonsense, foolishness.

6 *Pour un nouveau roman* (France), *For a New Novel* (US), *Towards a New Novel* (UK) by Alain Robbe-Grillet.

7 (1886-1956).

8 *Les éblouissements* (France).

9 Pierre Mertens, *Shadowlight*, trans. Edmund Jephcott (London: Peter Halban Publishers, 1997), vii.

10 One and the other, or each other.

23

Michael Lackey, Jay Parini, Bruce Duffy, and Lance Olsen

"The Uses of History in the Biographical Novel" from *Conversations with Jay Parini* (2014)

From a round-table conversation moderated by Michael Lackey at the University of Minnesota's Institute for Advanced Study (September 20, 2012): http://ias.umn.edu/2012/09/20/duffy-parini-olsen-biographies/. Reprinted by permission.

Lackey: Let me briefly start by telling you what led to this round-table conversation. Over the last couple years, I have read a number of biographical novels. What struck me is that there's virtually nothing written about this genre of fiction. I started to ask the question: why is this the case? One of the reasons—and I think there are many others—is that in the late thirties Georg Lukacs wrote an influential book called *The Historical Novel*. In that book, he makes the argument that the biographical form of the novel is a serious distortion of historical fiction and that it's actually something that should not be done. In essence, the biographical novel is by its very nature a flawed form. One of his arguments goes like this: the biographical novel could never rise to the level of a legitimate historical novel because the focus on "the biography of the hero" leads authors to overlook or misrepresent significant historical events and truths and thus "reveals the historical weakness of the biographical form of the novel." Most writers accepted this view. So before the 1970s, there were very few biographical novels. Three that immediately come to mind are Arna Bontemps's *Black Thunder,* which was done in 1936, Zora Neale Hurston's *Moses, Man of the Mountain,* which was published in 1939, and William Styron's *The Confessions of Nat Turner,* which came out in 1967. But starting in the 1980s, there was a veritable explosion of such novels. Let me mention just a few: Ron Hansen's *The Assassination of Jesse James by the Coward Robert Ford,* Gore Vidal's *Lincoln,* Bruce Duffy's *The World as I Found It,* Jay Parini's *The Last Station,* Irvin Yalom's *When Nietzsche Wept,* Parini's *Benjamin's Crossing,* David Mamet's *The Old Religion,* Anita Diamant's *The Red Tent,* Michael Cunningham's *The Hours,* Russell Banks's *Cloudsplitter,* Hansen's *Hitler's Niece,* Yalom's *The Schopenhauer Cure,* Lance Olsen's *Nietzsche's Kisses,* Edmund White's *Hotel de Dream,* Sherry Jones's *The Jewel of the Medina,* Olsen's *Head in Flames,* Parini's *The Passages of H.M.,* and Duffy's *Disaster Was My God.* There are many more. But how do we explain the proliferation of these novels? Why did so many writers disregard Lukacs's prohibition against the biographical novel? What changed in intellectual and political history that allowed these writers to write this kind of fiction? I contacted Jay, Bruce, and Lance in order to get some answers, and today I'm hoping that they will share some of their thoughts with us. Let me start by asking you three to define your novels. Would you call them biographical novels which also focus on history? Or, would you say that they are actually historical novels which just happen to use the life of a famous figure to illuminate a specific time in history? Or, would you agree with Lukacs and say that they focus almost exclusively on the biography of a specific person and, as such, are not terribly interested in history? Or, would you call them something entirely different?

Duffy: You first, Jay.

Parini: I go first? Oh dear. Well, I would say to hell with Lukacs. [Laughter] I did read that book when it came out. I was a graduate student at St. Andrews, in Scotland, where Lukacs was in vogue. When I got to writing *The Last Station* in the middle of the late eighties, I don't think I actually thought about his book or its argument. I tried to imagine what kind of piece of fiction I wanted to write. I didn't actually try to define it—not in theoretical terms—as I was writing *The Last Station.* I had become obsessed with Leo Tolstoy, and I wanted to look at his world really closely. I always believed that history is just a narrative. One of the greatest forms of fiction is called "history." History is fiction. As soon as we get into the business of putting reality into words, we're in the fictive realm. "Fictio" means shaping, and there's no such thing as an objective historian. I really believe that. Objective history is a piece of nonsense. Historians have tried to put one over on us over many centuries, going back to Thucydides. I'm more with Herodotus, who combined myth with history and understood that he was involved in a fictive enterprise. So when I write, I don't actually categorize my work. Yet I'm comfortable with the phrase "biographical novel" because three of the novels I've written are, in a sense, biographical. Most novels are autobiographical, and the truth is most biographies are forms of autobiography. [Laughter] So really, it gets confused very quickly. I simply would be more comfortable saying I'm writing a narrative. My narratives sometimes involve real people. I'm projecting on the screen, creating characters and trying to imagine what they're really like. I hope I'm getting closer and closer to the truth as I write about Tolstoy, as I write about Walter Benjamin, as I write about Herman Melville. I'm of course looking for gaps where I can fill things in, but trying to imagine the past involves a huge effort of fiction—deploying the techniques of fiction. In short: as soon as we begin putting things into words, we're involved in the action of fiction making. I think if we're going to write a history of the Peloponnesian War or a history of World War I or a life of Franklin Roosevelt—as a straight biography—or an imagined life of Leo Tolstoy, we're on some level engaging in the same work, which is putting into words. And as soon as we begin putting things into words, anything that's processed by memory becomes fiction. I'm in the business of processing memory. It might be my own memory or it might be a larger memory. How's that for a start?

Lackey: That's a good start. Bruce?

Duffy: I've always resisted titles for fiction—the "Coming of Age Novel," for example. That said, "the biographical novel" is probably a title that has some practical staying power. If I got to choose, I would probably prefer something in the realm of "the novel of life and ideas" because that, I think, is what I write—and what we all write—really, books about ideas. As far as history and Lukacs, he is really coming out of a deeply Marxist perspective, so it's a—to my mind—authoritarian, top-down sort of view of history, very deterministic, and trying to control things. Not me. I think writing a novel is not about control. Quite the contrary. For me, the novel is about letting yourself be uncontrolled, letting yourself be really open and driven by other events, really, being confused. Actively finding confusion rather than trying to find certainties, starting off with some laundry list of what you think a novel should be. That, to me, is—sorry—disgusting. I think such control has nothing to do with fiction. I don't think any writer would ever think in this our narrativization of the past goes. Afterwards, during the Q and A, someone asked: "Mr. Browning, what did you mean by that poem?" He said: "At the time I wrote that, only God and I knew what I meant. And now only God knows." [Laughter] That's sort of how I feel when asked questions like this. To harmonize with what you guys are saying: I believe there's an aesthetic logic that guides narrativity. Imagine trying to tell a story about Nietzsche or Wittgenstein or Tolstoy and not leave anything out, not shape it. That story would be tens of thousands—hundreds of thousands—pages long, and we would all stop reading pretty fast. I also want to frame my answer—and this goes to my earlier point about these kinds of narratives—by reminding us of Linda Hutcheon's notion of historiographic metafiction. She's talking about fiction that is highly aware of talking about pastness, we are always-already being written, rewritten, erased, reformatted and retold, edited. Her argument is—and I think it's an important one—that really these kinds of novels aren't about the past, but about the problematization of historical knowledge. Renarrativizing history points to history as a problem that writers are investigating. She makes an interesting distinction—I think it's one that we all sort of unconsciously as writers make—between facts and events. She defines facts as discourse defined, events as non-discourse defined. That is to say—and this goes back to what you guys are saying—as soon as you begin to tell a story, you move it from the real world into language. As soon as you move into language, you move into narrativity. As soon as you move into narrativity, you are talking about how you constellate facts around events. One can imagine, the Germans having won World War II, that the history of World War II would have been a quite different history than we now tell. All of which is to say: I left out what I needed to for aesthetic, but also, I think, epistemological reasons.

Lackey: In your novels, all three of you focus on figures who are deeply concerned with the condition of knowledge and formulate theories about knowledge. Lance, you focus on Nietzsche, specifically the role a will to power plays in the formation of a knowledge system. Bruce, you focus on Ludwig Wittgenstein, specifically how he initially rejected the role the Freudian subconscious played in the formation of knowledge but how he eventually came to understand and accept the power of the subconscious. And Jay, you focus on Walter Benjamin, specifically his rejection of metaphysical knowledge in favor of a de-essentialized, provisional form of fragmented and sometimes contradictory knowledge. Can you all briefly discuss what motivated you to focus on your particular writers, and specifically their theories of knowledge?

Olsen: My sense is that all theory, which is to say, all writing, is a form of spiritual autobiography. It has much less to do with the subject at hand than with the experience of the subject at hand filtered through a particular consciousness in the world. Or as J. M. Coetzee said: "All autobiography is autré-biography." As soon as you begin to talk about autobiography, you're narrativizing someone else. To your question, then. I want to say two events motivated me. One is that I spent the first few years of my life growing up in Venezuela. My dad was involved in setting up oil refineries. We lived in a jungle compound. It was just at that age when you're commencing to come to consciousness. I have a sister who was with me during that time, and, years later, as I was sitting with her, talking about these crazy events I remember experiencing—snakes in the washing machine kind of events, being chased through the jungle by a wild boar kind of events—I realized my sister was continuously getting it wrong. [Laughter] I was the only one who really remembered what had happened. [Laughter] That was fascinating to me—the slow understanding that we allegedly had these same experiences, but neither of us actually agreed on what the experiences were we had. We each narrativized them weirdly differently—to the point where stuff that my sister says happened to her, I vividly remember happening to me, and vice versa. The other thing that influenced me—well, you meet Nietzsche and, as Yeats says, you instantly become drunk on him. I did that as an undergraduate. I remember taking a course on existentialism and Nietzsche was on the syllabus, and, of course, to begin to read him is to never stop reading him. Also, to begin to read biographies of Nietzsche is immediately to realize how narrativized he is, how many versions of him exist in the universe. There's an existentialist Nietzsche, for example, a poststructuralist one, a crazy-man, a misogynist, a visionary, and so on. That intrigued me. Shortly after I graduated—in the late seventies, I think—maybe the early eighties—I wrote a story about Nietzsche, trying to capture the uncapturable, then thought I put him away. Maybe in 2001 I was walking by a bookshelf in my house and saw this line of Nietzsche books and thought, "I wonder if that guy still holds up?" [Laughter] I reached for . . . I think it was *Twilight of the Idols*, and started thumbing through it. Oh my God. I realized he had never left me. A way to deal with that unshakability turned out to be trying to write through his work.

Duffy: At some point, most novelists have a very humbling event—maybe several humbling events—and that is when a novel fails. You're writing a novel. You're spending a great amount of time on it, and you realize this is not going to work. You have to change your mind. So maybe this, with Wittgenstein, inspired me—I mean, in terms of realizing unconsciously what I so admired about him. Imagine. For years, Wittgenstein works with Bertrand Russell and G. E. Moore at Cambridge on a new philosophy. He goes to World War I, fighting for the Austrian army on the front lines. It's a terrible, demoralized army. Of course, they're defeated. Yet Wittgenstein comes away from this catastrophe with a slender manuscript called *The Tractatus*. And he thinks he's answered all the essential questions in philosophy. Thinking in his mind: "All the questions of philosophy have been answered now. We're done. We can all go home." Only to realize, years later, he was . . . wrong. A fool. Wrong about almost everything. So Wittgenstein quits philosophy and goes off to teach children. He goes into this Austrian mountain town and at first Wittgenstein is very idealistic. He thinks the children all like him. But, no, the children all hate him. [Laughter] The parents are horrible. Teaching—that doesn't work either. And so Wittgenstein comes to create another kind of philosophy. No grand truths. This is more a language philosophy looking at every particular thing that people say. Asking: Why do people say that? What does this expression really mean? Again, it's not about one incandescent overarching sort of system. It's about many different possibilities—more modern and chaotic. Well, I don't need to take you through all this, but the point here is what so amazes me about Wittgenstein as a great thinker. I mean, his bravery as a thinker, willing to do the very hardest thing. And this is to change your mind, to demolish what you have built and create something else. For me, that is what great thinking and—and art—are all about. Changing your mind. Simply changing your mind.

Parini: If I can build on what Bruce has said . . . I've always admired Wittgenstein myself. Just to imagine you had the whole world wrapped up in a ball in *The Tractatus* and then to spend two decades exploding or deconstructing your work by writing the *Philosophical Investigations.* That took courage, a kind of intellectual ferocity. I remember being first attracted to Benjamin when I was reading some letters he wrote to Gershom Scholem, his best friend who was a famous kabalistic scholar. He said, "You know, Gershom, you're always of two minds. I'm always of two dozen minds." [Laughter] What I loved about Walter Benjamin was the fact that he anticipated the fragmentation of postmodernity. That's what's most appealed to me. Pablo Neruda has a wonderful poem that begins, "My selves are many." I think this is true of all of us. I'm of about at least two dozen minds every day. I don't know which one to sit in. Or, I'm like Wallace Stevens with a mind "like a tree in which there were three blackbirds." My own tree is filled with many blackbirds. Benjamin seemed to me to anticipate this mentality. He both comes out of and resists the totalizing historical schools of Spengler or Lukacs or Erich Auerbach—the kind of positivism that gets summarized in a third-rate way by someone like A. J. Ayer in *Language, Truth, and Logic.* I find historical positivism, like philosophical positivism, somewhat old hat and false. For his part, Benjamin attracted me because he was an early thinker who was of many minds at once and who understood that there is no such thing as objective reality. There is only, as he said, the layering of subjective realities. My own work as a novelist has always involved the layering of subjective realities, trying to enter into these different subjectivities; letting each of the blackbirds in my tree to quack away for a bit. And hopefully by, as Benjamin suggested, the layering of these subjective realities, one approaches something like truth. But, you know, I love that line from Oscar Wilde's *The Importance of Being Earnest,* where he says, "The English are always degrading truths into facts." Historians and even the writers and the literary critics are so often degrading truths into facts. It's only when we start backing away from the facts and multiplying them and putting them against each other and creating not a dialogue, but an incredible cacophony of voices, that we begin to move through fragmentation toward an acceptance of the broken world that we actually occupy.

Duffy: Jay, there's one thing you said earlier. We were talking about Lukacs. And you were saying, "Well, Lukacs doesn't really speak to the postmodern world." I agree, it seems to me, Lukacs was creating this sort of battleship, this Maginot Line, of theories, all these brilliant super structures. Well, maybe that was true in his era, but I don't think it's how things operate today. It's not how people think today, and it's not true to the realities of today. Maybe I'm off course, but I think that's more or less what you were saying, Jay.

Parini: That kind of literal totalizing mentality's what got us into Iraq. I think we have to avoid that kind of thing.

Duffy: Yeah.

Lackey: Let's move to another topic. Anti-Semitism and the Holocaust are central to all of your works. Let me briefly address each one of your works individually at this point. Walter Benjamin and Gershom Scholem had a conflicted relationship. As a Jewish scholar, Scholem wanted Benjamin to embrace his Jewish heritage and to use his intellectual gifts to advance Jewish scholarship. But Benjamin understood that human identity is composed of many contradictory parts, so he could not enthusiastically embrace any single identity. What you, Jay, do so well in *Benjamin's Crossing* is to build up to that moment when Benjamin is dying and he is reflecting on his relationship with Scholem. While dying, Benjamin thinks about Scholem's theory of religious identity, which holds that Jews and Christians are essentially different. We have no way of knowing if this is what Benjamin was thinking at that time of his death. So why did your Benjamin have these thoughts on his deathbed, and how does this scene connect with the rest of the novel? Much of the novel is narrated by Scholem. Why is it significant that we get so much of the narrative from someone who was certainly close to Benjamin, but someone with whom Benjamin was in deep disagreement?

Parini: That was a way of setting a dialectic in motion. It's what I was trying to do there. Think of the trajectory of Walter Benjamin, how he begins as a kind of old school Hegelian, then he sidles his way into a kind of Marxism with some of his friends, such as Theodor Adorno. Then he gravitates, near the end, toward mystical kabalistic thought. Yet he never left any kind of thinking behind. He liked synthesizing everything. If we follow the traces of his various writings we notice that he was endlessly shape-shifting, finding different realities that wouldn't hold water and then abandoning them. Yet he kept returning to them, and then abandoning them again. On his deathbed, he was probably saying to himself: "Well, there's some truth in Marxism. There's some truth in Hegel. Maybe this dialectic is leading me somewhere." But I suspect he was moving toward a mystical understanding of reality. My sense is, looking at the letters between Gershom Scholem and Walter Benjamin, that on some level he was teasing and critiquing Scholem, suggesting to him by way of undertones: "You don't really understand what you're talking about. If you took this kabalistic mysticism seriously, you'd be living a different life." Benjamin was inherently a critic, and, like I say, he was of many minds. He allowed a play of voices—very different, even contradictory, voices—toward the end of his life. At least that's what happens in my novel. Who knows what really happened? The door is closed on history. So I'm trying—given what traces we have—to follow a path through the darkness, and see if I can arrive at some door, perhaps open it and peek in. It's my imagination peeking in.

Lackey: Nietzsche's sister married Bernhard Förster, who was a Christian anti-Semite. Elizabeth and Förster shared a dream of building a utopian community which would be free of Jews. In the late 1880s, they actually established such a community in Paraguay, and they called it Nueva Germania. Nietzsche despised Förster, and he passionately opposed his utopian community. Nietzsche did this in part because he hated anti-Semitism, as you make clear in your novel. And yet, Nietzsche's sister, who took charge of the Nietzsche Archive after Nietzsche's mental collapse, revised and even forged some of her brother's texts, thus making them acceptable—and even appealing—to Hitler and the Nazis. Your novel brilliantly builds up to the scene when Hitler visits the Nietzsche Archive and Elizabeth presents him with Nietzsche's walking stick. Why, in a novel about Nietzsche, did you shift the focus to Elizabeth, and specifically her meeting with Hitler? And why did you do all this in a novel rather than a scholarly study? Put differently, what does the novel allow you to communicate about this history-making event that you could not have communicated in a traditional biography or scholarly monograph?

Olsen: Okay. I think this is going to be my answer to why Lukacs is wrong. It's going to slant rhyme off of Jay's invocation of Wallace Stevens's poem "Thirteen Ways of Looking at a Blackbird"—that notion of needing to see reality in a multifaceted way, and also, you know, Jay's reading the poem as a postmodern. Ours is the age of polyphonic uncertainty, not the one Lukacs existed in at all, not the monologic, certain one he longed for. So, first, let me talk a little bit about the structure of *Nietzsche's Kisses,* and then quickly answer the questions you pose the best I can. *Nietzsche's Kisses* is structured in groups of three. Each chapter has a first-person section, a second-person, and a third-person. The first-person concerns the real time of Nietzsche on his deathbed, his last mad night on earth. The second-person sections are made up of Nietzsche's hallucinations, his dream states. The third-person sections are made up of Nietzsche trying to remember, to narrativize, his life. The structure of the novel, then, is insistently multivoiced—that is to say, it insistently privileges a plurality of perspectives simultaneously. The result of that structure is to bracket questions like truth, history, the world, not to mention Lukacs and his totalizing systems. [Laughter] In other words, the very structure of the novel works against any unifying view of, well, anything. It's all blackbirds all the way down. The short answer to the question of why I focused on Lisbeth and Hitler the way I did, then, is because very little is actually known about their meetings. It's historical blank space to be filled by the novelist, and the filling points to what can't be pointed to, to the moment of historiographic metafiction. You talk about the door closing on history? The door is often always-already literally closed on history. What I wanted to do was emphasize with the scene I wrote, in which Lisbeth gives Hitler Nietzsche's walking stick, Hannah Arendt's notion of the banality of evil; that you get one of the most evil guys in the history of the world behind closed doors, and he ends up talking about how nice dogs are. Who knows if that's what Lisbeth and Hitler actually talked about, of course, but if they didn't, they should have. That's the really terrifying part of Hitler: when he walked down the street, he looked just like a normal guy, except he also happened to be the leader of the Third Reich. What novels can do that scholarly studies can't? Every genre can do something that other genres can't do, or can't quite do. What's remarkable about the novel—the reason the novel exists, I think, as a genre—is that it can do three things astoundingly well that other genres can't. One is language: extended exploration of language's bliss. Poetry can do that, but for much shorter extents. Drama and film can't come close. But the more important thing is that the novel can do internal consciousness. It's a genre designed to explore internal modes of being, the circus of the mind in motion. Reading a novel, you live in another person's mind for three days, seven days, a couple weeks. What an extraordinary opportunity. What an extraordinary thing. A scholarly study can't do that, can't produce a thought-experiment about the experience of the experience of dying, the experience of a person's experience upon his deathbed if that person happens to be named Friedrich Nietzsche. The last thing novels can do that most other genres can't is bask in sense impressions. So there's that famous scene where Nietzsche protects a horse from getting whipped in Turin. We don't know anything about that day. We don't know if it was sunny, what it smelled like, what sounds were in the air. That's the novelist's job: to suggest what a moment might have felt like so a reader can imagine one version of that moment.

Lackey: Now for Bruce. Wittgenstein was Jewish. And yet he had a horribly conflicted relationship with his Jewish heritage, as you so brilliantly picture in *The World as I Found It*. This conflict manifests itself most poignantly through Wittgenstein's relationship with Max Einer, a fictional character who is a close friend of Wittgenstein's. Max, with Wittgenstein's unwitting assistance, develops some anti-Semitic views and eventually joins the S.S. Why is there this focus on anti-Semitism and the Nazis in a novel about Wittgenstein?

Duffy: One thing we do know about Wittgenstein—besides his ability to change his mind—and that's his relentless self-honesty. A quick example. One dark and stormy night, Wittgenstein called together some of his closest associates and confessed three awful things about himself. One was that he—a Jew—had been, at various times, guilty of anti-Semitism. The point is, no one could have been harder on himself. In fact, one thing that first drew me to Wittgenstein was his guilt, for example, as a guy with three brothers who committed suicide. Three. He's raised in Austria, in Vienna. He has a hugely wealthy family. And common for those times in Austria, he is a Jew whose family made the socially necessary decision to convert to Catholicism. So there was this great schism in who Wittgenstein was. I don't know all that much, to be honest, about what his personal conflicts were as far as being a Jew raised a Catholic. But I wanted to create that schism. I wanted to use this personal history as a way to explore the times, explore the dividedness, the neurosis that someone like him would have—the divided soul. As for Wittgenstein's friend Max, Max is definitely fiction. He is based on the fact that Wittgenstein was homosexual and had several muscular, working-class guys who were his friends, companions, whatever. In this way, Wittgenstein kind of reminded me of W. H. Auden, who also liked such "butch fruits," I believe they were called. Anyhow, Max is another divided soul, but more dangerous and unconscious, like Germany itself at that time. Max has come out of World War I. He was with one of the toughest fighting units that would advance offensives—men with Lugers, grenades, and flamethrowers who would lead the way. Max comes out of this, then becomes what they would call in those days "the wanderer." There was then this culture of being a hiker, a wanderer. So Max has his backpack. He's got all of his crazy, extreme religious views. And he's an anti-Semite. Here he reminded me of other people I've known who were like that . . . I had a close friend who I grew up with, really a brother when I was in high school forty years ago. Like his father, my friend hated black people—hated them. And yet, at the time, I never knew anybody better when it came to talking with black people and having a good time around them. Again, that schism. How the mind allows one kind of conduct—dreadful conduct—then somehow forgives it, creating a kind of amnesia? So in part, this was really what I was trying to do with Max—to give this very complex, I hope, portrait of a racist.

Lackey: At this point, what I want to do is segue into the question and answer section. But before I do that, what I'm going to do is get these three in a conversation with one another, and then we'll move to the Q & A. So my question for you three is this: How would you differentiate your approaches to the biographical novel from each other, and what questions do you have for each other?

Parini: I suspect we didn't quite answer a question you raised earlier, which does seem central to all of our enterprises. Why is it that all of our works often dwell on the Holocaust? *Benjamin's Crossing* is about a guy in 1940 running from the Nazis and being chased over the Pyrenees into Spain, where he is caught and commits suicide. But it's really about a man who represents, in a sense, the rational mind trying to retain a hold of rationality in an irrational world. Think of the brutality and chaos afoot: when you've got Hitler and the Nazi war machine killing millions of people in a systematic fashion—something not seen before, at least not on that scale. What I've been thinking as I've just been talking is that we, as human beings, are naturally a murderous people. Anyone who knows anything about the history of human beings knows that we club and slit each other's throats and kill each other all the time. It's what we do, one of our things, as human beings: we kill other human beings. At least a shocking number of us do, more often metaphorically than literally. What was exceptional about the Holocaust was simply the vast literal-mindedness of a regime dedicated to killing vast numbers of people: Jews, homosexuals, gypsies. Somehow systematizing that . . . Look at the number of genocides that belong to our fairly recent past. This whole country was based on the genocide of the Native Americans. Sixty million black people died in slavery. It's sad, but we're a country drenched in blood. With the Holocaust, you see this wild literalization: using the rational mind to systematize killing. And what kind of responses followed? We responded by dropping the atomic bomb on Hiroshima and Nagasaki—destroying innocent Japanese villagers. As writers, we try to come to grips with the fact that we are murderous human beings. Increasingly, since the Holocaust, we systematize this brutality. We allow our government to kill a hundred thousand Iraqis and don't even think about it much, just a few years after the fact. The terror of 9/11 gave us an excuse to commit murder on a large scale. We have assembled the largest killing machine that's ever existed—the U.S. military. There's never been an army remotely like ours, for size and destructive capability. And yet we move on, as a nation, as individuals, putting all of that to the side. We teach our classes. We study art and make pottery and make novels. But I feel like we're always living with this state of chaos, this underbelly of violence just out of view. Yet we have blood on our hands, all of us who live here and pay taxes. With the Benjamin novel, I focused on a man in flight from the murderousness of humanity systematized by the Nazis. But, you know, there's a Nazi in each of us that we're fighting. There's a state that grinds people under its wheels. We're having to contend with this all the time—or, more usually, ignore it. Fiction writing provides a way to deal with what lies beneath, out of sight: the fragmentation of our ghastly experience . . . How's that? [Laughter] Put that in your pipe and smoke it! [Laughs]

Olsen: [Laughs] I'm not going now! [Laughter]

Lackey: Maybe I should open it up for questions now. [Laughter] So do any of you have some questions for any of the panelists here?

Question 1: I'm a historian and I also try to write fiction—but not literary fiction. But I think that historians now, for the most part, are not really interested in finding out facts. I mean, we don't want to go into the unfactual, but we're more interested in, like, big patterns and how discourses construct how people think. The whole thing about the death of the author is very, very influential. And you all have been talking about "The Death of the Author" and you're kind of channeling things. But at the same time, you're talking about getting into the interiority of your characters, which I think is correct. That's what history can't do, but then what novels can do. So how do you reconcile the idea of the death of the author with your writing about the subjectivity of authors?

Olsen: This is going to take a second to answer, but I honestly think that it comes down to a grammatical misapprehension. Wittgenstein has this wonderfully instructive line that goes something like this: "One of the greatest misleading representational techniques in the language is the use of the word 'I.'" He goes on to talk about how Western thought has, by misreading grammar, created a faulty metaphysics. I'm really interested in what you're talking about: these weird authorial deployments of nouns and pronouns, and what their troubled relationship is to anything—the world, history, stable subject positions. I'm keenly aware of the problematics of the death of the author. Barthes talks about the text being a space where a number of other texts come together and clash, almost as though writers are just channeling other texts. That sounds right and not right and not-not right. I'm also interested in how, when we write a book (any kind of book) about somebody called Wittgenstein—when we write a book about somebody called Benjamin or Nietzsche—we generate a series of complications by using those nouns and pronouns. There's not really an answer in my answer, just a string of further questions and complexities. If Jay spends his time as a writer worrying about the blood we're all in up to our knees, I spend my time as a writer worrying about how nouns and pronouns misfire in interesting ways in fiction. [Laughter] And, essentially, it's the same problem. [Laughter]

Duffy: Exactly. [laughs] No doubt about it.

Lackey: Jay, do you want to respond to that?

Parini: I'm just wondering how any historians can justify their job. I mean, has somebody written the equivalent article, "The Death of the Historian"? How is it actually possible to write history in this age? I don't know how. I don't know what any historian imagines he or she is doing except creating a work of fiction. It may be based on facts, but the historians are arranging and rearranging and shuffling and building narratives and looking for patterns. When you look for patterns, it's like when you're looking at some rift in Africa. One person sees snails, the other person sees shale. Vision is ideologically grounded. So how is it possible to write history—or scientific history? You're just writing fiction without knowing it, or facing it directly.

Question 1: We spend most of our time thinking about that. [Laughter]

Parini: You make it all up.

Question 1: But also remembering the history of blood so we don't forget.

Parini: Sure.

Question 1: But also that it's all constructed.

Parini: It's the work of remembrance, which is always selective and always ideologically grounded.

Duffy: I'd say, I guess, one obvious thing, and that how we're living in an age of intense self-consciousness in which we see everything refracted in everything else. I think—if I may say so—that such a world can become crippling and overly self-referential. For example, I was talking to one of the students today in the French department who wanted to write a book, and she was going on and on and on, kind of in circles, worrying could she ever write this book. What would it be about? What would it all mean? Trying to help get her untangled, I said, "Imagine that you're in a vast library and there are all these books, every book ever written. And there's one space in that library for your book—for what you are uniquely going to create. Some small slot on the shelf." Yes, I do think that we're in a time when the book is in peril and the book industry is struggling to find another model. But I think there will always be a place for the author. The trick is to imagine that one special place—your place—in that universal library. Focus on that. Focus on the wire and not on how far you could fall.

Lackey: Did I see your hand here?

Question 2: Yeah. I'm a historian, too—a live one, not a dead one. Yet. [Laughter] I'm interested in the history of reading and the history of popular taste and the history in America in the twentieth century of popular taste for biography. I'm interested that this trend that you've identified, if you want to call it that, begins in the 1980s, and I wondered if you had any idea of why that should be. And secondly, if you saw any of your books as a part of a marketplace, in terms of an audience. I mean, did your books sell very many copies? Are they popular? And if not, is there a similar trend? Because all of your books are literary fiction. They would be classified as that, I assume, and not mass market popular fiction. Is there a similar trend or tendency towards the biographical novel in popular fiction, as well?

Duffy: [Everyone stares at Duffy.] . . . Oh. [Laughter] I don't know. You'd be better able to answer that one. Lance? Jay? Anybody.

Lackey: Well, you know, my project is very restricted because I'm focusing mainly on contemporary American biographical novels. So what's happening over in Europe is something that I'm not doing. And there have been a lot of biographical novels—Jay can talk about this—going back to the eighteenth century. The thing is that they've really started to proliferate in the last few years. Jay, is your *Last Station* a popular novel? It certainly has sold a lot. But when did it become that popular? Was it after the movie? Or was it before?

Parini: Well, it sold very well, once the movie came out. It was translated into twenty-five languages. So the bottom line was this: a lot of copies came into print!

Lackey: Is it a popular novel then?

Parini: I hope so. [Laughter] But, you know, you think back to the sixties and seventies, you had guys like Irving Stone writing *The Agony and the Ecstasy.*

Question 2: Yeah. That's a good one.

Parini: Or *Passions of the Mind* about Sigmund Freud. Those were number one bestsellers.

Question 2: *Lust for Life,* too, I guess. Vincent van Gogh.

Parini: *Lust for Life*! Vincent van Gogh! You often go back to Gore Vidal's *Lincoln.* That was a *New York Times* bestseller. It was a serious novel, and it imagines the life of Abraham Lincoln. Before that *Burr* was a huge bestseller, imagining the life of Aaron Burr. So yes, I think there's always been a kind of a public hunger for biographical fiction, at least of a certain kind. Readers like to think about other people's lives. Biography is, in many ways, one of the most ancient forms of literature. Suetonius's *Lives of the Noble Caesar* has been a bestseller for millennia, right? Or look at Vasari's *The Lives of the Artists.* The history of biography is long and deep. You'd also have to say that Suetonius was the first biographical novelist. His portrayal of Tiberius in that book has probably very little to do with the actual Tiberius, but it would make a hell of a good movie! So from that time of ancient Greece, writers have been trying to imagine lives. There were German writers working in the field of biographical fiction in the eighteenth and nineteenth centuries. It's not exactly new, but I do think that the novel after theory takes a very different turn. Even though I wasn't conscious of it, I would say that theory opened my eyes to the issue of perspective. When I started to write *The Last Station,* I thought about the fact that one could no longer adopt a positivistic, totalizing view of history. I couldn't do this, in any case. I couldn't say, "Here's what happened: Tolstoy's wife was in a bitchy mood and she started fighting with her husband. He said, 'To hell with you!' And they were throwing pots and pans at each other." That doesn't get anywhere near the complicated truth of that marriage, those lives. And it's difficult to see life steadily and whole, not now. Think of what happened in your family last weekend. Then ask the five different members of your family what happened last weekend and see what you get. This is where history comes in. This is real history. This is reality processed by memory. It becomes fiction.

Lackey: Anne?

Question 3: My question is kind of based off of two things. Last night, Jay, you mentioned that you did change a lot, but you didn't dare mess with Tolstoy's actual words. Today, you said that in some ways, we have a duty to change the past. I'm kind of struggling with those two concepts together. In what ways can we change the past and with which people? That also ties into my problems with how honesty and dishonesty function in this discourse of truth in fiction.

Parini: Last night I was talking in Morris [University of Minnesota, Morris] to some students. I mentioned the fact that when I wrote *The Last Station,* I felt shy about putting words in Tolstoy's mouth. I decided not to have Tolstoy be one of the characters speaking in the narrative per se, and I didn't want to write as Tolstoy. It wasn't possible. So whenever I had Tolstoy speak, I actually used quotations from Tolstoy. You might consider my novel the red letter edition of Tolstoy. I did, of course, make up conversations where he talked. Nevertheless, I put those conversations in created contexts, as some other character recollecting the dialogue. So that was a kind of idiosyncratic factor of *The Last Station,* that I decided to stick with the actual words of Tolstoy always. Because he happened to have a lot of people reporting what he said, I knew the sorts of things he probably said in reaction to situations. Sometimes I just took things from Tolstoy's fiction, as when I wanted to know what Tolstoy thought about death; I simply stripped out a page at the end of *The Death of Ivan Ilyich* and plugged it into my narrative. But you raise a very interesting thing here about truth or lies. I would say I'm more interested in whether something is authentic or inauthentic than true or false. I'm trying to create in my novels an experience for the reader that feels authentic. It's not "real." It's a made-up book, a novel. It's playing with reality. It's trying to imagine history, but in calling itself a novel, it gives you the license to create. By the time I turned to Benjamin and Melville, I felt at greater liberty to invent voices. I said to myself, "To hell with reporting actual conversations. I'm going to make it all up." [Laughter] So I made up their conversations based on what I thought they might have said. Even with the personal history of Melville, for instance, I asked myself: Does this seem to you like something that could have happened to Herman Melville? We know, for example, that Herman Melville briefly jumped ship in the South Seas on the island of Nuku Hiva and that he was kidnapped by a tribe of bisexual cannibals and that after several weeks he escaped. He writes about this in "fiction," which he calls a memoir, in *Typee.* He makes up names, but he says, "This is my own true experience." But he's making it up! When I was writing my novel, I thought, "What more fun could there be than imagining being kidnapped by a tribe of bisexual cannibals?" [Laughter] Melville goes there, in a sense, but doesn't go far enough. I took it further and played with it. There's an intentional playfulness there. The only truth I'm worried about is: does it seem authentic to the reader, as something that might have happened? What would it be like if you were kidnapped by a tribe of bisexual cannibals? What would you do? Go with it?

Duffy: Alas, I cannot speak to bisexual cannibals. In my case, I was being cavalier earlier when I said, "Do you really care how many sisters and brothers Wittgenstein had?" In other words, the fact is that I drastically reduced that number. On the other hand, I was obsessive with the tremendous amount of period detail required. I wanted the sort of details where the reader would think, "Wow. Where'd he ever find that?" The thing that was absolutely nonnegotiable was having the book be true to Wittgenstein's thought and to the trajectory of his thoughts. Here I wanted the reader not just to understand these ideas as "thoughts," but to feel them as real human problems. How did Wittgenstein come up with these ideas? Why did this idea occur to him? How did the realities of his life produce such unique thinking? Here I wanted the reader to experience, I hoped, the existential sense of being Wittgenstein, feeling that pain, that heat. In other words, realizing that ideas really do respond to life realities. Anxieties and many, many other things. So I guess I'm saying, in a long-winded way, that it's not all bullshit. [Laughs]

Olsen: I'm saying I don't know where literature ends and the bullshit begins. I would therefore answer in a faintly different way. A very strange thing happened in intellectual history after World War II. Think of Hemingway as the archetypal modernist macho guy who needed to write 500 words before he went out to fish. Then think about what happens after, say, the forties and fifties. There are suddenly whole generations of writers that want to write and do so, not by following Hemingway's path, but by going to college, perhaps even graduate school, and thereby become immersed in philosophy, aesthetics, and literary theory. That totally screws you up, because once you've read that stuff, you're infected. It's like biting the apple and being forced from the Garden of Eden. The flaming swords come down behind you, and you may want to get back in, but tough luck. Such knowledge gets you to think about certain problems in ways that, let's say, Hemingway would never have contemplated them. So I feel super uncomfortable talking about such ideas as "authentic" and "inauthentic," or "honesty" and "dishonesty," or "truth" and "untruth," because I honestly don't know what those words mean, can't point to their signifieds, can't think past a web of post-structuralist complications, nuancings, demythifications. I know what such words are supposed to mean, of course. But I'm not sure what they actually do. And I keep translating them from the realm of metaphysics into questions of narrativity—who's structuring the story, from what perspective, out of what ideology, for what reasons. That gives you a different set of questions to ask as you're moving into a novel. It isn't, of course, that I didn't do a lot of research on *Nietzsche's Kisses*. I read all the biographies I could get my hands on, read Nietzsche lots of times, traveled through Germany and Switzerland and Italy taking copious notes about the places that he spent parts of his life. But when I sat down to translate all of that into a novel—and this goes back to what I started off by saying—what I kept being metacognitive about was that what I was really doing wasn't getting at any "authenticity," any "truth," about Nietzsche. I was getting at what my sense of Nietzsche was at a certain time. And so we're back to those nouns and pronouns. For me, writing fiction amounts to exploring what we don't know. So I'm much more confused than Jay.

Lackey: Ande?

Question 4: I have been noticing some interesting parallels among how you each approached your subjects that you're writing about. In traditions of European thought, typically history and philosophy have looked at what is essential and what is unified about how we look at events, like identity having its central qualities. You've all looked at thinkers whose systems of thought have tried to de-essentialize reality and look at identity as being dynamic and fractious and not unified. Part of that has been each of them examining language as a symbolic system that is culturally embedded. I think that because each of you have looked at racism as well that there has been this sort of interesting thought that has been percolating as you were talking. As authors, you're in a unique position to use language to expose conflicts about how we interpret cultural meaning and show where we are in conflict, like looking at racism. There are ideas we have about people that to us are correct because we know things about ourselves and our culture, but are incorrect to those people. As authors, you've examined the nature of meaning, in a way. I'm wondering how, when you've approached your novels, if you've seen ways in which historical novels are in a unique position to help readers cultivate a multicultural consciousness. That was a gigantic question, for which I apologize. [Laughs] The last part is the part that I was really trying to frame properly.

Duffy: That's good, because you will probably not like the answer to this. I think, at least in the way I write, that I'm consumed with what's going on with the characters. In other words, without any cultural agenda. It's hard to write within the confines of any agenda. In fact, this is what I was objecting to in Lukacs. Anyhow, I don't operate in this way, and to be perfectly honest, I can't imagine that many writers do. But maybe you'll say that I'm wrong. [Laughs]

Olsen: I don't say that anybody's wrong. That was the most awesome question, by the way.

Duffy: That was a good question.

Olsen: I'm not sure that I was really thinking about this when I was writing the Nietzsche book, not sure that I really wasn't, but I am sure that the Nietzsche book was thinking about these things. So here's the short version of Nietzsche's narrative of Western philosophy: everything was just fine before Plato, then everything went to hell in a hand basket. The reason for this was Plato tried to essentialize, tried to categorize and stabilize. The thing Nietzsche found so alluring about the pre-Socratics like Heraclitus was their sense that essentializing simply didn't exist. [Alarm goes off] The constitution of reality, of lived experience for somebody like Heraclitus . . . Excuse me. My alarm's going off. I'll be right with you. Apparently I'm about to make a very important point about Western culture. [Laughter] The constitution of reality, of lived experience for somebody like Heraclitus is change. Transformation is the only thing that is consistent in the world. One of the things that I find really alluring about thinkers like Wittgenstein and Nietzsche is precisely their move to de-essentialize, to trouble assumptions, to challenge, to take nothing for granted. The result is always going to be of multiplicity. I would imagine race, then, to be a tremendously troublesome concept for Nietzsche, because race is a cultural attempt to essentialize in the face of a profuse, continuous changing pluriverse.

Lackey: Rachel, go ahead.

Question 5: You've all briefly mentioned your research process, either today or, in Jay Parini's case, last night at Morris. Then after mentioning your research process, you've all made comments about how "that wasn't what ultimately determined how you pictured the man you were writing about." So I'm wondering how important your research was to you, and what parts of it were the most important. What did really have an impact on your book?

Duffy: Was that to me?

Question 5: Any of you!

Duffy: Well, when I started *The World as I Found It,* it was before the Internet, so you didn't have all this ready digital access to the library. Luckily, I was living outside of Washington D.C., near the Library of Congress. So there my wife and I would go on Friday nights, off to the Library of Congress for a late-night Xeroxing party. Some date. I'd get $50.00 in dimes [Laughter] and we would go in there and start madly checking out books. Then we'd start photocopying them until I ran out of dimes. [Laughter] So I read all kinds of things. I also looked at a lot of period photos. I would just pore over photos, which just give you a tremendous amount of knowledge if you really look at them, for example, to imagine how the heat felt on the walls of Cambridge, what those bricks felt like. I read a number of period diaries and journals to really get a sense of what people were saying, how they really spoke, syntax and the like. Meanwhile, at the county library, I was checking out bags of books. Imagine that, having to stand behind this lunatic checking out seventy-five books. That's basically what I did with *The World as I Found It.*

Parini: I suspect that many of us really enjoy the idea of historical research. Although I make jokes about facts, I enjoy them, and I try in my biographical novels to stick with the agreed upon facts. So if I say that Herman Melville boarded a ship called *The Something* on this date, he will have done that. Melville took a train in the spring of 1857 from Rome to Florence. I went to the trouble of finding out what were the train schedules and how much did it cost for a ticket. I like to line up all the facts. You've got to get your marbles in your bag to write a novel. But then you arrange them; play with them. What did these things mean—facts on their own, the agreed upon facts? The date when Tolstoy left home matters, but what did it mean? And that's what you're trying to get at. You have to imagine those facts. You have to think of what they actually mean. That's what the writing in fiction is about. Fiction simply is about ordering the facts and imagining them: the motives, how things went down, and why they went down. As novelists, we're doing the same thing that historians are doing. They're just working slightly differently, with different genre restrictions and conventions. But I think we all build from research. Research is essential, and a huge amount of research is the baseline from which we begin to work.

Olsen: None of us could have written what we wrote without extensive sorts of research. Boots-on-the-ground research opens up an extraordinary number of doors. It's beyond richness to stand in the cramped room Nietzsche died in, for instance, and look at the bed, how the light fell. Fiction's all about what if. So I don't think any of us would deny how important the facts are, but the kinds of facts for me that are exciting are the ones that stimulate exactly those questions, rather than pin down any answers.

Duffy: One thing that I might add, talking about all of these facts. As I said, I'd check out all of these books, then pore over them, basically gorging myself. Then, almost closing my eyes, I'd write without looking at any of them. Why? Because you can be so seduced by the facts, so intimidated by the facts that you don't really reimagine the world as you must.

Lackey: It looks like our time is up, so let us end there. Thank you Jay, Bruce, and Lance for sharing your thoughts with us. And thank you, Ann, for having us.

PART FOUR

Interviews

24

Julia Alvarez

"Fixed Facts and Creative Freedom in the Biographical Novel" from *Truthful Fictions* (2014)

Lackey: Let me start by telling you about this project. I want to find out why the biographical novel came into being. Before the 1980s, there were only a handful of really good biographical novels by writers such as Arna Bontemps, Zora Neale Hurston, William Styron, and Gore Vidal. But starting in the 1980s this genre of fiction became very popular. Why did this start happening in the 1980s? And can we define the nature of this genre?

Alvarez: I wasn't aware of a trend developing. After all, we've always been writing about each other. Recently, I've been reading Horace's *Odes,* and he gives generic names to many of the people he addresses or writes about. But even though he's not using specific names, it is *very* obvious—as the footnotes often note—that the ode is about a particular, real-life figure. When Horace does use an actual name, it's in a complimentary ode. Perhaps in antiquity there were higher stakes: the temptation to disguise was due to the danger of banishment or death. Now we settle for litigation instead! But we human beings are curious critters, and writers are no exception: we are always trying to understand each other, and especially we want to understand figures who have had some renown, whether it's because they were so heroic or horrid. Perhaps this complicates your question, but I'm not sure that this is some new trend.

Lackey: But why not change the names? Why are we naming a character Virginia Woolf or Ludwig Wittgenstein in recent years? Why are contemporary writers more comfortable doing this? And why do authors feel like they can take this liberty more today than they could in the past?

Alvarez: *In the Time of the Butterflies* began with a blurb on the back of a postcard. A women's press was doing a series of postcards on women heroines around the world, and they asked me if I'd contribute a Dominican heroine. I chose three, the Mirabal sisters, who started the underground that toppled the dictatorship in the Dominican Republic. I realized I had more than a blurb to say about them! This led me to ask more questions and to collect information. At that time, not much had been written about them—a mention here and there in a history book. So, it was a process of discovery: finding and interviewing the people who had known them and who had survived the dictatorship, visiting the places that had been important in their lives. My initial objective was to write a biography about them. But as I went along, I realized that I had become interested in their characters—what made them become the figures they became, what made them stand up to the dictator at a time when so few men or—heavens!—women, dared to do so. Character, then, became my focus, and for me, that is the province of fiction: recreating what evolves in that character, the truth according to that character. At first, I kept all the names. But when the manuscript was finished, I got cold feet and I decided to make it a story about fictional characters in a fictional country. The person who actually talked me out of it was Minou, the daughter of Minerva, one of the murdered sisters. Minou said, "Julia, we've been behind you this whole time." She and Dedé, the surviving sister, had given me access to everything; Minou even sent me the original letters her parents had written to each other during their time in prison. "We want people to know their story," Minou insisted. "We want them to know about the Mirabal sisters; we want their story to get out." And I said, "*Bueno,* Minou, I'm a little nervous because I'm not holding anything back, and some of these people are still alive." Also, the last thing I wanted to do was upset Dedé, who had already been through so much. On the other hand, I wasn't writing to order, the airbrushed story. So the deal was that Minou would read the manuscript since she knows English, and anything problematical she would discuss with Dedé. If Dedé or the family were upset with my novel, I'd go back to the idea of a totally fictional world. Believe me, I sweated those couple of weeks not knowing what was going to be the verdict. Finally, Minou called me: "You have our blessing." Now that the novel has been translated into Spanish, Dedé has been able to read it for herself. When people ask her about the novel, she says: "Some things aren't exactly the way I remember, but Julia caught their spirit. She captured those times."

Lackey: So you started by writing a biography, but it eventually morphed into a novel?

Alvarez: You know, I didn't even know what it was going to be. I just knew I wanted to understand those sisters, to tell *their* story. But I didn't know how. Initially, I had this collage planned where I was going to use clippings from newspapers, telegrams, things that were happening around the world to create this kind of kaleidoscope around their story. I even wrote a number of poems in the voices of each sister to go between the chapters of this projected mongrel novel! It was going to be genre-bending. But as I got further and further inside the characters, the artistry started to fall away—the idea of using news clippings, the idea of using poems. I was captivated by their characters.

Lackey: This is the same strategy that Jay Parini uses in *The Last Station* with multiple narrators. He refers to it as a kaleidoscopic perspective.

Alvarez: Yes! The truth is complex, multi-faceted, and one person's truth might actually negate another's truth. I realized this as I interviewed more and more people: Dedé knew the three women as a sister, their revolutionary friends knew them as fellow revolutionaries, guards who remembered them knew them as prisoners. And so we have what I think of as a Native American moment where the truth sits in the center, but depending on where you sit around the circle, you see this or that aspect of the truth. As a novelist you can find ways to put all or many of those aspects into the narrative. But that's what makes literature trustworthy, rich, opposed to propaganda or what you have in a dictatorship, whether political or canonical, in which there's "one official story," the hegemony of one approved point of view and required allegiance to it. Once you're creating "real" characters you can complicate and present many aspects of the life and experience, because you don't have the point of view of just that one character. You can include other characters who bring out other aspects of your protagonist. And you also don't have just that single layer of character. You can also use setting, imagery, plot, the rhythms of your sentences, any number of elements to present other aspects of your character and his or her reality. By doing so, you are actually respecting the complexity of being a human being, including darker and hidden aspects of your character. I love what Terrence, the Roman playwright, once said, "I am a human being, nothing human is alien to me." That could be the motto of a novelist.

Lackey: And so it is through the creation of multiple characters that you can get to this more complicated perspective, whereas in traditional biographies and histories, a singular perspective dominates.

Alvarez: Not just multiple characters that complicate and enrich the perspective, but other elements of narrative, as I just mentioned. Of course, a good biographer would continue to complicate the material; however, there is the danger of a certain take on the character. You have to present the facts and perhaps draw a conclusion. Whereas, in fiction—and this is what I love about it—you can actually create *competing* truths. You can show multi-faceted dimensions—no truth trumps the other. Joseph Conrad makes this point in the preface to *The Nigger of the "Narcissus"* when he says: "Art itself may be defined as the single-minded attempt to render the highest kind of justice to the visible universe by bringing to light the truth, manifold and one, underlying its every aspect." That's what fiction does. He doesn't say *one* truth. He says the truth, *manifold and one*, underlying its every surface. It's that rich complexity we experience reading a novel, the feel of the texture of reality, a world as fully dimensioned and mysterious as our own. This is something that the facts can't get at by themselves. This representation of the truth, manifold and one, was for Conrad, and is so for me, the "*highest kind of justice*" we can render this universe. But it might not always be factual justice.

Lackey: Is it psychological justice? Is it political justice?

Alvarez: That's why I think it's a wonderful phrase: "The truth manifold and one." It's not just the psychological or the factual, it's "*manifold and one.*" All those layers of truths are woven into the narrative, which is why Conrad says that it is the way to render the highest kind of justice to our experience of being alive. Another quote I love is from Novalis, the German poet and novelist: "Novels arise out of the shortcomings of history." History can't explain the mystery of being a human being. It's not equipped to do that. But novels—that's what they do best. So when I want to understand the past, I go to them, I read them, I write them. Specifically, I write historical novels because I want to understand the past, or perhaps that is not totally accurate. I want to understand the *experience* of being alive in the past, which means being a human being alive in the past. With *In the Time of the Butterflies* I wanted to understand the dictatorship we had fled when I was a child, a dictatorship that had formed my parents, and thus the dictatorship which had indirectly formed me. I wanted to know why and how a whole generation and nation had tolerated this atrocious regime for thirty-plus years. Then, along come the Mirabal sisters. How and why did three women decide they could not bear it anymore? Where did they find this courage? How did they come to do this, given who they were, what no one around them had been able to accomplish? Many questions drove me to this material. People think that writers write because they know things. We write because we want to find things out.

But back then, there was hardly anything written about the Mirabal sisters. The fear and silence of those oppressive years were still with us. To find these things out I had to travel back to the Dominican Republic. I felt an urgency to contact the people who had known the girls, who could tell me the facts of what had happened to them. Originally, I intended to write a biography about the famous sisters, a factual document. But as I went along in my interviews, two things happened which moved me in the direction of a novel. First, I became more and more interested in character—the truth according to character, the province of novels, and second, the facts kept shifting depending who I talked to. I'll tell you about one instance: the legendary slap Minerva was supposed to have given the dictator at a dance when he got fresh with her. This story is told *everywhere*. There is even a popular merengue about the slap. I interviewed a handful of people who had been at the party. Some recalled the slap. Some remembered the pink imprint left on the dictator's right cheek. But Dedé, the surviving sister, told me there had been no slap. There had been words, an insulting remark on the dictator's part, a rebuff on Minerva's part that was "*como si le hubiera dado una galleta,*" as if she had slapped him on the face. The same happened time after time with one or another fact: someone's fact became another's fiction. I began to realize that "these facts" lay at the center, and the truth consisted of all these points around that circle. Everyone agreed there had been an insulting moment at the dance and a rebuff on Minerva's part. I chose to put in the slap because of the kind of truth that detail told. Facts are only a part of what really happened.

It's that kind of truth which is more than fact, but includes the facts, that I want to get to in a novel, the emotional, the *lived* reality of that moment and the drama, and the feeling of the character living it. And the fact is: the minute you start trying to capture an experience in writing, you begin making selections, leaving certain things out, highlighting others, even if you are writing biography. You want to create the *feeling* of that moment. But the feeling of that moment is not just the facts. If that were the case, just give people the transcript and have the deadpan camera record the information.

Even in our own experience of history, or what will be history to the future, and now it's just "our own times," we experience it as a story we tell ourselves of what is happening to us: we are a certain character, with our unique point of view, a certain background, living in a certain context, a particular setting, with a certain set of friends: all these elements are also the elements of storytelling, and they complicate and enrich the "facts" that are happening all around us. So when you are creating a character, and recreating moments in history through that character, you've got to create all that context on paper. For me, a novel is the best vehicle for conveying the feel of that moment, the drama of the moment, the emotion of the moment, the fact of the moment, the setting of the moment, the smells of the moment—for that particular character you are trying to make real. And sometimes, that reality can begin to seem more real than our own reality!

I've noticed that with the Mirabal family itself. I am now a part of the family; they have all read the novel. Sometimes, they start talking, and I think they're *remembering the novel*. There are things I recall in doing the research that Dedé said, "Oh, I don't know about that," or "I wasn't there," or, "I never knew that," but now she *remembers* the full-blown scene, which I made up from the details I got elsewhere. Or which I made up out of whole cloth because no one alive could tell me what exactly happened that resulted in said fact. So even our own memories are storytellers. We remember things that never really happened or that never really happened to us.

Lackey: Let me shift to another question. I've heard many professors criticize contemporary biographical novels. They say that creative writers are merely summarizing and paraphrasing histories and biographies and then calling their works novels. How would you respond to this critique?

Alvarez: It's not easier to write biographical novels; it's not a slacking off of the imagination, second-rate creativity, just a different set of difficulties and challenges. When you're writing within a certain set form you have to make it *breathe*. You have to make the sonnet sound like a real human voice speaking within that form. You've got to make it fluid, and you've got to move within its restraints. The same principle applies to biographical fiction. You have these set points that you can't change. There are certain things that are givens, and certain information which you intuit. You want to present your character accurately, authentically; you want to honor the truths, manifold and one. But you also have to create them on paper, render them real. I could have just reported on Dedé's Mirabal sisters, and that would have been just one perspective. But I found my challenge was to go around that circle and take in as many points of view as I could. I certainly had fixed facts: *this* happened and then *this* happened. But how did the character evolve from here to there? How did she who was here and reacted in this way become capable of doing this contradictory thing later? So that's where the truth according to character comes in. Maybe in a totally invented fiction, and I doubt there is such a thing, you yourself are fixing those points. But once those fixed points are there, you, too, have to work within the constraints you've set up. I suppose you can always go back and move this point over here, and then you'll have to recreate the whole web, because you tweak one thread and the whole weave changes. So you're just working with different kinds of difficulties and challenges. You still have to create that world and that life and that interior character on paper—that's still the same: bringing to life your characters (historical or not). And that's never easy. No shortcuts. Good writing is hard work.

Lackey: This reminds me of Virginia Woolf, who argues that the novelist's primary responsibility is to character. The author must use the imagination to create a figure that is brimming with life and authenticity. It is this obligation that explains why, according to Woolf, it is impossible to mix fact and fiction, to mix biography and the novel. In an effort to create a character's rich interior life the novelist cannot be restricted by the mundane facts of an individual's biography, which requires a person to focus primarily on representing a historical figure accurately. How do you respond to Woolf's critique? Can you offer some reason why she couldn't see her way toward the biographical novel? Or conversely, can you explain what has happened that has enabled so many writers like yourself to do what Woolf thought impossible?

Alvarez: One could argue that all of Woolf's novels are loose biographies of the world and the people who surrounded her. True, Woolf doesn't write about a particular known historical person, but she's writing about places and people and situations not all that different from her own. As a novelist, you write about a character because he or she intrigues you. You want to understand that character's interior life, what forms and informs that character. What was it like to be that character? If you have a historical figure, you already know some of the circumstances that shaped that character. If you have a totally fictional character, you invent those circumstances—it's just a different set of forces shaping your character, but character is what you are interested in. And in creating your character, real or fictional, you're always writing out of the material of your own life, your own biography. If you're writing about Napoleon, say, and you have him eat an orange, you never saw him do that, right? But maybe you had a father who was dictatorial and aggressive, and you remember how he used to devour oranges. So when you write about Napoleon eating that orange, you access that memory of your father to inform your description of Napoleon. The same goes for a totally fictional character, who is pushy, bossy. When you describe that character, you access what you remember from your own experience. And I also bet that your interest in Napoleon or a bossy protagonist has everything to do with your experience with that kind of character in your own life. That's what makes a particular character, whether historical or not, entrancing to you—your own biography. So I think.

Lackey: But here's the dilemma as Woolf represents it. In "Mr. Bennett and Mrs. Brown," she discusses the task of the novelist, which is to picture a Mrs. Brown. Arnold Bennett fails because he focuses on superficial externals rather than rich interiors. But for Woolf, if a novelist wants to make a character live, he or she must access the character's interiority; that's where the spirit lies. But to make a rich and living character, the novelist must abandon the impulse to represent Mrs. Brown accurately. The actual Mrs. Brown becomes insignificant, irrelevant. You make an important point by saying that novelists work within constraints. There is a form, like a sonnet, but within these constraints and restrictions, the artist can breathe life into the work. Woolf seems to be saying that the restriction of representing the character accurately would deaden the life of a character. But I think you would say that it is possible to have restrictions, and yet to breathe life into the character just the same.

Alvarez: Absolutely! But I think that it might be a misunderstanding of character here. It assumes that a character who is famous, a public persona, is a fixed entity who doesn't have all the variety, contradictions, and tremulous life and possibilities that the rest of us have. I think we're all telling ourselves a story in our head about who we are, a story that keeps changing as we get this bit of information. We also are telling ourselves a story about every person we encounter, from what we know about that person, what we've been told, and so on. And since we can't have every bit of information about that person, we are always connecting the dots, always creating them in our heads in order to understand them. This is what Woolf is so wonderful at doing with her characters. And that can be done with a historical character as well. There are the certain constraints with the historical figure, facts that shape the narrative, or his/her character, but once you've set up a fictional world, there are constraints on your protagonist as well; you have to work within that world you've created. The key thing for the novelist is to breathe life into that character.

Lackey: But doesn't that act of breathing life into a character take the novelist away from the actual reality of the historical figure?

Alvarez: Oh, I don't think so. That historical figure was not a statue, but as various, complex as we are. I don't think of it as moving away from my historical character, but moving deeper and deeper into that character, peeling the onion as it were. After a certain point, you feel you've touched bottom. That's why, after I had all factual information I needed to be able to connect the dots, I didn't want to keep talking to Dedé about her sisters. I didn't want to go checking back and forth because the characters had assumed their own momentum and their own voices, and their own interior life. They had begun to be real on paper.

Lackey: And yet, you were still committed to representing the actual figures as accurately as you could?

Alvarez: Yes, but this act of representing accurately should not be seen as a box. To clarify, let me tell you about Mate. I wanted each character to have a very particular voice. Mate was the youngest, and therefore, the most girlish of the sisters. But how do I convey that? What *form* would best embody her voice, her youth? And I thought, oh, a diary form because there is something very young and fresh and evolving about that form. I also needed a voice in this novel that would provide readers with the little details, the news of the day, what she had for breakfast, what so-and-so was wearing, the kind of information that a Minerva would probably ignore because she is so caught up in ideology. So I gave Mate this voice, and later, when Dedé read the novel, she said to Minou: "How did Julia know that María Teresa liked to keep diaries?" That gave me chills! Here, we're entering very different territory from the traditional, academic, analytical framework in explaining a writer's process! For me, it was an experience similar to *santería* in our Caribbean culture. In this animist religion, the *santera*, or priestess, is mounted by the spirit of a dead person, who uses the body of the *santera* to communicate to the living. The *santera*'s voice, walk, appearance are transformed by this possession. I was so involved in each Mirabal sister as I wrote her chapters that I could feel viscerally when I was straying away from that character or trying to take her in a certain direction she wouldn't go. I was taken over by the life of that character. It's this kind of obsession or possession which I can't explain, but I felt as I was writing the novel. This might be what Dedé meant when she said that I *captured* the spirit of her sisters. That was the best compliment I received. Dedé didn't say I had recorded every fact as she remembered it, but that I had *captured* her sisters' personalities.

Lackey: At this point, let me shift to another question. Many biographical novels include a preface, an afterword, or a postscript with a disclaimer saying that the work is fiction, which is not to be confused with biography or history. In your postscript, you say that, on one hand, you lack the talent of a biographer, which is why you cannot give us the Mirabal sisters of *fact*. But, on the other hand, you claim that the Mirabal sisters of your creation are true to the spirit of the real Mirabals. The distinction, as I understand, is between fact and spirit. Can you define what you mean by spirit? And can you discuss some of your research techniques for accessing and writing strategies for representing that spirit?

Alvarez: I did traditional research about the history of the era: I read histories of other dictatorships in Latin America. I conducted oral interviews. I visited all of the locations in the book, including the prison, the torture center, the church where they had gotten married, the houses they lived in. I felt I needed visceral contact with everything in order to get into the voices and inner lives of the characters. But I read things that were not immediately, directly relevant: diaries of young girls in war-torn places; memoirs by resistance fighters in Latin America and in France during the Second World War. It was also odd what made each sister come alive for me. When I first started writing in Patria's voice, I thought she was going to be the hardest for me because she's so religious. Conversely, I thought Minerva, because I love her revolutionary spirit, would be the easiest. But she was the most difficult to access. To get into Patria's character, I listened to a lot of organ music when I was writing her chapters. I wanted that sense of that spiritual soaring in her voice. I tuned into it by hearing that music and reading certain books, like Ron Hansen's *Mariette in Ecstasy*, which was very helpful. So, the research is not always direct information-gathering. But everything helped, researching *santería*, researching women who had been part of any number of resistance movements, including the resistance movement of French women during World War Two. Luckily, a whole book of their interviews and memoirs had just been published as I was working on my novel. It was very helpful to hear from these women, because they gave me insights about my own characters. These French women's admissions reminded me that even heroic women are complex, driven by fears, hopes, petty at times, brave sometimes by accident. I didn't want to create ideological pawns or stock historical figures, the prose equivalent of marble statues.

Lackey: Can I ask you a question about the Minerva character? Why was she so difficult to access?

Alvarez: Because she was driven, so idealistic. I knew there was more. But I couldn't seem to find my way inside her. That is, until I read Benazir Bhutto's memoir, *Daughter of the East*. Bhutto was Prime Minister of Pakistan, a heroic figure, a charismatic leader, a seemingly strong woman publicly, but in her memoir she confesses to panic attacks when she went out in public; at certain points in her life she's paralyzed by her fears, her fatigue, her flagging beliefs. Reading that memoir sprung open the character of Minerva for me. It explained some of the comments I would hear about Minerva, towards the end, as the pressures on her mounted. She wasn't just this flat, one-dimensional character, a total believer.

Lackey: Was she a broken character by the end? Or, could she recover?

Alvarez: I don't know. I think we die many deaths within our lives, and resurrection isn't always guaranteed. We do have the living dead, examples all around us. No done deals, at least not while we are alive. I think keeping parts of a character mysterious is part of the respect you render any character that you create. The complexity of a possibility; they're not a finished self, a set quantity…

Lackey: No formula.

Alvarez: Yes, right. That's such disrespect to your characters, when the plot is driving the story, and we just feel like the poor characters are yoked, carrying that plot forward. And I suppose that's what Virginia Woolf meant, that she didn't want to harness her characters to pulling the plot of what had really happened forward. She feared that she wouldn't have the license to create the full-dimensionality and complexity of the characters if that sort of burden of history were upon them. But I don't think that's even the way historical characters experience the history they're living as they're living it.

Lackey: In your postscript, you suggest that the imagination has the power to redeem the lives of the Mirabal sisters and the epoch in the life of the Dominican Republican. Can you clarify what that means?

Alvarez: You make meaning. It won't solve anything. The story won't save us, but the *telling* of the story is redemptive; we understand; we can bear the suffering. When everything has fallen apart, in that broken world, we learn how to be human again through the telling of the story. We are saying, this, too, is human; this, too, we can bear and understand. "These fragments I have shored against my ruins." I know the word *redemptive* has religious overtones, and I'm not trying to be hokey or self-aggrandizing, but telling the story can help us bear the unbearable.

I can think of two stories that explain this idea of redemption in the way stories can explain things, and explanations can't. One comes from Anna Akhmatova, that little piece she wrote, *Instead of a Preface*, about standing outside the prison where her son is incarcerated during the terrible years of terror. This weary woman who is also waiting in line recognizes Akhmatova and sidles up to her, and asks if she, Akhmatova, can describe this. And Akhmatova replies that, yes, she can. The last sentence, describing the weary woman's reaction, is something like, a smile passed over what once had been her face. For that moment, humanity is restored in that face and between the two women.

The other story is one that John Bartlow Martin, who was the US ambassador to the Dominican Republic after the dictatorship, tells about in his book, *Overtaken by Events*. He travels the country, asking people what kind of help they need to build a democracy. Martin meets with these teenagers in this one little outlying city, and when he asks them, they reply, "Build us a library so we can have some books." And he says, "Well, what books?" After a long pause, a thin, quiet one in a white shirt with large, brown eyes says, "Books about Trujillo." Martin is surprised. "Why?" And the young man replies, "So we can understand what happened to us." And that's what I think stories can help us do: make meaning so we can understand what happens to us.

My sister was a therapist for many years in Boston working with political refugees who had fled their countries, people who had suffered devastating losses, who had seen their families killed, whole villages destroyed. She said that many of them were suffering from post-traumatic stress disorder. They didn't even have the language to articulate their experiences. She told me that she knew they were coming back to the human fold when they could tell her the story of what had happened to them. The horror, the horror. I survived it. I'm here to tell you the tale. There's something about the telling of the story that makes it—even if it's inhuman—possible for us to hold its heartbreaking reality inside us and among us. We share in our common suffering humanity—that to me seems redemptive.

Lackey: Shifting focus, I would like to briefly discuss Dedé. There is a wonderful scene picturing Dedé undergoing a transformation. She has just read that Virgilio Morales is a communist, an enemy of the state. But then she reflects on the disparity of the representation of Lío and her experience of him, and this leads her to become more critically aware and, not coincidentally, immediately after this experience she begins to realize she has overlooked so much in all that she has read in the past. Do you think the biographical novel demands a more complicated form of literacy than the traditional novel, as it forces readers to engage and negotiate fiction *and* history? And can you discuss how the biographical novelist educates readers into more complex forms of literacy?

Alvarez: I have never thought of this before, a more complex form of literacy … I think that any good novel demands a new kind of literacy from us. A weak novel, historical or not, just confirms all our habits of thinking, speaking, seeing the world through the lens of clichés. But a great novelist creates a whole new kind of literacy, in part from the use of language. Think of William Faulkner, James Joyce, Gertrude Stein, Virginia Woolf. More recently novels like *The Buddha in the Attic* by Julie Otsuka or *Room* by Emma Donoghue. They teach us new ways of reading, of seeing the world. They push the parameters of being a human being by mapping areas of the human psyche that had been there before, but only as potential, as possibility. That Emily Dickinson line suddenly lit up in my head, "I dwell in possibility"! So I think the best writers widen our possibilities as human beings.

Lackey: Let me give you an example. I am teaching *In the Time of the Butterflies* right now, and in your novel, you address foreign policy, how the United States initially supported the resistance in the Dominican Republic. But then the United States withdrew its support. Part of the problem was Communism. If it is a choice between a dictator and Communism, the United States will let the dictator rule. For a teacher this is wonderful, because it gets my students into a conversation not just about what is going on in the novel, but also in the world around them. And in your work, especially in your postscript, you discuss the link between literacy and freedom, between the capacity to read and the ability to be free. It is through biographical novels that I have most success getting students to understand that link. Put simply, your novel demands not just that we read the text, but that we learn how to read our lives, how to read the political.

Alvarez: But don't you think that all good books force us to see and do that? Maybe the application to the political is a little fuzzier, but we learn to be critical thinkers, and that's why I think reading is so key. We develop the muscles of the imagination, which are also the muscles at work when we are compassionate, sensitive, and attentive. I think the best literature exercises our souls, perhaps even helps create them.

Lackey: I agree, but I think biographical novels resonate with students more powerfully than many other novels. Faulkner's *Light in August*, Woolf's *Mrs. Dalloway*, and Ralph Ellison's *Invisible Man* certainly teach us to read and think more critically and intelligently. But because your novel is so historically specific, my students can connect with the material in a way that many times they cannot in other excellent but less historically specific novels. I have been thinking about this because I have been teaching so many of these biographical novels and I have been stunned by the power they have over students.

Alvarez: What is it making them do what you say?

Lackey: It's getting them to think in more specific and complicated ways about domestic politics and foreign policy. This is something undergraduate students have a very difficult time doing. You have made characters and issues come alive for them, and in the process, the students want to understand these characters, these people, the Dominican Republic, and so much more. They want to understand how American foreign policy affects their lives and the lives of others, which is leading them to ask really smart and interesting questions.

Alvarez: This reminds me of the Middlebury mission to encourage students to go abroad for a year. One of the places they can come to, after graduation, is *Alta Gracia,* a sustainable coffee farm and literacy center in the mountains of the Dominican Republic that my husband, Bill Eichner, and I established in 1997. When students spend a year living there as volunteers, they begin to understand "underdevelopment," which up to then has been a textbook term. Poverty is no longer an abstraction. It wears the "human face divine," that wonderful Blake phrase. They are profoundly changed.

And I think that's the thing that happens when you read. When you enter a character, you see how issues affect a specific human being, one life, or one group of lives. I remember when I was writing *In the Time of the Butterflies*, being intrigued by the question: how do people come to courage? Reading those memoirs by women in the resistance in France, I was struck by how many came to their activism because of a specific person. A knock on their door, their neighbor from whom they had once borrowed butter, who had helped them when their baby had had colic, saying, "Can you help me? Can you hide my little daughter?" And although they hadn't wanted to get involved, it was no longer an issue, it was a human being whose life they understood and shared. Historical novels return us to the people the history happened to. We experience what it's like to be that person living at that moment. And that's the way we experience our own time—as I mentioned earlier—from our specific character. And that same complexity with which we are experiencing our moment in time, we have to accord to those characters in the past as well.

Your remarks made me think of something else. Years ago, I was working with the Poetry-in-the-Schools program. I called myself a migrant poet, because I would go wherever I was sent as a visiting writer, usually an elementary or high school. These were short six-week residencies. At one of these gigs, I met a British playwright who was having the students write up scenes about moments in history they were studying. Then the students acted them out. He had all these facts and figures that proved that, if students depicted a specific historical event, such as Lincoln deciding to go to war or Benedict Arnold siding with the Brits, they would retain the information much more readily. So when the final exam came, these students would all be able to write vividly about these events. But if these facts remained abstract and dry in a textbook, they just weren't interested. Somehow those moments that they had recreated were the ones they were apt to remember, think about, and want to learn more about.

Lackey: To conclude, do you have any final thoughts about the biographical novel?

Alvarez: I recently read a review of a new biography of Karl Marx, and the reviewer said that the author had provided a template of how we might approach great figures: "demystifying the words and deeds of those too often lazily deemed sacred." I think biographical fiction has been doing that demystification all along. It's part of a cultural shift, a new demand for transparency about our public figures. We see this shift when we compare figures like President Roosevelt and current politicians. In Roosevelt's time, the subject of his polio was *verboten*. Nowadays, if you are a public figure, your health records, your tax returns, your private life—it's our public right to know about. But no matter the talk shows and reality shows, the investigative reporting, there isn't anything that so powerfully recreates the interior life of a character, the complex stream of thoughts and feelings in response to whatever is happening as a good biographical novel. There is a natural kinship between biographies and novels, both are interested in character. Maybe, and I'm not sure about this, the biographer wants to get at the truth of a character, and the novelist at the truth according to character—it's a slight distinction but critical. But the minute we try to set up definite markers about where one genre ends and another begins, we're in trouble. It's a shifting landscape, just like it is inside the minds of every human being, as we live our lives, creating our internal world as we go along, part fact, part fiction, and all kinds of hybrids. It reminds me of that question people always ask me: do you dream in English or Spanish? They think they're going to catch me drawing a fixed line. But if I'm having a dream and the chair of my department comes to my door, she speaks to me in English. If my Papi comes in the same dream, he speaks to me in Spanish. There aren't these fixed markers. I understand the urge: we want to quantify, keep literature contained in neat little genre boxes, a kind of bad high-school English teacher's reductive need to nail down the winged life. We live in possibility, a messy landscape. We are trying to do the impossible, actually, to recreate life itself in language, and we need to range freely and creatively within the fixed contours of a particular character in order to make her or him come alive again in the imagination of our readers.

25

Russell Banks

"The Truth Contract in the Biographical Novel" from *Truthful Fictions* (2014)

Lackey: Let me start by telling you about this project. There have been many biographical novels written over the last thirty years, and my goal as a scholar is to figure out why this has happened, but it is also to define the nature of the contemporary American biographical novel. For this novel to be possible some major developments in literature had to occur. To indicate that this is the case let me briefly discuss Virginia Woolf's essay "The Art of Biography." For Woolf the novelist is free to create, while the biographer is tied to facts. Lytton Strachey and the new biographers of the early twentieth century revolutionized the biography by making liberal use of the creative imagination and fictional techniques in depicting a person's life, thus giving the artist/biographer the freedom to invent something new: a book that was not only a biography, but also a work of art. But ultimately, Woolf concluded, this combination proved unworkable because fact and fiction refused to mix. Can you explain why it is now possible to blend fact and fiction in the biographical novel as you do in *Cloudsplitter*?

Banks: It's difficult for me to explain because in a way the question, as you phrase it, presupposes that I was aware of there being an opening available for that kind of fiction. Or even that I was writing a kind of fiction when I was writing the novel. In fact, I have to say I wasn't aware that I was until you wrote me and sent me your questions. And I could then see, yeah, I guess you're right. Whether and how an occasion for the writing of biographical fiction, or a legitimization of it, preceded the writing I can't say. Not calling it by any name, I was aware of and had spoken about the biographical novel in public with other people, like Joyce Carol Oates with regard to her book *Blonde*, which is about Marilyn Monroe, and E. L. Doctorow and his work. It seemed to me a given that I could write from inside a historical figure. I could write a "life" of that figure, using that figure's life, but I would be writing a dramatic narrative, a work with a dramatic shape and intent, rather than a biography of that character.

Lackey: You get inside the character. Do you think this is one of the defining features of the biographical novel? That writers are now trying to get to the interiority of a character more?

Banks: Yes, but I don't think that is unique to our time. I think it's unique to fiction. What fiction does from Cervantes forward, really through the novel more than any other form of fiction, is validate and dignify the subjective experience of an individual human being. And the best way, of course, to do that is to get inside that person's head and see the world through that person's eyes. Until I started working with film about ten or fifteen years ago I thought that in the film world the director was the closest person to the novelist. But after I was working closely enough with everyone involved, I could see the differences between the director and the cinematographer, the screenwriter, the actor, and so forth, and I began to realize that the actor more than the director was like the novelist. Because the actor inhabits the characters, feels his or her way inside the character, and then looks out through the character's eyes. And that is essentially what a novelist has to do.

Lackey: Were you ever tempted to change the character names in order to give yourself some more freedom?

Banks: Not in the case of *Cloudsplitter*. I have done it in other works. I had a novel published recently that is clearly set in Miami, but I changed the name of the city so that it wouldn't be a novel about Miami. This is an interesting contrast perhaps. I realized, if I call it Miami, it is going to be strictly a story about the peculiarities of Miami. It won't be universal. It won't be a story about every city in the world, at least the Western world. And so I invented a new name for the city, even though I was at times describing Miami, Florida, and it gave me much more freedom to invent my story and also to universalize the story. The opposite is the case with the historical figure.

Lackey: But in doing that you are now tied to a lot of facts, right?

Banks: Yes I am, but there's so much also that isn't known and that's one reason why I've told it from the point of view of Owen Brown. The facts are so well-known I'd just be retelling them if I told it from the point of view of John Brown. But he is an emblematic and iconic figure, and it is much more difficult to penetrate and identify with a character like that than to tell a story from the point of view of his little-known son Owen. There are other reasons as well. But I'm not really answering your question. Can you rephrase it for me?

Lackey: I'm questioning here the kind of liberties you can take as a novelist when you decide to name a character after the original figure. There is a question of ethics here. On the one hand, you want to give your readers a story, a living character. But on the other hand, do you have the freedom just to alter history in any way you want?

Banks: My feeling is that I'm using history in order to tell a story. I could as easily use a journalistic account from yesterday's newspaper or another work of art. My real purpose is to generate and tell a story. It is not to correct history or write an addendum to the historical or biographical record. It is simply to appropriate the material that history has dropped at my door, somewhat the way Shakespeare certainly felt entitled to do or the way Homer felt entitled to do. This is something storytellers have done since the beginning of narrative. If history drops it on your doorstep, it's there to be used. I don't feel that I have any higher ambition in terms of using history than that provided by the requirements of story. My respect and use of historical facts are really based on my need for plausibility. I can't violate what is commonly known or I will lose the reader's suspension of disbelief, which depends on plausibility. It's the same with geography. If I set a story in New York City and I have Broadway running from the Upper East Side down diagonally across to the Lower West Side, I'm going to lose the suspension of disbelief that my reader has acquired from the plausibility of my description of New York. The same thing applies to historical figures. If I have John Brown not being executed in 1859, but living on to see Lincoln become president, I would lose my readers. My novel would lack the kind of suspension of disbelief that my kind of realism depends upon. That is the only concern I really have. I don't have any particular concern for the historical record as such. There are many things in that novel that are not part of the historical record but that a scholar or biographer of Brown would know didn't occur. He or she would know, for instance, that John Brown never heard Ralph Waldo Emerson deliver his talk on heroism at the Charles Street meeting house in Boston.

Lackey: Why did you include that scene?

Banks: I included the scene for dramatic reasons and for reasons of character in the story. I wanted to divide Owen Brown from his father John Brown over a figure like Emerson, who was an abolitionist, but a pacifistic man and nowhere near as radical as John Brown. And I knew, although I didn't have any text to confirm this, that Brown would probably take a critical view of Emerson. Even though Emerson's essay on heroism is calling for a man like Brown to rise up out of the population and deal with the issue of slavery. And Owen Brown would find him much more sympathetic. So it was in order to split the two characters in the story over the same figure, Emerson.

Lackey: There was a famous forum in 1968, run by the historian C. Van Woodward, with Robert Penn Warren, Ralph Ellison and William Styron. They talked about the ethics and wisdom of the biographical novel. Ellison was the most passionate. He said that the biographical novel is a mistake, and he had two separate reasons for this view. First, he said that there is no way you can get to the complexity of the original person. So if you make the decision to name the figure after the original, you're going to necessarily misrepresent the complexity of that person. Second, the moment you name the figure after the original, you are stepping into the historians' realm, and they are going to attack you. They are going to say that the mole wasn't on that side of the face or they're going to come back with some little detail and say you made this mistake. How would you respond to Ellison's critique?

Banks: I think he is flatly wrong about the complexity of character. That is a critique that doesn't make any sense to me. I don't even know what it means to say that a historical character has greater complexity than a fictional version of that historical character. Even a historical or biographical version is still, at best, an imagined portrait of the character. So who is to say that's more complex than a fictional character? He might as well say that fiction can't capture the complexity of a human being. It doesn't make any sense, that critique. His second critique, that you're making yourself vulnerable to criticism from so-called experts, also seems wrong. There is a case in *Cloudsplitter* where I ran up against a local historian—they're the worst. They really know their little square of the universe. I have an episode in *Cloudsplitter* where the Brown family for the first time in 1848 goes up to reside in North Elba, New York in the Adirondack Mountains and they are on an old road going alongside a long, narrow chain of lakes. They come to an opening between the mountains and there it is—the Plains of Abraham—and that is where they are going to live. After the novel was published, an elderly woman named Mary Mackenzie, the town historian for North Elba, wrote letters to newspapers, to *Adirondack Life* magazine, and to me personally, and then telephoned me, outraged that I had placed the Brown family on a road alongside those lakes in 1848 because that road wasn't built until the 1870s. I happened to know that fact because I had an old map and indeed there wasn't any road there then. There is now, it's been there since the 1870s. But I wanted the image in the novel relatively early of this family seen from above going along the edge of these narrow lakes that are like fiords, with mountains coming down directly into the water, so that

I could describe them as going along the blade of a scimitar and deploy the image as a prefiguration of the bloody swords that they would use much later—200 or 300 pages later—in Kansas in the Pottawatomie Massacre, which was an incredibly graphic part of the novel. I wanted to anticipate that with the image of the lake. So I violated history.

Lackey: So could we say that you subordinate historical truth at certain moments in favor of a certain kind of symbolic truth?

Banks: Yes, exactly. And in favor finally of a dramatic truth. And a story. That is really my primary concern, and I'm not concerned with history except insofar as I need it for plausibility. And, therefore, the small parts that only a local historian in upstate New York would know—it doesn't bother me that that fact was inaccurate. I did it deliberately because I wanted the image. The image was more important to me than the roadmap of North Elba in 1848.

Lackey: This leads to one of the more difficult questions I want to pose to you about history. In most of these biographical novels, there is a preface, an author's note, an afterword, or an epilogue, and they all have a disclaimer declaring that their work is fiction and it is not to be confused with biography or history. Of all these recent biographical novels you make the strongest claim by saying "*Cloudsplitter* should be read solely as a work of fiction, not as a version or interpretation of history." But this prefatory claim is difficult to square with your Owen's definition that he is giving us the secret history of John Brown. For those of us who have read your novel closely and carefully, we tend to agree more with your Owen Brown than with you. How do you respond to this?

Banks: What do you mean you agree more with Owen Brown? You think you are getting the secret history of John Brown? You are getting Owen Brown's, a fictional character's, version of the secret history of John Brown. There is still another, I'm sure, and there are still probably a hundred more secret histories of John Brown yet to be told. The historical Owen Brown had no awareness of Owen Brown the fictional character. Don't forget, too, that Owen Brown in the novel is telling this story from around 1903, when in fact he died in 1889. So right there, by authorial fiat, I violated history. Anyone who knows the story of John Brown well enough knows his son Owen, born in 1825, died in 1889. I let him live on into the twentieth century so that his story, John Brown's story, would lose some of the antique quality it might have had otherwise and would point toward the twentieth century, to our own time. Even to the twenty-first century, where it's now being read as a portrait of the terrorist that can be applied to our understanding of our present time. Owen Brown's claim to be telling the secret history of John Brown—his own and his father's secret history—is a fictional character's claim. It's not Russell Banks's claim.

Lackey: This gets to one of the central questions at the heart of this project. What is it that the novel can give us that traditional histories cannot? Someone like E. M. Forster says that the novelist can chart the subconscious short-circuiting into human action. This is something that the novelist is uniquely qualified to do. Milan Kundera has argued that the novelist can represent a phenomenological interior. Biographical novelists today have been charting a new way of understanding history. So when I read your disclaimer, it is a bit disheartening because these novels are hugely important in that they can unlock history in different ways than traditional history. But we have to be really systematic and precise by saying: this is what the novelist does, this is why it's different, this is what it is uniquely capable of achieving.

Banks: It might not be that easy to apply to history in the way that you are suggesting. I oftentimes argue with people who've said that in *Cloudsplitter* they've found some historical error, as it were. I don't regard it as error, just as a different use for history than a historian or a biographer might have. I'm not able, for instance, to understand the War of the Roses through Shakespeare or the Trojan War through Homer, or the Civil War through *Gone with the Wind*. I think you make a big mistake if you use literature in order to understand history. I would apply it instead to our understanding of humanity and what it means to be human. The novelist can humanize a historical figure by inhabiting the character in a way that a biographer and a historian can't. But that's in the interest of humanity, extending our understanding of human beings, not history.

Lackey: That might not give us a literal historical truth, but it does give us a certain kind of phenomenological truth, doesn't it?

Banks: Yes, so long as we the readers of the novel can test its claims for phenomenological truth against our own secret phenomenological truth and not find it inauthentic or wanting. In fiction, it's always the reader who validates the truth of the text, or lack thereof.

Lackey: Postmodernism has radically impacted the novel in recent years. We used to think that there was a clear distinction between fact and fiction. But postmodernists have argued that the moment we step into the realm of language, we are in the world of fiction. Traditional histories and biographies were once considered non-fiction, but postmodernism has exposed both as fiction. Thus, the dichotomy between biography and the biographical novel has collapsed in recent years.

Banks: And I think that's fine. I follow that collapse with a certain degree of enthusiasm actually. Maybe now we can claim that historians and biographers have no special claim to that material, that they have no reason to say this is their material and not mine too. History and biography are interpretive, and they're subjective. So there is no absolute historical or biographical truth that resides in the historical or the biographical record, the data. That material is up for grabs.

Lackey: And now that it is up for grabs, this gives fictional writers a new kind of license. Is this one of the reasons why the biographical novel has become so popular with prominent writers?

Banks: It could be. There is an increasing speed to the use of that material, and I think that it is simply because it gets justified and validated by all the writers that you're working with here. There's enough of them out there now so that some twenty-five year old kid coming along and writing his novel wouldn't feel in the slightest hesitant about going ahead and doing it. I could point to a dozen biographical novels today, but I couldn't when I was writing in the sixties and seventies. I couldn't point to a whole lot of books other than Styron's and one or two others.

Lackey: So one of your arguments is that because there are so many people doing this, it becomes more possible. But actually I would argue that there is a key turning point, which involves your novel. In 1999, your *Cloudsplitter* and Michael Cunningham's *The Hours* were both up for the Pulitzer. It seems that the literary establishment said in this year: these biographical novels are doing something unbelievably original, so original, in fact, that they are worthy of this country's most prestigious award.

Banks: That's what I was saying. There are enough models that have been validated by the critical and academic establishment that younger writers don't feel any hesitancy about extending and continuing that tradition, deepening it, which is great.

Lackey: Let me shift to a question about Jay Parini. Parini recommends that contemporary biographical novelists stop making the prefatory disclaimer that their characters are fictional. Rather, he recommends that authors say the following, "Everything in the following pages is authentic, which is to say that it is as true as I could make it—take it or leave it." Can you define your approach to the biographical novel in relation or opposition to Parini's approach?

Banks: I know Jay, he is a good friend, and I think he is being a little facetious there. But I also understand his desire to get rid of these little prefaces. I wish I hadn't put mine in. But given the time when the book was published, it felt necessary.

Lackey: Would you change it today if you had?

Banks: Yes, I think I would. I don't think I would leave it in. That is an interesting question and my answer is: unless my publisher insisted, I'd leave it out.

Lackey: But why would you leave it out today?

Banks: For the very reasons that you're pointing toward. Because there are so many other books using historical and biographical figures as characters, literary characters. If you call it a novel on the cover of the title page, that should be enough. What that implies is a contract with the reader. If it's called a memoir, it has a different contract. But my contract with the reader is that *Cloudsplitter* is a novel because it says so on the cover and title page: some of it is drawn from history, some of it is drawn from biography, and a lot of it is made up. Some of it is drawn from my own personal life. But for my purposes, the way it should be read is as a novel, and the books against which it should be measured are novels. The same way you read *Moby Dick* you read this—if I can be that grand. We don't apply the terms and standards of history or biography to it. If it were memoir, the author would have to say on the title page, "A Memoir of Owen Brown," or "The Autobiography of Owen Brown." That would bind him to a different contract with the reader. And if it was indeed the memoir or the autobiography of Owen Brown, and he invented large bits and pieces of it, like many recent and somewhat notorious memoirists, he'd be guilty of violating that contract.

Lackey: Let's turn to Owen for a moment. Assuming that your Owen is to be fictionally believed, that he is giving us the secret history of John Brown, can you explain the kind of history he can give us that traditional historians cannot? In other words, can you specify the kind of truth that the biographical novelist can access and/or represent?

Banks: What a novelist is doing in inventing a character out of historical and autobiographical material is creating an individual who is different from the character invented by the biographer or historian. What's the difference between the character I invent, John Brown, and the character Robert Penn Warren invented in his biography of Brown, for instance? Warren basically attacks Brown for being a horse thief and puts him down in every possible way. Now you could compare Warren's biography to W. E. B. Du Bois' biography, in which Brown is a hero of the highest order. In my version of John Brown, he is an incredibly complex human being: both good and bad. He is not cynical, but he is manipulative, controlling. He is slightly mad and is probably bipolar, but he is a character that is invented for the purposes of telling a story—entirely a larger and different purpose than a biographer would have. And you could also say Warren and Du Bois each had an agenda that was political with regard to the issue of race. I did not. The novelist does not have an agenda. The novelist does not have a message, doesn't have a historical truth to bring to bear on the book or on the character. The novelist is trying to present, in a sense I suppose, a higher truth, a truth of what it is to be a human being, period. A more universal truth, let's say. He uses the data of this character's life and embellishes it sufficiently and reorganizes it and restructures it in such a way that it can both be data and a portrait of human beings who are very different from John Brown. It could be a portrait of the reader. I'll give you an instance of how this works. I don't think a biographer of John Brown would receive a letter like one I got after *Cloudsplitter* was published. It was written by a woman who had served twenty-four years of a life sentence in Bedford Hills prison for women for crimes she committed as a member of the Weather Underground in the sixties and seventies. She was involved in a robbery in which two guards were killed back in the early seventies. She read the novel and wrote me the best fan letter I've ever gotten—a three-page, typed, single-spaced response to the novel—because she believed that Owen Brown's life and story were her life and her story. She is a late twentieth century person, Jewish, from New York, her father is a powerful and liberal lawyer. She was a radical person, but this was her story. I don't think she would have felt that if she had read a biography of John Brown instead.

Lackey: So you are saying that it is not necessarily that the biographical novelist accesses and represents a different truth, but that it engages the reader in a different way.

Banks: Absolutely. Yes, so that the reader believes the story is about the reader. I mean, we do that with every novel we read—call me Ishmael—we all are Ishmael when we pick that up and start reading it. We're not Ahab. We are the character who is telling us the story and whose story it truly is. And Owen Brown in many ways is like Ishmael. I was quite conscious of that in fact in the structure of the story and in the telling of the story. It is a different contract—I guess I wanted to go back to that term too—between the writer and the reader. My contract with the reader is that in some important way I want the novel to be about you, the reader, when you read it. Just as, when I'm writing it, it's about me; I'm living in that fictional world. I'm inhabiting these characters, looking out their eyes. There is an interesting interview I read some years ago between Michael Ondaatje and the actor Willem Dafoe, and it goes back to what I was saying before. After the filming of *The English Patient*, Dafoe was interviewing Michael for a magazine and Dafoe said: "What does it feel like to see your characters looking differently than the way you imagined them. Looking for instance like me, the actor." Michael said: "Actually, in the end, I don't know what my characters look like because I'm inside them looking out. I don't know what they look like any more than I know what I really look like. I know how tall I am and so forth, but I don't really know what it's like to be in a room with me, to look at me from outside." And it's the same thing with my characters. Michael is absolutely right: you're inside, you're inhabiting the characters the way an actor inhabits his. That's why actors are so insecure about their looks. They don't know what they look like, and unlike novelists, for them everything depends on their looks.

Lackey: At this point, I want to shift to a slightly different topic. One of the fascinating things for me throughout the novel was Owen Brown's homosexual desire, especially for Lyman Epps. There was this scene building up to this moment when Owen is going to tell Lyman, and it turns out horribly. Was there any documentary evidence to suggest that Owen was homosexual?

Banks: No. I had an interesting conversation about that with Ed White after the book was published. He was a big fan of the book and he said he thought it was a great portrait of a mid-nineteenth century homosexual, working-class man for whom there was no vocabulary to describe his own longings and desires. There wasn't even a vocabulary to describe him socially. I was quite aware of the fact that there was nothing in the record to suggest that he was homosexual, except for the fact that he was single his entire life, which wasn't that uncommon then or now. That is the secret history of Owen in a sense, but it's a secret even from himself. Because he has no language for it, he himself doesn't know. It's not available to him. He doesn't live on the streets, and he'd have to find it there. There's that big scene that takes place in Boston Common where he clearly is drawn to the heat and light of what is illicit sex or deviant sexual behavior of one sort or another, and he is drawn toward it and he doesn't know how to relate to it in any way. He is an extremely naïve and almost innocent man in that regard. But I was quite aware that I was using it, that I was tunneling my way into that aspect of the nineteenth century, in particular where religion and politics have no space for homosexuality.

Lackey: This is another common denominator among these biographical novels. An honest and open engagement with and discussion of homosexual desire has given us a whole new understanding of historical events, as in Bruce Duffy's *The World As I Found It* and *Disaster was my God*, Parini's *Last Station* and *The Passages of H.M.*, Cunningham's *The Hours*, and White's *Hotel de Dream*. Can you briefly discuss the role homosexual desire plays in *Cloudsplitter*, not just in terms of Owen's repressed and latent homosexuality, but in terms of the larger religious context and social structure?

Banks: It has freed up the novelist in a way. A biographer or historian wouldn't be able to describe from inside the experience of being homosexual in a repressed and sexually controlling society. There was no record of it, no letters—there couldn't be with someone like Owen, a working-class man in a deeply religious family. All the novelists you mention have felt that freedom and exercised it. And why not? These novelists are telling stories that a historian and biographer can't tell, because the historians and biographers don't have the records that would give them permission to do so. You know the biographers of Henry James stumble all over the place trying to avoid or confirm whether he was homosexual. But a novelist can go there and not be restricted the way biographers and historians are by the record, by the letters, notes, and recorded conversations. We have this freedom, so why not exploit and utilize it, why not exercise this freedom?

Lackey: But it also tells us something from a slightly different angle about this whole time period. And I think this is Ed White's point, isn't it?

Banks: The present time period?

Lackey: Well, no. What I'm thinking about is how your Owen struggles with no vocabulary for this experience inside of him? You're examining this character in battle with himself. There is no vocabulary for his experience and there are also stark prohibitions against his desire. He can't even really entertain this desire as a legitimate possibility. This gives us a new entrance into a nineteenth-century psyche.

Banks: I like that, but also a contemporary psyche. I know one of the thoughts I had initially, before I really ended up exploring his sexuality, was simply the question of plausibility. I knew that I would have maybe fifty male characters, and that I would deal with several of them up close. As a modern American in the late twentieth century, I cannot say I know fifty people and none of them are homosexuals. There is a certain percentage of the population that is homosexual. So it would be implausible for me to have fifty characters, and not one of them be homosexual. I can't tell a story about America and expect it to be believable if I don't have anyone in it except upper middle-class white people. The absence of black people and of poor people and so forth would be too telling. I'd have to acknowledge their absence in some way. I could have them absent, but I have to acknowledge that they're absent. I think that is what Toni Morrison is getting at in *Playing in the Dark*, the absence of blacks in nineteenth century American literature. It is the absence which is so telling. In *Cloudsplitter* I went there because I had something I wanted to say about homosexuality in the nineteenth-century. I went there because I knew it would be unrealistic for there not to be a homosexual among my major characters. And since Owen was the one I knew best and was most sympathetic to, and in a way the profile of his life as I had laid it out and was working with, the givens, it made it very possible—it didn't make it necessary—that he would be homosexual. The others married, the others had children, but he never did. The intensity of his attachment to his father was really something to consider too. And so I let it continue to develop as I went along in the writing of the novel, and it became increasingly important and interesting to me and ended up maybe telling something about the present. And here it goes back to your earlier thesis. Maybe my interest in it was contemporary. But as a result there is a dimension of nineteenth-century sexuality that comes into the novel that is not in the histories and not in the biographies of Brown. It's hard to imagine homosexuality in the mid-nineteenth century among working-class people without having a novelist guiding you.

Lackey: You also made this point that maybe John Brown was bipolar. That's a new category for explanation, and so a novelist has a little more freedom to go back and use that category to try and open up that character in a new and original way.

Banks: That is true, and it took me quite a while to begin to realize that. I would say to myself, "Oh I think I see what's going on here." And it wasn't because of what the biographies told me. It was because of what my character was doing and how he was unfolding in front of me in the novel. I began to see some of this behavior feels a lot like bipolarity. The depressions he would go through, the withdrawals, the mania, the grandiosity, the incredible physical energy and then lethargy, back and forth. So in a way it helped me to structure the story more plausibly in late twentieth-century terms—psychological, neurological, and medical terms. And we can begin to understand it through our present lens.

Lackey: Near the end of the novel your Owen makes a startling claim. He says that he believes that his and his father's actions would be a "history capable of establishing forever the true meaning of the nineteenth century in the United States of America." Styron makes a similar claim about his Sophie in *Sophie's Choice*, that her experience best represents the meaning and nature of the twentieth century. Can you talk first in the abstract about the way fiction functions to represent the nature and meaning of a century, and then can you specify how this functions specifically in *Cloudsplitter*?

Banks: That is a hard one to answer.

Lackey: Which is why I saved it for the end of the interview!

Banks: Well, you see it's really Owen Brown's claim, not necessarily mine. Who in *Sophie's Choice* made that claim?

Lackey: It is actually a claim Styron made in an interview like this.

Banks: I don't know that I would make that claim. Owen does. But I myself couldn't claim that. John Brown is an iconic figure that has been in the American imagination since 1856, really since the late 1840s in the Kansas Border War. He was a very famous figure when he was still alive all the way down to the present. Sometimes he is portrayed as a thieving madman, as by Robert Penn Warren, at other times he is a noble, sentimentalized, racial hero as in Du Bois's case. I was drawn to Brown initially because he is buried down the road from where I live in the Adirondacks, but also because of the fact that he was viewed by many African Americans as a heroic figure, even above Lincoln, by people like James Baldwin and Malcolm X and going all the way back to Du Bois. He was viewed by whites, however, even liberal whites, primarily as a madman, however well-intended. But neither side disagreed about the facts. The facts have been known from the day of his death. There has never been any real argument about the facts. And that was really interesting to me because that meant that he was basically a figure in our imaginations, and we could project our own historical version or vision on to him. So I went there with that in mind, and not because I wanted to tell the story of or create the lasting image of nineteenth-century America, except insofar I do believe that the story of race is the one story in American history and in our imagination that we cannot seem to get rid of.

Lackey: So you are claiming that this novel is not just about the past, but it's also about the present. And when we think about the 1850s, this is when—in the Christian imagination—we're going to flip on slavery. Christians before the 1850s almost exclusively support slavery because you have to believe in slavery since the Bible, in its literal sense, supports it. But in the 1850s Christians came up with new arguments and they flipped on the issue of slavery. We're going through that same flip right now, but it is about homosexuality. And so your introduction of homosexuality into the novel has resonance for the nineteenth century because it helps open up the nineteenth century, but it's very contemporary because we are seeing the flip happen right at this moment.

Banks: You are exactly right. I approached the theme of homosexuality in the novel not out of an attempt to be accurate about the nineteenth century, but out of what I see around me. This is not a secret. Every family has two or three members who are homosexual. This is the most normal thing. I mean, I just love this switch that Senator Portman from Ohio just made—he "discovered" his son was gay. That kid has to be in his twenties, and the father just figured it out. I just love that flip. And it's just fascinating to watch it happen, I mean, fascinating and sad too because we had to wait so long for this moment. But you're right, I was looking at Owen's sexuality through the lens of contemporary reality because it surrounds me and it had to exist then too. It can't be that different, but how it was expressed and how it was experienced had to be very different. And so I had to make that translation, and that took a leap of imagination really. That's why I was so gratified by Ed White's response to it. He said, this is a totally believable portrait.

Lackey: He created that in *Hotel de Dream* though.

Banks: Yeah, that's right. It's obviously something that concerns him enormously.

Lackey: Did you have that conversation with him before he wrote that novel?

Banks: Yes, I believe so.

Lackey: That's interesting and useful, because I'm going to be interviewing him in two days. And with that, let me thank you for sharing your thoughts with me, as I will pick up with Ed where I left off with you.

26

Bruce Duffy

"In the Fog of the Biographical Novel's History" from *Truthful Fictions* (2014)

Lackey: Let me start with a question about Georg Lukács's book, *The Historical Novel.* One of his central claims is that the biographical form of the novel is doomed to failure, because the focus on "the *biography of the hero*" necessarily leads authors to overlook or misrepresent significant historical events and truths. Given the nature of his claim, he would say both of your novels, *Disaster Was My God* and *The World As I Found It*, were not just failures, but that they were doomed to failure. How would you respond to that claim?

Duffy: Well, I guess I'd say Lukács has it backwards. The hero of the novel should be the foreground, and the history should be background. I think the point of a novel, any novel, is really to get inside some human beings—into their world in a way that history or biography can't duplicate, or rather in a way that delivers a different kind of authority and a different kind of pleasure. For me, very few biographers ever really take me inside someone's being in the masterful way a Richard Ellman does with Oscar Wilde, or Robert Caro does with LBJ. To that end, history may play a part, but it can't be the main focus. Facts will only take you so far. So, if you don't penetrate somebody, if you don't fully understand that character, if you don't really understand the political and social context of that world—meaning *your* fictional world—well, the history won't matter.

To me, Lukács has a very totalitarian, Soviet-style view of history, very out of step with the times. Just think of the Web in which ordinary people directly participate in the news process, with immediate access to almost any facts. True, they may be less scholarly in a classical sense, but they are also more savvy and cynical about the news and received history than they were in Lukács' day. That said, I am in no way saying that facts and history do not matter. I am just saying that in a post-Lukács world the novelist has a lot more leeway. And should take it, too.

Lackey: So is your critique that Lukács disengages history from human characters, from humans? That he makes history some sort of objective process that stands outside of humans? Is that what you're trying to say?

Duffy: He demands this imposed, matrix-like system, this historical overlay over the characters—a vast and an inflexible theater in which, I guess, he gets to sit as the judge. It's just so numbing—so *Darkness at Noon*. Honestly, I read Lukács and I feel numb, when I'm not bored. And what's really telling, the fact that I learn almost nothing from him. Read Walter Benjamin—also of that world—and I am *always* learning things and endlessly interested. Why? Because he is so much more alive than Lukács.

Lackey: So you think his view of history is too big, too overstated?

Duffy: Well, obviously, I like big concepts. But I think you can never lose sight of the *scale* of your characters, even the major ones. Most of us live in the fog of the day to day. We're not aware of giant sweeps of history around us in which we are the cogs. As a novelist, I want to put my characters into this fog of the day to day—into what is really going on right around them, the odd and even silly things. This to me is much more engaging and realistic to readers. Imagine a man fighting in the trenches during World War One, as Wittgenstein did. Wittgenstein is stuck in his small part of the war—in his part of the trench, his fear. He doesn't have some synoptic, God-like view from above. That is how people see things—at ground level. And this is what grabs readers, I think. Characters don't have the view of God. None of us does.

Lackey: While characters in the novel may not have a God's eye perspective of history, the historical novelist, coming years after the events in the novel, should—isn't that Lukács' point?

Duffy: As a novelist, I am not here to produce creaky newsreels or serve as some kind of handmaiden to history—you know, the dumb historical bee who can be relied upon to produce honey. But here is what is telling to me: It is very hard to artfully include a lot of history in a novel and not sound dumb or preachy. It really is. If you are not careful it can seem like a dramatic rendering of Wikipedia, or Michener throwing in all his packing crates of research, or Dos Passos with his self-conscious newsreel pauses.

The point for me is, the novelist is not here to *teach* anybody anything. And really, if somebody wrote something comparable to the painstaking history of *War & Peace*—well, would it even work today? I'm not so sure. This is not to in any way criticize the greatness of Tolstoy—written in Tolstoy's time. I just think Tolstoy's mode would feel very clunky in our time.

As we know, for example, we live in a time of profound self-consciousness and irony—meaning, that heavy, humorless use of history can seem earnestly dumb or just cheesy. In this sense, Lukács has not aged well. He is preaching to the wrong time in a church that no longer exists.

Lackey: What is your process of accessing the day-to-day consciousness of a character in the fog?

Duffy: A quick example. At the time I wrote *The World As I Found It,* I had never been to Europe, first because I was poor, and later because I thought my lack of exposure would make the book that much more fictional. And so I stared for days at period picture books. I pored over period letters and diaries. When possible I spoke to people who had been in Vienna, or knew what it was like to be a Jew in Poland in 1916. But what I realized finally was that I couldn't get bogged down in guide-book type detail. What I needed were the two or three killer details. Again, what really mattered was what the character was feeling walking down that foggy, cobbled street—the inner weather. Kafka doesn't have to paint Prague. He *leaks* Prague.

Lackey: Well, apropos of this, one of the things you insist on is that your work is fiction, that it's not history or biography. To my mind, this claim establishes a tidy division between fiction and history, fiction and biography, as if fiction could not be used to shed significant light on an historical period or a biographical figure. But when I read your work, I feel like you give me an inside perspective of history at a particular time or an inside perspective of these characters. Were you strategically dispensing with the overarching histories of the traditional historical novel? Or were you so immersed in the characters' lives that you simply considered the meta-historical perspective irrelevant?

Duffy: With *The World As I Found It* thirty years ago, I definitely arrived with a chip on my shoulder. I hated historical novels—they felt like the life-size talking Lincoln at Disneyland, way back when. Bodice rippers. History made nice.

But here suddenly was Wittgenstein. At that time, no one had written a biography on Wittgenstein. What I generally found were memoirs essentially painting Wittgenstein as this insane twentieth-century saint beyond the ken of mere mortals. Correctly or not, I felt these acolytes seemed to feel they owned his memory. At the same time, I was wildly unqualified for the task. I don't speak German, am not musically trained or a mathematician—and I could go on. And several writers I knew thought I was being insane, wrecking my career before I even had one, writing about some nut, and not even an American nut at that. So from the start, I felt I was doing something new and daring, if not begging for punishment. And I knew I was very consciously engaged in an act of provocation, like those Julian Schnabel pieces made of broken crockery, or Ezra Pound wanting to break the pentameter. I knew I had to break things. All my heroes—Wittgenstein and Rimbaud included—broke things. So I guess I started hurling.

I had no name for what I wanted to do, and no example, nothing I admired. What I was trying to do was draw some big lines around what I was doing to give myself some space—space in which to write about Wittgenstein not as some God but as a tortured, visionary, ridiculous, brave, flesh-and-blood man. To do this, I could not, and would not, be captive to the facts. Did anyone ever manage Wittgenstein? No way. So I came at it in that spirit.

Equally important, I had to invent a language, American and European, now and then, German and British, slang, passive, aggressive, poetic. With a lot of humor—to show the author was in control even when terrible things are occurring. For me the language and style were everything then, and always are, for each particular book. This is why my books are all stylistically different, the new one included. Style is the real hero, and it has to change constantly, especially in a book using history. Nimble—or dead. Funny—or boring. Otherwise, language is just this grey matrix holding stones of fact, like cement.

You know, I have great respect for history and biography—I couldn't do what I do without them. But yes, these are fundamentally different forms. As with anything, there is no clear, unambiguous division between them. Here the advantage that the fiction writer holds over the biographer or the historian is that he or she is not, as I said, so captive to the facts. Forced to color inside the lines. As a result, there are just things you can *say* as a novelist that a biographer or a historian might not feel empowered to say because the known facts won't safely support them. So the novel gives you tremendous power to go to where you really *imagine* these characters are; to *imagine* how they came to be, and who they are. And, like Aesop, how their ideas came to be—to create intellectual myths, as it were.

One thing that was hugely important to me in both these novels, *World* and *Disaster*, was to imagine: *Why* did these people think the things that they did? *What* was it about their life that caused them to think these things—that caused them to be so invested in these ideas, matters of life or death, some of them. I wanted this to be of the highest moral and human urgency. Not merely reporting the facts, as a researcher might. My goal is to put the reader inside the eye of the tornado.

In one of his journals, Wittgenstein wrote of his life, "I destroy, I destroy, I destroy." Similarly, Rimbaud as a teenager painted slanders on the wall of the church—a demon. Name me one writer or poet in the nineteenth century who writes and thinks like a twentieth-century being. Whitman, Dickinson, great as they are, they are all nineteenth-century creatures. All except one—Arthur Rimbaud. A teenager who produces modernism, like some kind of cold fusion, in his room on a dairy farm in the Ardennes. Then proceeds to attack Paris and the complacency of his time. Really, the first punk.

The point is, this kid was writing in the 1870s things that you wouldn't see until the teens or the twenties! I mean, *nobody* thought like that. Well, today, it's still hard to imagine how somebody—a schoolboy!—could be that far in advance of his time. Or how Wittgenstein, in the same way, could reinvent philosophy, or write *The Tractatus*, which for me is almost a severe, logical poem of high modernism. I want readers to feel that risk—that sheer recklessness—and this in part is what changing the facts does—it's dangerous, you bet it is. It unsettles readers. Jangles them. And again, that demands the overarching spirit of a style: poetic and visionary in the case of Rimbaud, formally logical in the case of Wittgenstein—then different, in an interior way, for every character. Style conveys facts not even named. Really, the history of what is *not* said.

Lackey: So you want people to understand the radical nature of the thinking of your characters. But do you offer an answer, and how confident are you in the answer that you supply in the novels? And why should we trust your judgment about these figures and their times more than, let's say, some biographer or some historian?

Duffy: I don't think these things come down to *an* answer—there are many different answers and many points of view, different forms of authority. Yes, I want you to believe the fiction, but otherwise, I'm not trying to convince you of anything—in fact, some conspiracy theory or something. It's various and nefarious, I guess. In fact, Wittgenstein makes the same point when he talks of "language games" in which different disciplines unwittingly play different kinds of language games. And this is how Wittgenstein himself changes the game, relentlessly looking for new things or things to break. "The avant garde is the history of people bored with other people's ideas." The point is, history is not sacred. Getting it right is not the mere facts. It's thinking deeply about these characters—about what they really thought, and why. All in a style that suggests how they might have thought, the way their stomach gurgled with fear, the processes of life.

Lackey: But tell me more about "getting it right." What does that mean to you?

Duffy: With both books I did a tremendous amount of research—and I was tremendously invested in getting a lot of facts right, even consulting authorities on the matter. At the same time, I was careful not to *over*-research to the point of becoming paralyzed in summoning the fiction. The other thing to acknowledge is my principal characters were, and are, damaged people, and without going into the particulars, I come from a very damaged background from the time my mother died when I was eleven. I've also very consciously had a tremendous amount of experience, including being in world danger spots. Meaning, a lot of possibilities as I create these characters, and a deep, first-hand understanding of danger and screwing up.

In the case of the Rimbaud book, I went to Ethiopia, to his town, Harar, then beyond into the tribal no-man's land near the Somali border. This was a smuggler-route, "Road Warrior" landscape littered with wrecked cars and tractor trailers. It's also a place in which every male over the age of fourteen is carrying an automatic weapon and a giant knife. But intense as this is, it is *nothing* compared to what Rimbaud knew in the 1880s. The point is, my trip made me realize—viscerally—the level of France-loathing and sheer alienation that kept Rimbaud penned up for ten years in what now is Ethiopia. Book knowledge won't convey something like that—that electrical charge, half fear and half thrill. I didn't want to over-focus, as usual, on Rimbaud's hashish-smoking teenage antics. I wanted to look at the terrible back half of his life, I mean when he abandons poetry and never once looks back on literature, bitter as an old gunslinger. Again, the point is not to be faithfully factual. It's to be authentic and compelling, even ruthless, in penetrating the impenetrable.

Lackey: Would you say that your strength, as a novelist, is that you've done all this research in order to understand the time period of the character? Or, would you say that your strength is that you understand the logical consistency of character itself, which enables you *ipso facto* to portray the time period of your protagonist?

Duffy: There is a term in symbolic logic called—I believe—"the truth sign." Well, Wittgenstein objected to the truth sign. Wittgenstein thought, "This is ridiculous, that any equation could declare itself true." In much the same way, as a writer, I can't be walking around with a giant truth sign over my head, claiming to know who the true Wittgenstein was. I don't.

Both these books took around seven years. Don't ask me why seven years. Prison sentences. But honestly I must have spent those first four or five years writing all the time and doing extensive research, while not really knowing *what* the hell I am doing. But then all of a sudden, with both books—just when I was about ready to throw in the towel—something clicked in, and I knew *absolutely* what I was doing: I knew absolutely who these characters were, much with a core of anger.

Lackey: Let's look more deeply at Rimbaud. How did you get inside of him and his world?

Duffy: Well, again, for going on five years, I wrote and wrote, hoping—stupidly—that I might make a prick palatable. Finally, I gave half of the manuscript to two close friends—both psychiatrists. And these two readers said, basically; "Hey, Bruce, nice writing. But honestly we can't feel or understand *who* this guy is or *what* he feels." It was crushing to hear—I was in London, on my way to Ethiopia to track him down, but I saw they were right. And why? Because unconsciously—as I think they realized as therapists—I was resisting the reality of Rimbaud, trying to dress up a snake.

Lackey: So what did you do then?

Duffy: Thank god I was on my way to Ethiopia. As I said earlier, Ethiopia was a huge help. It helped me mentally abandon what I had done, and it made me realize how alienated Rimbaud was to spend ten years there. Here's how it hit me. We're in the tribal areas. The heat was around 120 degrees. I'm dazed. We're stopped in the road. It's just me and my guide, and here we are surrounded by all these armed men. No law, no order, no ambulance, when I thought in this almost pleasant dream, *I wonder why they don't kill me?* And that was it. I was inside Rimbaud, a man numb to danger, floating in his own juice. I'd cracked the safe.

There was something else that helped me catch the scent. Something I had forgotten, and that was the fact that about ten years after Rimbaud's death, his mother, a tough old French farm woman of eighty or so, well, she had him exhumed. In fact, she sat in a carriage watching this man dig up her dreaded son and his beloved sister, who had died at age fourteen—really, the only thing she ever adored. Madame Rimbaud is awful, giving the gravedigger a hard time, loathing the gawkers now that her son is so famous. I thought, *this woman is a bitch*, and I was thrilled. So let her be a bitch! Let him be a prick! *Fuck'em*. The two most liberating words any writer should know. I thought, *he's not likable*. Amazing, visionary, many things, but not likable. And then it hit me: *This is the story of a monster raised by a witch*. Further concussions followed, one of the biggest being to treat him as the outlaw he was, rather than some fancy poet. What I loved was the idea of Rimbaud as a *poet with a gun*.

Lackey: Isn't there pressure to have likeable characters?

Duffy: Well, the truth is, your characters pick you. It's not about someone you'd like to invite for the weekend. The question is, does that character live or not? Feel real or not? *That's* what people want. Or so I like to believe.

Lackey: Why didn't you follow the lead of someone like Robert Penn Warren, who changes Huey Long's name to Willie Stark in *All the King's Men*? And was there any pressure from the editors for you to change the name? Or, were they okay with you using Wittgenstein's name right from the outset?

Duffy: I had a wonderful experience with my first publisher Ticknor & Fields—then part of Houghton Mifflin. I've actually got a funny story here. Ticknor never once tried to get me to change the name—to come up with some fictional name for Wittgenstein, like Silverstein. But about three or four months after they'd accepted the book, I got a worried call from my editor, who said, "We've got a problem here." Seems the editorial board at Houghton Mifflin had asked to see the book. Then they got greatly concerned, and wanted footnotes in it. Footnotes! Well, I had a fit. I told my editor this was just one of the stupidest things I could possibly imagine. The analogy I used was, "Does a general give away his battle plan?" "No way," I said, "I'm not here to pasteurize this thing for people, I'm not doing it." And my editor said "okay" and that was the end of it.

Lackey: But it makes sense because you were doing something unconventional in 1987. Most people would think of your book as a biography, but you're saying it's a novel. You can see that from an editor's perspective, they're confused.

Duffy: True. But you see confusion was the purpose. A purposeful confusion. The idea was not to create an Easy-Reader Wittgenstein. I wanted people to think, and actually I was hoping it would prompt them to consult other sources. Like the *Tractatus* itself, or Otto Weininger, who is a central figure at the end of the novel. The point for me was that I *wanted the reader to be in a state of anxiety* about what was true and what was not. And, being practical, I wrote a disclaimer explaining the spirit and aesthetic of the book. Besides mollifying the Houghton Mifflin editorial board, I didn't want readers so antagonized that they couldn't get beyond page five—or miss the whole point of the book playing fact detective.

Lackey: By the way, that's one of the key ideas in Wittgenstein's work—to unsettle and challenge the way words mean. This is central to his philosophy. So he becomes the perfect figure to unsettle established boundaries of fiction and thought.

Duffy: Wittgenstein has a great saying that philosophy is "showing the fly the way out of the fly-bottle." Out of common confusions. He was very provocative, and you're right. This is a big part of the spirit of the book. As far as my use of names, another brief anecdote. After the book came out I became good friends with a highly influential novelist who loved the book. But once we knew each other better, one day he told me that he believed my decision to use the real names was, as he put it, "a grievous aesthetic mistake." I'll never forget those words. "Grievous!" Like I should promptly hand over my sword or something. This was a brilliant man of immense sophistication, not some reactionary. We had kind of a fight about it, and of course we got over it. But my point was that, by using the real names—by mixing it up—I believed I was making an otherwise boring, costume-drama form aesthetically interesting.

Lackey: Getting back to the Rimbaud novel, you give readers something unexpected, which is a Rimbaud who becomes an anti-Rimbaud, someone who could no longer write, not even letters…

Duffy: It's as if Rimbaud had taught himself how to un-write. A lyric genius at fifteen years old, by age thirty-five, his letters home are excruciatingly awkward and formal. As if he had suffered a brain injury. And perhaps in a sense he had.

At this point late in his short life, Rimbaud is starting to become famous. His works are being published in Paris. Of course he thinks it's all rubbish. That's what's so frightening, I think. Rimbaud never once veered from his complete contempt for what he had done when he was a teenager, things the world would need another fifty years, at least, to learn. So, on one level, I found this horrifying. And yet on another level, I respected Rimbaud's integrity.

Lackey: And here late in the book he's dying and forced to lose his vanity.

Duffy: A prick gets his come-uppance. At the end of the book, we have to watch Rimbaud's leg get amputated, and we have to watch a man die and come to humanity like everybody else. Even take the sacraments late at the last minute. Everybody dies. Everybody has to go through this death process. For someone as proud—as arrogant—as Rimbaud this was a real comeuppance, to learn to be a mortal, as opposed to an *im*mortal. No happy ending, no change in heart, and a coming to death. It was here I came to like Rimbaud.

Lackey: Shifting to another topic, one of the things that has struck me about the contemporary biographical novel is that so many of you are dealing with both the Holocaust and anti-Semitism. You see the concern with anti-Semitism in David Mamet's *The Old Religion*, but you see the concern with anti-Semitism and the Holocaust in Jay Parini's *Benjamin's Crossing*, Ron Hansen's *Hitler's Niece*, Lance Olsen's *Nietzsche's Kisses*, and Irvin Yalom's most recent book, *The Spinoza Problem*. Why is there this obsessive concern about anti-Semitism and the Holocaust in so many of these novels? We certainly see this concern in *The World As I Found It*, especially in the character of Max, who is contradictory and complicated. That he becomes an S.S. member is really a stunning development within that narrative. Could you talk about the role of anti-Semitism in your novel?

Duffy: The Holocaust looms over my generation. I was born in 1951, just six years after the war. My father, an ex-naval officer, liked to watch *Victory at Sea* and World War Two TV documentaries. It was frightening to see little boys in short pants standing under Nazi guns. How could such a thing occur? How could you participate and return to normal life later? I'm not claiming I thought about it in any deep way as a child—it was just there. And so in the case of Max, the character you mentioned, I was struck by how a man could be so charming and also so frightening, and such a racist: how could all these temperaments be present in the same person? How could such a person be blind to these alter egos? Forgive himself, in effect.

I think I also saw this—obviously, on a smaller scale—when I was growing up in the D.C. area. Maryland was a pretty redneck place in the sixties and seventies, or at least around where I was living. So I had several friends who were racist and free with the N-word. People like to forget it but this was common. I just grew up with it. So in writing, I was trying to come through that mess. Racism, unconscious racism, whether it's black people or Jews or whomever—it's all part of it. My second novel, *Last Comes the Egg*, is full of racism. And I had a shift. My best friend in High School was Jewish. Both my wives are Jewish. But in the case of *The World As I Found It*, my first wife's grandmother was from Poland, and she spoke Yiddish. Nannie lived in this apartment in the Bronx where there were a number of old ladies, many concentration camp survivors with the tattoos inside their arms. And Nannie was just the sweetest old lady. I thought, "Well, I want to interview her." After all, Warsaw was close to where Wittgenstein was fighting in World War One. Nannie left in 1921, before the Holocaust, but she lost family to the Nazis. Well, Nannie started to talk about her memories. I have never seen such power and horror as in her rage against the Poles who routinely beat her family. One time Polish soldiers scalped off her grandfather's beard. Terrible things and not uncommon in many parts of Europe. Well, for me, that power, that anger was like being hit with an electric charge. It gave me a certain power, an inside privilege to speak these things, or so I thought. I should add that my first wife had a cousin, a man in his seventies very close to her grandmother, and a real tough guy. Moniek was an electrician in New York City, Brooklyn. But he had been in a Russian concentration camp, a German concentration camp, and had fought in the 1948 Arab-Israeli War. I have never seen a darker, angrier person in my life. Moniek even had a coiled way of standing that you could imagine inside the barbed wire, always looking behind his back. To talk to someone like him, well, that told me—beyond what any book could convey—about all these terrible emotions. The point is, with varying success, I was always looking for the shock of real experience. Not just the physical details, but the emotions. The emotions tell you everything—radar. They are your guide.

Lackey: So where did you get your conflicted Wittgenstein from, then? What sense did you have that he was so conflicted about his Jewishness?

Duffy: That was more made up. I can't really point offhand—this was more than twenty-five years ago—to some ready archival source. What astounded me was this whole Jewish dream of assimilation at the turn of the century, this lie that if the Jews converted to Christianity they would be accepted. And they believed: In Austria and Germany there was a period before the twenties when it was very common for Jewish families to assimilate and become Christians. Saying, if you become Catholic, things will be okay for you. And of course when Hitler takes power, things were not okay. The stain is ineradicable. And this is not just true over in Austria. To a lesser extent it was true in the US as well. Essentially, it was the same story of families trying somehow to purge themselves of their Jewishness or change their name. Or grandly overlooking the whole thing, say, as Robert Oppenheimer did pretty much. Many painful strategies and few successful.

Lackey: But getting back to the Wittgenstein character. In the novel, we get hints of him grappling with his Jewish heritage, the assimilation, becoming Catholic. But it's all leading up to the scene with G. E. Moore, when Wittgenstein goes to his house. It's a planned confession and Wittgenstein's going to finally tell him and several others that he's guilty—among other sins—of having denied his own Jewish heritage.

Duffy: And that *is* true, by the way.

Lackey: How did you approach Wittgenstein's confession, which is one of the last things one would expect him to do?

Duffy: In this scene, it was very hard for me to witness an incredibly proud man just scalding himself, just laying himself naked before other people. And who else would ever do such a thing? Tough as he could be on others, Wittgenstein was even harder on himself, to the point that friends feared him committing suicide if he failed in his own eyes. A sort of intellectual samurai. But I was very drawn to this, the idea that real thinking is a code with very real dangers—risks to the soul. That's the kind of world I wanted to capture. Ideas that carry real consequences. Integrity that will not be compromised.

Lackey: Is that part of what drew you to Otto Weininger? At age twenty-three in 1903, he made that sacrifice when the world rejected his book *Sex and Character*. Can you explain what led you to include the Weininger section in the novel?

Duffy: Looking back, I think on some level Weininger reminded me of Rimbaud. Not as a racist. I've never seen any evidence that Rimbaud was an active racist, or cared. Like Rimbaud, Weininger was a young genius with an intellect of an order that verges on insanity, even the demonic. For a certain kind of personality, such brilliance, so young, has to verge on insanity—10,000 volts pumped into a small fuse. Of course it blows. Few, if any, can withstand such power, such insanity. Rimbaud stopped writing forever. Weininger committed suicide. This is the kind of raw, seductive power than Weininger has, and I shrunk from it at first. It's like reading *Mein Kampf* or talking with the devil. But see, for a writer, the trick is not to open *Sex and Character* or *Mein Kampf* with contempt. The trick is to clear your mind and read *Mein Kampf*, say, as an out-of-work carpenter with a hungry family might have in 1929. That is my job as a fiction writer. Never to be superior to the material, but to use it, rather, like an Ouija board to find strange new places.

Lackey: But were there some specific ideas that drew you to Weininger?

Duffy: Well, Weininger had to have been the first, or one of the very first, to realize that none of us is purely male or female—that we fall somewhere on a continuum of sexual identity. Today, we can accept or at least uncomfortably entertain such an idea. But in 1903, this was frightening and revolting—terrifying. In short, like a nightmare, Weininger expresses many of the pathologies and nightmares of his time, from race to sex. Novelistically, Weininger's funeral—after his suicide—was a very dramatic and concrete way to show the toxic ideas that the young Wittgenstein was exposed to, again, in a time in which ideas could literally be a matter of life or death. Weininger's funeral made all these conflicts stand out.

Lackey: So if we think of *World* as illuminating the conditions under which Wittgenstein's philosophy came into being—specifically in the time period in which he lived—what does Wittgenstein's experience tell us? Why did you write about him in particular?

Duffy: Well, as far as why I wrote about him, I'd encountered a magazine article about this modernist house in Vienna that he had helped design and build for his sister. This was in the middle of the 1920s, when Wittgenstein had actually stopped being a philosopher. I think in that time, what attracted me was I had reached a point where my fiction wasn't going anywhere. At the same time, I was not very happy with what I saw being published in the so-called age of minimalism. So I think—I mean after the fact—that I felt a certain kinship with Wittgenstein, I mean as two displaced persons. Here I was, a writer hiding out as a Sunday painter, and here was Wittgenstein, a philosopher hiding out as an architect. So the book actually began as an idea for a painting. I was going to do this kind of collage with various prose poems in it.

So I did some drawings only to quickly realize that I didn't know much, or anything, about Wittgenstein. Worse, I'd minored in philosophy only to realize how meager my understanding really was, especially of symbolic logic. So I started to read about Wittgenstein, and here I soon had a revelation: At that time in the early eighties *there was no biography of Wittgenstein.* None. What an amazing situation! It was as if I had blundered into a treasure room. In other words, I could project my own story of Wittgenstein's life in advance of the inevitable biography. Scoop the story. So that was what led me—pure beginner's luck. I'm sorry, what was the second part of the question?

Lackey: It's about how Wittgenstein's personal life inflected his philosophy. I'm thinking here about the Golem scene, when he's at the theater. This turns out to be a very powerful scene—it resonates deeply.

Duffy: That was totally made up.

Lackey: But tell me, how can we use that to understand Wittgenstein or his philosophy? Or should we?

Duffy: In the Golem scene, he goes—with great arrogance—to a Jewish theater, to him a very grubby, ignorant thing. Here he confronts his true past, so upset by a seemingly garish simple-minded scene—and so unconscious of his deeper emotions—that he passes out. Anyhow, I can't make a direct connection to his Jewishness, or suppressed Jewishness, and his philosophy. I think the thing that quickly stunned me about Wittgenstein was the three brothers who had committed suicide. How do you come back from that, the sheer damage? But honestly, I didn't really know much about his family, and in a way I didn't want to. So I created characters. Knowing only the basics, I created Karl Wittgenstein. I created the other siblings that we have here. The trick was Wittgenstein, creating a character living on an edge in which *he* had to be perfect, with a sense of terrible peril if he wasn't absolutely perfect. A man on a tightrope. I wanted readers to feel that danger.

Lackey: It seems that he associated Jewishness with imperfection, and that's one of the reasons why he was constantly denying his Jewish heritage. Leading to that night when he made his confession to G. E. Moore.

Duffy: And I think you're right.

Lackey: So something happens there. Something happens that changes him when he's going to finally accept his Jewishness. Do we see that as a positive moment in his development? Is it a moment of self-acceptance?

Duffy: Well, there is a sense of self-acceptance—relief, I guess. But this is not a guy who then immigrated to Israel. But during World War Two—to acknowledge who he really was, to acknowledge his shame, even if he is too hard on himself—we all have a few of these secret griefs. But what I admire, for Wittgenstein it was always about what's right—about life as an obligation. Above all, Wittgenstein did not want to be a liar—ever. Or superior in a class way. As he said once, "All men are the same distance from God." There's a thought you can think about for a long, long time.

Lackey: Let's shift to the connections between Wittgenstein and Rimbaud, because these are two very different types of figures. Can you explain the logical connections between these two figures, and can you explain what makes these men in your novels so radically different from each other?

Duffy: At one point in Wittgenstein's journals, he says essentially, "If I have to describe my career, it's 'I destroy. I destroy.'" And Rimbaud had the same ruthless aesthetic. Rimbaud had very little respect for what he saw being published in his time, or for the thinking of his time. He, too, came to destroy. Both were also great writers, and so that was also the stylistic battle, to reflect in the writing Wittgenstein's precision, and Rimbaud's wildness and precision. For me in this sense, the writing is itself a character in these two books. Well, that was the aim, at least.

Lackey: Yet it seems that your Rimbaud was actually trying to build a better world in those early stages. He was destroying, but he also had this vision of rebuilding—maybe even the concept of love, reimagining it.

Duffy: Absolutely. In *The Illuminations,* Rimbaud's visionary prose poems, he invented a phantasmagoria of worlds colliding. Illogic. Events out of sequence. Dada and Surrealism long before they arrive. Even the montage style of early films that threw early movie audiences into fits with their different, jarring images. Nobody even dimly thought this way in 1872. This is how revolutionary Rimbaud was, and that is not a term I use lightly.

Lackey: Did he realize that it didn't work—that it was a utopic fantasy? Because he just gave up. Here I see a difference with the Rimbaud character—giving up in disgust.

Duffy: That's a really good distinction. Early on, when he's sixteen, Rimbaud is extremely idealistic. But by twenty, what I believe killed the poetry was the inevitable end of childhood. Still, Rimbaud's reaction was extreme. Poetry is barren, a lie. Every last word of it. And being the extreme person he is, Rimbaud never veers from that course, even at the very end of his life when his work is being discovered. For him the fruit is still rotten. And this is very modern, like Marcel Duchamp when he gave up painting for chess. Painting is like wallpaper—the pointlessness of painting in an age of mechanical reproduction. This is very much like Rimbaud, and it's disturbing. But welcome to our time.

Lackey: What else is modern about Rimbaud?

Duffy: He wants to create this brave new place in the world for women, in which woman also would be a Poet. In those days, so far as I know, nobody thought about the place of woman! Except to have children.

Lackey: That's why when I think about the Rimbaud character, one of the most intriguing parts of the novel is your analysis of the rational derangement of the senses, this intentional disordering of the mind. When I read the Wittgenstein novel, I feel like, "Wittgenstein's tearing things down—everything, including himself—but I rarely see him trying to build something up." Whereas the Rimbaud character thinks—and this is very Nietzschean—"I'm going to have this rational derangement of the senses. I'm going to disrupt all these comfortable, stable categories so that we can start to reimagine the world in a new way." But he gets so *terribly* disillusioned. It seems to me that, in his post-poetry world, he ultimately subscribes to a kind of corporate business mentality. Am I reading it right?

Duffy: I agree. I think the thing that is so touching about him is here he is, sixteen years old, and he's going to revolutionize love and have a systematic derangement of the senses. And by twenty, he gives it up, all of it forever, after doing some of the most—in my opinion—stupendous poems ever written, poems utterly unlike anything else. To have such an amazing body of work, to have such amazing integrity in what he did, then to just cast it aside—for me that was the story.

Lackey: Where are you going next? What book is on the horizon? Do you have one?

Duffy: It is still early in the game—less than a year into writing it. But the title is *A Towering Brilliance*, and it's built around the design, the dropping, and the aftermath of the first atomic bomb. It's really built around the physicists who built the bomb, mostly Jews, and many refugees from Hitler. It will have quite a cast of characters, very varied: Oppenheimer, the main character, as well as Einstein, Niels Bohr, Leo Szilard, and the rare woman in that world—Lise Meitner who coined the word "fission." We'll also be with General Curis LeMay, operationally in charge of the Enola Gay, the B-29 that dropped the bomb. And the Japanese writer Mishima, who dodged the war at twenty and then became an ultra-nationalist when Japan by then was a country of pacifists. In 1970 Mishima had his own private army and to protest the new Japan, he publically committed *seppuku*, had himself beheaded. Believe it or not, though, there will be a lot of humor in the book!

Quite aside from building the bomb, I want to look at the morality of the bomb. Robert Oppenheimer ran the Manhattan Project to build the first atomic bomb in World War Two. Oppenheimer was one of the most cosmopolitan scientists, ever, almost a pacifist in disposition. Yet before they drop the first atomic bomb, here he is giving precise instructions on how the bomb should be armed for maximum destructiveness. And he knows it's going to trigger an arms race. They all know it, some of the smartest people on the planet, yet they go ahead.

27

Joyce Carol Oates

"Enhanced Symbolic Interiors in the Biographical Novel" from *Truthful Fictions* (2014)

Lackey: Let me start by telling you about this project. I'm trying to figure out why, starting in the 1980s, so many prominent writers began to author biographical novels. I'm also trying to define the nature of this genre of fiction. Since the year 2000 you have become increasingly more interested in biographical fiction as you have written creative works about figures such as Edgar Allen Poe, Emily Dickinson, Mark Twain, Robert Frost, and Ernest Hemingway. Can you explain what motivated you to start writing this kind of fiction?

Oates: In terms of *Blonde*, I remember seeing a photograph of Norma Jeane Baker when she was about sixteen years old. I wasn't even sure when I saw the photograph that I knew who it was and then the caption of course said "Norma Jeane Baker." I was so struck by the fact that this girl was in high school at the time. She reminded me of many girls I'd gone to school with and she wasn't particularly glamorous. This made me think about the extraordinary metamorphosis that would transform an anonymous, unknown girl in a short time into this icon, this blonde goddess Marilyn Monroe. The idea came to me in a flash, that I'd like to write a novella, a postmodern treatment of this phenomenon of how a person loses her specific identity, becomes a cultural icon or artifact and loses her soul and identity. I had planned it to be quite postmodernist, an experimental narrative moving very swiftly through the years and ending with her being given her name. So the last line of the novella would be "Marilyn Monroe" with quotes around it.

Lackey: Was that the first time you authored biographical fiction?

Oates: Is there a difference between biographical fiction and fiction that just has historical figures in it? Because I had Mark Twain just briefly in a novel called *A Bloodsmoor Romance*.

Lackey: Biographical novels usually center the novel within the consciousness of a particular character, who is named after a historical figure like Twain, Marilyn Monroe, or Ted Kennedy.

Oates: I hadn't done that before. I didn't think at all of *Black Water* as biographical fiction. It is more like a ballad or an allegory, the elf knight riding in the forest. I wasn't thinking much of Ted Kennedy specifically. This is a very different sort of person, so I wasn't thinking at all that was biographical fiction.

Lackey: The standard view is that a work like *Black Water* would be considered a historical novel because you decided to change the name from Ted Kennedy to The Senator, which gives the character a more symbolic or allegorical significance. Changing the character's name and significant dates gives you more freedom, whereas in the biographical novel the character is named after the original figure, which supposedly limits the author's freedom. A lot of people are asking the question: "Why are so many prominent writers doing this kind of fiction now?" In the past, as is the case with Robert Penn Warren's *All the King's Men*, authors would change the name from Huey Long to Willie Stark. But they are not doing that as much anymore.

Oates: I've read and admired Gore Vidal's *Lincoln*, which is a deftly executed historical novel.

Lackey: That's right. And he also did *Burr*.

Oates: It never really seemed to me that unusual. There must have been many books about Lincoln, both fiction and nonfiction. I haven't read them. As for *Blonde*, I wasn't thinking about the biographical novel. I was thinking about the phenomenon of how the ordinary person grew, loses her name Norma Jeane Baker and becomes Marilyn Monroe. But then, when I got to about page 180, when she's about twenty, it just seemed really exciting to me that I would continue writing through her whole life. So ultimately, the novel is about Marilyn Monroe as she becomes more and more Marilyn Monroe. At first, she's always Norma Jeane. Then there's a certain point in the novel when she starts to be called "Marilyn" and a point when nobody remembers Norma Jeane and she's forgotten Norma Jeane herself. That's what interested me very much, to write about celebrity and fame. I didn't set out to write about Marilyn Monroe. It was more that I'd seen this photograph. I could have written about somebody else if anybody else had had quite that trajectory. You couldn't write about a fictitious person and get the same sort of resonance. Without specifying the name, it wouldn't mean anything. Willie Stark, is that his name?

Lackey: That's right, Willie Stark, who is based on Huey Long.

Oates: The name doesn't mean anything at all, but writing about Huey Long has a real charge, especially decades ago. Let's say you were writing about Shakespeare and inventing a kind of life for him, you'd be writing about Shakespeare as the phenomenon and the historical figure. And so why other people are doing this I don't know.

Lackey: There have been biographical novels, but not many until recently. Arna Bontemps did one in 1936 on Gabriel Prosser called *Black Thunder*, and Zora Neale Hurston did one on Moses in 1939. But before Styron's book about Nat Turner there are very few notable biographical novels. After *The Confessions of Nat Turner*, many prominent writers started authoring biographical novels. In 1968 Styron won the Pulitzer for *The Confessions of Nat Turner*, but in the Pulitzer's jury report, *The Confessions* is characterized as a historical novel. This is interesting because I don't think the committee had a category for making sense of the biographical novel at this time. The year 1999 is of crucial importance, because two were up for the Pulitzer: Michael Cunningham's *The Hours* and Russell Banks' *Cloudsplitter*. To my mind, something happened in the late nineties that made the literary establishment recognize this genre of fiction as legitimate.

Oates: I thought of *Blonde* as a historical novel. It's not that I really thought in these terms at all. It's basically just writing a novel.

Lackey: But when you say you thought of it as a historical novel, what does that mean? What does it disclose to us about history?

Oates: To me a historical novel is something I have to do a fair amount of research for because it may take place before I was born, before I knew anything. It inhabits a world that for me is history. It could be the year 1100 but you have to do research. Whether it's 1949 or 1970, we have to do research. We can't just start writing and remember and put things in. You actually have to go and do some real research. So to me that constitutes a historical novel.

Lackey: Shifting to another question, your character Henry James vows that no biographer would ever be able to plumb the depths of his secret and subterranean soul. Ironically as a novelist, James spent his career refining the technique of accessing the deepest levels of human interiors. What James could not have anticipated was the rise of biographical fiction, specifically biographical fiction about him. What is it that a writer of biographical fiction can give writers that a traditional biographer could not?

Oates: Novelists can speculate and be imaginative. I think of myself as an experimental and postmodern writer, so I can do things with the imagination that James would not have allowed, things that are mythic or parodistic. James was a psychological realist. He had a very rich concept of consciousness that is curiously devoid of the domestic, sensuous, or literal. He seems not to have much of a visual imagination. If you contrast him with somebody who has a strong visual consciousness like Vladimir Nabokov or D. H. Lawrence, there's a profound difference. Virginia Woolf doesn't have much of a visual consciousness either. It's all a shimmer of thought impressions and people don't actually have bodies. For instance, in *The Wings of the Dove* it is mentioned that Milly Theale has red hair. That's about it in this huge, long densely layered novel. You don't know what anybody looks like. All we get are reflections. It's a curious way of looking at life as only thought impressions rather than sense impressions. It's really quite extraordinary what he's trying to do. I thought of *Blonde* as a mythic novel. She's like Moby Dick. She's this figure that people all project onto and have different thoughts about.

Lackey: You mention your postmodern inclinations. Some argue that postmodernism made the biographical novel possible. The argument goes like this: We used to think there was a clear division between history and fiction, between reality and literature, but postmodernists argue that fact is already saturated with fiction. Given the blending of fact and fiction in postmodernism, many contemporary writers say to the historians: "You are not giving me anything that is *non*fiction even though you pretend that it is history and that it is somehow above or outside fiction." Would you say that postmodernism has contributed to the rise of the biographical novel?

Oates: Things start to shift and the bedrock of realism shifts. For instance, in the nineteenth century a reputable portraitist would paint a slightly flattering picture of a subject. It would be completely recognizable, very beautiful. Then something starts to shift and we have the work of Picasso and later in the twentieth century Francis Bacon and many others. They paint portraits of say, Gertrude Stein, but the portraits now are not at all real, not realistic. They have a glimmer of psychological realism. The one of Gertrude Stein is probably the most famous of these iconoclastic, experimental portraits. *Reputedly*, she said she didn't look like that, and Picasso said, "you will look like that." Francis Bacon has his "Screaming Pope" and portraits of his friends. He does portraits of people but in ways that are very disturbing and very private.

Lackey: Would you say that these artists are accessing a different kind of truth?

Oates: It's more a universal truth. When I write about Norma Jeane Baker I'm writing about a lot of people, even men. I'm writing about the biographical subject and smudging it a little to suggest that if you look in that mirror of Marilyn Monroe you will see something like yourself. Rather than her being this unique historical figure all by herself, I sense that there is a bond between us. And as I said before I felt drawn to write about her because she looked so much like girls I had gone to school with and even a little bit like my mother, a certain kind of girl in the 1920s or 1930s in America. She wasn't an "okie," but somebody like an "okie," a displaced American person who doesn't have any roots, who is washed up in California. The continent has shifted and she finds herself there. Monroe stands in stark contrast to someone like Elizabeth Taylor, who is more aristocratic.

Lackey: And the reason why so many men felt free to abuse Monroe was because of her background. They could manipulate and mold her and use her for their own particular purposes.

Oates: Yes, that is true, but she also manipulated and used people. She was one of these irresistibly wounded, infantile women that men are drawn to. They think maybe they might victimize them but then they end up like Arthur Miller and others being pretty much debilitated themselves. It is like being drawn to this beautiful flame, where the moth is drawn to the flame. Some men I'm sure did victimize her, but she also had power, a lot of power. And people like that who are borderline personalities are very deeply narcissistic and wounded. They can really hurt other people tremendously, which I think she did.

Lackey: Some prominent writers have either rejected or condemned the biographical novel. For instance, Virginia Woolf argued in a 1939 essay that the novelist is free to create while the biographer is tied to facts. For Woolf, writers have to choose between the art of representing a person's life accurately, which would lead them to produce a biography, or creating a living, breathing character, which would lead them to produce a work of fiction. Blending the two in the form of the biographical novel is not an option. Given this claim Woolf would say that your novel *Blonde* is a failure. How would you respond to this?

Oates: I just think that's silly. Virginia Woolf had so many misguided and foolish ideas about James Joyce, D. H. Lawrence, Arnold Bennett, and Katherine Mansfield. She thought that *Ulysses* was a failure; she never wrote anything approaching *Ulysses*. She's basically someone who was limited herself and when she saw what Joyce was doing, it is just so overwhelming and brilliant and way beyond anything she could think of, she just had to pronounce it a failure. I don't think that's important at all. But if you look at a novel that's very iconoclastic and experimental like *The Public Burning*, which is supposedly about Nixon and the Rosenbergs, you know that there is no way that that is a biography of Nixon or in fact the Rosenbergs. If Virginia Woolf read a novel like that she would not have been able to comprehend it because she lived at a different time. And I think that was her problem when trying to comprehend Lawrence and Joyce; she seemed to be in the vanguard of new techniques, but I don't think she was anywhere near the level of Joyce. She was basically trapped in her time.

Lackey: But that's the key to the question, isn't it? What was it about her time that made her incapable of imagining the biographical novel?

Oates: I have no idea. Shakespeare was writing great plays and using history and using historical figures and they certainly knew about Shakespeare. I have no idea why it was so limited. I think it was just her. She had very catty and nasty things to say about Katherine Mansfield who in many ways is a better writer than she is. Virginia Woolf couldn't begin to do the sorts of things that Katherine Mansfield did, let alone Lawrence. I don't particularly like her fiction. It is very over-rated I think. She's a great writer, but I think she is very over-rated.

Lackey: Your most recent novel is *The Accursed*, and it engages history.

Oates: Yes, it has lots of historical figures. Woodrow Wilson and Upton Sinclair are the main characters, one twenty-six years old and the other about forty-nine. But I wasn't thinking in terms of biography or history when I wrote that novel. It was more a postmodernist look at America. I was living in Princeton at the time and looking at the place I was living in 100 years ago. I don't really know why writers do what they do and I think most people don't really know the reason. Evolutionary psychology teaches us that people's motives are very obscure. People make war in other countries with the pretense of religion or democracy. But it is basically this Darwinian land-grab. They want the land, the fertile soil, and the waterways, but people never say that. In talking about literature, and that may include Virginia Woolf, they say things that sound plausible or maybe even impressive. But the real reasons that they are saying them may be different. And I think that Virginia Woolf is extremely anxious and envious. She even said something about James Joyce, that it is impossible for a living writer to judge another because it's too raw. That is a wonderful quote. She conceded finally that she couldn't really even read *Ulysses*. She was so put off by what she called the "soiled linen" and his schoolboy vulgarity. She looks down from a higher economic class, just basically not able to see that was a great work of art. Like somebody walking around an enormous mountain who just sees defects in this part of the mountain and just goes on. But I think that's true for most writers. So when I try to answer honestly, I say, "I don't think I really had a motive." I saw an opportunity.

Lackey: A number of the writers I have interviewed say that biographical novelists are unique because they can access and represent an undocumentable interior. According to this view, historians give us mainly externals, the facts. But the biographical novelist can access the motives and sometimes the subconscious. These writers say that they know the story, the external frame of the historical period, but their goal is to access and represent the motives. You as a writer might not be able to access what you are actually trying to do, but is it true that you're trying to get to the interiors of your characters? That you're trying to access them?

Oates: I suppose so, but the characters are fictitious. Trying to get to the inner self of a fictitious character is somewhat paradoxical. The effort of writing any kind of art is something that precludes explanation. I think there are poems of great exquisite beauty that are musical and profound but they can't be paraphrased. You can paraphrase most of Emily Dickinson's poetry, but that doesn't begin to approach it. I feel that I'm trying to express the mystery and the opacity of life. There are certain junctures in *Blonde* that are very raw and bleeding, like something has been broken and the marrow is exposed. Now Monroe is this blonde actress who slowly becomes this archetypal figure, and she wanders into a drugstore because she can't sleep, and she sees these Hollywood magazines. She sees her own picture on the cover and it's a beautiful picture. She is very made up and she's in some fancy dress and the real person standing there, the so-called "real" Marilyn Monroe—here is the image of what she is going to become. What would it be like to be on the eve of your death and you see how you're going to be remembered by posterity. And it's so far from being you. To me that was a poignant moment of great tragedy, but not really expressible in any other terms except as I'm telling you right now. So if the reader's reading that, the reader would have a certain feeling. But I'm not sure that it can be expressed in any other way.

Lackey: I want to discuss one of the approaches a number of biographical novelists use. Marilyn Monroe is an ideal subject for a biographical novel because she does in film what you do in the novel. Let me clarify what I mean. In *Niagara* Monroe plays the character Rose Loomis, and in order to access that character's interiority your Monroe surmises that Rose had a dark secret which in part explains some of the character's behavior. Is this a fictional scene or is this something that Monroe actually did?

Oates: That is fiction.

Lackey: When your Monroe specifies the nature of the secret, that Rose put a baby in a drawer which led to the baby's death, are we supposed to think that she intuits correctly? Or are we supposed to see this as a hypothetical that could serve to illuminate something about Rose's character?

Oates: She is working with an instinctive actress's approach to what she is doing. Monroe had actually been put in a drawer by her crazy mother, and she herself was nearly killed by her mother who was schizophrenic. Now I don't know *literally* in real life if any of this happened, but it might have happened. It is very plausible that that would have happened. It was very thrilling to go through the movies that I saw of Marilyn Monroe that are detailed in the novel and to look at the movie from the point of view of Norma Jeane, from the point of view of posterity. It was like seeing her from some vantage point in the future. She is dead and she is a posthumous voice narrating the movie of her own life.

Lackey: Anita Diamant uses what I think is a similar approach to the material as you in her novel *The Red Tent*. She bases her novel on the story of Dinah's rape from the Old Testament. In my interview with her, she said, if you read the Old Testament story closely and carefully, it doesn't sound like a rape, and the reason why is that the father offers a huge dowry because his son wants so badly to marry Dinah. In fact, the son loved Dinah so much that the father agreed to have the whole tribe circumcised in order to win this woman's love. Anita said she spent hours laboring over the logic of that story. She was concerned with the logic of character, culture, and history, and she ultimately concluded that the Old Testament story of a rape didn't make sense. My whole life I have been given one story about Marilyn Monroe, which is that she was a mindless bimbo, a dumb blonde. But you have given me a very different Marilyn Monroe. I wonder if this is what a lot of biographical novelists do. You all have a keen sense of character and story. Therefore, you can give us new access to history and culture, because you have a unique gift. It's not some sort of mystical, magical intellectual capacity. Rather, it is a hypersensitive awareness to the way character, story, culture, and history function. Is this what many good biographical novelists do?

Oates: That might be the case. Biographies have different interpretations of the same character. For instance, Jay Parini wrote a very positive biography about Robert Frost after Lawrence Thompson published his, which is very negative. And then Jeffrey Meyers has another biography following Jay Parini, which is in the middle. He's unsparingly critical, but he's sympathetic and forgiving. So it's like the three Robert Frosts you know. Frost would have liked Jay Parini's, and he would have been very upset at Lawrence Thompson's biography. It's basically that Robert Frost is seen doing the same things in all three books but the biographer has put a different light on it. One book is doing it for one reason, another biography is doing it for a malicious, selfish reason, and another biography, Jeffrey Meyers', is doing it because he's deeply unhappy and he can't help himself. So there isn't any sense that there is a fixed personality anywhere.

Lackey: So we could say it's all up for grabs. But the other possibility is that some of these biographies are just wrong.

Oates: Yes, they could be wrong. Or they weighed too much in one direction. That's true. I recently wrote a story about Robert Frost. It is an imagined interview with Frost, and it basically becomes clear that the interviewer is accusatory of Frost. She starts off flattering and fawning, but then she gets more and more personal, interrogating him, and finally accusing him. You realize that she's a fiction of his imagination. He is punishing himself with this sort of self-laceration. But he says at the end, "all these things may be true, but I'm a poet and my work is going to endure." He doesn't say it like that but the idea is that even though he's this contemptible person who did all these awful things, which he acknowledges, the fact is that he managed to write some poems that are beautiful and strong and are going to endure, and so the whole thing is justified by that. I didn't really know that I would come to that conclusion but maybe that's the basic bedrock of art. That Shakespeare or Milton or Chaucer and all these people worked out of different motives but what remains ultimately is that they were able to extract something great from their personal selves with all their failings and sorrow and tragedy. These works that are permanent, permanent as long as the language is permanent.

Lackey: So would you say that what leads you to write about certain people is not that you have a particular take on them but that there is some sort of mystery about them?

Oates: Yes, some sort of mystery. The most recent thing that I wrote is inspired by the Tawana Brawley case. But I don't use her name. A character who functions as Reverend Al Sharpton appears in the novel, but this character *is not Al Sharpton* in fact. So the historical individuals are not in the novel. Rather, their historical roles are the subject of the novel. I am very interested in events in our culture, and not much interested in the minutiae of individuals, which is the stuff of tabloids. I am interested in those events that have symbolic, ideally universal significance. This is a good example of changing the name because I wanted to change many things about it and work with different voices. This work becomes a dialogue about race, the confusions and blindness of race, and people seeing their own faces and things that are very subjective. But with that, it never would have interested me to write about Tawana Brawley or Al Sharpton. I'm interested in the symbolic possibilities of people who are *like* them. But my characters are more interesting, elastic and subtle than the real people. From my research, I discovered that these people were not nearly as nuanced or subtle as my fictitious characters. I don't know what the real Marilyn was like, but I don't think it is such a stretch to imagine a very poetic, sensitive, serious and earnest person. She writes little things in my novel, and in real life she did some writing. It wasn't very good. I have seen her writings and I didn't use most of it in the novel. I used maybe one line but I always enhance characters and make them a little more than they might have been in real life because I think that's what art is. King Lear may be a senile old man but he speaks so beautifully, and that's an enhancement of life.

Lackey: I interviewed Russell Banks, who wrote the biographical novel *Cloudsplitter*, and he deals with race in a similar way to what you're describing. His novel is narrated by John Brown's son Owen, and when doing the research for that novel, Russell discovered that, while everyone agreed about the facts of John Brown's life, there were two radically different interpretations of the man. From the perspective of many blacks, Brown is a hero and a saint, but from the perspective of many whites, he is a madman and a criminal. Russell realized that there is something problematic about taking an authoritative stance as is frequently done in biographies. So in *Cloudsplitter* he represents what happened, but he resists the impulse to take an authoritative stance in his fiction. Your task in *Blonde* is different because Monroe has so consistently been characterized as a mindless blonde. You obviously didn't want to make her such a mindless character, as you made her rich and complex. There are two possibilities here. First, art uses an historical event or character to make something much richer, as Lear becomes much more interesting than a senile old man. Second, art can revise our understanding of a biographical figure or a historical event, so your Marilyn Monroe is much richer and more complex than she is generally portrayed within the culture. Was one of your objectives to recover in part a more authentic and complex Monroe?

Oates: Yes, I felt that she was really a good actress. I thought that she was really like a genius. I thought she was much more sensitive and more thoughtful than she has been portrayed, much more playful, alive, and complex. She was always considered a "B" actress and everyone kind of condescended to her. Elizabeth Taylor was on this completely different plateau and Marilyn Monroe never even made much money compared to some of these other actresses. She was also very serious. She was always taking lessons, acting lessons, dance lessons, and other kinds of lessons. She was always trying to improve herself. When the actors were having lessons, acting class, she's the one who shows up in a crisply ironed white blouse and a skirt and they're all wearing jeans, and I think that was actually true. Many of these details are true. Many things I made up because they seemed plausible and insightful, but some things are actually real. She had many love affairs and abortions. I only deal with one of those abortions in *Blonde*. She was obviously a person of some compulsiveness and she had an addict's personality, much more than I gave her. She lived without thinking about the future. She was addicted to barbiturates and she was addicted to other things. She was a desperate person. I made her more an artist, because I think of her as an artist.

Lackey: But you charted very slowly and patiently how she moved towards addiction. At first, she is opposed to drugs, but she is slowly immersed into the Hollywood and drug culture.

Oates: The directors and movie people gave her drugs. The doctors injected her with amphetamines and barbiturates. You and I both teach in university departments. Suppose your English chair calls you in and says, "now it's time for your amphetamine shot." You have the choice of saying "no" and then you get fired or you take the shot and gradually you get addicted to it.

Lackey: Russell made a similar point in my interview with him. He said that when he's writing about something in the past, he is also writing about the present.

Oates: Oh yes, that's true.

Lackey: In the case of *Blonde*, the drug culture that we see in Hollywood is now painfully more apparent with so many young people dying.

Oates: That's right.

Lackey: And what is very useful in your novel is that you give us a way of understanding the dysfunctional psychology at work within this culture.

Oates: Yes.

Lackey: Did you feel yourself trying to lay out the nature of that dysfunctional psychology?

Oates: Oh yes. I wrote another novel about this idea, which is called *My Sister, My Love*. It is based on the JonBenét Ramsey case. I particularly look at the use of drugs given to children, like child athletes, and in this case a little girl figure skater. But there I changed the name and the family is different. But many things are different. My focus was on the exploitation of a child in *real* life and also in the novel.

Lackey: In *Blonde* you include a character that you refer to as "the Sharpshooter" and this character is very fascinating but also eerie. How does this character function? Is it an allegorical figure? And your narrator also makes the comment that this character does not know how to interpret. It's not that the character puts up false interpretations but that the character just doesn't know how to interpret.

Oates: One interpretation might be seeing the novel as a postmodernist, posthumous movie about Norma Jeane's life and Norma Jeane is watching her own movie and narrating it and she's going to die. So she invents this character the Sharpshooter who's going to come kill her at the same time that she's going to kill herself. It could be a postmodernist, posthumous movie that she's telling herself, and that she's created the Sharpshooter. Some people thought, and still think, that Marilyn Monroe had been killed, so this is a way of giving a dramatic form to that interpretation.

Lackey: The Kennedy family takes a big hit in your fiction as in *Black Water* as well as *Blonde*. Why is this?

Oates: I see them more as allegorical figures. I refer to JFK as The President. He did use Marilyn Monroe. The President and the Blonde Actress are sort of these figures like big puppets. She was so addicted to drugs at that point and he was such an exploiter of women. I'm sure he was a very nice person to his family and could be very wonderful to his friends, but he exploited people. He's exploiting Marilyn Monroe. The meeting between them is like a cartoon situation. At that point in her life, she left behind her own real life. When she was Norma Jeane, when she had real feelings toward her foster mother, that is one of the tenderer relationships that she has. And there is one of her foster mothers and she is so sorry to leave the woman. But she goes into this world where she's known as the Blonde Actress and people appropriate her, like the athlete Joe DiMaggio, who has seen her picture in the paper and wants to meet her. It's that sort of thing. But actually Joe DiMaggio is ultimately very nice to her. He's the one who paid for her funeral. That's not in the novel because you don't know that until after she dies. Her corpse was in the Los Angeles county morgue for a while because nobody had enough money to pay for a funeral director. But Joe DiMaggio came along and he paid for it and the funeral. He was so angry when all these Hollywood producers and all this scum of Hollywood came to her funeral. He didn't want them to come because he felt that they had killed her. All that I would have liked to have put in the novel, but I couldn't because it's after her death and that was sort of narrated by her.

Lackey: One last question. Of the biographical novels that have been written, can you tell me which ones you think are the best and why?

Oates: I like *Cloudsplitter*. Russell's my good friend.

Lackey: That's an extraordinary one.

Oates: Yes, it's very eloquent. The novels that mean the most to literary people are works of language and the biographical-historical elements are part of that. But it is more about the speech and language. I think that's why people write. If I'm writing a story it's because I'm basically trying to give voice to something that hasn't been said before. So that's why we like it. And Ralph Ellison's *Invisible Man* has wonderful language, this funny, unexpected sense of humor. Styron's *Nat Turner* I haven't read in so long but

I would sort of wonder whether it would hold up. People say that the voice of Nat Turner is not very good.

Lackey: A lot of people say that it's just not a believable novel.

Oates: That's what people say, yes. What about Norman Mailer's *Executioner's Song*?

Lackey: That is an interesting choice. That novel won the Pulitzer Prize for fiction, but there was some debate among the members whether it was actually a novel.

Oates: Sometimes when prizes are given by committees, there are connections between the people who win or lose and the jurors. That maybe people don't know about. When I was doing my research into Robert Frost, I found that he won three Pulitzer prizes. The problem is that his very best friend was on the Pulitzer committee. And I wouldn't be surprised if the same thing were true with Norman Mailer and other people who win and people who *don't* win like Stephen Jay Gould. I was on the Pulitzer committee, and Gould was our unanimous choice. But he didn't win. Gould was disliked for political reasons: He was an outspoken Marxist, and his theory of "punctuated evolution" was not the prevailing theory of evolution in some quarters. There could have been no doubt that Gould's book—*Wonderful Life*—deserved the Pulitzer Prize in non-fiction that year, but the Columbia committee, that votes upon the jurors' suggestions, must have been persuaded by someone on the committee who was anti-Gould. No doubt, the bias against Gould's politics was masked as some sort of "aesthetic" disagreement. It is a rare juror who speaks openly and honestly in such circumstances. A much lesser book was given the Pulitzer Prize. So one can look around for theories of what Gould was doing in intellectual theories, but it was really personal animosities that led to the decision. Somebody else got the Pulitzer Prize but there was no reason for that other person to win except that he *wasn't* Gould. So if anyone's trying to draw a conclusion from the person who won in that year it's going to be wrong because there's no conclusion to be drawn. It was a personal dislike of Gould. And that may be the case with fiction, poetry or drama. There are subterranean connections between people and somebody gets a prize for that reason. I'm on many committees, and I certainly see that. It's not that you necessarily give a prize to your best friend, but if you have an enemy, you just don't give it to that person. All these things are sort of shifting but I think maybe generally speaking there's some general theory to be drawn from all this.

Lackey: With regard to the biographical novel, it seems that people lack a vocabulary for articulating what this type of fiction is doing. For instance, a number of people have odd notions about the biographical novel. They say that many contemporary writers are merely summarizing and paraphrasing biographies and then calling their work fiction. They think that biographical novels require less in the way of creativity than what they would call "true fiction."

Oates: It is not so different from what I was saying about the twentieth-century portrait painters. It's much more subjective, a feeling that you're getting an original interior truth that just wasn't displayed before.

PART FIVE

Essays

28

Georg Lukács

"The Biographical Form and Its 'Problematics'" from *The Historical Novel* (1937)

The important modern historical novels show a clear tendency towards *biography*. The direct link between the two in many cases is most probably the contemporary fashion of historical-biographical *belles lettres*. But in the really important cases this is barely more than a formal link. The popularity of the biographical form in the present-day historical novel is due rather to the fact that its most important exponents wish to confront the present with great model figures of humanist ideals as examples, as resuscitated forerunners of the great struggles of today.

And given the conception, which we have analyzed, of the relations between historical protagonists and the people, it is inevitable that biography should appear as the specific form of the modern historical novel. If the great figure of the past is really the sole embodier of the great historical idea, if the historical novel is interested in the prehistory of the ideas which are being fought out today, then writers may understandably see the real historical genesis of these ideas and therewith of present-day problems in the development of the historical personalities who have championed and embodied these ideas in the past. Some overhasty and over-"sensitive" critics have a habit of creating a new aesthetic as soon as any new kind of writing appears. Thus any new manifestation of literature is immediately and uncritically raised into a criterion which is binding on literature in general. We have experienced this repeatedly from naturalism to expressionism, and now we fortunately possess a whole museum of such abortive aesthetic criteria. Yet the facts show that as a rule the few works which have survived the literary fashions of our time have done so *in spite of* such criteria. This should counsel caution and a look at mankind's artistic experiences during the past few thousand years. And there is every reason for such caution in regard to the present fashion of biography. The task of aesthetics and criticism in the case of a widespread practice like the use of the biographical form in the historical novel should simply be that of an impartial examination of the possibilities and limits of the form. Any artistic canonization of present-day practice is of no use either to theory or practice. If we derive the aesthetic criteria of a particular trend simply from the works belonging to this trend, then they have ceased to be criteria. And an aesthetic which is afraid to approach the question of criteria, of the rightness of a particular trend or genre, has abdicated from aesthetics.

Let us therefore look at literary practice rather more broadly and examine how the great writers of the past went about the problem of biography, how far they used a biographic method or presentation in their art. Goethe's practice is perhaps the most instructive here. In particular, because Goethe portrayed certain problems of his own life both as straight biography and as material for his novels. *Dichtung und Wahrheit* (*Poetry and Truth*) contains the material of both *Werthers Leiden* (*Sorrows of Werther*) and *Wilhelm Meisters Lehrjahre* (*Wilhelm Meister's Apprenticeship*). Now if one follows through these works from their inception, one sees that they verge away from the biographical. Since we now have the first version of *Wilhelm Meister*, we can see exactly how much more autobiographical it is than the final version.

The reasons for this trend away from the biographical are easy to see. The most conscious and planned life is full of accidents which cannot be portrayed. Certain features occur in a way that cannot be sensuously embodied. To give them the same significance as in reality, one would have to invent a whole new set of circumstances. The external appearance of dramatic collisions does not always correspond with their inner significance; sometimes collisions of slight significance in themselves lead to tragic consequences, sometimes the tragedy which would be the only adequate expression of a collision does not take place in life at all, the collision is blunted and leads to consequences which are only biographically, theoretically or creatively important, but not to a viable drama. The people, with whom the evolving hero of an autobiography has to do, come and go by chance, the outward history of the relations of the people to one another never corresponds really to their inner, dramatic or epic, significance. For this reason Hegel said with full justice of the epic constructed round biography: "In biography the individual admittedly remains one and the same, but the events in which he is involved can happen quite independently and retain the subject only as their quite external and accidental point of connection."

If one compares *Werther* with the Lotte Buff episode in the autobiography, one can see clearly what Goethe has added in the novel, where as a writer he has left the autobiographical behind. In *Werther* he has introduced the social element into the conflict and lifted the love collision onto a tragic plane. In a word, everything which gives *Werther* its lightning effect and eternal freshness is biographically untrue. No biographical account of the Lotte Buff episode could have remotely attained to the poetic greatness of *Werther*; for the elements of this poetry lay in Goethe's experience of this episode, but not in the episode itself as it actually occurred. But even then these were only elements and germs in Goethe's experience. It still required an enormous amount of poetic invention, the supplementing, extending and deepening work of generalization, before the story and the characters of *Werther* could take shape in the form we know them today.

This is the universal position of great writers in regard to reality in general and hence to the reality of their own lives, to their own biography. Since reality as a whole is always richer and more varied than even the richest work of art, no detail, episode, etc., however exactly copied, however biographically authentic, however factual, can possibly compete with reality. If one wishes to re-create the richness of reality, the whole context of life must be refashioned, one's composition must take on an entirely new structure. If biographically authentic details, episodes, etc., can be used here, just as they are, then this will be a particularly fortunate accident. Although even in these cases they cannot be left quite as they are, for their environment, what came before and after them, will have been decisively altered, and these alterations will transform the artistic quality of the biographical episode.

These are well-known facts, observable in the practice of the most important writers. However, they provide only the general premises of the problem which specially interests us here: namely the question of whether and in what way a biographical portrayal of *great men* in history is possible. Goethe portrays many things in *Wilhelm Meister* which he recounts autobiographically later on in *Dichtung und Wahrheit*. He makes of Wilhelm Meister a representative of those tendencies in life which were decisive for his youth and for his development to manhood, a representative of those trends among the best section of bourgeois youth at the turn of the eighteenth century which led to a new flowering of humanism. As such a figure Wilhelm Meister bears many personal traits of Goethe himself and his development contains innumerable episodes from the life of his creator. But apart from those basic alterations, the nature of which we have just analyzed in the case of *Werther,* Goethe undertakes one further correction of his hero's character: he deprives him of Goethean *genius*. Gottfried Keller does the same in his even more pronouncedly autobiographical novel *Der Grüne Heinrich* (*Green Henry*). Why? Because both great narrative artists—Goethe and Keller—clearly saw that a biographical portrayal of genius, a biographical account of the development of a man of genius and his accomplishments, conflicts with the means of expression peculiar to epic art.

One would have to portray the growth of the genius *genetically,* that is, by presenting, recounting, describing, etc., facts and episodes from his life, and this always involves some kind of "short circuit", as we shall soon show in detail. For the circumstances of life in which a quality of genius manifests itself, in which genius is kindled, and in which the achievements of genius make their first appearance (from a biographical-psychological standpoint) in fact do no more than provide a particular occasion against which such qualities or achievements may be revealed. And the connection between occasion and achievement cannot do other than appear accidental even in the best portrayal; the objective character of the accidental connection will not be dispelled by literary creation. The better the writer's work, that is, the more truthfully he portrays the particular occasion on the basis of scrupulously checked and selected material from the given life, the more noticeable and striking will its occasional and objectively accidental character appear.

If we deny the practicability of portraying genius by the biographical-psychological, genetic method we are certainly not denying that genius can be genetically explained, nor do we wish to surround genius with a mystery of inexplicability. On the contrary. We are denying that this kind of portrayal is possible because we know how very much the man of genius is bound up with the entire economic-social, political and cultural life of his time, with the struggle of the great movements, the class struggles, the development of the material and cultural heritage of his time, etc., and that he proves his genius by the originality with which he extends, concentrates and generalizes these most important tendencies in the life of an epoch.

But it is precisely *this* connection which cannot be made *immediately* evident in the biographical facts and episodes with which the *artistic* biographer or autobiographer has to work as a *creator* of character. These connections can only be brought to light on the basis of a broad, deep and very generalized *analysis* of an epoch. Not only must they be *investigated* by scientific means, it is *only* by scientific means that they can be adequately presented. If one looks at Goethe's *Dichtung und Wahrheit* in the light of these connections, then one realizes that every time Goethe wishes to clarify some synthesis between himself and the big movements of his time during certain stages of his development he forsook the means of narrative. In every such case Goethe uses scientific, historical means of the highest intellectual and artistic kind.

This scientific approach, as a method, needs to be quite specially underlined in our own day. For it has become increasingly the fashion to look down upon the scientific method with a kind of snobbish relativism, while sanctioning acknowledged scientific achievements by knighting them with the title of "art". Naturally the important works of historical science have often used artistic means, too. And this does not mean simply good and expressive prose, it means subtle description, plastic representation, forceful irony, satire, etc. None of this will undermine the basic character of scientific method, which is to disclose connections in accordance with the objective laws governing them. The destinies of individual persons, *experienced as individual destinies, cannot* provide a means for clarifying objective connections and laws. To create a really good historical portrait of an important figure one needs to show his personal singularity, his intellectual physiognomy, the singularity of his method, the objective significance of this method in the context of the most important movements which lead from past to future, at whose crossroads he stands and to whose development he has contributed in an original way—all of which must be shown in a very generalized and, because generalized, scientifically concrete, form using the correct scientific means.

This will produce a very high level of writing, but it will not be art. One of the comical aspects of our time is that the only praise one can find for works like Hegel's *Phenomenology of the Spirit* and Marx's *Eighteenth Brumaire* is to place them in the same category as Arthur Schnitzler or James Joyce. This is not only more-than-questionable praise for scientific achievements—it is also a sign of the diminishing understanding for the real principles of art.

We shall take a characteristic example to illustrate the tasks facing a scientific biography of a man of genius. One of the most important turning-points in the history of knowledge was Marx's description of the sole commodity which the wage laborer could sell as "labour power" instead of "labour". For any real biographer of Marx a central task would be to uncover the path which led to this brilliant insight which revolutionized economics. He would have to show how far pre-Marxist economics had got in this question, what contradictions it had become entangled in as a result of the unclearness of the category "labour" and the social reasons for these limitations. At the same time he would have to show against biographical material from Marx's life and career how this problem developed until it reached its conscious and clear formulation, how long Marx still used the old concept "labour" during his youth not only in word, but also in meaning, where he begins to attribute a new, enriched and precise meaning to the old term until the path is completely laid bare. However, even given that one knew the precise moment at which Marx reached this formulation, the representation of this moment could be of no more than episodic importance. For the discovery itself was a necessity of the class struggle between proletariat and bourgeoisie, a struggle which required the disclosure of the true character of capitalist economy—and which thereby paved the way for an adequate understanding of all forms of economy. From the standpoint of this objective necessity it is a matter of pure accident whether Marx came to his formulation in a conversation with Engels, on his own walking up and down his study or elsewhere.

Every biography of an important person will contain an abundance of such problems. And the biographical *belles lettres* of today, instead of showing the large social connections and their reflection in science and art, revel in pseudo-artistic, psychologically "deepened" portrayals of individual "occasions". Against this we must stress with all vigor the necessity of presenting the large objective connections. We must say there is no path which leads from Schiller's rotten apples to *Wallenstein* or from Balzac's black coffee, bust of Napoleon, monk's garb and walking-stick to the *Comédie Humaine,* etc.

But even the "deepest" psychological analyses of the various loves and friendships of great men do not really help us to understand their works any better. On the contrary, as far as really important human relations are concerned, these are much better explained by the large objective connections than by mere biographical psychology. The friendship of Marx and Engels was forged by the objective necessities of the revolutionary working-class movement. It was the complete devotion of both to the emancipation of the proletariat, their genius in founding and extending revolutionary theory, in leading the revolutionary working-class movement, which gave their friendship that human depth and inseparable unity which so moves us. The more intimately we know these objective connections and their material content, the more deeply can we comprehend the human character of the friendship between Marx and Engels. For only by understanding these connections can we really understand the personal part which each played in their common life's work and the so happily complementary character of their collaboration. The personal facts of their lives which have been transmitted to us provide an enormously important supplement to these connections. But it would be an illusion to think that one could start from these individual facts of life and produce an immediate picture of the large connections.

We repeat: the facts of a great man's life tell us at best the particular occasion on which something great was achieved, but they never give us the real context, the real chain of causation as a result of which this great accomplishment played its part in history. One could object to this that the historical novelist, too, can portray no more than the particular occasion against which his heroes perform their deeds. But this objection overlooks the difference in the relation of chance to necessity in the two cases. It is a characteristic of human life that the occasions which produce the most important feelings, experiences or deeds are accidental. If, however, the real character of the given literary figure is properly revealed in his deed, then although the occasion of the deed remains accidental it occupies precisely the position which would be required of it in reality. For it is part of life that necessity asserts itself through accidents of this kind.

Yet the true writer will keep the right proportions even in this case. That is, before introducing the occasion he will clarify the social forces encompassing his characters as a whole and at the same time indicate the psychological qualities of the particular character in question. The connection between the two will then be translated by the occasion into the deed. Thus the occasion will occupy a position in the given context of life appropriate to its corresponding position in objective reality; at the same time necessity, as is natural in literature, will make its appearance more clearly and deliberately than normally happens in life.

It is different with an historical achievement, the nature of which is to take mankind a step forward in a certain field. This is what gives every great historical achievement an objective and necessary character. Its essential quality is the fact that it accords with objective reality more richly and profoundly than previous such steps forward. Its significance therefore lies in this objective content and, as we have shown, can only be understood if the objective connections surrounding it are disclosed. Faced with these connections the immediate occasion loses all value. Whether we are acquainted with it or not has no effect, either in a positive or negative way, upon our knowledge of the real connection. Whereas with actions in the normal course of life it is quite indispensable to know the occasion in its right combination of chance and necessity in order to understand the deed.

Here we see the principal reason why the achievements of the great men of history *as achievements*, as works, lie beyond the reach of literature. Goethe once said of the poet's task:

> "Und wenn der Mensch in seiner Qual verstummt,
> Gab mir ein Gott zu sagen, wie ich leide."
> (And when man in his agony is dumb,
> God gave me a voice to say how I suffer.)

Naturally, it is not just a question of suffering if we are to define the mission of poetry. Nevertheless, Goethe describes its main task rightly—a task which only it can fulfill: it imparts to all manifestations of life a more distinct, more articulated, more understandable and essentially truer voice, closer to the essence of life, than these manifestations possess in life itself. It is precisely for this reason that the great achievement or work lies beyond the reach of literature. The writer cannot clarify it any further. He can show how it is connected with life and the effect it has on life, but he cannot portray the work itself. An important literary task might be to show how people at the time of the Church persecutions went bravely to the scaffold, bravely endured the tortures of the Inquisition for the truth of the newly arisen sciences, for the truth of the legitimacy of the godless universe; it would also be an important literary task to show the human, intellectual and moral foundations of such behavior, and in such a portrayal the world-historical significance of the scientific achievements of Copernicus, Kepler and Galileo would shine forth in a hitherto undreamt-of light. But even the greatest writer (and most learned in science) could add nothing to Galileo's law of falling bodies. He could only insert it into his work.

For this reason the great writers of the past, who knew the possibilities and limits of literature, always portrayed the achievements of great individuals *by their effects*. In the same way all great epic writers of the past always portrayed beauty by its effects—from Homer's Helen of Troy to Tolstoy's Anna Karenina—and never by direct description. Goethe once said of the conquest of Troy that it was unportrayable, "as a moment of fulfillment in a great destiny" it was "neither epic nor tragic, and in a true epic treatment" could "only be seen in the distance either from in front or behind". The achievements of great historical individuals also have this character of fulfillment.

It is a modern prejudice to suppose that the historical authenticity of a fact will guarantee its poetical effectiveness. This prejudice is strengthened when it is a case of the utterances and facts in the lives of men who are justly loved and revered by the masses. It is quite understandable that the liberated mass of workers in the Soviet Union should wish for lively, comprehensible and moving accounts of the lives of their loved and revered leaders Marx and Engels, Lenin and Stalin. These wishes can and must be satisfied. They can only be satisfied, however, by *scientific* biographies on a high literary level, intellectually thorough and at the same time popular. For it is only in the large objective connections, scientifically presented, that the features for which these men are loved and revered will emerge humanly as well. No assemblage of authentic documents can possibly satisfy these wishes, just wishes, of the masses.

If a writer, for instance, were to portray Marx, what would be the result? Marx would walk diagonally up and down his room, as we know from Lafargue's reminiscences, he would smoke cigars, his desk would be littered with books and manuscripts (see again Lafargue, Liebknecht, etc.); this would all be historically true, but would it bring us any nearer to Marx's great personality? Despite the authenticity of all the individual features this study could be that of any mediocre scholar or bad politician. Admittedly the writer would let Marx *speak* as well. And again we should get an authentic text—quotations, say, from the letters to Kugelmann. The ideas pronounced would, of course, be true, significant and important, but their origin in the given conversation, their character as intellectual manifestations of Marx's life could *not* appear convincing. In their original context they are both more powerful in themselves as well as more humanly immediate than they could possibly be in any such literary adaptation.

Now let us take a contrary example. Lenin's *State and Revolution* includes a large number of quotations from Marx, but obviously there is nothing remotely "literary" in the modern sense about Lenin's straightforward manner of presentation. Nevertheless, the reader of this magnificent work gets a powerful impression of the political and intellectual personality of

Marx. Why? Because Lenin sums up the major viewpoints of the European revolutions of the nineteenth century in a theoretically brilliant, lucidly outlined and popular way and this enables us to cast a glance, as it were, into the intellectual workshop of the founder of scientific socialism. We see how the great revolutionary events fructify his thinking on the central questions of revolution, how his bold and always correct generalizations bring to light the still hidden tendencies of historical development, how his insight into reality races prophetically ahead of historical development. Such presentations, but only such, bring out the human significance of Marx's personality which is not to be separated from his greatness as a thinker and politician. It is undoubtedly a major scientific and literary task to write biographies of the great leaders of the proletarian struggle of emancipation which really correspond to these demands, just demands, of the masses. But they can never be replaced by biographical *belles lettres,* by the insertion of authentic biographical facts into novels. Franz Mehring's biography of Marx contains many ideological errors and limitations. Nevertheless, it allows one to get to know Marx's human personality much more clearly and adequately than any belletrist treatment would.

Let us illustrate this by a further example which we quoted in the first section of this study—the fine passage from Lenin's *Will the Bolsheviks Retain State Power?* The example of the effect of a worker's remarks as to the better bread following the July rising of 1917 is not only a very convincing argument in Lenin's chain of thought, it also throws an unusually brilliant light into the workshop of his mind, bringing the leader of the Great October very near to us in a human and personal way. We suddenly see by this example how sensitively Lenin observed the apparently most insignificant facts in the lives of the working people and with what lightning speed and accuracy he drew far-reaching, generalizing conclusions from these experiences. But let us not forget that the powerful effect of this passage is due to the fact that Lenin had built it into the scientifically unbreakable chain of his argument. True, the passage would be just as correct and profound without the remarks preceding and following it, but it could not have this surprising, stirring and truly human impact.

This episode in Lenin has a very rounded effect. But were a writer tempted to reproduce it in a belletrist manner what would we have? A description of the room, an atmosphere of work; the table would be laid, the wife would bring in the bread, the man make his remarks about its good quality in connection with the July rising—and then "suddenly", like a pistol shot, Lenin's profound and correct reflections would follow. What in the context of the original pamphlet was humanly moving and intellectually inspiring would now have become a banal piece of montage. Can the genius, then, the great man of history, be portrayed artistically at all?[1] To this question we gave a clear and positive answer in the first two chapters of this work. We showed that the "world-historical individual" has his organic place in the novel as a minor figure and in tragedy as the chief figure. Our present arguments as to the impossibility of epicbiographic portrayal do not contradict this, but indeed confirm it from a different, negative angle. For why was this portrayal possible in the classics of the historical novel and historical drama? The reason was that they portrayed the great men upon the basis of their concrete historical mission, upon the basis of the totality of the objective social-historical determinants. The writers of the classical period, as a result of their broad and deep social experiences, saw the task of the great man in history clearly (however wrong they may have been at times in their theoretical pronouncements on this problem). From these experiences the classics of historical drama portrayed great, crisis-filled collisions of human history, and the "world-historical individual" appeared in their works as a great figure because in his own person he sensuously embodied the colliding social forces. From these experiences the classic of the historical novel portrayed a broad and rich picture of popular life and presented the "world-historical individual" as the supreme concentration and embodiment of the important tendencies of an important transition in popular life. The determination and genesis of the "world-historical individual" arises in the classics of the historical novel upon the basis of the unfolding and broadening of these tendencies. We experience in these novels the objective path of social-historical development which at a certain point causes Kutuzov or Pugachov, Cromwell or Mary Stuart to become those centers of force in which the social forces of a crisis are united. (And it should be noted that a "world-historical individual" by no means needs to be a genius).

Only in this way can the new, the qualitatively special that the "world-historical individual" represents be given expression. We experience in the most varied forms the movement of popular forces in a certain direction, we experience their inability to grasp adequately the content of this direction, their weakness in fulfilling the deeds required to transform this direction into a reality. When then the "world-historical individual" appears and—in accordance with the concrete historical circumstances and his own personal conditioning—finds an answer to this question and translates it into action, then and only then does the genesis of what is historically new become evident for us and so, simultaneously, does the role of the important man within this development.

In this kind of portrayal the occasion which gives expression in words and deeds to what is new receives a position which corresponds to its real character. Its accidentality is not eliminated. But the accidentality of the occasion here is no more than the irreducible accidentality of any individual event in human life: this individual event, however, exists in organic-historical connection with that infinite chain of individual events which in themselves are similarly accidental and in and through whose totality historical necessity always asserts itself. The necessity itself is produced by the complex inner social-historical unity of the popular movements over and above the immediate and psychological connections. The individual occasions which serve to portray the different stages at which historical necessity reveals itself need not be directly linked with one another. It is only necessary that the action, in its complex and intricate paths, should make the inner dialectics of this development clear to us.

It is easy to see what ideological inhibitions work against this kind of portrayal in modern writers. The development of capitalism inevitably alienates writers from popular life, they find it more and more difficult to see into the inner active forces of capitalist society, and as a result the same tendency comes to dominate their outlook as dominates the general philosophic development of the imperialist epoch. This tendency may be briefly stated: of all the factors which determine the complex context of life only the immediate causal connection between two related spatial-temporal phenomena is recognized.

Should there be dissatisfaction with the cognitive value of this conception it does not in general lead on to any deeper philosophical enquiry, to the discovery of the real and more complex connections where even causality, though more deeply conceived, appears as only one important category among many others. It leads rather to a doubting of the immediate causal connection itself (Machism) and, as a direct consequence of this, to a more or less mystical conception of the totality of society and of its total development. The literary greatness of the classics of the historical novel, who philosophically often stood at a relatively unadvanced level, lay in the fact that they were sufficiently intimate and well-experienced with popular life to be able to portray the real connections in life itself which went beyond immediate causality. In contrast to this the alienation which modern writers feel from popular life leads them to over-rate immediate causation, which they generally and inevitably see in terms of biographical-psychological causation, and so to acquire their preference for biographical form.

With the classics and their conception the historical figures practically never *develop before our eyes*. The genesis and development of the "world-historical individual" take place *among the people*. The great figures appear, as Balzac showed in the case of Scott, only at such points where the objective necessity of the popular movements imperatively requires their appearance. And then they appear as complete characters, as concentrations, as supreme forms of expression of this development. They are great because they possess this concentrating power, because they are able to answer the problems most deeply affecting the life of the people at this moment. Like the Homeric heroes physically, they are intellectually taller than the people by a head. But their historical greatness lies in the fact that they are taller *only* by a head and that they give the socially-historically possible and necessary concrete answer to the concrete questions of the people. In many cases this greatness is at the same time their limitation. If Vich Ian Vohr or Rob Roy, as well as being intellectually superior to the clan members, did not share with them a common attitude to life and hence certain common limitations, they could not be the leaders they are. Similarly, Cromwell or Burley in Scott are linked not only with the revolutionary tendencies of the Puritans, but also with their limitations. The same is true for Pugachov and the rebellious peasants in Pushkin and for Kutuzov and the patriotic spirit of the Russian army fighting Napoleon in Tolstoy.

It is this objective social context, portrayed in breadth and depth, which makes it possible for the characters to appear before us already complete, yet without producing any impression of lifelessness. Their inner vivacity and development is but an unfolding of the qualities which make them into the representatives they are of the popular movements in question. Their proof or failure in the given historic mission is thus essentially more a development than a genesis in the psychological-biographical sense. In most of the classical historical novels the prehistory of the important figures occurs before the action of the novel itself and is not recounted at all; we simply learn from a few scattered indications what is necessary for our understanding of the nature of their personal relations with the other characters. Where the personal prehistory is given at all, it is told only after we have long become familiar with the character concerned. And then our acquaintance with his past takes on a quite specific character: that of a special story inserted into the main narrative revealing to us the development of an important character with whom we are already familiar. This retrospective account is another of the artistic means used to put the accidental nature of any experience occasioning a deed or event into its rightful place.

May we again take an example from life. Say we have carefully followed the part played in Lenin's career by his fight against the Narodniks; we know precisely the enormous significance for the Bolshevik party of his two-front struggle against the Narodniks and Struvism; we then learn that after the execution of Lenin's dearly loved brother for his part in a plot against the Tsar Lenin immediately realizes the incorrectness of his brother's path, that it cannot lead to the liberation of the Russian people. Now let us reverse the picture. The Ulyanov family, Lenin's admiration for his elder brother, the news of the imprisonment and the execution—and then the theoretical reflections condemning the Narodniks. We do not deny that there is significant material here for a historical, literary portrayal of the great crisis of transition undergone by the Russian working people during the decline of the Narodniks. But if one were to use this material really effectively, one would have to rob the story's hero of Lenin's genius and make of him a still significant, but only typical, representative of this transitional period.

The portrayal of "world-historical individuals" from the standpoint of their success or failure in their historic mission frees them of all the trivial and anecdotic characteristics of biographical portrayal without making them forfeit any of their human aliveness. For, as we have seen, they have become "world-historical individuals" because the deepest personal core of their being, their most passionate personal aspirations are bound up in the closest possible way with the historical task they have had to fulfill, because their most personal passions tend towards precisely this goal. Thus his success or failure tells us in a concentrated manner all we want and need to know about such a personality. And a good writer who treats history not in the abstract, but as the complex destiny of the people, will be able to portray this central task so that it allows very different, very complex personal features in such a character to gain expression. But, as we have already argued from Otto Ludwig's apt pronouncement on Scott—only the humanly and historically *significant* features of his personality. He must not be placed on a pedestal in order to appear as a great figure, for the events themselves will raise him in imposing upon him their task: he appears only in situations which are significant, and hence only needs to unfold his personal qualities freely in order to appear significant.

This anti-biographical method at the same time provides an artistic answer to the question of why it was such a figure—why Cromwell or Burley, why Kutuzov or Pugachov—who took on this leading role. There is an irreducible element of chance involved. In a letter Engels examines the dialectic of necessity and accident which arises in this respect, the ultimate triumph of economic necessity in history: "This is where the so-called great men come in for treatment. That such and such a man and precisely that man arises at that particular time in that given country is of course pure accident. But cut him out and there will be a demand for a substitute, and this substitute will be found, good or bad, but in the long run he will be found. That Napoleon, just that particular Corsican, should have been the military dictator whom the French Republic, exhausted by its own war, had rendered necessary, was an accident; but that, if a Napoleon had been lacking, another would have filled his place, is proved by the fact that the man has always been found as soon as he became necessary: Caesar, Augustus, Cromwell, etc." In his further remarks Engels uses Marx himself and the rise of historical materialism to illustrate this relationship.

Belletrist biography, the biographical form of the historical novel sets itself—whether it likes it or not—the insoluble task of reducing this irreducible element of chance. It is the personality of the man portrayed which is to be the guide to his special calling, his biography will provide the inner, psychological proof of this calling. As a result the character is inevitably exaggerated, made to stand on tiptoe, his historical calling unduly emphasized while the real objective causes and factors of the historical mission are inevitably omitted.

A scientific treatment of history and also a scientific biography of important men assumes the *fact* that this element of chance has already established itself in life. The task of such writing is no longer to "deduce" this fact in some way or another, but simply to explain it by its presuppositions and consequences, and to show the necessity of development expressed in it. For this reason the objective achievement of the given figure must be at the center of a scientific biography. The theoretical significance and historical position of the achievement has to be *scientifically* demonstrated, and only in this way can the personality of the "world-historical individual" also be drawn humanly and brought personally close to the reader.

The classical historical novel also starts from the fact that in crises of popular life in past ages certain important figures have played a leading role—whether this was a profitable or harmful one. And the actual portrayal answers *artistically* why it should have been just this particular individual at this particular time who secured the leading role: he is capable of giving answers to the diverse problems of popular life, while both his shining qualities as well as his human limits and limitations are woven out of the same material as the popular movement itself. Chance is preserved here and there is no attempt to reduce it. The novel simply reflects, profoundly and authentically, how necessity and chance interlock in historical life. Thus chance is reduced here only in the sense in which history itself reduces it. It is reduced by our being shown in human terms how the concrete historical forces of a particular period have become concentrated in the life of this particular individual.

It would be both wrong and unjust to suggest that the important writers of our day do not see the connection between popular movements and historical figures. Heinrich Mann indeed states this connection very correctly in his novel: "'In short', said Agrippa d'Aubigné while they rode amongst the troop, 'you are no more, Prince, than what the people have made of you. And that's the reason why you can stand higher than they: a creation is sometimes higher than its artist. But woe betide if you become a tyrant!'" But unfortunately this correct insight gets no further than an insight even with Heinrich Mann and has no decisive influence upon the action and composition of his novel. Of all present-day writers he is the most deeply aware of this connection and of the need to portray it. Thus he gives Henri IV the national characteristics of the French people and portrays them in a most captivating way. In all the scenes where his hero comes into contact with the people his popular character comes across simply and convincingly. Yet these parts of the novel are the briefest; they contain the least action and are in the nature of reports. This of course is the right of every epic writer. No real narrative would be possible without such summaries of none-too important events and stretches of time. But the characteristic and decisive thing here is what receives detailed narrative treatment and what a brief report. In Heinrich Mann the role of the hero's relation to the people too often falls under the heading of report and even where it is really narrated remains largely episodic. Let us take an example from Henri's early youth. Heinrich Mann sums up briefly: "He slept with his people in the hay if necessary, neither undressed nor washed more often than they, stank and cursed as they did." This is then followed by a full portrayal of his relations with Condé and Coligny, although Mann knows quite well that it is Henri's new relation to the people which is at the basis of his differences with the admiral. We can see here how the biographical conception of the novel becomes an artistic obstacle to any real expression of the hero's popular characteristics. For the people, their joys and sorrows, their own spontaneous and conscious endeavors cannot be portrayed except through direct contact with the person of Henri IV. Thus very little can be shown of the popular movements which tend in his direction, which raise him to the heights he attains or which guarantee his ultimate victory in dangerous situations. Too little to explain his victory in terms of the lives of the French people. The biographical-psychological portrait of the hero, however fine in itself, provides too narrow and frail a basis on which to demonstrate this convincingly.

The position is similar with regard to Feuchtwanger's Josephus Flavius novels. In Josephus's conversations, particularly with Justus of Tiberia, one frequently finds shrewd and correct reflections on the relation between hero and people. However, when Josephus entering revolutionary Jerusalem in a spirit of compromise instead throws in his lot with the leaders of the extreme nationalist wing, Feuchtwanger has set himself a task which the biographical method cannot convincingly solve without defaming the person of Josephus. For let us imagine a classical portrayal of this episode. Through the lives of a number of individuals portrayed in the round we should be given a broad picture of the Jewish people with their different parties and trends. We should be humanly and politically enthralled by their determined national resistance, and Josephus's transformation would be made fully intelligible, personally and politically, by his interaction with this dynamic popular movement. But Feuchtwanger, as we have seen, portrays popular life in a very abstract and general way. When Josephus arrives in Jerusalem it is only his contacts with the conservative temple aristocracy which can be shown to us in concrete human terms. As a result his defection from them smacks unpleasantly of the behavior of a disappointed climber. And we find similar features in other crises of his life.

Those who defend the present biographical form of the historical novel will perhaps contend that it is only details such as these that have been transmitted to us about the lives of these characters and that we know too little about popular figures to be able to portray them as living characters. But the objection is invalid. If we know nothing about the popular life of a period, then we may say of it what Sainte-Beuve said of Flaubert's *Salammbô*—that it cannot be made to live for us artistically. But the great task of the historical novel is to *invent* popular figures to represent the people and their predominant trends.

It is natural that bourgeois historiography in general as a discipline of the ruling classes, should have consciously neglected, omitted or even slanderously distorted these factors of popular life. Here is where the historical novel, as a powerful artistic weapon in defense of human progress, has a major task to perform, to restore these real driving forces of human history as they were in reality, to recall them to life on behalf of the present. The historical novel of the anti-Fascist humanists sets itself the same task in intention. And it defends the principles of human progress against the slanders and distortions of imperialism as well as the attempts at total annihilation on the part of Fascism.

But at the present the task is conceived too abstractly. Given the conditions in which they live, it is natural for the leading intellectuals of the imperialist period to believe that the real bearers of humanist ideals are the isolated intelligentsia who take a stand against society. But however natural and socially explicable this belief, it is nevertheless burdened with liberal traditions of alienation from the people and its attendant distortions. The major charge undergone in recent years by the writers we are studying has taken them a long way from these traditions—Heinrich Mann most of all. In the intellectual problems posed in their historical novels this change is very clearly visible—again most clearly of all in Heinrich Mann. But the biographical method takes them back to the old conception of progress and humanism and prevents the full and adequate expression of their new revolutionary-democratic outlook.

The attitude behind the biographical form is one which views human progress exclusively or predominantly in ideal terms and sees its bearers as the more or less isolated great men of history. This raises the insoluble problem of how to connect in a direct way a detailed presentation of a character's private life with a convincing portrayal of the genesis of great, indeed "timelessly" magnified, ideas. Since these are important writers with whom we are dealing no detailed analysis is required to show that the personal life very often receives authentic and subtle portrayal. In this respect both Bruno Frank's *Cervantes* and Lion Feuchtwanger's novels attain to a not inconsiderable degree of human truth and psychological depth.

Here once again we must stress the quite special significance of Heinrich Mann. Henri IV much more than the characters of Mann's contemporaries is a concrete person, the son of his country and his age. He is also, as we have been shown, much more closely involved with the popular life of his time. As a result of this more pronounced and more vital popular element Heinrich Mann produces a wonderfully fine figure: Henri IV is full of personal charm, honesty, courage, intelligence, cunning; he is able to talk to every person in his own language; shows a broad vision, theoretically and politically, human tolerance and a strong will in carrying out his great designs. And the way the light-minded and easy-going youth is educated by the hard facts of life into this representative of the best and most popular traits of the French people is full of true poetic beauty. Heinrich Mann, moreover, is able to portray this development with all the psychological complexity of real life; it follows no didactic and pedantic straight line. Its way is intricate, full of doubt, despair and error. All this constitutes a peak of achievement in contemporary literature. And what must be specially emphasized is that Heinrich Mann has succeeded here in creating a really *positive* and vital figure who concentrates the best human qualities of those fighters who for centuries have struggled to extend human culture in the teeth of reaction and who today are defending this culture against Fascist barbarism.

But Heinrich Mann's novel is not simply an enchanting portrait. It sets itself the task of presenting a great historic turning-point in the history of the French people. This turning-point is embodied in Henri IV's conversion to Catholicism and the period of religious tolerance which succeeded the generations of civil war between Huguenots and Catholics and to which France owed its great resurgence right up to the age of Louis XIV. This turning-point is expressed much more weakly in Heinrich Mann than the personality of Henri IV himself. What is new and significant about Henri IV historically is that he ceases to be the mere leader of a party, i.e., the Huguenots, and with the help not only of the Huguenots but also of the other progressive elements in the country is able to consolidate national unity by means of religious tolerance. This great turning-point, however, is all too brief in Mann's portrayal. Because of the whole conception of the novel it is presented merely in a biographical-psychological manner—in the form of the hero's lonely reflections.

Admittedly it is biographically prepared. After the poisoning of his mother Henri meets Coligny in secret. The admiral says of Paris: ". . . 'They hate us because they hate religion.' And perhaps because you have plundered them too often, added Henri to himself, recalling the wretched inn . . . 'It should never have been allowed to come to this,' he said, 'we are all Frenchmen.' Coligny answered: 'But some have earned themselves heaven and others damnation. That must remain fixed—as truly as the Queen, your mother, lived and died in this belief.' The son of Queen Jeanne bowed his forehead. There was no reply once his mother's great companion-in-arms had brought her into the field. Both of them, the old man and the dead woman, stood together against him, they were contemporaries and shared the same unshakeable firmness in their opinions."

The deep difference between Henri and Coligny comes out very strongly here, especially as in the previous inn scene Heinrich Mann has given Henri a living picture of the Parisians' hatred. But here again this opposition escapes into the realm of lonely reflection and remains a dumb mental accompaniment to Henri's subsequent experiences at court which are recounted very extensively and vividly. And even after his flight from court, when he engages in open struggle, his opposition remains the lonely reflections of an isolated genius who—by a miracle of history—becomes the leader of his people. "He was to be leader of the Protestants: now another has taken his place, his cousin Condé, who was there before. He is zealous and rash, does not see beyond the war of the parties. You are putting your trust in a simpleton, good people of religion! He still lives in the times of the admiral. Does not realize that to divide up the kingdom for the sake of religion is tantamount to tearing it apart for one's own advantage like a will-o-the-wisp."

The times of Admiral Coligny are past: this is the great historical truth which Heinrich Mann has set himself to portray. For it is only against this change of the times that the thoughts of Henri IV can become more than the ponderings of a lonely eccentric, can assert themselves triumphantly in the civil wars and act as a guide to the history of France during a major period of resurgence. The secret of his victory then, as with every important historical figure, is his ability to understand the pressures of popular life in favor of some historic change, to give consciousness to these pressures and translate them into deeds.

In Heinrich Mann, however, this change remains a biographical fact in the life of Henri IV. For this reason his victory appears much less convincing than his psychological development and education. We think it unnecessary to repeat at length the reason for this weakness, namely that the biographical-psychological path to Henri's understanding is much too narrow a one. It is the understanding of a lonely great man, and however deep and correct, Henri IV cannot overcome all resistance in his own and the enemy's camp simply by understanding. This cannot appear convincing.

The victory of Henri IV's ideas could only appear convincing if we knew something about the varied trends in French popular life through the lives of individual characters travelling with greater or less consciousness, greater or less determination in the same direction; and if we experienced Henri IV as the leader of these trends. That is, if the difference between Coligny's period and Henri de Navarre's could be made clear to us in artistic terms as the difference between two phases in national life. This does not and cannot happen given the biographical form, despite Mann's fine psychological analysis of the spontaneous differences of temperament between Henri and his mother, between Henri and the Admiral.

Nevertheless this tendency of French development is visible even in its reflection among the ruling circles. However, certain abstract-humanist prejudices hinder Mann from seeing it. He does not see that the introduction of religious tolerance by Henri IV is only a step along the path to the then progressive establishment of absolute monarchy in France, that Henri's conquest of Coligny's period was a stage in the struggle between absolute monarchy and feudalism. This struggle in France proceeds in a very complicated, very uneven manner. It is certain that Catherine de Medici encountered similar problems and made similar endeavors, that she objectively was in some respects a forerunner of Henri IV and his endeavors. We are thinking of the period in which, with the help of the great bourgeois Chancellor L'Hospital, she used the Huguenots to break up the predominance of the Guises; in which supported by L'Hospital and the party of "politicians", she endeavored to exploit the balance between the religious parties in order to strengthen French absolutism. The historical causes which led to the collapse of these plans lie beyond our scope. What is important for us is the fact that the party of "politicians" and the figure of L'Hospital are completely absent in Heinrich Mann. That they should not receive a place in the *biography of the hero* is proper. But it is precisely this which reveals the historical weakness of the biographical form of the novel. Henri's psychological development has to do service for what was an important objective tendency of the time and the real precondition of his ultimate victory. (Obviously, we should expect an historical novel dealing with this period to have less to say about L'Hospital and his friends than about the real popular movements which to their activities gave political expression.)

Another consequence of this narrowing and abstract-making conception is that the so very contradictory and significant figure of Catherine de Medici does not receive her historical due in Heinrich Mann. She is made into a kind of stylized phantastic witch, an embodiment of the evil principle. Here Heinrich Mann's Enlightenment traditions create an obstacle to a really artistic grasp of historical reality. At the same time all this is cause and effect of the biographical form of the historical novel. The form itself is born out of these abstract tendencies, which it then reinforces by simplifying human character. Characters lose their individual concrete and complex dialectics; they become planets revolving round the sun of the biography's hero.

We have stressed the weak sides of this important work because they reflect not so much Heinrich Mann's individual failure, as the limits which the biographical method imposes upon even so outstanding a writer as him; particularly as he has now reached a point in his development where his extraordinary gifts of characterization are emerging in full maturity and strength. We may generalize this weakness of the biographical form of the novel by saying that the personal, the purely psychological and biographical acquire a disproportionate breadth, a false preponderance. As a result the great driving forces of history are neglected. They are presented in all too summary a fashion and relate only biographically to the person at the center. And because of this false distribution of weights what should be the real center of these novels—the given historical transformation—cannot make itself felt sufficiently strongly.

But this false proportion affects the psychological portrayal too. Here too it is less important features and episodes which gain predominance. And even in a work like *Henri* IV which on the whole is narrated in a masterly fashion there remains a certain element of the merely circumstantial. This is to be observed in all novels of a biographical kind. They abound in embellishments, with the effect that the big crises and turning-points, even in the hero's own life, are given too brief, too summary a treatment.

The important writers of today take exception—and rightly so—to an excess of the psychological. They try to translate the psychological development of their heroes into living action. This is a very healthy and progressive tendency. But again the biographical form with its inevitable constriction of action checks the unfolding of this tendency. For, as we have shown in the case of Heinrich Mann, the most important changes in the hero's life take the form of lonely rumination, of lonely discussion with himself. Hence the result of this justified dislike for the psychologism of declining bourgeois literature is a false curtailing of the big moments of crisis.

This failure at precisely the points where writers are trying to portray the most important historical changes in the lives of their heroes is no individual literary weakness and also no accident, but the necessary consequence of the biographical form in the historical novel, or rather of those ideological tendencies which still mislead writers into using this form.

Note

1 Note (written in 1953). To-day someone will perhaps take issue with the preceding remarks by pointing to Thomas Mann's portrayal of Adrian Leverkühn in his Faustus novel. I should be the last to question Mann's unique achievement; his characterization, both individual and typical, of a distinguished musician from the standpoint of his artistic career. (Cf. my studies on Thomas Mann). One must never forget, however, that Leverkühn was portrayed from the standpoint of his (typical) *'problematic'*; not as a genius, but as a *miscarried* great *talent*. Thus the unsurpassably portrayed genesis of this 'problematic' has inwardly nothing to do with the question we have been dealing with here, the biographically depicted genesis of genius. To which must be added in passing that Thomas Mann's biographical method turns out on closer examination to be hardly biographical at all. The genetic connections between the life and work of Adrian Leverkühn proceed only in the very rarest borderline cases from particular occasions in his life; in the main, the genesis of the stages of development, the works and crises of the central figure is Mann's broad and deeply grasped presentation of the social life from which—objectively historically—work, crisis etc. grow. The double time-sequence of the novel also serves to illuminate *these* connections: Zeitblom's reflections while writing Leverkühn's biography throw a genuine historical light on the real historical genesis from the standpoint of the consequences.

29

Carl Bode

"The Buxom Biographies" from *College English* (1955)

Poetry is more philosophical than history.
—ARISTOTLE

In the last ten years several prominent people have been doing their best to make an honest woman out of the biographical novel. One of them, who happens to look rather like Huey Long, is a New Orleans newspaperman. Another is an ex-college teacher with the face of a reasonably friendly faun. Both have made considerable progress but not, it must be admitted, quite enough. The biographical novel still goes its bosomy way, its flimsy clothing tattered and torn in exactly the wrong places. It has its reasons, though. After all, during most of its checkered history it sinned without knowing. It was ensnared by the fact that new and firmer notions of accuracy grew up. Actually the biographical novel deserves more to be pitied than censured.

For us it mainly started with Mason Weems. One of the most engaging liars that his time produced, he published the first edition of his life of Washington in 1800. He had been, he averred, the rector of Mount Vernon parish; and his readers needed no other credentials from him. The book throve like a weed. In the fifth edition appeared the fables of the cherry tree, the cabbage, and the colt. Before his death in 1825 Parson Weems had had the satisfaction of seeing some seventy editions of his supposedly biographical work in print. What he produced was not biography in any sense of the word as it is used today. Instead he created a myth. But it was a myth so suited to the American folk-hero pattern that it remains a model of its curious kind. Of the many ways in which the book satisfies popular

American demands, one example should be enough to illuminate the rest. That has to do with the rewards for being good.

Though it is part of the official American tradition to consider virtue as its own reward, we know that from the arrival of the Massachusetts Bay Puritans to the present, the average American feels unofficially that that is not enough. The renewed vogue of Lloyd Douglas' novels (*Magnificent Obsession* is again on the bestseller list), with their insistence that good deeds will return to the doer sevenfold, is sufficient proof of the continuing vitality of the feeling. To Parson Weems, Washington's career was crammed with incidents showing that when he did his duty, even though it might have been unpleasant at the time, he earned an ample recompense. In point then, because Washington put up, for instance, with the constant fretfulness of his ailing half-brother Lawrence, as was proper, he ultimately inherited nearly half of Lawrence's large estate. To use what Weems asserted were Washington's own words, "There exists . . . an inseparable connection between duty and advantage."

During the first half of the 19th century the imaginative parson was to find many imitators, and the biographical novel, though it would not yet be called that, would flourish. The American people steadily displayed a love for heroic life-stories which revealed itself not only in the printed book but in lyceum lectures and folk art as well. Notwithstanding, it is also true that throughout these same decades a few biographies were being produced which showed an earnest insistence on truth and historical accuracy. Though the wave of German scholarship with its ideal of citing a source for every statement was still to reach this country, we could nevertheless boast of several biographers who wrote the unadorned truth to the best of their ability. A noted and versatile New Englander, the Reverend Jared Sparks, became the most famous one before 1850. His lives of Washington and Franklin received wide though not unanimous acclaim. He was followed in the latter half of the century by an even more outstanding man, our first professional biographer, James Parton. If Sparks dominated the first fifty years, Parton dominated the second. Facile and conscientious at the same time, he not only proved that he could carry on meticulous research but also that he understood ideas and social forces. His three-volume life of Andrew Jackson, published in 1860, remains his masterpiece.

But its faults are likewise easy to see. They serve to show why the public often continued to enjoy a biographical novel more than a biography. Parton's book is too full of documents, too thorough, too complicated. What the average reader wanted in 1860, he had wanted in 1800—and still wants today. He wanted narrative drive, colorful anecdotes, and simple characterization. He wanted every sentence to move. And the reader with tastes above the average wanted still other things which even a Sparks or a Parton could not give. He wanted the motivations of the subject to be explored. Just why did Franklin or Jackson do this or that? He wanted the high points of the life to be described in full, without the disturbing gaps caused by the fact that the writer could not find some of the information he needed so badly. At the same time he wanted the dull parts omitted. And lastly he wanted an orderly, almost a symphonic, structure and a literary richness of style and metaphor to satisfy his esthetic interests.

In other words he wanted what is to be found in biography at its finest. Since he could get it only at rare intervals, he often—especially if he was the average reader—sacrificed his desire for accuracy in favor of some of those other things.

Because he feels the same today, he still buys a biographical novel more readily than he buys an accurate biography. Thus he encourages publishers to grant the biographical novel a permanent place on their annual lists. The book clubs frequently give the galley proof of such a work at least a calculating look, if not more. Several biographical novels have in fact been recent book club choices. Without doubt the biographical novel as a literary type has kept its vigor. Sometimes powerful, and often picturesque, it deserves much more attention than it has received from most critics. To let us understand it clearly, it should be seen in its context; we need to know what its literary landscape is like.

The best biographical novelist we have at present is Irving Stone (the ex-college teacher) and the next best is Harnett Kane (the newspaperman). To appreciate what those men, in particular, are doing, and to assess it accurately, we ought to look at the whole landscape now. In the center, for our purposes, we can put one book by each man, his most notable biographical novel so far. Each, incidentally, became a book club selection. One is Stone's story of Mrs. Abraham Lincoln; the other is Kane's novel about Mrs. Robert E. Lee.

To the left of them—and at some distance—we may locate *Whirlwind in Petticoats* (1947). It is the gamy life of a professional harridan of a hundred years ago named Victoria Claflin Woodhull and her overripe sister Tennessee. Dedicated to "all feminists" by its author, Beril Becker, it makes the most of the opportunities for sensationalism that the sisters' careers afforded. From the point of view of popularity, the selection of the subject proved a shrewd one. Women are interested in the suffering female, and most book buyers are women. (It is worth noting that even the best writers in the field like to write about a woman.) Furthermore, the Claflin sisters were reformers; they wanted to emancipate their sex. That too has a strong appeal for the dishpan and diaper trade. The scenes in the book are vivid; action is laid on with a trowel, and the joys of passion are abundantly discussed and described. From the time Victoria, afire, clung to the first male stranger (on page fifteen) to the time she kissed a giddy Henry Ward Beecher in triumph two hundred pages later, no possibilities are ignored.

If Becker's book represents the worst the biographical novel can do in one direction, two other books represent the best it can do in others. Both became

Pulitzer Prize winners. Robert Penn Warren's *All the King's Men* appeared in 1946. It was a novel, not a biography, yet it revealed the inwardness of Huey Long better than any of the several previous books about him. Warren called him Willie Stark and slightly shuffled the circumstances that surrounded him but that was all. To tell his story and to divine his character, Warren used all the rich devices of literary technique. The thoughtful management of scene, the illuminating dialogue, the characteristic action—all are there. And interwoven with them are searching symbols such as the long journey and the mirrored water. The whole story is driven along by the nervous vigor of Warren's style. The only weakness of the book lies in the hasty, huddled ending. It comes after Willie's assassination, and in its cursory assignment of rewards and punishments to the remaining characters it reminds us of a Victorian three-decker.

The other work, Carl Sandburg's study of Lincoln during the Civil War, won the 1940 Pulitzer Prize for history rather than for biography, because of its epic scope. It is primarily a set of books about a single man but the man was so great that he encompassed his time. To compose this biography Sandburg read everything about Lincoln, no matter how tenuously connected, that he could get. And when his mind had been steeped in Lincoln and Lincoln's life he sat down to write. He wrote without footnotes but there was no need for them. He transcended the outer forms of scholarship.

Because of his achievement as a man of letters Sandburg could add something else to his biography that is rarely found, and that was a felicity of style—a mingling of form and content beautifully suited to his subject. The love of mankind that marks Sandburg's poetry showed in his life of Lincoln. And it allowed him to rise to the heights of a great event in a way few other biographies could. When he described how the people felt about Lincoln's death and how the funeral train traveled its slow way through the country, he created a poem out of fact.

These three, then, Becker, Warren, and Sandburg—each in his own fashion—mark out the bounds of the field which Stone and Kane have occupied.

Harnett Kane started out as a legman for the New Orleans *Item*. His first book, *Louisiana Hayride* (1941), is a journalist's report on the Long regime. It is accurate reporting and nothing else. But after writing it he went on to publish three biographical novels, of which *The Lady of Arlington* (1953), about Mrs. Lee, is the latest and best. He has gradually improved in the thoroughness of his historical research and conveys his information with growing adroitness. He opens his book with a picture of Mrs. Lee shortly before her marriage, and the reader is caught up at once in the career of this long-suffering lady. Family love and family sorrows are movingly portrayed. Illness (Mrs. Lee's agonizing rheumatic fever), frontier hardships, the manifold worries of a soldier's wife, and the losses through death are shown as she encountered them. Kane's style is unobtrusive. His descriptions are accurate, the incidents correct. Most of Mrs. Lee's conversations as well as the things she thought are based on realistic inferences. Dialogue is often a stumbling block to the writer of the biographical novel. He is in constant danger either of making it sound like Sir Walter Scott or else like Sam Goldwyn talking to the Queen of England. Kane, though, manages to write it naturally and appropriately. There is one other test of a good biographical novelist which Kane passes with success. He is able to bring in several of the subsidiary historical characters and make them appear alive.

All in all, Kane can be commended for a book that combines historical research with a novelist's creativity. He does well, well enough to be widely recognized. But everything Kane does, Irving Stone does a bit better.

One would never have known it from Stone's first book, however. True, it was a biographical, or rather an autobiographical, novel but of the sort to make Stone squirm today. He himself is the hero, under the barest of disguises. *Pageant of Youth,* which found a publisher (now out of business) in 1933, is a panoramic college novel with the saxophone-playing Stone, there called Ray Sharpe, at its center. The theme seems to be sex on the campus. The book begins with Ray's freshman year and then takes him, and the people he meets, on through graduation. Several of the girls resemble the Claflin sisters; some of the young men show with gusto that they can be equally uninhibited. The faults in the book vary in gravity. One of the smaller is a sophomoric use of language which may on one hand confuse "ardent" with "arduous" ("he became arduous") and on the other describe a girl as "desperately quiet, with deep connecting rods of maladjustment soldered between her eyes."

A year after *Pageant of Youth, Lust for Life* appeared. Like the first book it had been forced to wait for a publisher but there the resemblance ended. Stone had learned an astonishing amount between the two books. Having once seen the paintings of Vincent Van Gogh, Stone became obsessed with the man and his turbulent art. He could not rest until he had written a life of him. The result was a carefully studied biographical novel striking enough to be reprinted several times and since included in the Modern Library. The writing is still clumsy in spots but the power of the events themselves in Van Gogh's tragic, blundering career holds the reader.

Five more biographical novels followed. They depicted Jack London, Jessie Benton Frémont, Eugene V. Debs, the painter John Noble, and Andrew Jackson's wife Rachel. Despite their variety, each volume showed advances in novelistic technique. The scholarship deepened too, though less steadily. The peak for the present-day biographical novel was approached last spring with the publication of Stone's book on Mary Todd Lincoln and her marriage. Rather flatly titled *Love Is Eternal* (from the inscription in the wedding ring Abe gave her), it is in every other way a notable piece of work.

The scholarship is just as sound, according to a leading Lincoln specialist, in *Love Is Eternal* as it is in the recent and respectfully reviewed historical biography of Mrs. Lincoln by a trained historian, Ruth Randall. It deserves to be called meticulous. Many an example can be found of Stone's deep scholarly concern with the life he was writing. Besides the most obvious ones, there are such additional tokens of his interest as the fact that he painstakingly prepared a floor plan of the White House of Lincoln's day—one had never been reconstructed before—as a piece of independent research and that he created most of his dialogue out of skilled paraphrases of historically accurate source material.

Furthermore, the handling of the data is judicious. Mrs. Lincoln is always a controversial figure, and Stone could be excused if he slanted his information one way or the other. But he does not. Rising above his declared intention to vindicate her, he portrays her bedeviled, neurotic character with fairness. As the book moves along through its many pages, she and Abe emerge as memorable human beings, one great and the other not, but human beings both. The minor characters, such as her cousin Logan and Stephen Douglas' wife, who surround them are as a rule still more carefully differentiated than in Kane; very seldom are they merely historical names. The scenes are well handled, with pace and even suspense to some of them in spite of the fact that historians already know how they came out. The descriptions give rich color to the picture Stone creates. The entire book, finally, is written in a style that is, though undistinguished, a smooth-flowing lucid medium for the story.

The aim behind the best writing of this kind is a noble one. It is to see beneath the surface reality of facts and to reveal the true reality to others. It is to use historical data more daringly but more penetratingly than the professional historian can. Of course it is an aim that is rarely achieved. Far too often, the padded and sensational books of the *Whirlwind* kind are all that appear. But every now and then among them there will be a book like Irving Stone's on Mary Lincoln, and then the potentialities of this interesting genre are realized.

30

Paul Murray Kendall

Excerpt from "Contemporary Biography" from *The Art of Biography* (1965)

If modern biography began with a book, Boswell's *Johnson*, contemporary biography in England and America began with a bang—the guns of the First World War blowing to pieces so many of the men and the states and the attitudes and the values of the Victorian world. The arts, already in ferment before the outbreak of that war, led the cry against Victorianism, proclaimed the arrival of liberation, experimentation, an exhilarating new day by the light of which man and his institutions would be reinterpreted, his enlarged powers given new expression. All sorts of *isms* burst into existence, expanded, and exploded—Dadaism and neo-expressionism and Freudianism . . .

Biography could not resist these volcanic forces. In the general upheaval of the arts, biography upheaved itself also. What Schoenberg and his twelve-tone system were doing for music, and Eugene O'Neill was doing for drama, Lytton Strachey did for biography in the publication of *Eminent Victorians* in 1917 and then, a few years later, his *Life of Queen Victoria.*

Strachey's brilliant, sophisticated attack upon Victorianism hoisted a shining banner in the wind of change. He demonstrated that biography, too, could be exciting, could express the personality of the writer, could join in the joyous iconoclasm, and could sell. A host of imitators sprang up. Debunking biographers laid low the heroic figures of the past, exuberantly proving that marble statues had feet of clay. Freudian biographers excitedly dug into the kitchen-midden of suppressions and complexes like schoolboys playing at archeology. Fictionizers sought to secure Strachey's effects, but lacking his genius, freely invented materials in order to demonstrate their talents and please the public.

It was a gay party while it lasted, but the favors were cheap and quickly shredded and the refreshments lacked sustenance. Before the end of the thirties, the "new" biography had lost its savor; critics like Bernard DeVoto and Allan Nevins exposed the shabbiness of amateurish psychoanalytical writing and the public turned its face away.

Meanwhile, the genuine accomplishment of Lytton Strachey had become recognized. His ironic detachment from his material, his lacquered style, his delicacy of selection and his dramatic touch, all left a permanent mark upon biography. Furthermore, biography had become a subject for serious literary examination. Harold Nicolson produced his perceptive little volume, *The Development of English Biography*; André Maurois joined the discussion with his *Aspects of Biography*; and dedicated people of letters like Virginia Woolf likewise responded to this critical interest in life-writing. In the United States, Gamaliel Bradford's impressionistic biographical sketches, which he called psychographs, stimulated interest in the possibilities of the medium, and Wilbur Cross in his *Lives* of Laurence Sterne and Henry Fielding had showed the academic world that scholarly biography need not lack grace and style.

The movement of criticism was of brief duration and has been followed only by sporadic sallies; but by the coming of the Second World War, the art of biography had steadied, had found its twentieth-century voice, and has since assumed a firmly recognized, if hardly dominant, place on the literary scene. Between 1916 and 1930, about 4800 biographies were published in the United States, averaging something like 300 a year. In 1929, at the height of the biographical boom, 667 new biographical works appeared, in a country of about 120 million people. In 1962, for a population of 180 million people, exactly the same number of new biographies was published, out of a total of 16,448 titles. In Great Britain in 1962, 577 biographies- appeared among the 18,975 new books which came from the presses. Biography is not often to be found in the best-seller lists, nor is it a notable winner of literary prizes; it has not produced an array of masterpieces. Yet it can be argued that life-writing at present, both in England and America, is practiced with a greater skill and devotion than at any time in its history.

The influence of Lytton Strachey, inspirational and technical, was quickly diffused into the biographical atmosphere. In the long run his work has served to reflect rather than to alter the intellectual climate which plays upon biography. The shape and quality of modern life-writing owes most to the large forces which have determined the destiny of all the arts.

Of modern self-consciousness I need not speak. We are the inheritors of scientific advances begun in the early seventeenth century and enormously accelerated in the early twentieth. To call this, even in irony, the Age of Freud, indicates our consciousness of, and doubts about, self and personality. All sorts of keys to human behavior have been handed to the biographer—which, it is true, he has sometimes used to open the wrong door, or has thrown away, or has played with like a small boy, uttering squeals of delight. As for an "official," socially imposed view of man—in all degrees of voice, profound to superficial, from all the licensed explainers of existence, philosophers and sociologists and preachers and economists and literary critics, society has been offered so many candidates for an official view of man, ranging from despair to euphoria, that, for biography, the field is wide open. There is no official view, as in the nineteenth century, to conflict with our level of self-consciousness. Yet, within this framework of awareness unrestrained, if not unharassed, two powerful forces have pressed upon life-writing: the force of science and the force of literature, one from without, as it were, and one from within.

Let us turn, for the moment, to two illustrative prophecies, written about 1930, regarding the course that biography was to pursue.

Hesketh Pearson, one of the most prolific of English professional biographers, declared exuberantly, "Already we have a school of biographers who are displacing the dramatists and novelists of pre-war days. . . . It is the day of the biographer; he is the dramatist, the essayist, the romanticist of the future . . ." Perhaps it is as well for literature that this bacchic augury has proved wide of the mark.

Towards the close of his *Development of English Biography*, Sir Harold Nicolson predicted that "the scientific interest in biography is hostile to and will in the end prove destructive of the literary interest. . . . The more biography becomes a branch of science, the less will it become a branch of literature. The literary element will, of course, persist, but it will be driven into other directions . . ."

With clairvoyance, he singled out the two forces, scientific and literary, which in the succeeding generation have indeed exerted a decisive influence upon biography. The influence, however, has not been so drastically or unrelievedly unfortunate as Sir Harold predicted. Both the force of science and the force of literature have turned out to be Janus-headed, malign *and* beneficial—and biography has in many ways profited from an invigorating, though dangerous, whipsaw of countercurrents.

In Great Britain, this split between science and literature in biography is much less severe than in the United States, just as, in the novel, the most spectacular adventures of modern fiction can be more clearly viewed here than in England. The steadier balance of English intellectual society, the slower metabolic rate of the English temperament, English reluctance to climb on the band-wagon of science, the continuing force exerted by the Oxbridge tradition of civilized letters, and the dedicated amateurism of the British—they play games, make indexes, and regard facts more casually than Americans—have all contributed, I believe, to reduce the extremes of the American biographical condition. The scholar, Miss C. V. Wedgwood, for example, writes so beautifully that we are not distracted by her learning, while the writer, Lord David Cecil, let us say, researches so meticulously that we are not played false by his style. Great Britain and the United States both have their share of distinguished works, competent biographical writing, and ephemeral or indigestible biographies; but the emphatic polarity of American biography reveals more vividly the impact of modern social-cultural forces.

The force of science has exerted a wide range of pressures on life-writing. It has, in general, stimulated the researcher behind the biographer to higher standards of precision and thoroughness than have hitherto been observed. In published source-materials—letters, journals, historical documents—no editions of the nineteenth or early twentieth century can be trusted; whereas today accuracy can be taken for granted in the work of all responsible scholars. Serious biographers have been spurred by the prevailing reverence for "the scientific approach" to seek out their evidences with dogged persistence, to eschew second-hand materials and concentrate upon the original document, the actual letter, to view with skepticism all doubtful information however attractive, and to interpret their findings with a rigorous regard for the elusiveness of truth.

Indirectly, science has provided aid and comfort for biography through that proliferating institution, the University, where the most intense scientific activity is concentrated and where its prestigious practitioners give the law. In the United States the writing of biography has been increasingly domesticated on the campus, as librarians, English departments, historians, have succeeded in diverting to themselves ever larger tributaries of the golden flow nourishing research. The professor-biographer—and most of the best American biographies are now probably written by professors—enjoys a financial support and technical aids that would have been a marvel to James Parton. Funds are available—after test tubes and reactors have been provided for—to buy microprinters, microfilm, xerographs, photostats, stenographic and research assistance, even leisure for study and writing.

Leaves-of-absence, with pay, are supplemented by grants from national bodies such as the American Council of Learned Societies; by fellowships from foundations, particularly the Guggenheim Foundation, which has done so much for so many scholars of all varieties, including biographers; and by aids and services of many sorts provided by the great libraries, like the Folger in Washington under the imaginative direction of that scholar-artist, Louis B. Wright. University librarians buy biographical materials right and left, hire people to catalogue them, install electronic retrieval systems to make them instantly accessible; university presses stand ready to print those biographies whose appeal is too limited for the commercial publishers; and university communities harbor the bookstores and the public on which the biographer mainly depends for his slender royalties.

Under the aegis of science, the American biographer, then, has received support and encouragement which are the envy of his fellows in the rest of the world.

On the other hand, the force of science has fastened biography in a bear-hug—dangerous today, perhaps frightening for tomorrow. Science, wittingly or no, has pressed us—and "us" includes biographers—to worship information as a thing-in-itself, to acknowledge the supremacy of facts and therefore to regard the accumulation of facts, no matter what kind, as the highest good; to confuse research—the ferreting out of facts—with scholarship, the understanding of them; to put our trust in methods, statistics, machinery. Attitudes proper to the physical sciences, and perhaps necessary to the newer ambitious sciences, have been diffused as standards of value for all manner of research. The vast collecting of data by, let us say, anthropology and by biology, the statistical measurements of sociology, garnering mass responses to experience, mass patterns of behavior, have stimulated a magpie competition in the weight, bulk, complexity of fact-compilation.

We pack into cavernous, air-filtered archives every scrap of information about ourselves, and we ransack the past for every scrap of information about our forebears. Indefatigable Frankensteins, in order to tame this monster before it crushes us, we organize scholarly "factories" and "laboratories" and "teams" in order to catalogue the precious detritus of the centuries and arrange it for publication. At Yale, proud plumes of smoke rise from the famous chimneys of the Boswell factory and the Johnson factory and the Walpole factory; many another university has, or is building, its historical and literary factories.

In themselves, the best of these enterprises offer humane services which mock mockery. The letters of Horace Walpole, the papers of Thomas Jefferson, given to the world in handsome volumes, admirably edited, offer an enrichment to life in general as well as immense aid to the labors of future scholars. Yet, for the art of biography, precariously perched between the demand of fact and the hope of illumination, this ambience of mass attack upon mass materials, of fact triumphant, has already posed, as we shall see, the threat of paralysis.

However, one branch of science, casting a spell on all the arts, has offered opportunities to the twentieth-century biographer which have wonderfully enlarged and enlightened the whole domain of life-writing. How could it be otherwise?—the science of human behavior speaks directly to him who seeks to puzzle out the unfolding of a life. Psychology and psychoanalysis have thrust fingers of light into the cave of the human mind, have deepened our sense of the complexities, the arcane tides, of personality, have enabled us to penetrate some of the dark corners of motive and desire, to detect patterns of action, and sense the symbolic value of word and gesture.

The biographer need not, fortunately, be a psychoanalyst, or even a student of psychoanalysis, to draw profit from the science. Merely as twentieth-century educated man he shares an insight into human nature veiled from his predecessors. Indeed, if he applies himself too intently to psychology, he runs the danger, unless he subdues his knowledge to his literary purpose, of producing a clinical exposition of a subject instead of the Life of a man. As Mark Schorer has observed, "A biographer, like any other civilized man, should know about the developments of modern psychology, but I do not think he should write as if he were a psychoanalyst."

Psychoanalysis is, after all, *analysis;* it explains, provides names for, classifies, deals in clinical record. But a biography is not *about* a man's life; it is the simulation of that life in words. When the biographer deploys his psychological knowledge or aspirations thereto, upon the page, he is telling instead of showing, he is transforming his subject into a specimen, he is blotting out the sense of a life being lived—the supreme object of biography—in order to deliver a lecture. The biographer's relations with psychology had better be platonic; she is an invaluable friend but as mistress, a *femme fatale.*

Psychology has also produced secondary radiation effects, probably slight, on the biographical climate. The bread-earning emphasis, in applied psychology, on psychic "types," frameworks and catch-alls of character, automatic diagnosis by psychological "profiles," has reinforced the general atmosphere of dehumanization exuded by statistical sciences like sociology; and that atmosphere, at the least, has made it harder for the biographer, one man at grips with one man, to catch his breath.

The force of literature, the "literary element," as Nicolson puts it, has not exerted nearly so dramatic an influence as the force of science; but that influence has, in all probability, been more steadily beneficial than baneful.

The biographer has been stimulated by the novelist—who in the United States is also likely to be a campus inhabitant—to develop literary as well as scholarly ambitions and to pay increasing attention to the formal problems of unfolding a life. Not infrequently these days the biographer is, like Mark Schorer and Leon Edel, a critic or writer of fiction, or, like Miss C. V. Wedgwood in Great Britain, an historian who is also a distinguished woman of letters. Professor-biographers have been moved to realize not only that Lives must be as artfully written as they are ardently researched but that biography demands not the exposition but the projection, the dramatization, of a life.

Yet literature, too, has played Mr. Hyde as well as Dr. Jekyll, or rather, has shown a temptress' as well as a help-meet's face. The modern novel has had an excitingly experimental career. It has generated all manner of new devices to tell old stories, has dared any manipulation of time, any violence of viewpoint, any innovations in narrative that offered possibilities of enriching, or enlivening, the domain of fiction. The serious biographer, on the other hand, is confined within the adamantine limits of the biographic oath to tell the truth. With enlarged means, it is true, and with an enlarged understanding of his medium, he is doing much the same thing that Einhard and Roger North were doing; whereas the present-day spinner of stories is working a much different vein, exploring quite another world, from those of the creator of Icelandic Sagas or even from those of Daniel Defoe.

The writer who is biographically inclined, eyeing the multi-coursed feast of the novelist, has reached for goodies beyond a biographer's power to digest, has sometimes indeed claimed the right to sit at the table and quaff the Falernian of invention. As the pressure of science threatens to smother the biographer in fact, the enticements of literature threaten to over-stimulate him with artifices.

This climate of attitudes and impulsions has done much to shape the three chief characteristics of modern American and British life-writing: (1) the decline of autobiography and the concomitant decline of biography springing from a life-relationship; (2) the extraordinarily wide range of biographical literature; and (3) the development of a mode of biographical composition, not hitherto entirely unknown perhaps, but new as a self-conscious practice.

Autobiographical *activity* has certainly not declined. "Ghosted" pot-boilers and artless effusions explore all latitudes from the doldrums of *Fifty Years in the Indian Civil Service* and the windy reaches of *Up the Ladder from Tot to Tycoon* to the hot breezes of *Footlights and Champagne: I Loved it All.*

I am referring to the decline of serious autobiography, autobiography as the form developed from the Renaissance to World War One: controlled retrospect, the recollected interaction of the *me* and the *not-me* deliberately shaped as a work of literature. A few such autobiographies have been written but none, so far as I know, of sufficient distinction to represent the substantial continuation of the great autobiographical tradition.

Instead, the autobiographic impulse has embodied itself in memoirs (recollection of the times), reminiscences (recollection of friends and family), collected opinions like Maugham's *The Summing-up,* and plain *res gestae*, chronicles of the events of a life. Sir Osbert Sitwell's highly polished volumes well represent the movement of autobiography outward to reminiscence-memoirs; as has been observed, this admirable work "tells us little about what it feels like to be in Sir Osbert's skin." The twentieth century is not the place to seek autobiography in the grand style, such as the *Commentaries* of Aeneas Sylvius Piccolomini.

The decline of the life-relationship as generating force of biography is equally marked. There are notable exceptions, like Ernest Jones' *Life* of Sigmund Freud, but the best modern American and British biographies have sprung from research, not from recollection. Life-relationship biography has, in general, now fallen to the vehicle by which the subordinates of famous military commanders express their admirations (*The Unknown Eisenhower; A Tentmate Looks at Monty*), and the friends of literary giants their frustrations, engendered by the great man—witness in the latter case the sad circle of works enclosing D. H. Lawrence, from Middleton Murry's *Son of Woman* to Richard Aldington's *Portrait of a Genius, But. . . .*

The link between the decline of formal autobiography and the decline of biography sprung from life-relationship—that tradition which until our day produced the world's greatest biographies—can be partly descried, it seems clear, in the force which science, particularly psychology, has exerted upon life-writing. Today the self is more exposed and yet more elusive, more comprehensible but less manageable, more fascinating but not so palatable. Undertaking an autobiography, under the aegis of modern psychology, is like signing a contract with the Devil: there is much to be won and everything, especially honor, to be lost. In the Age of Freud, to look no deeper than Gibbon looked in the Age of Hume is to perpetrate an anachronism; but to subject oneself to even amateur psychological scrutiny seems rather like performing an act of private therapy in public. Hence the autobiographer, skirting the sinister deeps of his personality, roams outward into the happier champaign of memoir-reminiscence.

For the writer contemplating the biography of a friend, as well as for the autobiographer, the fallibility of retrospect has been cruelly revealed; it is impossible to dodge the realization that memory recreates rather than regurgitates the past. Errors of fact may be checked against the record; but the complex of intimate feeling and fond recall, that dome of many-colored glass fragmenting the light of truth—to try to ignore or tinker with that is to confound the impulse willing the biography into existence. We have lost much in losing the brilliant images of memory, the living perception, the flashes of insight springing from intimacy; but, perhaps wisely, we have put our faith in the detachment which accompanies knowledge gained through research. The groper-from-without has fewer traps to fear than the borer-from-within. More practically, in this epoch of paper, a man accumulates so many documentary remains—again the force of science—that a coeval can hardly hope to live long enough to digest them into a biography.

In the second characteristic of modern life-writing, the wide range of biographical activity, we can see most clearly the partial fulfillment of Nicolson's prophecy, the split between the "literary element" and the "scientific element."

Stretched along a rough scale from the most literary-least factual to the most "scientific"-least literary, modern biographies display an infinity of gradations. These resolve themselves, broadly, into some eight perceptible types.

On the radical left appears the novel-as-biography, almost wholly imaginary. Then come the extensive and often marshy reaches of fictionized biography, which stretch from outright romancing to more or less serious biographical intentions. This popular form merges into the more carefully controlled and sometimes remarkably able genre, interpretative biography, running to the center of the scale. The Lives on the other side, all of them true to the biographic oath, range from the chief exemplars of modern life-writing, with the best scholarly biographies on the right flank, through the increasingly dense "research" biography, the "life-and-times" biography, what I venture to call the "Behemoth biography," and so to works of such high specific gravity that they are little more than compilations of source-materials. Hovering above the center of the scale appears the radiant-plumaged "super-biography," which seeks to be both ultimately literary and ultimately scientific.

To the force of literature, the "literary element," the art of life-writing is indebted for that twentieth-century phenomenon, the novel-as-biography—not the novel in the form of a life, *David Copperfield*, but the novel in the form of life-writing. Such works do not, like fictionized biography, masquerade as Lives; rather, they imaginatively take the place of biography where there can be no genuine biography for lack of materials. We have, in the autobiographical form, those brilliant re-creations of Robert Graves, *I, Claudius* and *Claudius the God,* and Mary Renault's *The King Must Die*; in the form of biography, Graves' *Count Belisarius* and Hope Muntz' study of Harold Godwinson, *The Golden Warrior.*

In fictionized biography the seductive influence of the "literary element" is all too apparent. Just as the compiler of biographical information risks no involvement, the fictionizer admits no limit to it. The heady airs of novelistic freedom encourage him to invent, transpose, as he will. The result is usually a flaccid compound of fact and fancy, ill-mated, a sort of mutant.

31

Ina Schabert

"Fictional Biography, Factual Biography, and their Contamination" from *Biography* (1982)

I

Recent tendencies in biography and biographical criticism convey the impression that biography as a whole is drifting toward fiction. Leon Edel invites the biographer "to be as imaginative as he pleases, so long as he does not imagine his facts."[1] David Gervais urges him to create "something truthfully intuitive and bold which will still be free of the false imaginativeness of the sort of *vie romancée* which Andre Maurois sometimes wrote."[2] But where is the line to be drawn between the novelist's imagined facts and the biographer's imaginative use of the facts? How are we to distinguish the biographer's intuition from both the novelist's truthful imagination and the false imaginativeness of belletristic lives?

Not even the categorizations for biography, as they have been proposed by James Clifford and Paul Murray Kendall, allow for a clear dividing line between biography and the biographical novel. Clifford discerns, among five gradations of increasing subjectivity, as a third type the "artistic-scholarly biography" where "the biographer considers his role that of an imaginative creative artist, presenting the details in the liveliest and most interesting manner possible," as a fourth type the "narrative biography" where the biographer "does allow some subjective imagination on his part to add color to his narration, though he does not indulge in pure fiction," as does the biographer of the fifth category. Here, "imagination is given full reign" and "the result reads like a novel, and largely is one."[3] Beginning with the subjective extreme, Kendall discerns as a first type the "novel-as-biography, almost wholly imaginary," as a second the "fictionalized biography" which "simulates life but does not respect the materials at hand," and as a third type the "more carefully controlled" "interpretative biography."[4] Jean-Paul Sartre offers his elaborate hypothesis on Flaubert's inner life as something between biography and fiction which he calls a *roman vrai*.[5] Richard Ellmann, sympathizing with Sartre's "adventurous conception, that it is really possible to map out every aspect of the mind and to verbalize processes largely inarticulate,"[6] gives us a *James Joyce* which has been characterized as a modern novel dovetailed into a biography.[7] A *novel biography*, combining factual and fictional statements, is recommended by Norman Mailer as the technique to capture the full, complex reality of a life.[8] As far as the more conventional types of biography are concerned, critical analysis in a number of cases has discovered features commonly associated with fictional rather than factual literature. The narratives have shown to be informed by personal and group prejudices, ideological assumptions and conventions of aesthetic patterning.[9] Consequently the German author Hans Magnus Enzensberger, feeling strongly about the inflected nature of biographical documentation and interpretation, has given the subtitle *Roman*, 'novel', to a mere selection of source materials interspersed with several comments of his own.[10] The reader of biographies thus finds himself in a plight similar to Mr Boffin's in *Our Mutual Friend* when Plutarch's *Lives* were being read to him:

> What to believe, in the course of his reading, was Mr Boffin's chief literary difficulty indeed; for some time he was divided in his mind between half, all, or none; at length, when he decided, as a moderate man, to compound with half, the question still remained, which half? And that stumbling block he never got over.[11]

Dickens spares his own readers such an embarrassment by presenting his works unambiguously as novels, that is, as statements offering not factual but imaginative truth. In our time, a refinement of the same logic has given rise to fictional biography as a separate literary genre. As expressly and consistently as Dickens, its authors proclaim their narratives to be novels. As novels on historical individuals, however, they have a more complex relationship with factual reality than the novel in general.[12] Virginia Woolf with *Orlando* (1928) and *Flush* (1933), and Robert Graves with the two Claudius novels (1934), *Count Belisarius* (1938) and *Wife to Mr Milton* (1944) were the pioneers in this mode of writing which by now has gained international importance. Hermann Broch's *Der Tod des Vergil* (1945), Thornton Wilder's *The Ides of March* (1948), Marguerite Yourcenar's *Mémoires d'Hadrien* (1951), David Caute's *Comrade Jacob* (1961), Anthony Burgess's *Nothing Like the Sun* (1964) and *Napoleon Symphony* (1974), William Styron's *Confessions of Nat Turner* (1967), George Garrett's *Death of the Fox* (1971), Peter Härtling's *Hölderlin* (1978) and Ludwig Harig's *Rousseau* (1978) are some of the genre's most interesting representatives. The authors are extremely self-conscious about their use of the fictional medium for the purposes of biography, and they have explained their specific aims in a number of theoretical statements.

While in factual biography the borderline which separates it from fiction seems no longer clear, the fictional biographies convey a precise idea of what constitutes a fictional statement on a historical life. This essay therefore adopts the point of view of the fictional medium in order to undertake a fresh assessment of factual biography as its non-fictional alternative. Part II sets out to state the features of fictional biography and to enumerate, by way of contrast, the specific qualities of its non-fictional, historiographic counterpart. Against this background of clear-cut distinctions, Part III discusses the "fictional" traits that have been attributed to non-fictional biography. They will be analyzed as contaminations either of terms or of techniques.

Contrary to a widespread notion, painstaking research concerning the facts of a life and fidelity to the facts are not qualities which necessarily distinguish non-fictional biography from the modern fictional form. Most of the novelists insist on scrupulous scholarship as an essential stage of preparation: "*tout apprendre, tout lire, s'informer de tout.*"[13] They may even claim superiority to the biographer proper: "the novelist," says Robert Graves, "needs to be two jumps ahead of the academic historian."[14] Some novelists confess to a superstitious adherence to as much historical detail as possible:

> They feel an urgent need to be exact, as precise as they are able to be, about the things of the time, feeling that by means of these they may manage to summon up the ghosts who used them. . . . novelists can be more pedantic than the most solemn cartoon image of the scholar.[15]

Novelists such as Yourcenar and Garrett spent many years of their life reading and meditating upon their subject in order to familiarize themselves with the historical world of the person they were going to write about.

Both non-fictional and fictional biographies are conceived in a process of interpreting the evidence. Not in all cases the fictional version is more selective or reductive than the non-fictional one: the organizing patterns of modern fiction are apt to accommodate the most heterogeneous materials. Whereas the scholarly biographer, bound to the rules of logical discourse, may have to reject part of the evidence as unreliable, novelists feel able and obliged to admit contradictory information:

> Lorsque deux textes, deux affirmations, deux idées s'opposent, se plaire à les concilier plutôt qu'à les annuler l'un par l'autre; voir en eux deux facettes différentes, deux états successifs du même fait, une réalité convaincante parce qu'elle est complexe, humaine parce qu'elle est multiple.[16]

Fictional and non-fictional biography thus represent the lives of historical persons by organizing as much factual evidence as possible within an interpretive context. The two modes of interpretation, however, are categorically different. The special claim of the fictional representation, often indicated by labels such as *novel* or *imaginative reconstruction* on the title page or in an introduction, is that the truth of poetry as opposed to the truth of an expository statement, that the essential rather than the factual reality is being expressed.

II

The organizing principles of the fictional and the non-fictional biographies differ accordingly.

Self-referentiality vs. transparency. The fictional representation of a life constitutes a self-referential unit. Its elements are linked together within complex schemes of correspondence, such as circular patterns of composition, leitmotif structures, musical arrangements imitating symphonic or counterpoint movements. The American version of Klaus Mann's *Symphonie Pathétique* (1948) with its four parts corresponding to the four movements of Tchaikovsky's work, and Burgess's *Napoleon Symphony,* which mirrors the structure of Beethoven's *Eroica,* are extreme examples of a general tendency. The introductory section of a fictional biography often anticipates the curve of the life which is going to be related; the last pages tend to resume, from the subject's or from the narrator's point of view, the major scenes, the dominant themes, the main achievements of the life, grouping them into an impressive finale. The outer world of biographical fact is seen in reference not to history but to an inner world which is the creation of the novelist: the external events find their counterparts in acts of expectation, planning, foreboding, of recollection and interpretation. The facts are thus made to operate as the constituent parts of an aesthetic structure; their function as factual information is suspended. In order to emphasize the aesthetic priority, the biographical novelist may confirm Livius's statement that he would have made Pompey win the battle of Pharsalia, had the effective turn of a sentence required it—having made sure, however, that his own aesthetic design does require no such thing.[17] By the organization of the work itself, as well as by the label of *novel,* the reader of a fictional biography is led away from asking himself whether and how the details of the narrative square with his historical knowledge; his primary concern is to understand how they are related to one another in the over-all design of the work. When, for instance, in Rhoda Lerman's fictional biography of Eleanor Roosevelt (*Eleanor,* 1979) the heroine is said to be in love with Charlotte Brontë's Mr Rochester, the reader would experience this as a truth confirmed by the tragic parallel to *Jane Eyre* into which Eleanor's married life eventually develops rather than as factual information that could be verified by external evidence. Not the detail, only the whole novel as an imaginative vision of the historical figure, is to be seen and judged against the background of biographical knowledge.

In non-fictional biography, on the contrary, the parts are items of information which cannot confirm each other by virtue of an intrinsic aesthetic pattern. Continually and separately, the statements of the narrative have to stand the test of factual verification. They must be justifiable as being inferred from the evidence, must be warranted as conclusions arrived at by means of historiographic, psychological, medical, economic, geographical and other knowledge. Accordingly, in the footnotes and the text itself the biographer refers to his source materials and to the results of previous research; he may discuss his interpretation of certain aspects of the evidence with relation to the theories of other scholars, may hint at possible consequences which things that are new in his biography will have for the body of biography and history. It is normal for the reader of a factual biography to agree with some parts of it while rejecting others. In the terms of William C. Dowling, "correspondence" to the world of historical knowledge, not aesthetic "coherence", is the first concern of a factual biography.[18] Roman Ingarden characterizes the scholarly text as "transparent" in the sense that it is immediately identified with and replaced by the objects it represents, whereas the fictional text would "conceal the corresponding, real, represented object by passing itself off for it."[19]

Essentiality vs. authenticity. Francis Steegmuller, author of a fictional biography of Ben Jonson, describes the genetic process in "A Note on Construction":

> After one has read the large mass of tradition and scholarship concerning the life and works of Ben Jonson, one emerges into the more vivifying air of independent meditation, and discovers that one has . . . evolved a definite conception of the man Ben Jonson, his friends, and his surroundings. This poetically true conception I have set down on paper.[20]

The fictional biography expresses what its author feels to be the characteristic, essential qualities of a particular individual in a particular historical situation. Whereas Steegmuller understands the poetic truth as Aristotelian, later novelists tend to stress the personal or collective subjectivity of their "poetically true conception." Writers such as Anthony Burgess, Ludwig Harig and Peter Härtling make it quite clear that the portrait they present is, inevitably, a self-portrait as well.[21] The subject of the fiction can be the life of a person as it has been reshaped and colored by myth: Burgess's *Napoleon Symphony*, Harig's *Rousseau* and Wallace Stegner's *Joe Hill* each depict a man "with his legend at his feet like a lengthening shadow."[22]

The criterion of poetic essentiality demands a creative use of the evidence. The selection of the material is controlled by the author's idea of what is characteristic of the person whose life he writes. The historical facts which he includes in the fiction as being representative are thereby transferred to metonymic or even symbolic status. They stand as details illustrating a whole way of life; they are taken as indications of an inner reality. Thus, for example, in Garrett's *Death of the Fox* the fact that Queen Elizabeth in her old age had all the mirrors in her state rooms covered with curtains, whereas at the same time large mirrors were installed in her private chambers, is made to stand for a code of behavior which separates the Queen and Sir Walter Ralegh from the world of King James.[23] Facts not pertaining to the novelist's vision of a life are "poetically false"[24] and have to be altered or discarded. On the other hand the novelist may invent episodes which elucidate the historical personality as he conceives it. As the extreme consequence of this liberty we have wholly invented lives such as Elinor Wylie's *Orphan Angel* (1926) and Woolf's *Orlando*, where the historical persons (P. B. Shelley, Vita Sackville-West) are allowed to develop their character, to realize their inclinations and aspirations in a series of fantastic adventures more fully than they ever could in the real world. In this respect, the fictional biography might be regarded as the highly sophisticated version of the anecdote which is known to be fictitious but which brings out a truth about a real person in a more poignant way than would a factual account.

Non-fictional biography can take no such liberties. It is a record of what, according to the evidence, must have happened in the course of a person's life. Selective principles may guarantee a certain degree of thematic unity; the evidence may be sifted with the intention to elucidate a person's role either in political, cultural or literary history, or it may be used with the view to reconstruct the private life of the individual. The selectiveness of factual biographies, however, tends to be mitigated by conventional, commonly shared ideas of what is historically important. No factual biography probably would, as Garrett's fictional life pointedly does, ignore Ralegh's activity as a poet. Some theorists admit the essentialist position, which characterizes fictional biography, as a legitimate basis for factual biography.[25] But they insist that this may be only a selective, never an inventive principle: the factual statements which are considered to reveal the character of a person are stressed, while features classified as "accidental" are played down.

No factually false statement may be introduced for the sake of essentiality; whereas in a novel this can lead to something "poetically true", in a factual biography the result is only bad, tendentious writing.

Novelistic structures vs. historiographic concepts of coherence. Up to this point it has been possible to uphold the dichotomy of factual and fictional writing on the assumption that there is a reality of history to which factual writing corresponds. Yet the most important insight of those who stress the affinities between biography and the novel is that the reality of past lives cannot be known. The composition of a factual as well as that of a fictional text is controlled by a concept of its author, a theory, a prejudice, a convention, a myth of coherence:

> There is little question that it is not primarily the materials, but the biographer's management of them, which determines the shape of a biographical life.[26] The discovery of order, pattern, structure, development and insight into a life are all achievements which relate to the biographer's triumph over accumulated data rather than any breakthrough in recapturing another's life.[27]

Both factual and fictional biographies thus are made up, and in this sense are fictions. The criterion of fidelity to the facts may still be useful as far as single parts of the evidence are concerned, but it can no longer be applied to the biographical narrative as a whole, because its coherence is always something which the writer has imposed upon the facts. Consequently, factual and fictional biographies can only be distinguished as two literary genres based on the biographical facts but governed by different laws of establishing coherence.

The fictional biographers create "lives" from the facts by working within the formal traditions of the novel. As far as they are to be taken seriously, they avail themselves of the structural techniques of contemporary fiction which have been developed in the attempt to convey human reality as it came to be understood since the discoveries of Bergson, William James and Freud. They use the forms of the stream-of-consciousness novel in order to imagine a complex inner life for the historical individual who is their subject, to suggest the plurality of the selves, the interplay of social roles, the internalization of the external world, and the potentialities lived out only in the mind, which make up the full reality of a life. A sophisticated technique of narrative perspective allows to present the dynamics of a person's changing views of himself and his world, as well as the different aspects of his personality as experienced by his contemporaries, and may also convey his historical otherness as it is perceived through the imaginative sympathy of a modern author/narrator. Some structural techniques have proved to be especially qualified for the purpose of writing a life according to the standards of the modern novel. In fictional biographies as different as Broch's *Tod des Vergil,* Wilder's *Ides of March,* Yourcenar's *Mémoires d'Hadrien,* Styron's *Confessions of Nat Turner,* Garrett's *Death of the Fox* and David Malouf's novel on Ovid, *An Imaginary Life* (1977), the introspective and retrospective mode of "the last days" has been exploited. This allows the events of a life to be related not chronologically, as "the series of gig lamps" derided by Woolf,[28] but within the rich and varying texture of personal remembrance.[29] The deathbed meditation is also easily adapted to the compositional ideals of self-referentiality and essentiality. Another favorite form of fictional biography is the biographer's/narrator's quest for the historical figure, whereby the subjective quality of biographical knowledge can be emphasized. The idea was suggested in Robert Penn Warren's *World Enough and Time* (1950) and is fully realized in Härtling's *Hölderlin* and Dieter Kühn's *Ich, Wolkenstein* (1978). Works such as these, which border on fictional autobiography, describe the hermeneutical process of biographical research as a continual mirroring of the biographer's and the biographee's consciousnesses within each other. The substitution of the chronology of the fictional quest for that of the historical life again allows to arrange the items of biographical information according to aesthetic principles.

The author of a factual biography establishes a context for the data according to conventions of historiography. This means that he evaluates the data, as well as the achievements of previous scholarship and scientific research which can be associated with it, as a well-informed, intelligent, understanding observer. Common sense, a "general knowledge of human behavior acquired through experience,"[30] "an intuitive 'logic of events'," "a quick awareness of what fits,"[31] "tact, empathy, empirical experience, and narrative flair"[32] have been named as the criteria according to which biographical data are fused into the totality of a life. Whereas James Clifford has demonstrated how little conscious biographers can be of their structuring activity,[33] and whereas among biographers themselves the equation of their vision with reality itself may go unquestioned,[34] theories of history, following R. G. Collingwood, emphasize the elements of subjectivity inherent in the procedure at its best. H.-I. Marrou, W. H. Walsh, A. C. Danto and others have shown that "factual" biography depends on the conceptual paradigms and the narrative patterns which are valid at the time of its composition. (In view of the comparison with modern fictional biography, it is interesting to observe that the narrative patterns of yesterday's novel, of late nineteenth-century "realism", function as the neutral medium for today's factual narrative.)[35]

Conventional, common sense biography usually keeps relatively close, in its processes of inference, to aspects of factual evidence. The alternative method of psychohistory resembles the novel in its ability to derive long sequences of inner events from single items of biographical information. Yet the latter is more scientific than conventional biography insofar as its texts are constructed along clearly defined hypotheses which are adopted from certain schools of psychology and socio-psychology. The pattern to be projected on the materials originates in a conscious choice. Retrospective evaluation, however, has come to the conclusion that in good psychohistories the onesidedness of the method is being controlled and complemented by common sense and intuitive historical understanding.[36] Thus, after all, they seem to be different only in degree from the more conventional types of life writing.

III

In fictional biography the biographical facts are arranged within a self-referential system of utterance, are used figuratively, as signs which stand for more or something other than themselves, and are seen together in a creative vision of inner experience conveyed with all the sophistication of the post-realist novel. Factual biography, on the contrary, opens out toward the whole of historical knowledge, its statements are meant to signify particular, authentic events, and they are placed within a narrative argument which follows generally accepted and/or scientifically established lines of reasoning. Hence the fictional qualities that have been observed in factual biography are of two different kinds. They may either consist in the only relative validity of the factual texts themselves, given the plurality of biographical paradigms, or they may pertain to hybrid texts composed simultaneously on historiographical and fictional principles.

The fiction of factual biography. Factual biography, insofar as it shapes the facts into a "life" according to a concept of human behavior, has come to be experienced as something akin to the novel as the subjectivity of the concepts has become more and more obvious. As soon as we have at our disposition several biographies on the same individual, which from roughly the same facts infer different lives and different personalities, their hypothetical status is undeniable. The several lives of Hart Crane, Jack London, Charlotte Brontë and Virginia Woolf have been discussed as illustrations of the plurality of biographical patterns.[37] The atmosphere of distrust generated by the rivalry between conventional biography and psychohistory also furthers the skeptical attitude toward biography, the unwillingness to accept any version as the real life. If the skepticism is expressed by referring to factual biography as fiction, it should be kept in mind that this fiction is categorically different from the imaginative, representative interpretation of the facts in fictional biography. Neither is, as has sometimes been assumed, the use of an unfamiliar scientific concept in biography similar to novel writing,[38] nor does it advance the critical spirit to call, as Enzensberger did, a composite biography plus commentary a *novel.*[39]

The word *fiction* in such contexts is not always meant to indicate merely the unavoidable relativity of factual biography, the plurality of versions which legitimately exist in a pluralistic and dynamic community of authors and readers. It may be used to characterize works degraded from the normal standards of biographical writing, works grossly tendentious, simplistic, inventive. Of course, such violations of the compositional rules of factual biography do not produce a work of the fictional genre, which has its own laws of composition, although degenerate factual biography tends to appropriate the biographical novelist's right to selection and invention for its own, different purposes.

The hybrid biography. When Richard Ellmann postulates that biography "make out of apparently haphazard circumstances a plotted circle," that it offer not only "a pattern of explanation and theme" but also of "symbol," and that it "describe the movements of the mind as if they were movements within the atom" and "label the most elusive particles,"[40] he sums up the program of the biography which combines elements of the novel and of factual writing.

The artistic, manneristic patterning which Ellmann recommends has been practiced since the times of the "new" biographers. The factual materials are subjected to a rigidly selective process which tends to reduce them to a set of highly significant events. Figurative titles may interpret the interrelations in terms of semantic contrast (*Sailor on Horseback; The Pen and the Sword,* etc.) or of a literary model (*Ariel*). While, owing to the scarcity or even total absence of references, the "coherence" of the factual statements with the body of historiography is weakened, figurative meanings are implicitly or even explicitly developed. Elaboration, amplification, repetitive devices and commentary work together in order to attribute to carefully selected details—an anecdote, a reported gesture, a statement made by the person whose life is being written—a representative status. The single fact is made to stand as a part for a whole to be imagined by narrator or reader, as an outward sign for a mental disposition. A quotation from Woolf's biography *Roger Fry* (1940) may serve as an example:

> "He sat at Rickett's feet," said Sir Walter Rothenstein. . . . Sitting at other people's feet was certainly a characteristic. Roger Fry had a great capacity all his life for laying himself open, trustfully, optimistically, completely to any new idea, new person, or new experience that came his way.[41]

Not only the evidence but also the lack of it tends to acquire a figurative meaning: the fact that nothing is known is taken to reveal a deficiency in the person who is the subject of the biography, is read as corresponding to a lack of information, interest, feeling, or belief on his part.[42] Imagery, especially iterative imagery, is another feature which in hybrid biographies undermines factuality, suggesting a second, more general level of meaning.

In Woolf's *Roger Fry* there are for instance a series of elaborate comparisons whereby Fry's extraordinary sensitivity is associated with the responsiveness of insects. The study of the individual is thus being transformed into a study of spontaneous empathy as a characteristic of the artist's mind in general. Symbolic overtones may crystallize into symbols comprehending the whole course of the life. As metaliterary elements, which mirror the biography itself, these symbols again intensify the self-referential tendency of a text. Woolf interprets Fry's studio where, in the middle of a disorder caused by his hectic activity, an arrangement of flowers or fruits is allowed to remain untouched, as a symbol of his life's double rhythm of action and meditation.[43] Another biographical item, an observation by Fry on the croaking of frogs, is used to indicate the modulations in the rhythmic movement ("Like the frogs at St Rémy, he broke the rhythm before it got quite fixed") and thus to complement the structural with a dynamic metabiographical image.[44]

The "new" biographers suggest an inner life for their characters mainly by a selective and figurative use of the evidence. Biographers of the avant-garde who agree with Ellmann's program of "describ[ing] the movements of the mind as if they were movements within the atom" and of "label[ing] the most elusive particles" go farther. They take some of the biographical facts as creative nuclei about which the accretion of an imagined, conscious and subconscious mental life is then going to take place according to patterns of the post-realist and post-Freudian novel. In Hildesheimer's *Mozart* (1977) this happens in small textual units; Sartre's biographies, especially *L'idiot de la famille* (1972), do it on a grand scale; Ellmann himself experiments in his *James Joyce* (1959) with more subtle ways of combining factual information with speculation bordering on such fiction; Mailer's *Marilyn* (1973) joins depth psychology and novelistic imagination in a simplistic, popularized form. The single particle of fact is not only, as in "new" biography, generalized into an iterative gesture and interpreted symbolically; it functions as determinant for a whole chain of imagined inner and known outer events. The passage where Mailer elaborates on the report that five-year old Marilyn's dog Tippy was shot by a neighbor may be quoted as a crude example of the procedure:

> So to the child, a catastrophic view of history must have begun. It is the view which assumes that at the end of every sweet and quiet passage of love, amputation or absurdity is waiting. Whole washes of the apathy that would sit upon her in later years, that intolerable dull and dead round she passed through in the year after her marriage to Miller was over, is probably sealed in the reflex of sorrowing for Tippy.[45]

Where the intuitive sympathy of the traditional biographer would not venture and psychological science is unable to operate because the historical evidence does not yield the kind and certainly not the quantity of data which are needed, the avant-garde biographer, combining their procedures with those of the modern novelist, constructs rather than re-constructs the complex working of a mind. In both "avant-garde" and "new" biography, the unqualified label of *biography* and the referential features of the text claim our factual belief, while at the same time the figurative, symbolic and purely imaginative elements create a closed semantic system which demands our willing suspension of disbelief. Biographies such as these may yield a certain Boffinesque charm as strange, unsettling reading experiences; their epistemological value, however, is doubtful.

Conclusion

Both fictional and factual biographies are based on the facts of history and of an individual's life, and both, in the sense that they are constructs made up from the facts, are fictions. Yet the constructs are different in kind. In some cases—prominent among them the "new" and "avant-garde" biographies—we find that the two modes of factual and fictional utterance are set side by side. The combination certainly does not produce, as a recent study on German biography assumes for the avant-garde type, an optimum of biographical knowledge.[46] Rather the fictional elements destroy the reliability of the text as a source of factual information whereas the factual narrative interferes with the imaginative vision. Macaulay's dream of the perfect marriage of fact and fiction—"we should not then have to look . . . for one half of King James in Hume, and for the other half in the *Fortunes of Nigel*"—[47] cannot come true.

While some techniques of the contemporary novel, such as the controlled multiperspectivism and the sophisticated handling of time schemes may be successfully adopted by factual biography and heighten its accuracy, the ambition to reveal an inner life, in the way the stream-of-conscious novel conceives it, cannot be fully realized in factual literature. This dimension of past existence is best suggested in form of a fictional hypothesis. The sympathetic imagination of the novelist, having assimilated the known facts about a historical person and his world, is able to invent a possible, plausible version of the experience which we can never come to know. Thus filling a void in biography of which a reading public familiar with the developments in depth psychology and in modern fiction has become increasingly aware, fictional biography by now prospers as a genre in its own right. It is most successful with obscure lives, where lack of material reduces the factual portrait to a mere sketch or silhouette: figures of the remote past, lower class heroes, artists about whose private lives little is known, and women.

Confronted with the achievements of the psychological novel, some critics of factual biography have begun to reformulate its functions in explicit juxtaposition to the fictional genre. Biographies of the future should, Edward

Mendelson suggests, focus their attention on the observable *effects* produced by an individual's actions on himself and others, not on the internal *affects* from which the actions might derive.[48] Oscar Handlin considers as their proper subject not the complete person but the sphere where the person and the society interact.[49] James Clifford, in an essay turning from descriptive to normative criticism, urges that the genre be redefined as "a narrative of transindividual occasions."[50] Rather than infringe upon the territory of the novel, factual biography should develop its own, different strengths.

Institut für Englische Philologie der Universität München

Notes

1 "Biography: A Manifesto," *Biography,* 1, i (1978), 1.
2 "Stories of Real Life," *Cambridge Quarterly,* 9 (1979), 62.
3 *From Puzzles to Portraits* (Chapel Hill: University of North Carolina Press, 1970), pp. 85–87.
4 *The Art of Biography* (New York: W. W. Norton & Co., 1965), pp. 15, 126.
5 "Sur *L'idiot de la famille,*" in: *Situations,* X (Paris: Gallimard, 1976), p. 94.
6 "Literary Biography" (1971), rpt. in *Golden Codgers* (New York: Oxford University Press, 1973), p. 7.
7 Edward Mendelson, "Authorized Biography and Its Discontents," in *Studies in Biography,* ed. Daniel Aaron (Cambridge, Mass.: Harvard University Press, 1978), p. 22.
8 *Marilyn: A Biography* (1973; rpt. New York: Warner Books, 1975), p. 15.
9 A. O. J. Cockshut, *Truth to Life* (London: Collins, 1974); Clarice Stasz, "The Social Construction of Biography: The Case of Jack London," *Modern Fiction Studies,* 22 (1976), 51–71; Margot Peters, "Biographies of Women," *Biography*, 2 (1979), 201–217; Carol Shloss, "The Lives of Hart Crane: Revision of Biography," *Biography,* 3 (1980), 132–146; James Gindin, "Method in the Biographical Study of Virginia Woolf," *Biography,* 4 (1981), 95–107.
10 *Der kurze Sommer der Anarchie: Buenaventura Durrutis Leben und Tod: Roman* (Frankfort: Suhrkamp, 1972).
11 Charles Dickens, *Our Mutual Friend,* ed. S. Gill (Harmondsworth: Penguin, 1971), pp. 537–538.
12 In this respect they differ from 19th century novels on historical figures as written by Scott, Bulwer-Lytton, R. F. Williams, Martineau, Ch. Kingsley, George Eliot and M. Hewlett, where the facts are replaced, rather than interpreted, by novelistic patterns.
13 Marguerite Yourcenar, "Carnets de notes," in *Mémoires d'Hadrien* (1951; rpt. Paris: Gallimard, 1974), p. 324.
14 "The Pirates Who Captured Caesar," in *Food for Centaurs* (Garden City, New York: Doubleday, 1960), p. 322.

15 George Garrett, "Dreaming with Adam: Notes on Imaginary History" (1970), rpt. in *New Directions in Literary History,* ed. Ralph Cohen (Baltimore: Johns Hopkins University Press, 1974), p. 259.

16 Yourcenar, "Carnets de notes," p. 324.

17 Cf. John Williams, "Author's Note" to *Augustus: A Novel* (Harmondsworth: Penguin, 1979).

18 "Boswell and the Problem of Biography," in *Studies in Biography,* ed. Aaron, pp. 73–93.

19 *The Literary Work of Art,* trans. G. G. Grabowitz (Evanston: Northwestern University Press, 1973), p. 245.

20 *O Rare Ben Jonson* (New York: A. A. Knopf, 1927), p. 153.

21 "Der vom Schreibenden Beschriebene erscheint im Geschriebenen, wie der Schreibende selbst im geschriebenen Beschriebenen erscheint: das Porträt wird so zum Doppelporträt." (Ludwig Harig, *Rousseau* [Munich: Hanser, 1978], p. 18).

22 Stegner, *Joe Hill: A Biographical Novel* (Lincoln: University of Nebraska Press, 1980), p. 13 (1st ed. 1950, entitled *The Preacher and the Slave*).

23 *Death of the Fox* (Garden City, New York: Doubleday, 1971), pp. 526–527; cf. Garrett's commentary, "Dreaming with Adam," pp. 249–250.

24 Steegmuller, *O Rare Ben Jonson,* p. 155.

25 Cf. Morton G. White, *Foundations of Historical Knowledge* (New York: Harper & Row, 1965), pp. 241–244, and also Robert Gittings' concept of biography implicit in his description of the genesis of his biography of Keats, in *The Nature of Biography* (London: Heinemann, 1978), p. 10.

26 Jeanne W. Halpern, "Biographical Images: Effects of Formal Features on the Way We see Life," *Biography,* 1, iv (1978), 7.

27 Peter Nagourney, "The Basic Assumptions of Literary Biography," *Biography,* 1, ii (1978), 101.

28 "Modern Fiction," in *The Common Reader,* First Series (1925; rpt. London: Hogarth Press, 1968), p. 189.

29 "Prendre une vie connue, achevée, fixée (autant qu'elles peuvent jamais l'être) par l'Histoire, de façon à embrasser d'un seul coup la courbe tout entière; bien plus, choisir le moment où l'homme qui vécut cette existence la soupèse, l'examine, soit pour un instant capable de la juger. Faire en sorte qu'il se trouve devant sa propre vie dans la même position que nous." (Yourcenar, "Carnets de notes," p. 314).

30 David E. Schwalm, "Locating Belief in Biography," *Biography,* 3 (1980), 17.

31 Jacques Barzun, *Clio and the Doctors* (Chicago: University of Chicago Press, 1974), p. 104.

32 Justin Kaplan, "The Real Life," in *Studies in Biography,* ed. Aaron, p. 1.

33 *From Puzzles to Portraits*, pp. 99–112.

34 "It is the exhilaration of modern biography to find how common sense and close to life it has become." (Gittings, *The Nature of Biography,* p. 92).

35 Cf. Barzun, *Clio and the Doctors,* p. 102; Savoie Lottinville, *The Rhetoric of History* (Norman: University of Oklahoma Press, c. 1976), p. 94.

36 Barzun, *Clio and the Doctors,* pp. 33–35; Donna Arzt, "Psychohistory and Its Discontents," *Biography,* 1, iii (1978), 23–24; Frank E. Manuel, "The Use and Abuse of Psychology in History" (1971), rpt. in *Varieties of Psychohistory,* ed. George M. Kren, Leon H. Rappoport (New York: Springer Pub. Co., 1976), p. 57.

37 Cf. the articles by Shloss, Stasz, Peters and Gindin cited in note 9.

38 Freud himself subtitled one of his biographical essays, *Moses and Monotheism* (1939): *A Historical Novel*; Oscar Handlin, in a polemical comment on Erikson's *Young Man Luther*, reads the *as if* of psychological hypothesis as the *as if* of (bad) fiction (*Truth in History* [Cambridge, Mass.: Belknap Press, 1979], p. 272).

39 Cf. note 10.

40 "Literary Biography," pp. 15–16.

41 *Roger Fry: A Biography* (rpt. New York: Harcourt Brace Jovanovich, 1976), p. 86.

42 In *Roger Fry,* statements such as p. 84 "The subject of the argument has disappeared," shift from description of the sources to description of the biographee's character. The device is exploited systematically in Wolfgang Hildesheimer's *Mozart.*

43 *Roger Fry,* pp. 201, 215.

44 *Roger Fry,* pp. 283, 296.

45 *Marilyn,* p. 43.

46 Helmut Scheuer, *Biographie* (Stuttgart: J. B. Metzler, 1979), p. 247.

47 "History" (1828), rpt. in *Miscellaneous Writings* (London, 1889), p. 158.

48 "Authorized Biography and Its Discontents," p. 24.

49 *Truth in History,* p. 276.

50 "'Hanging Up Looking Glasses at Odd Corners': Ethnobiographical Prospects," in *Studies in Biography,* ed. Aaron, p. 52.

32

Jay Parini

"Fact or Fiction: Writing Biographies Versus Writing Novels" from *Some Necessary Angels: Essays on Writing and Politics* (1997)

The relationship between fact and fiction is vexed. It's also a hot topic, as they say, and one that's bedeviled literary theory in particular, turning that once rather placid land into a charred battlefield where what is at stake is the nature of truth itself. The general drift of postmodern theory runs something like this: although truth may be in some sense objective, most attempts to reconstruct or reflect that objectivity, whether in fiction or nonfiction, history or biography, are tainted by both the medium itself—language, and ideology, that matrix of assumptions and preconceptions that underlies every gesture in the direction of signification. The extreme (if by now boringly commonplace) observation by Derrida, "*Il n'y pas de hors texte*" [There is nothing outside the text], has become a kind of poststructuralist mantra.

Like all revolutionary, or quasi-revolutionary, movements, poststructuralism served as a corrective, bending the proverbial board perhaps a little too hard in the opposite direction in the attempt to straighten it out. I suspect that few of us would be willing to posit an easy or (as they say) "unproblematic" relation between language and truth or, in the fields of literature and history, between narration and objective reality.

The assumption today is that the writer of any text—a critical essay, novel, biography, historical study—speaks from a particular point of view and that this viewpoint colors and to some extent shapes the content of the work. This is even, in important ways, true of science, as Stephen J. Gould points out in his reflections on natural history, *Eight Little Piggies* (1973). Gould spent a week with Richard Leakey at his field camp on early Miocene sediments near the western shore of Lake Turkana in Africa's Great Rift Valley, and he was present when the skull of *Afropithecus*—a new genus in the ape family—was discovered. Gould notes that try as he might, he could not see bone fragments or a skull anywhere in the sedimentation. What he could see, however—and this startled Leakey and his colleagues—was snails. Gould remarks:

> All field naturalists know and respect the phenomenon of "search image"—the best proof that observation is an interaction of mind and nature, not a fully objective and reproducible mapping of outside upon inside, done in the same way by all careful and competent people. In short, you see what you are trained to view—and observation of different sorts of objects often requires a conscious shift of focus, not a total and indiscriminate expansion in the hopes of seeing everything. The world is too crowded with wonders for simultaneous perception of all; we learn our fruitful selectivities.

I would argue that poems and novels, biographies and works of history, might also be thought of as "fruitful selectivities." To say that something is subjective, or (more properly) that it contains a "subjective element," is not to dismiss it. The subjective element is a product of necessary selection: we choose among the crowd of wonders, seeing what we are trained—or disposed—to see. Whether we like it or not, we have each been educated—trained, if you will—differently. We have read many of the same books but many different ones. Our experiences in life have shaped us too and so that we react differently to the same phenomena. It would be odd if we didn't. And rather boring. Furthermore, it is downright useful in the end for some of us to see skulls and others to see snails.

What interests me is how the poststructuralist shift toward subjectivity affects a novelist or biographer. I've written several historical or biographical novels, including *The Last Station* (1990), which looks at the last year in Tolstoy's life from several viewpoints. More recently, I've written a straight, that is, nonfictional life of John Steinbeck. As I worked on these books, my mind often turned to the relation of fact to fiction, and I want to share some of this thinking.

Not long after I began my research on the Steinbeck biography, my subject's widow, Elaine Steinbeck, told me that she had had a dream in which Steinbeck was sitting in heaven at dinner beside Leo Tolstoy. The famous American novelist told the great Russian writer that Jay Parini was about to write his biography. "Good luck, old man," Tolstoy exclaimed. "Have you seen what he did to me?"

This was funny but also not so funny. I take it for granted that all writers, in whatever genre, are trying to get at what we nervously call the truth. But how to do this?

I doubt whether anyone—even Tolstoy himself—could verify the reality summoned by me in *The Last Station.* Nevertheless, my method in that book still strikes me as a plausible one: I approached the story of that tumultuous last year at Yasnaya Polyana from a half-dozen viewpoints, hoping that by layering voice on voice something like the truth would emerge. I based those chapters on the actual voices of friends or relatives who were living with Tolstoy during this year; luckily for me, it happened that most of these people kept an intimate diary, so I had access to what my characters, who were after all real people, actually thought and felt. I did, however, take the novelist's option of invention when it seemed necessary. For instance, Tolstoy's young amanuensis, Valentin Bulgakov, mentions in his diary that he had a romantic affiliation with a young Tolstoyan woman; he alludes to her several times, intriguingly but unspecifically. I decided to invent her myself. I called her Masha—a typical Russian name—and had a wonderful time imagining her relationship with Bulgakov and making up their correspondence. In fact, I was quite pleased when an extremely well-known Tolstoy scholar wrote to me to say, "I thought your use of those letters between Bulgakov and Masha were particularly effective. I have indeed always admired those letters."

But did I get close to the truth about Tolstoy? Could I have come closer in a work of straight biography? What is indeed the relationship between the Yasnaya Polyana imagined in that book and the real place and lives that crisscrossed, often so tragicomically, in that house in 1910? Was it utterly corrupt of me to blur the distinction between fact and fiction so willfully? Instead of answering these questions directly, let me circle the subject like a fox around the henhouse. If the farmer is asleep, I may take a chicken or two.

It is interesting that, in modern Hebrew, no formal distinction exists between the genres of fiction and nonfiction. If you go into an Israeli bookstore, there is simply one category—*siporet*—which means 'prose narrative.' Although I would hate to lose the license to invent granted by the word *fiction,* I find it useful to dwell on the immense common ground shared by all forms of prose narrative. The areas of fiction and nonfiction overlap in suggestive ways, creating a kind of wild zone in which disbelief is suspended and the narrative itself becomes all consuming.

The term fiction, of course, has its origins in the Latin *fictio,* which means 'shaping.' The term, in this sense, suggests a process of selection and arrangement. Reality—that ongoing hail of sensation that pelts us from cradle to grave—is formless and, in its unmediated condition, without meaning. Random facts are not intrinsically interesting—rather like the sediment in Richard Leakey's dig. It takes a certain frame of reference, a shaping point of view, and, yes, an ideology, to make a fruitful selectivity.

One always begins, of course, with this thing called Fact or, as we say, "the agreed-upon facts." These are the bricks from which we must erect our house of fiction—or nonfiction. But what are facts?

The Bible is as good a place as any to search for truth, and one finds an early instance of the word *fact* in the Gospel of John. "And the word was made flesh" is a translation from the Vulgate: *verbum caro factum est*. The phrase "factum est" is, of course, not nominal but verbal in its construction. It wasn't until the late Middle Ages that, in Latin, factum began to creep slowly toward its modern, positivistic denotation. Even during the late Renaissance, the word fact retained a certain verbalness, as in the French *fait* or the Italian *fatto*. As late as the early nineteenth century, Jane Austen could describe a character as "gracious in fact, if not in word" and mean *deed* when she refers to fact. (It is at least intriguing to note that the Greek equivalents of the Latin *facio* would be *poieo*, 'to make', or *drao*, 'to do'—words that, as it were, evolved into *poetry* and *drama*, two of our main genres in the general category of fiction.)

In the nineteenth century fact was transformed into an ideal and thoroughly nominal category. So Thomas Carlyle would note with a lovely twang of irony: "How impressive the smallest historical fact may become as contrasted with the grandest fictitious event." Indeed, writers of the day were loathe to handcuff themselves to the mast of literalness that seemed to dominate the new ship of mental state. Dickens protested grandly and in *Hard Times* (1845), invented the schoolmaster from hell, Thomas Gradgrind, who has forever stood as the worst example of demonic adherence to mindless factuality. Oscar Wilde, that angel of wit, remarked near the turn of the century: "The English are always degrading truths into facts." Giving the aphorism that extra twist, he added: "When a truth becomes a fact it loses all its intellectual value." Lytton Strachey, the black prince of biography, observed wisely that history is "not an accumulation of facts but a relation of them."

Few except perhaps the most stalwart deconstructionist or philosophical idealist along the lines of Bishop Berkeley would go so far as to deny altogether the existence of a concrete reality: a world antecedent to both language and thought. Dr. Johnson, in his famous refutation of Berkeley, merely kicked a stone by the side of the road and said, "I refute it thus." Science, history, biography, and—yes—fiction, depend on the agreed-upon facts, and there is no point in denying that Napoleon was defeated at the Battle of Waterloo, that water is composed of two parts hydrogen to one part oxygen, or that sexual intercourse leads, in some instances, to pregnancy. It is the relation among facts that matters. So what the imaginative writer does is try to imagine Napoleon having sexual intercourse during the Battle of Waterloo while drinking a glass of water.

This relation among the facts assumes not only a narrative of events or repetition of facts but an imaginative revision and rearrangement—a mosaic that is, in effect, an interpretation. And so we return to fiction as shaping, a process that involves the manipulation of language and relies on similar tropes, turns, techniques, and sleights of tongue. This will be true, as I've learned, for the biographer as well as the novelist.

The task of the writer of biography (which is really a subgenre of history) is, I think, similar to that of the novelist and poet: to construct a version of reality, a fictio of events. And any construction involves a selection from the myriad parts of reality and then the creation of a relation of those selected parts to form a new whole. This is the crucial act of intellection as well as creation. "We compare, contrast, abstract, generalize, connect, adjust, classify, and we view all our knowledge in the association with which these processes have invested it," wrote Isaac Newton, emphasizing the associative nature of intellectual construction.

In his essay on the metaphysical poets, T. S. Eliot wrote what, for me, has always been a memorable description of the process of imaginative construction. Eliot is commenting on Donne in this passage, comparing Donne's verse to those of Tennyson and Browning, neither of whom Eliot especially liked. "A thought to Donne was an experience," he said, "it modified his sensibility. When a poet's mind is perfectly equipped for its work, it is constantly amalgamating disparate experience; the ordinary man's experience is chaotic, irregular, fragmentary. The latter falls in love, or reads Spinoza, and these two experiences have nothing to do with each other, or with the noise of the typewriter or the smell of cooking; in the mind of the poet these experiences are always forming new wholes."

The obvious source of Eliot's notion is Coleridge, who in his wonderfully ramshackle grammar of the creative mind, the *Biographia Literaria* (1817), distinguished between what he called the Primary Imagination and the Secondary Imagination. "The primary IMAGINATION," he wrote, "I hold to be the living Power and prime Agent of all human Perception and as a repetition in the finite mind of the eternal act of creation in the infinite I AM. The secondary Imagination I consider as an echo of the former . . . differing only in degree, and in the mode of its operation. It dissolves, diffuses, dissipates, in order to recreate." In another passage, Coleridge said, "Facts, you know, are not truths; they are not conclusions; they are not even premises, but in the nature and parts of premises."

Thus the primary act of perception involves facts: seizing the object by the senses, gripping it literally. It is an active motion, one of possession. It is a deed. And each time we see something and seize it and make it over into our own, we are repeating the eternal act of creation, participating in what Wallace Stevens in "A Primitive Like an Orb" calls "the essential poem at the center of things." And this essential poem is not any specific poem or story or novel or essay or biography, it is the sum of these acts. Stevens writes,

> One poem proves another and the whole,
> For the clairvoyant men that need no proof:
> The lover, the believer and the poet.
> Their words are chosen out of their desire,
> The joy of language, when it is themselves.
> With these they celebrate the central poem,
> The fulfillment of fulfillments . . .

Stevens's clairvoyants of the imagination—and I would include biographers and historians here as well as lovers, believers, and poets—take the image in the mind's mirror and shatter it, then reconstruct it. And so falling in love, reading Spinoza, listening to the clack of the typewriter, and smelling the garlic as it wafts in from the kitchen all enter into a new relation, and they become parts of a new creation, one that comments on and, ideally, informs the old creation. The writer's job, thus construed, is to take what God has given and to give back better.

Wallace Stevens is a useful poet for me, because he took as his main subject the complex negotiations between reality and the imagination that concern everyone who puts pen to paper. Stevens repeatedly paid homage to what he called "the necessary angel" of reality. Dr. Johnson may have kicked a rock to verify its existence, but what happens to that reality when we evoke it with a word? A subtle, almost invisible, textual maneuver occurs when we say "rock" and the hearer conjures the illusion of a specific rock. The better the poet, the firmer the sense of this reality. "How simply the fictive hero becomes the real," as Stevens says at the end of *Notes Toward a Supreme Fiction* (1942), in which the poet anticipates and out-deconstructs the deconstructer to the tenth power. But the reality of the imagined rock is not really real, not in the same way that the thing we lie down on by Otter Creek to enjoy a bit of sunbathing is real. A rock is a rock is a rock. But the word *rock* in Wallace Stevens's last great poem, "The Rock," is another thing. It takes its place in a grand procession of linguistic differentials.

What all this means for biographers or historians has interested many recent theorists, Foucault chief among them. He folds history into the realm of textuality, which brings it ever closer to fiction. In *The Archaeology of Knowledge* (1972), he writes that once we understand the true nature of history as a text, "the entire field is set free. A vast field, but one that can be defined nevertheless: this field is made up of the totality of all effective statements (whether spoken or written) in their dispersions as events and in the occurrence that is proper to them." Here I would simply call attention to the phrase "in their dispersions as events." These are the facts still in their active verbal phase: *verbum caro factum est.* Reality transmogrified into language and by language.

This view of history as textuality has seemed dazzling to some, though a moment's serious reflection suggests that little that is called new ever really is. The ancient Greeks, who seem at times to have understood everything, did not confuse facts with truth. Nor did they distinguish between fiction and nonfiction as we do. Their assumption was that narrative works contained elements of myth and legend, poetry, and fact. The *Iliad* was, in this regard, a fine prototype for later Greek historiography, represented by the imaginative, even fictive, histories of Herodotus and Thucydides.

Students of modern historical narrative often find Herodotus frustrating. There is no pretense to linearity in his work, for example. Herodotus was an early cubist, juxtaposing stories and points of view with artistic abandon, taking a scissors to the time line and rearranging events for dramatic purpose. He adored digressions too. There is a long digression, for example, about wildlife in Egypt in the middle of his history of the Persian Wars, and he intersperses this meander with gossip about Egyptian religious and social customs. He even includes a wonderful story-within-a-story about Helen of Troy and her supposed stay in Egypt during the Trojan War: a passage that assumes that both Helen of Troy and the Trojan War should be regarded with the same degree of historicity as the Persian Wars themselves.

Where did Herodotus get all his arcane information about the Egyptians and their beliefs and practices? In case we should wonder excessively, he tells us that he visited Egypt and interviewed a number of Egyptian priests. These priests, alas, talk about rival systems of Greek philosophy in explicitly Greek terms. They chat fluently about Greek culture with an awareness of nuance unlikely to be found in an Egyptian priest of that time, however learned. When Herodotus writes about the Persians, he plays similar tricks. At one point, for instance, he reconstructs a debate between Persian noblemen in 521 B.C. on the subject of whether the Persian Empire should remain a monarchy or try its hand at oligarchy or, even more shockingly, Athenian-style democracy. The debate is charged throughout with familiar Greek rhetoric about the pros and cons of the three rival systems, and the whole debate begins with these words: "A debate was held which some Greek readers may find hard to believe: but it was indeed held." Indeed.

Perhaps we should simply call Herodotus the father of the New Journalism. Like Tom Wolfe and others, he is constantly making up conversations between historical characters. So are we to assume that the Ionic-reading audience of this history of the Persian Wars actually believed that these conversations took place? Did the historian's readers really believe that Helen of Troy existed and had gone to Egypt—an account of the legend deeply at variance with that of Homer? Though I can't answer this question, I would like to assume that his audience simply regarded this history as a fiction—a well-shaped if somewhat idiosyncratic narrative that was open to debate. Indeed, future Greek historians would take issue with Herodotus and challenge him, as would generations of classical historians. But nobody in his or her right mind would accuse Herodotus of trying to deceive anyone. He was merely selecting and arranging his material in a pattern that seemed to him to be true.

The relationship between history and fiction is complex, and it would be churlish of me to suggest there is no difference. Fiction is in fact part of history. It both reflects and occasionally makes history. It is not, I suspect, for nothing that the rise of modern history parallels the rise of the novel. The Göttingen school of modern historiography and the novel were both flourishing by the 1770s, and the nineteenth century was pretty much the Age of History, for both history as a practice and the novel. The great novelists of that era—Scott, Dickens, Balzac, Flaubert, Stendhal—were all historians of a sort. Dickens's *Barnaby Rudge* (1841), for instance, provides an account of the Gordon riots more detailed and analytical than any yet produced by an historian. Stendhal's account of the Battle of Waterloo in *The Charterhouse of Parma* (1839) is superb military history. And Balzac's *Comédie humaine* (1841) offers a detailed social history of France between the years 1792 and 1840.

More so than any previous form of literature, fiction is history. But the story it evokes is not some remote idealized past; in a good novel, the past is not only our present but our future as well. We look to history for examples, for instances of what went wrong or right. And although some novels specifically ally themselves with the traditions of historical fiction, an argument can be made that any novel is by its nature historical, even those written in the present tense. Anything processed by memory is fiction. That is to say, anything that has been shaped and reconstructed is fiction.

Whereas only a few years ago any self-respecting novelist would cringe at the epithet *historical,* this seems to have changed. Writers have seized historical, often biographical, subjects and for good reason. In the old-style historical novels, such as *War and Peace* (1864–1869), history was a pictorial backdrop against which fictional characters played out their lives. We may catch a glimpse of Napoleon at the Battle of Borodino, but Napoleon is not the subject of the fiction. Recently, novelists have been foregrounding history and historical figures, thus redefining the genre. I have in mind here novels like *The General in His Labyrinth* (1990), Gárcia Márquez's study of the dying Simón Bolívar, or Peter Ackroyd's *Chatterton* (1987) or *Hawksmoor* (1985).

Novels are about lives, after all: about pieces of lives or whole lives. Traditionally, these lives have been made up, with half-believable disclosures at the outset that read, "The characters in this novel are entirely fictitious and any relation to persons living or dead is entirely accidental." I would prefer that novelists of the future write: "Everything in the following pages is authentic, which is to say it is as true as I could make it. Take it or leave it." One peculiarity of contemporary life, of course, is that so-called real lives often seem less true than the lives in novels. Could anyone have made up David Koresh, O. J. Simpson, and Newt Gingrich, for instance?

Prose fiction in the form of biography precedes the novel by centuries, gathering into its narrative streams the lives of great warriors, saints, and statesmen. Many of these biographies followed in the mode of Suetonius, who felt relatively free to imagine what he could not empirically know. It was taken for granted that what mattered was the story itself and that truth revealed itself in the process of narration. In *Dubin's Lives* (1979), Bernard Malamud's novel about a biographer and his problems, Dubin says, "There is no life that can be recaptured wholly, as it was. Which is to say that all biography is ultimately fiction."

The most fictitious form of biography from ancient times to the present is clearly autobiography, that mode of "true confessions" that begins with St. Augustine and proceeds through Rousseau and Erica Jong. The art of fiction has its origins there, I suspect, in a genre where subjectivity is, at least by the reader, simply assumed. (I once introduced Gore Vidal to Erica Jong, and Vidal asked what she was writing. "My memoirs," she said. Vidal replied, "At last, you're trying your hand at fiction.")

The autobiographical aspect of contemporary fiction could almost be called its defining feature. Saul Bellow, John Updike, and Norman Mailer, for instance, have been self-consciously autobiographical to the point of embarrassment. Updike's *Problems and Other Stories* (1979) is a searing example. This portrait of a family torn apart by divorce begins with an autobiographical preface in which Updike notes that the book describes "the curve of a sad time" in his personal life. The reader is thus invited to read the book as autobiography. *Problems* tells us what it's like for a family to go through a divorce, and one might argue that people can learn more by reading here about the infinitely complicated tensions, cross-purposes, and mixed feelings involved in such a crisis than by actually going through it. For mysterious reasons, it is hard to get a grip on what is happening in our lives while it is actually happening. We apparently need the mirror of fiction to see what lies in front of our noses. In a sense, we learn what our lives are like by reading about them as well as by living them, which is why fiction matters.

We read biographies for a similar reason: to find out how other people got through their lives. I, for instance, love to read about writers to see how they managed to get their work done in the course of busy lives. It's not easy to sit down to write when there are bills to be paid, children to ferry from one place to another, classes to teach, phone calls to answer, letters to respond to, and so forth. How did Dickens do it? Or Scott? Or Nabokov? In a good biography, one learns about a given subject's job difficulties, sexual conflicts, money problems, dental troubles, everything. If I'm interested in a writer, almost nothing about her or him can bore me.

Let me return to my novel, *The Last Station*. My longtime obsession with biography naturally spilled over into my fiction. Having read the diaries of the dozen or so people closest to him, I thought briefly about writing a straight biography of Tolstoy; I quickly, however, began to feel the limitations posed by conventional biography as a genre. One can describe events on the surface, but one can't get into them and under them in the same way that novelists can. What interested me in the case of Tolstoy was not the facts themselves—a half-dozen sound biographies already existed—but the emotional resonance of those facts. As I wrote, I found myself freely inventing, of course: how else can one write a novel? But I was working within the bounds of fact. Fact was the landscape and fiction the weather that played over that landscape and gave it color, texture, and mood.

I knew, for example, that Sofya Tolstoy on the night of July 23, 1910, threw herself into a pond with the intention of committing suicide. The "straight" biographer is stymied here by the fact that she did not mention this extremely significant act in her diary. Her husband merely notes it, rather dryly, as did a half-dozen other people. The agreed-upon facts are sparse. But these facts were productive for me as a novelist. I felt at liberty to enter her mind, to imagine her feelings. The conventional boundaries of biography may have prevented me from trying to put myself so fully into Sofya's shoes, although I was always keenly aware that if Sofya Tolstoy were to read this particular scene, she would say, "Give me a break, Parini. It was nothing like that." I would counter, "My dear Sofya, it never is."

Having written the Tolstoy novel and two other semifictional narratives, I began to wonder what it would feel like to write straight biography. No sooner had I begun to speculate along these lines than the chance to write John Steinbeck's life presented itself. I decided to go with it, and the experience of writing this book only confirmed what Malamud's Dubin asserts, that "all biography is ultimately fiction." The biographer, like the paleontologist, must reconstruct the extinct creature from a few scattered bone fragments; unless one wishes to erect a massive crate of air, one has no choice but to invent. Perhaps *invent* is the wrong word. To *envision*. Like the novelist, the biographer must summon the weather, the feel of a landscape, the texture of the subject's skin. A social fabric must be woven, made dense with conflicting motives, expectations, and anxieties. All the while, one realizes that the life of the biographical subject is not life at all: we do not live our lives in chapters, for example. The billion-faceted thing called human motivation must be simplified, often guessed at. One must choose a particular story from perhaps dozens of stories one could tell, which is why no single biography is ever definitive.

Elaine Steinbeck's dream about her husband's meeting with Tolstoy in heaven got me thinking. What follows is an interview I did recently with John Steinbeck himself, in heaven:

As I walked, ankle-deep in cloud, across the cool floor (heaven is rather like a geisha parlor that way: they make you take your shoes off), I could see Steinbeck sitting at a gilded table, reading. As I got closer, I saw the name of Charles Fourier, the Utopian socialist, on the cover.

"I never read this while alive," he said, without so much as introducing himself. "I should have. My notion of the 'phalanx'—you know, the idea that people act differently in group situations than they do on their own—it's all here."

Against my better judgment, I could not resist teasing him. "You were wrong about the etymology of the word, Mr. Steinbeck."

"Call me John," he said.

"Thank you . . . John. You see, it derives from a Greek word meaning 'spider', not a Latin word meaning 'turtle', as you thought."

"Does it matter?" he asked, rather wanly. I felt petty and, yes, pedantic. For a hideous moment I thought he was going to get up and go.

"You've come a long way," he said.

"There are some in Oxford," I said, "who would not agree with you."

He seemed mildly bemused. "I've read your book," he said. "Or most of it. I never like reading about myself. It never, you know, seems quite real."

"Was the book inaccurate in any way?"

"Look, son. May I call you Jay?"

"Of course."

"The point is, it only matters to a limited extent how 'accurate' a book like yours is. I picked up one or two mistakes, maybe half a dozen. This kind of thing is mostly irrelevant."

"Did you recognize yourself?"

"Sometimes," he said, scratching his darkly tanned scalp. "But it's not really me there. Biographies are always caricatures. It's why I don't like them."

"Can you be specific? I tried very hard to picture things as I imagined them."

"Ah, imagined! There you are! Your book is a fantasy of what you thought my life was like."

"What did you expect," I countered, "a videotape?"

"I suppose my quarrel is with the genre itself, not you. Biographies are really novels in disguise, aren't they?"

"Just as novels are autobiographies in disguise," I said. "I remember that letter to your editor, Pat Covici, where you said you always identified with one of the characters in each novel, and you called this the 'author-character.'"

He squinted at me through the bright haze. "Did you 'identify,' as they say in high school English classes, with me as you wrote your book?"

"Let's say I sympathized," I said, rather nervously. "You made it difficult for me at times."

"What upset you?" he asked. "That thing with Carol?"

He was referring to his first marriage, to Carol Henning. She wanted children, but he didn't. When she got pregnant accidentally, he insisted that she have an abortion. The procedure went wrong, and Carol could never again have children. Not long after, he insisted on a divorce—much to her chagrin.

"You behaved badly," I said. "Carol loved you. She typed your books, pushed you in all the right directions as a writer. She even gave you a title for *The Grapes of Wrath*."

He was scowling now. "You think your job as biographer is to sit in judgment, is that it? I didn't like your little asides about that marriage, in fact. You weren't there. You couldn't possibly know what went on between us."

He was right, and I felt horribly small.

"At least you uncovered that affair she had with Joe Campbell. Even I was shocked to read his diary. My God, the man was a cad."

"You tended to idealize women," I said, perhaps too boldly for someone in my position. "It was inevitable that you would be disappointed so many times in love."

"In life!" he said.

"I hope I didn't go overboard in attacking your mother," I said.

"Again, you simplified. But in general you got the right idea. She was a perfectionist, and I wasn't perfect. She used to say I'd either be president of the United States or go to jail. But you made my father into a weaker man than he really was. There was a quiet strength there: you'd need that videotape to see it. Even then, if you weren't inside me, you might have missed the exchange of energies between us."

"Perhaps I should have written a novel about you, not a biography," I said.

Wisely, he ignored my remark and leaned toward me now, his breath sweet with ambrosia. "I don't think my mother was half so upset with my academic failures as you made out. That was your mother you were writing about, not mine!"

I sat back, horrified. Perhaps in conjuring John Ernst and Olive Steinbeck I had really summoned the ghosts of my own parents! Biographers, like scientists, are subject to the phenomenon of "search image" as well. We see what we have been conditioned to see.

"You made one other big mistake," Steinbeck said gravely. "Like many of your colleagues in the field, you assume that oral testimony is accurate. You often try to prove points with quotations, forgetting that a dozen people have a dozen different versions of the same event. You were uncanny in ferreting out Carol's friends, and Gwyn's."

"Did they lie to me?"

"*Lie* isn't the word. These people didn't like me. They thought of me as somehow responsible for the misery of my wives."

I thought he was being awfully touchy. For the most part, my book is deeply pro-Steinbeck. The book is laced with quotations from his admirers.

"The people who could have really said something useful about me were Ed Ricketts and Dook Sheffield," he added. "And Pat Covici."

"They were all dead when I began my research," I said. "I'm not really one for seances."

He looked at me skeptically.

"Look," I said, feeling suddenly aggressive. "I knew quite a few things about you that I didn't say."

"I know, I know," he said. "I'm at least glad you were discreet. So many of your colleagues aren't. But I must complain about one thing. Your readers may well get the impression that I went all haughty and pompous at the end—that stuff about my staying in fancy hotels and owning a yacht and attending the theater in a top hat and tails. That stuff meant nothing to me."

I listened and inwardly acknowledged the truth of what he was saying. I think I had looked in some corners a little too hard for a story. It's not that what I said was untrue: Steinbeck had changed over time, and his values shifted. But everyone changes. Given Steinbeck's great financial success, he might well have gone over the top.

"And that stuff about the Vietnam War. You were one of them, weren't you? That antiwar gang?"

"I was," I said.

"You people really let down the side," he said. "There was no need."

I decided against rehearsing the arguments for and against the Vietnam War just now. Some issues are never resolved. "Was there anything about the book you liked?" I asked, feeling a bit let down by this interview.

He laughed that barrel-chest laugh of his. "Poor man," he said, "I've been rough on you, have I?" He looked at me warmly. "You must realize that no book is ever satisfactory. What was it Paul Valery said? 'A poem is never finished, only abandoned.' A biography is an invention, more or less true. You got some of it right. Tolstoy, you should know, is not especially happy about what you did to him. He was not nearly as bad to Sofya as you suggest."

I bit my lip. It still seems to me that I went easy on Tolstoy when it came to his marriage. The man was a dreadful husband in most respects: a bully and, in his most idiosyncratic way, a puritanical snob.

"I can assure you, however, I didn't like Jack Benson's biography any more than I liked yours. And I will probably dislike the next one as well."

The archangel who had escorted me through the gates was suddenly waving in the distance, and I knew I must go or forfeit my evening meals at Christ Church. "It was good of you to agree to this meeting," I said, standing.

"Fourier," he said, utterly ignoring my remark. "I was grateful to you for one thing: the tip on Fourier. He understood the phalanx better than I did. He was there way ahead of me, in fact."

I left him reading. I could see that no book I could have written would ever seem, to him, an accurate version of his life. A biography, like a novel, is simply one version of reality, more or less true depending on the depth of the author's knowledge and the extent of his or her imagination and sympathy. The "agreed-upon facts" in any given life are relatively few and fairly stable; what one makes of them is, as it were, another thing entirely.

33

Martin Middeke

"Introduction" from *Biofictions: The Rewriting of Romantic Lives in Contemporary Fiction and Drama* (1999)

Life-writing, historical consciousness, and postmodernism

The postmodern zeitgeist, as is well known, approves of uncertainty, ambiguity, and fragmentation; it distrusts the ideas of totality, synthesis, or binary oppositions. Instead, the collage is preferred to the unifying whole, the paradox to the logical, subjectivity to objectivity, relativity to truth, difference to identity, duration to origin, metonymies to metaphors, the signifier to the signified. These features give evidence of the linguistic turn which the humanities and, especially, epistemology have taken in the twentieth century, and which has evolved radical constructivism and the structuralist and poststructuralist philosophies of Michel Foucault, Roland Barthes, and Jacques Derrida. Derrida's notorious statement of "il n'y a pas de hors-texte" has become proverbial in the context of a theory in which all knowledge and experience are considered as language-based, in which any perception of the world is regarded as being always preceded by language. This language-centered epistemology has entailed the deconstruction, the demystification, and, ultimately, the death of any authority, be it god, the author, or the canon. Such authorities have been replaced by concepts of intertextuality; the unity of signs has been displaced into differences; meaning, truth, and knowledge have been decentered by a radically subversive language whose potential spin-offs may hover between the dead end of ideological radicalism and the avenue of a politics of difference. The emphasis of difference, then, may give expression to off-center minorities and to the de-marginalization of those marginalized by the traditional, authorial, canonical forces of power.

Postmodernism sets out to challenge the occidental idea of enlightenment and, especially, the cognitive and epistemological values which the concepts of a historical past, a cultural heritage, or tradition have conveyed right into our present. Indeed, "whatever means are used to make sense in postmodern times, history does not seem to be one of them."[1] A post-historical impression is reinforced by a socio-cultural condition which Jürgen Habermas called "die neue Unübersichtlichkeit": a cultural state of affairs which has sprung from the alienating experience of socio-economic pluralization and segmentation. The twentieth century has witnessed the reversal of those eschatological promises made by the processes of nineteenth-century modernization, a *Frankenstein*-like turning of the monster against its creator. And in the face of disillusionment, unemployment, amorphous bureaucracies and sophisticated technologies which render global self-destruction possible, there are not a few who grieve over the loss of utopian belief in the future.[2] In the face of such an historical situation it would seem paradoxical that postmodernism (or any other philosophy) should forego the orientation inherent in the historical mode of thinking, which relates the potential of human action and identity to the encompassing correlation of past, present, and future.

According to Jörn Rüsen, three essential questions arise here which concern the human understanding of reality and also, by extension, of art: firstly, we may ask whether a historical identity which has become precarious is able to initiate changes in our historical thought and in our modes of interpretation. Secondly, we may question the traditions which define identity and, in reaction to this, demand a new way of historical thinking aiming at the renewal of the old structures. And thirdly, we may want to know the extent to which a new mode of historical thought can incite radical innovation.[3]

It goes without saying that what is asserted here about the condition of history also applies to the *writing* of history and the writing of the history of lives—biography. Thus, the burden of the "nightmare of history" (Nietzsche), which lies at the heart of both the historiographical and fictional discourses of postmodernism, may easily be projected onto biography. With reference to life-writing—no matter whether of the authoritative or the fictional kind—we may suspect a postmodern emphasis on the indeterminacy of biographical knowledge and the laying bare of epistemological uncertainties and blanks within the context of the representation of biographical facts. Especially, we may gather that the biographer, like the historian, is likely to be mistrusted for his declaration of neutrality and the assertion of the objective nature of what he is recounting.[4] Indeed, as Hayden White puts it,

> most contemporary thinkers do not concur in the conventional historian's assumption that art and science are essentially different ways of comprehending the world. It now seems fairly clear that the nineteenth-century belief in the radical dissimilarity of art to science was a consequence of a misunderstanding fostered by the romantic artist's fear of science and the positivistic scientist's ignorance of art.[5]

A new revisionist historical consciousness would therefore have to accentuate that fiction and historiographic/biographical discourse are not mutually exclusive.[6] That is to say, such a consciousness would have to be aware of the fact that fiction and biography/historiography have affinities which are based upon the narrative nature of both genres. Hence, taking into account the epistemological findings of the linguistic turn in philosophy, both the deconstructive and the heuristic potential of fiction would have to be acknowledged. Yet to acknowledge the fact that linguistic representations create reality and may even change it does not mean that, in turn, we have nothing but linguistic representations. And to assert that there are structural parallels between fiction and biography is not necessarily to say that they are the same, that fact and fiction are indistinguishable, or that they are characterized by the same functions.[7] In fact, readers and critics of biofictions will find themselves reminded of the distinction between fact and fiction every time they consult the factual biographies in order to trace fictional deviations from the factual accounts of the lives at issue, deviations which may be considered relevant, that is, symbolic. No matter whether readers or critics are trapped into pursuing red herrings or whether biofictions entangle them in a game with the historical material, the factual world may be suspended, but hardly done away with. For the writer of biofictions this means that a fictional or empathic/sympathetic approach to the subject may make use of the historical material, may play with it, may even invert it, if necessary, and still arrive at a heuristically impressive and plausible interpretation of that life. As a consequence, the artist may incorporate and reflect upon epistemological uncertainties caused by the aporias of time and language, *without* obliterating historical consciousness.[8]

This holds true of all the novels and plays discussed in this volume, fictional rewritings of the lives of British Romantic writers for which we suggest the generic term "biofictions." Their artist-protagonists constitute a poetological and self-reflexive *conditio sine qua non* in that they focus our attention on what it means to be an artist and on the attendant circumstances in the creation of art. Contemporary biofictions may vary individually in the degree to which the novels and plays either comment self-reflexively on the processes of writing, or metabiographically center on the epistemological problem of recounting a life. Biofictions cast doubt on "our beliefs in origins and ends, unity, and totalization, logic and reason, consciousness and human nature, progress and fate, representation and truth, not to mention the notions of causality and temporal homogeneity, linearity, and continuity,"[9] but they do not deny the respective historical foil on which they are written—indeed, how could they without missing their point?

All the novels and most of the plays discussed here in poetological terms belong to what Linda Hutcheon calls historiographic metafiction; they are characterized by their overt historical referents (Blake, Chatterton, the Shelley-Byron circle, etc.). Since the carrier of this reference is language, the reference of the signifier to the signified, the relationship between the subject of contemplation and its object is seen as problematic. Even so, the valid historical foil counteracts a postmodern "anything goes" and thus transcends a purely autoreflexive, hedonistically autonomous or narcissistically solipsistic concept of art which is self-sufficient. However, the hermeneutic emphasis on interpretation, which is the aim inasmuch as it determines the structural principle of postmodernist biofictions, keeps these works of art from being mere chains of factual information. As Andreas Höfele has convincingly argued, the situation is fairly paradoxical: the texts *de*construct and, at the same time, *re*construct historical knowledge, and

> the concept of history as a consistent, teleologically streamlined process has broken down under the onslaught of deconstructionist theory proclaiming an era of 'posthistoire,' and the notion of the self as a clearly defined ontological entity has dissolved under the dissecting lens of psychoanalysis and role-theory, yet we find a conspicuous flourishing of the historico-biographical clement in contemporary English literature.[10]

One fairly obvious explanation for both the aesthetic paradox at work here and the prominence of life-writing is the assumption that the classical modernist dilemma between cut-up forms and the perception of a fragmented reality on the one hand and the hunger for the mythically objective and stable on the other is more archetypically essential to human beings than postmodernists and poststructuralists would have us believe.

In order to make this point clearer, the works of postmodernist biofictions discussed here clearly have to be set apart from the aesthetically dubious but sociologically and anthropologically highly interesting phenomenon of countless sequels to the novels of another Romantic writer: Jane Austen. These sequels testify to a prevalent sense of nostalgia and a retrogressive desire—"retro-fashions" as Jean Baudrillard sardonically called the trend[11]—on the part of their readers. Julia Barrett (a.k.a. Julia Braun Kessler and Gabriella Donelly) concludes her sequel to Jane Austen's *Sense and Sensibility* after two-hundred-and-forty pages of fake Austen characters, fake Austen landscape and fake Georgian architecture as follows:

> To sanction ideal attachment—to argue, in effect, for love, and love alone—may be ill-advised in this or any age. Yet when all is said, the inclinations of the heart *will* prevail, whatever the consequences. And, steadfast Reader, what association for Margaret Dashwood could have been as exquisite as that which she presently contemplated?[12]

Here, the juxtaposition of historical past and Barrett's present brings about a vulgar nostalgia for emotion in the face of alienation, a ludicrous, grossly idealized Arcadia lulling readers into a sense of existential belonging in the face of disintegration, striving towards continuity in the face of isolated fragments. Yet even without the embarrassing address to a "steadfast" reader this retrospect idyll is unintentionally ironical.

Leaving the desire for sequels apart, the immense popularity of biography must be attributed to a similar desire to get to know others in what have become anonymous social environments. As Ira B. Nadel indicates, biography as a "verifiable fiction" has become the heir of the nineteenth-century realist novel. Founded upon the Aristotelian pattern of a beginning, middle, and end, as well as on a straightforward development of character, biography provides links to individual stability: it has become "an essential element of modern survival. Through its account of the lives of others, it shows us how to live. The popularity of biography exists in direct proportion to our need to feel that life, in a world of disharmony, dishonor and strife, must have value."[13] With regard to an analysis of biofictions in contemporary English literature a related question may be asked: does not a desire for life, authenticity, originality paradoxically underlie all fictional efforts to deconstruct the same? And can we not speak of a biographical desire essential to all human beings, the manifestation of an ineradicable subjectivity especially in times when philosophy and the experience of the world around us suggest the death of the self? We will therefore have to specify how writers of biofictions react to historical relativism, epistemological uncertainty, and twentieth-century aesthetic experiments and, at the same time, satisfy their own as well as their readers' desire for historical and biographical background. We will also have to ask if this revised historical consciousness reintroduces chances for enlightenment in seemingly posthistorical times.

De-romanticized? The relevance of romanticism for a poetics of contemporary biofictions

The prominence of the biographical mode and the artist-protagonist within historiographical metafiction and contemporary drama has not remained unnoticed on the evidence of novels such as D. M. Thomas's *The White Hotel*,

Julian Barnes's *Flaubert's Parrot,* Peter Ackroyd's *The Last Testament of Oscar Wilde,* and plays like Christopher Hampton's *Tales From Hollywood,* Peter Shaffer's *Amadeus,* Barry Kyle's *Sylvia Plath: A Dramatic Portrait,* Pam Gems's *Stanley,* and Tom Stoppard's *Travesties* or, most recently *The Invention of Love,* to name but a few representatives of the genre not dealt with in this volume.[14] The fact, however, that in many contemporary biofictions the historical referents are writers of the Romantic period has largely been neglected. This is astonishing insofar as both the common ground and the differences between the Romantics and the contemporary novelist or playwright are obvious and, indeed, form an interesting link to the understanding of contemporary poetics.

Turning back to the Romantics as the historical foil of contemporary biofictions is a far from arbitrary gesture. The reason why Romantic lives like those of Shelley and Byron have not lost their mythical fascination is, of course, that they were simply interesting, unpredictable, and often notorious lives. Moreover, the Romantics were probably the first artist-figures in the modern understanding of the word. Similar to what Hegel conceived of in *The Phenomenology of Spirit* [*Die Phänomenologie des Geistes*] as the "inner revolution," the Romantic artists fashioned themselves after the ideal of a non-conformist, independent consciousness that strives to arrive at absolute freedom and, thereby, became icons of the artist. David Morse points out that, when one thinks of Blake or Shelley, the Romantic artist becomes the visionary, yet also the outsider, as the vision and the real world hardly ever match:

> In his attempts to communicate his vision to the world the artist faces the problem that the vision, because hypothetical, lacks credibility; the artist has no credentials that can validate his claims to prophetic status; in the act of communication itself the vision becomes warped, fragmented and distorted, while there is equally the danger that the artist was mistaken and that his vision was nothing more than a delusion, and a dangerous one at that. The artist veers between megalomania in his intoxication with his own ideas and impotence and despair at his inability to maintain his own sense of the visionary and to bring it into some kind of meaningful relationship with the everyday world. The Romantic protagonist, whether anachronistic hero, artist or hypocrite, becomes a law unto himself. Estranged from the world and at variance with it, he has no choice but to assume that he is right and that the world is wrong. He increasingly figures as a Superman—a man who moves beyond ordinary criteria of good and evil and enters the world of moral relativity in which he knows no law but that of his own will.[15]

The variety in the representations of Romantic artists' lives in contemporary biofictions testifies to the fact that there is no one definition of Romanticism.

Such aspects as the power of the artistic imagination, the return to nature, the emphasis on wonder, strangeness, and beauty, as well as the Faustian yearning for the infinite still may best be summarized by the keyword "subjectivity." Romantic subjectivity relates to the various manifestations of individuality and especially to the historicization of human existence. Romantic thought envisaged a potentially changing universe as a continuum of past, present, and future, and Romanticism set this view of an organically changing world against the traditionally rigid concepts of neoclassicism. That is why the Romantic era constitutes the starting point of a mode of historical thought that is based upon dynamic instead of static categories, and in which relativistic conceptions of truth replaced absolute and timeless ones. The idea of reforming society and setting human beings free from the fetters of external influences or the belief in things as they are [*Die Dinge an sich*] was prevalent in philosophical discourse ranging from Kant's *Critique of Pure Reason* [*Kritik der reinen Vernunft*], Fichte's *Foundations of Transcendental Philosophy* [*Wissenschaftslehre*], Schiller's *On the Aesthetic Education of Man* [*Über die Ästhetische Erziehung des Menschen*], and Schelling's *Of the Ego as Principle of Philosophy* [*Vom Ich als Prinzip der Philosophie*] to Hazlitt's *The Spirit of the Age,* Hegel, and John Stuart Mill's *On Liberty.*[16] The Romantics therefore began a process which late twentieth-century postindustrialism can hardly claim to have brought to a close. Moreover, the epistemological problems of how to connect, interrelate, and unify subjective points of view with objective reality and thereby arrive at an autonomous existence were central issues of the idealism of Kant, Schelling, and Fichte, and were also a dominant subject matter of Romantic poetry and Romantic theories of art. To give but one example, Samuel Taylor Coleridge, who was influenced by (and at times thoroughly mistaken about) German idealism, thought that the subject can only know and understand the object of contemplation when subject and object merge, dissolve, become one. This, however, would presuppose that the subject can self-reflexively become one with itself and, besides, suspend and escape temporality. In his *Biographia Literaria,* Coleridge put the epistemological problem in a nutshell when he commented on the infinite regress at work here:

> We can never pass beyond the principle of self-consciousness. Should we attempt it, we must be driven back from ground to ground, each of which would cease to be a ground the moment we pressed on it. We must be whirled down the gulf of an infinite series.[17]

The position of the artist as an outsider and the epistemological difficulties involved in linguistic representation and, accordingly, in self-knowledge are obviously reflected in Romantic heroes such as Wordsworth's Marmaduke, Byron's Manfred and Don Juan, and, of course, Coleridge's ancient mariner. They are all marginalized outsiders, lonely wanderers on a quest for a vision, who at the same time know that this vision is out of reach and indeed lost forever. Thus, Morse is right when he emphasizes that "the Byronic hero is not cause but consequence: he is always encountered *after*—a perennial fifth-act Hamlet or Macbeth."[18] With reference to twentieth-century poetics Coleridge's epistemological and poetological insight into the infinite regress inherent to understanding foreshadows the extremes of Beckett's minimalism, and it shows that the Romantics might well be considered proto-deconstructionists—albeit to a varying degree which would have to be analyzed.[19] However, Coleridge insisted on establishing art and the imagination as the *causa sui* in the processes of understanding in order to sidestep the infinite regress: compared with postmodernist biofictions, Romanticism, then, is radically different, since it sets out to bridge the gap between subject and object. Yet the emphasis on fiction as imaginative truth, the re-establishment of historical consciousness, and the symbolic relevance of the past for the present within postmodern biofictions can certainly not deny traces of Romanticism.[20] To give another example illustrating this: in the "Second Manifesto of Surrealism" André Breton points out that Romanticism constitutes an important part of the cultural heritage of contemporary art. Like those of the Romantics, the visions of the surrealists cannot at once be those of every man, or, in other words, a temporary outsider position of the artist paves the way before intellectual stances can broadly be taken for granted. Furthermore, like the Romantics, the surrealists denounce a "ridiculous illusion of happiness and understanding." However, in contradistinction to the Romantics' turning to the imagination as the *causa sui,* as an instrument of unifying subject and object, the surrealists—like the postmodernists—"appear in the midst of, and perhaps at the cost of, an uninterrupted succession of lapses and failures, of zigzags and defections which require a constant re-evaluation of its original premises [. . .]." Thus, for Breton, Romanticism represents the ultimate beginning of contemporary art, yet only in the sense of the "first cry of a newborn child."[21]

As regards another side of the Romantic view of the artist: Wordsworth defines "good" poetry as "the spontaneous overflow of powerful feelings"; poetry, he argues, "takes its origin from emotion recollected in tranquillity [. . .]."[22] Percy Bysshe Shelley sets poetry apart from reasoning: "A man cannot say, 'I will compose poetry.' The greatest poet even cannot say it: for the mind in creation is as a fading coal which some invisible influence, like an inconstant wind, awakens to transitory brightness [. . .]."[23] In much the same vein and drawing largely on Coleridge, John Keats characterizes the poetic imagination as a matter of instinct rather than of quantitative, intellectual reasoning. "O for a Life of Sensations rather than of Thoughts," he pleads. Whereas reasoning offers an outward view, the imagination sympathetically looks inward, focussing on hidden intentions and realities of life. Hence the poet who, according to Keats, identifies momentarily with the object of his contemplation may neither pursue an "irritable reaching after fact and reason" nor ever have preresolved upon his object. Uniquely merging with that object of contemplation, the "camelion [*sic*] Poet" is different from "the virtuous philosopher," the poet "has no identity—he is certainly the most unpoetical of all God's creatures."[24] In their entirety these statements reflect the Romantic view of the artist-genius:

> A cardinal axiom of Romanticism was that of the uniqueness, singleness and particularity of everything in the universe, and such an assumption has pervaded modern literary criticism with consequences so catastrophic that they verge on deliberate mystification and anti-intellectualism. In this view every artist is an entirely original and unique genius who creates a wholly idiosyncratic perceptual field that we name Blake, or Wordsworth, or Lawrence, or James, and which we interpret as the construction of a personal identity.[25]

The Romantic belief in the originality of the artist-genius and the nature of art as divine creativity has been contradicted by the postmodernist insistence on narrative structure, writing, the conventionality of signification, and on the status of texts as intertexts. History and society are seen as being constantly read and interpreted, as Julia Kristeva emphasizes:

> Nous appellerons INTERTEXTUALITÉ cette inter-action textuelle qui se produit à l'intérieur d'un seul texte. Pour le sujet connaissant, l'intertextualité est une notion qui sera l'indice de la façon dont un texte lit l'histoire et s'insère en elle.[26]

This implies that the text contains a productivity beyond that of its creator: of course, the more such productivity is ascribed to the text itself, to reading, and to intertextual play,[27] the more the linguistic concept of the sign loses its transcendental signified in the process of signification, the more the idea of the Romantic genius begins to vanish. Hence the crucial problem that emerges from the juxtaposition of Romantic and postmodernist concepts of the artist within biofictions is how to encounter infinite regress, the never-healing wound of the subject-object difference within the process of human understanding. As mentioned above, the Romantics took refuge in the realm of poesy and made imagination—at least temporarily—overcome that gap.[28]

> Romanticism is the attempt to heal the break in the universe, it is the painful awareness of dualism coupled with the urge to resolve it in organic monism, it is the confrontation with chaos followed by the will to reintegrate it into the order of the cosmos, it is the desire to reconcile a pair of opposites, to have synthesis follow antithesis.[29]

Not only do poststructuralism and deconstruction seek to devalue such Romantic logocentrism, they also relish the very differences the Romantics suffered from. Thus, insofar as the re-writings of Romantic artists' lives within postmodernist biofictions are highly self-conscious and intertextual writings, they imply an ironic deconstructive distancing between the past and the present. The artists are no longer unreachable heroes; rather they arc debunked, ironicized, or dethroned to textual trickster figures, anti-heroes, or, more realistically, to human beings who have common desires—for instance, Mozart in Shaffer's *Amadeus*—and, as Howard Brenton's Mary Shelley puts it, "lungs of mucus and blood."[30] But as I have stated above, as long as a revisionist historical consciousness, that is, ultimately, reality-reference, re-enters works of art that Werner Wolf accordingly describes as "moderate experiments,"[31] there is no reason to declare the Romantic cause as lost.

"If Winter comes, can Spring be far behind?"[32]—Shelley's reservedly utopian vision in the "Ode to the West Wind" is a political statement that draws on the necessity of political change in the context of the French Revolution and England's conservatism. It also hints at the socio-political relevance of Romanticism for our "posthistorical" times. As M. H. Abrams has said, "we continue to live in an era of conflict, revolution, inordinate expectation, recreancy, and counterrevolutions that was inaugurated by the Romantic age of revolutions."[33] Blake's and, particularly, Godwin's and Shelley's vision of creating a New Jerusalem characterized by a free personality in a free society is very much likely to have had a political impact on the contemporary political British playwrights and their attempts to set up theater (e.g. the London fringe movement) as a counter-culture to middle-class establishment. Indeed, the political and social criticism inherent in Blake, the young Wordsworth, Burns, and Shelley in particular render these four also proto-socialists, paradigmatic angry young men—a characteristic feature that accentuates the parallels to contemporary political playwrights and their refusals to conform to the pressures urged on them by mass culture and commercialism.[34] As expressed in Shelley's *Alastor,* the self-referential introversion of the artist should not exclude caring for the human race,[35] art should not outrun reality, and, in poetological terms, proto-deconstructionist art should not surpass the proto-socialist utopian vision.

This tension is further evidenced by the observation that a representative number of the works discussed in this volume center on one literary figure who has traditionally lived in the shadow of the canonized "great" six: Mary Shelley. Contemporary women writers have paid much attention to her life and her novel *Frankenstein,* both have also been widely discussed within feminist literary criticism. In the context of an opposition between a radically aesthetic, deconstructive approach on the one hand and a radically political or realist approach on the other, Mary Shelley and feminist criticism would somehow have to take up a middle position. Feminist theory has paid attention to the results of a deconstructive analysis which lays bare the conventionality of power structures which have enabled a few and disabled many. At the same time, feminist criticism would be expected to be politically relevant; a theory which has justifiedly not tired in pointing to the fact that women have been denied historical agency cannot afford to surrender a utopian perspective to purely deconstructive pluralization, let alone give in to an impression of posthistorical resignation and nothingness. The discussion of Mary Shelley and *Frankenstein* within contemporary biofictions and feminist criticism focuses on such aspects as female sexuality, the opposition between public man and private woman, guilt, alienation, orphanhood, intellectual activity. Mary Shelley's life and intellectual background including the influences of her parents William Godwin and Mary Wollstonecraft, her husband Percy Bysshe Shelley, and Byron, as well as the mythical genesis of *Frankenstein* imply the problems of motherhood and child-bearing; they underline the relationship between birth and death, and the crucial tension between a dangerous solipsism and the humanistic responsibilities of science; and, most of all, Mary Shelley and *Frankenstein* embody the fact that the Romantic universe, or, to be more precise, Percy Bysshe Shelley's and Victor Frankenstein's universe, was a highly gendered construction, too. As Anne K. Mellor has aptly remarked, by controlling the biological functions of human reproduction, "Frankenstein has eliminated the necessity to have females at all." Mellor points out that Mary Shelley's ideal was to look upon nature as a "sacred life-force in which human beings ought to participate in conscious harmony." Obviously, Frankenstein's patriarchal cult of the individual, his egotism and selfishness are rejected in favor of an ideal, a life led in harmony between men and women. This also touches upon questions of aesthetics, as Mary Shelley "purposefully identifies moral virtue, based on self-sacrifice, moderation, and domestic affection, with aesthetic beauty."[36] Clearly enough, *Frankenstein* is an overt rejection of the radically subjective and, consequently, egocentric aspects of Romanticism. And likewise, the monster's narrative account of his existence reinforces the necessity of individual rationality and agency.

> Delivered at the top of Mont Blanc—like the North Pole one of the Shelley family's metaphors for the indifferently powerful source of creation and destruction—it is the story of deformed Geraldine in "Christabel," the story of the dead-alive crew in "The Ancient Mariner," the story of Eve in *Paradise Lost,* and of her degraded double sin—all secondary or female characters to whom male authors have imperiously denied any chance of self-explanation. At the same time the monster's narrative is a philosophical meditation on what it means to be born without a 'soul' or a history, as well as an exploration of what it feels like to be a 'filthy mass that move[s] and talk[s],' a thing, an other, a creature of the second sex.[37]

In much the same way as doubts are cast on radical individualism and solipsism, the Romantic male concept of free love is questioned here. Mellor is right in asking whose interests free love serves at all, and she does not hesitate to say that although Percy Bysshe Shelley is widely looked upon as a feminist, neither he nor any other Romantic poet "ever imagined a utopia where women existed as independent, autonomous, different, but equally powerful and respected authors and legislators of the world."[38] Howard Brenton puts it bluntly when he has his Byron accuse Shelley of hypocrisy:

> Y'bloody hypocrite! Where is your legal wife? In England! The two women you are with, Mary y'call your wife, Claire y'friend—concubines, sir! Y'mistresses, sir! All your idealism, revolution in society, revolution in your personal life, all trumpery! The practice of it, sir, the practice doth make us dirty, doth make all naked and bleeding and real! [. . .] Y'damn theorising! All you want to do is get your end away.[39]

In order to counteract male Romantic ideology Mellor suggests the term "feminine Romanticism" for discussions of women writers of the period. This feminine Romanticism is characterized by a moderate subjectivity that acknowledges its individual rights, but also subscribes to an "ethics of care." It does not delegate social reform and the utopian change of society to the actions and visions of a small number of megalomaniac men, but rather to "communal exercise of reason, moderation, tolerance and the domestic affections that can embrace even the alien Other."[40]

Notes

1 Rüdiger Kunow, "Making Sense of History: The Sense of the Past in Post-historic Times," in *Making Sense: The Role of the Reader in Contemporary Fiction*, ed. Gerhard Hoffmann (Munich: Fink, 1989), 169.

2 Jürgen Habermas, *Die Neue Unübersichtlichkeit* (Frankfurt am Main: Suhrkamp, 1985); see also Jörn Rüsen, *Zeit und Sinn: Strategien historischen Denkens* (Frankfurt am Main: Fischer, 1990); Christian Meier, "Vom 'fin de siècle' zum 'end of history'? Zur Lage der Geschichte," *Merkur* 44 (1990): 809–23.

3 Jörn Rüsen, "Die Kraft der Erinnerung im Wandel der Kultur: Zur Innovations- und Erneuerungsfunktion der Geschichtsschreibung," in *Der Diskurs der Literatur- und Spachhistorie: Wissenschaftsgeschichte als Innovationsvorgabe*, ed. Bernard Cerquiglini and Hans Ulrich Gumbrecht (Frankfurt am Main: Suhrkamp, 1983), 29–46.

4 Linda Hutcheon, *A Poetics of Postmodernism: History, Theory, Fiction* (London and New York: Routledge, 1988), 88.

5 Hayden White, *Tropics of Discourse: Essays in Cultural Criticism* (Baltimore, MD: Johns Hopkins UP, 1992), 28.

6 There can be no doubt that a good biography must be more than a compilation of facts: Phyllis Rose is unequivocal about the fact that "biography—and I mean by that the highest reaches of biographic art, self-conscious, artful biography, composed and not compiled biography—aspires to the condition of the novel" ("Biography as Fiction," *Tri-Quarterly* 55 [1982]: 111); Dennis W. Petrie comments upon the degree to which design plays a role within life-writing: "Although criticism should concern itself less with the historical authenticity of a biographer's facts *per se* and more with the manner in which the biographer has presented them, the two factors are—and should be—irrevocably entwined. And a biographer's purpose will surely affect the structure and style of his work. For example, hagiographers violate facts to achieve their adulatory aims: and directly because of this, their art becomes pattern-molded and cliché-ridden. On the other extreme, Lytton Strachey manipulates literal truth to construct brilliantly formalized, compact portraits of subjects whom he loathes. Thus, the circumference of truth in biography is always design—design in function, form, and fashion. Ideally, the biographer can wrestle with the problems that these three elements encompass and manage to strike a fair and pleasing equilibrium." (*Ultimately Fiction: Design in Modern American Literary Biography* [West Lafayette, IN: Purdue UP, 1981], 16–17). See also Helmut Scheuer, "Kunst und Wissenschaft in der modernen literarischen Biographie," in *Literatur und Sprache im historischen Prozeß: Vorträge des Deutschen Germanistentages,* ed. Thomas Cramer (Tübingen: Niemeyer, 1983), Vol. 3, 287–300, and Malcolm Bradbury, "The Telling Life: Thoughts on Literary Biography," in *The Troubled Face of Biography,* ed. Eric Homberger and John Charmley (New York: St. Martin's Press, 1988), 131–40. A slightly ironical remark was made by Katherine Frank: "In contemporary literary biography it seems that it requires two books by two authors to approach biographical completeness, and that we must reconcile ourselves to the fact that the narrative and analytic biographical modes are very different impulses. There will continue to be biographers who want to tell us a life story, and others who will want to tell us what the story means, but few of them will attempt to do both" ("Writing Lives: Theory and Practice in Literary Biography," *Genre* 8 [1980]): 513).

7 Ina Schabert is right in pointing to the "unavoidable relativity of factual biography." And Schabert has made an important distinction when she points to the fact that even though a factual biography may itself be "degraded from the normal standards of biographical writing, grossly tendentious, simplistic, inventive," "such violations of the compositional rules of factual biography do not produce a work of the fictional genre." "Both fictional and factual biographies," Schabert continues, "are based on the facts of history and of an individual's life, and both, in the sense that they are constructs made up from the facts, are fictions. Yet the constructs are different in kind." These differences touch upon the degrees of self-referentiality in factual and fictional biography, the aim of the factual being "correspondence to the world of historical knowledge" rather than "aesthetic coherence." Furthermore, the differences are matters of essentiality: while the factual elements within biofiction gain metonymic status and thus, as Schabert asserts, make fictional biography resemble a sophisticated anecdote, selectivity within factual

biography hints at thematic unity. Moreover, "no actually false statement may be introduced for the sake of essentiality; whereas in a novel this can lead to something 'poetically true,' in a factual biography this is only bad, tendentious writing" ("Fictional Biography, Factual Biography, and Their Contaminations," *biography* 5.1 [1992]: 1–16; quotations: 10, 13, 5, 7). Franz K. Stanzel points to reception theory: he sees the difference between fictional and factual biography in the way the reader reacts to the appeal-function of the blanks in the text ("Historie, Historischer Roman, Historiographische Metafiktion," *Sprachkunst* 26.1 [1995]: 113–23).

8 Cf. Marianne Dekoven, "History as Suppressed Referent in Modernist Fiction," *English Literary History* 51 (1984): 137–52.

9 Hutcheon, *A Poetics of Postmodernism,* 87.

10 Andreas Höfele, "The Writer on Stage: Some Contemporary British Plays about Authors," in *British Drama in the 1980s: New Perspectives,* ed. Bernhard Reitz and Hubert Zapf, *anglistik & englischunterricht* 41 (1990): 79–91.

11 Jean Baudrillard, *Kool Killer oder der Aufstand der Zeichen* (Berlin: Merve Verlag, 1978), 49.

12 Julia Barrett, *The Third Sister: A Continuation of "Sense and Sensibility"* (London: Michael O'Mara Books, 1996), 240. Rolf Breuer is currently preparing a list of all the completions, continuations, and adaptations of Jane Austen's novels, together with an essay on "The Poetics of the Sequel."

13 Ira B. Nadel, "Narrative and the Popularity of Biography," *Mosaic* 20.4 (1987): 134, 136.

14 See Ina Schabert, *In Quest of the Other Person: Fiction as Biography* (Tübingen: Francke, 1990); Annegret Maack has published two important essays on the subject "Charakter als Echo: Zur Poetologie fiktiver Biographien," in *Klassiker-Renaissance: Modelle der Gegenwartsliteratur,* ed. Martin Brunkhorst, Gerd Rohmann, and Konrad Schoell (Tübingen: Stauffenburg, 1991), 247–58, and "Das Leben der toten Dichter: Fiktive Biographien," in *Radikalität und Mässigung: Der englische Roman seit 1960,* ed. Annegret Maack and Rüdiger Imhof (Darmstadt: Wissenschaftliche Buchgesellschaft, 1993), 169–88. See also Barbara Schaff, *Das zeitgenössische britische Künstlerdrama* (Passau: Stutz Verlag, 1992).

15 David Morse, *Romanticism: A Structural Analysis* (Totowa, NJ: Barnes & Noble, 1982), 6–7.

16 See M. H. Abrams, "Revolutionary Romanticism," *Bucknell Review* 36.1 (1992): 19–26.

17 Samuel Taylor Coleridge, *Biographia Literaria,* in *Samuel Taylor Coleridge,* ed. J. Jackson (Oxford and New York: Oxford UP, 1985), 301. On the interdependence of language and consciousness, see also Harold Bloom, *Romanticism and Consciousness: Essays in Criticism* (New York: Norton, 1970).

18 Morse, *Romanticism,* 289; on the irreconcilable subject-object difference highlighted by the Romantic/Byronic hero see especially 284–92.

19 For a more detailed analysis of the correlation between Romanticism and deconstruction see J. Drummond Bone, "Historicism and Deconstruction: Two Contemporary Perspectives on Romanticism," in *Beyond the Suburbs of the Mind: Exploring English Romanticism: Papers Delivered at the*

Mannheim Symposium in Honour of Hermann Fischer, ed. Michael Gassenmeier and Norbert H. Platz (Essen: Die Blaue Eule, 1987), 212–24, and Christoph Bode, "Romanticism and Deconstruction: Distant Relations and Elective Affinities," in *Romantic Continuities: Papers Delivered at the Symposium of the "Gesellschaft für Englische Romantik" held at the Catholic University Eichstätt,* ed. Michael Gassenmeier and Günther Blaicher (Essen: Die Blaue Eule, 1990), 131–59. Bode's important essay contains a rich bibliography on the issue. On the reception and popularity of Romanticism within deconstructive theory, see also Hubert Zapf, "Dekonstruktion als Herausforderung der Literaturwissenschaft: Das Beispiel der englischen Romantik," *Anglia* 106 (1988): 360–79.

20 Coleridge pointed out that a symbol "is characterized by a translucence of the Special [the species] in the Individual or of the General [the genus] in the Especial or of the Universal in the General. Above all by the translucence of the Eternal through and in the Temporal. It always partakes of the Reality which it renders intelligible; and while it enunciates the whole, abides itself as a living part in that Unity of which it is the representative. The other [allegories] are but empty echoes which the fancy arbitrarily associates with apparitions of matter." Quoted in Aidan Day, *Romanticism* (London: Routledge, 1996), 110.

21 André Breton, *Manifestoes of Surrealism,* trans. Richard Seaver and Helen R. Lane (Ann Arbor: U of Michigan P, 1972), 152, 152–53, 151, 153. On the relationship between Postmodernism and Surrealism, see also Elizabeth Deeds Ermarth, *Sequel to History: Postmodernism and the Crisis of Representational Time* (Princeton: Princeton UP, 1992).

22 William Wordsworth, "Preface to *Lyrical Ballads,*" *William Wordsworth,* ed. Stephen Gill (Oxford and New York: Oxford UP, 1986), 598, 611.

23 Percy Bysshe Shelley, *Shelley's Poetry and Prose,* ed. Donald H. Reiman and Sharon B. Powers (New York and London: Norton, 1977), 503–04.

24 John Keats, letters of November 22, 1817 [first quotation] and December 21, 1817 (to George and Thomas Keats) [second and third quotation], in Maurice Buxton Forman (ed.) *Letters of John Keats* (New York: Oxford UP, 1935), 227–28 and 72.

25 Morse, *Romanticism,* 2.

26 Julia Kristeva, "Narration et transformation," *Semeiotica* 1 (1969): 443.

27 See Mikhail M. Bakhtin, *Rabelais and His World* (Bloomington: U of Indiana P, 1988); Roland Barthes, "From Work to Text," in *Image Music Text,* ed. and trans. Stephen Heath (London: Fontana Press, 1977); Jacques Derrida, *Of Grammatology,* trans. Gayatri Chakravorty Spivak (Baltimore: Johns Hopkins UP, 1976), 50.

28 John Keats's thoroughly deconstructive lines in the concluding stanza of his "Ode to a Nightingale," for instance, dismantle the merely temporary soothing the imagination is able to bring about: "Forlorn! the very word is like a bell/ To toll me back from thee to my sole self!/Adieu! The fancy cannot cheat so well/As she is fam'd to do, deceiving elf." (*Poetical Works,* ed. H. W. Garrod [Oxford: Oxford UP, 1986], 209). Similarly to this, Keats called the capacity of human beings to endure half-knowledge—or, in other words, difference—"negative capability," an important philosophical as well as poetological

principle for Keats's most mature work. See Walter Jackson Bate, *Negative Capability: The Intuitive Approach in Keats* (Cambridge, MA: Harvard UP, 1939).

29 Henry H. H. Remak, "A Key to West European Romanticism?" *Colloquia Germanica* (1968): 44. I am grateful to Rolf Breuer for drawing my attention to Remak's essay. For a similar diagnosis, see also Catherine Belsey, "The Romantic Construction of the Unconscious," in *Literature, Politics and Theory: Papers from the Essex Conference 1976–1984,* ed. Francis Barker, Peter Hulme, Margaret Iveson, and Diana Loxley (London and New York: Methuen, 1986), 68–69. A concise overview of the debate is provided by Day, *Romanticism,* 107.

30 Howard Brenton, *Bloody Poetry* (London: Methuen, 1989), 13. See also Höfele, "The Writer on Stage," 81, 85, and Dieter A. Berger, "Künstlerdethronisierung als Dramatisches Prinzip: Zur Ästhetik des Gegenwartstheaters in Großbritannien," in *Studien zur Ästhetik des Gegenwartstheaters,* ed. Christian W. Thomsen (Heidelberg: Winter, 1985), 209–24.

31 Werner Wolf, "Radikalität und Mässigung: Tendenzen experimentellen Erzählens," in *Radikalität und Mässigung,* ed. Maack and Imhof, 34–53 (esp. 45–51).

32 Percy Bysshe Shelley, "Ode to the West Wind," *Poetical Works,* ed. Thomas Hutchinson (Oxford and New York: Oxford UP, 1986), 579.

33 Abrams, "Revolutionary Romanticism," 31.

34 See Catherine Itzin, *Stages in the Revolution: Political Theatre in Britain Since 1968* (London: Methuen, 1980).

35 See Day, *Romanticism,* 161–62.

36 Anne K. Mellor, "Possessing Nature: The Female in *Frankenstein,*" in *Romanticism and Feminism,* ed. Anne K. Mellor (Bloomington: Indiana UP, 1988), 220, 228, 229. See also Elisabeth Bronfen, *Over Her Dead Body: Death, Femininity and the Aesthetic* (Manchester: Manchester UP, 1992), 130–39.

37 Sandra M. Gilbert and Susan Gubar, *The Madwoman in the Attic: The Woman Writer and the Nineteenth-Century Literary Imagination* (New Haven and London: Yale UP, 1979), 213–47 (esp. 234–235).

38 Anne K. Mellor, *Romanticism and Gender* (New York and London: Routledge, 1993), 28.

39 Brenton, *Bloody Poetry,* 43.

40 Mellor, *Romanticism and Gender,* 209–10.

34

John Keener

Chapters Four and Five from *Biography and the Postmodern Historical Novel* (2001)

Chapter four

The problem of genre I: Biography and/as history

I cling to the tangible, to visible reality and to history.

JEFFREY MEYERS. *The Spirit of Biography*

These studies of Schultz, Oswald and Nixon have shown that certain historical figures—and perhaps all historical figures, to a certain extent—baffle our conventional distinctions between narrative which is "historical" and that which is "fictive." Yet, it is this very boundary that must be the base, the control to any experiment in reconceptualizing biographical narrative. Despite their various crossings, and despite the fact that image-systems make for strange generic bedfellows, each of the texts discussed in the previous three chapters could be argued as being more history than fiction, or vice versa. In other words, biographical narrative operates somewhere between what we might call "historical" and "novelistic" discourse. A text that tackles the full biographical scope of an historical figure might take the form of either historical or novelistic narrative, as a comparison of

John Banville's novel *Doctor Copernicus* and Angus Armitage's biography *Copernicus* shows. The same applies to texts that contain perfunctory biographical information, as with the Jack Kennedy of Walter Abish's short story "The Istanbul Papers" (*Minds Meet,* 1975) and Taylor Branch's history *Parting the Waters* (1988). In my discussion of Schultz, Oswald and Nixon, I have at once assumed and troubled the difference between these two general ways of narrating. The matter is, of course, far from simple. To discern more precisely between the "historical" and the "fictive," I turn now to an extended definition of biography as distinguished by its (albeit equivocal) endeavor to maintain an "historical" mode of discourse while narrating, or insinuating, biographical time, for biography's problematic role as "historical" discourse indeed mirrors that of biographical narrative in general. The issues discussed below directly affect the way that we "read" the lives of "real" people in any text.

What qualifies biography as "historical" discourse? According to Hayden White, "all written discourse is cognitive in its aims and mimetic in its means," and so "history is no less a form of fiction than the novel is a form of historical representation."[1] But biography—again, by virtue of its concern with *people*—often takes this reciprocity with fiction further than other modes of "historical" narrative, or far enough to provoke considerable critical retrenchment. Benjamin Hrushovski's distinction, for example, is simple: the literary (i.e. the non-historical) text possesses an interdiegetic frame of reference and the historical text an extradiegetic one. Likewise, Ina Schabert differentiates between fictional and historical biographical forms by the nature of referentiality with regard to their "systems of utterance":

> In fictional biography, the biographical facts are arranged within a self-referential system of utterance . . . and are seen together in a creative vision of inner experience conveyed with all the sophistication of the post-realist novel. Factual biography, on the contrary, opens out toward the whole of historical knowledge, its statements are meant to signify particular, authentic events, and they are placed within a narrative argument which follows generally accepted and/or scientifically established lines of reasoning.[2]

Schabert provides some extreme examples to back her argument, most notably Anthony Burgess' biographical novel of Beethoven, *Napoleon Symphony,* whose structure references its content by actually mirroring the arrangement of Beethoven's *Eroica*.

Since binary divisions like this—basically restatements of Aristotle's "real/imaginary" distinction—break down when referential systems (or "systems of utterance") are aped (as with Burroughs' *The Last Words of Dutch Schultz*) or compounded (as with DeLillo's *Libra*), more multifold taxonomies have emerged from biographical theorists like Paul Murray Kendall and

James Clifford. Kendall proposes three speculative types of biography: "interpretative biography," which controls its use of fictional discourse; "fictionalized biography," which, as its name suggests, takes liberties with information as well as discourse; and "novel-as-biography," which is "almost wholly imaginary."[3] (This last type was pejoratively labeled "biografiction" by Durling and Watt in 1941's *Biography: Varieties and Parallels*) Clifford's five biographical types are: Objective Biography (which gives the "impression" of completeness and no imagination of form, style, etc.); Scholarly-Historical Biography (which allows for selection, but no guesswork or "fictional devices," including psychology); Artistic-Scholarly Biography (in which "the biographer considers his role that of an imaginative creative artist"); Narrative Biography (which is "a running narrative, almost fictional in form"); and full-blown Fictional Biography (in which "imagination is given full rein. The fictional biographer thinks of himself almost as a novelist . . . The result reads like a novel, and largely is one").[4]

Clifford regards generic differences as crucial to the biographer's task ("He cannot select his evidence or choose a style, or make any of his difficult choices, until he knows just what form his work will take"[5]). But none of this prepares us for works like Vladimir Nabokov's *The Real Life of Sebastian Knight* (1945), Steven Millhauser's *Edwin Mullhouse: The Life and Death of an American Writer, 1943-1954. By Jeffrey Cartwright* (1972), R. M. Koster's *The Dissertation* (1975), or Wolfgang Hildesheimer's *Marbot: A Biography* (1981). All these authors upset the standards of biographical form by writing what must be considered, structurally, as a collection of *biographies*; but in terms of content, nothing *biographical* occurs within these books because none of their subjects, strictly speaking, are "real." In *Marbot,* Hildesheimer does test the parameters of the "fictive" subject by borrowing the rudiments of identity from the margins of history (one Sir Andrew Marbot [1801-1830]) to affix to an essentially fictional character. It is difficult to tell where this kind of practice stops and more pointed borrowings, like John Barth's abduction of Ebenezer Cooke in *The Sotweed Factor* (1960), begin. When so little is known about figures like Marbot (and to a lesser extent. Cooke), a single narrative can create an image-system with a single resonance frequency, obviating any question as to its "fictiveness" and at the same time resulting in a figure less discursively "real" than Dutch Schultz, Richard Nixon, or Lee Harvey Oswald. Perhaps this is the definition of the fictional character.

The fact is, biography has undergone four hundred years of criticism and still nobody is entirely sure what it is; William Epstein lists as one of its characteristics a "resistance to criticism."[6] Persistent uncertainty about the criteria for "biography" *per se* is the reason lives like Schultz's, Oswald's, and Nixon's offer such puissant examples of the contested zone between fiction and history. If there were a sanctioned definition of biography in place, the qualities of fictional narratives would be easier to determine (and things would be much less interesting). That the line between fictional and historical biographical narratives remains so intransigently difficult to define is a consequence of biography's formal interaction with both fictional and historical narrative modes, and this interaction, in turn, complicates the problem of defining what biography is. These problems are further exacerbated by the postmodern interrogation of historical truth, essentialist identity, and the relationship between the two. All this suggests that biography is more a *practice* than a genre, which strengthens my general description of biographical narrative but does little to define biography as a baseline for narrative comparison. Nevertheless, it would be worthwhile to attempt a few working distinctions between biography's "fictional" and "historical" elements. Three of these—structure, the narrator, and language—are particularly interesting and troublesome.

Biography and form

My first question is whether the *structure* of biography can be manipulated (usually in the interests of narrative unity) while still avoiding "contamination" by other narrative modes. Aristotle pointed out that "infinitely various are the incidents in one man's life which cannot be reduced to unity; and so, too, there are many actions of one man out of which we cannot make one action."[7] Subsequently, the conflict is between proponents of what Milton Lomask calls "the narrative biography, in which you carry an individual from cradle to grave, though not necessarily in that order . . . [and] the topical biography, in which you try to suggest the whole of your subject by splitting it into its parts"[8] . . . in other words, linear and non-linear narrative. Partisans of the former maintain that, since temporal linearity most nearly approximates the "reality" of experiential time, it also parallels the evolution of the "essence" of the subject, as when Kendall declares that "the manipulation of time, regardless of its novelistic associations, ruptures the essential dimension of life."[9] The autobiographical narrator, meanwhile, appears to have been allowed to "rupture" his or her own "essential dimensions" with impunity. Even when the Aristotelian maxim (that the various incidents in a life cannot be reduced to unity) holds firm, unity in autobiography is not only allowed but expected. The autobiographer is free, if not obligated, to provide the kind of structural unity that is taboo in strictly objective biography.

Many critics defend non-linear biographical structuring not only as an artistic prerogative but a pragmatic (if not a psychological) necessity. Milton Lomask, for example, insists that "no human life is so tidy, so uncomplicated, that you can reconstruct it by simply reciting the events of it in sequence,"[10] thus echoing Berthoff's idea that history itself must be "recovered by inquiry and assembled according to some cohering fiction (in the non-narrative sense) of intelligibility."[11] The emphasis on linearity in biography assumes an aspect of historical writing that is self-evidently false: that historical/biographical discourse, being linear, always matches story-time (also linear), event-for-event. In other words, linear structuring can eliminate the distinction between the two levels of narrative analysis, story and discourse, collapsing the two as Stephen Ambrose does in his methodical *Nixon*. Cohn argues that "the story/discourse dichotomy has remained marginal at best for the analysis of historical (or generally nonfictional) narrative," and therefore disregards it as one of her "Signposts of Fictionality."[12] The most cogent refutation of this idea appears in the same number of *Poetics Today* as Cohn's essay. There, Gérard Genette insists that "no narrative, including extrafictional and extraliterary narrative, oral or written, can restrict itself naturally and without special effort to a rigorously chronological order," and that anachronies—disruptions of linearity like prolepsis and analepsis—are operative in both kinds of narrative (even if fiction does declare its anachronies with more flourish).[13]

Of course, few critics insist upon linearity in the strictest sense. Indeed, it is all but impossible to maintain. The biographer's impulse to essentialize the life, usually requiring an atemporal survey of selected evidence, or even the reference to evidence outside the present moment, normally supersedes the mandate for linear structuring. An expository "idea" of the subject transcends the calendar. The essentialized "idea" can remain potent even when the birth-to-death life course remains intact. Johnan Galtung, for example, has identified a recurrent sequence in biographies of the modern West: Childhood, Education, Work, and Retirement.[14] Such structuring suggests a biographical model with a capitalist ideology: that the development of the individual reflects a progressive integration into, mastery of, and eventual liberation from, the market. Such progressive staging reinforces the convention by which "a man's entire youth is treated as nothing but a preliminary to his maturity."[15] Bakhtin describes this doctrine as originating in the classical concept of *entelechy*, the philosophical ideal of actuality as opposed to potentiality. In other words, the very act of linear narrating necessitates temporal sectioning, which betrays an "idea" or ideology. In Epstein's words, such narratives "reproduce and celebrate in biographical discourse the straight lines of moral rectitude and professional careerism already inscribed in cultural discourse."[16] Linear structures, then, implicitly reinscribe this cultural pattern, and the "high points" or crises of biography occur either at the seams between these divisions or at moments where one of its roles is fortified or exchanged. Steven Millhauser, in his pseudo-biographical novel *Edwin Mullhouse,* satirizes this when he arranges the short eleven-year life of his subject into three divisions: The Early Years (birth to age 6), The Middle Years (6 to 9) and The Late Years (9 to 11).

In superimposing it upon an eleven-year life-span, Millhauser reveals chronological compartmentalization—linear as it is—to be a form of artifice, if not a calculated agenda. In that this kind of structuring is a function of biographical "careerism." it points toward another presupposition of conventional biography: that linear structuring redefines the subject as inherently *public*. Subjects like Nixon and Schultz are validated in biography by their steady, progressive mastery of the public world around them. The narration of this mastery both infers and implies the "outer man" and appears in the reader's mind as a kind of graph.[17]

Biography and the narrator

A second problem in distinguishing biography as "historical" narrative involves the narrator, that (fictional) agent who makes night visits across the border. The biographical narrator has been called both fictional and historical, often at the same time. Ira Bruce Nadel's three types of biographical narrator, for example, span the entire range of forms; they include "the dramatic/expressive, the objective/academic and the interpretative/analytic. The first emphasizes participation, the second detachment and the third analysis."[18] This distinction reinforces the idea that the biographical narrator is at times fictional, conventional wisdom holding that, through the narrator, fiction is "mediated." One of Dorrit Cohn's "Signposts of Fictionality" is the presence of such mediation, "the doubling of the 'narrative instance.'" This "doubling" is especially obvious, Cohn continues, in homodiegetic fiction (in which the narrator is also a character), although "we are compelled to accept that the language transmitted to us in heterodiegetic fiction cannot be imagined by analogy to *any* plausible real-world discourse situation, no matter whether we personalize or depersonalize its origin."[19]

Genette has offered a straightforward test for the fictionality of narrative involving a series of algebraic relationships between the author (A), the narrator (N) and the interdiegetic character (C), which he qualifies with a simple axiom: "What defines narrative identity . . . is not legal identity as the Census Bureau understands it, but the author's serious adhesion to a story for whose veracity he assumes responsibility."[20] In other words, Paul Sann's *Kill the Dutchman!* is a factual narrative because the reader can only presume that Sann himself "assumes responsibility" for the veracity of his story. On the other hand, the "reporter" in *Miami and the Siege of Chicago* is a *character* (and so the text is a fictional narrative) because it is the "reporter," not "Norman Mailer," who assumes that responsibility. Tamar Yacobi would say that Mailer's "reporter" is a true fictional subject, and therefore that *Miami*'s narrative is "fabricated," since:

> Between the two extra-fictional parties to the communication act—the implied author and the reader—there stands at least one fictional subject (a speaker, narrator, reflector, channel of information) and often more

> than one. By whatever name it is called, such mediacy of transmission necessarily attaches not to discourse in general or even to narrative, as most theorists appear to believe, but to fabricated discourse and narrative . . . Only the maker of fictions must in principle speak through the voices of others, and these voices all of his own making.[21]

We might therefore read any fictional text as being set between large, invisible quotation marks, even in those cases where paratextual markers ("a memoir," for example) ostensibly eliminate the narrator by equating him or her with the author of the text. The impact of this on the text's real-world truth value is profound. The critic and the "ordinary" reader alike perceive "the opposition between the relative, indirect, and partial knowledge of the historian and the elastic omniscience enjoyed, by definition, by someone who invents what he narrates,"[22] but they also tend to consider the "partial" knowledge as more credible than the "omniscience" of a narrator. Many biographical novels revel in fictional mediation and even use it to explore the very truth values that they undermine. But these narratives are never (or rarely) mistaken for historical discourse, except when they use parody to create the rare "hoax" text.

In so far as it is mediated by a narrator, then, fictional discourse is *diegetic,* in the Jamesian sense that a narrator diegetically "tells" while an author mimetically "shows."[23] Literally speaking, no narrative of any sort is less mimetic than any other. With reference to the narrator, fictional and historical discourse are in many cases practically distinguishable, but only by the *degree* to which (to borrow Plato's terminology) the author "takes a role or personality," or (to borrow Cohn's) there is a "doubling of the 'narrative instance,'" or (to borrow Genette's) "A=N." It is in fiction rather than history that this generally happens. In Yacobi's words, "only the maker of fictions must in principle speak through the voices of others."[24] Barthes has identified the growing integration of historical forms in all modern narrative—which he calls its "reluctance to declare its codes"—as a movement toward the mimetically "dramatic."[25] As with linear structuring, then, the opposition between mimetic and diegetic narrative has distilled into a fairly straightforward convention: historical texts are *dramatically re-enactive,* and fictional ones are *diegetically expressive.* But this is a diaphanous quality indeed.

With this in mind, one of the great ironies of biography is that, even when the author does attempt to submerge the "narrator" *per se,* a curious thing frequently happens: the author fills the narrator's role, or falls into it. He or she "takes a personality" within the text, and in so doing assumes a diegetic voice. This voice is sometimes empathetic, sometimes hostile, but it always speaks with some urgency to the uninitiated from the standpoint of one who uniquely comprehends a particular life. The potential for personal agenda is the primary reason that biography must continually argue for its historical legitimacy. There is a danger of subjectification when the author "gets too close," when there is too much correspondence between subjective historian and objectified historical subject. Many theorists deplore the absence of the author-as-narrator, as when Joseph Gold argues that the lack of narrative voice "detracts from, rather than enhances, the believability of a life-story."[26] Precepts like this one have devolved from the epigrammatic writings of Leon Edel, whose own portrait of the biographer is itself ambiguous. On the one hand, Edel insists, "the biographer may not substitute his . . . fantasy for that of the subject." On the other, "an 'impersonal' biography is tasteless and without character, force, or authority."[27] Many biographers, like Edel, consider biography a special, humanistic form of history, and so liberties in narrative point of view are a lurking, ambiguous danger.

In most pre-Modem biographical theory, it had been considered indecorous for the biographer to show much personal interest in her subject, although it did happen (consider the wrath heaped upon Shakespeare biographers George Brandes and Frank Harris near the turn of the century). After Lytton Strachey inaugurated the "debunking" period of biography with its aggressive biographical stance, a theoretical literature arose that combined apologetics with admonishment. Today, biographers alternately defend and warn against identification, in language that is often moral in tone and imperative in syntax. On one hand, Doris Kearns expresses the "need to get away, to leave, not to be owned" by the subject ("Angles of Vision," in *Telling Lives: The Biographer's Art,* ed. Marc Pachter [Philadelphia: University of Pennsylvania Press, 1981], 92.), and Richard Holmes identifies "peculiar and perilous identification" as "the first crime in biography" (*Footsteps: Adventures of a Romantic Biographer* [New York: Viking, 1985], 264). In *Writing Lives,* Edel describes the impulse toward and against identification as a complex psychological reaction to Freudian transference, against which he somewhat cryptically cautions. On the other hand, Catherine Drinker Bowen permits that the biographer "falls in love" with her subject, "slowly, after deep acquaintance and many arguments back and forth" (*Biography: The Craft and the Calling* [Boston: Little, Brown, 1969], 42). During research for his biography of John Brown, Stephen Oates claims to have become "utterly and completely immersed in his [Brown's] life" (*Biography as High Adventure: Life Writers Speak on Their Art.* [Amherst: University of Massachusetts Press, 1986], 129-130). For Gamaliel Bradford, the increase in biography writing in the middle part of the century can be attributed to "the desire to get out of ourselves and into the lives of others" (*Biography and the Human Heart* [Boston: Houghton Mifflin, 1932], 3). The so-called "new biography" is essentially an attempt to reconcile suspicion and acceptance of biographical identification. Like the patron of the "new biography," Leon Edel, Robert Gittings aims at a self-consciously ambiguous reconciliation of the two stances, by remarking that identification is a matter "of which the most conscientious biographer must be continually and actively aware" (*The Nature of Biography* [Seattle: University of Washington Press,

1978], 59.), which is to say that identification is useful, even vital, but must be the object of continual vigilance.

I am describing a conflict within the biographer herself, one that often goes unrecorded, what Richard Holmes (*Footsteps,* 66-67) calls a "pre-biographic" narrative:

> [The] fictional or imaginary relationship between the biographer and his subject . . . [is] not merely a 'point of view' or an 'interpretation,' but a continuous living dialogue between the two as they move over the same historical ground, the same trail of events. There is between them a ceaseless discussion . . . a steady if subliminal exchange of attitudes, judgments and conclusions . . . This form of identification or self-projection is pre-biographic and in a sense pre-literate . . . But the true biographic process begins precisely at the moment.

Of course, biography as we normally conceive it exists far beyond this "pre-biographic" stage, where all the "subliminal exchange of attitudes, judgments and conclusions" between the biographer and subject have been written out, or *over,* although this is certainly not always the case.[28]

Biography and style

Structure and narrative point of view are only the most macrotextual elements by which historical and fictional discourse are distinguished in biography. Differences in *language* work on a more clandestine, microtextual level, for in biography language is assumed to be inextricably connected to content. In Hughes and Horowitz's conception of "organic biography," for example, "thought and style are not and cannot be separated."[29] Nadel characterizes this organic quality as the biographer's quest for the ideal metaphor through language. "In a biography," he writes, "referential and figurative language interact as the biographer locates a pattern or image that develops metaphorical qualities to shape the life of the subject."[30] Meanwhile, despite lingering echoes of York Powell's argument in the 1890's that "style has no more to do with history than it has with law or astronomy,"[31] recently updated in Hayden White's well-received claims of a "poetical understructure" to all supposedly "factual" discourse,[32] there is still a common preconception of an historical discourse that biography should, but does not always, adhere to.

Because of ideas like these, and the prevalence of texts that apply them, biographical language has come to be viewed in narrative theory as formless, intuitive, and somewhat recalcitrant. The perceived danger is that the reader might find himself taken in by fictive language in biography without fair warning.

Semiotics answers this problem by disregarding the analytical "how" of fictional discourse in favor of a simple, descriptive "what." But the result tends to be abortive circular reasoning: fiction is fictive because it uses fictional syntax. "On the face of it," Benjamin Hrushovski writes, "fiction can be described as language offering propositions which make no claim for truth values in the real world."[33] Even Genette feels compelled to note that "factual narrative and fictional narrative behave differently toward the story which they 'report' by the mere fact of this story's (supposedly) being in one case 'truthful' (as Lucian put it), in the other case fictional, that is, invented by someone."[34] Barbara Herrnstein Smith's influential distinction between "natural" and "fictive discourse" begins with the definition of "natural discourse" as the utterance "that can be taken as someone's saying something, somewhere, sometime, that is, as the verbal acts of real persons on particular occasions in response to particular sets of circumstances . . . A natural utterance is a historical *event*." In other words, real-world, "historical *event*" makes redundant the ambiguities of language: no matter "how eloquent its style, or how culturally significant and otherwise estimable it is, the composition must still be regarded as a *natural utterance* so long as it may be taken as the verbal responses of a historically real person."[35]

Hair-splitting over Herrnstein Smith's terminology is tempting. For instance, we might note that many satirical novels do, in fact, respond to "particular sets of circumstances." We might also question the "naturalness" of the political text whose agenda is not entirely clear. Although she does not say as much, Herrnstein Smith's distinction between "natural" and "fictive discourse" actually involves the presence of a narrator. If a narrated text is diegetically mediated by someone other than the author, then "natural" discourse must be that which is unmediated—that is, direct. This is, incidentally, the standard most often born by those who seek to historicize autobiography, in which, as Genette has shown, the author and narrator can be equated by virtue of the fact that autobiography refers to the past of a *real* speaker. This factor is not to be disregarded, but at the same time it should be acknowledged that a convergence upon the "historically real person" is a quality that exists independently of structural or narratorial dissimilarities. Cohn makes a useful point: "If the genre [autobiography] is defined by way of the reality of its speaking subject, then it remains no less real when that subject lies or fantasizes about his past than when he utters verifiable truths."[36]

Certainly none of these writers are naive enough to believe that real-world verbal responses cannot be imitated in fictive situations, but they do imply that the single, incontrovertibly fictive quality in narrative betrays the lack of an extradiegetic message. There have, however, been attempts to draw distinctions within the message itself. Käte Hamburger's *The Logic of Literature,* for instance, divides language into "creative" and the "non-creative" types.[37] The latter comprises a "statement-system" or "reality report" that bears some resemblance to Herrnstein Smith's "historical event." but diverges from "creative" language also along syntactical lines. I should point out that Hamburger omits first-person narration—both the autobiographical and the fictive—from "creative" discourse. In that she is concerned solely with linguistic and syntactical truth-value, Hamburger argues that the first-person "is not fiction in the sense . . . [of] language and poetology"; for Hamburger, the "I" is the prime historical "statement-subject" (59). The first-person point of view, though, produces a "feigned reality statement whose degree of feint is subject to variation" (328). Cohn agrees that "in contrast to the distinctively fictional discourse that creates the mind of an imaginary 'he' or 'she,' there is nothing distinctively fictional about the discourse of an imaginary 'I.'"[38] This suggests two things: first, that novels written in the first-person, regardless of the presence of other fictional qualities, are not linguistically false, and so Hamburger's ideas are useless for identifying fictionality in these texts; and second, that autobiography, which as we have seen passes the narratorial "mediation" test, is fictional only its structural liberties, which are often justified as a by-product of the author-as-narrator. This is why Michal Glowinski refers to first-person narration as "an imitation by means of a given form, of other forms of literary, paraliterary, and extraliterary discourse."[39] and this appears to be the case regardless of the author's intentions.

In Hamburger's view, fictional narration (which she also calls "mimetic" narrative so as to distinguish it from the direct transcription of the "reality report") exhibits six qualities, three of which have to do with temporal leveling resulting from the ambiguous use of verb tenses, one with the description of fictional space, and the final two with the narrative of consciousness. Since Hamburger's six points invoke most of the issues involved in biography's use of language, I examine them one at a time.

First, Hamburger outlines fiction's contradictory use of tense indicators ("*This* evening the King *intended* to play the flute"), by which the fictional preterit "loses its grammatical function of designating what is past" (66). This occurs with such frequency, Hamburger observes, because the fictional past and present are often conflated into a kind of fictional non-time, resulting in the fictional preterit's tendency to induce the illusion of "being there" ("The noonday sun stood over Julier Pass" is cognitively equivalent to "the sun is standing" over Julier Pass) (98). One reason that the fictional preterit seems so immediate may be that the preterit in general is often considered to be an "historical tense." Cohn calls it the "inferential past tense": "It gives his view an air of logic, of inevitability, without giving him airs of omniscience . . . No matter how fanciful its content, the *form* of an inferential statement puts a stamp of historicity on the text that contains it."[40]

Hamburger holds that the presence of this fictional preterit negates the truth claim of any narrative in which it appears, regardless of the historicality of the subject. Furthermore, this ambiguity between the preterit and present tenses makes for a jarring effect when the present tense actually *is* used; the present tense naturally creates a sense of immediacy (a literal "being there"), but the artifice becomes apparent when the reader realized on some level that he or she is not there at all. Only in first-person accounts is this problem mitigated, which is why first-person narrative like autobiography are not treated in depth by Hamburger.[41] They are, regardless of their truth value, syntactically "historical."

Another element of Hamburger's "creative" language involves "spatial deictics," a kind of intensified subjectivity in the spatial presentation of objects, in phrases like "to the right" or "in the distance." Hamburger points out that parallel phrases that invoke *temporal* relationships—"after that" or "previously"—tend not to produce the same subjectivity as spatial deictics. since time is *communal* and space is *personal*. Spatial subjectivity, she adds, can be circumvented through the insertion of a fictive-neutral element: "When *one* enters the room, *one* finds a sideboard on the right." She also notes that not all spatial directions are necessarily subjective (Washington is *east* of West Virginia regardless of one's location).

More important are Hamburger's final pair of "creative" markers, both of which involve the narrative description of the internal states of human figures. First, "verbs of inner action" ("to believe," "to think," "to intend," or even "to be" when followed by an internal adjective) betray fictionalization. Additionally, "narrated monologue," a conflation of internal monologue and stream-of-consciousness, constitutes for Hamburger "the uttermost consequence of the verbs of inner action" (84). Taken together, these two practices fall under the standard rubric of "focalized narrative." When focalized narrative goes unflagged by a "verb of inner action," the result is "free-indirect" discourse or speech, containing a deliberate "confusion between the speech (uttered or inner) of the character and that of the narrator" (Genette *Narrative* 172).

Here is a brief example containing both straightforward focalized narrative and free-indirect speech, taken from Pietro Citati's biography *Kafka*:

> Kafka could not endure happiness: he feared that the joy of living might make him inattentive to the voice of destiny. His obligation was to listen to anguish and despair and go wherever they advised. No one was as wretched as he.[42]

Although Citati's first two sentences betray focalization by their use of "verbs of inner action" ("feared," "could" and "was" in conjunction with the adjectives "happiness" and "obligation"), the last sentence of the narrative is syntactically indeterminate as to *who* considers Kafka to be uniquely wretched. But the implication exists that Citati is describing Kafka's own self-perceptions. Genette claims that such free indirect discourse is the most characteristic element of fictional narrative, "for at its maximum extent it can saturate the entire discourse, insidiously assimilating the whole of it to the character's consciousness."[43] Some critics incorrectly assume that focalized narrative must be indicated by a linguistic marker or "verb of inner action,"[44] otherwise the material is simply being narrated from without.

Cohn asserts that focalization is the *only* reliable means of identifying fictional narrative. "Fiction is recognizable as fiction only if and when it actualizes its focalizing potential," she argues.[45] This attitude clarifies for Cohn the problems created by genre-inspecific forms like the New Journalism and the "non-fiction novel": "Closer study of these works," she believes, "would affirm that their fictionalizing devices boil down to nothing more nor less than the consistent application of focalizing techniques . . . In this perspective, biographies that act like novels, far from erasing the borderline between biography and fiction, bring the line that separates them more clearly into view."[46]

Although only the most "energetic" biographies try to eradicate all syntax that assigns thought processes, the extent to which focalization constitutes bona fide fictional narrative is understood to be a function of documentation and depth. Joseph Blotner's meticulous *Faulkner,* for instance, often ascribes to the writer various strategies and motivations ("One of the reasons Faulkner had not revised 'This Kind of Courage' [in the summer of 1934] was that he had a new story on his mind"[47]). But Blotner makes certain to document assertions like this one (in this case with letters and canceled checks from the *Saturday Evening Post*). But even documentation cannot historicize focalized narrative that probes beyond a certain psychological depth. In such cases, the biographical subject becomes a fictional figure in Cohn's sense: "the minds of imaginary figures can be known in ways that those of real persons cannot"; biography is more historical, then, when it shows restraint, employing what she calls the "language of nescience," or a kind of calculated un-knowing.[48] That such restraint is part of the generic definition of biography *per se* only reiterates its intransigence as a genre, as well as its interdependence with other modes of biographical narrative.

Chapter five

The problem of genre II: Fictional reality and modes of biographical narrative

I am what is around me.
One is not a duchess
A hundred yards from a carriage.

These, then are portraits:
These are merely instances.

Wallace Stevens, "Theory"

I have observed that generic labeling only buttresses the old border between history and fiction, and I have dedicated the preceding chapter to exploring the complexities of biography as the historical standard against which biographical narrative is measured. Things remain complicated. Perhaps a new taxonomy is needed, one that takes into account the unique challenges of narrating a life. This chapter theorizes new patterns in biographical writing in order to make some sense of the contrarieties that exist within the field: the realistic and fantastic, the linear and anachronistic, the syntactically objective and fictional, the full-blown life-span and the brief appearance of an historical figure in a larger narrative framework. In order to make some sense of how these issues distill into identifiable *types* of texts. I define four modes of writing—biographical novel. biographical travesty, autobiography and biography—that function across three different categories of biographical time. On a more general level I show that, since each mode performs similar biographical work a different way, what might be viewed as contradiction is actually a productive (if "disturbing") tension.

It would be reckless to assume that every mode of biographical narrative performs the same function or has the same discursive effect with respect to a given historical figure, any more than that all modes of narrative *narrate* in the same way.[1] Still, whether they address them or not, all writers of biographical narrative do provoke the generic anxieties of readers like Michiko Kakutani:

> The point . . . is not that literary categories as such are desirable. The point is that they possess inherently different conventions and create different expectations, and that mixing the forms makes for certain problems of veracity . . . What is true and what isn't.[2]

Rüdiger Kunow puts it another way: "Both the text as an organized/organizing structural unity and its elements . . . are to be understood not only for their aesthetic function but also for the way in which they define or impinge on the version/vision of history presented."[3] Such critics worry that a destabilized border between fictional and factual modes will irrevocably trouble not only "what is true," but *what is what* in terms of "historical" or "fictional" form.

Differences do exist even when conventional boundaries are called into question. One concerns the degree to which a given text can be considered overtly *biographical.* Extremely important is the simple fact that an historical figure can appear in a variety of kinds even within a particular mode. What I call biographical *scope,* then, depends on the extent to which a text approximates comprehensive, birth-to-death biographical time. (Of course, the scope of a text is not always indicative of its overall impact on an image-system. Can anyone doubt the weight of Scott Fitzgerald's relatively brief appearance in *A Moveable Feast* or Lee Harvey Oswald's on *Assassins*?) If we combine them with the variable of biographical scope, all the (supposed) qualities of "historical" discourse discussed in Chapter Four prepare us to draw some distinctions between historical and fictive biographical narratives. If, as I have argued, each representation of an historical figure implicates all its companion representations, then the entire collection of biographical narrative might be arranged into a manageable taxonomy, based on both scope *and* method of discourse.

As we know, temporal scope (with respect to the historical individual, *not* to the story-time of the text as a whole) can extend from birth-to-death biographical time all the way down to the fragmentary episode. A general rule is that a broader biographical time-frame betokens a greater biographical focus, although this is not always the case. Consider, for example, Nancy Cardozo's biography *Maud Gonne,* which encompasses, but does not focus upon, the life of W. B. Yeats, or Frederick Busch's novel *The Mutual Friend,* which delineates a segment of Charles Dickens' life, but ostensibly focuses upon the broader lifespan of Dolby, Dickens' fictionalized companion and tour manager.

As for a text's discourse, I have shown in Chapter 4 that there are any number of ways by which we might distinguish between subdivisions of "fictive" and "historical" in biographical narrative. For the purposes of this study, I will identify two *fictional* ways of writing—"fiction" *per se* and the more specialized "anatomy"—and two *historical* ones: "historical" *per se* and the more specialized "autobiographical." When these modes are applied back to the life-span, biographical narrative can be arranged thus, and the following four (bold-faced) biographical modes established:

	Mode of Discourse	*Temporal Scope of Biographical Narrative* Life-Span	Life-Segment	Cameo
FICTION	Novel		BIOGRAPHICAL NOVEL	
		Libra	*Billy Bathgate*	*Jailbird*
	Anatomy		BIOGRAPHICAL TRAVESTY	
		Dirty Tricks	*The Public Burning*	*Illuminatus Trilogy*
HISTORY	Autobiography		AUTOBIOGRAPHY	
		Last Words of Dutch Schultz	*Six Crises*	*The Collective*
	History		BIOGRAPHY	
		Oswald's Tale	*St. George and the Godfather*	*Murder. Inc.*

In the chart above, I designate three temporal categories: the complete life-span, the life-segment, and the episodic cameo. There is one interesting precedent for my tripartite model. As long ago as 1605, Francis Bacon divided history into three classes: those which deal with "a *time*, a *person*, or an *action*" (emphasis mine).[4] Adapting Bacon's model to human-centered biographical time means rearranging it: my "complete life span" focuses on Bacon's *person*; my "life segment" involves an *action*; and my "cameo" submerges the individual into a larger *time*.

As Bacon was certainly aware, such classifications are essentially arbitrary, denoting relative proportions, rather than specific quantities, of human time. Furthermore, the two extreme poles of biographical temporality are idealized: a thoroughly complete life-span can never be represented any more than an historical figure can appear episodically in a way that is entirely disassociated from that life-span. Thus a narrative that tends toward the complete *life span* will usually commence at some point recent to the subject's birth and close at some point closely before the decease of the subject. Omitted segments are, in such cases, usually covered by analeptic or proleptic narrative; the comprehensive story-time of these texts, once all forms of narrative anachrony are considered, effectively narrates the life-span, even if the narrative structure is non-linear. Likewise, the amorphous designation *life-segment* can describe any amount of biographical time that insinuates—but does not explicitly narrate—the complete life span. A large number of biographical narratives occupy this temporal zone. Jacobs has observed the particular efficacy with which "postmodernist literary techniques overcome the traditional obligations to completeness" in biography,[5] and has argued that this temporal tightening allows for more in-depth probing of biography's "dark areas."[6]

Finally, the *cameo* occurs when an historical figure appears in a text without any overt narrative reference to his or her life-span. The cameo is a kind of biographical shorthand. It ranges from an appearance with significant impact upon the plot to a mere "brush with greatness" by someone else, and from status as character to status as symbol or literary element. In other words, the cameo can produce either a brief displacement of the image-system, or merely historical verisimilitude in human form. Therefore, any friction between the biographical subject and the textual diegesis depends on biographical semes recognized by the reader. This is why only our more prominent historical figures occur with efficacy in episodic time (although the cameo appearance of a relatively obscure historical figure may reflect the postmodern proclivity for esoteric subjects). McHale believes that in texts like these, "highly 'charged' figures are often preferred, figures rich in associations for most readers, able to excite strong reactions."[7]

Although many cameos, especially those in travesty, are satirical, the cameo is necessarily no more or less historically accurate than any other kind of biographical narrative. It can function as an element of mimesis, speculation, or downright subversion. Consider, for example, the benign presence of Joseph Goebbels and Adolf Eichman in Vonnegut's *Mother Night,* or William and Christina Rossetti as they appear near the end of Fowles' *The French Lieutenant's Woman,* or John F. Kennedy in the film *Forrest Gump.*[8] Some figures, Pearl Bell reminds us, serve only "to underscore the pertinence of . . . [the] narrative to the political and social reality" of the novel's context.[9] But even these hint at the writer's notion of a figure's image-system. Often the cameo figure is so isolated from his or her larger life-span that the text's contribution to the larger biographical narrative must be ascertained not straightforwardly, but more inferentially by the manner in which the subject acts upon, and is acted upon by, the diegesis itself. Others—as with the Jack Kennedy or Malcolm X of Thomas Pynchon's *Gravity's Rainbow* or the Freud and Jung of E. L. Doctorow's *Ragtime*—create, in McHale's words, "a certain *tension* between the internal and external fields [of reference]." He mentions a specialized form in which two or more historical figures meet in absurdly ahistorical combinations. These meetings, he writes, "compound the ontological offense" described above.[10] Examples include Kafka and Wittgenstein in Guy Davenport's "Aeroplanes at Brescia" and Kennedy and Mailer in Walter Abish's "The Istanbul Papers." The cameo's value as biographical narrative is often a function of this tension. We can learn from the way the character is "used," as I have shown in my discussion of Richard Nixon.

Thus each of my four narrative modes—biographical novel, biographical travesty, autobiography, and biography—works along the temporal distance between life-span and cameo. I have already defined *biography* by distinguishing it from history. In the process of that discussion, as well as in my treatment of the last words of Dutch Schultz, I have also explored the nature of *autobiography* as a distinct narrative mode. That leaves us with the *biographical novel* and *biographical travesty* as the pair of modes that employ "fictive" as opposed to "historical" discourse. Since not all fiction works in the same way, further explanation of the differences between the two is necessary.

Biographical fiction encompasses all narrative that applies "novelistic" discourse to the representation of an historical life. I use the term "novelistic" not in its generic sense, but in its common acceptance as realistic narrative of fictional events. This can include not only prose narrative, but also film, drama, or even narrative poetry. As such, novelistic discourse is implicitly biographical. Lukács' description of the novel can apply to all novelistic discourse:

> The outward form of the novel is essentially biographical . . . The novel in itself and for itself is by no means bound to the natural beginning and end of life—to birth and death; yet by the points at which it begins and ends, it indicates the only essential segment of life, that segment which is

> determined by the central problem . . . When the beginning and the end of this segment of life do not coincide with those of a human life, this merely shows that the biographical form is oriented towards ideas: the development of a man is still the thread upon which the whole world of the novel is strung.[11]

Written in 1914, this passage has stood up so well because it assumes what later writers would argue for at greater length: that, like all narratives dealing with the lives of women and men, the novel insinuates the biographical, if not structurally then in the form of a "central problem" of identity functioning as the "thread upon which the whole world of the novel is strung." Televised narratives also approximate the novel's biographical "central problem," as do the essentially novelistic techniques of most film, short story, and narrative poetry.

However, the way a novel takes, manipulates, and returns an image-system to its cultural home is different from the anatomy. To spotlight the differences between, say, the Ernest Hemingway of William Henderson's novel *I Killed Hemingway* and Keith Abbott's travesty *Rhino Ritz,* an understanding of the differences between the two modes is crucial. Both authors invoke the man whom we know as Hemingway, but the *worlds* into which they place their Papas are very different. To use a more complicated example, the trio of Richard Nixons we find in Seelye's *Dirty Tricks.* Roth's *Our Gang,* and Coover's *The Public Burning* are different from one another by virtue of the diegetic environments in which they function; one exists in a world of literary parody, one in a world of rhetorical parody, and one in a kind of cultural/historical carnival world. But all three are fundamentally different from the verisimilar worlds of Ehrlichman's *The China Card,* Condon's *The Death of a Politician,* and Vonnegut's *Jailbird* (even if the verisimilitude of these three texts itself varies). This essential disparity cuts to the heart of the idea of novel as "*realistic* narrative of *fictional* events," a difference great enough to create two separate modes.

The difference between biographical novels and travesties is ontological. The "worlds" of novelistic and anatomical discourse have a direct impact upon how we "read" the historical figure as a textual element. Therefore, with reference to biographical fiction and travesty, both worlds are fictive. However, novelistic worlds are, in the words of Umberto Eco.

> . . . parasites of the actual one . . . They are in effect 'small worlds' which bracket most of our competence of the actual world and allow us to concentrate on a finite, enclosed world, very similar to ours but ontologically poorer.[12]

Anatomical worlds, on the other hand, occupy a "'never and nowhere' that nevertheless faithfully reflects the essential characteristics," but not the "specific qualities," of their cultural source.[13] Many critics have noted that postmodern texts tend to exaggerate the "never and nowhere" as fictional context, creating ontologies that Eco calls "self-voiding."[14] However, while this may weaken the biographical value of the *actions* of historical figures, it actually serves to heighten their value as contributions to a biographical "idea." This is why I adopt the term "anatomy" directly from Northrop Frye (who in turn borrowed it from Burton as a replacement for the more cumbersome "Menippean satire"). With Frye, my conception of anatomy has in common with Menippean satire a world whose raw material is ideas rather than specific, verisimilar events. It includes, but is not limited to, "encyclopedic narratives," which Mendelson says "attempt to render the full range of knowledge and beliefs of a national culture, while identifying the ideological perspectives from which that culture shapes and interprets its knowledge."[15]

To claim that ontology can so affect narrative that it bisects biographical fiction is to suggest that there is more to the idea of diegetic worlds than a mere contrast between the "fictive" and the "real." That is, our usual notion of two kinds of narrative world—the simply real and the simply fictive—clashes with all the grades of "reality" that we see embodied in the pseudo-fictional and pseudo-historical narrative that makes up literature in general and biographical narrative in particular.

Television defines the problem. The last decade has revived the "Dramatic Reenactment," words we had seen superimposed across the bottom of the television screen before, underscoring everything from didactic religious programming to advertising spots. But the popularity of this new "Reality TV"—shows like "Cops" or "Real Stories of the Highway Patrol" that feature authentic video footage of domestic scenes, public events and especially law enforcement situations—has given the words "dramatic reenactment" a new utility. The same footage of a Chicago drug-bust might appear on a newscast and the entertainment program following it, and our ability to discriminate immediately between the formal "truth" of the news and the "lies" of entertainment programming has become enervated. Meanwhile, "Reality TV" continues to exercise its prerogative as entertainment by fashioning "historical narratives"—that is, "dramatic reenactments"—to augment factual material. Naomi Jacobs has likened contemporary television to the eighteenth-century "news/novel matrix" described by Lennard Davis.[16] Television *needs* the "Dramatic Reenactment" caption in the same way that the British print media needed the Stamp Act revision of 1724 to differentiate between taxable "news" and non-taxable "fiction."[17]

In some cases, actor and agent are cognates. When documentary footage of an event is unavailable, the producers may employ the original "newsmaker" in the fictive dramatization. A Los Angeles policewoman is asked to portray *herself* in the recreation of an arrest; or, a Detroit autoworker hurries down the hallway of a Hollywood set to dial "911" on a prop telephone, as he had done in his own home weeks previously. In either case, "dramatic reenactments" are at the same time "real people in real situations." But how "real" are these narratives? Their subjects are certainly historical individuals, and they do constitute extradiegetic referents, which is to say that they possess identity outside the boundaries of the story. In this respect they are by no means fictional characters. Still, the caption "Dramatic Reenactment" serves to remind us that we are not watching "news."

It is, therefore, not the *subject* of such a narrative that fictionalizes so much as the *world* in which that subject operates, whether the narrative actually occurs alongside the real Interstate 605 in Los Angeles or on a Hollywood soundstage. Regardless of veracity and verisimilitude, identifiability and recognizability, narrative "reenactment" creates a fictional world.

We might say, then, that every mode of biographical narrative *surrounds* the historical figure in a different way, in an analog to reception theory's "horizon of expectations." Some methods of representation (biography, autobiography) being more conventionally "historical" than others, the worlds they create are analogous to the "dramatic reenactment" undertaken in its original setting. (Thus biographical and autobiographical worlds *are* liable to fictionalization. but as the result of the structural, narratorial and linguistic elements discussed in Chapter Four, not as an ontological *a priori.*) Conversely, when biographical fiction and travesty "reenact" an historical figure—in the literal sense that a narrative causes the figure to "act again"—they are dehistoricized not so much by incongruity between textual and real-world identity or behavior (although such incongruity may occur) as by the disparity between fictional worlds and the "real" one. The fictional world is a "heterocosm," a self-contained universe separate from the one in which "news" happens. The criteria for historical validity is different in fictional texts than in historical ones, even when a fictional world *seams* real.

Practically speaking, the difference is absolute. The sensationally-fictive world (like that in the anatomy) is just as "false" as a verisimilar one. Toni Morrison's Cincinnati (the setting of much of *Beloved*), John Irving's Derry, New Hampshire (respelled "Dairy" and fitted out with an eponymous hotel), Thomas Pynchon's European "Zone" (*Gravity's Rainbow*) and Kurt Vonnegut's Tralfamadore (which exists in works like *Slaughter-House Five* as a temporally and spatially obscure space), are all equally fictive, although the texture of their fictiveness varies. Biographical travesties create "self-voiding" worlds, in which truth claims are especially "dubious" because the entire narrative structure undermines itself.[18] But ontological self-nullification can be accomplished in verisimilar texts as well, especially those that undermine themselves through metafictional devices (as in Fowles' *The*

French Lieutenant's Woman). All fiction, McHale points out, operates in a "possible world"; more paradoxical ones he calls "zones," using a term extracted from Appollinaire via Pynchon (the "zone" is a "topos that becomes ontology . . . The result is a kind of between-worlds space").[19] This is more or less a high-brow, intellectual form of science fiction, but it is still only fictive.

The effort to draw a clear boundary between the fictional and historical text-world thwarts conventional criticism, but the absence of this boundary allows for ambiguity that is unbearable to some readers. As John Searle has expostulated, "how can it be the case in 'Little Red Riding Hood' both that 'red' means red and yet that the rules correlating 'red' with red are not in force?"[20] Searle's question points beyond structural, narratorial, or syntactical markers, which, as we have seen, are problematic in themselves. The ontological difference between the real and unreal world is abstruse. Kendall Walton writes that the two are mutually "insulated and isolated in some peculiar way," as if there were "a logical or metaphysical barrier between them."[21] Precise distinction has therefore been undertaken largely by semiotics, which has, so to speak, explored fictional versus historical "redness" in all its variations. Beginning in the 1970's and drawing from the work of Frege, Russell, Wittgenstein and Heidegger, a long parade of critics—Eco, Pavel, Mink, Hrushovski Searle, Plantinga, Kaplan, and Walton among them—have studied the real-world validity of fictional "redness," and vice versa. With the exceptions of Eco and Pavel, few of these critics have much to say on the issue of literary fiction itself; one non-existent semiotic referent (Never-Never Land) is often as good as another (Yoknapatawpha County) for exemplifying the "false" seme. Ironically, many of these semioticians eventually come full circle, working their way back up from the semiotic depths to reaffirm a familiar verdict: that history refers to the real world and fiction does not. We have already encountered this idea in Hrushovski and Herrnstein-Smith. Here, Louis Mink simply couches it in more specialized language: "History *does* of course differ from fiction in so far as it is obligated to rest upon evidence of the occurrence in real space and time of what it describes and in so far as it must grow out of a critical assessment of the received materials of history."[22]

With reference to *people* rather than abstractions like "redness," the problem is: "In what sense are we committed to the existence of Raskolnikov?"[23] A still more relevant question for biographical narrative is: in what sense are we committed (or resistant) to the existence in fiction of, say, Henry Ford (i.e. the one in *Ragtime*)? One position (Hrushovski, Searle and Mink) considers the fictional Henry Ford as a completely different referent than the historical one, therefore possessing no substance at all outside its ontology. These critics affirm Walton's "metaphysical barrier." The second position (Eco, Pavel and McHale) resists the binary ontological model with its "true/false" polarity in favor of a range of textual worlds that allows for the exchange of common referents.

The first position evolved as an element of classic realism, and seeks to gather non-realistic or "anti-realistic" texts within the ontological model of this rubric. The characters of classic historical fiction, according to Lukács' definition, "always represent social trends and historical forces" but never specific elements of the historical milieu.[24] Hrushovski, for example, argues that fiction possesses one overarching "internal field of reference," although more complex narratives can have numerous interlocking ones within the whole. Metafictional devices only exaggerate this; such texts "build the boat under their own feet while rowing in the sea."[25] Fictions can incorporate "referents and/or frames of reference from Fields external to them," but when this occurs, "the literary text selects elements and reshuffles their hierarchies while creating its own autonomous Field."[26] Most importantly, to Hrushovski, "even when historically known persons appear in individualized [fictional] situations . . . either no claim can be made that they actually happened or such a claim is irrelevant."[27]

But how can we tell an irrelevant frame of reference? Mink offers a provocative theory about biographical narrative. In considering narratives of "real" people, he juxtaposes the two cognitive reading-acts of "following a story" (fiction) and "having followed a story" (history). We can, Mink writes, understand a single referent either way, but with varying real-world validity:

> In the case of human actions . . . to know an event by retrospection [historically] is categorically, not incidentally, different from knowing it by prediction and anticipation [fiction]. It cannot even, in any strict sense, be called the "same" event, for in the former case the descriptions under which it is known are governed by a story to which it belongs, and there is no story of the future.[28]

Fictional worlds exist in an equivocal, perpetual future, a state of unrealized possibility, and therefore do not exist in real time. Here, Mink is essentially making the same presupposition of fictional self-evidence as Hrushovski does. The same can be said of Searle, who considers the fictional world to be an act of "pretending" (but not a "lie," there being in most cases no intention to deceive).[29] To Eco, the fictional world is a harmless pretense and the reader is like the Italian King who attended a painting exhibition, looked at a picture of a village, and asked the director of the exhibition, "How many inhabitants does it have?"[30]

One can only conclude that Hrushovski, Mink and Searle all assume the presence and certainty of paratextual flags ("a novel," "based on . . .," or our "Dramatic Reenactment"), and therefore that a fictional ontology is one that *declares* its fictiveness. This is by no means a negligible part of a text's identity.

As Genette has observed, regardless of what is *in* a book, its ultimate effect depends on "the official status of the text and its reading horizon."[31] But while these writers describe fictional worlds, they are of little use in demarcating differences between ontologies "mirrored" by history and those "created" in fiction.[32] In any case, as McHale as remarked, "there is an ontological scandal when a real-world figure is inserted in a fictional situation . . . [that] sends shock-waves throughout that world's ontological structure."[33] These shockwaves are evidence of biographical narrative at work.

Thus the writer of the anatomy, like Coover's Cecil B. DeMille, works to produce meaningful historical *spectacle.* In the twelfth chapter of *The Public Burning* (titled "A Roman Scandal of Roaring Spectacle"), DeMille explains his approach in this way:

> See, life and real stuff of life aren't always the same thing . . . like, one don't always give you the other, you follow? So sometimes, to get your story across, you gotta work a different angle or two, use a few tricks, zap it up with a bit of spectacle—I mean, what's spectacle? it's a kind of *vision,* am I right? (281)

Rhetorically, the postmodern anatomy is characterized by its replacement of novelistic narrative with a discursive gumbo that draws parodically from any number of narrative and non-narrative modes. In Thomas LeClair's words, such fictions "take large rhetorical risks with the reader who knows traditional fiction and who is saturated with the other media that have largely replaced fiction as a source of information and entertainment," and so they "move beyond the limits inherent in the conventions [of traditional realistic fiction] to a new kind of communication" drawn from popular culture and media.[34] Structurally, anatomical discourse is often atemporal. As one critic observed in a review of Ishmael Reed's *Flight to Canada,* "time becomes a modest, crazy fluid . . . The cluttered past, present and future are interchangeable."[35]

In fictional anatomy, the incongruities of discourse make for irreverence where the historical figure is concerned. This is why I use the term "travesty" to describe its incorporation into biographical narrative. If travesty treats a serious subject frivolously, then biographical travesty treats the historical figure in historically-frivolous ways. It also thumbs its nose at biographical truth, as with Philip José Farmer's *Riverworld* series, whose governing deity arbitrarily plucks figures from the annals of history, *after* their "deaths." Biographical travesty trivializes history for its own ideological and didactic purposes—why Strout calls them "Antihistorical Novels." He defines these as "pastiches that spoof the historical novel and cast doubt on the intelligibility of history as either a process or an interpreted record."[36] In McHale's view, such anti-historicism manifests itself as either "apocryphal" or "alternative" history: "Apocryphal history operates in the 'dark areas' of history, apparently in conformity to the norms of 'classic' historical fiction but in fact *parodying* them. In the second case, alternative history spectacularly violates the 'dark areas' constraint."[37] In either situation, although the historical figure is the object of travesty, it still affects, and is affected by, the historical agenda of the text as a whole. At the very least, the function of historical figures in anatomy is directly related to that figure's extradiegetic biographical identity; at most, some element of that identity tropes and "magically disturbs" history itself. Thus biographical travesty—in all its implausibility—contributes to biographical narrative at the same time that it contributes to the "magical disturbance" of history that characterizes most postmodern anatomies. But biographical travesty does not, as critics have claimed, merely "reduce historical figures to simplified types,"[38] in order to "patronize the past and thus set it aside."[39]

Despite their ontological differences, biographical novel and travesty share several of the vicissitudes of fictional narrative. One immediately apparent variation is in point of view. Both William Styron's biographical fiction *The Confessions of Nat Turner* and Coover's travesty *The Public Burning,* for example, are narrated in the first-person by the biographical subject (Turner narrates Styron's book, Richard Nixon half of Coover's), while other recent fictions—like Jay Cantor's novel *The Death of Che Guevera* or Carlos Fuentes' travesty *Terra Nostra*—are narrated in third person. Conversely, the life-segment narrative of Kennedy's *Legs* (1975) is undertaken by Diamond's fictionalized attorney Marcus Gorman, while similar texts assume the form of first-person narratives (as with Peter Ackroyd's *Hawksmoor,* most of which is narrated by Restoration architect Nicholas Hawksmoor, renamed Dyer). Meanwhile, biographical narrative can be nested, as when John Updike's *Memories of the Ford Administration,* manages an intermittent, third-person speculative biography of James Buchanan within the modern "memoirs" of its protagonist. Narrative perspective and distance vary widely within biographical fiction and travesty, though both *always* create their own worlds, regardless of the authority of the third-person narrator or the immediacy of the first. As Berthoff has commented, "*history* is descriptive, and its problem is verification. *Fiction* is constitutive or inventive, and its problem is veracity."[40] Veracity can be achieved through any number of means, none of which approaches (or attempt to approach) historical "verification" more than any other.[41] Realizing this eliminates the need for pedantic distinctions between, say, third-person "novels written between the lines of modern biographies" and first-person "fictionalized biographies." These, Jacobs continues, tend to "establish the tentativeness of their interpretations through passages of fantasy or direct authorial intrusion, through conflicting perspectives on the subject, and in some cases through deliberate and easily-detectable lies."[42] There is no single narrative method that we can call "realistic," but rather an amalgam of realistic effects (such as third-person narrative, structural linearity, "unpoetic" language, the footnote, etc.) and therefore of biographical tributaries to the image system.

In other words, the multifold spectrum of biographical fiction assumes that "the past is not an 'it' in the sense of an objectified entity that may . . . be neutrally represented in and for itself."[43] No single fictional point of view approximates "neutrality" more than any other; therefore, all biographical fiction functions, practically, in the same way. The main difference is that postmodern biographical novelists, unlike their predecessors (such as Woolf, Graves, Fast and Stone) are no longer "extremely self-conscious about their use of the fictional medium for the purposes of biography."[44] They *contribute* to biographical narrative rather than merely departing from it in generically conspicuous ways.

In this chapter I have theorized the differences between various modes of biographical narrative—differences of a formal, narratological, stylistic, and temporal nature—so that I can demonstrate in later pages how biographical narratives cross these lines as they work together toward the delineation of the historical life. If human identity is, as Barthes has suggested, an *image-system* that can be inscribed only through "the effects of resonance," then its delineation requires a *discourse-system,* each of whose components vibrates on its own frequency, and none of which modulates the resonance of the whole. Historical narrative predicated upon inertia makes for a static figure: quiescent, manageable, historical only in the sense of its permanence. Biographical resonance, however, is beyond mere insult or information—it is a magical disturbance of History—so that in the end we learn not only about the individual in question, but through that individual we learn more about such American myths as gangsterism, politics and assassination than we could have by reading an undisturbed History. Just as Doctorow's Billy Bathgate, through his exposure to Dutch Schultz, discovers that "I was living in even greater circles of gangsterdom than I had dreamed, latitudes and longitudes of gangsterdom" (320), we tap into the image-systems of our historical figures in order to have access to the "latitudes and longitudes" of American culture.

This is not to merely repeat the postmodern cliché that personal identity is in the final analysis unstable, subject to disappearance beneath a variegated cloak of discursive selves, but only that contemporary American culture creates, reifies, and sustains this ongoing process of biographical inscription and erasure as a means of interrogating the role of the individual in a very, very complicated world. There is no reason to believe that socio-historical agents like Schultz, Oswald and Nixon should remain exempt from the process simply by virtue of their prominence in it. They are no safer than we are. On the contrary, that they thrust themselves—or are thrust—onto the stage of national events renders them uniquely susceptible to inscription, erasure, and reinscription, along with other figures from J. Edgar Hoover and John F. Kennedy to James Dean and Marilyn Monroe. Such sacrificial lambs (or wolves, depending) both attract and generate discursive insult and information, and beyond that, magical disturbance. The bigger they are, the harder they fall.

Notes

Chapter four

1 Hayden White, *Tropics of Discourse: Essays in Cultural Criticism* (Baltimore: Johns Hopkins University Press, 1978), 122.
2 Ina Schabert, "Fictional Biography, Factual Biography, and Their Contaminations," *Biography* 5 (1982): 9-10.
3 Paul Murray Kendall, *The Art of Biography* (London: Allen & Unwin, 1965), 15.
4 James L. Clifford, *From Puzzles to Portraits: Problems of a Literary Biographer,* (Chapel Hill: University of North Carolina Press, 1970), 85-87.
5 Ibid., 83.
6 William Epstein, *Recognizing Biography* (Philadelphia: University of Pennsylvania Press, 1987), 7.
7 Aristotle, *Politics & Poetics,* trans. Benjamin Jowett and S. Butcher (New York: Heritage, 1964), VIII.
8 Milton Lomask, *The Biographer's Craft* (New York: Harper & Row, 1986), 2.
9 Kendall, *The Art of Biography,* 136.
10 Lomask, *The Biographer's Craft.* 42.
11 Warner Berthoff, "Fiction, History, Myth: Notes Toward the Discrimination of Narrative Forms," in *The Interpretation of Narrative: Theory and Practice,* ed. Morton W. Bloomfield (Cambridge: Harvard University Press, 1970), 275.
12 Dorrit Cohn, "Signposts of Fictionality; A Narratological Perspective," *Poetics Today* 11 (1990): 777.
13 Gérard Genette, "Fictional Narrative, Factual Narrative," *Poetics Today* 11 (1990): 758.
14 Johnan Galtung, "Macro-History as a Metaphor for Biography: An Essay on Macro and Micro History," *Biography* 13 (1990): 284.
15 Mikhail Bakhtin, *The Dialogic Imagination: Four Essays,* ed. Michael Holquist, trans. Caryl Emerson and Michael Holquist (Austin: University of Texas Press, 1981), 140.
16 Epstein, *Recognizing Biography*, 143.
17 Thus an emphasis on linearity leads to a further distinction: between biographical subjects who lend themselves readily to linear structuring, and those (like Oswald) who appear to demand—or whose biographers must resort to—liberties in structural arrangement, who defy the graph (in Oswald's case, this creates a discursive space that conspiracy narrative fills). Bakhtin calls these two biographical types "Energetic" and "Analytical." The "Energetic" subject, as exemplified by Plutarch, is realized

> . . . not by his condition, but by his activity, his active force . . . Therefore human life and character may no longer be portrayed by means of an analytical enumeration of the characterological qualities of the man (his vices and virtues) . . . Rather, one must portray him by means of his deeds, his speeches and other extensions and expressions. (*Dialogic* 140-41)

Meanwhile, "Analytic" biography involves private phenomena: "social life, family life . . . virtues, vices, physical appearance, habits and so forth . . . In this way, the temporal progression of the biographical sequence is broken up" (Bakhtin *Dialogic* 142). (John Garraty has made a provocative, but as yet uninvestigated, claim with regard to these two types: "Biographies by *contemporaries,*" he writes, "tend to be weak on career and strong on character" [64; emphasis mine].) Lomask calls texts that are strong on character "topical biographies"; they are more discursive and expository than those that "carry an individual from cradle to grave" (2-3). In an apparent contradiction, such exposition is often accomplished by a further manipulation of linear time, through "scenes" that manipulate the linear flow of "summary" through "anisochrony." or irregularities in speed or rhythm. Although linearity, energy, and isochrony (that is, regularity) are interrelated, none necessitates the others, nor do any of the three ensure a definite degree of truth value, regarded as a function of structure. The identification of "insidious" subjectivity or bias in biography (as opposed to more apparent narratorial or linguistic "danger" flags) often rises from these three qualities, but the presence of subjectivity defies systematic criteria. There are certainly a pair of extreme ideals at work: biographies that strive for reportage on one hand and "understanding" on the other, linearity suffering as we make the transition from the former to the latter, Between them fall such controversial forms as the psychobiography, intuitive biography, comparative biography, debunking biography, laudatory biography, and life history.

18 Ira Bruce Nadel, *Biography: Fiction. Fact, and Form* (New York: St. Martin's, 1984), 170.

19 Cohn, "Signposts of Fictionality," 800, 796.

20 Genette, "Fictional Narrative, Factual Narrative," 768. Genette's schematic differentiates author (A), narrator (N) and interdiegetic character (C), where the symbol "=" signifies equivalence of identity. For Historical Narrative like biography, A=N≠C≠A (the author is narrator but is disconnected from the characters); but for Autobiography, A=N=C=A (the author, narrator, and character are one). As for Fictional Narrative, with homodiegetic fiction, A≠N=C≠A (the narrator is a character, but neither have any connection to the author); with heterodiegetic fiction, A≠N≠C≠A (the author, narrator and character are in no way equivalent); and in heterodiegetic autobiography (as in some of Mailer's work), A≠N≠C=A (the author is a character, but the identity of the narrator is disconnected from these). Strictly speaking, then, historical narrative (Genette calls it "factual narrative") occurs only when the author of a text is indistinguishable from the narrator, which is to say, when there *is no* narrator, at least not an easily identifiable one. Genette's schematic raises further issues with regard to biography, such as this one: if historical narrative is distinguished by the divergence of both author and narrator from character, where does that leave biographies whose authors appear, even slightly, in the text? We might also bear in mind, as Genette does, that the "A=N" relationship can be feigned, as in the Millhauser novel mentioned above (which "looks like" biography), or in such "autofictions" as Borges' (which "looks like" autobiography).

21 Tamar Yacobi, "Narrative Structure and Fictional Mediation." *Poetics Today* 8 (1987): 335.

22 Genette, "Fictional Narrative, Factual Narrative," 772.

23 This tension between the author's "partial knowledge" and the narrator's "omniscience," incidentally, most effectively isolates autobiography from both fiction and history. It is impossible to demonstrate that autobiography is defined by either; the autobiographer seems to be allowed mastery of the text, but not the fallacy of self-awareness. (According to Genette's schematic, autobiography is not fiction because "A=N.") Bakhtin agrees that "there could not in principle be any difference between the approach one took to another's life and to one's own, that is, between the biographical and the autobiographical points of view" (*Dialogic* 132). But when "approach" becomes practice, things are bit more tricky, especially when the autobiographical narrator appears as a *nameless* "I," in which case the link between author and narrator is no more tangible than in fiction. Such a persona "condemns us to vacillate or allows us to oscillate . . . between fictional and referential readings" (Cohn "Fictional" 15). (Has anyone who has taught an American literature survey not encountered the student who refers to *Walden* as a "novel" and been stymied as to how to correct this label?) Ultimately, there can be no doubt that autobiography often *reads* like a first-person novel, and so we may be left with such reader-response distinctions as this one from Jerzy Kosinski: "Autobiography emphasizes a single life: the reader is invited to become the observer of another man's existence and encouraged to compare his own life to the subject's. A fictional life, on the other hand, forces the reader to contribute: he does not simply compare; he actually enters a fictional role, expanding it in terms of his own experience" (*The Painted Bird,* 2nd Edition [Boston: Houghton Mifflin, 1976], xiv).

24 Yacobi, "Narrative Structure and Fictional Mediation," 335.

25 Roland Barthes, "Introduction to the Structural Analysis of Narrative," in *Image, Music, Text* (New York: Hill & Wang, 1977), 116.

26 Joseph Gold, "Biography as Fiction: The Art of invisible Authorship," in *Reflections: Autobiography and Canadian Literature,* ed. K. P. Stich [Ottawa: U Ottawa Press, 1988], 335-36.

27 Leon Edel, *Writing Lives* (New York: Norton, 1984), 16, 17.

28 A few biographies exist at just this stage. We might call them "self-conscious biographies" because their narrators are unusually cognizant of themselves as being engaged in the biographical act. They not only experience but narrate the struggle to "know" their subjects and to produce a text that communicates this. Ruth Hoberman calls them "mediated biographies" because they actually accentuate the perceptions of the biographer, who is himself "experienced dramatically" (*Modernizing Lives: Experiments in English Biography, 1918-1939* [Carbondale: Southern Illinois University Press, 1987], 103). The modem prototype of the form is generally considered to be A. J. A. Symons' *The Quest for Corvo* (1934), which Norman Birkett has described as a quasi-literary "quest . . . [which] hold[s] the attention by sheer fascination of the pursuit" (*The Quest for Corvo: An Experiment in Biography* [London: Folio Society, 1952], xi).

The self-conscious biographer, like Symons as characterized by Birkett, is a hero on a quest for "clues." This is an idea that has always been implicit in biography, a fact that many biographers have attempted to modify retroactively by writing essays about *how they came to write* their biographies. The 1980's saw a crest in this sort of retrospective, solipsistic biographical theory. Richard Holmes' *Footsteps: Adventures of a Romantic Biographer* (1985) is a record of the author's literal, geographic journeys through which he accessed the "physical past" of his subjects. In *The Spirit of Biography* (1989) Jeffrey Meyers offers essays called "The Quest for Katherine Mansfield," "The Quest for Wyndham Lewis," and "The Quest for Hemingway." Meyers' *The Craft of Literary Biography* (1985) is comprised almost entirely of retrospective quest narratives, as are Zinsser's *Extraordinary Lives* (1986), Pachter's *Telling Lives* (1981), and Oates' *Biography as High Adventure.* The practice may have been modeled on Robin W. Winks' *The Historian as Detective* (1969), which contains twenty-eight accounts of various historians' "quests," and which may have been influenced, in turn, by books like Catherine Drinker Bowen's autobiographical *Adventures of a Biographer* (1959) and essays like Mark Schorer's "The Burdens of Biography" (in *To The Young Writer: Hopwood Lectures, 2nd Series,* ed. A. Bader [Ann Arbor: University of Michigan Press, 1965]). Essays like these, obviously, are separate and distinct from the biographies themselves. One is subjective and personal and the other is not. It is another thing entirely to integrate the "quest" with the "biography," as self-conscious biographers do. The self-conscious biographer goes beyond identification, toward what Donald Winslow calls the "biographical fallacy," which is "analogous to the 'pathetic fallacy,' [and constitutes] a reading into a life one's own life . . . using the subject of a biography as a means of autobiography." ("A Glossary of Terms in Life-Writing, Part I," *Biography* 1.1 [1978]: 65).

Winslow's definition points toward an issue even more fundamental than identification with the subject: whether biography is *art,* into which the artist can and must intrude, or *history,* in which the historical narrator per se has no active role. When biography is considered to be art, Wilde's notion that "the only portraits in which one believes are portraits where there is very little of the sitter, and a very great deal of the artist" comes into play (*The Complete Works of Oscar Wilde* [New York: Harper & Row, 1966], 316). The result is an approach like Schorer's ("Biography has two subjects . . . the figure whose life is being created . . and the mind that is creating it" ["The Burdens of Biography," 147]), or Edel's ("An artist in biography is present in his work in the same way that a painter is present in his portraits" [*Writing Lives,* 65]). When biography is considered to be an historical litany of events, the result is like Blotner's: "All you can do is try your best not to write your own biography in the process of writing someone else's" ("On Having Known One's Subject," in *Leon Edel and Literary Art,* ed. Lyall H. Powers [Ann Arbor: U.M.I. Research Press, 1938], 61). The practical truth of the matter lies somewhere in between. Nadel points out the simple fact that we discovered in Chapter Four, that "whatever role the biographer consciously chooses, his or her presence in the text is inescapable through tropes, narrative style, and language of the work. And this reveals the essential secret of the enterprise: that the biography is fundamentally self-reflexive" ("The Biographer's Secret," in *Studies in Autobiography,* ed. James Olney [New York: Oxford University Press, 1988], 25). In fact, Nadel continues, the whole debate about the presence of the biographer in the narrative is "a diversion, a cover-up . . . deflecting the reader from the inadequacies of the facts or lack of comprehensiveness. The biographer, to cover up his secret, then places himself in the foreground of the narrative" (25). For Joseph Gold, no biography can be written that is not about the biographer as much as the subject. Any attempt to disguise the presence of the biographer is illusory. "Biographers," he believes, "are people who want to write, who need to express themselves, but who for some reason cannot write about themselves or be otherwise visible" ("Biography as Fiction," 134). His advice is to "own what you write, for the story of another's life is certainly in some way the story of your own" (139).

There are many gradations of this self-reflexivity in the self-conscious biography. John Garraty believes that biographers who use a great many footnotes, in so far as they are meant to underline the fruits of the biographical process, have "devoted more space to describing their problems as biographers confronted with the lacunae and the contradictions in the evidence than to judging the meaning of the evidence" (*The Nature of Biography* [London: Cape, 1958], 82). Or a biographer may simply couch biography within personal reflections about the subject, as Robert Penn Warren does in *Jefferson Davis Gets His Citizenship Back* (1979). Or he may fashion an ongoing narrative of his struggle to comprehend the subject, as Norman Mailer does in *Oswald's Tale* and also in *Marilyn,* which is a record not only of Monroe's life but also of how Mailer himself (in another third-person persona) comes to create her.

29 K. J. Hughes and Peter M, Horowitz, "Organic Biography: The Death of an Art," *Journal of British Studies* 12.2 (May 1973): 87.

30 Nadel, *Biography: Fiction, Fact, and Form,* 158.

31 William R. Siebenschuh, *Fictional Techniques and Factual Works* (Athens: University of Georgia Press, 1983), 105.

32 White, *Tropics of Discourse,* 105.

33 Benjamin Hrushovski, "Fictionality and Fields of Reference: Remarks on a Theoretical Framework," *Poetics Today* 5 (1984): 229.

34 Genette, "Fictional Narrative, Factual Narrative." 757.

35 Smith, Barbara Herrnstein, *On the Margins of Discourse: The Relation of Literature to Language* (Chicago: University of Chicago Press, 1978), 15, 20.

36 Dorrit Cohn, "Fictional Versus Historical Lives: Borderlines and Borderline Cases," *Journal of Narrative Technique* 19 (1989): 13.

37 Hamburger, Käte, *The Logic of Literature,* trans. Marilynn J. Rose (Bloomington: Indiana University Press, 1973).

38 Cohn, "Fictional Versus Historical Lives," 13.

39 Michal Glowinski, "On the First-Person Novel," *NLH* 9 (1977): 106.

40 Cohn, "Fictional Versus Historical Lives," 10.

41 Generally, autobiography has two faces, one looking askance at the first-person novel and the other at biography, both expressions being combinations of antipathy and kinship. For my purposes, it is more profitable to define

autobiography against biography rather than against fiction, mainly because of a lack of equivocation where the "reality" of the subject is concerned.

42 Citati, Pietro, *Kafka,* trans. Raymond Rosenthal (New York: Knopf, 1990), 221-22.

43 Gérard Genette, *Narrative Discourse: An Essay in Method,* trans. Jane E. Lewin (Ithaca: Cornell University Press, 1979), 762.

44 See Hrushovski, "Fictionality and Fields of Reference," 228.

45 Cohn, "Fictional Versus Historical Lives," 9.

46 Ibid., 11.

47 Joseph Blotner, *Faulkner: A Biography,* One-Volume ed. (New York: Random House, 1984), 332.

48 Cohn, "Signposts of Fictionality," 785.

Chapter five

1 My definition of narrative in this essay falls somewhere between Thomas Pavel's "weak or literary mythocentrism," which he characterizes as "the strategy of *focusing the literary inquiry* on narrative phenomena, so as to marginalize other aspects of the text and make them appear dependent on plot," and his "stronger or more generalized mythocentrism," which "postulates the existence of a narrative level *in every meaningful event*, be it a story, a nonliterary text, or even a nonlinguistic semiotic object" (*Fictional Worlds* [Cambridge: Harvard University Press, 1986], 5; emphasis mine). Since most "nonliterary texts" or "nonlinguistic semiotic objects"—portraits, cartoons, or the lasting folklore of political agenda—serve only to echo more explicitly narrative texts, I focus for the most part on *textual* narratives (novels, short stories, stage and screen drama, biographies and autobiographies, and some narrative contained within expository commentary).

2 Michiko Kakutani, "Do Facts and Fiction Mix?," *New York Times Book Review,* January 27, 1980, 3.

3 Rüdiger Kunow, "Without Telos of Subject? Coover's and Doctorow's Presentations of History," in *Reconstructing American Literary and Historical Studies,* ed. Günter H. Lenz, et al. (New York: St. Martin's, 1990), 375.

4 John A. Garraty, *The Nature of Biography* (London: Cape, 1958), 71.

5 Naomi Jacobs, *The Character of Truth: Historical Figures in Contemporary Fiction* (Carbondale: Southern Illinois University Press. 1990), xix-xx.

6 Naomi Jacobs. "Michael Ondaatje and the New Fiction Biographies," *Studies in Canadian Literature* 11 (1986): 4.

7 Brian McHale, *Postmodernist Fiction* (New York: Methuen, 1987), 85.

8 By way of demonstrating that every cameo constitutes its own biographical narrative (even when more than one are contained in the same text), we might note that Rudolf Hess does not receive the same mimetic treatment in Vonnegut's novel as his fellows, Goebbels and Eichman. Vonnegut's Howard Campbell meets Hess at a 1944 New Year's Eve Party, during which Hess is revealed ironically satirized as having been an introspective would-be writer.

"How I envy you creative people," he tells Campbell. "Creativity is a gift from the gods" (*Mother Night* [New York: Dell, 1966], 26).

9 Pearl K. Bell, "Coover's Revisionist Fantasy," *Commentary,* October 1977, 67.

10 McHale, *Postmodernist Fiction,* 85, 86.

11 George Lukács, *The Theory of the Novel,* trans. Anna Bostock (Cambridge: MIT Press. 1990), 77, 81.

12 Umberto Eco, *Six Walks in the Fictional Woods* (Cambridge: Harvard University Press, 1994), 85.

13 Georg Lukács, *The Historical Novel,* trans. Hannah and Stanley Mitchell (Lincoln: University of Nebraska Press, 1962), 20.

14 Eco, *Six Walks in the Fictional Woods,* 81.

15 Edward Mendelson, "Encyclopedic Narrative from Dante to Pynchon," *Modern Language Notes* 91 (1976): 1269.

16 Jacobs, *The Character of Truth,* 23.

17 Lennard J. Davis, "A Social History of Fact and Fiction: Authorial Disavowal in the Early English Novel," in *Literature and Society: Selected Papers from the English institute, 1978,* ed. Edward W. Said (Baltimore: Johns Hopkins University Press, 1980). 128.

18 Eco, *Six Walks in the Fictional Woods,* 81.

19 McHale, *Postmodernist Fiction,* 33, 58.

20 John R. Searle, "The Logical Status of Fictional Discourse." *New Literary History* 6 (1975): 319.

21 Kendall Walton, "Appreciating Fiction: Suspending Disbelief or Pretending Belief," *Dispositio* 5.13-14 (1980): 2.

22 Louis O. Mink, "History and Fiction as Modes of Comprehension," in *New Directions in Literary History,* ed. Ralph Cohen (Baltimore: Johns Hopkins University Press, 1974), 111.

23 Walton, "Appreciating Fiction," 2.

24 Lukács, *The Historical Novel,* 34. Scott, for example, argued merely against anachronism in costume and landscape—"the character of the age must remain inviolate"—while excusing some revision of language (*Ivanhoe,* Waverly Novels Vol. XVI [Edinburgh: Black, 1860], xxxix), a practice which, to Cooper, was necessary for the creation of the historical *"beau-ideal"* (*The Last of the Mohicans* [New York: Oxford University Press, 1990], 398). McHale characterizes such methods as an effort at "camouflaging the seam between historical reality and fiction" (*Postmodernist Fiction*, 90), a feat accomplished, we might say, by avoiding that seam altogether. McHale also points out that the difference between the general and the specific depends largely on the going idea of the historical "dark area," which changed greatly from Scott to Tolstoy (for whom the inside of Napoleon's head is such an area).

25 Benjamin Hrushovski, "Fictionality and Fields of Reference: Remarks on a Theoretical Framework," *Poetics Today* 5 (1984): 232.

26 Ibid., 236.

27 Ibid., 237.

28 Mink, "History and Fiction as Modes of Comprehension," 112.

29 Searle, "The Logical Status of Fictional Discourse," 325.

30 Eco, *Six Walks in the Fictional Woods*, 75.

31 Gérard Genette, "Fictional Narrative, Factual Narrative," *Poetics Today* 11 (1990): 757.

32 Wolfgang Iser has discarded altogether the Aristotelian binary model by which history tells what happened and literature what might, replacing it with a "triad" comprised of the "real," "the "fictive," and the "imaginary." The "real" is a referential aggregate comprised of all the text's mimetic elements, not only particular objects and people, but also "thought systems, social systems, and world pictures as well as other texts" (*The Fictive and the Imaginary: Charting Literary Anthropology* [Baltimore: Johns Hopkins University Press, 1993], 305) Meanwhile, the "imaginary" is a *quality* that exists apart from those real elements, even though the "real" is used semiotically to "point" to the "imaginary." The "fictive," in Iser's conception, is therefore not a quality of mendacity, but is the *act* by which this semiotic process occurs; it "has all the qualities of pertaining to an event and thus relieves the definition of fiction from the burden of making the customary ontological statements regarding what fiction is" (*The Fictive and the Imaginary,* 305). According to Iser's model, fiction's imaginative alteration of reality is a communication between, not a contradiction of, ontologies. Those elements of the "real" that "point to" the "imaginative" are in Iser's view referentially equivalent to the same elements in an historical work. In reconciling historical referents with fictional devices, Iser provides our best explanation for why historical and fictive ontologies can and do share referential material. Even when Iser's "fictive" process results in a fantastic world, the historical individual within it can be seen to interact with the "imaginary" while retaining its semiotic historicity. That is, if we were to remove the paratextual barriers that Hrushovski, Mink and Searle have observed between the worlds of, say, Pynchon's *Gravity's Rainbow* and Stephen Ambrose' *Rise to Globalism,* we might find between them a "semipermeable membrane" (McHale, *Postmodernist Fiction,* 35), through which run the V-2 rocket and the U-boat, the Volga and the Rhine, various parts of London and elements of Pavlovian psychology. Not to mention Richard Nixon, who therefore possesses what Eco calls "transworld identity," because Pynchon's and Ambrose's Nixon are, for all intents and purposes, "identical" (*The Role of the Reader: Explorations in the Semiotics of Texts* [Bloomington: Indiana University Press, 1979], 230).

The impact that proper names, as opposed to nominal camouflage in the tradition of the *roman-á-cléf,* has on transworld identity is complicated. McHale alleges that "transworld identity between real-world persons and fictional characters depends upon identity of proper names; this is part of its definition." In the *roman a cléf,* he continues, "transworld identity between real-world persons and fictional characters have been deliberately *occluded*" (*Postmodernist Fiction,* 206). I agree that a degree of "occlusion" occurs when names are changed, but I would not go so far as to say that, by virtue of such a change the historical figure is no longer present in the text. After all, many early cléfs were republished later with a key to names and places printed at the beginning of the book, a practice that tends to reinforce them as biographical narratives. Furthermore, the policy of disallowing an historical figure based on the presence or absence of a particular appellation creates serious problems of admissibility: is "Nixon" or "Richard" or "Dick" (or even the culturally-meaningful "Tricky Dick") any less indicative of the historical 37th President of the United States than "Richard Milhous Nixon"? Ultimately, the degree to which a text can be read as a biographical narrative depends more on the degree of identifiability than on the presence of a name. Conventional disclaimers of "resemblance to persons living or dead" therefore do little do dissuade the interrogation of a text as biographical narrative. On the other hand, the use of an historical name in a fictive text unavoidably invokes the biographical personage in so far as that name is recognizable by the reader. This is true even when the historical figure seems to be present in name only (as in Barthelme's "Robert Kennedy Saved from Drowning"). Thus, statements like Keith Abbot's at the beginning of Rhino Ritz, that character "names have been used independently of their actual bodies," do little to divert their inclusion in biographical narrative.

33 McHale, *Postmodernist Fiction*, 85.

34 Thomas LeClair, "Robert Coover, *The Public Burning*, and the Art of Excess," *Critique* 23.3 (Spring 1982): 6.

35 Jerome Charyn, review of *Flight to Canada* by Ishmael Reed, *New York Times Book Review,* September 19, 1976, 5.

36 Cushing Strout, *The Veracious Imagination: Essays on American History: Literature, and Biography* (Middletown: Wesleyan University Press, 1981), 185.

37 McHale, *Postmodernist Fiction*, 90.

38 Jacobs, *The Character of Truth*, xx.

39 Paul Fussell, review of *Gossip from the Forest* by Thomas Keneally, *New York Times Book Review*, April 11, 1976, 7.

40 Warner Berthoff, "Fiction, History, Myth: Notes Toward the Discrimination of Narrative Forms," in *The Interpretation of Narrative: Theory and Practice*, ed. Morton W. Bloomfield (Cambridge: Harvard University Press, 1970), 272.

41 One peculiar exception to this rule is the published screenplay of Oliver Stone's film *Nixon,* whose numerous scholarly notes are meant to validate the film *outside* its diegesis. That this device is flawed and ultimately unsuccessful indicates that the film is a more sound biographical statement without the notes.

42 Jacobs. "Michael Ondaatje and the New Fiction Biographies," 3, 5.

43 Dominick LaCapra, *History. Politics, and the Novel* (Ithaca: Cornell University Press, 1987), 10.

44 Ina Schabert, "Fictional Biography, Factual Biography, and Their Contaminations," *Biography* 5 (1982): 3.

35

Ansgar Nünning

"Fictional Metabiographies and Metaautobiographies: Towards a Definition, Typology and Analysis of Self-Reflexive Hybrid Metegenres" from *Self-Reflexivity in Literature* (2005)

1 Introducing the paradox of 'Life-Writing' and the genre of the metabiography

In one of his incisive essays, in which he sings the praises of a more distanced stance towards the objects and texts we study, Rolf Breuer makes an observation that provides a particularly good starting-point for an article that sets out to gauge new developments in contemporary genres: "Natürlich muß das Handwerkszeug der Literaturwissenschaft, die Begrifflichkeit usw. angesichts neuer Gattungen und Gattungsmischungen geschärft und erweitert werden, aber deswegen müssen nicht etwa die Kategorien aufgeweicht werden."[1] As anyone familiar with Rolf Breuer's pioneering works will know, the academic standards that they have set—both in terms of terminological precision and analytical rigor—are very high, and anything but easy to meet or emulate. Instead of softening up the categories of criticism, he has always insisted on the importance of the distinction between the 'object language' we encounter in works of art and the 'meta-language' we use as critics and theorists.[2]

Both this distinction and Breuer's suggestion that we need to enlarge and refine our analytical and terminological toolkit provide a timely reminder for anyone who tries to come to terms with the complex field of the plethora of hybrid new genres in contemporary literature. More and more novels not only cross the boundaries between fact and fiction, they also tend to blur genre distinctions. As a result, an increasing number of postmodernist novels seem to resist generic classification all together, or at least test the limits of it. This blurring of genre conventions has resulted in the emergence of new hybrid forms like the travelogue, historiographic metafiction and other postmodernist variants of historical fiction, and the fictional biography. In his hilarious satire on poststructuralism and deconstruction, *Mensonge,* Malcolm Bradbury makes an observation that encapsulates some of these trends: "Alas, what with the Death of the Author and the Disappearance of the Subject, even an ordinary biography is bound to be a problem these days. Biographies are said to be fictions revealing more about the biographer than they do about their subjects, who of course do not exist anyway."[3]

Bradbury's witty observation not only has a peculiar appropriateness to novels like Peter Ackroyd's *Chatterton* (1987), Julian Barnes's *Flaubert's Parrot* (1984) and Antonia S. Byatt's *The Biographer's Tale* (2000), but it can also be read as an allusion to the increasing degree of self-reflexivity that is characteristic of postmodern novels in general and fictional biographies and autobiographies in particular. Ackroyd's *Chatterton,* for instance, is indeed anything but an ordinary biography, be it fictional or not, featuring the Death of the Author as one of the more prominent leitmotifs.[4] What novelists like Ackroyd, Barnes, Byatt, and a host of others (e.g. Patricia Duncker, Alison Lurie, Steven Millhauser, Michael Ondaatje, Carol Shields, and Barry Unsworth,[5] to name but a few) have done instead of accumulating evidence and writing a conventional narrative biography is to juxtapose several stories that present the reader with highly self-reflexive intertextual, or rather intermedial, biographical quests for the respective biographee. Best-selling novels like *Chatterton, Flaubert's Parrot* and *Possession: A Romance* are therefore not so much fictional biographies than ingenious meta-biographies, providing various fictions that indeed reveal more about the individual biographers than they do about their elusive subjects.

A great part of our interest in these novels arguably derives from the fact that not only their content, but also their complex structures, intertextual networks, and metabiographic self-consciousness foreground the paradoxical relation between life and writing which the somewhat oxymoronic term 'biography' somewhat unsuccessfully tries to conceal. Michel de Certeau has made a succinct observation on 'historiography' which clarifies what is at issue here: "Historiography (that is, 'history' and 'writing') bears within its own name the paradox—almost an oxymoron—of a relation established between two antinomic terms, between the real and discourse. Its task is one of connecting them and, at the point where this link cannot be imagined, of working *as if* the two were being joined."[6] Taking my cue from de Certeau, I shall argue that the term 'biography' also "bears within its own name the paradox—almost an oxymoron—of a relation established between two antinomic terms," between 'life' and 'writing.' Whereas the task of conventional biographies, factual and fictional alike, "is one of connecting them and, at the point where this link cannot be imagined, of working *as if* the two were being joined," a fictional metabiography emphasizes that there will always be an ineluctable and insurmountable difference between a life and a book.

Setting out from this point of departure, the present article will examine postmodernist modes of challenging the conventions of biography and autobiography in a paradigmatic novel, Antonia S. Byatt's *The Biographer's Tale* (2000), and the changed attitudes to the possibilities and problems involved in life-writing that this novel expresses. Illustrating de Certeau's thesis that "the past is the fiction of the present,"[7] Byatt's novel can be read as an expression, in theme and form, of the constructivist view that biography, just like historiography, is a subjective and constructive process which does not reproduce the past but is only an intellectual construct. In what follows I will argue that this highly self-conscious and self-reflexive novel can be seen as a paradigm example of new generic variants of the fictional biography which I suggest should be designated 'fictional metabiography' or 'fictional metaautobiography' respectively in that it is concerned with the manifold problems involved in any attempt to write either a biography or an autobiography. The remarkable achievement of this ambitious novel can be found in the ways in which it conveys a sense of the complexity and perplexity of the problems attached to any auto/biographic enterprise. In addition to questioning the very possibility of truthfully representing a person's life, Byatt's novel self-consciously examines the problems of auto/biographic reconstruction, exemplifying the paradoxes of 'life-writing.'

After a brief preliminary discussion of the crossing of traditional genre boundaries characteristic of fictional biographies or biographical fictions, the second part of the article provides some steps towards a typology of biofictions, arguing that novels like *Chatterton, The Biographer's Tale* and *Flaubert's Parrot* can be seen as paradigms of the fictional metabiography,[8] while Dave Eggers's *A Heartbreaking Work of Staggering Genius* (2000) provides an equally paradigmatic example of the fictional metaautobiography.[9] The third section analyzes the structure and themes of the intertextual quests for the biographees in Byatt's novel, with an eye to illuminating and assessing the epistemological and metabiographic ideas implicitly and explicitly asserted in the novel. Some observations on the constructivist view of biography and on the notion of generic memory exemplified not only in Byatt's novels, but also in a wide range of other postmodernist English, American and Canadian metabiofictions conclude this essay.

2 Towards a typology of biofictions: Antonia S. Byatt's *The Biographer's Tale* and Dave Eggers's *A Heartbreaking Work of Staggering Genius* as paradigm examples of the fictional metabiography and metaautobiography

Being located on the border between historiography and literature, fact and fiction, postmodernist biofictions show a pronounced tendency to cross boundaries and to blur genre distinctions. In his seminal survey of the modern British novel, Malcolm Bradbury repeatedly draws attention to what he calls "generic crossovers, crossings of borders, easy passage between the high and the popular forms, or the literary and the media arts" and to the resulting "breakdown of the conventional borders of genre and narrative type."[10] The resulting proliferation of hybrid genres located on the borderline between factual and fictional biographies bears witness to the fact that the conventional dichotomy between 'fact' and 'fiction' has of late been called into question.

Yet the ways in which genre conventions are blurred as well as challenged in contemporary (meta-)biofictions are so multifarious that it does not make much sense to subsume all the novels in question under one label, be it 'historiographic metafiction' or 'fictional biography.' The great variety of biofictions dealt with in a groundbreaking volume edited by Martin Middeke and Werner Huber[11] sufficiently testifies to the need to devise a typology of the different generic variants of the genre known as the fictional biography, and, one might add, for the use of biographical material in drama, poetry, and film as well.[12]

Such reservations notwithstanding, novels like *The Biographer's Tale* and *A Heartbreaking Work of Staggering Genius* are, of course, paradigm examples for a volume dedicated to exploring the intricate issue of self-reflexivity in literature, in more ways than one even. First, these novels exemplify not just the current renaissance of 'life-writing,' i.e. the recent trend in postmodern literature to fictionalize the life of historical personages in the form of a fictional biography, but also the increasing degree of self-reflexivity which is characteristic for many of the novels that belong to this trend. Second, these novels are revisionist in at least two ways: they question and revise the official biographical record of the respective biographees, and they also express revisionist notions of auto/biography and auto/biographical fiction. Thirdly, and arguably most importantly, *The Biographer's Tale* and *A Heartbreaking Work of Staggering Genius* are paradigmatic in that they cross traditional genre boundaries and shift the emphasis from the mere writing, or rewriting, of an historical individual's life to the epistemological and methodological problems involved in any attempt at life-writing itself.

Consequently, like a great number of other postmodernist historical novels and biofictions, Byatt's and Eggers's novels seem to resist generic classification altogether, or at least to test the limits of it, because they are characterized by a blurring of genre conventions and by an intense degree of self-reflexivity. This crossing of traditional genre boundaries is not confined to a blurring of the fact/fiction boundary but extends to hybrid new forms of biofiction. As these and many other novels serve to show, this blurring of genre conventions has resulted in the emergence of such new generic variants of the fictional biography (which is in itself a hybrid form) as the revisionist fictional biography, the fictional metabiography, and the fictional metaautobiography.

Paradoxically enough, however, one of the results of this genre blurring and self-reflexivity is that the concept of genericity becomes more, not less, important, as Perloff rightly observes: "It is the paradox of postmodern genre that the more radical the dissolution of traditional generic boundaries, the more important the concept of genericity becomes."[13] The more often generic borders are crossed and the less secure habitual categories stand, the more important it becomes to identify the genre conventions that a given work adapts, transforms, and subverts. Despite the fact that generic categories have multiplied, little sustained attempt has been made to discuss the impact of generic cross-references in postmodernist biofictions, let alone to provide a systematic typology of the recent proliferation of various subgeners of biofictions and similar hybrid genres.[14]

Determining the generic status of novels like *The Biographer's Tale* and *A Heartbreaking Work of Staggering Genius* is thus not quite as easy as one might expect. At first sight, like many other contemporary novels, they seem to belong to that generic crossbreed known as fictional biography or autobiographical fiction respectively. In her seminal monograph, Ina Schabert defines this genre as follows: "FICTIONAL BIOGRAPHY is engaged in the comprehension of real historical individuals by means of the sophisticated instruments of knowing and articulating knowledge that contemporary fiction offers."[15] Like the historical novel, the fictional biography is a hybrid genre in that it blurs the fact/fiction boundary. On closer inspection, however, they turn out to be fictional, or even metafictional, *meta*(auto)biographies rather than just a fictional biography in that they do not really represent the life of an historical individual but challenging and problematizing the issues of representation and life-writing. Undermining the basic assumptions of positivist historiography and biography, these novels focus on the perception and reconstruction of the lives of various auto/biographees rather than on representing their lives as such. In doing so, Byatt's and Eggers's novels raise a number of important metabiographic problems. In contrast to the genre that Linda Hutcheon christened 'historiographic metafiction,' however, which addresses problems related to the writing of history explicitly in metafictional comments, fictional metabiographies incorporate such issues into their narrative structure. Like many other metahistorical novels and fictional metabiographies, *The Biographer's Tale* and *A Heartbreaking Work of Staggering Genius* focus on the continuity of the past in the present, on the interplay between different time-levels, on forms of historical consciousness, and especially on the reconstruction, rather than representation, of the lives of real historical individuals. They are thus a far cry from such fictional biographies or autobiographies as Robert Graves' *I, Claudius* (1934) and *Wife to Mr. Milton* (1979), Robert Nye's *The Memoirs of Lord Byron: A Novel* (1989), or John Banville's *Doctor Copernicus* (1976) and *Kepler* (1981) which are somewhat more traditional specimen of the genre.

Given the great number of differences in themes and techniques that appear in postmodernist fictional biographies, a typology of biofictions seems to be needed that takes into account both the thematic innovations and the narrative devices that distinguish different kinds of this subgenre from one another. Along the lines of a typology of historical fiction that I developed elsewhere,[16] I would suggest designating these main subgenres, which are of course merely 'ideal types' (in the sense of Max Weber), as 'documentary fictional biographies,' 'realist fictional biographies,' 'revisionist fictional biographies,' 'fictional metabiographies,' and explicit forms of 'biographic metafiction.'[17] Documentary fictional biographies tend to have a great number and wide scope of reality references and to foreground the conventionally backgrounded factual world. Realist fictional biographies, by contrast, represent the life of a real historical individual, using conventional fictional devices and foregrounding the plot against the backdrop of some identifiable historical context.

Although the documentary fictional biography and the realist or traditional fictional biography belong to the group of generic hybrids which integrate factual with fictional material, it is the other three types that are of particular relevance as far as self-reflexive generic variants are concerned. The fact that the majority of the historical novels and fictional biographies that have won, or been shortlisted for, the Booker Prize represent these postmodernist manifestations of historical biofiction is indicative of the high critical esteem which metafictional modes have enjoyed since the end of the Seventies.

Revisionist fictional biographies, by contrast, *rewrite,* rather than just represent, the life of real historical individuals. They reinterpret the biographical record and revise the formal conventions of traditional biofictions, but in contrast to biographic metafictions they lack any elements that break the aesthetic illusion and that foreground either the process of biographic reconstruction or the fictionality of the text. Like the postmodernist historical novel,[18] the revisionist fictional biography revises both the content of the biographical record and the conventions of biographical fiction. It often does so by violating one or even all of the constraints on the insertion of reality references that realist fiction adheres to.[19]

Fictional metabiographies (as well as metaautobiographies) also explore, revise, and transform the conventions of the traditional biography and autobiography, but what they formally foreground are the problems of 'life-writing' and the forms of historical consciousness. Rather than focusing primarily on the past, they make use of the interplay between different time-levels, emphasizing the continuity of the past in the present. In contrast to the indirect mode characteristic of fictional metabiographies, biographic metafiction explicitly thematizes and undermines the conventional boundaries between biography and fiction by deploying the devices of metafiction. The latter two postmodernist variants of biofictions have one important feature in common: they deal not so much with biographical facts as with the epistemological, methodological, and ontological problems associated with 'life-writing.' They differ in that the latter directly thematizes the problems that the reconstruction and representation of the life of historical personages in the form of a biography, be it fictional or factual, inevitably entails, whereas the former incorporates these issues into the structure.

Given these theoretical and typological underpinnings, it can be argued that *The Biographer's Tale* and *A Heartbreaking Work of Staggering Genius* represent curious generic hybrids of biofictions, or, more particularly, of the kinds that I have designated as the metabiographic variants of the fictional auto/biography. They can be considered as paradigm examples of the typological variants designated 'fictional metabiography' and 'fictional metaautobiography' because metabiographic reflections become one of the main issues, if not the key issue, of these novels. In contrast to documentary, realist, and revisionist fictional biographies, Byatt's and Eggers's postmodernist fictional metabiography and metaautobiography are not confined to narrating the life of the biographee. Foregrounding the seam between fiction and historical reality in various ways, they rather set out to explore problems involved in the writing of history and biography and their representation.

In addition, it seems to be useful to differentiate between the various forms that both historiographic metafiction and biographic metafiction—just like other types of metafiction—may take. It may either be explicit, that is it may use the devices of metafiction to self-referentially explore and overtly thematize the epistemological, methodological, and linguistic problems connected with any attempt to construct coherent accounts of the past. But historiographic and biographic metafiction may just as well be implicit, that is incorporate its metahistoriographic and metabiographic concerns formally in the structure of the novel.

Fictional metabiographies like the one that will be examined in the next section represent significant innovations in the treatment of biography and autobiography as a literary theme because what they highlight is the process of biographical reconstruction and the protagonists' consciousness of the past rather than a represented historical world as such. Instead of focusing on and portraying the life of real historical individuals on the diegetic level of the characters, fictional metabiographies are generally set in the present but concerned with the appropriation, reconstruction, and transmission of the biographee's life. Such novels typically explore how characters try to come to terms with the past. What is highlighted in *The Biographer's Tale* and *A Heartbreaking Work of Staggering Genius* are the auto/biographical endeavors of the protagonists living in the present rather than the past itself. Moreover, like many other fictional metabiographies, these novels do not portray the past as a self-contained and complete world, but as liable to the distortions that subjective reconstructions and recollections entail. It might therefore be profitable to explore the possible connections between the structural properties of Byatt's self-reflexive novel and its epistemological and metabiographic implications.

3 "[A]n experiment in the nature of biographical narrative:" Epistemological and metabiographic implications in Antonia S. Byatt's *The Biographer's Tale*

As in many other self-reflexive fictional biographies, it is not the representation of a biographee's life itself that provides the focus of Byatt's novel *The Biographer's Tale* but rather the process of biographical and historical reconstruction, which takes the form of a biographical quest conducted by the unfortunate postgraduate Phineas G. Nanson. Being fed up with criticism and "postmodernist literary theory,"[20] and yearning for facts, the protagonist, who also serves as the I-narrator of the novel, sets out to write a biography of a great biographer, Scholes Destry-Scholes. Talking to Ormerod Goode, one of the two joint Heads of the Department, he explains why he no longer wants to be a postmodern literary theorist: "'I need a life full of things,' I said. 'Full of facts.'" (p. 4)

The protagonist soon realizes, however, that what he needs is indeed more difficult to come by than he may have thought. What Phineas finds instead of a life full of facts is nothing but textual fragments and a great number of gaps. What is more, these disconnected type-scripts and other remnants of the past fail to add up: facts do not "slot together" (p. 10). What is needed to make them do exactly that is "Destry-Scholes's resourceful marshalling and arranging of *facts*" (p. 15). Facts are not 'out there,' ready to be found or discovered by the eager biographer, Phineas learns, they have to be made, invented, or constructed by the writer himself: "This faceless writer constructed this edifice of style, of facts" (p. 20). Since it is the biographer himself who has to do "the construction-work" (p. 99), Phineas gradually realizes that the "threads of connection are my own" (p. 227).

The impossibility of synthesizing the contradictory remnants and accounts of Destry-Scholes's life serves to undermine the belief that biographical events and facts can ever be objectively known. The structure of Byatt's novel shows that there is not one authentic representation of the past but a plurality of competing versions. Highlighting the fact that biographers subjectively process the information they encounter in their sources, *The Biographer's Tale* lays bare the impossibility of producing an objective, totalized, and true account of the life of an historical individual.

Although the relationship of history to the present is an important factor underlying the complex structure of Byatt's novel, there are several formal and thematic features which serve to direct the readers' attention from the past and Destry-Scholes's life to the present, to Phineas's biographical quest. Foregrounding unresolved contradictions between different versions of the biographee's life and death, the pattern of the intertextual quest serves to raise important metabiographic issues. The structural features of Byatt's novel bring to the fore the constructivist insight that subjectivity and constructivity are ineliminable features of historical knowledge and of biographic constructions.

Focusing on the pattern of an intertextual quest, *The Biographer's Tale* draws the readers' attention to epistemological and methodological problems of 'life-writing,' problems which are inseparably connected with any attempt to construct coherent accounts of the lives of historical individuals. Byatt's novel is not only closely concerned with the epistemological and methodological problems of auto/biography, it also displays the sort of high degree of metafictional self-consciousness characteristic of historiographic and biographic metafiction in general. The central question implicitly raised by the complex quest structure and the dense intertextual network of *The Biographer's Tale* is formulated by the protagonist himself when he asks himself, "How, one may ask, does such a man set about constructing another human being, in some sense *ex nihilo,* an individual who was not there before, and now exists." (p. 84)

Byatt's novel can be read as a fictional metabiography in that it expresses constructivist notions of knowledge and life-writing through literary means. By showing how auto/biographers actively structure the information they encounter in their sources, *The Biographer's Tale* scrutinizes both "history in the making" and "historiography in the making."[21] Whereas the various historical sources, type-scripts and fragments shed light on "history in the making," the protagonist's biographical quest and reconstruction are primarily concerned with biography in the making, with the making of biographical images.

The fragmentary and densely intertextual montage structure of *The Biographer's Tale* emphasizes the discrepancy between the biographee's allegedly real life in the past and the remembered and textualized versions of his life, foregrounding the insurmountable gap between a person's life and any written representations thereof. The inability to grasp and narrate the complex processes that make up another person's lives is implicitly expressed through the juxtaposition of heterogeneous fragments. The problems of the biographer are enhanced by the questionable authenticity of sources and documents as well as by the possible risk of the distortions of facts (cf. p. 164). Phineas becomes more and more self-conscious about both the problems inherent in his biographical project and his own inclination to digress: "I have managed to trap myself in digressions, if there can be digressions in a project that appears alternately to have too little and too much form." (p. 168)

Concerning itself with the question of how much we can ever know about the past, *The Biographer's Tale* calls into doubt positivist notions of objectivity and factual truth, showing that any biographical representation is an intellectual construct. Both through its complex structural layering of historical reconstruction and its metabiographic self-consciousness, Byatt's novel shows that what is commonly regarded as a biographical fact inevitably depends on the selective bias of the individual biographer. More specifically, both the protagonist's quest and the intertextual structure of *The Biographer's Tale* draw attention to the distorting effects of selecting sources, to the biographer's problem of having to rely on scanty evidence, to the partiality, contradictoriness, unreliability, and questionable authenticity of historical sources and documents, and to the close affinity between history and stories. The intertextual network of Byatt's novel and the many metabiographic comments it contains serve to foreground the fact that subjectivity, relativity, selectivity, and constructivity are ineliminable features of biographic (re-)constructions.

Far from relying mainly on indirect or structural modes of poetological self-reflexivity as intertextuality and the juxtaposition of different fragments from Destry-Scholes's life and work, *The Biographer's Tale* also features a wide range of self-reflexive comments in which a great number of the epistemological and methodological problems faced by biographers and historians are explicitly thematized. There are, for example, many self-conscious references to different kinds of biography, ranging from "the Victorian conventions of respecting privacy" to "the first wave of Freudian biography" (p. 15), the "second wave psychoanalytic biography" (p. 16), and "the modern critical, or psychoanalytical, biography" (p. 165) as well as "what we currently call group biographies" (p. 236). Moreover, the narrator repeatedly comments on the discrepancy between life and writing, between history as it is experienced and history as a written record of something that happened in the past. Like the gaps and unresolved tensions between conflicting sources, such comments expose the epistemological problems faced by any biographer.

Byatt's novel not only abounds in self-reflexive comments on the conventions of biographies, to a certain extent it resembles, and almost reads like, "a theoretical enquiry—for aspiring biographers" (p. 25), or like "an experiment in the nature of biographical narrative" (p. 165). What is probably more indicative of the high degree of generic self-reflexivity characteristic of Byatt's novel than anything else is the fact that almost every convention relevant for the genre of the biography is explicitly thematized, foregrounded, and called in question in the narrator's discourse. When the narrator refers to Destry-Scholes's "detached narrative tone" (p. 16), for instance, he adds in parentheses that Destry-Scholes "was fortunate enough to live before the idea of 'objectivity' was deconstructed" (p. 16). The narrator also mentions in passing "that identity, that the self, is a dubious matter" (p. 97) and "that objectivity is an exploded and deconstructed notion" (p. 98), thereby questioning two more key notions on which the art of life-writing is based and foregrounding "the hopeless nature of the project of biographical accuracy" (p. 236). The overt skepticism of such reflections serves to underline that *The Biographer's Tale* is a fictional metabiography rather than just a fictionalized recreation of a famous biographer's life. Despite the high degree of uncertainty and skepticism that Byatt's novel projects, however, it is not the factual existence of past events that is called in question, but only man's ability to ever know or faithfully represent the true facts of a person's life.

Like such other metabiographies as *Flaubert's Parrot* and *Chatterton, The Biographer's Tale* is particularly concerned with the incommensurability between an experience and any recording or representation of it in writing, and with the concomitant contingencies of historiographical and biographical endeavors. Byatt's novel alerts the reader to the idea that our models of both another person's life and of biography as a genre are as much an intellectual construction (albeit not necessarily a fiction, as Hayden White maintains) as the fictional worlds projected in the novel. The epistemological and metabiographic implications of Byatt's novel suggest that historiographic and biographic representations may offer a mediated form of access to the past but that they can never provide a transparent reflection or a reliable account of an historical individual's life. The actual and chaotic dynamics of other people's lives and historical events eludes every attempt at delineating them comprehensively in writing or any other medium. In the end, an insurmountable gap remains between the life of a person and any representation thereof.[22]

Since what is foregrounded instead in *The Biographer's Tale* is "the relation of biographer to subject" (p. 162), Byatt's novel turns out to be as much of a metaautobiography as a metabiography. It suggests that a biography tells us as much about its author as it does about its subject, the biographee. Phineas not only realizes that there "were also odd moments where the professional biographer revealed his own preoccupations" (p. 97), he even begins to fear that his biography might turn into an autobiography: "And the last thing I have any interest in writing—I mean this—is an autobiography." (p. 99) The reader, however, gets the impression that the narrator is protesting a bit too much: "I am not writing an autobiography. I am writing in the first person for the sake of precision, because this procedure allows me to say certain things I am reasonably sure of." (p. 100) In the end Phineas realizes that he seems to have failed to match "Destry-Scholes's real achievement in describing a whole individual, a multi-faceted single man, one life from birth to death. I appeared to have failed to find Destry-Scholes himself" (p. 214). The narrator's comments remind the reader that the genres of the biography and the autobiography are much more closely intertwined than one might think and that Malcolm Bradbury might well have a point when he flippantly characterized biographies as "fictions revealing more about the biographer than they do about their subjects:"

> I have to respect him for his scrupulous *absence* from my tale, my work. It will be clear that I too have wished to be *absent*. I have resisted and evaded the idea that because of Destry-Scholes's *absence* my narrative must become an account of my own presence, id est, an autobiography, that most evasive and self-indulgent of forms. (p. 214)

4 Conclusion: On a constructivist view of auto/biography and generic memory

What emerges in such self-reflexive postmodernist auto/biofictions as *The Biographer's Tale* and *A Heartbreaking Work of Staggering Genius*, then, is biography and autobiography as patterns of retrospective projections. Byatt's and Eggers's novels suggest that there is not one truth about a biographee's life, only a series of versions which are dependent on and constructed by the auto/biographer rather than retrieved from the past. Moreover, Byatt's and Eggers's novels show that biographers cannot check whether there is any correspondence between their versions of history and the real events of the past because the latter are inaccessible except through textualized or visual representations, the authenticity of which is shown to be dubious at best. Fictional metabiographies and metaautobiographies like *The Biographer's Tale* and *A Heartbreaking Work of Staggering Genius* thematize and cross the boundary between history and writing, because they draw attention to the "process of turning events into facts through the filtering and interpreting of archival documents," "of turning the traces of the past [. . .] into historical representation."[23] The reader can compare the different fragments and versions of Destry-Scholes's life delineated in Byatt's novel, but he or she cannot compare any of these versions to what they are supposed to depict, that is the enigmatic events of the life and death of the great biographer that are not directly presented. The structure of both the biographical quest and the intertextual network also serves as a means of foregrounding the textual form through which history is mediated, of highlighting the fact that it is impossible to know the past by any other than textualized means.

By undermining the notions of truth and objectivity, fictional metabiographies and metaautobiographies like *The Biographer's Tale* and *A Heartbreaking Work of Staggering Genius* call into question the ontological boundary between fact and fiction, the real and the imaginary. Both the complex structure of the two novels and the metabiographic and metaautobiographic self-consciousness of the protagonists overtly bring to the fore the creative and interpretive role of the auto/biographer, who constructs rather than reconstructs history or his story. Exploring, crossing, and undermining the border between fiction and (factual) biography, these fictional meta(auto) biographies problematize the whole issue of representation. Like many other postmodernist historical novels and fictional metabiographies, *The Biographer's Tale* displays that "crisis in representation" which Hans Bertens in his brilliant survey *The Idea of the Postmodern* has identified as the "common denominator to all these postmodernisms [. . .]: a deeply felt loss of faith in our ability to represent the real."[24] Byatt's and Eggers's novels illustrate that narrative, as the narrativist school of metahistorians has convincingly demonstrated, is not a transparent medium for representing historical reality but imposes a specific narrative shape on events.

In sum, fictional metabiographies and metaautobiographies like *The Biographer's Tale* and *A Heartbreaking Work of Staggering Genius* exemplify a constructivist view of both biography and autobiography in that they expose both the incommensurability between an experience and any recording of it, and the concomitant contingencies and constructivity of 'life-writing.' By highlighting the distance between historical events and written representations, such postmodernist auto/biofictions testify to what de Certeau regards as the central paradox of historiography, the insurmountable gap between historical reality and historiography. Despite the fact, then, that the term biography suggests that the biographer creates a nexus between a past life and writing, postmodernist self-reflexive biofictions remind the reader that the gulf between the real past and discourse, between life as it is experienced and as it appears in the form of a biography, is, in the end, unbridgeable.

A more detailed analysis of *The Biographer's Tale* and *A Heartbreaking Work of Staggering Genius* could show that these novels are far from confined to merely revealing a constructivist view of auto/biography. On the contrary, the metafictional questioning and self-reflexive staging of the conventions of auto/biography in these works serve to foreground what one, for want of a better term, may call the 'generic memory' of the two genres in question, i.e. of the biography and autobiography respectively. Like any other genres, these two literary genres and their formal characteristics are closely related to conventionalized expectations (or, to use a term from cognitive psychology: schemata). Repertoires of forms specific to particular genres are elements of the collective memory and as such belong to the common knowledge of societies, which individuals acquire through socialization processes. Metabiographies and metaautobiographies serve to foreground the main characteristics of the two genres in question, while also showing that these conventions are elements of the literary memory and elements of the collective memory (shared by authors and readers alike), crystallized in schemata, and that they guide the interpretative strategies and expectations along certain paths.

One might even go so far as to argue that fictional metabiographies and metaautobiographies like *The Biographer's Tale* and *A Heartbreaking Work of Staggering Genius* can be seen to represent a particular kind of literary self-reflexivity that has, curiously enough, not received the amount of attention that it arguably merits: i.e., generic self-reflexivity. The latter has arguably led to the establishment of new hybrid and highly self-reflexive genres of which fictional metabiographies and metaautobiographies are two of the most prominent examples. Like its autobiographical counterpart, the fictional metabiography constitutes a particularly interesting species of generic self-reflexivity, one that critically explores the generic conventions and memory of the genre to which it belongs, viz. the art of biography or life-writing.[25] Other examples would include, for instance, the postmodern meta-romance as well as new variants of metadrama and metapoetry.[26] Given these interesting new developments in contemporary literature, which arguably call for new descriptive and analytical tools, one can only hope that future critics and theorists will continue to heed Rolf Breuer's call that, rather than softening up our categories, we should strive to enlarge and refine them.

Notes

1 Rolf Breuer, "Lob der Distanz. Ein wissenschaftspolitischer Essay," *Merkur: Deutsche Zeitschrift für europäisches Denken* 48.3 (1994): 199–210, at 207.

2 Rolf Breuer, *Literatur: Entwurf einer kommunikationstheoretischen Theorie des sprachlichen Kunstwerks* (Heidelberg: Winter, 1984), p. 12.

3 Malcolm Bradbury, *Mensonge* (Harmondsworth: Penguin, 1993 [1987]), p. 29.

4 For a detailed reading of Ackroyd's novel as a fictional metabiography, see my article "An Intertextual Quest for Thomas Chatterton: The Deconstruction of the Romantic Cult of Originality and of the Paradoxes of 'Life-Writing' in Peter Ackroyd's Fictional Metabiography *Chatterton*," *Biofictions: The Rewriting of Romantic Lives in Contemporary Fiction and Drama*, eds. Martin Middeke/Werner Huber (Rochester, N.Y.: Camden House, 1999), pp. 27–49.

5 For the first book-length study of the genre referred to as 'fictional metabiographies,' see Julijana Nadj's forthcoming dissertation, "Gattungsgedächtnis und Gattungskritik: Studien zur fiktionalen Metabiographie in der zeitgenössischen englischsprachigen Erzählliteratur."

6 Michel de Certeau, *The Writing of History*, trans. Tom Conley (New York: Columbia UP, 1988), p. xxvii.

7 de Certeau, *The Writing of History*, p. 10.

8 Since I have analyzed Ackroyd's and Barnes's novels elsewhere, this essay will focus on *The Biographer's Tale*. Cf. also my article "'How do we seize the past?' Julian Barnes' fiktionale Metabiographie *Flaubert's Parrot* als Paradigma historiographischer und biographischer Metafiktion," *Literatur in Wissenschaft und Unterricht* 31.2 (1998): 145–171.

9 Cf. Dave Eggers's *A Heartbreaking Work of Staggering Genius* (London: Picador, 2001 [2000]). Though limitations on space preclude the possibility of providing a close reading of Eggers' novel, references to his idiosyncratic work may at least serve to show that an analogous argument to the one I am trying to make about fictional metabiographies can and should be made concerning fictional metaautobiographies.

10 Malcolm Bradbury, *The Modern British Novel* (Harmondsworth: Penguin, 1994 [1993]), pp. 344, 407.

11 Cf. *Biofictions: The Rewriting of Romantic Lives in Contemporary Fiction and Drama*, eds. Martin Middeke/Werner Huber (Rochester, N.Y.: Camden House, 1999).

12 See, however, Stephanie Kramer, *Fiktionale Biographien: (Re-) Visionen und (Re-)Konstruktionen weiblicher Lebensentwürfe in Dramen britischer Autorinnen seit 1970: Ein Beitrag zur Typologie und Entwicklung des historischen Dramas* (Trier: Wissenschaftlicher Verlag Trier, 2000).

13 Marjorie Perloff, "Introduction," *Postmodern Genres*, ed. Marjorie Perloff (Norman/London: University of Oklahoma Press, 1988), pp. 3–10, p. 4.

14 A number of recent studies of postmodernist fiction have, however, demonstrated that the destabilization of generic distinctions and the blurring of the fact/fiction boundary have indeed become the hallmarks of contemporary fiction. For a survey of recent approaches to the relationship between 'fact' and 'fiction' in contemporary literature cf. my article "Mapping the Field of Hybrid New Genres in the Contemporary Novel: A Critique of Lars Ole Sauerberg, *Fact into Fiction* and a Survey of other Recent Approaches to the Relationship between 'Fact' and 'Fiction,'" *Orbis Litterarum* 48 (1993): 281–305. For a first attempt to outline a typology of biofictions, see my essay (an essay in the original sense of that word, i.e. an attempt) "Von der fiktionalen Biographie zur biographischen Metafiktion: Prolegomena zu

einer Theorie, Typologie und Funktionsgeschichte eines hybriden Genres," *Fakten und Fiktionen: Strategien fiktionalbiographischer Dichterdarstellungen in Roman, Drama und Film seit 1970: Beiträge des Bad Homburger Kolloquiums, 21.–23. Juni 1999,* ed. Christian von Zimmermann (Tübingen: Narr, 2000), pp. 15–36.

15 Ina Schabert, *In Quest of the Other Person: Fiction as Biography* (Tübingen: Francke, 1990), p. 4.

16 Based on a systematic set of parameters I have tried to show that traditional as well as postmodernist manifestations of the historical novel can be organized under a limited number of typological rubrics; see A. Nünning, *Von historischer Fiktion zu historiographischer Metafiktion, Bd. 1: Theorie, Typologie und Poetik des historischen Romans* (Trier: Wissenschaftlicher Verlag Trier, 1995).

17 The use of the term 'biographic metafiction' is meant to stress the analogies that exist between this generic variant of the fictional biography and what Linda Hutcheon in her influential study *A Poetics of Postmodernism: History, Theory, Fiction* (London/New York: Routledge, 1988) calls 'historiographic metafiction.' For a completely different typology of fictional biographies, see Schabert, *In Quest of the Other Person.*

18 Cf. Brian McHale, *Postmodernist Fiction* (New York/London: Methuen, 1987), p. 90, according to whom the postmodernist historical novel is revisionist in two senses: "First, it revises the *content* of the historical record, reinterpreting the historical record, often demystifying or debunking the orthodox version of the past. Secondly, it revises, indeed transforms, the conventions and norms of historical fiction itself."

19 Cf. McHale, *Postmodernist Fiction,* pp. 87–88, who has shown that in the traditional historical novel the insertion of historical facts is governed by a number of constraints which he calls "the 'dark areas' constraint" (p. 87), "a constraint on anachronism," and a third constraint which postulates that the "fictional world obeys real-world physics and logic" (p. 88).

20 Antonia S. Byatt, *The Biographer's Tale* (London: Chatto & Windus, 2000), p. 4. All subsequent page references will be to this edition and appear in brackets following quotations.

21 Cf. Elisabeth Wesseling, *Writing History as a Prophet: Postmodernist Innovations of the Historical Novel* (Amsterdam/Philadelphia: John Benjamins, 1991), pp. 135ff., 120ff., who provides one of the most comprehensive and succinct accounts of the "metahistorical dissection of historiography" (p. 135) that goes on in postmodernist historical novels.

22 Cf. Schabert, *In Quest of the Other Person,* p. 184: "The historical person is not identical with the images which people have made themselves and continue to make of him. He is the mysterious source, the essence from which they derive, the final reality of which they constitute varying reflections and different views."

23 Linda Hutcheon, *The Politics of Postmodernism* (London/New York: Routledge, 1989), p. 57.

24 Hans Bertens, *The Idea of the Postmodern: A History* (London: Routledge, 1995), p. 11.

25 For an excellent analysis of these hitherto largely unexplored issues, cf. Julijana Nadj, "Die fiktionale Metabiographie als kritisches Gattungsgedächtnis," *Literatur, Erinnerung, Identität: Theoriekonzeptionen und Fallstudien*, eds. Astrid Erll/Marion Gymnich/Ansgar Nünning (Trier: Wissenschaftlicher Verlag Trier, 2003), pp. 211–226.

26 Cf. Eva Müller-Zettelmann, *Lyrik und Metalyrik: Theorie einer Gattung und ihrer Selbstbespiegelung anhand von Beispielen aus der englisch- und deutschsprachigen Dichtkunst* (Heidelberg: Winter, 2000).

36

Valentina Vannucci

"The Canon and Biofiction: The Subjects of History and New Literary Worlds" from *altri canoni/canoni altri: pluralismo e studi letterari* (2011)

1 Foreword

The neologism "biofiction" currently indicates the genre of postmodern rewritings with one or more figures of the past as protagonists whose biographies (*biographical histories*) are consciously hinted at and at the same time removed through a witting integration of literature and historiography all within the realm of fiction. It has the effect of dismantling in one fell swoop the canonical ideas of identity, historical identity and history, giving life to a contemporary hybrid that deconstructs, while pretending to revisit, the canonical historical novel.

Biofiction appears to contradict the most radical formulations of poststructuralism and constructivism which theorize the suspension of the concepts of identity, referent and content into a purely semiotic model inasmuch as they are revisions of historical subjectivities that challenge history, yet use it as a referential intertext. They reject canonical biographies but set up their hypotheses on recognizable biographical elements. They also discredit an essentialist conception of identity, but exploit at least a 'part' of it before its disintegration into the relentless flux of discourse. The relationship between language and self seems, indeed, an appropriate beginning for analyzing this genre that opposes and together overlaps with biography, traditionally conceived as the resurrection of a person's spirit through word.

1.1 'Bio'. The postmodern era between reality and representations: History as a literary intertext

Biography is fundamentally a narrative
which has as its primary task the enactment of a character
and place through language – a goal similar to that of fiction.
NADEL (1984), *Biography: Fiction, Fact and Form*

I don't care what people say: biography is here to stay.
FISH (1991), *Biography and Intention*

The canonical biography is based on an epistemological faith in the notion of the subject's unity and knowledge: biographers can capture the essence of a person, who later appears embodied in their work (*the flesh made word*). According to this view, language is mimetic – it mirrors reality – and the death of a person authorizes the biographical writing not only in a legal sense, but also for its claims of completeness. Indeed, only after the terminal event can a life be wholly represented and its meaning be definitively grasped. In other words, we might say that the end of existence can establish the true public resonance of subjects and their eventual inclusion in the canon of the personalities deserving mention, allowing a linguistic transformation (bio-*graphy*) of an individual life into a mythical experience. It is for this reason that Ira Bruce Nadel underlines the ambiguity of the word "myth," suggesting on the one hand the essence of a person and, on the other, the attached legend. Therefore, he entrusts biography with a double activity: "The first is the desire to correct or revise the myth; the second is its own unconscious creation of new myths."[1]

The possibility of dividing the public from the private personality and facts from myth has been believed for a long time. After Lytton Strachey and his battle against the "ill-digested masses of materials"[2] which featured in the Victorian biography, New Biography has raised attention specifically toward the biographical subject's personality; in the meantime, the subjective and biased point of view of the biographer has gradually started to be ever more recognized. Nonetheless, until recent times biography has been continually thought of as a truthful genre. It was believed that, though being consciously based on a hypothesis, the unknowable "ultimate truth" only concerned the inner life of the recounted subject; within this framework, any inaccurate information about events could be totally removed from the biography. The goal of biographical representation could be achieved either by leaving inaccurate information out of the text or by contesting it through documents, photographs, objects or other evidence attached to the historical reality of the subject. The biography's achievement will therefore be affected by the best possible research, where "best" is to be read as a quantity and by the best possible presentation of facts, where the adjective suggests, instead, a screening and selection process necessary to realize an organic, causal and teleological project.

If we accept this canonical idea of biography, which considers historiographical contents as scientific data, biofiction is to be considered a completely different genre, whose literary contents are freed from the criteria of objectivities that have been regulating the historiographic production since the 19th century. Biofiction assumes figures of the past as protagonists, set up hypotheses on their personality and, yet, do not bother to separate historically documented biographical data from inventions. A text like *The Mistressclass* (2003)[3] by Michèle Roberts, for instance, where Charlotte Brontë is able to survive her pregnancy, belongs to a fictional genre, whereas *The Life of Charlotte Brontë* (1857) by Elizabeth Gaskell,[4] just to mention a text with the same biographical subject, is intentionally truthful. The evident gaps and manipulation in Gaskell's work, together with the excessive involvement of the biographer in her subject and object of analysis, have the declared purpose of correcting the mythos of an unfeminine *Jane Eyre*'s author while substituting it with another mythos, that of a Brontë "angel of the house." Still, since it is invariably the authorial choice to define the genre of the written text, Gaskell's angiographic narrative, even if overtly corrective and considered very unreliable today, is not enlisted in the canon of fictional works, but in that of biographies.

We have discussed true facts (biographical data), lies (legends, myths), and intentions. These seem to be the elements distinguishing the canonical biography from the contemporary genre of biofiction. Traditional biography distinguishes between truth and invention and proposes a hypothesis among the many possible; this hypothesis is overtly subjective, but supported by elements that are thought to be objective (the "facts"). Even if some or many of these facts are then contested by other biographies or historiographical studies, inaccurate biography do not become fictions as happens for most discredited scientific studies.

Biofiction casts everything – biographical facts, inventions – into the same ontological order of fictional creation, demanding not to be taken literally. Because of its fictional status, the genre appears to also be allowed to include fictional autobiographies without any further distinction; biography, on the contrary, is based on a non-coincidence between the narrating and the narrated subject, whose life is reconstructed by the former. The traditional autobiography, canonized in the pre-romantic and romantic era, could and should also turn to memory, whose "material," believed to be more biased and unreliable than biographical research for a long time, was to be considered an expression of one and only one identity.

The most recent theories have, however, denied this distinction: how is it possible to state that the writer's subjectivity is, during the writing process, the same as that of the narrated subject? And, more generally speaking: what is subjectivity? What is the role of language in the construction of self? In short, Paul De Man asks: are we sure that autobiography is based on reference?

We assume that life *produces* the autobiography as an act produces its consequences, but can we suggest, with equal justice, that the autobiographical project may itself produce and determine the life and that whatever the writer *does* is in fact governed by the technical demands of self-portraiture and thus determined, in all its aspects, by the resources of his medium?[5]

The issue at stake is the ontological priority of self or of language. Every cognition, we read later in the essay, underlies a tropological structure, and knowledge of self is no exception: "the specular moment of the autobiographical work is not a situation or an event that can be located in a history, but [...] the manifestation, on the level of the referent, of a linguistic structure."[6] Paul L. Jay, discussing both these statements and an essay by Rodolphe Gasché,[7] focuses his attention on the contradictions inside the very idea of writing, the locus of an unavoidable "radical disappropriation"[8] of identity from language:

> We have become accustomed, when thinking about the concept of a thinking or a writing 'subject', at once to demystify and problematize that concept, to understand it as having reference less to a Natural, privileged, and potentially unified psychological condition, than to a historically constituted set of ideas and assumptions whose referents are complexly dispersed in the very language which seeks to constitute them.[9]

There is no contradiction between identity and discourse, self and representation, because 'I' can exist only as a representation. The critique of the subject as a unique entity, the recognition of language's non-transparent nature and the consequential end of the correspondence between "words" and "things," are topics that have been extensively discussed by Barthes, Foucault, Derrida, and other exponents of (post)structuralism, deconstructionism and of post-Freudian psychoanalysis. They have elaborated critical and philosophical theories contesting some humanistic assumptions like the centrality of the human being in the universe and the instrumental use of literature as a medium able to reproduce reality and subject to a human hegemonic purpose.

It is, however, almost superfluous to observe that, even if the subject has begun to be conceived as dissolved, fragmented, created and not described by language, a kind of surface-effect with a Nietzschean resonance, rather than a conscience endowed with unity and purpose that a certain kind of philosophy (from Descartes to Kant) has transmitted to us, the genre of biography has not vanished. On the contrary, it has exponentially increased, and the interest in individuals seems to have been boosted so much that a widespread variety of postmodern literature, such as biofiction, not only does not repudiate human subjects, but even nourishes itself with personalities of an extra-textual past, identities who have been canonized by official biographies and whose historical reference we are asked to recognize. Hence, if we compare the two genres according to these assumptions, many of the differences previously identified seem to disappear. The critical, philosophical and historiographical debate on the impossibility of reproducing people's lives, and, by and large, on the way reality can be perceived and known, shows that the two genres are joined by the inescapable filter of narrative, which organizes materials in a literary structure and imposes a meaning in order to make them understandable at all. As a result, the traditional distinction between true and false has been delegitimized, the irreducible fictional status of every enunciative context laid bare. If canonical identity has been dismantled, denied, and dissolved into a linguistic construct that is neither transparent nor referential, it is worthwhile to look for new descriptive categories which can define the semiotic subjects of biography and biofiction.[10]

William Epstein has proposed some definitions that appear to admit the pre-existence of human subjects with respect to their linguistic codification. The fictional subject is different from the biographical subject because the first can only exist in and through discourse, being thoroughly encodable (*trans-discursive*). Biographical subjects, instead, can be defined as figures pre-existing their own biographies, thus owning an existence that cannot be completely or ultimately reduced to semiosis (*extra-discursive*).[11] Such a terminological choice allows us to identify a gap in the process of biographical recognition, a discontinuity between discursive and non-discursive which is impossible to fill.[12] It is in this gap, in this unbridgeable distance between reality and representation that, I believe, a space for new biofictions and biographies opens up. Both of them are, indeed, cultural practices whose aim is to add their own truth to the "cumulative biography"[13] of a given historical figure: something discursively built up, layer upon layer, out of a combination of political, economic and social representations whose sum has fixed the canon of the biographical subject.

Accepting this view, the conflict originated from the conventional distinction between fiction and non-fiction is strictly a political one, since it reflects the tension between an "authority" in charge to stabilize subjects and a "divergence" that, instead, questions "sanctioned identities" both esthetically and polemically.[14] Rewriting (or profaning?) historical identities, in a way that has variously been defined as ironic, violent, or regenerative, means to accordingly reflect on the authorial structures that define the tradition (the so-called contexts of meaning), to identify the distribution of extra-discursive figures as they have been set up by power, and to prevent any abducting or burying of the subject into a fixed, sanctioned and unchanging identity. If in Foucaldian and Barthesian theoretical elaboration biographic recognition is always a subjugation, a violence committed under the pretext of interpretation, biofiction finds its space in the creases (or, rather, gaps) that the ideological, fragmented and discontinuous narration of canonical history has neglected, oppressed, shown as it were out of the "Discourse"; even if we know gaps are necessarily linked to the rhetorical and syntactical laws of the discourse of history.

Canonical identities, seen as essentialist and ideologically connoted, are therefore being appropriated by biofiction only to be subsequently betrayed. So it happens, for instance, that the name of Catherina de' Medici, figured in hundreds of documents, literary texts, official biographies, and plays that shaped her identity during centuries, is evoked in the paradigmatic even if rather unknown *The Stars Dispose* (1997) and *The Stars Compel* (1999) by Michaela Roessner[15] only to show in the end that we do not know her, and another version of this figure will be forever possible: an equally powerful representation which, later, we may be able to consider. In these kinds of texts, whose fictionality is declared by paratextual framings, the romancing elements of the plot suggest an idea of history as discursively structured; while revealing how facts acquire meaning, they activate a metafictional reflection that can be seen as "progressive."[16] Indeed, the known historical and biographical data of the above mentioned biofictions have been faithfully reconstructed in detail: there is not a single historical event in the time ranging from 1519 to 1533 that cannot be checked in any historiographic narration on Italian Renaissance. For these reasons we can hypothetically wonder during the reading if the extra-textual Catherina (who, inasmuch as past, is today unknowable) should be moved *only* by ambitious and selfish aims, and if her predilection for occultism could not be an instrument of rule. Also, even more unreasonably, if her young personal cook (to whom documents make little reference because he was peripheral to the centers of power in charge of discourse) could not really have had an affair with the artist Michelangelo. Such is a story lost in the fragments buried by other *stories* that History has not included in her narrative project.

Preference granted to true historical personalities but decentered because of age (in Roessner's biofictions Catherina is caught in her childhood and prime), class, sexual orientation (both categories are relevant to the young cook Tommaso), or, elsewhere, gender, ethnicity and other "markers" of identity, points out a kind of subject that has not, or at least not necessarily, been merged into a surfacing effect. They can still show a so-called wholeness while revealing that their coherence is consciously an illusion,[17] discursively shaped by a writer in the same way the canonical unmarked subject – inductively Occidental, male and heterosexual – has been a non-innocent filter in the process of canonization of official history, whose ideology is recognized and laid bare by biofiction.

Identity, which has never been considered as marginal as today, is therefore utilized to deconstruct history, and alternative notions of subjectivity challenge the literary dominion of the historiographic canon, conceived as a power system that can have some representations emerge and others submerge. It has been argued that biofiction writers do not deny historical consciousness, but exploit our epistemological uncertainties (our ability to know 'the ultimate objects' of the past) by manipulating historical material in order to obtain a somewhat plausible interpretation of life.[18]

However, the very genre of biography, traditionally proposed as a credible hypothesis, has faced decades of experimentations in the last part of the nineteenth century that have developed alongside its enduring traditional structure.[19] From the pioneering fictionalized biography by Marguerite Yourcenar *Memoires d'Hadrien* (1951),[20] to the "anti-biography" by David E. Nye *The Invented Self: An Anti-Biography, from Documents of Thomas A. Edison* (1983)[21] (whose sources mentioned in the title appear not to have been ordered into a coherent synthesis, with the effect of producing not just one, but many Thomas Edisons), biography has tried to account for a multiple, decentered and unknowable self, including the limiting and provisional character of the adopted perspective ("whose truth is told") in its aesthetic project. The recent proposals for a non-conclusive, multi-perspective, non-linear feminist biography, even for living female-authors (meaning, not yet canonized nor canonizable),[22] disclose the resonance that postmodern theoretical reflections, especially deconstruction and the Lacanian psychoanalysis, had on this genre, too. Moreover, as far as the more circumscribed field of literary criticism is concerned, the long path began by Wellek and Warren in 1948 (and, even earlier, by Boris Tomaševskij in 1923), has contested authors' literary lives as the only authoritative tool to understand their works, freeing their biographies from the condition of a privileged hermeneutic voice and debasing them to the status of mere intertexts, paving the way for a multi-methodological critical approach.

We have insofar observed the many affinities shared by postmodern biography and biofiction. Yet, the last one is an even more "hybrid" genre: every text is a pastiche of different narrative strategies and, if sometimes the distinction between "fiction biographies" and "fiction histories"[23] seems to be fading away, other biofictions show more overtly manipulated biographical data. We might suggest that a boundary is probably when the rewriting originates from the assumption that the biographical subject has not died in the circumstances we know, as it happens in *The Mistressclass* by Michèle Roberts or in *The Ghost Writer* (1979) by Philip Roth.[24] This brings about a *double* resurrection/anachronism, one of which is fatally subsumed among the strategies of this literary genre (we might say that "resurrection" is one of biofiction's aesthetic conditions). The other is, instead, part of the plot of particular works like the ones mentioned above: fictions that are even further menacing the agreement of "willing suspension of disbelief," which had already been spoilt by assuming a historical figure among the main characters (Coleridge's formula is, indeed, importantly overturned by Naomi Jacobs, who uses the definition "suspension of *belief*").[25] In these kinds of texts, rewriting a subject of history may appear less justified and also raise ethical issues (Roth's work, which evokes such a symbolical personality as Ann Frank, has an especially disturbing effect).[26] As a result, literary criticism's statements to maintain the "historical consciousness" is much more difficult to share.

Martin Middeke, editing an anthology of essays on postmodern narratives that he first calls "biofiction," observes in the Introduction that critics and readers of these narratives "will find themselves reminded of the distinction between fact and fiction every time they consult the factual biographies in order to trace fictional deviations from the factual accounts of the lives at issue," [27] specifying :

> Biofictions cast doubt on "our beliefs in origins and ends, unity, and totalization, logic and reason, consciousness and human nature, progress and fate, representation and truth, not to mention the notion of causality and temporal homogeneity, linearity and continuity," but they do not deny the respective historical foil on which they are written – indeed, how could they without missing their point?[28]

Biofiction originates from knowledge and awareness of some assumptions about the past into whose narrative strategies they inscribe their own. Based, as we have seen, on the linguistic nature of reality as a consequence of the epistemological change after the linguistic turn of the last century, it does not seem to deny the historical event (the "referent"), but rather reflect on the epistemological limits caused by the ontological status of the footprints of the past, even if its scattered remains must be built more than re-built.[29] The confusion of factuality and representation, according to this view, remains in the fictional world of representation, in other words, the rewriting does not deny the past, but asserts its unknowable, provisional and indeterminate nature as a consequence of the textual modality we can access: we are far from stating that there is nothing "outside the text," or no reality beyond representation. The past recreated by the rewriting of life in biofiction is non-conclusive and, since linguistically shaped, discourages the reader to identify with the historical setting and a purely psychological, apolitical reading, meaning just information and evasion. But this is still to maintain a historical awareness, not to embrace a radical constructivism, a historical relativism or even revisionism.

The Second World War, the Holocaust and other tragic events of the twentieth century have discredited a positivistic conception of history, its progressive aim: absurdity originated by using history and historical identities as intertextual referents and the self-reflexivity implicit in the very concept of anachronism forbid an uncritical immersion of the reader into the fictional world, and the subsequent necessary process of suppression of a past perceived as such. Refusing this kind of automatic reaction, biofiction obliges a rethinking of the past from a point of view in the present, in a progressive (present-oriented) and not self-aimed, "retrogressive" (past-oriented) way.[30] Literary anachronisms, like the microphone showing up in the framing of the filmic rewriting of *Marie Antoniette* (2006),[31] compel consumers to internalize implications, engaging them in the interpretative process that relates their contemporary experience to the one they have received. Naomi Jacobs, in this regard, writes:

> In the Greek, anachronism means "against time," a definition that might be expanded to read "against history." For one must know history to be able to recognize anachronism; indeed, history must exist before anachronism exists, because a judgment that something is anachronistic assumes that certain objects or ways of thinking belong to a particular time and to no other. The writer who purposely uses anachronism is subverting that assumption, arguing "against time" by rejecting the historicist assumption that every time is unique.[32]

Anachronism establishes the equivalence between an original, correct context and a new, incorrect one, forcing us to recognize the similarities between the two ages and the authoritarian impulses in the process of the creation of meaning. As for traditional biography, there is an operation of unveiling: only, what biofiction discloses is not the essence of an identity, but the chorus of the voices that have formulated it. They disclose the path of codification of a canon which is created and not found, opposing their apparently a-historical representations as liberating strategies.

2 '-fiction'. A possible variety of historiographic metafiction

The indeterminate nature of historical knowledge, the discursive fragmentation of the concept of identity, and the contestation of a canon perceived to be ideologically shaped are not discoveries of biofiction or, more broadly, of postmodern narrations; nonetheless, contemporary narratives foreground such problematizations[33] by appropriating canonical strategies of representation. These are thus subverted by a parodic mode so as to determine an actual "abuse" of the tradition. [34] Biofiction shows all the features of postmodern writing, first and foremost a crossing of genre boundaries that gives life to infinite hybridizations and contaminations. It proposes itself as a peculiar genre while containing all the variegated literary forms ascribable to a novel or a romance. Although some stylistic features may be dominant with respect to others in a single work, a linear development of the biography may serve as a model.

However, the infinite variety and possibility of combining styles and textual modalities are sometimes evidence of an ideological collision between genre and gender, bringing up a rather paradoxical issue. We assumed that the genre is to be defined by the presence of a biographical and historical rewriting in the narration, even if this is equipped with self-reflective elements. And yet, the genre of the historical novel[35] sometimes seems, at least in these texts, not only revisited, but the most changed tradition, or rather, dismantled from its very foundations. It is, indeed, the flexible romance in all its sub-genres that is often the most suitable form to absorb the changed historical consciousness and its literary representations.[36]

Ornella De Zordo, while noticing the varied narrative strategies in *Fair Exchange* (1999) by Michèle Roberts,[37] makes some general observations that are quite relevant here:

> the text intertwines the romance, that is to say the most underestimated form of storytelling, the one that has pertained, since ancient tradition, to imagination, to the romantic reverie, to the inconsistent and even to the absurd, with the opposite form, the high-brow storytelling of the historical novel. This has for a long time been seen as the privileged genre for the representation of reality: a serious, reliable form endowed with realistic strategies, shaping itself up through an accurate gathering and reconstruction of data.[38]

The relationship between the realist historical novel and liberal humanism with its codified connection between the male gender and the ideas of action, power and History[39] has been largely discussed by literary criticism; the unbridgeable gap of the former and the contemporary historiographic metafiction, to which biofiction would seem to belong, could therefore hardly be neglected. Linda Hutcheon has noticed, among the many differences between the two genres, the non-assimilation of the historical data in postmodern narratives, whose deception/lies lay(s) bare, as we have already seen, the artificiality of every enunciative context. Moreover, she focuses on the function of the authentication of the details and of the renowned personalities in the traditional historical romance.[40] These, in the famous theorization on the genre written by György Lukács, can never be central figures in the plot because of the universalistic quality implied in the realistic strategy.[41]

Actually, nothing more of the social nonconformity of biofiction's main characters could be more distant from the typifying claims than those by Walter Scott, conceived as embodiments of historical forces in a particular time. Their traits are, on average, characteristic[42] and show a synecdoche-like relationship between the individual and the national state.[43] As we have noticed, in biofiction it is not only canonical identity that is no trope of history, but the very canonical history is also dismantled by an idea of non-normative identity. In these narrations, characters that are too marginal to be representative coexist with the renowned ones, who are protagonists or somewhat important to the plot. Moreover, they are seen from an unusual point of view,[44] the very point of view that originates the rewriting.

The foreshadowing of known personalities is, furthermore, what seems to distinguish biofiction from the more unspecific historiographic metafiction. The latter arranges historical and fictional characters in the same order of representation; however, they do not grant them enough space to have their biographical trace not only recognized but also discussed, along with the central issues of the narration. This clarification seems to allow us not to include some historiographic metafictions among biofiction like, for instance, *The French Lieutenant's Woman* (1969)[45] by John Fowles, where Gabriel and Christina Rossetti only fill cameo roles. These names, unchanged with respect to the tradition, have a destabilizing effect on the fictional world; nonetheless, the largely canonized lives to which they are bound are discussed very shortly in the text.[46]

Middeke's definition of biofiction as metafiction with "overt historical referents"[47] is, indeed, inherently ambiguous. It could refer both to fictions where historical correlatives obey the designation semantics and to texts where the characters' identities are definitively attributable to that of renowned personalities. That is, for instance, the case of *Fair Exchange*, where a "Wordsworth family" is mentioned, yet some events of William Wordsworth's life are instead narrated in the story of the character "William Saygood." Moreover, in this biofiction the personality of Mary Wollstonecraft is shared both by her namesake character and by her fictional pupil Jemima Booth.[48]

The relationship between name and identity raises many critical issues for generic recognition. Indeed, there are many contemporary texts where historical names that have been inhabited by true people are actually protagonists of the plot; nevertheless, they sometimes show no association at all with the subjectivity of their extra-discursive referents. This is particularly true in some science fiction or science fantasy works.

In conclusion, since we assumed a "part" of the true subjectivity as fundamental to biofiction,[49] it is important that consumers be able to locate a relevant connection to the narrative's main characters (no matter if these names be exactly after the biographical ones or not) with the historical intertext, otherwise we should not be allowed to discuss these texts in terms of biographical rewriting.[50] If that is not the case, if names of historical characters are only evoked to be re-collocated in the most disparate fantastic contexts, I believe that we are to encounter other genres of fiction where the *absolute* negation of historical identity, substituted by a fictional one, entails the turning of history into pure language.[51]

3 The revival of the subject and contemporary literary criticism. An anti-anticanon?

Defining biofiction as a specific literary genre has entailed some reflections about deconstructed realistic strategies, an idea of a character with a clear and pre-established link to an extra-discursive entity, and the fundamental role of the consumer in identifying, examining and delimiting an extra-textual connection: a cooperation that is, therefore, also decisive for generic recognition. Biofiction is, in this sense, a very contradictory literary practice, as it assumes an external reference for its characters; all the same, a reading that does not recognize the referential connection is also, hypothetically, possible.[52] However, even once the connection with the past has been established, it continues to be unstable, since it depends on the fictional alterations of the plot, made by the *writer*, on the variegated pre-knowledge of consumers regarding the narrated historical period, and on their reactions during the various points in the rewritings.[53] All this suggests an eccentric collocation of biofiction in the contemporary criticism, since it is a genre that upsets tradition and, at the same time, also the very critical trends that has declared this tradition "dead."

As is widely known, Barthes and Foucault's theorizations about the so-called "death of the Author" (a concept elaborated by the former as a dissolving of authors into the text itself, who would be, therefore, cut out from history and condemned to a circle of endless semiosis and, by the latter, as a questioning of a certain social function of authors)[54] has entailed a shifting of emphasis from the idea of the originality of art works to that of *writing*: an amalgamation of different subjectivities whose wholeness is the literary intertext.[55] Afterwards, the poststructuralist debate on the narrative character, inaugurated by *The Character of Character* (1974) by Hélène Cixous,[56] has contested the repressive quality implicit in the canonical idea of character. That, for the critic, displays a stable, pre-established meaning to be investigated by an anthropocentric criticism that evaluates fiction according to an exploration of the protagonist's psychology, which seems to be both characterized and criticized along the lines of real people.

As late as the eighties this kind of methodological approach describes Modernist and Postmodernist characters as having become "absent" from the text, which is extensively discussed in Thomas Docherty's monograph with its revealing title *Reading (Absent) Character.*[57] According to this view, they should have become verbal constructs that, from Beckett on, substituted their "anthropomorphic" forefathers with "fragmentary 'instant of subjectivity', none of which seems to be related to one another, and none of which seem to develop in a more stable Self."[58] Such a fragmentation and dispersion of the character's subjectivity would correspond to a similar mobility of the reader,[59] who would be released by an authoritative authorial intention and, as such, now freed to move around spaces in which codes and seeds mix, with no transcendence or depth to be found.

Nonetheless, even though biofiction's precariousness between intention and receptive context has been noted here more than once, scholars of this genre have found themselves uncomfortable with theories assuming absent characters, an elimination of authorial subjectivity[60] and a disappearance and/or multiplicity of proper names in contemporary fiction, since "the fixity of the name endangers the suppositious freedom to change in the character, and it is this freedom which contributes in no small measure to the illusion of the character's real ontological existence."[61]

Modern linguistics' tenets, and especially the description of grammatical subjects as empty shifters lacking empirical reference, have appropriately called our attention to the dangers of ignoring in a critical approach the purely artificial nature of every narrative character, "evaluating" them instead according to the parameters adopted for real people. Now, it is surely undeniable that a *purely* psychological reading would be limiting for biofiction's characters, let alone assuming a perfect coincidence between protagonists and their historical referent. However, we should consider the fact that in these texts a kind of an ontological antecedence of an original is assumed by the very genre; and, if this reference is then problematized by a conscious use of critical theory, its "intentionality" cannot be disregarded. As we have noticed, the biographical forgery is a symbolic, ideological device for new subjective and oriented re-readings, aimed to contest the tradition.

To put it another way, if the author and character's contestation turns out to be a contestation of the traditional and realist authors and characters, whose hypothesized authorial *voleur dire* was then to be decoded by the only authority of biographical criticism, we need critical models for biofiction that are able to consider not only an instability of meaning, but also its eventual limitations. Even if assuming epistemological skepticism, which is relevant for fictional biographical rewritings whether or not these narrations make use of intradiegetic characters, it is not so much the person "who speaks," rather, as Lucia Boldrini argues,

> the very possibility to ask the question; since it is important to know not so much the person but the textual, social role which is attributed to the ethical responsibility of transforming reality; which discursive modalities have allowed such a role and the fact that such alteration of reality is acclaimed as a good literary work, instead of being condemned as falsity, distortion or spreading of private and confidential facts. [62]

Taking for granted that no narrative protagonist even in the most mimetic fictional creation may be human-like, the critic proposes a definition for biofictions' characters that may be accountable both for the *explicit* linguistic nature of its subjects and, at the same time, their eventual behavior as any other of the traditional protagonists, in other words, as beings endowed with a stable psychology and characteristic traits. She then calls for an integration of what defines a purely semiotic model, usually adopted for the *nouveau roman* and Beckett's works, and the possible-worlds semantics (nonetheless a semiotic model), as elaborated, among others, by Uri Margolin. According to his view, a narrative protagonist is a "possible non-actual individual," and therefore ontologically different from a real ("non-actual") person; he then concedes such protagonists an eventual attribution of mimetic elements ("possible"), whose procedures can be interpreted by readers through a limited number of textual statements.[63] However, Boldrini argues, biofiction's characters are fictional recreations of historical referents, and as such (in this certain sense) "real"; their existence is "impossible" in the way we find it in narratives, as it has finished and it has been canonized by cultural practices from which the rewriting can move away more or less radically.[64] Margolin, furthermore, defines literary characters as "ontologically thin,"[65] but the name introducing biofiction's personalities does not change in the course of the narration, and reminds us immediately of historical identities.[66] Having been alive, these are, at least initially, ontologically "full," and their assumptions will be transformed by the specific discourse of the single rewriting.[67] For all these reasons, Boldrini suggests that biofiction's characters may be referred to as "actual but impossible individuals."[68]

Her weird (and rather unknown) proposal of terminology which overturns the well-known definition of the possible-worlds semantics has, in my opinion, some rather interesting advantages. It may, indeed, as it has been insofar noticed, emphasize biofiction's historical derivation with respect to other kinds of texts; and also, even more importantly, it appears more suitable to describe those figures who seem to belong to worlds that are not, from a narratological perspective, self-voiding. This aspect will be explored in the next section.

4 Possible-worlds semantics of fictionality and some observations

We now have to investigate how fictional re-creations of the biographical canon may affect the single literary works, or rather, the way characters can weaken, or strengthen, the illusion of verisimilitude of the writing (and vice versa), and the problems in interpretation posed by the authentication function in this kind of narrative. The issue is much more complex than it may appear, as it is in the interaction of the concepts of subjectivity, character and proper names that every single text places itself into a specific position, different every time, and this interaction produces an almost infinite range of textual effects.[69] Nevertheless, some general considerations may be useful.

Firstly, it would be legitimate to state that in biofiction the relation between character names and their historical referents is placed at an interval not including the extremes. In other words, it cannot be a perfect coincidence (or that would be, as previously discussed, an impossible reflection of self) nor a perfect split-up; the latter characterizes "recombinant fiction" analyzed by Jacobs where names only have the purpose to create the experience of the marvelous and betray both immediately and definitively the expectations of the reader.[70]

In between these two end points there is a range of miscellaneous contexts where historical identities, even if necessarily re-shaped, may appear more or less displaced with regard to the one that readers perceive to be their own "canonical" model, according to their pre-knowledge. It should be noticed that historical subjects' approaches or movements away from our specific ideal model are not directly related to a status of character opacity. In biofiction, one aspect of the dual nature (mimetic or semiotic) of subjects might prevail over the other, and even if characters do not appear in our eyes too distant compared to their historical counterparts, their linguistic features may however be remarked by textual devices (for instance, a narrator's speech reminding us of their artificiality in a digression, an unreliable first-person narrator, two or more conflicting versions of an event, and so forth).[71] Among these, the impossible world of *Lord Byron's Doctor* by Paul West (1989) stands out, because the character Polidori narrates his own death.[72]

In other biofictions, the character's alignment strategy with their canonical protoworld does not discourage the reader's immersion into the fictional world, which can therefore be read as any other fiction and also relay a specific, even if temporary, biographical and literary plausibility. *Dr Copernicus* (1976) by John Banville and *An Imaginary Life* (1978) by David Malouf,[73] just to mention two well-known works, do not contain any logical violations, or rather, they do not lay bare the authentication procedures in a way that might invalidate the whole fictional world. This is also the case in *Mab's Daughters* (1991) by Judith Chernaik[74] or in the already mentioned *The Stars*, whose plausibility is not, interestingly, menaced even from the magical elements in the plot, as they appear justified by the documented esotericism to which the historical character was devoted. This shows that even if readers are necessarily aware of the linguistic nature of the characters, which forbids them to assimilate the historical data in the fiction, a somewhat mimetic reading is not to be completely excluded *within* the narration before we close the book and begin wondering what was true and what was not. Moreover, these texts show that we cannot claim, as some critics do (Jacob among them), that biographical characters of postmodernism are always "reduced" to "cultural types," universal tendencies without any details or internalization.[75]

It may, therefore, appear reasonable to conclude, as Lubomír Doležel does, that the impossibility of a fictional world rewriting is to be judged with the same criteria applicable to all kinds of fictional worlds: only the ones describing or implying contradictions are impossible.[76] His theoretical frame is particularly relevant here, as it allows us to describe biofiction (biographical rewriting) critically. At the same time, however, we need to investigate his approach further, and, in particular, his conception of narrative characters to see to what extent they can meet with our observations about biofiction's variety and their effect on the biographical and literary canon. In *Mimesis and Possible Worlds* (1988), the critic encourages a "possible-worlds semantics of fictionality"[77] denying the necessity for a double semantics of fictionality, one "for worlds of the 'realistic' type and the other one for 'fantastic' fiction."[78] The worlds of realistic literature, Doležel argues, "are not less fictional than the worlds of fairy tales and science fiction."[79] "Mimetic criticism" may work, he continues, "if a particular prototype of the fictional entity can be found in the actual world (Tolstoy's Napoleon – historical Napoleon, a fictional story – a fictional event)," but fail when there are characters like Hamlet, who do not represent any actual individuals. The impossibility to find an "actual universal" real prototype for any fictional entity (psychological types, social groups, existential or historical conditions) forces, therefore, mimetic criticism to an "interpretative detour," altering its mimetic function into a "universalistic version."[80]

A very important point, according to Doležel, is that if we assume the one-world model frame, as in the case of "shared proper names," the distinction between characters and real people becomes blurred; conversely, a possible-worlds semantics allows us to protect fictional identities "by the boundary between the actual and the possible worlds."[81] Fictional worlds are accessible from the actual world only trough "semiotic channels," by means of information processing that allows us to go across world boundaries.[82] As a consequence, all fictional entities are, as already mentioned, "non actualized possibles," and a view which presents fictional individuals as a mixed bag of "real" and "purely fictitious" characters is explicitly refused by the critic as "naïve."[83] Postmodern semantics accepts the transposition of a non-essentialist concept of identity across worlds, and, since the rewriting does not invalidate the canonical protoworld, criticism should not emphasize its delegitimizing effects toward the narratives of the "masters":[84] The rewriting develops alongside the original world without obliterating it, asserting itself as an alternative and sovereign world which expands the fictional world and, hopefully, will enter the literary canon in turn.[85]

Such a theory of fictionality, which has been purposely elaborated for postmodern textual criticism without any distinction between historiographic metafiction and what we have here called biofiction, raises a first, almost superfluous, observation. While contesting the supposed excessive emphasis attributed to a subversive revision effect which would be granted by some critics of postmodern rewritings (Hutcheon in the front line, even if she is not mentioned), Doležel is proposing an interesting and integrative-aimed approach, which is very useful to us. However, we may also overturn the perspective and notice that the very formulation of his theory is the consequence of a need to account for a boom in publications that explicitly thematizes textual access to the past, the provisional quality of any historical (and not just literary) representation. Then, if the possible-worlds semantics of fictionality (by now definitely included into the contemporary canon of criticism) apparently makes no difference among various kinds of "narrative reference" (an historical or a fictional text), the author himself specifies that a rewriting with Napoleon as a subject and another with an alternative incarnation of Edward Rochester do differ: in the first case the cross-world identity transmissibility is originated from the actual world, whereas in the second one it originates from the fictional world created by Charlotte Brontë.[86] He says that this is the only distinction, even if it turns out to be highly significant "at the semantic level."[87]

This may be the single distinction, but that does not mean it is a little one. As we have insofar suggested, it qualifies the biographical rewriting (biofiction) with respect to other postmodern genres, also confirming, therefore, both the premises and the implications of this generic recognition, that is, the need to identify and discuss the alignment of the fictional world with an "extra-discursive" reference. Doležel has a point when he says that the final purpose of criticism must be that of interpreting a literary work.[88] However, this essay has tried to raise attention to the great variety of biofiction, and the possible need for history as one of its interpretants. This is especially true, in my opinion, for some kinds of "mimetic" biofiction, whose individuals are surely "non-actual individuals/possibles," as Margolin and Doležel claim, but mostly show us characteristics of "actual but impossible individuals," as previously noted.

Biofiction presents itself as fiction. As such, even if the concept of narrative identity has been assumed as a constant in this hybrid genre, it should not modify our historical consciousness in the same ways that other postmodern rewritings have not extinguished the life of their literary protoworld. At the same time, texts of this genre differentiate sensibly from one another, according to their strategies and purposes: some of them seem more possible than others, their world containing a symbolic twist with respect to the historical, canonized one. While fictionally altering the boundary between reality and representation, this kind of biofiction reveals the discourses that have traced that line, suggesting that some of them may be still at work.

Notes

1 Nadel (1984), *Biography: Fiction, Fact and Form*. New York: St Martin's Press.

2 Strachey (1986), *Eminent Victorians*. Harmondsworth: Penguin: 10.

3 Roberts (2003), *The Mistressclass*. London: Little Brown.

4 Gaskell (1877), *The Life of Charlotte Brontë*. Harmondsworth: Penguin Books.

5 De Man, "Autobiography as De-Facement," *Comparative Literature*, 94 (5) (1979): 920.

6 De Man (1979): 922.

7 Gasché, "French Issue: Autobiography and the Problem of the Subject," *Modern Language Notes* 93 (4) (1978): 573-574.

8 Jay, "Being in the Text: Autobiography and the Problem of the Subject," *Modern Language Notes* 97 (5) (1982): 1045.

9 Jay (1982): 1045-1046.

10 For a discussion of the elements of biography traditionally considered fictional – structure, language, narrator – see John Keener (2001), *Biography and the Postmodern Historical Novel*, New York: Mellen: 159-73.

11 Epstein, *(Post)Modern Lives: Abducting the Biographical Subject*, in Epstein (ed) (1991), *Contesting the Subject: Essays in the Postmodern Theory and Practice of Biography and Biographical Criticism*. West Lafayette: Purdue University Press: 223.

12 Epstein (ed) (1991), *Contesting the Subject*: 234, note 10.

13 "Each biographical text, depending upon its temporal scope, contributes more or less to a cumulative 'biography' of a given figure." Keener (2001): 8.

14 Keener (2001): 4.

15 Roessner (1998): *The Stars Dispose*. New York: Tor Books; Roessner (1999): *The Stars Compel*. New York: Tor Books.

16 Martin Middeke, *Introduction*, in Middeke, Huber (eds) (1999), *Biofictions: the Rewriting of Romantic Lives in Contemporary Fiction and Drama*. Rochester (NY)-Woodbridge: Camden House: 18. His idea is examined in depth in the conclusion of the paragraph.

17 "The illusion of unity is always experienced by the reader and biographer but not the subject"; Nadel (1984): 181.

18 "a fictional or emphatic/sympathetic approach to the subject may make use of historical material, may play with it, may even invert it, if necessary, and still arrive at a heuristically impressive and plausible interpretation of that life. As a consequence, the artist may incorporate and reflect upon epistemological uncertainties caused by the aporias of time and language, *without* obliterating historical consciousness": Middeke, *Introduction*, in Middeke, Huber (eds) (1999): 3.

19 After Strachey's innovations in biography and literary Modernism, the twentieth century has witnessed a new shifting of the biographical genre toward fiction, with the effect of making the methodological choice of the biographer ever more conscious. Among the experimentations of the twentieth century, Nadel chooses to include the *psychobiography*, the *group biography*, the *metabiography*, the *segment biography*, and the *contextual biography* in his study; Nadel (1984): 183-205.

20 Yourcenar (1974), *Mémoires d'Hadrien. Suivi de Carnets de notes de Mémoires d'Hadrien*. Paris: Gallimard.

21 Nye (1983), *The Invented Self: An Anti-Biography from Documents of Thomas A. Edison*. Odense: Odense University Press.

22 I refer here to the suggestions of Sharon O'Brian, whose contestation of "unitary, representable self" originates from her conception of the idea as inseparable from the social construct of the feminine gender: "From the perspective of deconstruction, to posit a female voice or a woman writer's creation of identity is to confuse the social construction of 'woman' with an experiential reality; it is also to accept the patriarchal ideology of individualism." Sharon O'Brian, *Feminist Theory and Literary Biography*, W. Epstein (ed) (1991): 127 and 123-133.

23 I use here Naomi Jacobs' terminology because it emphasizes more than others the relevance of the fictional elements that biofictions (for Jacobs, "fiction histories") share with non-traditional biographies, which she calls "fiction biographies" (these are usually known as "fictionalized biographies") as opposed to "straight biographies," meaning canonical biographies. In fact, she explains that: "The familiar label 'fictionalized biography' seems to imply that the fictional component is superficial, a thin overlay; I prefer to call these works fiction biographies as a way of emphasizing the primacy of fiction in their makeup." Naomi Jacobs (1990), *The Character of Truth: Historical Figures in Contemporary Fiction*. Southern Illinois University Press: Carbondale: 28. Other scholars prefer to use a different and, often, larger, range of categories, thus confirming both the difficulty to label more and more hybrid genres, and the tendency of biography and novel to converge in the same literary practice: see, for instance, Keener (2001), *Biography and the Postmodern Historical Novel*: 181.

24 Roth (1979): *The Ghost Writer*. New York: Farrar, Straus &Giroux.

25 Jacobs (1990), *The Character of Truth*: 69.

26 The issue is, indeed, central in the novel, focused on the controversy between Doc Zuckermann and his son, Nathan, a writer who has the opportunity to publish a short-story which revolves around an old family dispute caused by an inheritance. Turning Nathan's actual "greedy" relatives into fictional characters brings with it the danger of stereotyping Jews just as it was tragically done by anti-Semitic propaganda. The whole point is that there difficulty for readers to distinguish "between the historical and the artificial [...], if only when identity is at stake" (in other words, fictional characters are symbol-laden, and if a few fictional Jews are greedy, then all the real Jews are greedy). Readers are not concerned about art, reminds the father to the writer son, and postmodern criticism seems to echo him: "If a text – any text – involves a potential human figure, the reader will instinctively look beyond the framing text [...] to read the human text within"; Keener (2001), *Biography and the Postmodern Historical Novel*: 6.

27 Middeke, *Introduction*, in Middeke, Huber (eds) (1999): 3.

28 Middeke, *Introduction*, in Middeke, Huber (eds) (1999): 3-4.

29 We can have access to history only through texts, that means, through the narrative form which assembles a series of historical events into a narrative with a plot (*emplotment*); emplotments are arbitrary and follow literary models of configurations (comedy, romance, tragedy and satire). It is from these models, from these configurations that the meaning of history originates, rather than from the original events (*primary referent*). Even insisting on the

reality of "facts," the canonical distinction between literature and history collapses in the work of narrative historians like Hayden White, whose elaborations have been here shortly resumed. On this subject: Hayden White (1973), *Metahistory: The Historical Imagination in Nineteenth-Century Europe*. Baltimore and London: Johns Hopkins University Press; White (1978), *Tropics of Discourse: Essays in Cultural Criticism*. Baltimore and London: Johns Hopkins University Press. White (1987), *The Content of the Form. Narrative Discourse and Historical Representation*. Baltimore and London: Johns Hopkins University Press.

30 "Contemporary biofictions are not characterized by a retrogressive but by a decisively progressive movement to explain and interpret the present": Middeke, *Introduction*, in Middeke, Huber (eds) (1999): 18. Jacobs, for instance, describes the appearance of characters based on Nazis in these terms in fiction histories: "Modern history may be no more insane than ancient history, but we can know about it in much greater and more distressing detail, a fact that has helped to produce these urgent absurdist fictions suggesting that the human race has learned no lessons, made no progress, and hoping that if we cannot see the idiocy of the present day, perhaps we can recognize the same idiocy in its earlier appearances." Jacobs (1990): 76.

31 Sofia Coppola et al. (2006), *Marie Antoinette*. France/USA. As is well known, the genre of biographical motion picture ("biopic") has considerably increased since the eighties.

32 Jacobs (1990): 75.

33 "The provisional, indeterminate nature of historical knowledge is certainly not a discovery of postmodernism. Nor is the questioning of the ontological and epistemological status of historical "facts" or the distrust of seeming neutrality and objectivity of recounting. But the concentration of these problematizations in postmodern art is not something we can ignore." Linda Hutcheon (1999), *A Poetics of Postmodernism: History, Theory and Fiction*. London: Routledge: 88.

34 "Postmodernism signals its dependence by its *use* of the canon, but reveals its rebellion through its ironic *abuse* of it"; Hutcheon (1999):130. This modality is defined by Hutcheon as "paradoxical" because it settles the very norms that it then criticizes, engendering an "authorized transgression"; Hutcheon (1999): 129. On parody see also Hutcheon (1985), *A Theory of Parody. London*. London: Methuen, and Mirella Billi (1993), *Il testo riflesso: la parodia nel romanzo inglese*. Napoli: Liguori, which also conceives the concept of parody as difference and emphasizes its quality of "transformation that is both sacrilegious and productive, at the same time, and at many levels"; Mirella Billi (1993), *Il testo riflesso*: 41, translation mine.

35 It is interesting to observe that, according to Ira Bruce Nadel, the heir of the realistic novel of the nineteenth century is the traditional biography, because of its quality as *verifiable fiction*. While validating the consequences of his statement also for the postmodern rewritings, Middeke concludes: "does not a desire for life, authenticity, originality, paradoxically underlie all fictional efforts to deconstruct the same?". Middeke, *Introduction*, in Middeke, Huber (eds) (1999): 5; Nadel, "Narrative and the Popularity of Biography," *Mosaic* 20 (4) (1987): 134.

36 On the subject see Diane Elam (1992): *Romancing the Postmodern*. London: Routledge.
37 Roberts (1999): *Fair Exchange*. London: Little, Brown.
38 De Zordo: "Le finzioni della storia," in M. Roberts (2000): *Lo scambio*. Translated by Giorgia Sensi. Ferrara: Tufani: 242, translation mine.
39 Ibid.
40 Hutcheon (1999): 113-117.
41 According to Lukács, the large and variegated representation of the reality of an age can emerge only by beginning at the daily life of the common people, of their joys and pains, of the average man's crises and their confused incidents. The important figure that leads events and summarizes a trend of history will necessarily summarize it at a certain level of abstraction. Lukács (1977), *Il romanzo storico*. Translated by Eraldo Arnaud: 37. Lukács (1957), *Der historische Roman*. Berlin: Aufbau-Verlag.
42 Lukács (1977): 33.
43 Lukács defines the universal historical human being as a man representative of one of the many classes and social strata fighting against each other. Nevertheless, if they must fulfill their pinnacle functions and successful completion of such a poetic world, they cannot fail to make clear, directly or indirectly, the progressive traits of the whole society and of the whole age; Lukács (1977): 49.
44 Hutcheon (1999): 114.
45 John Fowles (1996): *The French Lieutenant's Woman*. London: Vintage.
46 Beside the Fowles-like texts, there are other peculiar cases which may need to be distinguished. These are narrations where historical characters are actually relevant to the plot, but recounting subjects' lives is overlooked by the question of life's representation, causing the writing's shift into the genre of the "metabiography." Although a unique definition is sometimes very difficult, we might assume as paradigmatic for this purpose Julian Barnes's *Flaubert's Parrot* (1984) or Peter Ackroyd's *Chatterton* (1987), which are focused on an investigation of the elusive existence of the historical characters; a biographical quest, which, moreover, often changes its target in the course of the reading. All this, with the additional inclusion of critical theory into the plot, emphasizes the immeasurable gap between experience and its narration, the subjectivity and artificiality involved in every attempt of life-writing. If postmodernism has by now been peacefully defined as a continual process of re-shaping and hybridization, it seems nonetheless reasonable to suggest that a biographical fiction should, at least, *pretend* to tell a story whose agents are historical characters; this surely does not happen in *Flaubert's Parrot,* even though the ambiguity of the first person chronology in the second chapter may raise ontological issues. Julian Barnes (1985): *Flaubert's Parrot.* London: Picador. Other metabiographies/metafictions, like Ackroyd's *Chatterton* (1987), could also be collocated near the edge of the biofiction genre in the most opaque fictional worlds. Peter Ackroyd (1988): *Chatterton.* London: Abacus; contrast that with the same author's previous text, *The Last Testament of Oscar Wilde* (1983): Ackroyd (1984): *The Last Testament of Oscar Wilde.* London: Abacus.

47 "All the novels and most of the plays discussed here in poetological terms belong to what Linda Hutcheon calls historiographic metafiction, they are characterized by their overt historical referents." The content of the anthology is, however, focused specifically on the life-rewriting of English Romantic authors, whose artistic quality is, according to Middeke, "a poetological and self-reflexive *conditio sine qua non* in that they focus our attention on what it means to be an artist and on the attendant circumstances in the creation of art." Middeke, *Introduction*, in Middeke, Huber (eds) (1999): 4 and 3.

48 On this subject, see also the already mentioned Afterward to the Italian edition of the text De Zordo: "Le finzioni della storia," in M. Roberts (2000): 233-234.

49 According to Lucia Boldrini, "the historical or biographical fiction needs reference [...], even if (or, rather, because of) reference takes place to problematize the whole issue of 'how' we can have access to reality; and even if the writing then distances itself from the referent; what is important, in any case, is that a referential link has been established." Lucia Boldrini (1998), *Biografie fittizie e personaggi storici*. Pisa: ETS: 171, translation mine.

50 As we will see later, according to Lubomír Doležel, the non-essentialist semantics of identity is based on the constant proper name as a rigid determiner. Nonetheless, postmodern rewritings do not always obey such semantics. In the transpositions from one world to another, individuals might be re-baptized and their counterparts might acquire pseudonyms. Doležel (1999), *Heterocosmica. Fiction e mondi possibili*. Translated by Margherita Botto. Milano: Bompiani; 227-228. Doležel (1998), *Heterocosmica Fiction and Possible Worlds*. Baltimore: Johns Hopkins University Press.

51 I refer here, embracing Jacob's perspective, to those science fiction and science fantasy narrations discussed in the chapter *The Speculative Self: Recombinant Fiction*: Jacobs (1990): 105-148. The connection between biofiction and science fiction is also explored by Christine Kenyon Jones in Middeke's volume. Her interesting essay, mentioning some recent "cyberculture novels" and "biofictionals fantasies," investigates the affinities among Romantic authors, the content of their works and contemporary science fiction, which often choose these characters as protagonists. Christine Kenyon Jones, *Poetry and Cyberpunk: Science Fiction and Romantic Biography*, in Middeke, Huber (eds) (1999): 175-186.

52 Conversely, the same may happen for biography "characters." In both cases, an unaware reader may infer by the cover whether the narrative subjects are biographical, fictional or "both." For a definition of biographical subjects as "characters" see Phyllis F. McCord, "A Specter Viewed by a Specter': Autobiography in Biography," *Biography* 9 (3) (1986): 219.

53 We may suppose, for instance, different possible receptions of the Catherina de' Medici's rewritings by readers living in Italy or in the United States, where Roessner's works were published. Moreover, if we consider the case of *Fair Exchange*, figures like Annette Vallon and Mary Hutchinson ("Annette Villon" and "Fanny Skinner" in the biofiction), have a different historical resonance with respect to their historical lover and husband William Wordsworth, whose surname is, in addition, turned into "Saygood" by Roberts. The instability of cultural solicitations is an essential condition of the genre; all the same,

as it happens in Roberts's mentioned book, there are levels of the polemic discourse which are potentially accessible to all the literate public: the irony of the pseudonym "Saygood" is here, indeed, also raised by its simple and direct interaction with the plot, which turns out to be an effective force of propagation of complex issues of feminist criticism.

54 Roland Barthes (1967), "The Death of the Author," *Aspen*, 5-6 (1967): 849-855. Michel Foucault (1969), "Qu est-ce qu'un auteur?," in *Dits et écrites 1954-1988. Edition établie sous la direction de D. Defert et F. Ewald.*, *Vol I: 1954-1969*. Paris: Gallimard: 789-821.

55 Julia Kristeva, "Bakhtine, le mot, le dialogue, le roman," *Critique* 33 (239) (1989): 438-465.

56 Cixous, "The Character of Character," *New Literary History*, 5(2) (1974): 383-402.

57 Docherty (1983), *Reading (Absent) Character: Towards a Theory of Characterization in Fiction*. Oxford: Clarendon.

58 Docherty (1983): xv.

59 Docherty (1983): 8.

60 Docherty (1983): xv.

61 Docherty (1983): 45.

62 Boldrini (1998): 153 (translation mine). However, she immediately adds that some of these problems are also to be shared with biography, therefore implicitly denying the specificity of the "truth" of the work of art in respect to that of biography (Ibid.)

63 Margolin, "Structuralist Approaches to Character in Narrative: The State of the Art," *Semiotica* 75 (1989): 1-24, qtd in L. Boldrini (1998): 166.

64 Boldrini (1998): 168.

65 "Possible INDS are constructs [...] introduced and sustained exclusively by means of a set of semiotic procedures or operations. As a result, all the information that can be had about them is 'in'. [...] Such INDS are hence ontologically 'thin' and not maximal, having only a limited number of properties and relations"; Margolin, "Individuals in Narrative Worlds: An Ontological Perspective," *Poetics Today* 11 (4) (1990): 847.

66 Boldrini (1998): 174.

67 Boldrini (1998): 168. "In these kinds of texts the name is already there at the beginning of the narration; often, it is even in the title. Therefore in what Genette defines as 'paratext', which is not the text yet; when this name shows up in the text, it is not an emptiness to be filled, but something which is already full"; Boldrini (1998): 174, translation mine.

68 "But our characters, if we look at them carefully, are not as much as 'possible non-actual individuals', rather 'actual but impossible individuals'. 'Actual' as they are real, 'impossible' as their life has already been lived, documented, narrated in biographies, and it is from this official biography that biofictions distance themselves with more or less strength"; Boldrini (1998): 168, translation mine.

69 There are many subjectivities at stake, and each biofiction shows its originality in the specific combination among the fictional character characterization

(ascribable to the author) and the historical referent mythos. This last is, in turn, to be thought of as the meeting place between the reader's idea and the writer's about that "cumulative biography," shaped in part by the historical subject. However, can narrative characters really and ultimately move away from the author's writing style? I refer here, in particular, to *The Master of Petersburg* by Coetzee, where the character Dostoyevsky seems, to me, to also show the typical traits of the many Coetzeean protagonists who persistently look for "signs" (the Magistrate in *Waiting for the Barbarians*, 1980, the doctor in *Life and Times of Micheal K*, 1974, the teacher in *The Age of Iron*, 1990); John Maxwell Coetzee (1994): *The Master Of Petersburg*. New York: Penguin.

70 "At once unrealized and unrealizable, historical figures float in and out of these stories as if dreamed or hallucinated, serving a college-like vision that may be satiric, speculative, magical, or mythical. The effect is disjointed, disorienting: the factual and the fantastic battle for predominance and the fantastic triumphs [...]. Readers go to science fantasy and science fiction alike for an experience of the marvelous, whether based on futuristic technology or on magic. The presence of recognizable figures in new contexts is one means of creating that experience of the marvelous"; Jacobs (1990): 105 and 111.

71 Doležel adopts the Austinian theory of performative speech acts to explain the literary text's world-constructing capacity, so that "the genesis of fictional words can be seen as an extreme case of world-change, a change from nonexistence into (fictional) existence"; this genesis is produced by the especially illocutionary force of literary speech acts ("the force of authentication"). According to this theoretical approach, "A non-actualized possible state of affairs becomes a fictional existent by being authenticated in a felicitously uttered literary speech act [...]. The theory of authentication assumes that the force of authentication is exercised differently in different literary text types (genres). In the particular case of the narrative text type [...], the force of authentication is assigned to the speech acts originating in the so-called narrator [...]. The mechanism of authentication is best demonstrated in the case of the 'omniscient,' 'reliable,' authoritative Er-form narrator. Whatever is uttered by this source automatically becomes a fictional existent. Other types of narrators, such as the 'unreliable,' 'subjective', Ich-form narrator, are sources with a lower degree of authentication authority"; Doležel, "Mimesis and Possible Worlds," *Poetics Today*, 9 (3) (1988): 490, followed by an investigation about skaz narrative and the self-disclosing narrative (which he identifies as "metafiction"), where the authenticating act loses its performative force. It should be noted that Doležel's selection of "self-disclosing narrative ('metafiction')" includes the *nouveau roman* and John Barth and John Fowles' works; Doležel (1988): 491-492.

72 West (1989): *Lord Byron's Doctor*. Chicago: University of Chicago Press. The narrator's unreliability has been invalidated since his telling of his visit to the character Claire Clairmont in England after the separation from Lord Byron, as in the fourth part we come to know that the protagonist has remained in Italy until April 1817. Despite the many quotations from historical sources, the anguished West's Polidori belongs to an impossible world, appearing "a ghoul, a revenant [...] who, like the vampire of his story, can transmute into a deathless voice bound neither by time nor place," Annegret Maak, "The Life

We Imagine": Byron's and Polidori's Memoirs as Character Construction," in Middeke, Huber (eds) (1999): 142.

73 Banville (1990): *Dr Copernicus*. London: Minerva; Malouf (1978): *An Imaginary Life*. New York: Braziller.

74 Chernaik (1992): *Mab's Daughters*. London: Pan Books.

75 Jacobs (1990): 70. In analyzing some of Doctorow and Reed's works whose implications she generalizes, Jacobs argues that a detailed presentation of the character's inner being would preclude the past-present analogy. Therefore, fiction histories' protagonists are, in her view, affected by a process of simplification and universalizing that turn them into "cultural types," "comic cut-outs," "common citizens," which are more important as ideas and concepts than as individuals. If one agrees with her observation about biofiction's possibility to disclose that shapes processes' repeatability, her conclusions about a supposed absence of psychology in historical characters seem to be contradicted by many texts which agree with my definition of "biofiction." It is important to notice that her selection of "fiction histories" covers a wide range of texts, including narratives that, according to the perspective of the presented work, belongs to the more general category of historiographic metafiction, to which, in my personal opinion, biofictions may or may not belong. Jacobs (1990): 84, 70, and 73. Edgard Lawrence Doctorow (1975): *Ragtime*. New York: Random House. Ishmael Reed (1972): *Mumbo Jumbo*. Garden City: Doubleday.

76 Doležel (1999): 226.

77 Doležel (1988): 481.

78 Doležel (1988): 483.

79 Ibid.

80 Doležel (1988): 477. Mimetic criticism, taking fictional particulars as representations of actual universals, makes them "disappear" from semantic interpretations; Doležel (1988): 478. What the critic is contesting here is Auerbachian criticism, whose "specific interpretant" is secular history, and "especially the changing forms of 'everyday life'" (Ibid.). A slightly different alternative to such "mainstream of mimetic criticism from Aristotle to Auerbach" is represented, in his view, by *The Rise of the Novel* (1957) by Ian Watt, actually another "best seller of mimetic criticism" explicitly indebted to Auerbach. Here, the mimetic function is replaced by a "pseudomimetic" one that, by identifying the source of representation with the "author," presupposes that fictional particulars somehow pre-exist the act of representation. Pseudomimetic interpretations, for Doležel, also dominate contemporary "textual practices," where the source of representation is specified in terms of narrative genres of modes, narrative discourse types, stylistic devices; Doležel (1988): 477-480.

81 Doležel (1988): 483. It should be noted that his position is, even if from different approaches, the same as Middeke's, who defends the distinction between "facts" and "fiction" in readers' awareness (see paragraph 1.1).

82 Doležel (1988): 485.

83 Doležel (1988): 483.

84 Doležel (1999): 225.

85 Ibid.
86 Doležel (1999): 226-227.
87 Doležel (1999): 226.
88 "The need of semiotic mediation in the access to fictional worlds explains why fictional semantics has to resist all attempts at 'decentering,' 'alienating' and by-passing the literary text"; Doležel (1988): 485.

Works cited

Primary Sources

Ackroyd, Peter (1984): *The Last Testament of Oscar Wilde*. London: Abacus.
— (1988): *Chatterton*. London: Abacus.
Banville, John (1990): *Dr Copernicus*. London: Minerva.
Barnes, Julian (1985): *Flaubert's Parrot*. London: Picador.
Chernaik, Judith (1992): *Mab's Daughters*. London: Pan Books.
Coetzee, John Maxwell (1994): *The Master Of Petersburg*. New York: Penguin.
Doctorow, Edgard Lawrence (1975): *Ragtime*. New York: Random House.
Fowles, John (1996): *The French Lieutenant's Woman*. London: Vintage.
Malouf, David (1978): *An Imaginary Life*. New York: Braziller.
Reed, Ishmael (1972): *Mumbo Jumbo*. Garden City: Doubleday.
Roberts, Michèle (1999): *Fair Exchange*. London: Little, Brown.
— (2003) *The Mistressclass*. London: Little, Brown.
Roessner, Michaela (1998): *The Stars Dispose*. New York: Tor Books.
— (1999): *The Stars Compel*. New York: Tor Books.
Roth, Philip (1979): *The Ghost Writer*. New York: Farrar, Straus & Giroux.
West, Paul (1989): *Lord Byron's Doctor*. Chicago: University of Chicago Press.

Secondary Sources

Barthes, Roland (1967), "The Death of the Author," *Aspen*, 5-6 (1967): 849-855.
Billi, Mirella (1993), *Il testo riflesso: la parodia nel romanzo inglese*. Napoli: Liguori.
Boldrini, Lucia (1998), *Biografie fittizie e personaggi storici*. Pisa: ETS.
Cixous, Hélène, "The Character of Character," *New Literary History*, 5(2) (1974): 383-402.
De Man, Paul, "Autobiography as De-Facement," *Comparative Literature*, 94 (5) (1979): 919-930.
De Zordo, Ornella: "Le finzioni della storia", in M. Roberts (2000): *Lo scambio*. Translated by Giorgia Sensi. Ferrara: Tufani: 231-243.
Docherty, Thomas (1983), *Reading (Absent) Character: Towards a Theory of Characterization in Fiction*. Oxford: Clarendon.
Doležel, Lubomír, "Mimesis and Possible Worlds," *Poetics Today*, 9 (3)(1988): 475-496.

— (1999), *Heterocosmica. Fiction e mondi possibili.* Translated by Margherita Botto. Milano: Bompiani. (1998) *Heterocosmica. Fiction and Possible Worlds*, Baltimore: Johns Hopkins University Press.
Elam, Diane (1992): *Romancing the Postmodern*. London: Routledge.
Epstein, William (ed) (1991), *Contesting the Subject: Essays in the Postmodern Theory and Practice of Biography and Biographical Criticism.* West Lafayette: Purdue University Press.
Foucault, Michel (1969), "Qu est-ce qu'un auteur?," in *Dits et écrites 1954-1988. Edition établie sous la direction de D. Defert et F. Ewald.*, *Vol I: 1954-1969.* Paris: Gallimard: 789-821.
Gasché, Rodolphe, "French Issue: Autobiography and the Problem of the Subject," *Modern Language Notes* 93 (4) (1978): 573-574.
Gaskell, Elizabeth (1877), *The Life of Charlotte Brontë.* Harmondsworth: Penguin Books.
Hutcheon, Linda(1985), *A Theory of Parody*. London: Methuen.
— (1999), *A Poetics of Postmodernism: History, Theory and Fiction.* London: Routledge.
Jacobs, Naomi (1990), *The Character of Truth: Historical Figures in Contemporary Fiction.* Southern Illinois University Press: Carbondale.
Jay, Paul L., "Being in the Text: Autobiography and the Problem of the Subject," *Modern Language Notes* 97 (5) (1982): 1045-1063.
Keener, John F. (2001), *Biography and the Postmodern Historical Novel*, New York: Mellen.
Kristeva, Julia, "Bakhtine, le mot, le dialogue, le roman," *Critique* 33 (239) (1989): 438-465.
Lukács, György (1977), *Il romanzo storico.* Translated by Eraldo Arnaud. Torino: Einaudi.
— (1957) *Der historische Roman.* Berlin: Aufbau-Verlag.
Margolin, Uri, "Structuralist Approaches to Character in Narrative: The State of the Art," *Semiotica* 75 (1989): 1-24.
—, "Individuals in Narrative Worlds: An Ontological Perspective," *Poetics Today* 11 (4) (1990): 843-871.
McCord, Phyllis F., "'A Specter Viewed by a Specter': Autobiography in Biography," *Biography* 9 (3) (1986): 219-228.
Middeke, Martin, Huber Werner (eds) (1999), *Biofictions: the Rewriting of Romantic Lives in Contemporary Fiction and Drama.* Rochester (NY)-Woodbridge: Camden House.
Nadel, Ira Bruce (1984), *Biography: Fiction, Fact and Form.* New York: St Martin's Press.
—, "Narrative and the Popularity of Biography," *Mosaic* 20 (4) (1987): 131-141.
Nye, David E. (1983), *The Invented Self: An Anti-Biography from Documents of Thomas A. Edison.* Odense: Odense University Press.
Strachey, Lytton (1986), *Eminent Victorians.* Harmondsworth: Penguin.
White, Hayden (1973), *Metahistory: The Historical Imagination in Nineteenth-Century Europe.* Baltimore and London: Johns Hopkins University Press.
— (1978), *Tropics of Discourse: Essays in Cultural Criticism.* Baltimore and London: Johns Hopkins University Press.

— (1987), *The Content of the Form. Narrative Discourse and Historical Representation*. Baltimore and London: Johns Hopkins University Press.

Yourcenar, Marguerite (1974), *Mémoires d'Hadrien. Suivi de Carnets de notes de Mémoires d'Hadrien*. Paris: Gallimard.

Filmography

Coppola, Sofia et al. (2006): *Marie Antoinette*, France/USA.

37

Monica Latham

"'Serv[ing] under two masters': Virginia Woolf's Afterlives in Contemporary Biofictions" from *a/b: Auto/Biography Studies* (2012)

This essay sets out to explore Virginia Woolf's afterlives portrayed by four contemporary authors: Robin Lippincott (Mr Dalloway), Michael Cunningham (*The Hours*), Sigrid Nunez (*Mitz: The Marmoset of Bloomsbury*), and Susan Sellers (*Vanessa and Virginia*). They have resurrected the figure of Woolf, used her own narrative tools and style to portray her, and put into practice her own theory of "new biography," which serves two "masters," fact and fiction.

"Let it be fact, one feels, or let it be fiction; the imagination will not serve under two masters simultaneously" (V. Woolf, "Biography" 478). Woolf's common reader's imaginary outcry is for her an opportunity to assess the state of Victorian biography, before pioneering a new genre that shows that imagination can successfully serve these two masters simultaneously. In the wake of Woolf, contemporary authors have continued to extend the limits of biography, incorporating other forms and ingredients to produce new generic literary products. The "continued proliferation of the producing and the consuming of auto/biography" (Saunders 286) on our contemporary literary market has given birth to numerous subcategories of the genre of life writing, among them biofiction, which has proved as fertile and popular a territory as biography and fiction—the two genres it seeks to fuse.

Traditionally, the art of fiction consists of giving life to imaginary characters and simulating believable lives for them in order to make them look and sound "real" in the fictitious universe in which they evolve. The phenomenon that transforms a historical figure into a character in fiction is also a common writing practice. The most successful fictitious biographies are those which combine a savvy amalgamation of documentary evidence and poetic license, plausibility, and imagination, "no more than a pinch of" "the truth of real life and the truth of fiction" (V. Woolf, "Biography" 477); this specific life-writing genre lies at the confluence of authenticity (conferred by biography) and imagination (as authors explore other possible avenues and give their readers access to the imagined inner lives of the characters). Biographical fiction relies on biographèmes[1] that lend verisimilitude to the character's life story, but it also explores the "swarm of possibilities" usually rejected by conventional biographies (James, qtd. in Edel 29).

"Biofiction,"[2] a portmanteau, indicates that reality and fiction, likeness and imagination, blend in this kind of literary work. It reveals the transfers that operate from biography to fiction and the crossover genre, which fuses two opposed poles when narrating the imaginary lives of people who really existed. This transgeneric life writing offers the reader a simulacrum of a real life: writer-biographers' subjective representation of their subject's life. Such a strategy is part of the current postmodern cultural and literary practice that manipulates the real as well as plays with different layers of truths and pluralism of realities.

Given her tragic death, Virginia Woolf's life and work have been "variously and passionately idealized, vilified, fictionalized, and mythologized" (Lee, *Nose* 39). Biographers[3] and fiction writers have re-imagined and reconstructed their own versions of the modernist author and made her come alive on their pages. In this essay, I examine several imaginary versions or facets of her life that also incorporate her work. Various contemporary authors haunted by Woolf—Robin Lippincott, Michael Cunningham, Sigrid Nunez, and Susan Sellers—have all fictionalized Woolf's life through the prism of her novels. They have transposed biographical elements and shaped a poetic trajectory of her life by using her own literary structures. Thus, in their representation of the biographized Woolf, the subject becomes a Woolfian character depicted with Woolfian narrative tools.

Mr. Dalloway, The Hours, Mitz: The Marmoset of Bloomsbury, and *Vanessa and Virginia,* all depend on minute factual research but also require an imaginative and creative dexterity in order to open up infinite possibilities, prolong the true facts, or fill in the nebulous blanks left by biographies. In their respective works, the contemporary authors transcend the limits and constraints of traditional biography. As historical figures become characters in a fictitious work, poetic license allows them to go off the beaten track and give the reader a different image of the subject from the one contained in the standard biographies. Fictional narratives map a wider territory and present greater potential: for example, as her biographers put Virginia Woolf in fictional situations, they can delve into her imaginary inner life, construct an "as if," and bring the reader into her psyche.

The major formal challenge of the four novels is how to integrate into the contemporary text the subject's oeuvre, and how to fuse (more or less) seamlessly two different styles, the writer-biographer's and the biographized's. Lippincott, Cunningham, Nunez, and Sellers are all highly influenced by their subject's experimentation with hybridized genres, their novels being an amalgamation of biographical, historical, and scholarly research. If the production of such generic works is based on familiarity with iconic cultural references, so must be their reception; only readers whose prior cultural, literary, and aesthetic knowledge of the subject's life and work allows them fully to understand the writer-biographer's skillful endeavor successfully receive and acclaim these biofictions. In these four recent excursions into the genre, the authors have selected from the substantial quarry of biographical material and completed these facts with imaginative details. However, their novels are more than life-writing hybrids combining fact and fiction, as they could also be considered sequels, variations, spin-offs, pastiches, parallels, imitations, or homages to Woolf's works.

Robin Lippincott's *Mr. Dalloway,* which takes place on June 28th, 1927—three years after the events in *Mrs. Dalloway*—traces this particular day. It is Richard and Clarissa Dalloway's thirtieth wedding anniversary and also a day of scientific significance (the sun's total eclipse). Lippincott's postmodernist rewriting of Woolf's *Mrs. Dalloway* plays with the distinction between reality and fiction while reinventing the "real" as he brings together different layers of characters and multiple degrees of fiction. For this, he relies on an ingenious and intricate mixture of different sets of characters: new ones invented by Lippincott, fictitious ones who seem familiar given that they have been borrowed from *Mrs. Dalloway,* and real, historical figures who become characters. One of them is Virginia Woolf, who appears as the author of the recently published *To the Lighthouse* (1927). Richard buys a copy of it as a gift for Clarissa, thus giving Lippincott's novella a metafictional twist. In addition, Woolf, her husband Leonard, and Vita Sackville-West make cameo appearances in the novel as they come to see the eclipse along with the other characters in the story. This scene is based on the actual event described by Woolf herself in her diary (3:142). The Woolfs, Sackville-West, and her husband Harold Nicolson, travelled by special trains and coaches from Euston to Yorkshire to see the eclipse from Bardon Fell. In *Mr. Dalloway,* Richard has organized a special, thirtieth wedding anniversary; he will take his guests from King's Cross Station by train to North Yorkshire, then by bus to Bardon Fell, a spot where they will view the total eclipse of the sun, "something bigger and more profound" than "their meagre day-to-day existences" (136).

The Virginia Woolf portrayed by Lippincott is a Dalloway-esque character seen from a multiplicity of points of view and through the eyes of various characters: Robbie notices that she is a "tall, thin woman"; Lady Vallance recognizes a "tall, elegant figure"; she is a "beautiful" woman—an ironic compliment given by her own character, Clarissa Dalloway. Thus, Woolf's eponymous character and Virginia Woolf herself both become Lippincottian characters who evolve in the same fictitious universe during a short secondary scene within Lippincott's novella which offers an extension of Woolf's own novel. This constitutes a typical example of fictitious embroidery upon a biographème documented by autobiographical material. The character of Virginia Woolf is absorbed in a complex network of new and old characters in a story that plays with the multiplication of fictitious and realistic stances to create a vertiginous narrative game that combines not only biography and fiction, but even more convolutedly so, biography and different levels of fiction.

Lippincott, the pasticheur who brings Woolf to life here, draws her portrait in a novella that closely mimics her style. However, this technique is more elaborate in Michael Cunningham's *The Hours*. Woolf is also given life in this postmodern novel based on the day-in-the-life format of *Mrs. Dalloway.* In one of *The Hour*'s triptych of stories, Woolf is portrayed as a tormented author grappling with her own novel, *The Hours* (the initial title of *Mrs. Dalloway*). During one specific day in 1923, the reader follows the character of "Mrs. Woolf" waking up at Hogarth House, planning her new novel, writing its first lines, musing over the fate of her character, Clarissa, welcoming her sister Vanessa and her children, sharing a kiss, taking a walk, contemplating escaping the suburbs, and going to London on the train.

Cunningham takes the reader into the subject's mind during the composition process of her novel and applies her technique of portraying characters to the author-writer who becomes his character, "Mrs. Woolf." Cunningham probes her "liquid mind" and fluidly transcribes her train of thoughts on the page. Compared with Lippincott's fleeting portrait, Cunningham's more sustained palette describes the richer portrait of her inner landscape. He borrows Woolf's tools and techniques and paints her in the same way she painted the complex inner lives of her own characters. Through a skillful *mise en abyme* device, Woolf becomes a Woolfian character—thinking and behaving like her own characters, especially like Clarissa Dalloway, the key figure upon whom Cunningham's three plots all hinge in a novel about creation, writing, and reading.

Cunningham ironically starts Woolf's afterlife with her death staged in the "Prologue," in which he recreates the last moments of her life. The author uses biographèmes that support and validate his imaginative recreation of Woolf's death. For example, in the suicide scene he incorporates the real content of Woolf's farewell letter to her husband. The letter, transcribed by

Hermione Lee in her biography of Woolf, follows Woolf's organization of words and sentences, and translates her state of mind just before committing suicide.[4]

> *Dearest,*
> *I feel certain that I am going*
> *mad again: I feel we can't go*
> *through another of these terrible times.*
> *And I shan't recover this time. I begin*
> *to hear voices, and can't concentrate.*
> *So I am doing what seems the best thing to do. You have*
> *given me*
> *the greatest possible happiness. You*
> *have been in every way all that anyone*
> *could be. I don't think two*
> *people could have been happier till*
> *this terrible disease came. I can't*
> *fight it any longer, I know that I am*
> *spoiling your life, that without me you*
> *could work. And you will I know.*
> *You see I can't even write this properly. I*
> *can't read. What I want to say is that*
> *I owe all the happiness of my life to you.*
> *You have been entirely patient with me &*
> *incredibly good. I want to say that—*
> *everybody knows it. If anybody could*
> *have saved me it would have been you.*
> *Everything has gone from me but the*
> *certainty of your goodness. I*
> *can't go on spoiling your life any longer. I don't think two people*
> *could have been happier than we have been.*
> *V.* (Lee, *Virginia Woolf* 747)

Cunningham mimetically reprints the letter in the same way and uses italics to confer on the whole scene a "reality effect."[5] This poem-like letter, the kernel of truth at the core of Cunningham's suicide scene, is framed by a prose characterized by close pictorial detail of the surrounding scenery and cinematic attention given to the unfolding events, which constitutes Woolf's own narrative trademark. The narrator accompanies Woolf from the moment she leaves Hogarth House to the river Ouse where she drowns herself and records the "myriad impressions" received by the character. The immediacy and progress of the scene is created by present tense, simple verbs detailing her movement and perceptions and by a meticulous description of the character's slightest gestures, doubts, hesitations, and thoughts. The narrative voice focuses on the tiniest details, such as the last impressions she absorbs before she commits suicide: the shape and the color of the stone in her pocket, which becomes her final anchor, the movement and temperature of the water, the reflection of the light and shade in the water and on the river banks, the weeds caught in her hair, and the texture and color of the mud, which all compose Virginia's final resting place. While the stream takes away her body, the reader follows the "stream" of her consciousness. The scene staging her state of mind and her death is thus depicted with tools borrowed from the subject of the biography; Cunningham's colorful prose contains Woolfian refrains, precise digressive thoughts contained between brackets that constantly interrupt the flux of main thoughts, and a complex syntax whose articulations are kept precariously together by flexible, intermediary punctuation that temporarily and incessantly rejects the final full stop.

The fictitious portrait of Woolf is more detailed after the prologue set in 1941, in the chapters that take place in 1923, entitled "Mrs. Woolf." These fragments constitute facets of the writer during one working day—Cunningham evokes a Woolf in the process of living an ordinary day, during which she imagines an ordinary day in the life of her characters—peppered with domestic obstacles that prevent her from writing but also with prolific descriptions of states of mind that propel the advancement of her novel. The narrator infiltrates her mind and gives the reader the portrait of a writer racked by headaches, tormenting voices, and moments of depression. This is the aggrandizement of the inner landscape often described by Woolf herself in her diary. Cunningham turns factual autobiography into poetic narration and manages to give us a pictorial *mise en abyme,* as if when drawing the portrait of his character, Mrs. Woolf, he used her self-portrait as a model.

Thanks to a privileged access in this novel to the character's interior monologue, the reader follows the fictitious process of composition of *Mrs. Dalloway.* Little by little, the outlines of the plot take form, from fragments issued from premonitory dreams as the author falls asleep during the day or reveries during her afternoon walks. Cunningham's portrait of Woolf is that of a writer whose material environment and the constraints linked to her illness can prevent her creative impulse. On the other hand, her rich, tumultuous, and tormented inner life imagined by Cunningham—in the way Woolf imagines the inner lives of Clarissa Dalloway or Septimus Smith—counterbalances her constraining, sterile, domestic life and favors creativity. Ideas that simmer and develop in her mind become the foundations that support the future novel. The way Woolf envisages the unfolding of her novel throughout the day reflects a heuristic method based both on a prospective vision of her novel (she constantly adjusts the trajectory of her novel) and a retrospective one (she is always prey to doubts about the pages she has already written). The reader witnesses the writer's groping with her novelistic material and her juggling with both a program and process writing.[6] The Virginia Woolf that Cunningham imagines lives mainly for her writing and gives little time and attention to her social environment. Her thoughts are constantly occupied by the fate of her characters; she is completely absorbed by the creative effervescence and the interior life that inspires her, even during verbal exchanges with her family. The movement of her consciousness is thus interrupted by external events, some of them becoming material for her fiction.

In the passages where the character of Woolf is composing her novel, Cunningham engages in mapping a speculative genetic progress or a simulacrum of the genesis of *Mrs. Dalloway*. He condenses factual elements from the period of time in which she wrote *Mrs. Dalloway* (two years) into one imaginary day in which she begins the creative process, focusing on the thinking process that leads to writing the first lines of the novel. The poetic depiction of her genesis of *Mrs. Dalloway* consists of a mixture of (auto)biographical proofs—in her letters and diary, Woolf often describes the advancement of her imaginative work, her findings, and dead-ends—and Cunningham's fertile imagination, restrained by Woolfian stylistic imperatives, part and parcel of his DNA.[7] *The Hours* allows Cunningham to express his kinship with Woolf, whose work has had a considerable impact on his personal and artistic development.

Cunningham successfully makes Woolf a believable character with a full artistic life and a tragic death. Her portrait "rings true" according to Woolf's biographers and scholars, who have an intimate knowledge of Woolf's life and work (Lee, "Ms. Brown" 19). Cunningham gives life to a Woolf who, without a doubt, resembles both Woolf as described by biographers and auto-portrayed in her own autobiographical works and her own fictitious characters. He recreates a life by borrowing facts, details, and events from the author's real life—especially concerning the medical history, visions, and hallucinations described in her diary—but also from the fictional universe of *Mrs. Dalloway*. While Woolf had "cover[ed]" Clarissa Dalloway "very remarkably with herself" (V. Woolf, *Diary* 3: 32) since she had poured into her fiction many of her own emotions and experiences, we could argue that Cunningham, in turn, covers his Mrs. Woolf very remarkably using Clarissa Dalloway herself.

The author's afterlife is thus depicted with the stylistic and narrative tools of the writer herself. Cunningham puts into practice the artistic credo and the theory of modernist fiction—expressed by Woolf in her critical essays—in a postmodernist novel, which seems to suggest that there are no new stories, just new ways to retell, again and again, the same story. Cunningham feeds on Woolf's work and draws a portrait of Woolf in accordance with it. This is an example of a cannibalization of Woolfian prose. The use of pastiche calls into attention Cunningham's postmodernist practice of the mimicry[8] of an idiosyncratic modernist style. Several recognizable Woolfian features appearing in *Mrs. Dalloway* and constituting its trademark are successfully employed by the author of *The Hours*: the free indirect speech, the change of focalization, the pictorial and poetic quality of descriptions, the particular use of punctuation, and the incantatory-like effect of repetition.

"Tiny deviations from fact" that some Woolfian critics complained about are not what matters in this novel (Lee, "Ms. Brown" 19); Cunningham is not a biographer, but a fiction writer whose method consists in fictionalizing biographical events. He breaks free from biography, distorts it, and fabricates new events that seem authentic as they encroach on real, biographical material. Although some of Cunningham's imagined details, such as Woolf's tone and specifics of class, "don't always ring quite true" (Lee, *Nose* 50), biofiction does successfully "serve two masters simultaneously" in this case.

Virginia Woolf's portrait in Sigrid Nunez's *Mitz: The Marmoset of Bloomsbury* is indirectly drawn through Mitz's "unauthorized" (115) biography written in the tradition of Woolf's *Flush* (1933), the biography of Elizabeth Barrett Browning's cocker spaniel, whose model was the Woolfs' own spaniel, Pinka. *Flush* was inspired by other biographies, just like *Mitz* was inspired by *Flush*. The chain of inspiration may go back to Lytton Strachey's dignified biographies, *Eminent Victorians* and *Queen Victoria*. *Flush* and *Mitz,* which chronicle the lives of pets, are mocking imitations of the genre. In her "mock biography" ("mockiography"), Nunez continues Woolf's tradition while portraying the author who inspired her. The starting point of Nunez's novel is the real fact that between 1934 and 1938 the Woolfs owned a marmoset.[9] Mitz's burlesque biography relies on the invention of a life story and imagined biographical detail for this pet; between the lines, it writes a biofiction of the Woolfs supported by "published fact" and events collected by the author from different (auto)biographical sources listed at the end of the novel (Nunez 115).

Mitz's saga offers the reader insights into the Woolfs' social, domestic, and private life. Vignettes describing their routine abound: Virginia divides her day into compartments, and has a passion for street-haunting, which provides her inspiration for her novels and allows her to sift her sentences through her mind. The author reconstructs the marmoset's impressions of the Woolf household in the troubled five years preceding World War II. The Woolfs write, entertain friends, travel, mourn their relatives' and friends' deaths, worry about their health and mortality, and apprehend the imminent war. *Mitz* is an evocation of a couple during a specific period of their lives: the wane of Bloomsbury and the looming presence of Nazi Germany.

Like *Flush,* Nunez tells us, *Mitz* combines documented biographical material with invented details and dialogue. The real quotes extracted from authentic sources are delimited by inverted commas and mark the frontier between "the two masters," reality and imagination. The typographical marks signal the actual fragments, like a frontier between real scraps and imaginary prose. In her "Acknowledgements," Nunez explains her research methods and the way she has fused biographèmes with invented conversations. In order to shape the pet's mockiography, Nunez has combed through voluminous heaps of Bloomsbury lore, the countless biographies, memoirs, diaries, and letter collections,[10] and culled her facts and quotations carefully, adding invented conversation.

One iconographic piece of documentary evidence in the 2007 *Mitz* re-edition published by Soft Skull Press, is a very blurred picture of Pinka and Mitz on the last page of the novel. Based on this photograph, which creates an effect of reality within the mockiography, Nunez invents an amusing relationship between the two animals. In addition, the dust jacket picture on the 1998 edition designed by John A. Parks illustrates the hybridity of the novel and highlights the phenomena of its fabrication, manipulation, and distortion of reality in general. The picture is a montage of Gisele Freund's famous photo of Leonard and Virginia Woolf, in which the marmoset is irreverently added in the middle, between the couple, symbolically holding Leonard's hand and turning its back to its rival, Virginia. The image reflects a comical triangular relationship that constitutes the very core of Nunez's novel.

Quentin Bell, Virginia Woolf's nephew and later her biographer, loathed Mitz, and claimed that its face resembled Joseph Goebbels's (*Bloomsbury* 125). The marmoset, wrote Bell with uncharacteristic venom, "seemed to be in a perpetual state of vicious fury; ugly at all times, it became hideous when it vented its spite at the world. It was deeply in love with Leonard and would spit out its jealousy upon the rest of humanity" (42). Nunez's more affectionate, fictitious portrait is a mix between the real animal and Flush, the Woolfian character. The author describes the marmoset's perceptions—especially in the scene where one August night in Rodmell someone leaves the door open and Mitz spends the night in the fig tree. When Mitz finally comes back home, the Woolfs' relief is expressed at the end of the chapter in a very Dalloway-esque manner: "For there she was" (65).

Nunez's hesitant narrative voice evinces the enthralling power of the "two masters" and the constant wrestling between fact and fiction. The first master, the omniscient narrator, is didactic and informative in adopting the dry and factual voice of a biographer:

> Already Virginia had begun *Three Guineas*, the political pamphlet she had been itching to write for some time and which she had once thought of calling *On Being Despized*. It had begun as a sequel to *A Room of One's Own*, the pamphlet she had published in 1929 and in which she discussed the fate of the woman writer in a patriarchal world. In the sequel she planned to discuss education and professions for women. But now, with the threat of fascism and war always present, she began thinking of it also as her "war pamphlet": a meditation upon the reasons for war and what might be done to prevent it. Virginia believed that fascism, the

> pursuit of war, and the oppression of women were all connected, and in *Three Guineas* she meant to show how. (79)

On the other hand, Mitz's fanciful point of view and its imagined voice give a humorous portrait of Woolf and her circle: "And here was another mystery of Bloomsbury: people were called one name when they were present and other names when they were not. The 'uncastrated cat' coming to dinner was in fact Ethel; the 'great toad' and the 'dear old ass' both turned out to be Tom. And who were Mr. Bennett and Mrs. Brown?" (68–69). Through the animal's limited understanding, the reader gets an amusing indication of Woolf's famously gossipy nature and irreverent attitude towards her guests. A bewildered Mitz ponders Woolf's food issues: "Of all things strange about humans to Mitz this was the strangest: how Virginia would not eat" (69). Mitz reveals another facet of Woolf's character and draws an endearing portrait of her, "a fragile mind in a fragile body" (27) who has doubts, fears, insecurities: her "thorns" that Leonard tries to "get out" in patient discussions (35).

Mitz sketches for the reader the portrait of a creator absorbed by her art and a prolific writer engaged in different projects. The marmoset hears the comforting sounds of pen on paper as Woolf writes, but also hears her mutter, struggling to complete *The Years*. Through Mitz's eyes, we witness Virginia's painstaking writing process, "the near-breakdown under the strain of finishing her novel," (49) and the intensive work sessions she inflicts on herself: "Once Virginia did get back to work, it was with a vengeance. She saw her novel finished by the end of summer, but still she had not found a title to please her" (61). Woolf's painful writing and revising processes are followed by her fear of reviews. Mitz can decipher the noises made by her mistress and read the signs that betray Woolf's mental torments. Mitz sees that the "mysterious activity" that consumes her can have a contradictory effect on her: "From a distance, then, Mitz observed Virginia. And she saw how this mysterious activity that could bring such a flush to Virginia's check could also have quite the opposite effect" (75). Woolf's writing process is intrinsically linked with her changing moods, and her mental unbalance can quickly become a barrier to creation.

Mitz's mistress is permanently inhabited by her mission as a writer. Highly observant, Woolf pays close attention to the smallest of natural details around her: "Though she shared in the conversation and heard every word, Virginia never stopped taking in what was happening around them. A writer, said her father's old friend Henry James, must be someone who notices everything. (So avidly did Virginia observe this rule, Leonard sometimes had to chide her in public for staring.) The changing light, the changing colors of the sky, the flight of swallow and bat, when the nightingale sang and when it did not—none of this was missed by Virginia" (2–3). Woolf is a sensitive writer whose eyes always focus on details and whose ears are attuned to the slightest sounds and noises. She constantly penetrates minds, people's but also animals', and wonders about inner lives: "Leonard never indulged in speculations about Mitz's inner life. It was not his way. But for Virginia this habit of musing and 'making up' came as naturally as breathing" (46).

The biographèmes Nunez uses to support a fictitious version of Woolf's life may seem to consist of stereotypical details, often repeated by biographers and expected by readers who have an *a priori* implicit image of the modernist writer. However, beyond the actual events, accurate historical landmarks, and private information that Nunez has extracted from primary sources (letters, diaries, and memoirs) and woven into her biofiction, the main purpose of such a novel is to offer the reader an ingenious fictional reconstruction, a slice of life built in the spirit of Virginia Woolf by borrowing from her real life and by imitating her imaginative tools.

This phenomenon can be observed in author-cum-critic Susan Seller's *Vanessa and Virginia*. Sellers's novel serves more than two masters and is more than just a sophisticated blend of biography and fiction, given its passages of informed literary and art criticism (metafictional and metapictorial descriptive snippets). As the title indicates, the novel contains the portraits of the two artist sisters and their relationship—their strong affection but also their fierce jealousies. Their intertwined life stories unveil their sisterly complicity, the artistic collaboration between "the one with words" (14) and the one with colors; the novel also explores their rivalry, often expressed in terms of painting. The main portrait (an auto-portrait in prose) is of Vanessa Bell in her multiple roles as sister, wife, mother, lover—and above all, artist. The story is told using her first-person narrative voice and with her eye for symbolism, balance, and color. The novel is unique in giving voice to Bell, one of the most influential figures in Woolf's life.

Woolf appears in an oblique, peripheral portrait in the background. Gradually, the two artists' destinies end up looking more and more alike: Sellers merges the portraits so that the two sisters reflect one another in a series of meaningful episodes taken from their childhood, when they fight for their parents' attention and strive to find artistic ways to do so (such as writing their family newspaper, *Hyde Park Gate News*), and from their lives until Woolf's suicide. These episodes form a chronological but also a kaleidoscopic portrait made up of disconnected vignettes and sketchy memories. Bell lovingly reveals that her "intellectually agile, eloquent and daring" sister shines among the Bloomsbury set (45). It is a very emotional paean to her sister, one in which she praises Woolf's talents but also points out her fragility and weaknesses.

Vanessa and Virginia is a portrait of a writer by a painter and an intimate glimpse of an emotional and artistic war. Bell constantly compares their two arts, often concluding that her sister's talent is unmatched, even by her own: "I lack your subtlety and skill" (16). Being ill-at-ease with words and in awe of her sister's poetic skill, Bell takes up painting instead of writing and Sellers portrays her using painterly language: "We placated each other by exaggerating our differences, renouncing all claim to the other's field. I, always less skilful with words than you, relinquished them to you entirely. I took painting for myself" (36). Each with her own tools—words and colors—expresses herself in her specific art, but each also keeps an attentive and jealous eye on the other's artistic productions.

Bell knows how to detect in her sister's novelistic technique the tools and concepts borrowed from painting. Woolf absorbs them and puts them into practice, thus creating a revolution in the art of fiction: "You will apply [Clive Bell's] precepts to your writing. For all your affected disdain, it is my art that is showing you the way" (48). Woolf acknowledges the supremacy of painting in depicting emotions: "You hold the light. Then there are lonely moths like me circling the lamp, searching for away in" (143); "There is no doubt painting is leading the way. Fiction has forgotten its purpose" (74). It is Bell who opens the way to artistic experimentation and innovation and thanks to her sister and other artists with whom she is in close contact in Bloomsbury, Woolf "unlearns" (74) the purpose of conventional fiction and gropes her way towards what proves to become the essence of her writing. Her new method of writing contains the pictorial principles of fluidity, dynamism, choice and distribution of colors and light.

This novel, which is ultimately about borrowings, imitations, and mirror effects, reflects the sisters' arts, its aim being to capture the point of view of a painter and at the same time to express this vision with the words of a writer. Sellers's biofiction constitutes the scriptural space in which the two arts converge. Like Lippincott, Cunningham, and Nunez, Sellers draws the portrait of the eponymous sisters in the spirit of their arts—which is to say by borrowing their styles and artistic tools. For instance, Sellers adopts the Woolfian narrative method which consists of plunging into the characters' meandering thoughts—the movement of each woman's consciousness and inner life is closely followed and observed—evoking the complexity of domesticity and rendering the throb and minuteness of their private lives. Similarities to Woolf's own prose style—the rhythm of her lyrical prose, the use of arresting, overworked images, the intensity of syntactically complex sentences, the attention conferred to details, magnifying close-ups on minute objects and trivial events that have a significant impact on the subject's consciousness, motifs and refrains that resonate at precise moments throughout the narration, and so forth—are immediately detectable in this biofiction. Woolf's life and art are depicted with her very own palette, resurrecting the figure of the author in the twentieth-first century, and prolonging her modernist writing in its postmodernist literary heir. Sellers masters the art of the light pastiche,[11] a looser form of literary imitation than the detailed and meticulous close imitation practiced by Lippincott or Cunningham, for example. Her prose is proof of an intimate knowledge of the Woolf's corpus, and the result evinces her literary skill in mimesis, adapting Woolf's style and Bell's point of view in a novel that fuses the portraits of the two artists.

Like Cunningham, Sellers re-imagines and reconstructs the most famous and iconic event in twentieth-century British literature, and the most dramatic episode associated with Woolf: the drowning scene. Sellers recasts Bell in Woolf's role, allowing the fateful moment to be indeed witnessed through Bell's haunting thoughts. She visualizes the suicide scene, imagining her sister filling her pockets with stones, vicariously feeling the "paralyzing cold" and the weight of the wet clothes as Woolf "force[s] [herself] forward": "The water is in my mouth, my lungs, as the river drags us under" (177). The first-person plural pronoun, "us," grammatically marks the ultimate fusion between Woolf and Bell: the latter feels her sister's sensations of the tragic gesture in her own flesh and body.

Fiction gives writer-biographers the freedom to play with chronology and be selective: time is elastic and fluctuant, allowing prolepses and analepses as well as close-ups and freeze-frames on details or epiphanic moments laden with utmost significance. Fiction also allows them to flirt with the truth, to fill in the gaps left by traditional biography, to prolong facts mentioned in historical documents, and to explore the characters' thoughts in order to imagine what they might have felt. Authors of biofiction do not contradict historical events, but the genre they adopt authorizes them to incorporate new, original, and personal elements, such as their own experiences. In the case of *Vanessa and Virginia,* Sellers confessed in an interview that she poured her sisterly feelings into the novel to represent the privileged relationship between her two protagonists.[12] Consequently, Woolf's life as portrayed by Sellers resembles both the writer-biographer's and the biographized's, thus creating a strong affiliation between Sellers and Woolf. Sellers has compared the relationship between biography and biofiction to photography and painting, two arts that contain similarities in terms of representation, the difference being that a photograph is strictly mimetic while painting always allows room for interpretation, expressed in the form of added lines, colors, or shades, that are not necessarily in the model, but that are summoned by the composition to offer an original vision of the model.[13]

Lippincott, Cunningham, Nunez, and Sellers all have a deep knowledge of their subject and the biographèmes they have selected are used as solid factual scaffolding upon which to base their novels in order to confer authenticity to their biofictions. Sellers is comfortably intimate with Woolf's life and work, and Woolf's erudition is distilled in Sellers's fiction in a more subtle and sophisticated way than in Nunez's work, where highly didactic and explicit passages erupt in the narration: Nunez's novel bears the heavy, overpowering imprint of documentary evidence. Indeed, *Mitz* discloses too much the threadbare fabric of biography. Sellers seems to "serve extremely well under two masters"; she is better at the art of processing real details and fusing them with imagination. Stitches, hems, and hinges between biography and fiction—roughly visible in *Mitz*—are hardly distinguishable in *Vanessa and Virginia*. The fusion is smoother, more fluid, effortless, and the result is a coherent, seamless, fictitious memoir.

Biofiction is a flourishing genre appreciated by readers and critically successful on the English-speaking literary scene. In a traditional biography, the reader is confronted with a multitude of raw and arid facts and information that are difficult to process and assimilate. Enveloping lives in a layer of fiction brings along the comfort and the pleasure of reading a different kind of story that appeals more to the modern reader, as the resulting literary product has a more accelerated narrative rhythm and contains dialogues and a plot.

The readers' passion[14] for this genre confirms the fascination they have for the lives of figures who have had an important impact on our literary, cultural, or artistic traditions. Based on minute and rigorous biographic research, biofiction goes beyond the constraints of traditional life writing to provide an engrossing afterlife or a riveting reconstruction of the larger-than-life historical figure. The examples given in this essay tend to make Virginia Woolf more accessible to a wider reading public, not only by popularizing her literary style, but also by portraying her as a fragile writer fighting her tormenting demons. These biofictions revalorize the biographized who is resuscitated in the twenty-first century: Woolf comes back to life in contemporary novels that, in turn, use her own oeuvre and idiosyncratic style as a backbone. The reinvention of Woolf amounts to a continuous renaissance and reassessment of her life and work. Thanks to these biofictions, the figure of the author is constantly updated to adapt to new readers and reading practices. The biographized becomes the reflection of the writers-biographers, their epoch, and their readers.

Though biofiction is popular and pleasurable to read, as a genre it has created some difficulties for its critics. They suggest it might only select and reinforce stereotypes conveyed by a handful of biographèmes that may caricature shortcuts of the subject's life, particularly those well-known facts expected by readers. In contradistinction to readers and the authors themselves, critics argue that such books offer the reader only a simplified figure of the complex author ("Virginia Woolf lite" [Rubenstein 3]) as well as watered-down versions of her novels. In addition, these novels rely heavily on the reader's ability to recognize the specific borrowed and recycled Woolfian stylistic and generic *topoi*. However, what happens at the reception level when less-knowledgeable readers do not recognize them? What does their pleasure in reading consist of? This is the reason why the literary product offered by the author of a biofiction must necessarily combine the right amount of erudition and vulgarizing. The author must feel constrained "not by his own free will but by some powerful and unscrupulous tyrant who has him in thrall" (V. Woolf, "Modern Fiction" 160)—that is to say by the necessity to meet the readers' expectations—to throw in the stereotypical, recognizable ingredients which compose the common reader's implied image of Virginia Woolf. Especially after the release of Stephen Daldry's adaptation of *The Hours,* Woolfian critics pointed out the clichéd representation of the modernist author as a restless, tormented and neurotic artist.[15] Lastly, critics question the practice of writing such books, some of them castigating the lack of creativity of authors who engage their efforts in a genre that relies on other works and that appropriates historical figures. Jonathan Dee has considered ten recent novels, by biofiction writers such as Michael Cunningham, J. M. Coetzee, Norman Mailer, and Don DeLillo, that employ flesh-and-blood people who become characters. Dee has pronounced the trend a "veritable epidemic" which has spread "in the last twenty-five years or so" (77).

However, biofiction reflects deeper writing practices and current cultural phenomena. The novels I address here use postmodernist techniques similar to sampling in music, or recycling and collage in the visual arts; these intertextual practices consist of selecting fragments from previous works and integrating them in contemporary productions. Besides, the fundamental process at the heart of biofiction is manipulating the truth and recreating a reality that can appear "hyper-real"—more real than reality itself—an understanding that corresponds to the contemporary view that absolutely objective historical truth does not exist.

Moreover, biofiction constitutes our modern myths: the mythmaking process depends on the extraordinary stories of the historical figures and the writer-biographer's ability to combine fact and fiction. Like Roman and Greek myth writers in the past, our contemporary writers tell the stories of the heroes or gods who captivate and intrigue them. The role of the biofiction I have examined in this essay is to reconstruct and expand the myth around Virginia Woolf: Lippincott, Cunningham, Nunez, and Sellers, by exploring the modernist author's imaginary lives, keep alive the public's fascination with her personality, her tormented life, and premature death.

Université de Lorraine

Notes

1 See Barthes's notion of biographèmes as kernels of truth or biographical shortcuts that condense a whole life. (Barthes, *Chambre* 54).

2 In French, Buisine coined this neologism.

3 Among the numerous biographies of Woolf, see Bell, *Virginia*; Lee, *Virginia Woolf*; and Briggs.

4 "I was struck by the organization of the words on the page. Woolf had written them in short, jagged half-lines, as if she could hardly get to the end of the

sentences. I reproduced the letter in my book as it looked on the page, almost like a poem" (Lee, *Nose* 40).

5 See Barthes for a discussion of this term.

6 "Écriture à programme" (writing according to plan) and "écriture à processus" (writing that is open to any contingency along the way) are Hay's terms (313).

7 "I read it [*Leaves of Grass*] in college, and I loved it. It didn't enter my DNA the way *Mrs. Dalloway* did—I lost my virginity to *Mrs. Dalloway*, and that can only happen once" (Cunningham, Interview).

8 See Jameson's definition of pastiche: "Pastiche is, like parody, the imitation of a peculiar or unique, idiosyncratic style, the wearing of a linguistic mask, speech in a dead language. But it is a neutral practice of such mimicry, without any of parody's ulterior motives, amputated of the satiric impulse, devoid of laughter" (17).

9 The motto of the novel is a biographème: "At that time I had a marmoset called Mitz which accompanied me everywhere, sitting on my shoulder or inside my waistcoat" (L. Woolf 16).

10 Virginia Woolf left nearly four thousand letters and a thirty-volume diary.

11 However, in an interview, Sellers states that by having adopted Bell's point of view, she was attempting to avoid literary pastiche:

> Virginia Woolf's style is so distinctive and I know her work so well, that I think if I had written from her point of view I might well have ended up with literary pastiche. Vanessa, on the other hand, was often described by contemporaries as the silent sister—a woman of relatively few words. We do have many letters by Vanessa and a few essays, but their style is more prosaic and not as familiar to me as Virginia's. I also liked the idea of writing from the viewpoint of a painter. (Interview by Lisa Glass)

"Given the sister's close relationship, I wanted to evoke Virginia's interior, poetic, lyrical writing style; but I did not want to produce a pastiche—and because I wanted to tell the story from Vanessa's viewpoint I knew I had to write with a painter's voice" ("US Interview").

12 "I know that I brought some of my own life-experience to the sisters' relationship. I've always been fascinated by the way our early dealings with our siblings mould who we are and continue to resonate in our adult relationships. Like Vanessa Bell, I'm the eldest in my family and could empathize with Vanessa's sense of responsibility towards the younger Virginia—as well as her pleasure in and at times intense resentment of her sister's success!" (Interview by Caroline Leavitt).

13 "I imagine the differences between straight biography and what I have done with the sisters' story are similar to those between a photograph and a painting: where the photographer aims for a true likeness, the painter offers an individual view—refocusing, highlighting, and sometimes adding lines or colors that are not in the original but which the composition appears to call for" (Sellers, "Writing").

14 My contention about the popularity of biofictions is based on their profusion on the book market. Some of them (for instance, Hilary Mantel's *Wolf Hall* and *Bring Up the Bodies*, and Colm Toibin's *The Master*) have been highly

acclaimed by critics and have won prestigious book prizes, and as a result have become bestsellers. Besides, the literary critics' growing interest in this genre is evinced by the numerous studies in the field. See, for example, Middeke and Huber.

15 See, among others, Lee, *Nose* 37–62.

Works cited

Barthes, Roland. *La Chambre Claire, Note sur la Photographie*. Paris: Gallimard, 1980. Print.

—. "The Reality Effect." *The Rustle of Language*. Trans. Richard Howard. Oxford: Blackwell, 1986. 141–48. Print.

Bell, Quentin. *Bloomsbury Recalled*. New York: Columbia UP, 1996. Print.

—. *Virginia Woolf: A Biography*. London: Pimlico, 1996. Print.

Briggs, Julia. *Virginia Woolf: An Inner Life*. London: Allen Lane, 2005. Print.

Buisine, Alain. "Biofictions." *Revue des Sciences Humaines* 224 (1991): 7–13. Print.

Cunningham, Michael. *The Hours*. New York: Picador, 2000. Print.

—. Interview by David Small. *Same Old, Brand New Michael Cunningham. PowellsBook. Blog*. Powell's City of Books, 11 Jun. 2005. Web. Jan. 2011.

Dee, Jonathan. "The Reanimators: On the Art of Literary Graverobbing." *Harpers* June 1999: 76–84. Print.

Edel, Leon. *Henry James: A Life*. 2 vols. London: Flamingo, 1996. Print.

Hay, Louis. "La Troisième Dimension de la Littérature." *Texte* 5/6 (1986–1987): 313–28. Print.

Jameson, Frederic. *Postmodernism, or, the Cultural Logic of Late Capitalism*. Durham: Duke UP, 1991. Print.

Lee, Hermione. "Ms. Browns Secret." Review of *The Hours* by Michael Cunningham. *Times Literary Supplement* 8 Jan. 1999: 19. Print.

—. *Virginia Woolf*. London: Vintage, 1997. Print.

—. *Virginia Woolf's Nose: Essays on Biography*. Princeton: Princeton UP, 2005. Print.

Lippincott, Robin. *Mr. Dalloway*. Louisville: Sarabande, 1999. Print.

McNeillie, Andrew, ed. *The Essays of Virginia Woolf: 1925–1928*. Vol. 4. New York: Harcourt, 1994. Print.

Middeke, Martin, and Werner Huber, eds. *Biofictions: The Rewriting of Romantic Lives in Contemporary Fiction and Drama*. Rochester, NY: Camden House, 1999. Print.

Nunez, Sigrid. *Mitz: The Marmoset of Bloomsbury*. London: Harper Collins, 1999. Print.

—. *Mitz: The Marmoset of Bloomsbury*. New York: Soft Skull, 2007. Print.

Rubenstein, Roberta. "Outlook." *Washington Post* 26 Jan. 2003: 3. Print.

Saunders, Mark. "Biography and Autobiography." *The Cambridge History of Twentieth-Century English Literature*. Ed. Laura Marcus and Peter Nicholls. Cambridge: Cambridge UP, 2005. 286–303. Print.

Sellers, Susan. Interview by Lisa Glass. *"Interview with Novelist and Virginia Woolf Expert, Susan Sellers + Giveaway." Vulpes Libris*. Wordpress, 17 Feb. 2009. Web. Jan. 2011.

—. Interview by Caroline Leavittville. "*Read This Book: Vanessa and Virginia.*" *CAROLINELEAVITTVILLE.* Blogspot, 25 June 2009. Web. Jan.2011.
—. "US Interview." *Susan Sellers.* Wordpress, n.d. Web. Jan. 2011.
—. *Vanessa and Virginia.* London: Two Ravens, 2008. Print.
—. "Writing Vanessa and Virginia." *Two Ravens Press.* Two Ravens Press, n.d. Web. Jan. 2011.
Woolf, Leonard. *Downhill All the Way: An Autobiography of the Years 1919–1939.* London: Hogarth, 1967. Print.
Woolf, Virginia. *The Diary of Virginia Woolf.* 5 vols. Ed. Ann Olivier Bell. London: Penguin, 1979–1985. Print.
—. "Modern Fiction." McNeillie 157–65.
—. "The New Biography." McNeillie 473–80.

BIBLIOGRAPHY

Primary source material

Ackroyd, Peter (1987), *Chatterton*. New York: Grove Press.
Ackroyd, Peter (2006), *The Lambs of London: A Novel*. New York: Nan A. Talese.
Ackroyd, Peter (1983), *The Last Testament of Oscar Wilde*. New York: Harper & Row.
Alexander, Robert (2006), *Rasputin's Daughter*. New York: Viking.
Allende, Isabel (2006), *Ines of My Soul*. New York: HarperCollins.
Alvarez, Julia (2001), *In the Name of Salome*. Chapel Hill: Algonquin Books.
Alvarez, Julia (1994), *In the Time of the Butterflies*. Chapel Hill: Algonquin Books.
Asch, Sholem (1939), *The Nazarene*. New York: Carroll & Graff.
Atkins, Eileen (1995), *Vita and Virginia*. London: S. French.
Attenberg, Jami (2015), *Saint Mazie: A Novel*. New York: Grand Central Publishing.
Atwood, Margaret (1996), *Alias Grace*. Toronto: McClelland & Stewart.
Bainbridge, Beryl (2001), *According to Queeney*. New York: Carroll & Graff Publishers.
Balfour-Paul, Jenny (2015), *Deeper than Indigo: Tracing Thomas Machell, Forgotten Explorer*. Surrey: Medina Publishing.
Banks, Russell (1998), *Cloudsplitter*. New York: HarperPerennial.
Banville, John (1976), *Doctor Copernicus*. New York: W.W. Norton & Company.
Barber, Ros (2012), *The Marlowe Papers*. London: Sceptre.
Barker, Pat (1991), *Regeneration*. New York: Plume.
Barnes, Julian (2005), *Arthur and George*. New York: Alfred A. Knopf.
Barnes, Julian (1984), *Flaubert's Parrot*. New York: McGraw-Hill.
Barnes, Julian (2016), *The Noise of Time: A Novel*. New York: Knopf.
Barrett, William E. (1938), *Woman on Horseback: The Biography of Francisco Lopez and Eliza Lynch*. New York: F.A. Stokes.
Barron, Stephanie (2009), *The White Garden*. New York: Random House, 2009.
Beattie, Ann (2011), *Mrs. Nixon: A Novelist Imagines a Life*. New York: Scribner.
Bell, Madison Smartt (1995), *All Souls' Rising*. New York: Vintage Books.
Bell, Madison Smartt (2009), *Devil's Dream*. New York: Vintage Books.
Bell, Madison Smartt (2000), *Master of the Crossroads*. New York: Pantheon.
Bell, Madison Smartt (2004), *The Stone That the Builder Refused*. New York: Pantheon.
Benjamin, Melanie (2010) *Alice I Have Been: A Novel*. New York: Bantam Books.
Benjamin, Melanie (2011), *The Autobiography of Mrs. Tom Thumb*. New York: Bantam Books.

Benjamin, Melanie (2013), *The Aviator's Wife: A Novel*. New York: Bantam Books.
Bergman, Megan Mayhew (2015), *Almost Famous Women: Stories*. New York: Scribner.
Binet, Laurent (2013), *HHhH*. London: Vintage Books.
Bontemps, Arna (1936), *Black Thunder: Gabriel's Revolt: Virginia, 1800*. Boston: Beacon Press.
Boyle, T. C. (2004), *The Inner Circle*. New York: Penguin Books.
Boyle, T. C. (2009), *The Women: A Novel*. New York: Viking.
Bradbury, Malcolm (2000), *To the Hermitage*. New York: Overlook Press.
Broch, Hermann (1945), *The Death of Virgil*. New York: Grosset & Dunlap.
Brooks, Geraldine (2011), *Caleb's Crossing*. New York: Penguin Books.
Brooks, Geraldine (2015), *The Secret Chord: A Novel*. New York: Viking.
Buck, Pearl S. (1956), *Imperial Woman*. New York: J. Day Co.
Buechner, Fredrick (1993), *Son of Laughter*. New York: Harper One.
Burgess, Anthony (1977), *Abba Abba*. Boston: Little, Brown and Company.
Burgess, Anthony (1988), *A Dead Man in Deptford*. New York: Carroll & Graff Publishers.
Burgess, Anthony (1974), *Napoleon Symphony*. New York: W.W. Norton and Co.
Burgess, Anthony (1964), *Nothing Like the Sun: A Story of Shakespeare's Love Life*. New York: W.W. Norton and Co.
Burnett, Constance Buel (1955), *The Silver Answer: A Romantic Biography of Elizabeth Barrett Browning*. New York: Alfred A. Knopf.
Burns, Mary F. (2013), *Portraits of an Artist: A Novel about John Singer Sargent*. San Mateo, CA: Sand Hill Review Press.
Busch, Frederick (1975), *The Mutual Friend*. New York: Harper & Row.
Cantor, Jay (1983), *The Death of Che Guevara*. New York: Vintage Contemporaries.
Capote, Truman (1965), *In Cold Blood: A True Account of a Multiple Murder and Its Consequences*. New York: Random House.
Carey, Peter (2000), *True History of the Kelly Gang*. New York: Vintage International.
Caute, David (1961), *Comrade Jacob*. New York: Pantheon Books.
Cezair-Thompson (2007), *The Pirate's Daughter*. New York: Random House.
Charyn, Jerome (2014), *I am Abraham: A Novel of Lincoln and the Civil War*. New York: Liveright Publishing.
Charyn, Jerome (2010), *The Secret Life of Emily Dickinson*. New York: Norton.
Chase-Riboud, Barbara (2003), *Hottentot Venus: A Novel*. New York: Anchor Books.
Chase-Riboud, Barbara (1994), *The President's Daughter: A Novel*. Chicago: Chicago Review Press.
Chase-Riboud, Barbara (1979), *Sally Hemings: A Novel*. New York: St. Martin's Press.
Chevalier, Tracy (2009), *Remarkable Creatures*. London: Harper.
Chiaverini, Jennifer (2013), *Mrs. Lincoln's Dressmaker*. New York: Plume.
Coetzee, J. M. (1994), *The Master of Petersburg*. New York: Viking.
Cooke Newman, Janis (2006), *Mary: Mrs. A. Lincoln*. Orlando: Harcourt.
Coover, Robert (1976), *The Public Burning*. New York: The Viking Press.
Cullen, Lynn (2014), *Mrs. Poe*. New York: Gallery Books.
Cunningham, Mark Allen (2007), *Lost Son: A Novel*. Denver: Unbridled Books.

Cunningham, Michael (1998), *The Hours: A Novel*. New York: Picador.
Cutter, Kimberly (2011), *The Maid*. New York: Houghton Mifflin Harcourt.
Dalby, Liza (2001), *The Tale of Murasaki: A Novel*. 2000. New York: Anchor Books.
Davenport, Guy (1979), *Da Vinci's Bicycle: Ten Stories by Guy Davenport*. Baltimore: Johns Hopkins University Press.
Davenport, Guy (1970), *Tatlin!* Baltimore: Johns Hopkins University Press.
Davis, Kathryn (2002), *Versailles*. New York: Houghton Mifflin.
Dawson, Jill (2001), *Fred & Edie*. New York: Welcome Rain Publishers.
Dawson, Jill (2009), *The Great Lover: A Novel*. New York: Harper Perennial.
Dawson, Jill (2011), *Lucky Bunny*. London: Sceptre.
Dawson, Jill (2003), *Wild Boy*. London: Sceptre.
De Chellis Hill, Carol (1993), *Henry James' Midnight Song*. New York: Poseidon Press.
Delbanco, Nicholas (2008), *The Count of Concord: A Novel*. Champaign: Dalkey Archive Press.
Del Giudice, Daniele (1983), *Lo Stadio di Wimbledon*. Torino: Einaudi.
DeLillo, Don (1988), *Libra*. New York: Penguin Books.
Diamant, Anita (1997), *The Red Tent: A Novel*. New York: Picador.
Diliberto, Gioia (2004), *I am Madame X: A Novel*. New York: Lisa Drew Book/ Scribner.
Dobbs, Michael (2008), *Churchill's Triumph: A Novel of Betrayal*. Naperville, IL: Sourcebooks Landmark.
Doctorow, E. L. (2009), *Homer and Langley: A Novel*. New York: Random House.
Donoghue, Emma (2004), *Life Mask*. London: Virago.
Duffy, Bruce (2011), *Disaster Was My God: A Novel of the Outlaw Life of Arthur Rimbaud*. New York: Doubleday.
Duffy, Bruce (1987), *The World As I Found It*. New York: New York Review Books.
Dunmore, Helen (1993), *Zennor in Darkness*. London: Penguin Books.
Dyer, Geoff (1996), *But Beautiful: A Book About Jazz*. New York: Picador.
Ebershoff, David (2000), *The Danish Girl*. New York: Penguin Books.
Ebershoff, David (2008), *The Nineteenth Wife*. New York: Random House.
Ehrlich, Leonard (1932), *God's Angry Man*. New York: Simon and Schuster.
Ellison, Ralph (1952), *Invisible Man*. New York: Vintage Books.
Endore, Guy (1934), *Babouk*. New York: Monthly Review Press.
Endore, Guy (1956), *King of Paris: A Novel*. New York: Simon and Schuster, 1956.
Endore, Guy (1965), *Satan's Saint: A Novel about the Marquis de Sade*. New York: Crown Publishers, Inc.
Endore, Guy (1961), *Voltaire! Voltaire!*. New York: Simon and Schuster.
Enright, Anne (2002), *The Pleasure of Eliza Lynch*. London: Vintage Books.
Fermi, Sarah (2006), *Emily's Journal*. Cambridge: Pegasus.
Fish, Laura (2008), *Strange Music*. London: Jonathan Cape.
Fitzgerald, Penelope (1995), *The Blue Flower*. New York: Mariner Books.
Flanagan, Richard (2001), *Gould's Book of Fish: A Novel in Twelve Fish*. New York: Grove Press.
Ford, Ford Madox (1963), *The Fifth Queen*. New York: The Vanguard Press.
Forster, Margaret (1990), *Lady's Maid*. New York: Doubleday.
Fortin, Roger A. (1990), *One Man's Justice: George Remus, a Cincinnati Legend*. Cincinnati: Ohio Bookstore.

Foulds, Adam (2009), *The Quickening Maze*. London: Jonathan Cape.
Fowler, Therese Anne (2013), *Z: A Novel of Zelda Fitzgerald*. New York: St. Martin's Press.
Frank, Bruno (1935), *A Man Called Cervantes*. New York: Popular Library.
Freeman, Gillian (2006), *But Nobody Lives in Bloomsbury*. London: Arcadia Books.
Gael, Juliet (2010), *Romancing Miss Bronte*. New York: Ballantine Books.
Galloway, Janice (2002), *Clara: A Novel*. New York: Simon & Schuster.
Garrett, George (1971), *The Death of the Fox*. New York: Doubleday & Company, Inc..
Gedge, Pauline (1977), *Child of the Morning: A Novel*. Chicago: Penguin.
Gee, Maggie (2014), *Virginia Woolf in Manhattan*. London: Telegram.
George, Margaret (1986), *The Autobiography of King Henry VII, With Notes by his Fool, Will Somers: A Novel*. New York: St. Martin's Press.
George, Margaret (2011), *Elizabeth I*. New York: Viking.
George, Margaret (2006), *Helen of Troy*. New York: Viking.
George, Margaret (2002), *Mary, Called Magdalene*. New York: Viking.
George, Margaret (1992), *Mary Queen of Scotland and the Isles: A Novel*. New York: St. Martin's Press.
George, Margaret (1997), *The Memoirs of Cleopatra: A Novel*. New York: St. Martin's Press.
Gerson, Noel B. (1960), *The Yankee from Tennessee*. Garden City, New York: Doubleday & Company.
Glancy, Diane (2004), *Stone Heart: A Novel of Sacajawea*. New York: Overlook Press.
Graves, Robert (1938), *Count Belisarius*. New York: Penguin Books.
Graves, Robert (1960), *Food for Centaurs: Stories, Talks, Critical Studies, Poems*. New York: Doubleday.
Graves, Robert (1934), *I, Claudius*. New York: Modern Library.
Graves, Robert (1944), *Wife to Mr. Milton: The Story of Marie Powell*. New York: Noonday Press.
Griffith, Nicola (2013), *Hild: A Novel*. New York: Farrar, Straus and Giroux.
Groosman, Austin (2015), *Crooked*. New York, Boston, and London: Mulholland Books.
Gross, Joel (1987), *Sarah: A Novel of Sarah Bernhardt*. New York: William Morrow and Company.
Hall, Brian (2008), *Fall of Frost*. New York: Viking.
Hall, Brian (2003), *I Should Be Extremely Happy in Your Company: A Novel of Lewis and Clark*. New York: Penguin Books.
Halter, Marek (2007), *Lilah*. New York: Crown Publishers.
Halter, Marek (2008), *Mary of Nazareth: A Novel*. New York: Crown Publishers.
Halter, Marek (2003), *Sarah*. New York: Crown Publishers.
Halter, Marek (2006), *Zipporah, Wife of Moses*. New York: Crown Publishers.
Hamer, Mary (2012), *Kiping & Trix*. Twickenham: Aurora Metro Books.
Hansen, Brooks (2003), *The Monsters of St. Helena*. New York: Picador.
Hansen, Ron (1983), *The Assassination of Jesse James by the Coward Robert Ford*. New York: Harper Perennial.
Hansen, Ron (1969), *Desperadoes*. New York: Harper Perennial.

Hansen, Ron (2008), *Exiles*. New York: Picador.
Hansen, Ron (1999), *Hitler's Niece*. New York, Harper Perennial.
Harig, Ludwig (1978), *Rousseau: Der Roman vom Ursprung der Natur im Gehirn*. Augsburg: Carl Hanser Verlag.
Hartling, Peter (1976), *Holderlin: Ein Roman*. Munich: Luchterhand.
Hawkes, Ellen, and Peter Manso (1983), *The Shadow of the Moth: A Novel of Espionage with Virginia Woolf*. New York: St. Martin's.
Hickey, Elizabeth (2005), *The Painted Kiss*. New York: Washington Square Press.
Himmich, Bensalem (2011), *A Muslim Suicide*. Trans. Roger Allen. Syracuse: Syracuse University Press.
Himmich, Bensalem (2004), *The Polymath*. Trans. Roger Allen. Cairo and New York: The American University in Cairo Press.
Himmich, Bensalem (2005), *The Theocrat*. Trans. Roger Allen. Cairo and New York: The American University in Cairo Press.
Holden, Craig (2002), *The Jazz Bird*. New York: Simon & Schuster.
Horan, Nancy (2007), *Loving Frank*. New York, Ballantine Books.
Hughes, Glyn (1996), *Bronte: A Novel*. New York: St. Martin's Press.
Humphreys, Helen (2002), *The Lost Garden*. New York: Norton.
Hunt, Samantha (2008), *The Invention of Everything Else*. New York: Houghton Mifflin.
Hunter, Evan (1984), *Lizzie*. Westminster: Arbor House Publishing Co.
Hurston, Zora Neale (2011), "from HEROD THE GREAT." Edited by Michael Lackey. *Callaloo* 34(1) (Winter): 121–25.
Hurston, Zora Neale (1939), *Moses, Man of the Mountain*. New York: Harper Perennial.
Hustvedt, Siri (2014), *The Blazing World: A Novel*. New York: Simon & Schuster.
James, Syrie (2008), *The Lost Memoirs of Jane Austen*. New York: Avon.
James, Syrie (2009), *The Secret Diaries of Charlotte Brontë*. New York: Avon.
Johnston, Wayne (1998), *The Colony of Unrequited Dreams*. New York: Anchor Books.
Jones, Sherry (2012), *Four Sisters, All Queens*. New York: Gallery Books.
Jones, Sherry (2008), *The Jewel of Medina: A Novel*. New York: Beaufort Books.
Jones, Sherry (2009), *The Sword of Medina: A Novel*. New York: Beaufort Books.
Jong, Erica (2003), *Sappho's Leap*. New York: Norton.
Kanner, Rebecca (2015), *Esther*. New York: Howard Books.
Kanner, Rebecca (2013), *Sinners and the Sea: The Untold Story of Noah's Wife*. New York: Howard Books.
Kazantzakis, Nikos (1960), *The Last Temptation of Christ*. Trans. P. A. Bien. New York: Scribner Paperback Fiction.
Keane, Mary Beth (2013), *Fever: A Novel*. New York: Scribner.
Kehlmann, Daniel (2005), *Measuring the World: A Novel*. New York: Vintage Books.
King, Susan Fraser (2009), *Lady Macbeth*. Istanbul: Artemis.
King, Susan Fraser (2010), *Queen Hereafter*. New York: Crown.
Kobek, Jarett (2011), *Atta & The Whitman of Tikrit*. Cambridge: The MIT Press.
Kohn, Rebecca (2004), *The Gilded Chamber: A Novel of Queen Esther*. New York: Rugged Land, LLC.
Korda, Michael (1993), *The Immortals*. New York: Simon and Schuster.

Kramer, Kathryn (1998), *Sweet Water.* New York: Alfred A. Knopf.
Kristeva, Julia (2015), *Teresa, My Love: An Imagined Life of the Saint of Avila.* Trans. Lorna Scott Fox. New York: Columbia University Press.
Kulyk Keefer, Janice (2004), *Thieves.* Sydney: Harper Collins.
Lappin, Linda (2008), *Katherine's Wish.* La Grande, Oregon: Wordcraft of Oregon.
Larsen, Deborah (2002), *The White.* New York: Alfred A. Knopf.
Lefland, Ella (1990), *The Knight, Death and the Devil.* New York: William Morrow & Company.
Lerman, Rhoda (1979), *Eleanor: A Novel.* New York: Holt, Rinehart, and Winston.
Leveen, Lois (2012), *The Secrets of Mary Bowser.* New York: William Morrow.
Levin, Janna (2006), *A Madman Dreams of Turing Machines.* New York: Alfred A. Knopf.
Liebmann-Smith, Richard (2008), *The James Boys: A Novel Account of Four Desperate Brothers.* New York: Random House.
Lodge, David (2004), *Author, Author.* New York: Viking.
Lodge, David (2011), *A Man of Parts.* New York: Viking.
Lourie, Richard (1999), *The Autobiography of Joseph Stalin.* Washington, DC: Counterpoint.
Lyon, Annabel (2009), *The Golden Mean: A Novel of Aristotle and Alexander the Great.* New York: Vintage Books.
Mack, Karen, and Jennifer Kaufman (2013), *Freud's Mistress.* New York: Berkley Books.
MacKenna, John (1993), *Clare: A Novel.* Belfast: The Blackstaff Press.
Maguire, Elizabeth (2008), *The Open Door.* New York: Other Press.
Mailer, Norman (1994), *The Armies of the Night: History as a Novel, The Novel as History.* New York: Plume.
Mailer, Norman (2007), *The Castle in the Forest.* New York: Random House.
Mailer, Norman (1979), *The Executioner's Song.* New York: Vintage Books.
Mailer, Norman (1997), *The Gospel According to the Son.* New York: Random House.
Maine, David (2006), *The Book of Samson.* New York: St. Martin's Press.
Maine, David (2005), *Fallen.* New York: St. Martin's Press.
Maine, David (2004), *The Preservationist.* New York: St. Martin's Press.
Mallon, Thomas (1994), *Henry and Clara: A Novel.* New York: Picador.
Mallon, Thomas (1997), *Dewey Defeats Truman.* New York: Pantheon Books.
Malouf, David (1978), *An Imaginary Life: A Novel.* New York: George Braziller, Inc.
Mamet, David (1997), *The Old Religion.* New York: The Free Press.
Manguel, Alberton (2002), *Stevenson Under the Palm Trees.* New York: Canongate U.S.
Mann, Heinrich (1935), *Die Jugend des Konigs, Henri Quatre.* Berlin: Aufbau-Verlag.
Mann, Thomas (1943), *Joseph and His Brothers.* New York: Alfred A. Knopf.
Mann, Thomas (1939), *Lotte in Weimar: The Beloved Returns.* Oakland: University of California Press.
Mantel, Hilary (2012), *Bring up the Bodies.* New York: Henry Holt and Company.
Mantel, Hilary (2009), *Wolf Hall.* London: Fourth Estate.
Markovits, Benjamin (2008), *A Quiet Adjustment.* New York: Norton.
Markovits, Benjamin (2007), *Imposture: A Novel.* New York: Norton.

Marquez, Gabriel Garcia (2003), *The General in his Labyrinth*. New York: Vintage Books.
Matthiessen, Peter (1990), *Killing Mr. Watson*. New York: Vintage Books.
Maugham, W. Somerset (1946), *Then and Now: A Novel*. New York: Vintage Classic.
May, Antoinette (2015), *The Determined Heart: The Tale of Mary Shelley and Her Frankenstein*. Seattle: Lake Union Publishing.
McCann, Colum (2003), *Dancer*. New York: Picador.
McCann, Colum (2013), *TransAtlantic*. New York: Random House.
McCunn, Ruthanne Lum (1988), *Thousand Pieces of Gold*. Boston: Beacon Press.
McLain, Paula (2015), *Circling the Sun: A Novel*. New York: Ballantine Books.
McLain, Paula (2011), *The Paris Wife*. New York: Ballantine Books.
McMurtry, Larry (1988), *Anything for Billy*. New York: Simon & Schuster.
McMurtry, Larry (1990), *Buffalo Girls*. New York: Simon & Schuster.
McMurtry, Larry (1997), *Zeke and Ned*. New York: Simon & Schuster.
McMurtry, Larry, and Diana Ossana (1994), *Pretty Boy Floyd*. New York: Simon & Schuster.
Melville, Herman (1854 [1982]), *Israel Potter: His Fifty Years of Exile*. Evanston and Chicago: Northwestern University Press.
Mercurio, Jed (2009), *American Adulterer*. New York: Simon and Schuster.
Mertens, Pierre (1997), *Shadowlight*. Trans. Edmund Jephcott. London: Perter Halban.
Michener, James (1990), *The Eagle and the Raven*. Austin: State House Press.
Min, Anchee (2001), *Becoming Madame Mao*. New York: Mariner Books.
Min, Anchee (2004), *Empress Orchid*. New York: Mariner Books.
Min, Anchee (2007), *The Last Empress*. New York: Mariner Books.
Moehring, J. R. (2012), *Sutton*. New York: Hyperion.
Monk Kidd, Sue (2014), *The Invention of Wings*. New York: Viking.
Moran, Michelle (2011), *Madame Tussaud: A Novel of the French Revolution*. New York: Broadway Paperbacks.
Morgan, Clare (2011), *A Book for All and None*. London: Weidenfeld and Nicolson.
Morgan, Jude (2009), *Charlotte and Emily: A Novel of the Brontes*. New York: St. Martin's Press.
Moses, Kate (2003), *Wintering: A Novel of Sylvia Plath*. New York: Anchor Books.
Motion, Andrew (2003), *The Invention of Dr. Cake*. London: Faber and Faber.
Mujica, Barbara (2013), *I am Venus: A Novel*. New York: Overlook Press.
Mujica, Barbara (2001), *Frida*. New York: Overlook Press.
Mujica, Barbara (2007), *Sister Teresa: A Novel*. New York: Overlook Press.
Muntz, Hope (1949), *The Golden Warrior: The Story of Harold and William*. New York: Charles Scribner's Sons.
Murphy, Yannick (2007), *Signed, Mata Hari: A Novel*. New York: Little, Brown and Company.
Najmi, Hassan (2014), *Gertrude: A Novel*. Northampton, MA: Interlink Books.
Naslund, Sena Jeter (2007), *Abundance: A Novel of Marie Antoinette*. 2006. New York: Harper Perennial.
Nunez, Sigrid (1998), *Mitz: The Marmoset of Bloomsbury*. New York: Harper Flamingo.

Oates, Joyce Carol (1992), *Black Water* New York: Plume.
Oates, Joyce Carol (2000), *Blonde*. New York: Harper Collins.
Oates, Joyce Carol (2008), *Wild Nights: Stories about the last days of Poe, Dickinson, Twain, James and Hemingway*. New York: Harper Perennial.
Olds, Bruce (2001), *Bucking the Tiger*. New York: Picador.
Olds, Bruce (1995), *Raising Holy Hell: A Novel*. New York: Picador.
Oliveira, Robin (2014), *I Always Loved You: A Story of Mary Cassatt and Edgar Degas*. New York: Viking.
Olsen, Lance (2007), *Anxious Pleasures: A Novel After Kafka*. Emeryville: Shoemaker & Hoard.
Olsen, Lance (2006), *Nietzsche's Kisses*. Tallahassee: Fiction Collective Two.
Oman, Carola (1929), *Miss Barrett's Elopement*. New York: Henry Holt and Company.
O'Reilly, Sally (2014), *Dark Amelia: A Novel of Shakespeare's Dark Lady*. New York: Picador.
Parini, Jay (1997), *Benjamin's Crossing: A Novel*. New York: Henry Holt.
Parini, Jay (2009), *The Last Station: A Novel of Tolstoy's Final Year.* 1990. New York: Anchor Books.
Parini, Jay (2010), *The Passages of H.M.: A Novel of Herman Melville*. New York: Anchor Books.
Parmar, Priya (2014), *Vanessa and Her Sister*. New York: Ballantine Books.
Pepper, Curtis Bill (2012), *Leonardo: A Biographical Novel*. Chambersburg: Alan C. Hood & Co.
Phillips, Caryl (2005), *Dancing in the Dark*. New York: Vintage International.
Phillips, Caryl (2007), *Foreigners*. New York: Vintage International.
Poniatowska, Elena (1996), *Tinisima: A Novel*. Trans. Katherine Silver. New York: Farrar, Strauss & Giroux.
Pullman, Philip (2011), *The Good Man Jesus and the Scoundrel Christ*. Edinburgh, London, New York, Melbourne: Canongate.
Pynchon, Thomas (1997), *Mason and Dixon*. New York: Picador.
Renault, Mary (1969), *Fire From Heaven*. New York: Vintage Books.
Renault, Mary (1958), *The King Must Die*. New York: Vintage Books.
Renault, Mary (1972), *The Persian Boy*. New York: Vintage Books.
Renault, Mary (1978), *The Praise Singer*. New York: Vintage Books.
Roberts, Michele (2003), *The Mistressclass*. New York: Henry Holt.
Robuck, Erika (2013), *Call Me Zelda: A Novel*. New York: New American Library.
Roessner, Michaela (1999), *The Stars Compel*. New York: TOR.
Roessner, Michaela (1997), *The Stars Dispose*. New York: Tor.
Roiphe, Katie (2001), *Still She Haunts Me*. New York: Dell Publishing.
Rosenthal, Amy (2008), *On the Rocks*. London: Oberon Books.
Russell, Mary Doria (2011), *Doc*. New York: Penguin.
Russell, Paul (2011), *The Unreal Life of Sergey Nabokov*. Berkley: Cleis Press.
Schmitt, Gladys (1961), *Rembrandt: A Novel*. New York: Random House.
Scott, Joanna (1990), *Arrogance*. New York: Picador.
Scott, Joanna (2014), *DePotter's Grand Tour: A Novel*. New York: Farrar, Strauss and Giroux.
Sellers, Susan (2009), *Vanessa and Virginia*. New York: Houghton Mifflin Harcourt.
Sharratt, Mary (2013), *Illuminations: A Novel of Hidegard von Bingen*. Boston and New York: Mariner Books.

Shiba, Ryotaro (1998), *The Last Shogun: The Life of Tokugawa Yoshinobu*. Trans. Juliet Winters Carpenter. New York, Tokyo, and London: Kodansha International.

Simmons, Dan (2009), *Drood*. New York: Little, Brown and Company.

Slotkin, Richard (2000), *Abe: A Novel of the Young Lincoln*. New York: Henry Holt.

Slouka, Mark (2002), *God's Fool*. New York: Knopf.

Sontag, Susan (1992), *The Volcano Lover*. New York: Picador.

Spargo, R. Clifton (2013), *Beautiful Fools: The Last Affair of Zelda and Scott Fitzgerald*. New York: Overlook Press.

Stacton, David (2011), *The Judges of the Secret Court*. New York: New York Review Books.

Stanush, Claude, and Michele Stanush (2003), *All Honest Men: A Biographical Novel*. Sag Harbor: Permanent Press.

Stead, C. K. (2004), *Mansfield*. London: The Harvill Press.

Stead, C. K. (2006), *My Name Was Judas*. London: Harvill Secker.

Steel, Byron (1927), *O Rare Ben Jonson*. New York: Alfred A. Knopf.

Stegner, Wallace (1971), *Angle of Repose*. New York: Penguin Books.

Stegner, Wallace (1950), *Joe Hill: A Biographical Novel*. New York: Doubleday & Company.

Stone, Irving (1961), *The Agony and the Ecstasy*. New York: Signet.

Stone, Irving (1985), *Depths of Glory*. New York: Doubleday.

Stone, Irving (1944), *Immortal Wife*. New York: Doubleday.

Stone, Irving (1961), *Love is Eternal*. New York: Doubleday.

Stone, Irving (1934), *Lust for Life*. New York: Plume.

Stone, Irving (1975), *The Greek Treasure*. New York: Doubleday.

Stone, Irving (1980), *The Origin: A Biographical Novel of Charles Darwin*. New York: Doubleday.

Stone, Irving (1971), *The Passions of the Mind*. New York: Doubleday.

Stone, Irving (1951), *The President's Lady*. New York: Doubleday.

Stone, Irving (1965), *Those Who Love: A Biographical Novel of Abigail and John Adams*. New York: Doubleday.

Strauss, Darin (2000), *Change and Eng*. New York: Plume.

Strauss, Darin (2002), *The Real McCoy*. New York: Plume.

Styron, William (1967), *The Confessions of Nat Turner*. Vintage International.

Sultan, Rosie (2012), *Helen Keller in Love*. New York: Viking.

Taylor, Alienora Judith (2015), *Riding at the Gates of Sixty: A Fictional Account of Virginia Woolf's Death – and Life*. CreateSpace Independent Publishing Platform.

Tennant, Emma (2001), *Sylvia and Ted: A Novel*. New York: Henry Holt and Company.

Todd, Kim (2007), *Chrysalis: Maria Sibylla Merion and the Secrets of Metamorphosis*. Orlando: Harcourt.

Tóibín, Colm (2004), *The Master: A Novel*. New York: Picador.

Tóibín, Colm (2012), *The Testament of Mary*. New York: Scribner.

Tripp, Dawn (2016), *Georgia: A Novel of Georgia O'Keeffe*. New York: Random House.

Troyanov, Iliya (2008), *The Collector of Worlds*. Trans. William Hobson. London: Faber and Faber.

Truss, Lynne (1996), *Tennyson's Gift*. London: Hamish Hamilton.

Tsypkin, Leonid (2001), *Summer in Baden-Baden*. Trans. Roger and Angela Keys. New York: Quartet Books, Ltd.
Tuck, Lily (2004), *The News from Paraguay*. New York: HarperCollins.
Uribe, Kirmen (2014), *Lo que mueve el mundo*. Barcelona: Planetas de Libros.
Urquhart, Jane (1993), *Changing Heaven*. Boston: David R. Godine.
Vargas Llosa, Mario (2010), *The Dream of the Celt*. New York: Farrar, Strauss and Giroux.
Vidal, Gore (1973), *Burr: A Novel*. New York: Ballantine Books.
Vidal, Gore (1962), *Julian: A Novel*. New York: Vintage International.
Vidal, Gore (1984), *Lincoln: A Novel*. New York: Vintage International.
Vincent, Norah (2015), *Adeline: A Novel of Virginia Woolf*. Boston: Houghton Mifflin Harcourt.
Vlasopolos, Anca (2007), *The New Bedford Samurai*. Kingsport, Tennessee: Twilight Times Books.
Vreeland, Susan (2012), *Clara and Mr. Tiffany*. New York: Random House.
Vreeland, Susan (2001), *The Forest Lover*. New York: Viking Books.
Vreeland, Susan (2003), *The Passion of Artemisia*. New York: Penguin Books.
Waite, Helen Elmira (1953), *How Do I Love Thee?: The Story of Elizabeth Barrett Browning*. Philadelphia: Macrae Smith.
Wallace, Carol (2011), *Leaving Van Gogh*. New York: Spiegel and Grau.
West, Paul (1989), *Lord Byron's Doctor*. Chicago: University of Chicago Press.
Wheeler, Richard S. (2002), *Eclipse: A Novel of Lewis and Clark*. New York: Tom Doherty Associates.
Wheeler, Richard S. (2003), *The Exile*. New York: Tom Doherty Associates.
White, Edmund (2003), *Fanny: A Fiction*. New York: Harper Collins.
White, Edmund (2007), *Hotel de Dream: A New York Novel*. New York: HarperPerennial.
Wiggins, Marianne (2007), *The Shadow Catcher*. New York: Simon & Schuster.
Williams, John (2004), *Augustus: A Novel*. 1971. New York: New York Review of Books.
Woolf, Virginia (1933), *Flush: A Biography*. New York: Harcourt, Brace, & World, Inc.
Woolley, Bryan (1981), *November 22*. New York: Seaview Books.
Yalom, Irvin D. (2006), *The Schopenhauer Cure*. New York: HarperPerennial.
Yalom, Irvin D. (2012), *The Spinoza Problem*. New York: Basic Books.
Yalom, Irvin D. (1992), *When Nietzsche Wept: A Novel of Obsession*. New York: Perennial Classics.
Yourcenar, Marguerite (1954), *Memoirs of Hadrian*. New York: Farrar, Straus & Company.

Secondary source material

Barber, Rosalind (2010), "Exploring Biographical Fictions: The Role of the Imagination in Writing and Reading Narrative." *Rethinking History* 14(2) (June): 165–87.
Belling, Catherine (2016), "The President's Glands: Somatic Interiority and the Referents of Biographical Fiction in *American Adulterer*." *a/b: Auto/Biography Studies* 31(1) (Winter): 59–82.

Bird, Stephanie (1998), *Recasting Historical Women: Female Identity in German Biographical Fiction*. Oxford: Berg.

Bode, Carl (1995), "The Buxom Biographies." *College English* 16(5) (February): 265–69.

Boldrini, Lucia (2012), *Autobiographies of Others: Historical Subjects and Literary Fiction*. New York: Routledge.

Buisine, Alain (1991), "Biofictions." *Revue des Sciences Humaines* 224: 7–13.

Carnes, Mark C. (2001), *Novel History: Historians and Novelists Confront America's Past (and Each Other)*. New York: Simon & Schuster.

Clifford, James L. (1970), *From Puzzles to Portraits: Problems of a Literary Biographer*. Chapel Hill: University of North Carolina Press.

Cohn, Dorrit (1989), "Fictional versus Historical Lives: Borderlines and Borderline Cases." *The Journal of Narrative Technique* 19(1) (Winter): 3–24.

Cooley, Elizabeth (1990), "Revolutionizing Biography: 'Orlando', 'Roger Fry', and the Tradition." *South Atlantic Review* 55(2) (May): 71–83.

Cooper, Katherine, and Emma Short (2012), *The Female Figure in Contemporary Historical Fiction*. New York: Palgrave Macmillan.

Danto, Arthur C. (1981), *The Transfiguration of the Commonplace: A Philosophy of Art*. Cambridge, MA: Harvard University Press.

Davis, Lennard J. (1996), *Factual Fictions: The Origins of the English Novel*. Philadelphia: University of Pennsylvania Press.

Dee, Jonathan (1999), "The Reanimators: On the Art of Literary Graverobbing." *Harpers* 298(1789) (June): 76–84.

Doctorow, E. L. (1977), "False Documents." *American Review* 1(26): 215–32.

Ellison, Ralph (1969), "The Uses of History in Fiction." *Southern Literary Journal* 1(2) (Spring): 57–90.

Fischer, Heinz-D., and Erika J. Fischer (2007), *Chronicle of the Pulitzer Prizes for Fiction: Discussions, Decisions and Documents*. München: K.G. Saur Verlag.

Foley, Barbara (1986), *Telling the Truth: The Theory and Practice of Documentary Fiction*. Ithaca: Cornell University Press.

Frus, Phyllis (1994), *The Politics and Poetics of Journalistic Narrative: The Timely and the Timeless*. Cambridge: Cambridge University Press.

Hollowell, John (1977), *Fact & Fiction: The New Journalism and the Nonfiction Novel*. Chapel Hill: The University of North Carolina Press.

Hutcheon, Linda (1988), *A Poetics of Postmodernism: History, Theory, Fiction*. New York: Routledge.

Iggers, George G. (1997), *Historiography in the Twentieth Century: From Scientific Objectivity to the Postmodern Challenge*. Hanover: Wesleyan University Press.

Jacobs, Naomi (1990), *The Character of Truth: Historical Figures in Contemporary Fiction*. Carbondale and Edwardsville: Southern Illinois University Press.

Kaplan, Cora (2007), *Victoriana: Histories, Fictions, Criticism*. New York: Columbia University Press.

Karla, Grammatiki A. (2009), *Fiction on the Fringe: Novelistic Writing in the Post-Classical Age*. Leiden: Brill.

Keener, John F. (2001), *Biography and the Postmodern Historical Novel*. Lewiston: The Edwin Mellen Press.

Kendall, Murray Paul (1965), *The Art of Biography*. New York: W.W. Norton & Company.

Kohlke, Marie-Luise (2013), "New-Victorian Biofiction and the Special/Spectral Case of Barbara Chase-Riboud's *Hottentot Venus*." *Australasian Journal of Victorian Studies* 18(1): 4–21.

Lackey, Michael (2016), *The American Biographical Novel*. New York and London: Bloomsbury.

Lackey, Michael (2014), "Introduction," in Jay Parini's *Conversations with Jay Parini*. Editor Michael Lackey. Jackson: University Press of Mississippi: ix–xxi.

Lackey, Michael (2016), "Locating and Defining the Bio in Biofiction." *a/b: Auto/Biography Studies* 31(1) (Winter): 3–10.

Lackey, Michael (2016), "The Rise of the Biographical Novel and the Fall of the Historical Novel." *a/b: Auto/Biography Studies* 31(1) (Winter): 33–58.

Lackey, Michael (2014), *Truthful Fictions: Conversations with American Biographical Novelists*. Editor and Interviewer Michael Lackey. New York and London: Bloomsbury.

Lackey, Michael (2014), "The Uses of History in the Biographical Novel: A Conversation with Jay Parini, Bruce Duffy, and Lance Olsen," in *Conversations with Jay Parini*. Editor Michael Lackey. Jackson: University Press of Mississippi: 125–48.

Latham, Monica (2011), "*On the Rocks*: Women (and Men) in (and out of) Love," in *Études Lawrenciennes* 42. Paris: Presses Universitaires Paris Ouest: 281–317.

Latham, Monica (2015), *A Poetics of Postmodernism and Neomodernism: Rewriting Mrs. Dalloway*. New York: Palgrave Macmillan.

Latham, Monica (2012), "'Serv[ing] under two masters': Virginia Woolf's Afterlives in Contemporary Biofictions." *a/b: Auto/Biography Studies* 27(2) (Winter): 354–73.

Latham, Monica (2014), "Thieving Facts and Reconstructing Katherine Mansfield's Life in Janice Kulyk Keefer's *Thieves*." *European Journal of Life Writing* 3: 103–20.

Latham, Monica (2008), "Virginia Woolf's Suicide Notes: Michael Cunningham's Art of Transposing a Life's Epilogue into a Fictitious Prologue," in *Last Letters*. Editor Sylvie Crinquand. Newcastle: Cambridge Scholars Publishing: 37–55.

Lodge, David (2006), *The Year of Henry James or, Timing is All: the Story of a Novel*. London: Harvill Secker.

Lukács, Georg (1937), *The Historical Novel*. Lincoln: University of Nebraska Press.

Lyotard, Jean-Francois (1979), *The Postmodern Condition: A Report on Knowledge*. Minneapolis: University of Minnesota Press.

Mallon, Thomas (2001), "The Historical Novelist's Burden of Truth," in *In Fact: Essays on Writers and Writing*. New York: Pantheon Books: 291–95.

Malmgren, Carl Darryl (1985), *Fictional Space in the Modernist and Postmodernist American Novel*. Lewisburg: Bucknell University Press.

Marcus, Laura (2014), *Katherine Mansfield's Afterlives*. Bath, England: Katherine Mansfield Society Publications.

Middeke, Martin, and Werner Huber (1999), *Biofictions: The Rewriting of Romantic Lives in Contemporary Fiction and Drama*. Suffolk: Camden House.

Mujica, Barbara (2016), "Going for the Subjective: One Way to Write Biographical Fiction." *a/b: Autobiography Studies* 31(1) (Winter): 11–20.

Nadel, Ira Bruce (1984), *Biography: Fiction, Fact & Form*. New York: St. Martin's Press.

Novak, Julia (2011), "Biographical Fiction to Historiographic Metafiction: Rewriting Clara Schumann." *Brno Studies in English* 37(2): 145–58.

Novak, Julia (2012), "Father and Daughter across Europe: The Journeys of Clara Wieck Schumann and Artemisia Gentileschi in Fictionalised Biographies." *European Journal of Life Writing* 1: 41–57.

Novak, Julia (2014), "Nell Gwyn in Contemporary Romance Novels: Biography and the Dictates of 'Genre Literature'." *Contemporary Women's Writing* 8(3): 373–90.

Novak, Julia (2016), "The Notable Woman in Fiction: The Afterlives of Elizabeth Barrett Browning." *a/b: Autobiography Studies* 31(1) (Winter): 83–107.

Novak, Julia (2014), "The (Re-)Making of Clara Wieck-Schumann: Celebrity and Gender in Biofiction," in *Search for the Real: Authenticity and the Construction of Celebrity*. Editor Andrew J. Sepie. Oxford: Interdisciplinary Press: 97–112.

Novak, Julia, and Sandra Meyer (2014), "Disparate Images: Literary Heroism and the 'Work vs. Life' Topos in Contemporary Biofictions about Victorian Authors." *Neo-Victorian Studies* 7(1): 25–51.

Nünning, Ansgar (2005), "Fictional Metabiographies and Metaautobiographies: Towards a Definition, Typology and Analysis of Self-Reflexive Hybrid Metegenres," in *Self-Reflexivity in Literature*. Editors Werner Huber, Martin Middeke, and Hubert Zapf. Würzburg: Königshausen & Neumann: 195–209.

Parini, Jay (2014), *Conversations with Jay Parini*. Editor Michael Lackey. Jackson: University Press of Mississippi.

Parini, Jay (1997), *Some Necessary Angels: Essays on Writing and Politics*. New York: Columbia University Press.

Parini, Jay (2016), "Writing Biographical Fiction: Some Personal Reflections." *a/b: Autobiography Studies* 31(1) (Winter): 21–26.

Perkin, J. Russell (2010), "Imagining Henry: Henry James as a Fictional Character in Colm Tóibín's *The Master* and David Lodge's *Author, Author*." *Journal of Modern Literature* 33(2) (Winter): 114–30.

Popkin, Jeremy D. (2005), *History, Historians, & Autobiography*. Chicago and London: The University of Chicago Press.

Ryan, Judith (2012), *The Novel after Theory*. New York: Columbia University Press.

Savu, Laura E. (2010), *Postmortem Postmodernists: The Afterlife of the Author in Recent Narrative*. Madison: Fairleigh Dickinson University Press.

Schabert, Ina (1982), "Fictional Biography, Factual Biography, and their Contamination." *Biography* 5(1) (Winter): 1–16.

Schabert, Ina (1990), *In Quest of the Other Person: Fiction as Biography*. Tubingen: Francke Verlag.

Scott, Joanna (2016), "On Hoaxes, Humbugs, and Fictional Portraiture." *a/b: Autobiography Studies* 31(1) (Winter): 27–32.

Sellers, Susan (2008), "Writing *Vanessa and Virginia*." *Two Ravens Press*, UK Website.

Southgate, Beverley (2009), *History Meets Fiction*. Harlow: Longman/Pearson Education Limited.

Stone, Irving (1957), "The Biographical Novel," in *Three Views of the Novel*. Washington, DC: Library of Congress.

Tóibín, Colm (2010), *All a Novelist Needs: Colm Tóibín on Henry James*. Editor Susan M. Griffin. Baltimore: Johns Hopkins University Press.

Vannucci, Valentina (2011), "*Canone e* biofiction: *i soggetti della storia e i nuovi mondi letterari*," in *altri canoni/canoni altri: pluralismo e studi letterari*. Editors Ornella De Zordo and Fiorenzo Fantaccini. Florence: Firenze University Press.

White, Hayden (1987), *The Content of the Form: Narrative Discourse and Historical Representation*. Baltimore: Johns Hopkins University Press.

White, Hayden (1973), *Metahistory: The Historical Imagination in Nineteenth-Century Europe*. Baltimore: Johns Hopkins University Press.

White, Hayden (1992), *Tropics of Discourse: Essays in Cultural Criticism*. 1978. Baltimore: Johns Hopkins University Press.

Wilde, Allen (1981), *Horizons of Assent: Modernism, Postmodernism, and the Ironic Imagination*. Baltimore, Johns Hopkins University Press.

Woolf, Virginia (1942), "The Art of Biography," in *The Death of the Moth and Other Essays*. Editor Leonard Woolf. London: The Hogarth Press: 119–26.

Wright, Terry R. (2007), *The Genesis of Fiction: Modern Novelists as Biblical Interpreters*. Hampshire: Ashgate Publishing Limited.

Yalom, Irvin D. (1998), *The Yalom Reader: Selections from the Work of a Master Therapist and Storyteller*. Editor Ben Yalom. New York: Basic Books.

Zavarzadeh, Mas'ud (1976), *The Mythopoeic Reality: The Postwar American Nonfiction Novel*. Urbana: University of Illinois Press.

INDEX

Note: Locators with letter "n" refer to notes.